The Library of Scandinavian Studies

COUNT HANS AXEL VON FERSEN

Portrait by Peter Dreuillon, Düsseldorff, 1793
Photo courtesy of Svenska Porträttarkivet, Nationalmuseum

Count Hans Axel von Fersen

COUNT HANS AXEL VON FERSEN

Aristocrat in an Age of Revolution

H. Arnold Barton

TWAYNE PUBLISHERS

A DIVISION OF G. K. HALL & CO., BOSTON

The Library of Scandinavian Studies

Erik J. Friis, *General Editor*

Volume 3

Count Hans Axel von Fersen, by H. Arnold Barton

Copyright © 1975 by G. K. Hall & Co.

MANUFACTURED IN THE UNITED STATES OF AMERICA

Library of Congress Cataloging in Publication Data

Barton, Hildor Arnold, 1929–
   Count Hans Axel von Fersen.
   (The Library of Scandinavian studies; v. 3)
   Bibliography: p.
   I. Fersen, Hans Axel von, greve, 1755–1810.
I. Series.
DL750.F4B37   355'.0092'4 [B]   74–22113
ISBN 0–8057–5363–X

Contents

About the Author

H. Arnold Barton was born in Los Angeles, California. He received his B. A. from Pomona College in 1953 and, following service with the U. S. Coast Guard in the Mediterranean and Pacific, took his Ph.D. at Princeton University in 1962. He has taught at the University of Alberta, Edmonton, and the University of California, Santa Barbara, and presently is professor of history at Southern Illinois University, Carbondale. He is the author of *Letters from the Promised Land: Swedes in America, 1840–1914* (Minneapolis: University of Minnesota Press, 1975) and of numerous articles, principally on eighteenth- and nineteenth-century Scandinavia. He also edits the *Swedish Pioneer Historical Quarterly*.

Preface

A remarkable amount has been written about Count Axel von Fersen, yet there is much about him that has remained little known. The bibliography to this present study shows how vast has been the production of that breed M. Charles Kunstler has in all seriousness referred to as "*les férsenistes.*" Yet most of the existing literature on Fersen is devoted specifically to his problematical relationship with Queen Marie-Antoinette of France, to the neglect of other aspects of his life. It is mainly the work of French *littérateurs* with little interest in political affairs, lacking knowledge of Fersen's native Sweden and of the Swedish language. Most of these writings are highly romanticized and thus of little historical value. There are, meanwhile, some important collections of published documents, but these have not previously been fully utilized in exploring Fersen's career. To date, there has not been a detailed, balanced, and scholarly study of his public and private life.

It is, however, precisely because Fersen has so long attracted interest—for whatever reasons—and because so much material has already accumulated concerning him, that a full biography seems called for. The deposition of the great majority of the voluminous Fersen papers in the Swedish State Archive in 1954, the completion of the work of ordering and cataloguing them by 1965, the appearance in recent years of a number of important monographs on revolutionary Europe and on Sweden, as well as the publication in 1956 of Bengt Hildebrand's valuable article on Fersen in *Svenskt biografiskt lexikon* XV, with its wealth of bibliographical leads, have all made this time a propitious one for the task.

Axel von Fersen deserves more consideration that he has ever received for the significant personal parts he played in various important episodes of his time, in particular in connection with the flight to Varennes, the counterrevolutionary diplomacy of the monarchical powers of Europe in 1791–93, and Sweden's participation in the War of the Third Coalition, to say nothing of the revolutionary situation in Sweden in 1809–10 which led to his tragic death at the hands of an enraged Stockholm mob.

At the same time, however, Fersen proves to be a highly representative figure of his era, his nationality, and perhaps above all of his social class, in a time of crisis and upheaval. The circumstances of his life make him a remarkable example of a high aristocrat caught in an age of revolution and it is in this viewpoint that I find the main unifying theme of my study.

Fersen was deeply involved in areas of late eighteenth-century life and activity which though of great significance in themselves, have generally been overlooked in favor of other, more established and traditional topics of study. The French and international Counterrevolution has until recently been relatively neglected. Its leaders have on the whole received from historians little attention in comparison to their opponents, the leaders of the Revolution. If one accepts, however, as does the present author, the thesis that there took place in this period a very real struggle between determined and closely matched antagonists, that its outcome was by no means predetermined, and that it did not end by 1799 or 1815 in a clear-cut victory of the Revolution over the Counterrevolution, then the importance of such figures as Calonne, Breteuil, Mallet du Pan, and Fersen himself emerges in truer perspective. There was at the same time relatively little concern with revolutionary or quasi-revolutionary disturbances in countries outside France before and during the Revolution, regarded in a European or Western context, until the appearance of Jacques Godechot's *La grande nation* in 1956 and Robert R. Palmer's *Age of the Democratic Revolution* in 1959–64. The internal histories of several European countries are not widely known for this period, not least of all that of Fersen's Sweden. The reigns of Gustav III (1771–92) and of his son, Gustav IV Adolf (1792–1809) comprise one of the most interesting eras in all of Swedish history—the Gustavian Age— yet it is almost unknown outside of Scandinavia. The last and only detailed treatment of Gustav III in English is R. Nisbet Bain's two-volume work, *Gustavus III and his Contemporaries*, published as far back as 1894, which in many respects is badly outdated. There is, meanwhile, virtually nothing in English touching on Gustav IV Adolf. Works in other non-Scandinavian languages on this period of Swedish history are almost as scarce.

Preface

In studying Fersen's life and times, one is by necessity much concerned with these and other generally unfamiliar aspects of the period. There are meanwhile two themes which I have in particular sought to elucidate in this biography: first, the attitudes and actions of that element within the Counterrevolution, in France and abroad, known to contemporaries as the "Party of the Tuileries," which sought above all to establish a strong monarchy in the face of both the aristocratic and the democratic factions, and which centered around Marie-Antoinette, the Baron de Breteuil, and Fersen; and secondly, the relationship of Sweden to the whole of the revolutionary age in the West, between in this instance Gustav III's revolution of 1772 and that which in 1809–10 cost his son, Gustav IV Adolf, his throne, and Axel von Fersen his life.

Over the years the search for Axel von Fersen has brought encouragement and help from many persons, which I am grateful to acknowledge. Professor R. R. Palmer, then of Princeton University, was the mentor of my first, preliminary venture into the subject. Since that time, the late Professor Bengt Hildebrand of Stockholm, Professor Sten Carlsson, Uppsala, Professor Emeritus Gerhard Hafström, Lund, *Landsarkivarie* Jöran Wibling, Härnösand, Herr Arne Forslund, Stockholm, and Baroness Blanka Klinckowström, Stafsund, have given valuable suggestions or have provided research materials.

I owe a special debt to the unfailing helpfulness of *Förste bibliotekarie* Olof von Feilitzen of the Royal Library, as well as to *Förste arkivarie* Nils F. Holm, *Arkivarier* Ingemar Carlsson, Sven Astrand, and their colleagues of the Swedish State Archives, during my research trips to Stockholm. The interlibrary loan and acquisitions personnel of the libraries at Princeton University, University of Alberta, Edmonton, and University of California at Berkeley and Santa Barbara gave dedicated assistance.

Mr. Erik J. Friis, the general editor of this series, has rendered many valuable services, for which I am most grateful. Publication of this book is partially subsidized by a grant from the Swedish State Humanistic Research Council.

Finally, my earliest investigations into this subject led me to Aina. When she married me she in a sense married this project as well. It is to her that this book is affectionately dedicated.

H. A. B.

Tyresö, Sweden

CHAPTER I

The Upbringing of a Grand Seigneur, 1755–1780

1

The house of Fersen was an illustrious one. Its descent is documented back to the thirteenth century in Pomerania, though family tradition traced its origins to the time of Christ in Thuringia and Scotland. In the sixteenth century, a branch established itself in Estonia. During the Swedish rule in the Baltic provinces, several of its members rendered distinguished service to the crown and at the end of the seventeenth century, Axel von Fersen's great-grandfather was made a Swedish count and settled in Sweden proper. Among his forefathers, Axel could count three field marshals and three royal councillors in Swedish service and he was related by blood or marriage to the foremost families of the Swedish and Baltic aristocracy. His father, Count Fredrik Axel von Fersen, since 1755 the leading figure of the aristocratic "Hat" party, was probably the most powerful man on the Swedish political scene in the third quarter of the eighteenth century and was sometimes called the Cato or Cicero of his country. He was as well one of the richest men in Sweden and his house in Stockholm was regarded as the city's finest after the royal palace itself. He was master of the estates of Steninge, Ljung, Mälsåker, Lövstad, and Älgö in Sweden, Wuojoki and Harwila in Finland. He owned ironworks at Ljung and Finnåker, and was a director and major stockholder in the Swedish East India Company. The Fersen household was the favored gathering place during Axel's youth of Sweden's highest

1

society and of foreigners of distinction. So impressed was one courtier that he divided all mankind into "Frenchmen, Fersens, and rabble."[1]

Hans Axel von Fersen was born on 4 September 1755, in Stockholm, the second of the four children of Fredrik Axel von Fersen and his wife, Hedvig Catharina, née De la Gardie. The eldest of the four was Hedvig Eleonora, later married to Baron Thure Leonhard Klinckowström. Next after Axel was Eva Sophie, later Countess Piper, throughout Axel's life the member of the family closest to him and one of his few real confidants. The youngest was Fabian Reinhold, who held high court positions until his death in 1818. With Fabian's son, Gustav Hans von Fersen, the family name died out in 1839, though descendants of Axel's two sisters are still living in Sweden.[2]

Axel's mother was first lady in waiting to Queen Lovisa Ulrika. From childhood, he, his brother, and sisters held honorific court positions and would continue to do so throughout their lives. Their uncle, Count Carl von Fersen, was court master of the hunt, later director of the court theater, and his five daughters were among the principal ornaments of a court renowned for feminine beauty.[3]

Fredrik Axel von Fersen was in principle one of the most eloquent proponents of the "aristocratic republicanism" of the Era of Freedom in Sweden, hence a firm opponent of royal absolution. In 1756, he had taken the lead in crushing a royalist coup d'état centering around Queen Lovisa Ulrika. His was the political philosophy to which Axel was exposed since childhood. The victory of the pro-Russian, anti-aristocratic "Cap" party in 1765, however, convinced the elder Fersen of the necessity of strengthening the crown to some degree and encouraged by the French ambassador, the Baron de Breteuil, drew closer to the court. He nevertheless sought to avoid too close a connection, which might limit his freedom of action. When his daughter Sophie reached marriageable age, she was courted by King Gustav III's brother, Duke Fredrik of Östergötland. Field Marshal Fersen—now a state councillor—forbade the match and betrothed his daughter to Count Adolph Piper of Engsö, whom she married in 1777.[4] Both the court and the party chieftain sought to use their relationship to their own advantage. There were clearly political motives behind the extraordinary favor Axel would enjoy at court until Gustav III's death, especially as relations between the king and the elder Fersen grew strained and eventually reached the breaking point.

Axel received an education befitting his station from a private tutor, Jacob Johan Forslund; according to the tradition of his descendants, he was a natural son of Fredrik Axel von Fersen, and was thus an elder half brother to his pupil. Forslund apparently fulfilled his duties well and the elder Fersen was well pleased with him.[5] During this period, the cultural life of the Swedish court and nobility was patterned after France and French was the language of polite society. The Fersen family habitually spoke and corresponded in French among themselves and Axel always kept his diary in that language.[6] Naturally, Axel received a military appointment at an early age: in 1770 he was made corporal in the Mounted Life Guard.[7]

2

In the spring of that year, when Axel was fifteen, he departed on a grand tour to finish his education, accompanied by a tutor, Jean Bolemany, a Protestant Hungarian baron.[8] They traveled by way of Elsinore, Copenhagen, and Hamburg, to Brunswick, where Axel attended the Kriegsinstitut Carolinum. Already in Elsinore, he began to keep a diary, a habit he would follow for most of the rest of his life, and wrote home faithfully to his family.[9] Commenting on a letter from Copenhagen, the elder Fersen wrote with worldly amusement to Jacob Forslund in June 1770:

He seems to me quite astonished by all he sees there and yet there is nothing astonishing there; but I recognize in this the way of young voyagers, like the mouse who climbing upon a clod of earth found the world to be very great.[10]

What nevertheless impresses the reader of Axel's diary and letters is the equanimity and poise with which from the beginning he faced this great new world.

At Brunswick, Axel studied history, German, the clavichord, and exercise at arms. He was presented to Duke Ferdinand of Brunswick, with whom he would have fateful dealings in the future.[11] After some eight months, he and his tutor resumed their travels through Germany, being everywhere well received by princely houses. In May 1771, they arrived in Strasbourg, where Axel studied natural law, fortification, drawing, German history, and military exercises. Everywhere his father was known and respected, he wrote home, adding, "the air of France agrees well with me."[12]

In October, the travelers continued to Switzerland, where Axel was impressed with the mountain scenery and the uninhibited behavior of the young girls.[13] The following month they arrived in Turin, where the French ambassador entered Axel in the Royal Military Academy. He remained a year and a half, studying Italian, fortification, and drawing.[14]

In the spring of 1773, Fersen and his mentor quit the Piedmontese capital, "not without regrets," and visited Milan, where Axel was presented to the Archduke-Regent and noted the plainness of the local ladies. He thereafter discontinued his diary, kept up only spasmodically in Turin, but brief notes for intended entries show that he and Bolemany continued to Rome where, his father informed Forslund, the Pope presented him with a gold medal and "warmly welcomed him in my behalf." Axel assiduously visited the monuments of antiquity and Christianity, and met both the engraver Piranesi and the finest Swedish sculptor of his day, Johan Tobias Sergel. In Naples, he visited Pompeii, the grotto at Posilippo and "the mouths of Vesuvius." Here he renewed acquaintances with the French ambassador, the Baron de Breteuil, who had served from 1763 to 1767 in Stockholm, where he had frequented the Fersen household, and his young widowed daughter, Mme. de Matignon. Breteuil wrote flattering things to the elder Fersen about his son, which, Fredrik Axel commented with good-natured skepticism to Forslund, "I only believe in part. I know the vivacity of the French and the quickness with which they are infatuated with anything new." Axel was a frequent visitor in the home of the British ambassador, Sir William Hamilton, the well-known collector of antiquities, later husband to the better known Lady Emma. Turning northward, he and his tutor made their way to Florence, thence to Paris, where they arrived in November 1773.[15] They remained there for the next five months. During this time, Axel continued his studies, though his occasional diary entries give a picture mainly of the gay social whirl into which he found himself readily accepted.

Axel's rough notes reveal that he first visited Versailles on November 18 and was presented to the French royal family the next day. On December 6, he attended "the ball of Mme. the Dauphine." At this time then, he apparently first saw Marie-Antoinette, with whose memory his name would remain forever linked. On New Year's Day, 1774, he resumed his diary with a visit to Versailles and a call on Mme. du Barry. It thereafter recounts a tireless round of balls of all descriptions. On 30 January, a masked woman conversed with Axel for some time at an opera ball in Paris before he discovered her to be Marie-Antoinette. Balls were so numerous that by February he noted he now attended only those given by the dauphine. Meanwhile there was a constant succession of spectacles, operas, theater, card parties, picnics in the open air, dinners, *salons* and *soupers dansants*. There were excursions in and around the city, on the boulevards or *chaussées* that surrounded it, to suburban vauxhalls, to palaces and gardens. Fersen also met notables of all kinds, both French and foreign.[15a]

In early May, a few days after Louis XV's death, Fersen and Bolemany departed for England. Shortly thereafter, the Swedish ambassador, Count Gustav Philip Creutz, wrote from Paris to his master, Gustav III, praising the young count for his success in Parisian society and "the singular nobility and elevation of his mind."[16] The king was doubtless watching young Fersen's progress with interest.

In England, Axel noted "a total difference of customs, of food, in manner of thinking, even in the construction of houses, in fact in everything" from France and the comparison did not in his mind favor England. He was presented at the Court of St. James, where "nothing proclaims the grandeur of a king" and was little impressed by George III. In general, he considered English-women plain and the social functions he attended dull. He nevertheless used his four months in England to good effect in conscientious sightseeing.[17]

Fersen and Bolemany set out in September on the return voyage to Sweden. Traveling through Lille and Brussels, they proceeded to Berlin and Potsdam, where Axel was presented to Frederick II. From Dresden, he wrote enthusiastically to Sophie of a Miss Leyel, an English girl whose family he had met in Paris and London, and who knew the Fersens in Stockholm.[18]

Finally, in December 1774, after four and a half years abroad, Axel Fersen returned to his father's house. On the grand tour he had seen and experienced many strange and wonderful things. What was more important, he had completed an education suitable for a brilliant place in society and the state by learning languages and manners, and by forming widespread personal acquaintance-ships within the charmed circle of those who controlled the destinies of Europe.

3

For a little over three years, Axel remained in Sweden. He was immediately received at court and was promoted to captain in the Light Dragoons.[19] He seems to have spent most of his time at court in Stockholm and the summer palaces at Drottningholm, Gripsholm, Ulriksdal, and Ekolsund. He kept no diary during these years, which is regrettable as this was the most brilliant era of the court of Gustav III, reputedly one of the gayest in Europe, which has left its strongly nostalgic imprint upon Swedish culture and historical consciousness. A few brief notes to Sophie give glimpses of the pleasures and gossip of the courtiers, but it is mainly through the accounts of others that his activities can in some measure be reconstructed. He was clearly among the inner circle of the king's favorites and accompanied him on various excursions through the country. Gustav III's passion was plays and spectacles, in which he participated as impresario, actor, and often playwright. Along with more serious fare went a constant round of court divertissements, masquerades, and pageants in which Axel Fersen was a regular participant, with his brother and sisters.[20] Piquant descriptions of these events in the memoirs of the time recall an elusive and long-vanished world of rococo fantasy and make-believe. In August 1776, Axel participated in Gustav's III's splendidly staged medieval tournament at Ekolsund and the next year in another on Adolf Fredrik Square in Stockholm.

All of this could be quite wearing and Axel wrote Sophie complaining of having to wear a 40-pound suit of armor for days on end while tilting at rings and Turks' heads. He was not, however, always happier away from court, and he sighed with boredom while visiting in the country with his parents, whose pleasures were "not very lively."[21]

The elder Fersen strongly disapproved of the waste, frivolity, and lack of dignity of Gustav III's court, above all disliking the carefree and irreverent crowd of young noble fortune hunters with which the king surrounded himself. The court at this time was evidently divided between the older, high-aristocratic faction, in which the elder Fersen held a prominent place, and the younger courtiers around the king's brother, Duke Karl of Södermanland, and the latter's wife, Duchess Hedvig Elisabeth Charlotta, Sophie Fersen's bosom friend.[22] Axel doubtless found himself in a difficult position between the two factions, particularly when his father became involved in a sharp dispute with the king during the winter of 1777 over Sophie's participation in a court divertissement together with young women of doubtful reputation. Thus caught in between, it is not surprising that in the spring of 1778 Axel sought leave to travel to England. His expressions of weariness with the amusements of the court need not be taken too seriously; others too complained of Gustav III's untiring search for pleasure and novelty. Axel's letters and diary show, both earlier and later, how much he appreciated social and esthetic pleasures while in his later years he frequently felt nostalgic for the court of Gustav III. Like his father, however, he had little but disdain for the younger courtiers.[23] He departed Stockholm in April 1778, little realizing that it would be six years before he would return.

4

Axel went to London to seek the hand of Miss Catherine Leyel, of whom he had written so enthusiastically from Dresden three years before. She was not only charming but heiress to a fortune in the English East India Company. Fredrik Axel von Fersen, sometimes accused of too great a fondness for money, was only too aware that his son's upbringing had been costly and welcomed a chance to fill the family coffers.[24]

Axel lost no time in seeking Miss Leyel's hand. But his efforts proved vain: she could not be persuaded to leave her parents. Once out of Sweden, however, he felt little inclined to return and remained in London for nearly three months, learning English and sightseeing. He was "in despair" over his courtship, he wrote Sophie—now Countess Piper—on 30 June, but mainly, it seems, because of the "intolerable unpleasantness of being subjected to mockery and witticisms" if he returned home. He thus proposed to his father that he be permitted to seek experience as a soldier or learn diplomacy under Count Creutz in Paris.[25]

In August 1778, Fersen recrossed the Channel and made his way to Paris. There was no opening at the Swedish embassy; a young diplomat, Baron Erik Magnus Staël von Holstein, was just then beginning his service there. Staël was an old friend—one of the few Axel ever used the familiar *tu* with—and was delighted to see him. The following year and a half, Fersen spent much time at the embassy and Creutz taught him the rudiments of diplomacy. Meanwhile, his thoughts naturally turned to the alternative of going to war.[26]

It was natural that he should consider this. For generations Swedish officers and soldiers had served abroad in times of peace at home. In particular, they had sought service in the French forces, in keeping with a long tradition of friendship and alliance between France and Sweden since the Thirty Years' War. For certain noble families, including the Fersens, service in France had become customary, their members holding commissions in both armies. Fredrik Axel von Fersen had spent thirteen years with the French army, commanding his own German mercenary regiment; he had served with distinction in the War of Austrian Succession, eventually attaining the rank of brigadier. Doubtless as a tribute to him, Axel had been made an honorary *lieutenant à la suite* in a French regiment, Royale-Bavière, at the age of fifteen in 1770.[27]

The year 1778 was a propitious time. Since the beginning of his journey, Axel's diary and letters show his keen interest in European affairs. Shortly after he arrived in London, war broke out between Britain and France over the rebellion in North America. Meanwhile, hostilities between Austria and Prussia over the Bavarian succession appeared to threaten a general European conflagration. Fersen obtained permission to seek a place as aide-de-camp with either the emperor or the king of Prussia. He particularly hoped to serve under the great Frederick, but not even Creutz's influence with the philosopher d'Alembert, who enjoyed the confidence of the Prussian monarch, produced an appointment. Axel now sought a place in the French army, asking his father in November to put off thoughts of matrimony for a few years at least.[28]

Meanwhile, Axel quickly found his way back into Parisian society. In August he was presented to Marie-Antoinette, who exclaimed, "Ah, here is an old acquaintance!" He became a frequent visitor to Versailles and one of the intimate circle of the queen's friends at the Trianon.[29] Marie-Antoinette showed such favor toward the young Swedish count that it soon gave rise to rumor.

Among the intimates of the Trianon, Fersen met an older compatriot in French service, the popular Curt von Stedingk, a native of Swedish Pomerania. The two became good friends and in September attended army maneuvers in Normandy under the

Duc de Broglie. Urged by Ambassador Creutz, they somewhat grudgingly had uniforms made in the new "Swedish" style designed by Gustav III himself and Marie-Antoinette insisted on seeing them so attired.[30] They were well received at the encampment; the duke and other senior French officers remembered and esteemed Axel's father, a recommendation that served him well during his whole time with the French army. The Swedes observed with interest the trial of the controversial new infantry tactics of Du Mesnil-Durand, involving attack in column rather than in line formation. Large numbers of young noblemen were on hand, "all aides-de-camp." Fersen and Stedingk took part in the social amenities of the camp, where Broglie held "a kind of court," well attended by ladies from local and Parisian society. At the end of September, Fersen and his friend returned to the capital.[31]

Fersen now busied himself with negotiations for a military appointment, excursions, and social engagements of all kinds. He made new acquaintances, among them the Russian Countess von Stegelmann and her widowed daughter, the Baroness von Korff, who showed great hospitality to the Swedes in Paris.[32] Axel discontinued his diary after October, except briefly in March 1779, but his letters show he was ill during much of the winter and spring, with digestive troubles and, for the first time apparently, that bane of his future existence, hemorrhoids. In January, he despaired over the "bad news" of imminent peace in Germany. Stedingk meanwhile obtained a French brigade and distinguished himself at the storming of Grenada and the siege of Savannah.[33]

Fersen had to wait a year before a place in the French army could be arranged for him. In September 1779, he was appointed, thanks to the combined interest of his powerful connections, aide-de-camp to the Marshal de Vaux, who commanded a force gathering at Le Havre for a projected landing in England.[34] Before long, however, Axel feared the expedition would never take place, despite immense preparations. After five months of waiting, Vaux's force went into winter quarters and Axel returned to Paris after a visit to Brest, where he enviously witnessed the return of Curt von Stedingk, wounded and covered with glory.[35]

Fersen now had to try all over again to secure an appointment. He besought his father's permission to remain another winter in Paris, shared less expensive quarters and made detailed accounts of his economies. He thus reported to his father in January 1780 a monthly expense of 1,102 *livres* for rent and table, a valet, lackey and stable boy, three horses and incidentals. He was well received at Versailles, where he went "two or three times a week" and was much in the company of the Baron de Breteuil and his daughter. At length, in February, he received a brevet as *colonel en suite*, attached to the Régiment Deux-Ponts (Zweibrücken), thanks largely to the influence of the queen herself. This aroused the jealousy of all the young men at the court, especially since he was a foreigner, and he concluded that only the older people understood the obligation France owed Field Marshal Fersen and "find this favor just and merited." Soon after he was appointed an aide-de-camp to his father's old comrade-in-arms, General de Rochambeau, then preparing an expeditionary force for service in America. In late March, Axel departed for Brest and a month later sailed for America.[36]

5

Before turning to the young nobleman's first experience in the new world of revolutionary ferment, it would be well to gain some impression of him as an individual. Axel Fersen's appearance was perhaps best described by two contemporary sobriquets: *"Långa Axel"* ("Tall Axel") and *"le beau Fersen."* Tall and slender, with blue eyes and light brown hair, his handsomeness was legendary. His face, as depicted in a number of portraits, was somewhat long and narrow, with an air of elegance and reserve, a hint of irony, and a certain hauteur.[37]

At the time of his departure for America, Axel was 24 years old. Not only had he by this time already made the acquaintance of most of those persons who would be most important in his life, but his personality, attitudes, and values were formed in all essentials, as shown in his letters and diary. The impression these give agrees on the whole with that created by his portraits. He tended to be formal, correct, and somewhat aloof in dealing with others, so that his natural reserve could at times be taken for arrogance. He was discreet often to the point of secretiveness, though he could be outspoken when convinced the occasion demanded it. He was fastidious in his personal habits, ate and drank sparingly, and tended toward somewhat hypochondriac broodings over his bodily functions and the state of his health. His constant notations on personal matters in his diary give on the whole the impression of a self-contained, indeed often self-centered, and rather isolated individual, which in contrast to the old, romantic Fersen legend has produced some disillusionment on the part of recent critics.[38]

Axel Fersen was perhaps best described by his contemporary, the Duc de Lévis, who while no friend, wrote the following:

> . . . [he was] tall and his features regular without being expressive. His manners were noble and simple. His conversation was not very animated and he showed more judgment than spirit. He was circumspect with men and reserved with women, serious without being melancholy. His countenance and manner belonged perfectly to the hero of a novel, though not a French novel; for this he lacked both brilliance and levity.

Another contemporary, the Comte de Tilly, observed that this air of cool detachment with a hint of mystery accounted in large part for the extraordinary impression he created upon women.[39] A long succession of them may be glimpsed in discreet and laconic notations in his dairy and in his record of the letters he wrote. Yet beneath this rather cold exterior lay the ardor which once aroused by Marie-Antoinette would turn into a powerful and sustained passion. Mme. von Korff, who herself seems not to have been immune, said he had "a burning soul beneath a crust of ice."[40]

In matters of taste, Axel Fersen was an aristocrat of the aristocrats. He dressed with care and elegance, and with the resources of his later years attired his retainers in splendid liveries and drove fine carriages, drawn by well-matched horses in magnificent harness and trappings. Indeed, his strong interest in horses and *équipages* remained notable throughout his life. Just as he was himself fastidious about appearances, he tended to judge others largely by their outward attributes, placing great importance on grace, elegance, and *savoir-faire,* and was ever mindful of the distinctions of social rank. With his own peers, he was always impeccably correct, with persons of common origin generally affable and condescending, while those in whose company he felt least comfortable were bourgeois with pretentions beyond their station.

By the same token, Fersen had a keen appreciation and good knowledge of the visual arts, particularly architecture. Wherever he traveled, he judged cities in terms of well laid-out plans, imposing prospects, and handsome public buildings. He was also well versed in painting, sculpture, and the decorative arts. As was characteristic of his generation, he was fascinated with the theater and even more with music, particularly opera.[41] He appreciated courtly dress, behavior, and ceremonial. It is not surprising that the France of that day represented to him the pinnacle of elegance and taste, and aside from other considerations, his reaction to the revolution there must have been largely determined by what he can only have seen as the disappearance of so much he esthetically admired.

In his mind nothing could match the splendor and refinement of Versailles. During his first visit to Paris, he had criticized the *ennui* of the French that poisoned all their pleasures.[42] This, as it happened, became all too characteristic of Axel himself. From his earliest travels, he appraised all he saw with a keen and critical eye, quickly losing interest in anything that did not measure up to his own uncompromising standards. Thus, time and time again he criticizes the courts of Vienna, London, Stockholm, and the various German and Italian principalities for lack of taste and elegance, and the Germans, English, Italians, and not least his own countrymen for lack of appreciation and understanding for what he considers the finer things. Still, he was not unqualifiedly enthusiastic for France and the French.[43] In all things he was always critical and usually dispassionate. Neither chauvinist nor expatriate, he was a true eighteenth-century cosmopolitan.

If Axel had a lively appreciation for things esthetic, he had little for purely intellectual pursuits or the realm of ideas as such. He showed little interest in literature or the sciences, apart from some of their practical applications, and next to none in philosophy. His remarks on the British Museum in 1774 are revealing:

It is like all the museums of the world and there is nothing extraordinary about it if not that it is very well arranged and that it is complete enough in all its parts. What I did see that was extraordinary was one of those stones from Egypt with water inside which you can feel by shaking it a little in your hand. I believe that of all the museums of the north it is the one with the most beautiful collection of Etruscan vases, which the Chevalier Hamilton, minister in Naples, collected there and gave them as a present.

Here he met a Swede, Daniel Solander, one of Linnaeus's most outstanding disciples, who had been on Captain Cook's expedition around the world in 1768–71 and showed Axel weapons and implements from "Otahiti," which to him simply proved "how far these peoples are behind in the arts." Solander also took him to one of the weekly dinners of the Royal Society, which he found "neither gay nor instructive" and after two hours of learned papers he took some consolation in noting that half of those present had fallen asleep.[44]

Alma Söderhjelm has asserted that Axel Fersen's library was a very meager one, though it is not clear on what basis. The libraries of Lövstad and Stafsund, containing most of the Fersens' holdings, include good collections of eighteenth-century works, though it is usually uncertain which belonged to the family. There is no itemized list of books in Axel Fersen's estate inventory of 1810 and only a small number can definitely be identified as having been his. It nevertheless stands to reason that he had at his disposal not inconsiderable library resources. He meanwhile complained in 1797 that he had lost most of his own books in Paris at the time of the revolution.[45]

It is true that Fersen speaks little about books in his diary and letters, and seldom gives titles or sources for specific ideas. Yet he frequently mentions reading newspapers, journals, and pamphlets from different countries and he conscientiously compiled large and valuable collections of such material. At the same time, he wrote copiously, particularly between 1790 and 1800. His diary alone amounts to some 20,000 closely written pages while his letter register shows that scarcely a day passed during those years when he did not write one or several letters or dispatches.[46] Fersen's reading and writing—which in the 1790s must have occupied most of his active time—was, however, concentrated on concrete, above all political, problems, usually on a day-by-day basis. His ideas thus appear to have derived less from books than from journalistic or publicistic materials, the stage, private conversation, and the very language and rhetoric of his time. Writing under such circumstances, he did not develop a graceful and polished literary style like his father's; the real value of his diary and letters is documentary rather than literary.

It would seem that those persons who exercised the greatest influence on Axel Fersen during his youth were all warmly attached to the ideas of the Enlightenment. His father was much interested in the intellectual currents of the times and was one of the original members of the Swedish Academy when it was founded in 1786. His tutor on the grand tour, Jean Bolemany, was evidently an enthusiastic adherent of the philosophic camp. That Axel was warmly attached to him is shown by their frequent correspondence until the latter's death in Germany in 1806 and his attempt to secure favor for him with Gustav IV Adolf in 1797.[47] Gustav III had wide intellectual interests and was much attracted to the French *philosophes*, especially the physiocrats, in the early years of his reign.[48] Count Gustav Philip Creutz was a habitué of philosophic *salons* in Paris and friend to many of the leading figures of the Enlightenment.[49]

A number of experiences brought Axel into contact with the Enlightenment during his formative years between 1770 and 1780. During the first days of his grand tour in 1770, he noted a long conversation about Holbach's *Système de la Nature* between Bolemany and a traveling companion in Denmark, which seems to have impressed him.[50] While in Brunswick, he was initiated at his own wish into the Order of Freemasons by Duke Ferdinand and the Swedish Duke Karl of Södermanland.[51] In Strasbourg in 1771, he studied "natural law" with a certain "Professor Reiseisen."[52] That October, while visiting Switzerland, Bolemany took him to Ferney to meet Voltaire.[53] In Paris during the winter of 1774, he attended lectures on "physics" at the Sorbonne, where Diderot's daughter, the only lady present, struck up an acquaintance with him.[54] He also visited on a number of occasions the celebrated hostesses of philosophic *salons*, Mme. Geoffrin and the Marquise du Deffand, both of whom he found rather dull, and in 1778 was graciously received by Gustav III's confidante, the Comtesse de Boufflers.[55] He does not, however, note having met any of the philosophers in their homes. In Sweden in 1774–78, he doubtless attended the customary evening readings from edifying books at Gustav III's court.[56] In Paris in 1779–80, Axel wrote his father of doing much reading under Creutz's guidance, including evidently Mably's *Droit publique de l'Europe* and doubtless the Abbé Raynal's enormously popular *Histoire des établissements des européens dans les deux Indes*, that vast compendium of the most characteristic ideas of the Enlightenment. In America he was on friendly terms with the Chevalier de Chastellux. He was also acquainted with Baron Grimm and with Marmontel, editor of the *Mercure de France*.[57]

After the outbreak of the revolution in France, Axel Fersen was not long in blaming the ills he saw around him on the pernicious effects of "philosophy."[58] Such comments should not however lead to the conclusion that he was not himself influenced by the dominant attitudes, values, and ideas of the Enlightenment, as an examination of material from his letters and especially his diary—most of it not previously published or cited—will show.

Axel's visit to Switzerland in 1771 was a kind of reverent pilgrimage as Bolemany had apparently been there before and admired the country. Axel wrote rapturously of the majestic mountain scenery and moralized, "Here the philosopher will find men who are the least degraded and who hold most strongly through the simplicity of their manners and usages to the primitive existence of the reasonable being." Of the Bernese:

. . . the men are generally large and handsome, endowed with an understanding perfectly suited for the sound cultivation of the spirit; they also organize themselves into printing societies at their own expense which encourages many to translate and even write books.

Axel was pleased to make the acquaintance of some of these Bernese writers and savants. The Swiss, he wrote, were brave warriors and proud, but did not seek to change their "fate" except for the Vaudois, who "are more influenced by French blood"; the German-Swiss worked hard, knowing their land to be their own, and often tripled their incomes. Switzerland had a republican government, "less mysterious than those of Geneva and Venice, and more solid than that of Holland," while the public buildings of Berne "impress with their grandeur and characterize the noble pride of a republican," though he noted aristocratic traits in the canton. Here, too, he admired the law code, based on custom, thus avoiding the "chicanery" of Roman law.[59]

Bolemany had evidently prepared his pupil well. Axel's image of Switzerland would appear to reflect both Montesquieu's ideas about republics in the *Esprit des Lois* and Rousseau's idealization in the *Nouvelle Heloïse* of the wild grandeur of the Swiss mountains and noble simplicity of their inhabitants. In October 1778, Axel visited the park at Ermenonville where Rousseau had been buried only three months before. Two years later in New England, he would again write of a people living in rude plenty amid a benign nature, uncorrupted by luxury and vice, though here his direct inspiration may have been Raynal.[60]

During his visits to England, Fersen revealed much interest in and admiration for British institutions. In May 1774, he visited Westminster Abbey,

... where there are buried the kings and many persons who have distinguished themselves, as much in the sciences as in other ways, and to whom tombs have been erected, which does great honor to the English nation which seeks to perpetuate the memory of great men and does justice to merit wherever it is found.

He attended a Quaker meeting, assiduously visited the law courts, and while attending a cavalry review at Blackheath, noted that only two regiments participated, "for the King is forbidden to assemble a greater number for fear he will misuse them."[61] In all, his sightseeing and comments here recall Voltaire's *Lettres philosophiques.*

Returning to London in 1778, Axel wrote in his diary a lengthy and sound description of the structure and function of Parliament, the judicial system, and the military forces. He appreciated the manner in which Parliament's power of the purse held in check the seemingly autocratic powers of the king and admired the Magna Carta as "the basis of English liberty."[62] His views on English political life in actual practice were, however, ambivalent. In June 1778, he witnessed George III's opening of Parliament:

When the king drove through the streets, there were people right next to the carriage who told him that he ought to watch out for his head, dismiss his ministers and take others instead. This is what the English call liberty; it is the presumptuousness of being able to insult the king, the ministers, and Parliament with impunity.[63]

In August he wrote with greater detachment:

Opinions are strongly divided on the question of English liberty. Some maintain that it exists, others that it is only the license of being able to abuse the Parliament, king, and ministers in the public papers without punishment. I am rather of the opinion of the latter but I believe that the English people is destined by the form of its government to be the freest people in the world and the happiest in its liberty, but that it is only through abuses that it is not.[64]

Fersen's admiration in these years for the free traditions and institutions of Switzerland and Great Britain stand in striking contrast to the strong preference for autocratic forms he expresses repeatedly after 1789 in discussing the politics of France and Sweden. The importance of intervening experience is clear. Yet one may also discern something of the influence of Montesquieu's conception of the relativity of political institutions and their varying suitability to different nations. Not the least of Montesquieu's services to his aristocratic admirers was a rationale for being liberal abroad while remaining conservative at home.

Montesquieu based this idea on the concept of strongly differing national types, determined in the first instance by climate and terrain. Like other Swedes of their time, both Axel and his father speak repeatedly of the vivacity, imagination, ardor, impetuosity, fickleness, and frivolity of the French. Meanwhile, scattered comments over the years show that he regarded his own countrymen as phlegmatic and coarse, lacking in grace and fantasy, but he himself took pride, in America and elsewhere, in his own hardiness, energy, cool-headedness, and constancy of purpose, which he also clearly conceived as natural Nordic qualities. Occasional remarks concerning Italians, Germans, Dutch, English, and others further confirm these views on the existence of rigid national types.

Montesquieu's *Esprit des lois*, with its emphasis on aristocratic "intermediary bodies" as the bulwark against tyrannies of the one or the many, surely provided Fredrik Axel von Fersen and his friends with their theoretical gospel in mid-eighteenth-century Sweden. Both Fersens, father and son, reflect the high-minded ideals of noble service and obligation upon which Montesquieu's conception of monarchy was based; while Axel gravitated increasingly toward the ideal of a nobility serving as the strongest support of a benevolent autocrat, his father continued to hold to an ideal of "enlightened aristocracy," opposed to the concept of "enlightened despotism," but no less characteristic of the century. It was from the viewpoint of such idealism that Fredrik Axel criticized the frivolity of Gustav III's court and that both he and his son were repelled by many of its younger courtiers. On his way to England in 1778, Axel was highly embarrassed by his traveling companions, two loutish young Swedish noblemen, who bullied the peasants at the post stations, "persons much more useful to the state than themselves." Later, after months of frustrating inactivity, when the Marshal de Vaux's camp disbanded in late 1779, Axel besought his father to be allowed to remain in France until the next campaigning season, to profit from the opportunity "to rise out of the class of the lazy and idle, and to acquire the knowledge and experience necessary in order one day to be useful to my fatherland and to serve worthily, as you have done, ... a master who so deserves it."[65] He could never, throughout his life, accept the irresponsibility and recklessness of so much of the European nobility and his complaints, while attending army maneuvers in England in August 1778, that the officers were worse than the men they commanded, foreshadow many of his later criticisms of incompetence among his peers.[66] In his personal and public life, he held faithfully to the ideal of *noblesse oblige.* His own most admirable virtues—like his father's—were the aristocratic ones of loyalty to persons, steadfastness to principles, and courage and dignity in the face of danger to life, fortune, or reputation.

Somewhat paradoxically, Montesquieu himself may well have contributed to Axel Fersen's reserved and doubtful attitude toward the *philosophes* in France. Even his father, who took obvious pride in "our enlightened time," was apprehensive of the influence of the Paris philosophers and their taste for "innovation" upon Gustav III.[67] For both, as for many Europeans, these persons were somewhat suspect because they were Frenchmen—with all the levity and inconstancy Montesquieu implied to be their nature —not because they were the champions of reason applied to human problems. Regardless of what he would say about "philosophy" and "philosophers," Axel Fersen himself never repudiated a fundamentally rational and pragmatic approach to life. His attitude toward religion, in common with his family, was distinctly skeptical. During his younger years he not infrequently expressed irony and indignation over religious superstition and fanaticism, especially in Catholic lands.[68] Though prepared on occasion to observe the forms of the Lutheran faith he was baptized in, he did so for reasons of propriety. Meanwhile, he remained unaffected by other "enthusiasms" of a pseudo-religious or secular nature. He apparently had little or nothing to do with Freemasonry after his initiation in 1770 and regarded with amusement the bizarre occultism and emotional mysticism that luxuriated within the myriad secret societies of the time. He thus never underwent the kind of conversion from rational skepticism to religious orthodoxy or some kind of romantic mystique that so many of his generation experienced.

In all this, the rationalism and anti-clericalism of Voltaire shows through. Axel's comments on meeting the Sage of Ferney in 1771 are revealing:

He was dressed in a scarlet vest with old embroidered buttonholes which his father and grandfather had worn, an old uncurled wig, old-fashioned shoes, woolen stockings pulled up over his breeches, an old dressing gown. All of this harmonized admirably with his face, which is all shriveled but in which the eyes are very beautiful, and altogether the face has a quite satyric air. . . . M. de Voltaire does much good in his village. He attracts here all the watchmakers of Geneva who work for him. He uses his theater building to provide lodging for them without consideration for anything else.[69]

Axel makes no mention of what was discussed. His keen eye for outward detail meanwhile provides a charming vignette of the aging philosopher. But most particularly, Axel's attention was drawn less to Voltaire's words than to his deeds, the cultivation of his own garden in the world of practical affairs. What made Axel Fersen a child of his own age was above all his pragmatic concern over concrete human problems coupled with a tempered optimism concerning well-considered institutional improvements.

Such an attitude would suggest that the physiocrats were that faction among the *philosophes* whose views were most congenial to Fersen's own. Their ideas were widely influential. Raynal espoused their doctrines and Gustav III was much influenced by them. Even Fredrik Axel von Fersen, who had played a substantial role in the mercantilist ventures of the Era of Freedom, wrote in his memoirs that "freedom is the soul and mainspring of all commerce."[70]

Axel Fersen's diary and letters from his travels meanwhile constantly reveal his typically eighteenth-century love for system and order, and his conscientious desire to observe and learn about practical and useful institutions. His somewhat theatrical exclamations over the Swiss Alps aside, the landscapes which most strongly impressed him were those most fertile and best cultivated, as for instance in the Austrian Netherlands, which he described in 1778 as "the most beautiful country in the world, rich and well-tilled, the roads excellent, straight as a ruler and bordered with a double row of great trees; it seems as though one journeys through a garden."[71] He was greatly interested by manufactures, as witnessed by his discussion of textile weaving in Amiens and Abbéville in his diary for May 1774.[72] He disliked Milan with its "very narrow and tortuous streets" and the old part of Brussels with its houses "badly built in the German fashion" but found the new part, built by the Archduke-Regent Charles, "very beautiful."[73] He admired London, where he found "all the streets illuminated with lanterns at each quarter of a league which is a mark of the opulence of the city, but the impression of these prospects, drawn straight as a string and so well lit struck me. . . ." The Chelsea and Greenwich Hospitals for old soldiers and sailors, he wrote, "do honor to the nation." Paris, of course, profoundly impressed him, and he noted particularly the Place Louis XV with its symmetrical architectural framework, "the most beautiful square one could see," the broad, straight prospect of the Champs-Élysées from the Tuileries Palace and Gardens, the spacious, tree-lined boulevards that marked the limits of the city, the bridge at Neuilly and *les Halles*, the central food market, especially the new *Halle au Bled*, which he felt could not be more ingenious, commodious, or beautiful.[74] He admired Brest for its harbor, "unique and worthy of the grandeur of the French monarchy," and Lille, a handsome and well-planned city, with its great *Hôpital Général*, whose inmates enjoyed good living conditions and practiced useful trades, and the clean, spacious—and odorless—barracks which housed the garrison, where the beds, twenty to a room, were "two feet wide and each soldier has his own so that they no longer have to sleep together."[75]

Axel Fersen never lost interest in such useful establishments, as his role in the Swedish government between 1799 and 1810 would show. His ideas as to what constituted the proper concerns of government were expressed in 1778 in his appreciation of the significance of the Magna Carta:

. . . It established the same weights and measures throughout the country, it protects merchants in their commerce, it forbids depriving peasants of their tools of cultivation . . . , finally, it proclaims that no subject may be exiled or molested in any way whatsoever in person or property except by judgment of his peers and in conformity with the ancient laws of the land.[76]

Utility, material well-being, justice for all, order and security under law for the individual and his rightful possessions: these remained throughout his life the consistent core of his political thinking.

If then, Axel Fersen was neither a profound nor an original thinker, his attainments were of a different sort. He not only appreciated music but could perform on the flute and clavichord. He knew in addition to French and his native Swedish, English, Italian, and German, in approximately that order of fluency, and kept a good command of Latin.[77] Above all, he was a keen and critical observer of political and military events. If in the light of subsequent history, his judgments often seem unjustified and even blind, in the context of his own time he shows much perceptiveness, objectivity, and balance. His letters and diary show he was anything but hasty in passing judgment, though stubborn in holding to opinions once formed.

The Duc de Lévis had said Fersen's countenance and manner "belonged perfectly to the hero of a novel" though he lacked the "brilliance and levity" necessary for a French one. He was indeed endowed with little of that wit which distinguished so many of his contemporaries; the occasional touches of humor that enliven his earlier years are quietly ironic, not light-hearted or ebullient. He inclined rather to melancholy than to anger. Yet here, too, he shows something of the feeling of his age, which was that of sensibility as well as sense. His delighted descriptions in the fall of 1778 of the English parks at Ermenonville and Chantilly show how receptive he was to the pre-romantic mood.[78] The fervent yet wistful idealization of the bonds of eternal friendship that infuses some of the letters of his younger years to his sister Sophie and their mutual friend, Evert Taube, and his brooding fascination with the question of destiny and the tragedy that seemed ordained to be his lot expresses the same spirit. If later generations have seen Axel von Fersen as a romantic and tragic figure, it was surely in part because he himself viewed his fate in such a light.

CHAPTER II

Fersen and the War of American Independence, 1780–1783

1

Through judicious influence, Axel Fersen had secured a place on General Rochambeau's staff and was now on his way to America. Paradoxically, in this first encounter with revolution, the young nobleman had in effect volunteered his services for an expedition in support of a group of subjects in open revolt against their legitimate monarch.

Why had he gone? It is first of all clear that he had been anxious for the past two years to find military employment. At the same time, there was a reason which made it wise for him to leave France for a time. Count Creutz wrote Gustav III in April 1779 that the queen showed an unmistakable "penchant" for Axel which offended many at court, but in resolving to go to America, he had shown "a firmness beyond his years."[1]

It has also been asserted that Fersen was fired with enthusiasm for the American ideals of freedom and democracy. He was clearly delighted to go on the campaign. By 1780, the American colonies had been in revolt for five long years, drawing the attention and admiration of Europe. When France entered the war, young noblemen flocked to the colors, many of whom could not find places. Axel wrote his father in March that he was at the height of his desires and felt a joy he could not express.[2]

Yet what were his feelings toward the conflict itself? Before attempting to answer, it would be well to consider the impact of the American Revolution on his native Sweden.

22

2

Here as elsewhere, the situation in America aroused great interest, being much discussed in the press, the popular stage, in taverns and coffee houses. Many expressed sympathy for the Americans. Even Gustav III wrote in December 1776 to Mme. de Boufflers in Paris, praising their proud spirit and speculating that the new republic, like ancient Rome, might one day "put Europe under tribute." The Swedish people, moreover, during their Era of Freedom, had become used to much the same political vocabulary as they now saw used across the Atlantic.[3]

Yet such indications can easily lead to a false impression of unbounded enthusiasm while in actuality reactions to the American Revolution were largely mixed. The king's momentary admiration for the colonists quickly passed. The newspapers, while filled with news from America, were by no means agreed in their attitudes toward the revolution. Many were pro-British and others, showing no attachment to Britain, disapproved of the "usurpation" of power by the rebellious colonists. Only by 1780 did two or three small journals appear that openly espoused the American cause.[4]

Much apparent enthusiasm can be explained on other grounds. One was Sweden's traditional pro-French orientation. Together with this was the general resentment in Continental countries, Sweden included, against British high-handedness in trade and maritime rights. Fersen, in London in July 1778, reflected this view when he wrote that the English spoke "'with their usual conceit and fanfaronade.'" Despite shortages and difficulties, they

. . . bluster and swagger incredibly, their reasoning is destitute of good sense and is based on their unlimited pride. They consider it fundamental that all the powers must lower their flags to them. And in the state in which things are now . . . there are people who despite all maintain that France has more to fear if its fleet is destroyed than England. . . .[5]

The Swedish commercial community was enthusiastic over new opportunities for trade with the former British colonies, previously closed to them; with the anti-British allies in the New World a profitable trade likewise developed. While interest in the event was widespread, enthusiasm was much more limited.

Some, of course, there were who from the start hailed the American Revolution as a milestone of human progress. As the conflict neared its successful conclusion, however, discontent with Gustav III and his policies began to develop for various reasons and from this time on important segments of Swedish opinion tended increasingly to idealize the event in retrospect. Even when in later years "democratic" opponents of the regime became disillusioned with the excesses of the French Revolution, they retained their enthusiasm for America. Writing in 1790, the editor of the radical journal, *Medborgaren*—"The Citizen"—Karl Fredrik Nordenskiöld, looking back proclaimed: "America has taught nations to know their rights and the equal protection which a benevolent nature affords to all. *All men are born free and equal;* this was the first meaning of the actions of the American states."[6]

A considerable number of Swedes participated in the War of American Independence. This might seem the most convincing argument for widespread enthusiasm in Sweden for the cause of the American patriots. Nevertheless, the particular group of Swedes who actually served in the war was probably that least likely at the time to be inspired by American ideals.

Over 100 Swedes served in the French forces, 116 with the Dutch and over 30 in the Continental navy or on American privateers.[7] Only after France entered the war, however, did any great enthusiasm develop among young Swedes to take part. Thereafter, they turned up in such numbers in Paris that Creutz hardly knew what to do with them. Fersen noted many Swedes in Paris in the winter of 1779–80 and no less than twelve serving in Brest. Most of the Swedish officers, seeking army commissions, were turned away, though a few may eventually have found places in the Continental forces. Fersen spoke in December 1780 of the arrival in Boston of "several Swedish officers who have come to the American army, from what I am told, and a M. Söderström to look after commercial matters."[8] Naval officers, meanwhile, were most welcome in France. Most of the Swedish officers were noblemen and officers in Swedish or in some cases French service when the war began. Most were dependent upon military employment and like other foreign officers who sought service in the war they were in straitened circumstances following a long period of peace in Europe. Stedingk wrote indignantly that the importunate demands of many of his countrymen for French commissions were "nothing more than disguised begging."[9] The largest group of Swedish officers served in the Dutch navy, which offered the greatest opportunities for foreigners.

Meanwhile, some fifty Swedes held commissions in the British navy, into which over 370 Swedish seamen were either enlisted or impressed. Few if any of the Swedish officers remained in America or later returned there. In general, they distinguished themselves in later life through loyal service to their king. As for Swedes below officer rank, their part in the war may on the whole be attributed to the vagaries of life at sea. In sum, the participation of Swedes in the war owed little to the attraction of American ideals.[10]

For his own part, Gustav III quickly overcame such early admiration as he might have felt for the American colonists. Thereafter, his correspondence repeatedly condemns the Americans as rebels against their rightful monarch.[11] He nevertheless sought to use the diplomatic situation created by the war to raise Sweden's strength and prestige among European nations following her long eclipse in the Era of Freedom. He took part in the League of Armed Neutrality of 1780 and encouraged his officers to serve in the French forces to increase the goodwill of his French ally, to prepare against a possible war in the North, and to restore respect for Swedish arms in Europe.

Gustav's correspondence with his ambassador in Paris reveals yet another ambition. In April 1779, Gustav directed Creutz to inform Count Fersen he was commissioned to "explore, quietly and under pretense of personal curiosity, the possibility of obtaining from the United States some district on the Continent of North America or some island in the vicinity." Gustav was at this time exerting influence to gain a commission for Fersen with the French army, presumably to go to America. Creutz believed a continental colony would be unfeasible, as the Americans desired to be "the sole masters there," and that a West Indian island would be preferable, to serve like Dutch St. Eustatius, as a depot for Swedish trade in the New World. The following spring, when Axel was departing for America, Creutz felt he should be able to act on this matter in concert with the French envoy in Philadelphia, the Chevalier de La Luzerne. Although Fersen gathered some information and saw La Luzerne in March 1782, if not before, Gustav III's project drops out of sight until 1784, when he obtained the island of St. Barthélemy from France.[12]

What then were Axel's own views toward the struggle in which he was to take part? Unfortunately, his diary for this period no longer survives. Years later, after the execution of Marie-Antoinette during the French Revolution, Fersen, then in Brussels, complained:

This terrible event makes me regret all the more the loss of my memoirs since the year 1780. I had written them day by day. I left them in Paris in 1791; when I left there, I did not dare take them with me, and the person with whom I left them burned them, in the fear that they might be seized while in his possession. They were precious notes on the Revolution which might have served . . . to write the history of that epoch. I regret their loss all the more because my memory is bad and I no longer remember what I did myself.[13]

The loss is scarcely less regrettable for what they might have revealed about the War of American Independence and events in Sweden in the 1780s.

Axel's letters to his family before his departure for America make no mention of the American Revolution as such or the reaction to it in France. Count Creutz was a close friend of Benjamin Franklin; Fersen's letters frequently speak of Creutz but never mention Franklin. Axel's joy over going to America can be adequately explained by his military ambitions and it does not appear that he concerned himself with events there until actually on the scene. His observations in the summer of 1778 on the anarchical consequences of British liberty, however, reveal little natural affinity for the American cause.

3

Fersen spent three years in America. The convoy carrying Rochambeau's small force sailed from Brest on 4 May 1780 and following a brush with five British warships, arrived on 11 July in Newport, Rhode Island, where it was promptly blockaded. It was not until the next summer that Rochambeau was able to attack the British.[14]

Meanwhile, Fersen thrived very well in Newport, where he lived in the home of Robert Stevens on New Lane (now Mary Street).[15] His closest comrades were the Duc de Lauzun and an Englishman in French service named Sheldon. Together they spent much time in the home of Mrs. Deborah Hunter, a widow with two charming daughters, one of whom, Axel wrote his sister, was "a pretty girl of eighteen years, gay, amiable, witty, who plays the clavichord and sings perfectly. I spend every evening teaching her French." He later mentioned the girl was helping him with English, which proved useful, for by September he served General Rochambeau as an interpreter. By this time too, the Marquis de Laval, colonel of the Bourbonnais Regiment, was teaching him to exercise a platoon.[16] Clearly, despite his study of military science in Brunswick, Strasbourg, and Turin, and his Swedish commission, Fersen, like many high aristocratic officers of the time, had little experience with the actual command of troops. He nonetheless deserves credit for making the most of his opportunity to learn all he could about the military profession. His letters to his father are filled with detailed and accurate accounts of military operations and his own speculations on the shifting strategic situation. When many of the French officers took passage home to spend the winter of 1781–82 in Paris, Fersen wrote:

I will stay here, I would have no other reason to go to Paris except my amusement and pleasure; I must sacrifice them.... I should prefer ...to make one more campaign here and to finish what I had begun. When I made the resolve to stay here, I foresaw all the boredom I would have to put up with; it is proper that the experience which I may acquire here should cost me something.[17]

Meanwhile, Fersen seems to have filled a responsible position. Before sailing from Brest, he had written his father that he was one of six aides, the only one with the rank of colonel. "As there is no general staff worth speaking of for his army, the general's aides-de-camp will fulfill its functions." Fersen's conception of his own importance at this time was apparently rather sanguine, for later he complained he was not given enough responsibility. Of the aides, however, he still seems the one on whom the general relied the most.[18]

Although Axel was usually reticent about describing his personal part in the operations, his letters give occasional glimpses of his activities. He accompanied Rochambeau to meet General Washington in Hartford on 22 September 1780 and at Weathersfield, Connecticut, on 22 May 1781. He was sent to Washington again in January 1781 to smooth out some minor friction between the allied commanders. In August 1781, after the French had joined the Americans at Phillipsburg, New Jersey, they received word of the arrival of their fleet under Admiral de Grasse from the West Indies. Fersen was immediately sent to Newport to direct Admiral Barras to proceed from there with his small squadron to join de Grasse and to arrange sea transportation for the French siege artillery to Chesapeake Bay.[19]

This mission completed, Fersen returned to the French army, which began its march southward, feinting toward New York and Sandy Hook to throw the British off the scent. "We crossed Jersey," Fersen relates, "which is one of the most beautiful provinces in America and one of the best cultivated." In Philadelphia, the army paraded for the inhabitants, "who had never seen so many men uniformed and armed alike, nor so well disciplined." The expedition took ship in Annapolis—where Fersen was involved with the embarkation—for Virginia. Fersen took part in the siege of Yorktown, but though he wrote a detailed account, he characteristically included next to nothing about himself. Next month, however, Creutz wrote to Gustav III from Paris:

The Duc de Lauzun who has returned with the news [of Yorktown] has given a flattering testimony of honor about the young Count Fersen. He told me that in all the operations where the fighting was intense, Fersen was present, now in the trenches and now in the midst of the attack, and that he exhibited the most brilliant proofs of valor.[20]

After the fall of Yorktown in October 1781, the war on the North American continent was virtually over. The French army wintered at Williamsburg, "an ugly little town which is more like a village."[21] Early in 1782, Fersen took a sightseeing tour around Virginia with the Chevalier de La Luzerne, noting its topography, its tobacco cultivation, its inhabitants, both black and white, and not least of all the wretched inns, where one could drink only rum or hard cider and eat only salt pork and corn pone, the preparation of which he described in detail. Fortunately the travelers carried their own supply of "*pâtés*, ham, wines, and bread."[22] Some months later, in August 1782, Fersen spoke of attending a conference between Rochambeau and Washington, this resulting in his being sent to Yorktown to arrange the secret removal of the French siege artillery by sea without escort to Baltimore.[23] Already in October 1780, Fersen had written his father that he hoped for a command of his own. The Duc de Lauzun was considering turning his personal "legion" over to him, without the customary payment, for, as he said, "I do not sell men."[24] After interminable delays, however, the project fell through by early 1782, in Axel's view, due to intrigues at Versailles, and because Lauzun, despite his proud gesture, changed his mind. Possibly Lauzun, who never mentions Fersen in his memoirs, was jealous of Fersen's favor with the queen. Meanwhile, Axel's fellow aide on Rochambeau's staff, Baron Ludwig von Closen, wrote in August, "Through Comte de *Fersen's* and the Duc de *Lauzun's* connections with the *leading figures at the court,* some of us were educated in all the particulars concerning *politics, intrigues and cabals* in Paris."[25] In September, Fersen was appointed to a field post as *colonel en second* of the Régiment Royal Deux-Ponts, to which he had until then been attached as a supernumerary officer, to the chagrin of its veteran lieutenant colonel. In Closen's view, "The Comte de Fersen was too well liked at Court!!!"[26]

The French expeditionary force sailed from Boston in December 1782 for Porto Caballo in the Spanish captaincy-general of Venezuela. Here it waited nearly two months to be joined by a Spanish expedition preparing in Cadiz, to undertake a new venture against the British in the West Indies, presumably an attack on Jamaica.[27] From Porto Caballo, Axel wrote Sophie:

We are dying of boredom here, we are growing thin, drying out, aging, turning yellow with heat and monotony. In this wretched country there are no amenities; one cannot here satisfy any of the five senses. One sees nothing but black here—not a trace of white anywhere. Man is not made to live here but it is so much the better suited for tigers, bears [*sic*], and crocodiles. They say Caracas, which is 36 leagues from here is a beautiful city, that there is society there, pretty women, who have nothing black about them except their eyes. . . .

He planned to leave on 14 March for a two-week visit to Caracas— as most senior French officers managed to do—though there is no later mention of this intended excursion. Meanwhile, the Spaniards —who Fersen sourly commented, "never hurry"—never arrived. Instead came the news of the peace settlement in Paris and on 3 April 1783, the French sailed for home. After stopping a fortnight at Cap Français in Santo Domingo, they arrived in Brest on 17 June and Fersen hurried back to Paris and a hero's welcome.[28]

4

Throughout the war, Axel wrote, as seen, frequent and extensive letters to his father. For the most part, his comments are limited to military matters. Here and there, however, they give glimpses of Fersen's own views of what was going on around him.

Since returning to the Continent in 1778, Axel had been keenly observant of military affairs and his comments on the French army already show his views on the nation and army with which he served. In Normandy in 1778, he praised the smartness with which the French troops carried out "the new tactics of M. de Ménil-Durand." He noted their admirable discipline, fine appearance, and good behavior, as well as the excellent feeding and lodging of the men. It was, however, characteristic that Fersen considered a German mercenary brigade "the finest, as much by the appearance of the men as by the precision and attentiveness in the exercise." To Fersen, himself a foreigner seeking appointment in the French service, nationality meant nothing among soldiers. The exercise meanwhile revealed weaknesses in the organization and leadership, and certain French officers complimented Field Marshal Fersen's service to France by saying he had been "the first to introduce order and discipline."[29]

In Fersen's eyes, the greatest problems affecting the military emanated from the civil government and the court. He strongly criticized the confusion surrounding the preparations for the Marshal de Vaux's expedition in 1779. "Nobody knows what will be done; it is said that the ministry knows nothing about it." In the face of this, the army did its best though the navy was, in Axel's view, "an undisciplined and undisciplinable corps." He made similar criticisms of the preparations for Rochambeau's force at Brest. "No order in the operations," he wrote his father, "no set plan; they only take council of the moment.... the means are always lacking because they are not anticipated..."[30]

During the American campaign, he at first admired the correct behavior of the French troops in Newport, "which astonishes the inhabitants, who are accustomed to the pillage of the English and their own troops," but later expressed disillusionment over what he considered the characteristic lack of discipline in the French army. As for the noble courtiers who had vied so hard to obtain places in it, Fersen commented ironically on their despair at being forced to winter in Newport, far from the delights of Paris, which only an order to march against the enemy could console.[31]

Considering Fersen's own place in French society, he could hardly be considered anything but one of the *gens de cour* himself. In America, despite high prices, he provided himself with amenities suitable to his rank and station, including a *valet de chambre* and two grooms, one of whom had some practice in "bloodletting and a bit of medicine," and for a time a cook, borrowed from Lauzun. He estimated his monthly expenses in 1782 at 420 *livres* or in round figures, 6,000 per year.[32] Yet he prided himself on his Nordic stoicism in the face of hardship, considering this quite beyond the French courtiers in the army. During the Yorktown campaign, he slept on the ground under an ordinary soldier's blanket. In April 1782, he rode from Williamsburg to Philadelphia and back, 700 English miles, in eight days, including a whole day in Philadelphia and "at least four or five hours sleep each night," astonishing everyone, especially the Americans, and establishing his reputation as the speediest man in the French army. From Williamsburg, he wrote proudly that Rochambeau pointed him out to the young French courtiers as an outstanding example of hardihood and when the latter hastened to return to Paris for the winter after the siege of Yorktown, expecting to be promoted to brigadiers for their exploits, Axel took pride in remaining with the army.[33]

Fersen's relations with the general had their ups and downs. He at first regarded Rochambeau as ideal for his position, though later, when he had served with him for some months, he became more critical. He was often offended by the general's brusque manner, secretiveness, and suspicion, as well as his reliance for advice upon certain old veterans of unprepossessing social origins. At times, Fersen complained that Rochambeau would make a good subordinate but was a mediocre commander. Doubtless much of the friction was inherent in Fersen's position as aide-de-camp, especially during the early months when the army languished in unwelcome inactivity and he himself still lacked experience. After Yorktown, Fersen's attitude toward his chief softened considerably and when Rochambeau returned to France in late 1782, he wrote that the whole army sincerely regretted his departure, having been glad to serve under him.[34]

Fersen's views on America underwent a marked change. Durand Echeverria gives him as a prime example of those officers in the French expeditionary force who were strongly anti-American in attitude.[35] It would, however, be a mistake to assume that Fersen held such views from the start.

At first, he showed considerable enthusiasm for America. As

we have seen, he enjoyed Newport and on his way to Boston and
the West Indies two years later, made a detour to take leave of his
friends there. The latter did not forget him. In 1818, his nephew,
Baron Axel Leonhard Klinckowström, visiting Washington, D. C.,
met a Mr. Hunter from Rhode Island who remembered Count
Fersen well and said his family still possessed letters from him.[36]
Witness also the following, from a letter from September 1780:

We had excessive heat here during the month of August; I never felt
anything like it in Italy. Now the air is cooler. It is a superb climate
and a charming country. We were on the mainland eight days ago
with the general . . . and we saw the most beautiful country in the world,
well-cultivated, charming views, comfortable inhabitants, but without
luxury and without ostentation; they content themselves with those bare
necessities which in other countries are reserved only for an inferior
class; their dress is simple but good and their manners have not yet
been corrupted by the luxury of the Europeans.[37]

As noted, the influence of the Abbé Raynal here seems manifest.
A few days later, Fersen accompanied Rochambeau to Hartford to
meet General Washington:

M. de Rochambeau sent me on ahead to announce his arrival, and I
had time to see this man, illustrious, if not unique, in our century. His
countenance, beautiful and majestic, but at the same time, gentle and
honest, corresponds perfectly with his moral qualities; he has the appearance of a hero; he is very withdrawn, speaks little, but is polite
and genteel. An air of sadness adorns his physiognomy, which is not
unbecoming to him and which makes him more interesting.

This description sounds rather like an idealized picture of Fersen
himself. Perhaps he saw in the American hero something of his
own self-image. Washington, for his part, was apparently well
impressed with the young Swede.[38]

Fersen's enthusiasm for America and the Americans, however,
soon cooled. In particular, he found fault with what he considered
their poor showing as soldiers and what struck him as their
exceptionally mercenary nature.

As an officer accustomed to European armies, Fersen was
naturally baffled by the nondescript forces of the rebellious
colonials and was not overly impressed with their military qualities
by his own standards. His letters from Newport in 1780–81 are

filled with reports of the lack of discipline and the cowardice of the American militia.[39] He meanwhile frankly admired the British. While in England in 1778, he had observed their military exercises with great interest. He did not then find their troops impressive-looking; they did not march or hold formation well, nor did they show much subordination to their officers, who were so inept that noncommissioned officers instructed them and even maneuvered whole companies. Nevertheless, the men impressed Axel with their toughness and good morale, qualities he could not but admire in them in America. Like many of his fellow officers in the French army, he was deeply moved by the execution of the unfortunate Major André in 1780. The war, he wrote, did honor to the British.[40] His admiration for them was that of a professional soldier for a professional army he could often feel was fighting a better war than his own or that of his allies. His professional pride shows in all his letters at this time and from Porto Caballo he wrote concerning the impending peace, "I do not know whether to rejoice over this; I like war very much," though, he added, "I do not like the theater where it is taking place."[41]

Fersen's criticisms of the fighting qualities of the Americans were, however, based on a dark period for them in the war, while the French remained inactive. After he had fought beside them at Yorktown, he must have formed a higher opinion of them, for he no longer made the same accusations.

Meanwhile, Fersen took the Americans severely to task for their hardheaded mercenary demands. Since he spoke English, which was rare among the French officers, he was probably often required to bargain with local farmers and merchants over army purchase contracts, a task for which he was fitted by neither taste nor background. The French, he wrote in October 1780, were forced to observe great economies "in a country where one must always have money in hand." By the following winter, he was complaining that the Americans were both lazy and selfish, that they were as ready to sell to the British as to the French and that in general, "they take more after the Dutch than the English." When General Rochambeau left the army in the fall of 1782, Fersen praised him above all for the tact with which he had maintained harmony between two allies who basically had little liking for each other. The Americans, he added, had "taught us neither to love them nor to respect them." It was with such comments that Fersen departed America. For many officers in the French force, the experience had been a very different one and they left with sincere regrets.[42]

There remains the question of Fersen's reactions to the political revolution going on around him. In September 1780, he described the struggle as he saw it:

[America] . . . is a country which will be very happy, if it can enjoy a long peace and if the two factions which divide it at present do not cause it to suffer the fate of Poland and of so many other republics. These two parties are called the *whigs* and the *tories*: the first is entirely for liberty and independence, it is composed of people of the lowest origin who possess no property; most of the country people are in it. The *tories* are for the English, or, more properly speaking, for peace, without worrying themselves too much whether they are free or dependent; these are people of a more distinguished class, the only ones who own property in the country; some have relatives and property in England, others, in order to keep what they have in this country have embraced the English cause, which was the strongest. When the Whigs are the strongest, they pillage the others as much as possible. This gives rise to a hatred between them and an animosity which will be difficult to extinguish and will always be the germ of a thousand troubles.[43]

Fersen naturally saw the struggle in terms of European experience. The recent example of Poland might well be uppermost in a Swedish mind at that time and among the "other republics" was doubtless Sweden itself before Gustav III's coup of 1772. To Fersen's mind, the American Tories and Whigs, backed by Britain and France, must have looked like the Russian and French parties in the Polish diet or the French-backed "Hats" and Russian-backed "Caps" in the Swedish Riksdag.

He thus viewed the American Revolution as essentially a civil war between domestic factions backed by foreign powers, yet at the same time recognized a class conflict between the propertied and unpropertied elements of society, albeit in oversimplified form. He saw that what was taking place was not simply a war for independence but a real revolution.

A few months later, Fersen wrote to his father:

. . . the spirit of patriotism is only to be found among the leaders and principal people of the country, who make great sacrifices; the others, who are in the majority, think only of their personal interest . . . everyone is for himself, no one for the public welfare. . . . This is not to say that there are not admirable men, whose character is equally noble and generous; there are many, but I speak of the nation in general. . . .[44]

Here again Fersen's background as a Swede, a nobleman, and the son of his father comes to the surface and reveals the social and political beliefs underlying his mistrust of "republics." He believed among the "principal people of the country" were men whose integrity, disinterestedness, and devotion to the public weal made them a natural elite best fitted to rule. These would, however, always be in the minority in any society, thus unable to prevent the majority from forming irresponsible and self-interested factions, harmful to the nation as a whole. In these views, he resembled his father, who though a strong upholder of parliamentary liberties had by 1772 accepted Gustav III's curtailment of the unlimited power of the estates and the establishment of stronger monarchical power in Sweden.[45]

Perhaps the example of Poland was again in Axel's mind in June 1781, when he suspected the British of wishing to partition America, keeping the southern colonies, where they were spending money and making friends, and letting the northern colonies go. His remarks on the Virginians almost a year later meanwhile show the centrifugal forces which he saw as inherent in "republics":

It seems in effect that the Virginians are another race of people; instead of occupying themselves with their farms and with commerce, each proprietor wishes to be a lord. . . . All of those who engage in commerce are regarded here as inferior to the others; they say they are not gentlemen and they do not wish to live in the same society with them. They have all the aristocratic principles and when one sees them, one can scarcely understand how they have been able to enter into the general confederation and to accept a government based upon a perfect equality of condition; but the same spirit which has brought them to free themselves from the English yoke might well lead them on to new undertakings, and I would not be surprised to see Virginia detach itself after the peace from the other states. I would not even be surprised to see the American government become a perfect aristocracy.[46]

The ways in which Axel reacted to the Americans, their society and revolution were thus conditioned by his own family background, noble status, and Swedish nationality. On the one hand, he showed a patrician distaste for American materialism and utilitarianism; on the other, a natural fear for a "republican" or "aristocratic" form of government—in his mind nearly synonymous—considering the experiences of Sweden and Poland in the middle years of the century. A French nobleman, inspired by the ideas of the Enlightenment and far from the example of the northern European "republics," might well show greater enthusiasm for that form of government. Yet whatever his opinions about American political principles, he was deeply impressed with what was taking place. When in the fall of 1782, his father entreated him to return to Sweden, Axel wrote back:

Everyone would find it extraordinary that at the moment when it is about to finish, at the moment when this new continent is on the point of obtaining through a glorious peace the liberty for which it has fought, I should choose this moment to quit. I myself would despair at not being witness to so memorable an event.[47]

CHAPTER III

Fersen, Gustav III, and Sweden, 1783–1789

1

Fersen's participation in the American war brought its rewards. In 1781, Gustav III presented him *in absentia* with the Order of the Sword, the following year promoted him to colonel in the Swedish army, and in 1783 made him lieutenant colonel in the Light Dragoons with the right of reversion to the post of "captain-lieutenant" in the *Livdrabantkår* or Life-Guards. As seen, he was made *colonel en second* or second in command of the French Royal-Deux Ponts regiment. After his return to France, Louis XVI presented him with the order, *Pour le mérite militaire.*[1]

One thing remained to satisfy his military ambition: the command and ownership—after the usage of the day—of his own regiment. The idea was not new. A note apparently dating from late 1778 or early 1779, inserted into his diary, shows even then he had been thinking of this for some time.[2] It was natural that he should wish to climax his military career in France in the way his father had done before him.

Axel wrote his father on this matter already from Santo Domingo. While he avowed his pleasure at the prospect of seeing him again, he requested that he be allowed to defer his return to Sweden until the following spring, not wishing to lose the advantages earned in French service before seeking his own regiment. He maintained that such an appointment would be mainly "honorific and profitable," and would not require that he remain abroad permanently. To sweeten the pill, he broached the idea of marriage. He had

37

occasionally written to Miss Leyel while in America and would renew his suite. If this match should fail, there was another possibility, Mlle. Gérmaine Necker, who was both rich and Protestant, though if his friend Staël at the Swedish embassy in Paris had any prospects with her, he would not stand in his way. At the same time, he wrote Gustav III, requesting permission to enjoy the "fruits of three years of war" by obtaining a regiment in France, assuring him that this would not keep him from serving in Sweden as well.[3]

Arriving in Paris, Fersen found neither marriage match was possible. Catherine Leyel had married the Earl of Delawarr and Staël had hopes with Mlle. Necker, who herself was apparently not uninterested in Axel. He wrote his father that he felt in no hurry to marry and that bachelorhood suited him very well. He was given lodgings by the hospitable Staël and urged his father to use his influence to help obtain for his friend the position of successor to Count Creutz at the Paris embassy. Meanwhile, Fersen set about procuring a regiment with zest and determination. He still hoped to acquire Lauzun's Legion, but found the duke no longer interested.[4]

Fersen thus turned to the Royal-Suédois regiment, founded in 1690 with mercenary troops in Dutch service who had been taken prisoner in the War of the League of Augsburg. It was now composed mainly of German mercenary troops but was from the beginning officered by the sons of illustrious Swedish noble families. The regiment was at this time the property of Alexandre and Ernest Sparre, members of a French branch of their family.[5]

The brothers Sparre were willing to part with their regiment for 100,000 livres from Fersen and the *Cordon bleu* of the Order of the Seraphim from Gustav III. Fersen thought the decoration an "exorbitant extravagance," but did his best to persuade both Fredrik Axel and the Swedish king to provide for these demands. He wrote repeatedly to his father, pointing out the advantages of such a regiment. It would be a profitable source of income and would provide training, experience, and revenue, not only for himself, but for his brother Fabian and their children in future years. He had no intention to expatriate himself. Count Creutz and the Baron de Breteuil were doing their best to expedite matters. There was only the matter of money. Axel besought his father to advance the necessary funds from his future inheritance.[6]

By August, Axel began to receive replies from his father, strongly opposing his project, claiming he could not spare the money, that his son had been expensive enough already and admonishing him not to put hopes in the favors of monarchs, for "if ever your fortune is dissipated, your esteem is also and you will find neither friends nor protector."[7] Axel continued to plead his case with a show of ardor unusual for him. His letters to his father since leaving Sweden in 1778, with their constant discussion of his economic circumstances, appeals for money, and protestations of the strictest economies, doubtless explain in large part his determination for an "existence" of his own, independent of the family fortune. Playing on his father's mistrust of monarchs, he shrewdly argued that with appointments and incomes in two countries, he could always withdraw from one or the other if not rendered "justice" and would thus enjoy greater "consideration" in both. The anticipated income of 12,000 livres from the regiment would provide for amortization of his debt and together with his Swedish appointments, allow "an agreeable existence." He wrote Gustav III and Sophie, urging them to support his cause with his father.[8]

Correspondence with his father became heated. Fredrik Axel suspected his son of being simply attracted by the pleasures of Paris and of wishing to expatriate himself, which Axel bitterly denied. Gustav III meanwhile sent him a letter for the French king, recommending Axel for the position of colonel of the Royal-Suédois, which Axel delivered at Versailles in September. He meanwhile arranged a loan upon the security of the Baron de Breteuil before his father could write—as he did—forbidding him to contract financial obligations. The same month, Axel received the appointment and arranged for his friend, Curt von Stedingk, to serve as his *colonel-commandant,* or lieutenant colonel in charge. He meanwhile still hoped to get the 100,000 livres from his father. "What use is it, at the age of 60, to have a considerable fortune," he wrote bitterly to the sixty-four-year-old Fredrik Axel. "That is no longer the time when one wishes to enjoy it and it is not possible to do so."[9]

2

Meanwhile, Axel decided he should return to Sweden without further delay, to straighten out his affairs with his father; he set out in September. After visiting Fabian, studying in Strasbourg with Bolemany, he quickly crossed Germany, arriving in Wismar, where he visited his brother-in-law, Baron Thure Klinckowström, an official in the Swedish administration there, who gave him a letter from the king. In it, Gustav III announced he was undertaking a grand tour on the Continent and requested Axel's presence in his entourage. Axel immediately wrote his father of his disappointment that after so long a separation their reunion should be further postponed, but that duty demanded he heed a master "who has never ceased to heap benefits upon me."[10]

By the fall of 1783, Fersen had been away from his native land for five and a half years, during which time great changes had been taking place on the Swedish political scene. His diary (until 1779) and letters during his absence seldom mention Sweden and almost never political developments there. His frequent letters to his father during Gustav III's grand tour give the first real insight into his own personal relationship with the king and reactions to the new state of affairs in Sweden.

What then was the situation there?[11] On 19 August 1772, a year after his accession, Gustav III carried out a *coup d'état* which by strengthening the power of the crown, brought to an end the tumultuous and perilous Era of Freedom. The king's action was generally accepted with relief by all orders of society. Even Fredrik Axel von Fersen put his hopes in the change and accepted appointment to the new state council.[12] From Turin, Axel wrote his father that October:

Your last [letter] . . . overjoyed me with the ample and at the same time instructive account that you had the kindness to give me of the felicitous revolution of 19 August. Together with you, I cannot admire enough the tranquility with which it passed and the prudence, benevolence, and courage of our young king, who offers his life to the good and the liberty of his subjects, and who instead of abusing his power, uses it only to make them happy and to secure for them a stable government.[13]

A little over two years later, when Axel returned to Sweden, he found Gustav III and his regime still at the height of their popularity, and he departed abroad again just before the first signs of friction began to appear at the Riksdag of 1778.

Gustav III's new constitution of 1772 provided a system of checks and balances much admired in philosophic circles. The king and the estates shared in legislation while the latter controlled taxation. Among other things, the king was forbidden to undertake offensive war without their consent. He was meanwhile bound to consult with the *råd* or state council on important matters of state.[14]

The king stated his ideal to be the balanced polity of the great Gustav Adolf and in the new constitution proclaimed his abhorrence of "a king's despotic power, or the so-called sovereignty."[15] Acute observers were not, however, long in perceiving loopholes in the new system which gave the monarch greater room to maneuver than appearances would suggest, and as time passed, Gustav gave cause for grievance to various groups within his realm. It seems doubtful that he originally drafted his constitution without intending eventually to subvert and bypass it; certainly he revealed from the start a strong inclination for personal rule.[16] Seven months after his appointment, Fredrik Axel von Fersen resigned from the council, ostensibly because of "diminishing strength and increasing years."[17] At the Riksdag of 1778, however, he formed the natural focal point for the hopes of the opposition, despite his stated intention simply to maintain the inviolability of the new constitution. This brought him into strained relations with the king, which Axel wrote in January 1779 aroused great interest in Paris society: "Mme. de La Marck and Mme. de Boufflers censure you strongly but Mme. d'Usson has taken your side." All wanted further details which Axel was unable to provide.[18]

Thereafter, Gustav III's reforming zeal, which had met with general approval, became increasingly overshadowed by his desire to make a mark on the international scene. In this he was abetted by Ambassador Creutz in Paris, who in 1779 suggested an ambitious plan for Sweden to seize Norway from Denmark, an idea Gustav himself had long cherished. Creutz's proposal gave rise to a chain of events leading eventually to the king's tour on the Continent in the fall of 1783, at which time Creutz returned to Stockholm to take charge of foreign affairs.

The American war and Sweden's rapprochement with Denmark and her ally, Russia, in the League of Armed Neutrality of 1780 intervened, but Gustav did not lost sight of Creutz's project. He sought to wean Catherine II from her Danish alliance through a show of warm affability, meanwhile making secret military preparations with the help of certain of his favorites. To avoid suspicion, he planned a journey to the Continent, ostensibly to visit the thermal waters of Pisa. To accompany him, he gathered his current group of favorites. These included Baron Evert Taube and his younger rival, the Finnish Baron Gustav Mauritz Armfelt, Barons Jacob Cederström and Hans Henrik von Essen, Carl Peijron, and the diplomat Ulrik Gustaf Franc, the sculptor Johan Tobias Sergel, the littérateur Gudmund Göran Adlerbeth, and Baron Fredrik Sparre, the member of the royal council responsible for military matters, who was thus conveniently removed from Sweden. There, certain of the king's confidants, among them Creutz, remained behind to prepare for "The Great Affair."[19]

3

Fersen caught up with the royal suite at Erlangen in mid-October 1783, where, as he wrote his father, Gustav III received him like a long-lost brother and singled him out for special distinction among the group. Fredrik Axel, disappointed that his son's return should thus be delayed, grumbled that Axel's *"corvée"* would be a hard one, since the king had such a talent for wearing out his courtiers that he had already "sent several of them to the other world."[20]

Though Gustav was doubtless delighted to see Axel again, political motives were hardly absent from his choice of him as a traveling companion. By 1783, the elder Fersen's relationship with the king had cooled considerably and Gustav probably wished to assure himself of the goodwill of his son before he could return to Sweden following his years abroad and there be won over to the growing opposition.[21]

Axel's personal relations with the king had always been very good. He soon, however, began to tire of the journey. He had to accompany Gustav constantly as an interpreter: "It seems that I am destined for this task; I already did it for M. de Rochambeau for three years, but that was more instructive and more interesting."[22] He became increasingly critical of his traveling companions and of the king himself. He complained of the dreariness of Italy during the winter and the lack of diversion. Others in the party, such as Armfelt and Adlerbeth, less blasé than Fersen, left more enthusiastic accounts. The group spent some time in Pisa, where the king, traveling as the "Count of Haga," visited the thermal baths and where they met the Grand Duke Leopold of Tuscany, whom they at first mistook for a valet. From here, the party continued to Florence, where they met Emperor Joseph II, then also traveling incognito as the "Count of Falkenstein," who impressed Axel with his seriousness and simplicity of manner. Here also they visited Prince Charles Edward Stuart, the aging pretender to the British throne, who was understood to possess Freemasonic secrets of the most esoteric nature and whom Armfelt described as full of romantic sentiment and possessed of a dignified grace, worthy of his race and rank. Gustav III granted the unfortunate prince a small pension from his privy purse. In Florence, too, Axel became involved in a brief, but to all appearances, intense affair with an English Miss Gower.[23]

In Rome, the group again encountered Emperor Joseph. The two monarchs attended a high mass at St. Peter's where, according to Fersen, "it was an extraordinary sight to see a king and an emperor mixing with the people, attending the Mass, and to see the pope pass with all the appearance of a sovereign. This would be a good lesson for a young prince; he would learn by this the nature of human grandeur." The Swedes were put in an even more somber frame of mind when they witnessed the acceptance of a 17-year-old girl into a nunnery and the philosophical Adlerbeth inveighed against the tyranny of popery and superstition.[24]

Axel complained in Rome, "We live in a perpetual state of giddiness, and although we have nothing to do, it seems that we do not have enough time to do everything. It is a useless activity, which is discouraging." The Swedes were presented to the pope in the "Swedish dress" the king had designed, but Fersen was relieved that they were usually allowed to dress "*à la française*."[25]

A few weeks later, Axel wrote his father a letter which summed up his feelings for the king and his traveling companions:

We have a principle of disorder and irresolution which is rare; we change our minds twenty times a day, and each idea is more extraordinary than the last. I am at the point of despair to be on this voyage; . . . it has obliged me to be the witness, each day, of new follies, of new extravagances, and of new absurdities. We have nothing else to do, Baron Taube and I, but to try to prevent them and to repair them; but that is not always possible, and it is very unpleasant to be here.

All of this had affected his feelings toward the king:

It is quite extraordinary, that with so many talents, so many attainments, and so much spirit, one could have so many failings. I am very sorry about this, for I am and I should be attached to him for my whole life; he has done everything for me and one cannot know him without being very attached to him and without lamenting his weaknesses.

Certainly Axel still felt deeply attached to his king through bonds of affection and gratitude, but was disillusioned by what he now saw of him. Sadly he compared Gustav III and his retinue with Joseph: "The great simplicity of his manners, of his discourse and of his dress, contrasted sharply with the elegance and levity of our own; he had a solid appearance and we a frivolous one. I do not know whether the contrast was altogether to our advantage. . . ." The real source of trouble, in Axel's view, lay in the king's young companions, whom travel had not edified in the least. Except for the older Baron Taube, he felt little in common with any of them.[26]

Among the king's favorites, the one most feared and criticized in Sweden was Gustav Mauritz Armfelt, whose own letters from the journey reveal a friendly enough attitude toward Axel. "Fersen and I rage like madmen against the voyage, the roads, and human caprice," he wrote his fiancée in December. Their relationship would undergo many vicissitudes in the years to come and would never be a close one as far as Axel was concerned. Evert Taube, on the other hand, became thereafter his closest personal friend. Meanwhile, though Gustav continued to treat Fersen with special distinction, his patience was sometimes put to the test. "It is known here," Elis Schröderheim wrote the king from Stockholm in March 1784, "how Your Majesty's suite is divided into two parties: Baron Taube, Count Fersen, Councillor Sparre in the one; Baron Armfelt, Baron Essen, Peijron in the other, and Baron Cederström neutral." To a friend, Schröderheim confided in July, "The king has been quite disgusted with Fersen during the whole voyage and several times with Taube." Leopold of Tuscany informed his brother Joseph II in November 1783 that Gustav III showed "much suspicion" toward those who accompanied him, and a fortnight later:

He has not been greatly applauded in Italy up to the present, nor has his suite. Councillor Sparre, a man of parts, does not conceal at all his disapproval of the voyage and the conduct of the king, and the young men, his favorites, and especially Baron Armfelt, make themselves scarcely agreeable through their hauteur and their ways, and particularly Count Fersen, who even gives witness to contempt in public for the king.

The political aspect of the favor Axel enjoyed emerges yet more clearly: Creutz could write Gustav III in November 1783 that the elder Fersen was "keeping quiet," meanwhile Axel wrote nothing during the royal tour to indicate that he was aware of its diplomatic purposes. Indeed, considering who he was, Gustav surely did his best to keep him from finding out.[27]

In January, the "Count of Haga" and his party arrived in Naples for the *Carnivale,* which Gustav III, Armfelt, and their host, King Ferdinand IV, enjoyed with gay abandon. On more than one occasion, Armfelt wrestled with His Sicilian Majesty and he became fast friends with both Ferdinand, whom Fersen regarded as something of a diamond in the rough, and Queen Caroline, the sister of Emperor Joseph, Grand Duke Leopold, and Queen Marie-Antoinette, who, Fersen noted, "like all of the house of Austria," had spirit, liked to govern, and did so. Gustav was rather overwhelmed by Ferdinand's passion for boar hunting. As for Fersen, he soon became acquainted with Lady Elizabeth Foster, daughter of the Earl of Bristol, and the recent victim of a broken marriage, with whom he soon developed a warm and lasting friendship.[28]

While still in Rome, Axel, having learned of the new American Order of the Cincinnati and his eligibility for it, wrote Staël, now ambassador in Paris, to make sure he was not overlooked. In Naples, he learned from General Rochambeau that he was included and wrote Staël for copies of the relevant documents. On 14 February, he wrote Stedingk, the only other Swede eligible, that Gustav III was displeased he had not requested permission to wear the order and that it was "necessary that he should write an antedated letter and simply request that he be permitted to wear it in Sweden as though this were beyond doubt in France." Gustav meanwhile urged Louis XVI not to allow his subjects to accept the American order and flatly refused to permit either Fersen or Stedingk to wear it. Fersen was highly incensed, remonstrated vigorously with the king, and wrote Creutz, urging him to persuade Gustav III to change his mind. Creutz did his best but the king wrote him from Turin on 26 May:

As far as the American order is concerned, I remain adamant in my position. This mark is intended to commemorate a rebellion which, although crowned with success, is still criminal in the eyes of a king. It is not for the sake of the king of England that I will not allow my subjects to wear it; it is for my own sake, for that of all kings, whose cause this is. It is in order not to show before the eyes of my nation that Swedes may decorate themselves with such a mark.

He objected moreover to the idea that anyone but princes could create "knights," which "neither mighty Venice nor proud Holland in their time of glory considered themselves competent to do." Perhaps more to the point, he wrote Stedingk on 26 March: "Too recently having ourselves escaped from our troubles that there should not still exist, no doubt, some germs of our former divisions, it is my duty to avert anything that could reawaken such ideas." Fredrik Axel von Fersen, meanwhile, characteristically saw no reason why the Order of the Cincinnati could not be worn in the same way as those of other "republics," such as that of the Maltese Knights, and held it an honor to receive such a distinction from men who "dared all to free themselves from the oppression of royal power."[29]

From Naples, the royal party returned to Rome, then proceeded to Parma, with the king riding by preference in Axel's light German *chaise*. Here the ducal house regaled them with balls, masquerades, concerts, and *"contredanses à cheval."* "It seems to me," Axel wrote his father on 27 April, "... that balls, assemblies, fêtes, and divertissements are more beautiful and pleasant in the gazettes and from afar than from close by. For some time now all these things bore me and I prefer to the noise and excitement of the great world the tranquility and charm of a small society." The king, he added, persisted in his absurd refusal to permit him to wear his Order of the Cincinnati, which, to add insult to injury, had been stolen from him by a pickpocket in the Vatican. On 3 August, however, he noted in his letter register that he had ordered a "small Cincinnatus" in Paris.[30]

The "Count of Haga" next visited Venice, where the *Carnivale* was postponed until his arrival. Gustav was fascinated with its fairy-tale atmosphere and myriad delights, though by now even the exuberant Armfelt was beginning to flag. Most of the entourage now returned to Sweden, while the king, with Taube, Armfelt, Peijron, and Fersen, left for Paris, arriving in early June.[31]

The five weeks Gustav III now spent in Paris were surely one of the high points of his life. He visited the Académie Française, the Parlement, the park at Ermenonville, the porcelain manufactory at Sèvres; he watched Franz Anton Mesmer demonstrate "animal magnetism" and the ascent of a Montgolfier balloon in his honor. He attended theater and opera tirelessly, and visited the notables of the cultural world, especially the *grandes dames* who reigned over the Parisian literary *salons*. Axel complained that the king's insatiable search for pleasure amounted to a "mania."[32] The climax was a magnificent fête given by Marie-Antoinette at the Trianon, including a lavish performance of *Le Dormeur éveillé* by Marmontel and Grétry, followed by a supper in the open air and the illumination of the English garden. The only incident that marred the king's stay was the death of Peijron in a duel with the Comte de La Marck. Meanwhile, Gustav III's personal relationship with the French royal family was not improved by the visit. His affability toward Mme. du Barry and the Comte de Provence while in Paris in 1771 had offended Marie-Antoinette and it would seem his pretentions in 1784 did not help to ingratiate himself; Gustav was meanwhile apparently irritated by the French queen's coquettishness.[33] In years to come, each would have reason to wish for the other's support, a circumstance of decisive importance for Axel Fersen.

Gustav III's secret plans had in the meantime not fared as he had hoped. Catherine II, having solved her Crimean problem and learning of Gustav's true intentions, sharply reminded him of her obligations to her Danish ally. It was probably at this point that he began to think of a showdown with Russia at the first opportunity, rather than the immediate conquest of Norway. On 19 July 1784, he concluded at Versailles a new defensive and subsidy treaty with France, which included the cession of the small West Indian island of St. Barthélemy, finally realizing Gustav's dream of a New World colony.

The king also took the opportunity to settle the details of Fersen's appointment as proprietary colonel of the Royal-Suédois regiment, upon which an annual pension of 20,000 livres was settled. Axel could now return home with something to show for his efforts.[34] During his travels, his relations with his father had again become amicable and they were soon corresponding over details of regimental administration.[35]

The royal party left Paris on 19 July and arrived in Stockholm on 5 August. Thus Axel returned to his family after an absence of over six years. Not long after, his father wrote to him, "I avow to you that I have not yet forgiven the king for having held up your return for ten long months and for no other reason, for you, than to be the witness of his amusements."[36]

4

There remain few documents for that period in Fersen's life between his return to Sweden in the summer of 1784 and the outbreak of Gustav III's war with Russia, four years later. His diary for these years no longer exists while his letters to his family were relatively few and concerned mainly with personal affairs. They do, nonetheless, contain interesting references to Marie-Antoinette and developments in France, to be considered later.

His movements may be traced through his account and correspondence books. He remained in Sweden from August 1784 until April 1785, spending most of his time at court, to judge from Fredrik Axel's complaints to Fabian in Strasbourg. Axel was among other things present at the last of Gustav III's festive winter sojourns at Gripsholm Castle.[37]

When war threatened in the spring of 1785, between the Dutch and their French allies, on the one side, and the Austrians on the other, over the opening of the Scheldt River, Axel left Sweden, earlier than intended, to join his regiment at Landrécies in French Flanders, where he remained several months. Not long after, Gustav III reminded him that while he did not expect him to remain in Sweden the whole time, he desired at least "an equal share" of his time. Meanwhile, Count Ulrik Scheffer, a brother-in-law to Sophie Piper, wrote to Baron Taube:

I know how hard it will be for M. and Mme. de Fersen as well as for my sister-in-law to see the departure of a son and a brother who is so tenderly loved and who so well merits to be. The father I truly pity. He had hoped for all the consolation of his own age in enjoying the company of his son. He will now regard him as lost to him forever. I hope that he will not be so affected to become inconsolable. My sister-in-law will not be less affected with all the sensibility of her character. . . .[38]

In France, Axel was reunited with Fabian and his old mentor, Bolemany. His brother came to Paris and during the winter shared his quarters at Ambassador Staël's residence. Axel spent much time and effort on the tangled finances of a maiden aunt living in Paris. Meanwhile in Sweden, Count Creutz died in the fall of 1785 and for some months his position as *kanslipresident* or foreign minister remained unfilled. It was rumored that Gustav III was considering Axel Fersen for the post, though Axel's own letters say nothing of this. In April 1786, the king put the direction of the *kanslikollegium* into the hands of Baron Malte Ramel and Count J. G. Oxenstierna. Concerning the latter, Axel wrote his father in March, "You know the king's weakness for names," but unfortunately Gustav was not Gustav Adolf nor was the count Axel Oxenstierna. The king's real intention was, however, to manage foreign affairs himself.[39]

On 14 January 1786, Axel attended the long-awaited wedding of Gérmaine Necker and Baron Staël. Of the bride, he had written his father the previous fall that she "is not pretty, on the contrary. But her wit, amiability, and character make up for beauty. It would be difficult in effect to be more pleasant or intelligent." His ideas about Mme. de Staël would later be less charitable. That summer, Axel returned to Sweden via England, where he visited his old comrade, Sheldon, from the American war, which caused a stir among the Devonshire House coterie to which Lady Elizabeth Foster belonged. He remained in Sweden from July 1786 to May 1787. Here again, little is known of his activities. He returned to Paris in time to represent his king at the christening of Staël's first child. On 17 December 1787, he was appointed "captain lieutenant" in command of one of the four companies of the Life Guard—the Finnish—by right of reversion, and on the same day, lieutenant colonel of the honorary noble guard, *Adelsfanan*. His letters to his father in 1787–88 show that he was not, however, anxious to obtain command of a regular line regiment in Sweden in addition to that he held in France but that he speculated over possibilities for recruiting soldiers in Sweden and Swedish Pomerania for long-term enlistments in the French service.[40]

When Fersen arrived in Sweden in July 1786, only a few weeks had elapsed since the closing of the Riksdag of May and June, in the course of which Gustav III discovered the full magnitude of the opposition to his regime among all classes, which had developed during the past few years. Particularly since the last diet in 1778, the king had succeeded in alienating large and important segments of opinion. All classes were disappointed at the flagging pace of internal reform. The nation as a whole was alarmed by the king's extravagance and tended to agree with the diarist R. F. Hochschild that he encouraged "arts and sciences that a poor country ought rather to do without," particularly since poor harvests in the early 1780s threatened famine in the countryside and the end of the American war reduced foreign trade. Gustav's tour abroad with his favorites in 1783–84 was significant for the development of that neoclassical late Gustavian style in architecture and the visual arts that is a perennial source of inspiration in the

Swedish cultural tradition. But it was regarded at the time by many as a dangerously wasteful folly when serious problems demanded the king's presence at home.[41] Many too, were alarmed by worsening relations with Russia and Gustav's continual warlike preparations. Each of the estates had particular grievances and the Finns complained both of the government's demands and its neglect of their interests.

The main seat of opposition was, however, the aristocracy. Largely a service nobility, dependent upon state employment, they had rallied to Gustav III's new regime in 1772, which offered them protection against the anti-aristocratic attacks from the lower estates of the preceding years.[42] While favoring them, however, Gustav increasingly alienated them by seeking to turn them into a court nobility on the French model and by the prominence he gave his favorites, to the prejudice of legally constituted organs of government. Under these circumstances, the nobility tended to revert to their traditional role as guardians of the constitution, threatened by the king's willful exercise of power.

When, in April 1786, Gustav III suddenly issued a summons for a Riksdag, he himself was hardly prepared for the magnitude of the opposition in all four estates. Its natural leader in the house of the nobility was Fredrik Axel von Fersen and bitter confrontations took place between him and the king. Almost all of Gustav's proposals were rejected by the estates, regardless of merit, mainly at the instigation of the nobility, and the grant of revenue was both reduced and limited to four years, necessitating another diet at the end of that time.

This outcome came as a profound shock to a monarch who gloried in the love, if not the adulation of his people. Gustav was now faced with two possibilities: either he could adhere more scrupulously to the constitution, thereby mollifying the nobles; or he could sacrifice the nobles and, while continuing his personal rule, win over the lower estates through the satisfaction of their individual practical demands. Although it ran counter to his own strongly aristocratic inclinations, he chose the latter course, thereby playing to the traditionally monarchical sentiments of the mass of the Swedish people. Meanwhile, his relations with the nobility worsened until the final showdown in 1788–89.

Axel Fersen's own direct reactions to the Riksdag of 1786 are not preserved but no doubt during his ten-month stay in Sweden following its conclusion, he became thoroughly imbued with the constitutional arguments of the opposition. On his way back to France in May 1787, he wrote of his growing respect to his father, "since I have learned to know you better." It is in his reactions to later occurrences that Axel reveals something of the effects of the political conflict in Sweden. In August 1787, for instance, he agreed with two other company commanders in the Life Guard to resign if Gustav III gave a company in that corps to one of his favorites, suspected of theft. The maneuver succeeded and the favorite left the country. Fersen's reluctance to take a regiment in Sweden has been noted and in January 1788, he wrote his father about the possibility of leaving the Life Guard without retiring from the Swedish service.[43] Between 1787 and 1789, Fersen's comments on events in both France and Sweden evidence an aristocratic and anti-monarchical leaning, as will be seen, doubtless deriving from his months at home in 1786–87.

Axel returned to France, as noted, in May 1787 and remained there nine months. Meanwhile, Gustav III prepared a scheme of epic proportions: he planned to attack Russia. Since Catherine II's sharp reminder of her commitment to Denmark in the spring of 1784, relations between Sweden and Russia had rapidly deteriorated. Catherine had never reconciled herself to Gustav's strengthening of royal power in 1772 and she now instructed her ambassador in Stockholm to prepare opinion for the time when Russia could attack Sweden so swiftly that Gustav would have no time to prepare his defenses, thereby destroying the new regime and reestablishing the old, weak constitution of the Era of Freedom. Among those the ambassador strove hardest to win over was Fredrik Axel von Fersen.[44] Meanwhile, discontent was growing dangerously in Finland, giving rise to a movement for local autonomy. Though this was generally conceived within the framework of the Swedish monarchy, its leading proponent, Göran Magnus Sprengtporten, after falling out with the king, began to think of independence under Russian protection and in 1786 entered Russian service.

Gustav III's Russian war of 1788–90 was the final blow which set the Swedish nobility irretrievably against him, and it came in then and later for a storm of criticism. Still, Gustav was well enough aware of Russia's designs. It was a question of attacking or being attacked and the king's war plan was not as fantastic as it might seem. The idea was to attack St. Petersburg swiftly and decisively while Russia was deeply involved in war with Turkey.

If successful, Sweden could end, once and for all, Russian interference in Swedish internal affairs and the threat to the present
regime. And if Gustav's most sanguine hopes were realized, Sweden
might regain those Baltic and Finnish territories surrendered to
Russia in 1721 and 1743.

5

In December 1787, Turkey declared war on Russia, as expected.
Gustav hurried his preparations, seeking diplomatic support from
Paris, Berlin, and London. Among other things, he apparently
sought to profit from Axel Fersen's favor at the court of Versailles.
France, however, opposed a Swedish venture against Russia,
Prussia was cool, and Britain noncommittal. An attempt to persuade the Danes to break their defensive alliance with Russia
likewise proved fruitless.[45] Gustav, with characteristic optimism,
still considered British and Prussian support and Danish neutrality
almost assured, while Turkey promised subsidies that in the end
were never paid.

As the Swedish council was strongly opposed to war with
Russia, Gustav could only strengthen his armed forces ostensibly
for defensive purposes. His true intentions were still widely suspected and his favorites were soon rashly predicting a speedy
victory. His commanders in Finland warned of the poor condition
of the troops and the fear of war among the people. The French
ambassador strove to dissuade him from his plan, but Gustav
would hear of no impediment and continued his preparations
with high optimism.

In the spring of 1788, Gustav III recalled his officers from foreign
service, including Fersen and his lieutenant colonel, Stedingk.
Axel departed Paris in mid-April to take up his post as captain
lieutenant of the king's body guard. Though he had planned a visit
to Sweden that summer, he returned with reluctance and evidently
shared from the start his father's strong opposition to the war.
Fabian was appointed a captain in the Guards. In the middle of
June, Axel wrote his father from Stockholm that the king was
determined to leave for Finland even though nothing was yet
ready, "nor could it be." "This makes one feel horror and pity. . . .
In the streets one sees nothing but officers out of breath trying to
procure necessities and unable to find them." The king nevertheless
sailed with his fleet for Finland, "as though leaving for a festivity."

His army and navy, comprising some 40,000 men, was the largest ever assembled by the Swedish nation.[46]

There remained the matter of provocation for a war. The Russians should appear the aggressors so that the Danes would not be forced to recognize a *casus belli* under their alliance with Russia and since the Swedish constitution of 1772 forbade the king to make aggressive war without the consent of the estates. The Russians carefully avoided provocation and in the end Swedish soldiers disguised as Russians staged a border incident. Gustav submitted an impossible ultimatum and without awaiting an anwer, commenced hostilities.

Despite the Swedish preparations, the Russians seem genuinely taken by surprise, causing a near-panic in their lightly defended capital. Yet from the start, things began to go wrong. The Swedish fleet under the king's brother, Duke Karl, upon which the descent upon St. Petersburg depended, was fought to a standstill in the Finnish Gulf in mid-July. In Helsingfors, Gustav celebrated the encounter as a victory, but Axel Fersen who witnessed the festivities painted a dark picture of the disaffection of the Swedish-Finnish army. The king's pretense that the war was defensive deceived no one. Numerous officers sought to resign and the army was crippled by confusion and inexperience.[47]

With landing operations impossible, Gustav attempted to attack overland, across the Karelian Isthmus. By early August, however, the assault was frustrated at the Russian border fortress of Fredrikshamn, partly through the king's shortcomings as a military commander but even more through the hostility of his own officers. A few days later, the Russians blockaded the Swedish fleet at Sveaborg, in the Helsingfors Archipelago, giving them free access to the Baltic. By 5 August, Gustav wrote dejectedly to his favorite, G. M. Armfelt, that the best he could now hope for would be a peace with honor that would permit him to appear without shame in his own capital. On the same date, Axel Fersen wrote to Sophie:

Here are two letters for the ambassador [of France], my dear friend, which must be sent him immediately. This is to engage him to come here for he is charged with conciliating everything, if that is possible, and if he does not come here he will do nothing. If he has already left for here, you may read them and then burn them.[48]

This unofficial approach to the French ambassador and the admonition to destroy the enclosed letters if they did not reach him may well have originated with Gustav III himself. On the other hand, the possibility that Axel Fersen acted on his own, is not to be overlooked. His future activities in the diplomatic field would show that he was prepared on occasion to decide for himself where the public interest lay.

Meanwhile, more serious problems of discipline were brewing. The failure before Frederikshamn and the ensuing retreat served to reinforce the officers' constitutional objections to the war with defeatism, especially among the Finns. On 9 August, a group of Finnish officers turned to desperate measures, drafting a note to the Empress Catherine, expressing opposition to the war and the resolve to fight only in actual defense of their homeland, and urging her to compel the king of Sweden to convene the estates before making peace with him.[49] Not far away, that same evening, Axel wrote his father that the spirit in the army "would make all decent citizens shudder" and that the king was so discouraged he was "inclined to put an end to everything." The following day:

Everything is finished here. The king sees that he has been misled in everything. He is in despair. He has decided to end everything as quickly as possible, and if he does not, all the army will leave him. The proposals that are being made would make one's hair stand on end. There is much talk of a Riksdag; it is hoped that this may be avoided. At this time people are too hot-headed. The king has requested that the ambassador [of France] should come. He is hoping to broach the subject of negotiations through him. He had me come to him yesterday. He has treated me with kindness and confidence. It was pitiful to see. He began by saying, "You indeed warned me about this, my dear count, at Karlskrona, and you were right. I have seen well enough since that you were not happy about all of this. I would have done better to believe you, but I have been cruelly misled." The king is in despair. If this could correct all of his follies, it could serve some useful purpose; but I believe he is incorrigible.[50]

Gustav, hearing suspicious rumors from the Finnish army, demanded an oath of allegiance from its officers. In response, the insurgents, encamped at Anjala, prepared a declaration on 12 August, stating their opposition to the unlawful war and their resolve to prevent future misfortune by demanding a Riksdag and appealing to the empress for peace. This declaration was widely circulated and an unsigned copy sent to the king. Thus was formed the so-called Anjala Confederation.[51]

The king, through his attack on Russia, had thus provided his aristocratic opponents with both justification and means to call him to account by revising the constitution in favor of the estates and especially the nobility, the army, the bureaucracy, and Finland, through the traditional device of the anti-royalists of the Era of Freedom: the appeal to St. Petersburg. Axel described the situation to his father on 17 August, suspecting the complicity of the Russians and their desire for Finland, and expressing his fear of a Riksdag, "which at any other time would be a desirable thing." He continued:

The king has had me come many times to him. He has spoken to me of his position. I have hidden from him none of his faults. He has seemed to feel things, but not as much as I should have wished. As he is always false and dissimulating, I do not know what decision he will make, but I would not be surprised if he were to abdicate. . . .[52]

Helpless in the face of the officers' mutiny, Gustav III could only offer amnesty to anyone renouncing it. Yet circumstances soon played into his hands. Influenced by Sprengtporten and her ministers, Catherine replied to the Finnish officers' appeal in such a way as to reveal her desire to separate Finland from Sweden with their help, which was farther than most of them were prepared to go. Disconcerted, they still continued to press for their program, which called forth numerous anonymous writings opposing the war and demanding a diet.[53] Widely publicizing their cause in Sweden itself, they naturally sought the support of Fredrik Axel von Fersen as the dominating figure in the parliamentary anti-royalist opposition.[54]

In his memoirs, Fredrik Axel later wrote that the Anjala Confederation was "in conflict with law and the articles of war, criminal as well as contrary to sound reason." His position at the beginning of the war nevertheless appears ambivalent. During the months preceding, he was observed among the growing circle from the Swedish opposition around the Russian ambassador, Count Andrei Razumovsky. Jean Bolemany was evidently suspected of mysterious dealings, including espionage, for the Russians, and in August made his way from Stockholm via Copenhagen to St. Petersburg. He spent his later years in Russia and Germany, and Fredrik Axel at his death in 1794 willed him a small pension. In 1807, Count Hans Gabriel Trolle-Wachtmeister, the son of Gustav III's chancellor of justice, noted that Fredrick Axel von Fersen was suspected in 1788 "with reason" of being aware, if not more directly involved, in a plot that summer to arrest Gustav III at

Sveaborg fortress, after which a "revolution" should take place "through the convening of the estates" in Stockholm. The elder Fersen's role in these months remains obscure but it evidently involved more than his memoirs imply. To what extent Axel shared his knowledge, views, and intentions at this point is also open to conjecture, though his strong opposition to the war is clear enough and most of the political writings in his voluminous collection of materials relating to it are hostile to the king.[55]

Meanwhile, Gustav III received news of what should have been the final blow: Denmark had honored her alliance with Russia and was preparing an offensive from Norway. In actuality, this gave the king a welcome opportunity to escape the pressure of the insurgent officers in Finland and to return to the surer ground of Sweden. His attitude immediately stiffened and he was gratified on his way home to receive touching protestations of loyalty from the non-noble classes in Finland.[56]

Axel too was determined to return to Sweden, as he wrote Sophie, if not with the king, then on his own.[57] In any event, he accompanied Gustav back to Sweden, where opinion among the mass of the people was by now aroused to fever pitch against the aristocratic officers. The country was flooded with pamphlets accusing them and indeed the entire nobility of cowardice and treason.[58]

The king knew how to profit from his position. With a theatrical flourish, he appealed to the Dalecarlian peasantry to help him drive the hated "Jute" into the sea, as Gustav Vasa had done over three centuries before. The gesture was a great success. The Dalecarlians raised a volunteer corps with its own elected officers, inspired as much by resentment against the nobility as by hatred for the Danes. Deputations from many provinces offered to do likewise to aid the king against his enemies, foreign and domestic, and the cry was raised to "break the gentry." After a few weeks, G. M. Armfelt, to whom the king largely entrusted the volunteer corps, wrote to Gustav, "The time has come when we are more embarrassed by the zeal of your subjects than by the treason of the factious," while to his wife, he wrote:

The bitterness among the lower orders against the nobility is so great that one hardly dares to admit to being a baron or a count. They are talking of nothing less than killing and uprooting the whole pack of them. God help us out of this confusion![59]

It was feared among the nobility that the king might march on Stockholm with his peasant army and there was talk among the opposition of bringing over insurgent units from Finland to defend the capital. Civil war seemed imminent.[60]

Instead, Gustav went to the defense of Göteborg against the Danish-Norwegian offensive. At this point, two of his assumptions proved at least half right and to his advantage: Britain and Prussia were unwilling to see Turkey and Sweden go down in total ruin and Denmark was only lukewarm in her attachment to Russia. Mainly through the initiative of the British minister to Copenhagen, Hugh Elliot, Britain and Prussia brought pressure to bear on Denmark and arranged an armistice, followed shortly by a declaration of neutrality for the duration of the Swedish-Russian conflict. From Göteborg, Axel described the situation to his father. Elliot and the Prussian minister to Denmark "lord it over us completely, as if they were the masters of unlimited power." They wanted peace, however, and pressed Gustav III to convene the estates, which he said he would do but which Axel, knowing his deviousness, doubted. "I have found the king no more reasonable than usual and there is nothing that can be done with him"; he was still filled with "grand projects and follies."[61]

By this time, Axel prepared to return to France. Learning the king wished to charge him with a mission to Copenhagen, he let it be known that he intended to go by way of Ystad instead. To Sophie, he confided he would take the shortest possible route, even if this led straight through the Danish army, to which he was prepared to give his parole.[62] He could not, however, evade a final consultation with the king in Göteborg, where he was shocked by the "domineering and superior tone" of the British and Prussian ministers, who now "decide the pettiest details" and continued to insist on a diet, which the king clearly sought to avoid. Gustav, Fersen continued,

... had nothing to say to me, for I had prevented him from telling me what he wanted, namely that the nation was to blame for everything that had happened. I had been able to find out that this had been his intention, but I forestalled him and he did not dare to speak of it any longer, although he wished to do so. Finally, he bade me make a sort of defense for what had happened during the time in question [to the French government], also to maintain the necessity of accepting the mediation which England and Prussia had offered. I thereupon answered him that I was going to speak the truth. . . .[63]

While still in Finland, Axel had written his father that the new army reforms in France required that he return to his regiment, as well as financial details connected with its purchase. By early October, Gustav III had granted him permission to return and entrusted him with letters for the French court.[64] He thus seems to have been charged with some sort of mission there and like many others, to have been granted leave for the winter when campaigning in the North was considered unfeasible. Meanwhile, he felt deeply the widening gulf which separated the king from the nobility in his country, as well as the special position of his own family.

His letters just before his departure show the strain of his situation. His father was a natural leader for the opposition, regarding the war as aimed not only against Russia, but likewise against Sweden's constitutional liberties.[65] A final showdown between the king and the nobility, with the proud old count at their head, seemed inevitable. Axel's letters show the depth of his disillusionment with Gustav, whom he had always held in affection. Perhaps the king sent him off to France for the winter to keep him from turning into an outright enemy rather than a disenchanted friend; perhaps to keep him from bringing to bear an influence which could be considerable among the younger nobles, in support of his father's cause during the coming months.

At any rate, Axel returned to France and did not return for the next campaign, in 1789. Lars von Engeström, later Swedish foreign minister and a man with whom Axel's future relations were generally cool, wrote in his memoirs not only that Fersen had not participated at all in Gustav III's Russian war, but that he had even tried to prevent his Swedish officers in the Royal-Suédois from doing so, which had brought him a sharp rebuke from the king. Unfortunately, this, like certain other of Engeström's allegations about him has never been questioned, although it clearly rests upon a misunderstanding. Apparently in the spring of 1790, an officer in the Royal-Suédois gave such an idea to the king who thereupon reprimanded Fersen. The latter immediately informed Baron Taube in May that he had been assured of a year's prolongation of leave for all Swedish officers in French service, adding that the young officer in question was a troublemaker and should be watched. The following month, Fersen wrote Gustav III that although there had never been any question of withholding leave from any of the Swedish officers, the formalities had been delayed by the inefficiencies of the French war office, whereupon the king acknowledged the falseness of the imputation.[66]

In his letters to his father and the king in the winter and spring of 1789, Axel spoke of poor health as his main reason for not returning to Sweden himself. Doubtless, however, developments both there and in France during these months played a greater part, while Gustav III would soon consider his presence more valuable in Paris, close to the French royal family, than in Finland. Axel's letters nevertheless show with what deep concern he followed events in his homeland.

Meanwhile, anti-aristocratic propaganda poured forth in Sweden, inspired from on high. One pamphlet from Göteborg caused a particular furor in Stockholm society, where Gustav III feared the elder Fersen was seeking to "envenom spirits," and prompted Hedda Klinckowström to an outburst of fury. "My friend," she wrote Fabian in Finland, "if it is possible, counsel patience. The moment of vengeance and truth has not yet come. It is not yet time to attack the author. . . . God damn for ever the authors of all the sufferings, all the enemies, and all the sorrows we have. If there is a divine justice, it will not spare them." By February 1789, the king's own sister-in-law, Duchess Hedvig Elisabeth Charlotta, wrote in her diary that the history of no age could reveal a counterpart to the horrors Sweden was now undergoing and that their author must remain for all time "an object of dread and abomination, not only for his own land but for the whole world."[67]

6

The epilogue to the events of 1788 was one of success for the king on every side. The Anjala Confederation fell apart over the question of cooperation with Russia, which most of its adherents opposed, and by early 1789, Gustav III arrested most of its leaders. These were tried and condemned to death, though the king subsequently pardoned all but one. Only a few escaped to Russia.

In the winter of 1789, the long-awaited Riksdag convened, but with radically different results from those foreseen by the insurgents the previous summer. Capitalizing on the anti-aristocratic passions of the lower estates, Gustav III secured passage for an Act of Union and Security, which both reduced the powers of the estates and the privileges of the nobility. Though couched in deceptively moderate language and carefully qualified clauses, the act was at once more authoritarian and more egalitarian than it appeared, as the king's opponents did not fail to note. It shows, indeed, striking similarities to the Declaration of the Rights of Man and the Citizen in France the following July and would be of epoch-making importance for the dissolution of the old corporate society in Sweden and its replacement by a modern class society based on wealth and accomplishment. Thereafter, there was a steady advance of men of common origin into the higher dignities of the realm; Axel's old tutor, Jacob Forslund, was, for instance, the first commoner to become a chancellery councillor. The abolition of restrictions on the purchase of most categories of noble land meanwhile led to that great growth of wealth and social mobility among the Swedish peasantry that ultimately provided the broad base for the democratization of Swedish society.[68]

Gustav III's victory over the aristocracy proved, however, a Pyrrhic one. The Act of Union and Security did not establish a complete autocracy, the claims of his opponents notwithstanding, yet three years later he paid for it with his life at their hands. Twenty years later, his son, Gustav IV Adolf, was deposed and both the constitution of 1772 and the Act of Union and Security replaced by the constitution of 1809, which once again strengthened the estates and which has remained Sweden's fundamental law until this day.

For the sake of this concentration of power—incomplete and transient as it proved—Gustav III resorted to drastic means when, in contrast to Louis XVI that same year, he deliberately leveled those privileges which underlay the whole aristocratic way of life he himself so dearly loved, to win the support of the unprivileged orders. In the end, it was nevertheless this expedient, rather than the end he sought to gain by it, that proved his most lasting accomplishment.[69]

In the brief time that remained to him after the diet of 1789, Gustav III became increasingly captivated by the ambition of leading a European crusade to crush the hydra of revolution in France, which he saw as a menace to all crowned heads and all orderly society. Yet on one occasion at this time, he said with a prescience he himself could hardly have appreciated, "I am myself a democrat."[70]

CHAPTER IV

Fersen and France: The Coming of Revolution, 1785–1790

1

In his letters to Sophie in the summer and fall of 1788, Axel alluded to a powerful reason for returning to France as quickly as possible, quite aside from the situation in Sweden. This was the queen of France, whose relationship with him had already attracted much attention.[1] At this point, one enters into that intriguing question which far more than any other has perennially drawn interest to Axel Fersen. A seemingly endless debate has concerned itself with the nature of this affair from his day to the present, which will doubtless continue, barring the unlikely discovery of some new and indisputable evidence.

The question is closely tied to that of the Fersen letters. Though it was long suspected that Fersen's papers might include correspondence with the French queen, the historical world saw these letters in printed form only when Fersen's grand-nephew, Baron Rudolf Mauritz Klinckowström, published them in 1877–78.[2] His collection of sources includes 29 letters from Marie-Antoinette to Fersen, some written by herself, some by others—principally her secretary, the Baron de Goguelat—some partly or wholly in cipher, from the period, 28 June 1791 to 1 August 1792. It also includes 33 letters from Fersen to the queen, based on his own rough drafts. Some of Marie-Antoinette's letters were, however, published in abridged form, with deletions indicated by rows of dots. This seemed suspicious, all the more so when Baron Klinckowström denied access to the originals. His son, Baron Axel Klinckowström, saw the letters and noted certain passages were already inked over. Alma Söderhjelm later showed this to be the work of Fabian Fersen, following his brother's death in 1810. Axel Klinckowström intended in time to subject the letters to scientific tests to determine what had been struck out, but his father apparently sought to prevent further examination of them, for after his death, the envelope which had contained them was found empty and it is believed that he burned them. Although no deletions are indicated in the published version of Fersen's letters to the queen, the drafts for these have likewise not been located.[3]

The letters of Axel Fersen and Marie-Antoinette preserved and published by R. M. Klinckowström naturally comprised only a small part of their total correspondence. It is estimated from Fersen's letter register that he wrote close to 200 letters to the queen and that she wrote something like the same number to him. All their letters prior to mid-June 1791, however, were doubtless destroyed during the preparations for the flight to Varennes in that month.[4] The deletions in Klinckowström naturally stimulated controversy over the nature of their relationship. The baron himself wrote to Maxime de La Rocheterie and the Marquis de Beaucourt, editors of an edition of Marie-Antoinette's correspondence that appeared in 1895–96, that nothing among the Fersen papers "could throw a shadow upon the conduct of the queen." Klinckowström claimed that after answering her letters, Fersen sent them to Gustav III, after first eradicating certain expressions "on delicate points," concluding rather unconvincingly, that "the friends of this august martyr will find these [reasons] sufficient to banish any spiteful interpretations . . . ." Auguste Geffroy sought in 1878 to demonstrate that the deleted passages were of a political and not of a personal nature. There is, however, no indication that Fersen sent any of his letters from the queen directly to Gustav III, though he occasionally copied extracts from them into his letters to the king. The position of the deleted passages in relation to undeleted material as well as their usual occurrence at the end of the letters makes it doubtful that they dealt with politics.[5]

According to one view then, Fersen was never actually in love with the queen and his devotion was motivated by his sense of honor, by admiration, pity, gratitude, and the confidence she accorded him. If he were more a partisan of Marie-Antoinette than of Louis XVI, it was because he rightly respected her abilities more than his. Advocates of this theory believed that Fersen himself edited the queen's letters to preserve for posterity a picture of her at her best, unmarred by occasional lapses from regal dignity.[6]

A more widely held view was that Fersen and the queen loved each other, but holding to the ideals of courtly chivalry, never expressed their love. Thus Fersen could only show his devotion through self-sacrifice and service. Most of the older writers on the subject conceived it in this way, thus generally producing highly romanticized accounts.[7]

It is now clear that Fersen and Marie-Antoinette loved each other with a very real and human love, which they did not seek to hide from each other. It is nevertheless argued by some that their relation did not extend as far as physical intimacy.[8] Others have asserted that they were lovers in the full sense.[9] Finally, the charge has even been made that Fersen not only made the queen his mistress, but did so for entirely cynical and egotistical reasons.[10]

Most of the writing on Fersen and the French queen is unscholarly and of little historical value. The conclusions these works draw—often with a surprising air of certainty—generally derive less from concrete evidence, which is in any case incomplete, than from the preconceptions of their authors about human nature and what they consequently feel Fersen and Marie-Antoinette would or ought to have done under the circumstances in which they found themselves.

In the face of so much controversy, what can be said with any reasonable certainty about their relationship? Its development over the years can be reconstructed with fair accuracy through Axel's correspondence, especially with Sophie, and his account and correspondence books. This is what Alma Söderhjelm did in her *Fersen et Marie-Antoinette*, published in 1930, necessarily the basis of all work on the subject since then.

It has been seen that Marie-Antoinette, then dauphine, showed interest in Axel during his first visit to Paris in 1773–74 and remembered him as "an old acquaintance" when he returned in August 1778. Thereafter, she asked Creutz in September why Fersen did not attend her Sunday card parties and insisted on seeing him in his new Swedish uniform. According to the Comte de Saint-Priest, it was on this latter occasion that Marie-Antoinette was visibly affected at the sight of him. Fersen meanwhile wrote his father more than once that the queen was "the most amiable princess I know." He neglected his diary from early October 1778 through 1779, except in March 1779, but during this period it is clear that he was much in evidence at the Petit Trianon.[11] The evident favor he enjoyed played a part in his decision to go to America. "The queen says a thousand obliging things to me," he wrote his father in February 1780,

. . . she later said to the Baron de Breteuil that if there were anything I desired in this country, I had only to tell her and she would try to obtain it. She is a charming princess. . . . she has almost always promenaded with me at the Opera balls. . . . Her kindnesses to me and the post of colonel have attracted the jealousy of all the young men of the court. They can neither suffer nor understand that a foreigner can be better treated than they.

In March he supped several times in the royal *cabinet*, "to the great astonishment of the French." Creutz wrote Gustav III on 10 April 1779 that Marie-Antoinette surely had a "penchant" for Axel: "The queen could not take her eyes off him during the last days; in looking at him, they were filled with tears." The Duchess de Fitz-James had asked him outright if he thus intended to abandon his "conquest" for America. According to an oft-repeated anecdote, Marie-Antoinette sang the couplet from *Didon*,

> Ah, que je fus bien inspirée
> Quand je vous reçus dans ma cour

while fixing Axel raptly in a gaze that left no doubt about her emotions in the minds of those present.[12]

While in America, however, Axel did not write anything that showed nostalgia for Versailles. He enjoyed the Hunter sisters in Newport while his letters to Sophie show a continuing interest in a certain "charming countess" in Sweden. In March 1783, however, he wrote Sophie from Porto Caballo, that he was counting upon remaining permanently in French service, as colonel-proprietor of a regiment, though he besought her to keep this secret. Some weeks later he approached his father more cautiously on the matter. It is impossible to say how great a role the French queen played in this project, which Axel had considered even before leaving for America. Most likely his motives were still mainly military and professional.[13]

It is clear, however, that in the summer of 1783, Marie-Antoinette helped procure the Royal-Suédois regiment for him and it seems their relationship quickly developed at this point. On 31 July, he wrote Sophie:

Despite all the pleasure I will have in seeing you I cannot leave Paris without regret. You will find this quite natural when you know the reason; I will tell you about it for I do not want to hide anything from you. I am very glad that Mlle. Leyel is married. They will not talk to me any more about her and I hope that they will not find any other. I have made my decision. I do not wish ever to form conjugal bonds; it is contrary to nature.

Thus Sophie should eventually become the mistress of his household. "I cannot belong to the sole person to whom I would wish to belong, the only one who truly loves me; thus I wish to belong to no one." To his father he wrote that a regiment in France was "the only thing that could make me happy for ever," for many reasons, some of which he could not confide to paper.[14]

Fersen began to keep a letter register in November 1783, while with Gustav III in Italy; from that time it records frequent letters to Marie-Antoinette, usually under the covering name of "Josephine," during his absences from Paris. It may, however, be recalled that Axel was not adverse to a passing affair or two in Italy. After visiting Paris with his king in the summer of 1784, he returned for some months to Sweden where among other things he purchased a small dog for the French queen and undoubtedly told all to Sophie.[15]

Returning to France in the spring of 1785, he wrote his sister on 15 May, "I arrived at Versailles this evening at 6:00 o'clock and I will remain here until tomorrow to pay my court tomorrow morning." An undated fragment of a letter to Sophie, presumably from the same period, reads, "It is 8:00 in the evening, I must leave you. I have been in Versailles since yesterday. Do not mention that I am writing from here for I date my other letters from Paris. Adieu, I must go to the queen's card party." In October, he wrote his father from Fontainebleau that there were not enough days in the week for all the pleasures of the court. When Fersen left for England and Sweden in May 1786, an anonymous letter from Versailles informed its recipient, "The departure of the Swedish Comte de Fersen has created some sensation within the queen's society; but the clouds spread by this absence will soon be dissipated."[16]

The Comte de Saint-Priest probably had in mind Fersen's next
sojourn in France, in 1787–88, when he wrote in his memoirs:

... Fersen rode into the park, near the Trianon, three or four times a
week; the queen, alone, did the same on her part, and these rendezvous
caused a public scandal, despite the modesty and discretion of the
favorite, who never showed anything publicly and was, among all the
friends of a queen, the most discreet.

Marie-Antoinette, according to Saint-Priest, frankly told her husband of the gossip concerning Fersen and herself, apparently to
show the extent of ill-will toward her, thus insinuating that the
foreign count was the only person on whom she could rely; she
then offered to stop seeing him, which Louis XVI declined, and
he himself came to share her confidence in Fersen.[17] Saint-Priest
maintains that already in 1778-79, the queen's favorites, Mme. de
Polignac, the Baron de Besenval, and the Comte de Vaudreuil
encouraged her interest in Fersen, feeling that "an isolated foreigner, little ambitious by character, would suit them better than a
Frenchman, surrounded by relatives, who would win all the favors
for them and would in the end become the head of a clique which
would eclipse them all."[18]

Axel's letters to Sophie from Finland in 1788 show his extreme
impatience to return to Marie-Antoinette. He would take good
care of himself, he wrote on 3 July, "to see them again, and you,
my tender friend. Therein lies all my happiness." Whom he meant
by "them" is clear. "I have only time enough to tell you that
everything that is taking place gives me great pleasure," he wrote
on 10 August, "for all this will end. You will be reassured, she
also, and I will see you both again. Ah, God, could I but see you
both together. . . ." When at last he returned to Paris, he wrote
Sophie on 6 November, "I am delighted to be here and that my
voyage is over. God, if only I could see you—nothing would *at this
moment* be lacking for my happiness."[19]

Difficult times were to follow. Yet when Marie-Antoinette was
by the summer of 1789 abandoned by most of her former intimates
who emigrated abroad at an early date, Axel Fersen remained
by her side. Danger and adversity served only to draw them closer
together until separated by the onward rush of revolution and war.

Enough has been said to reveal not only the narrative outline of
the relationship but its emotional nature as well. This clearly

eliminates the older conception that Fersen was inspired by respect and gratitude only. One ought not, to be sure, be misled by the extravagant protestations of emotional friendship with which letters in those days customarily ended. Yet surely Marie-Antoinette's enciphered letter, which Fersen received on 4 July 1791, is something altogether different: "... I can tell you that I love you and have only time enough to do that." She "cannot live" without being able to write to him, and ends, "Adieu, most loved and most loving of men. I embrace you with all my heart." As this note was deciphered in Fersen's hand, Baron Klinckowström probably failed to recognize it as coming from the queen and it thus survived. The old legend of the Swedish "Tristan" and his French "Iseult"—to use Henry Bordeaux's description—must likewise fall by the wayside.[20] At the same time, the hostile picture of Fersen as a cynical profligate who egotistically exploited the queen's love is untenable in the face of the accumulated evidence, not least that giving insight into Fersen's psychology.

What remains is a relationship beyond question based upon a very real and natural love which may or may not have led to physical intimacy. It is upon this latter point that an inordinate amount of speculation has centered. What evidence is there that Fersen was the queen's lover in the full sense? Certainly he himself never said so in any of his surviving papers. Auguste Geffroy wrote toward the middle of the last century of the caution that was always so characteristic of him:

Those of our contemporaries who have known M. de Fersen report, in effect, that he possessed a rare discretion; they say one could indeed get him to respond to one question, to two perhaps, but not to a third, for he immediately became mistrustful of himself, if not of others.[21]

It is doubtful that he would ever have committed evidence on the most intimate details of his affair with the queen of France to writing. Even so, Fabian Fersen went through his papers after his death, eradicating certain passages and probably destroying various documents. Almost all the letters Axel received from women other than his sister—and his correspondence book shows they were numerous—have disappeared. There remain only a few brief notes from Marie-Antoinette; the most revealing of these, the one that Fersen received on 4 July 1791, has been noted above.[22]

Much meanwhile has been made of the passage in Fersen's diary describing his hazardous secret visit to the Tuileries in February

1792: "Went to *her*, went by my usual way, fear of National Guards, her lodging marvelous, remained there." The last words, *"resté là,"* are inked over in the manuscript but it has been possible to make them out. Fersen further notes that he did not see Louis XVI until 6:00 o'clock the following evening.[23]

A number of Fersen's contemporaries furthermore implied or stated outright that he was Marie-Antoinette's lover. The Comte de Saint-Priest, minister of the *maison du roi*, who mentions Fersen's secret visits to the queen between about 1787 and 1791 in a number of places in his memoirs, strongly suggested that they were physically intimate and referred to him once as the *"ami en titre."* Henry Richard Fox, Lord Holland, long after took the queen's *première femme de chambre,* Mme. Campan, to task for not speaking of Marie-Antoinette's love affairs in her memoirs. "These amours were not numerous, scandalous or degrading," he wrote, "but they *were amours.*" He further claimed that Mme. Campan had privately told mutual acquaintances that Fersen had been in the queen's boudoir at Versailles on the famous night of 5 October 1789, from whence he was forced to escape in disguise, which M. A. de Bacourt later disproved on the basis of Mme. Campan's own memoirs. Lord Holland's wife, Lady Elizabeth, wrote in her diary in 1793, "M. de Fersen, the lover of the unhappy Queen, came to see me. He is tall and stately, and has the pretention in his manner of a favourite." "See for the first Time since I arrived in Europe Count Fersan [*sic*] whose Merit consists of being the Queen's lover," Gouverneur Morris, the new minister of the United States in Paris, wrote with republican bluntness in his diary on 25 September 1789, adding, "He has the Air of a Man exhausted." Fersen himself noted with resignation in November 1797 that General Bonaparte had told a German diplomat "that I had gone to bed with the queen," to which the latter replied that he believed these periods of ancient history to have been forgotten. There is, finally, a cryptic and pathetic passage in Louis XVI's testament in which he assures his wife that "she may be sure that I hold nothing against her, if she should think she had anything with which to reproach herself."[24]

Remarks like these suggest how widespred the idea was on the level of everyday gossip that Fersen was the queen's lover. It was widely rumored in 1785 that Axel was the father of Charles Louis, later the second dauphin and so-called Louis XVII, born that year. In 1791, Quentin Craufurd, with whose own mistress

Fersen was at the time involved, described him to William Pitt as "Her Most Christian Majesty's prime favourite," who was "generally supposed to be the father of the present Dauphin." Fersen himself noted without comment in February 1793, how the French revolutionaries "intended to declare the dauphin a bastard."[25]

On the basis of her painstaking investigation, Alma Söderhjelm concluded in 1930 that Fersen was indeed the queen's lover, in her view, from 1789 onward. Lacking conclusive proof, she put much emphasis on the editing of Marie-Antoinette's letters by Baron Klinckowström and the disappearance of the originals, otherwise basing her conclusions on total impression and surely, on woman's intuition. This view has been shared by Stefan Zweig and Bengt Hildebrand and more recently by Stanley Loomis and Kjell Strömberg.[26]

A number of recent authors meanwhile hold that Fersen and the queen were, in the words of André Castelot, only "limited lovers." Their arguments gain cogency by being practical rather than moralistic. Thus they point out the astonishing lack of privacy of a queen of France, the danger of scandal of the gravest sort, the threat of *lèse-majesté* through the birth of a child out of wedlock, and not least of all, Fersen's liaisons with other women. The deletions in the letters they consider probably occasioned by misleading or ambiguous references which might lead the reader to construe more in the relationship than existed.[27] Indeed, despite all the controversy over the vanished letters, it seems unlikely in the extreme that they would have revealed anything more than is now amply demonstrated through other sources: namely, that Fersen and Marie-Antoinette loved each other. They could hardly be expected to prove conclusively physical intimacy between them.

What comments may be added to this much-discussed question? In the first place, certain arguments should not pass uncriticized. Too much should not be made, for instance, of the queen's undoubted lack of privacy. Saint-Priest speaks repeatedly of her secret meetings with Fersen at the Petit Trianon, Saint-Cloud, and the Tuileries, and he even maintains that she accustomed Louis XVI not to disturb her at such times. On Christmas Eve, 1789, Fersen to his delight was able to spend the whole day with her.[28] Thus, if they were not lovers, it was not for lack of opportunity. The most notable instance of this kind was surely Fersen's secret visit to the Tuileries Palace on 13–14 February 1792. Yet what does that actually prove? If Fersen remained hidden somewhere in the queen's chambers for a night and the following day, he had come at extreme peril both to himself and to the royal family and could hardly move about freely. Considering how closely watched the king and queen were, it does not seem likely that he could see the queen very long for fear of discovery and he probably could not have seen Louis XVI unobserved any sooner than he did. Many factors are involved here so that the visit can hardly be taken as an *a priori* proof of physical intimacy between Fersen and the queen. Fersen was furthermore hidden for the next several days in Quentin Craufurd's house, where he undoubtedly did engage in such intimacies with the latter's mistress, Eleanore Sullivan.[29] That he should have done so with the queen of France as well strains one's credibility. Stefan Zweig's comment, that Joseph II discovered that his sister wished to withdraw from her husband's embraces after the birth of her fourth child, if true, may indicate nothing more than a desire to stop bearing children. The same author's suggestion that Fersen tacitly admitted the truth of General Bonaparte's remark in 1797, that he had gone to bed with the queen, by failing to challenge the general to a duel, is astonishing when one considers that Fersen was then the ambassador of his king at the Congress of Rastadt, where such quixotic behavior would have been out of the question. Fersen, incidentally, was equally laconic in recording in 1791 the rumor that Barnave, the revolutionary, was sleeping with the queen.[30]

There are, however, psychological considerations that also deserve attention. As far as Marie-Antoinette is concerned, there seems no real reason to believe that she ever had any lover—except possibly Fersen—despite malicious rumors which can readily be explained by the vociferous ill-will toward her both within the court and beyond. During the Affair of the Diamond Necklace in 1785, public opinion easily believed that she had sold her favors to the Cardinal de Rohan while from 1789 on, she was accused in public print of having had as lovers well over a dozen prominent personages and even of practicing Lesbianism. In actuality, she showed, especially after the birth of her first child in December 1778, a conscientious attitude toward marriage and family, even a certain prudishness that recalls her mother and various of her numerous brothers and sisters, such as Joseph II and particularly

Leopold of Tuscany, though admittedly not the notoriously licentious Marie-Caroline of Naples.[31] Mme. Campan called special attention to her mistress's temperance in personal habits and great physical modesty. Above all, Maria Theresia's daughter showed a great sense of her identity and dignity as a queen which grew impressively in the face of adversity during her last years. Her strength of character shows through in the constancy of her devotion to Fersen, the one great love of her life.[32]

In the case of Axel Fersen, the problem is more complex. He too possessed a strong sense of propriety, yet at the same time a highly erotic nature. Marie-Antoinette was neither the first nor the last woman in his life and even at the time of his relationship with her there seems no doubt that he indulged in physical intimacies with other women, notably with the Italian-born Eleanore Sullivan, a prominent figure in the European *demi-monde*. This woman—so totally unlike the queen of France—would, incongruously enough, be the object of the second great affair of his life. All this has not surprisingly caused much disillusionment in its striking contrast to the old, romantic Fersen legend.[33]

Yet perhaps this very circumstance provides the psychological key to the situation. Regarding relations between men and women, as with much else, Fersen showed a curious mixture of cynicism and idealism. The two brief affairs he had in Italy while accompanying Gustav III in 1783–84 here prove revealing. It will be recalled that they took place after Axel had written Sophie that he did not intend to marry since he could not belong to the only person he would wish to have. In Florence, in November 1783, he met Lord Cowper's sister, Emelie Gower, to whom his letter register shows he wrote frequently during the next four months in response to her even more frequent letters to him. His brief notations here show that he regarded the affair as a passing fancy and gently sought to disengage himself, which he accomplished by the end of April by insinuating that "that can never take place" because of his father's opposition. Though he also wrote Lord Cowper, urging that he console his sister, he nonetheless canceled a visit to Spa two years later to avoid "a certain *Miss* from Florence."[34]

If Fersen took a wordly view toward affairs of this sort, his lack of malice does him credit. Throughout his life, he was tactful, considerate, and discreet in his relations with women. They in turn used him as he used them and he evidently suffered as many disappointments in love as he caused. Considering his natural reticence, women frequently seem to have pursued him much more aggressively than he did them and he appears on occasion to have drifted into affairs without much effort or desire. During the 1780s he became involved with the Duchess Hedvig Elisabeth Charlotta in Sweden, later his brother Fabian's mistress; during his visit to Sweden in 1794–95, she made determined efforts to entice him back, which he carefully avoided.[35] In October 1790, Axel wrote Sophie concerning Mme. de Saint-Priest:

She has become crazy over me and continued in spite of everything I have been able to say to her. It is truly folly.... The details are incredible. There is no kind of humiliation to which she has not submitted herself.... as far as the refusal on my part to profit from everything a woman can offer a man.

She continued to write passionate letters to him the following spring.[36] The Comte de Saint-Priest's coolness toward Fersen in his memoirs is probably not unrelated to this situation.

In Italy, however, Axel also became involved in a second affair, with Lady Elizabeth Foster, a young and appealing victim of a broken marriage, whom he met in Naples in February 1784. Both his letters to Sophie and hers to her confidante, Georgiana, Duchess of Devonshire, show a warmly sentimental relationship, which is later substantiated in both of their diaries and by the fact that they continued to correspond until the year of Axel's death. Elizabeth's real passion, however, was even then Georgiana's husband, the Duke of Devonshire, whom she later married. This was a situation Fersen could well enough understand and on 7 December 1784, he wrote a letter to her in which, according to his correspondence book, he "declared everything," doubtless about his own great affair.[37]

All of this suggests a distinct separation in Fersen's mind between physical love and the institution of marriage, which he regarded realistically and cynically, and friendship, which inspired in him the most genuine idealism. It is hardly surprising that he should consider matrimony, in his day and among his social class, to be "contrary to reason," as he told Sophie, a matter of convenience and fortune, not of passion, nor that he should commit adultery with married women without qualms of conscience. Of such affairs, he speaks without dissimulation in his diary, showing a matter-of-fact recognition of his own and others' erotic needs, mingled with a certain irony, not least toward himself.

He meanwhile possessed a highly exalted conception of friendship, which doubtless underlay his feelings toward Lady Elizabeth Foster. But it is above all with Sophie and with Baron Evert Taube, who from about 1787 on was her devoted lover, that Axel revealed his capacity for warm and emotional friendship. To Taube, for instance, he wrote in August 1789 that his sister dreamed

> ... of a charming future ... when we will be all three reunited, when we will never leave each other, when we will live only for each other. Ah, my friend, how happy we will then be ... the idea alone gives me pleasure.... Concern yourself only with that future and preserve yourself in order to enjoy it. My house, my lands, all that I shall possess will contribute to embellish it and to make it more pleasant.... The happiness of my friends will be my own and I shall enjoy it even more than they....[38]

He was meanwhile deeply touched by Marie-Antoinette's interest in Sophie and fervently looked forward to the day they might meet.[39]

It seems above all that it was this ideal of perfect friendship that formed the basis of Axel Fersen's love for Marie-Antoinette. In matters of love and friendship, he appears to typify his age, with its striking mixture of rococo frivolity and irony, on the one hand, and preromantic emotional fervor and yearning moral idealism, on the other. It would be too much to conclude that such attitudes ruled out the possibility of a physical relationship with the French queen. But they do suggest that they could very well have remained "limited lovers," and even, possibly, that Fersen's attitude toward the relationship might not have been the same had it been otherwise. At the same time, this separation in his thinking between erotic love and friendship seems to reconcile the views—demonstrable in both cases—of Fersen as a romantic idealist and as a cynical and egotistical Don Juan: he was in actuality both, though with different women and in different relationships. There could be no greater contrast than between Marie-Antoinette and Eleanore Sullivan. Agonizing over his position with regard to them both as the queen's tragic end approached, he wrote in his diary in October 1793 that he needed both "sacred and profane love." His love for Marie-Antoinette surely revealed his most idealistic side.[40]

At this point, the author must emerge from seemly obscurity to add, somewhat reluctantly, his own pronouncement on the relationship to those of his many predecessors. I am inclined, mainly for the psychological reasons given here, to range myself with the consensus that Fersen was not her lover, yet at the same time to add, with M. Vallotton, that he was in truth more than that.[41] In retrospect, the whole matter of physical intimacy becomes relatively insignificant. The really important question has been answered beyond any doubt: that Fersen and the queen loved each other deeply, sincerely, and honestly. It was this which was of such profound significance in the lives of both of them.

2

As we have seen, Fersen divided his time almost equally between France and Sweden between 1784 and 1788. These were hard years for France and his letters reflect the growing crisis.

He returned to his regiment at Valenciennes, as noted, in April 1785, at the time of the Scheldt crisis, after delivering to Versailles an offer by Gustav III to provide the Dutch with an auxiliary corps of 6,000 men in return for increased subsidies from their French ally.[42] This would not be the last time Gustav would offer armed assistance to His Most Christian Majesty.

The French government, however, preferred to negotiate with Austria. Since the American war, its power was increasingly undermined by two problems in particular: the mounting financial crisis and the growing hostility to the queen. Axel wrote home, describing the Affair of the Diamond Necklace, which he felt to be an especially hard blow to a government laboring under a serious deficit. Naturally taking the queen's side, he considered the behavior of the Cardinal de Rohan infamous.[43]

Again returning to France in 1787, once more at the prospect of war, this time between France and Prussia over revolutionary disturbances in the United Netherlands, he reached Paris in time to witness the end of the first Assembly of Notables, which greatly impressed him "and probably will not be seen again in our days." He approved too, of the numerous economies the Assembly resolved to make, especially in the royal household.[44]

If anything, his remarks show that he did not feel these reforms had gone far enough. He had recently returned from Sweden, where following the diet of the previous year there was much concern over financial problems, especially court extravagance. He was a member at this time of the fashionable Valois Club at the Palais-Royal, which consisted largely of liberally-minded noblemen and included La Fayette, the Lameth brothers, the Abbé Sieyès, Saint-Priest, the Vicomte de Noailles, and Ambassador Staël.[45] Fersen himself became much absorbed in practical reform in preparing a new "capitulation" for his regiment in accordance with the new requirements of the Council of War. To be sure, he was not anxious to have his recently awarded pension as colonel-proprietor reduced by the new economies, but after making attempts, as he wrote his father, to gain exemption, he economized as much as he could.[46] One gains the impression that he simply made such representations *pro forma*, to allay Fredrik Axel's perpetual financial anxieties. His accustomed style of living cannot meanwhile have fared too badly, as comments to his sister in 1788, on the remarks of a mutual acquaintance in France, show:

The marquise's description is a little exaggerated, especially regarding my equipages. They are good and proper but nothing magnificent or extraordinary; it is that which I avoid with care. My livery is simply a blue habit with silver boutonnières and a collar of crimson velvet. You see that this is not so superb. The rest is also a bit exaggerated, although there is some truth to it.

During the summer of 1789, he maintained a staff of ten servants.[47]

Axel rejoined his regiment at Maubeuge in 1787 at a time when Joseph II's reforms were causing serious disturbances a short distance away in the Austrian Netherlands. Axel wrote to his father with keen interest how in Mons "all in bourgeois dress" sported cocardes in red, white, yellow, and black, how the local garrisons were insubordinate and the Austrian governor in Brussels was afraid to show himself in the streets. The instigators were the local clergy and nobility, "while the good bourgeoisie and prosperous farmers" feared only "great evils and great losses" from the revolt.[48] Fersen again shows himself in favor of reform, but that distaste for the insubordination of subjects against rightful authority he had revealed in America comes to the fore.

In the meantime, France, after some show of support for the Dutch "patriots" backed down when faced with Prussia, Great Britain, and financial collapse. He would be glad, Axel wrote Sophie, if this would relieve her worries about him, but he regretted losing the chance to cut a figure at the head of the regiment he had taken such pains to train.[49] He returned to Paris in the fall of 1787, where the American painter John Trumbull was sketching portraits for his painting of Cornwallis's surrender at Yorktown in 1781. He worked in the home of the American minister, Thomas Jefferson, and was fortunate in finding in "this capital of dissipation and nonsense," in his words, all his subjects, including Count "Phersen."[50]

At the end of December 1787, Fersen wrote at great length to Gustav III on the situation in France, where for the past six months "most extraordinary and distressing things" had been taking place, noting that the king had wished him to keep him thus informed. The humiliation of "the affair of Holland" was the result of problems caused by the finances and especially the *parlements*. The latter

... appear to have formed the project of opposing in everything the will of the king and of creating in the monarchy a power that counterbalances his, which would be a monstrous thing. It cannot be imagined what their goal is, if not the desire of five or six individuals, men of spirit and eloquence, to talk and to make themselves famous no matter at what price. They induce the others to follow—which is only too easy in a century in which philosophy has made so much progress and in a country where anglomania has gone so far as to affect attitudes and ways of thinking about the administration; but they have been able only to grasp these things imperfectly and in their least applicable aspects. One hears nothing from the mouths of everyone but liberty, conservation of property, contempt for the court, and he who seeks to be fashionable by affecting disregard toward the court and its favors secretly stoops to a thousand base expedients in order to obtain them. Here, Sire, are what I believe to be the true reasons for the conduct of the Parlement [of Paris]. They should seem frivolous, but in considering a little the character of the French, they will not be so in their effects.

The *parlements* showed "bad faith" and "little patriotism" in rejecting the government's proposed territorial subvention and stamp tax; they posed as the "defenders of the people" but considered only their own advantage,

... since the stamp tax would naturally bear more heavily on the rich, who account for the greatest consumption, than upon the poor, and the territorial subvention, in making each province responsible for the sum that should be submitted to the royal treasury, would oblige the members of the *parlements* to pay like the rest; while under the present system the majority pay little or nothing through abuses and because it would be too dangerous to call to account a man who would serve at once as judge and defendant.

Several of the *parlements* refused to recognize the newly established provincial assemblies:

This resistance by the *parlements* to an administration that is the pride and joy of the provinces and which had often been demanded by them revolts almost everyone. Their poor faith and self-interest is too clear not to strike all men of good-will who truly love their country. The English system is worth nothing in France: the one is a free country, the other is not at all suited to be that.

He took Calonne to task for having revealed the state of the government finances, a branch of administration that "'ought to remain secret." As a result, government credit was ruined. "The philosophers and the admirers of English liberty say the opposite, but philosophy and liberty are incompatible with monarchy." The reduction of pensions and other economies had caused much protest, but the *premier ministre*, Archbishop Loménie de Brienne, was securely backed by the crown. Though a man of good intentions, however, it was regrettable that Brienne was somewhat "weak and frivolous" and besides, "a man of system," an *"économiste."* It would have been well if the archbishop had appointed M. Necker controller-general; "People have a high opinion, and with reason, of the talents and honesty of this man." Since the departure of Calonne, the Polignac circle was losing its influence with the queen, who, he wrote, "is generally detested; to her are attributed all the evils that are taking place and she is given no credit for anything good." "The king is always feeble and suspicious; he confides in no one but the queen. It appears it is she who does everything. The ministers go often to her and inform her on all matters." It was even rumored that she encouraged the king to drink to bend him to her will. "Since anglomania has crept into all minds, Versailles is more deserted than usual...."[51]

Axel meanwhile kept his father well advised on the political conflict in France, which no doubt delighted the old parliamentary leader. There was much talk of convening the Estates General. Fersen again attacked the *parlements* for their self-interest. Their "principal aim" was "to avoid paying taxes by constantly refusing all measures that would make their distribution more equal by making the rich pay more than the poor." On the whole matter of privilege, a comment from a letter in January 1788 is also worth noting: "I do not believe it to be useful or necessary in Sweden as in France for there to be persons destined for the highest ranks by reason of their birth alone."[52]

These first observations by Fersen on the political crisis in France already reveal attitudes he would hold throughout the revolution that followed: his mistrust of abstract system building, of popular enthusiasms, of ambitious and unscrupulous individuals, of weakness in governments. He shows himself distinctly on the side of a strong royal authority—a "monarchical system"—as opposed to one limited by entrenched corporate privileges or aroused public opinion. Meanwhile, however, the situation in Sweden, particularly Gustav III's war with Russia, proved a sobering and disillusioning reminder to Fersen of the abuses to which royal absolutism was prone.

He returned from that war in November 1788 to a situation in France very different from what he had left in May. The principal conflict was no longer between the government and the *parlements* over royal despotism. The king had given way and called the Estates General for the following spring. The real struggle now lay between the privileged orders and the Third Estate. The Royal-Suédois regiment was stationed for a time that fall in Rennes to preserve civil order. Returning to France, Fersen tended to view the increasing social antagonisms there as analogous with those he had just observed in Sweden and Finland. Deeply pessimistic about his own country, he tended to regard the situation in France with greater optimism.[53] He was nonetheless much concerned over the effects of the press upon public opinion, as he would continue to be thereafter; in January 1789, he wrote his father:

> ... the public is inundated with writings, brochures, and pamphlets. Not a day passes when five or six do not appear and most of them show no common sense; they contain nothing but words void of meaning or ideas that are entirely seditious. Everyone is author or administrator, and especially the women. You know as well as I the extent to which they set the tone here and how much they like to meddle in everything. They are now occupied with nothing but the constitution, and the young men, to please them and be fashionable, speak of nothing but Estates General and governments, though often their waistcoats, their cabriolets, and their morning coats provide them with diversion. I do not know whether the kingdom will profit from all these changes but society has suffered by them.

"This country is still in a state of great ferment," he continued in the same letter, "but here, in a short while, great passions pass and reflection follows." There was much dispute over doubling the Third Estate at the forthcoming Estates General but the king had decided on this course, which Fersen felt was "actually what appears to be most just." Confidence in Necker's talents and honesty, he wrote later the same month, reconciled many to this decision, "which was desired by a part of the nobility and does much good." The *parlements* were losing through their "follies" what little prestige they still possessed. Finally, although the unusually cold winter caused much suffering in Paris, "the aid being given to the poor and to charity are being carried to extraordinary lengths and nothing is more common than to see individual persons keeping warm and feeding 50 to 100 poor people."[54] Surely, in Axel's thinking, a society capable of such humanitarian concern must have seemed fundamentally sound.

On 1 March, he wrote Gustav III that he believed "goodness, decency, frankness, and loyalty to the king" would "calm spirits" and restore to France that "weight and influence" in Europe naturally bestowed by her position and "inexhaustible resources." On 10 April, however, less than a month before the opening of the Estates General, he showed somewhat less assurance to his father:

Spirits are furiously aroused. You know how this nation is: the madder ideas are the more passionately they are welcomed. All speak of liberty without knowing anything about it, without having any conception of it, and always confound it with license. The Third Estate, blind with having obtained an equality in numbers to those of the other two orders combined, believes that it consequently should obtain everything and conceives the most ridiculous and extravagant pretentions. But decisions on these matters are being deferred until the meeting of the Estates General and it appears that this will be less unfortunate than was first believed.[55]

3

Meanwhile, Axel received grievous news from Sweden. In the Riksdag convened in February, his father had taken his accustomed place as leader of the anti-royalist opposition in the house of the nobility. Axel wrote that he hoped his health would not suffer from "the grief of seeing the total ruin of our fatherland. That sorrow is quite just and I share it most acutely." To prevent opposition from the nobility to his Act of Union and Security, Gustav III had 19 of its representatives arrested on the night of 19 February, including the elder Fersen. Forewarned of the king's intention, some one hundred nobles gathered at the old count's house, intending to "oppose force with swords in their hands." Fredrik Axel dissuaded them, pointing out that such resistance would result in a bloodbath at the hands of the enraged populace and would brand the entire nobility as "treasonable and rebellious" in the eyes of the nation. He thereupon submitted quietly to arrest and imprisonment.[56]

Axel was in Valenciennes when he received the news, with orders to return to Paris, apparently from the queen herself, who wished to console him.[57] In Sweden, his sisters pleaded with the king in vain for their father's release. Many nobles resigned government and court posts in protest, including Hedda Klinckowström. Fabian, Sophie, and Axel wished to do likewise, but were forbidden to do so by their father himself, who maintained that in such perilous times their country had the right to expect their brave and loyal support. His letter to Axel in this regard so moved Marie-Antoinette that she copied it out in her own hand. It was also much admired by Breteuil and others, but caused Axel much embarrassment when a club, "of which there are many in Paris in imitation of the English," made public an alleged copy of it, filled with distortions and exaggerations, "in brief, a letter arranged according to the situation and French spirits at the moment." Axel thus felt compelled to send copies of the actual letter to many of his friends.[58]

Though Fredrik Axel's patriotic sentiments were unquestionably real, he also had more political reasons for preventing his children's resignations. The nobility must not, he later wrote, leave state service at the very time when as a class they were threatened by the three lower estates, for by so doing they would renounce their influence in government and, replaced by men of common origin, lose the basis for their existence. "The lower estates regard noblemen as parasites in society, and that is what they will become when they cease to serve their fatherland with knowledge or with arms." Through the ruin of the nobility, he believed, the king sought to destroy the constitution and the liberties of the nation.[59]

Axel sought to remonstrate. The time had come, he wrote on 25 May, after his father had been released, to take a step he owed them both by resigning from the Life Guard. While he praised his father's example of "moderation and submission," to retain his post would be "a tacit consent to lend myself to the will and designs of the king, whatever they might be." When Fredrik Axel persisted in his refusal, Axel's letter of 8 June made clear his moral predicament. Gustav III's behavior seemed to show that he regarded "the good of the state" as "a secondary goal." "How is one to chose between these two obligations? What will be the line of demarcation where one of these duties must give way to the other? Must one serve the king? Must one serve the state?"[60] It was a question many European noblemen were compelled to face in these years.

He nevertheless agreed to "defer" his resignation and urged Sophie to emulate their father's noble behavior rather than the "exaggerations" of their intransigent sister Hedda, warning her furthermore to consider "the example of France."[61] In the face of the situation there, his disillusionment with Gustav III was already beginning to give way to his old monarchical preferences.

Fredrik Axel was released after only a few weeks. Gustav III thereupon turned his considerable charm to the task of reconciling him, and the old count responded with a quiet dignity that chagrined the king's more extreme opponents. "A king may be capricious toward his subjects," he had written to Fabian in 1787, "but a subject cannot show ill humor toward his master. One may hold to one's rights even so—firmness and loyalty can very well be combined. . . ." Axel, now increasingly anxious to gain Gustav III's support for the hard-pressed French royal family, was greatly relieved.[62]

For Gustav, the price of his final victory over the noble opposition came high. He never ceased to sorrow over the loss of the good-will of his nobility.[63]

4

Scarcely a week after Gustav III dissolved his Riksdag in Stockholm, the Estates General convened at Versailles, on 4 May 1789. Axel Fersen, who divided his time that winter and spring between his regiment at Valenciennes, his house in Paris, and the court at Versailles, witnessed the event, which he described as "superb." "You know, my dear father, how imposing the elegance and magnificence of the court of France makes such ceremonies." Ambassador Staël considered it the greatest day in France's history, but Axel felt the novelty would soon wear off and the French people gladly divest themselves of the burden of self-government. The situation seemed more serious after the formation of the National Assembly: "three or four madmen" were behind the whole affair, and God alone knew where it would all end.[64]

In July, he described the storming of the Bastille and uprisings in provincial towns, which he considered "only a parody" of what took place in Paris. All this he regarded as the work of the "vilest rabble," but "the bourgeoisie has been armed everywhere, which has reestablished order right away." Axel and his regiment helped suppress rioting in Valenciennes and pillaging of abbeys and manors in the surrounding countryside. All the bonds were broken, he wrote, and he doubted that everything could be restored as easily as it had been torn down.[65]

The following month, he wrote how Paris, the center of the trouble, was filling up with vagabonds and numerous deserters from the army, who increasingly intimidated the "Estates General." Persons of quality hastened to leave the capital. "There remains neither laws, nor order, nor justice, nor discipline, nor religion," which was the effect of "anglomania and philosophy." "Anglomania" was at this time associated particularly with the Duc d'Orléans, thus with a Whiggish, aristocratic opposition to royal absolutism. It still seemed largely a matter of outward display to Axel, who in October complained to his father that "a great many young men, self-styled Patriots or Jacobins, have cut their hair completely and look like English grooms, without powder. Here you have the French!" "No one dares to command and no one will obey," he wrote in September. "There is the liberty of France. . . . I have always been of your opinion, my dear father, about a national assembly. I have always envisioned it as one of the most dangerous things for this country, but it was impossible to foresee that it would be so disastrous." At the end of that month, Axel moved to Versailles to be near the royal family, like many others from Paris.[66]

Axel thus failed entirely to see the Revolution in France as a great national movement. He had long considered the French as a people to be excitable, unstable, and impractical, and felt all groups in French society responsible in some degree for the present impasse, through selfishness, irresponsibility, or naiveté. But these were only sins of omission. He did not believe that the Revolution itself had arisen from any of the established orders of society: he held the bourgeoisie no more to blame than the nobility. Nor did he consider the National Assembly responsible for the excesses of the Revolution or guilty of anything worse than its appalling weakness. Thus he saw in the Revolution simply the work of a handful of malcontents who had placed themselves at the head of the dregs of society. Most people, though misled by "anglomania and philosophy," would be brought to their senses by the violence and anarchy he felt inherent in the attempt to put abstract principles into actual practice.

What surely impressed him more than anything else with the seriousness of the situation were the "October Days"—5 and 6 October 1789—when the palace at Versailles was beset by an immense crowd from Paris, a wild attempt was made on the queen's life, and the royal family was forced to return with the mob to Paris. "I was a witness to everything," Axel wrote his father, "and I returned to Paris in one of the carriages of the king's suite; we were six and a half hours on the road. God preserve me from ever seeing such a distressing spectacle again as that of those two days." He himself gave no further details but was observed by others who, due to the confusion of the moment, later gave varying accounts of his activity. According to a rather questionable recollection of Mme. d'Adhémar, Fersen mingled with the crowd outside the Hôtel de Ville in Paris to find out its intentions before galloping to Versailles to warn the queen. From this tale may derive Lady Holland's assertion that Fersen the following day "disguised himself as a *démocrate,* and cried out with the mob, 'Vive la nation,' so that he might remain close to the Queen's coach," which is disproven by Fersen's own letter to his father. Lord Holland later claimed that Fersen fled in disguise from the queen's bedchamber, as noted, which likewise has been shown to be false. More trustworthy is doubtless the Comte de Tilly's and the Comte de Narbonne's testimony that Fersen was among those who stood guard in the anteroom to the queen's apartment when La Fayette arrived that night from Paris. When the crowd demanded that the queen appear on the balcony alone, according to this version, she hesitated but at a sign from Fersen, went; La Fayette then joined her and kissed her hand, to the delight of the crowd. Axel was doubtless among those keeping vigil over the royal family throughout that long night. What advice might he have given them? It seems not unlikely that he might have joined the Comte de Saint-Priest, with whom he was then closely associated, in urging them to flee to the protection of loyal troops at Rambouillet; less than two years later it would be Fersen who arranged their escape from Paris. Meanwhile, on the evening of 6 October 1789, Saint-Priest found Fersen among those gathered at the Tuileries to attend the king, following his arrival there, and fearing that at such a moment Fersen's presence could provoke further dangers, persuaded him to leave. "It is certain," Saint-Priest wrote, "that if some ill-intentioned person had pointed him out to the populace that milled about, he could have been massacred."[67]

For the time being, Fersen strove to keep up a kind of determined optimism. Yet the events of those days left their indelible impression. On 5 October 1798, he wrote in his diary, "I remembered that day vividly. It was nine years ago, all our agonies at Versailles. Had they but departed, all would have been saved."[68]

Fersen now moved back to Paris. In the period that followed, according to Saint-Priest, he saw Marie-Antoinette privately at the Tuileries almost every day. Saint-Priest even claimed that La Fayette, commander of the Paris National Guard, allowed this by leaving an entrance unguarded and suspected this as a means to increase the queen's unpopularity.[69]

In November 1789, Baron Taube arrived in Aachen to recuperate from a wound received in Finland. Axel wrote him of his concern that the foreign regiments in French service might soon be dissolved, which would not only affect his own livelihood but deprive the king and queen of their only reliable military support.[70]

There was more to Taube's arrival than met the eye. The baron was in many ways his monarch's political alter ego. His appearance in Aachen revealed Gustav III's growing concern over events in France.

5

Gustav had been watching the situation there for some time. His interest was both military and financial, since France had traditionally supplied Sweden's need for a strong ally and foreign subsidies. Though he had not been averse to profiting from diplomatic support from France's rivals, Britain and Prussia, in his war with Russia and Denmark, and toyed with the idea of an alliance with them, his letters to Stedingk and Armfelt reveal how deeply he was concerned over the state of affairs in France, one which he felt he himself had only narrowly avoided in his own realm through a show of firmness that stood in contrast to the weakness and indecision of Louis XVI and his government.[71] By December 1789,

Gustav sought an alliance with Britain, "in view," he wrote Taube, "of the little assurance which the whole existence of France gives me." He would thus only consider a renewed French alliance as a second alternative, in which case he would provide, in return for the stiffest conditions, 12,000 troops and 15 vessels "to aid the king." Ultimately, neither the British nor the renewed French alliances worked out and the next year, Gustav had nowhere to turn but to his erstwhile enemy, Catherine II. In the meantime, he concerned himself increasingly with plans to render some sort of aid to the French crown.[72]

When he learned of the Paris insurrection of July 1789, Gustav III wrote Armfelt, inquiring where "*le grand Axel*" had been "during all of this excitement." Axel, the latter replied, had been with his regiment at Valenciennes. "Always careful and aloof, he watches the total overthrow of France, the court and his humiliated benefactress, without stirring from the spot." As one of the few who had stood by Gustav III during the dark days of 1788, Armfelt was no doubt contemptuous of Axel's divided sentiments and timely escape from Sweden. Fersen's own biting comments from Italy five years earlier show there was little love lost between them. Fersen nevertheless seems to have intentionally avoided too much contact with Marie-Antoinette during the summer of 1789 to keep from compromising her popularity.

Evert Taube in Aachen served as a sort of unofficial agent for French affairs. For some months, Gustav had suspected Ambassador Staël in Paris of too great a sympathy for the Revolution. This was not altogether fair to Staël, who sought conscientiously to carry out his duties and whose dispatches show much insight, judgment, and balance. It was, however, his misfortune to be son-in-law to Necker, whom he praised to the skies, and whom Gustav considered a charlatan. Furthermore, Mme. de Staël's vigorous intervention in the affairs of the Swedish embassy became increasingly embarrasing. Staël and his wife, who also wrote on her own initiative to Gustav, while deploring the excesses of the extremists and the mob, were outspoken in condemning the follies of the court, including the princes and the queen herself, and of the aristocratic party in the National Assembly. Meanwhile the hapless Staël, who for all his good intentions was riddled with debts, thus fell increasingly under the domination of his rich and imperious wife. Already by August 1789, Gustav had secretly instructed the first secretary in Staël's embassy, A. I. Silfversparre, to submit his own reports on events in France without the ambassador's knowledge.[74]

On 12 July 1789, Staël wrote, "This revolution has been made by the queen," adding, "... I do not doubt that it is the queen's wish to obtain M. de Fersen's appointment as Your Majesty's ambassador here." As will be seen, Fersen himself hoped—by August 1789, if not earlier—to replace Staël in Paris.[75] If Gustav had already begun to suspect Staël at this point, however, Axel's own favor with the king after leaving Sweden the previous fall was evidently still precarious.

In December, Axel briefly visited his regiment in Valenciennes to quell a mutiny among the troops stationed there. On 7 January 1790, Taube wrote Gustav III from Aachen:

Le grand Fersen came here from Valenciennes to see me. The scenes that have passed before his eyes in France have been a good school for him and have done him a great deal of good for the future, he now recognizes the great evils of a popular government, and he said to me, and I heard this with joy from his lips, that of all the ways in which the different events of life might be conducted, he would have none in which it was possible to forget that one had a king, that of all the possible forms of government, anarchy was the most horrible, the most tyrannical and always destructive for all countries—this is not the sentiment which they have always tried to impart to Axel.

In April, when it was expected Staël would accompany the ailing Necker to Switzerland, Taube recommended Fersen for the position of ambassador in Staël's place or any other official position. He continued:

... if Your Majesty wished to employ *långa Axel* in one way or another, Your Majesty would infinitely oblige The Person who is interested in this now more than ever. It is all the same, Sire, under what title Your Majesty might wish to employ him at present, but Your Majesty would be assured forever of the gratitude of The Person who is interested. I dare, Sire, to assure you that Axel would serve us with fidelity and attachment; he is at this moment more anxious to serve you, Sire, than anything else, and Your Majesty may count on his everlasting gratitude.

It is clear who "The Person" in question was.[76]

Axel's relatively easy return to the good graces of Gustav III and the king's forbearance with him during 1789 were without doubt largely due to Axel's unique position in the confidence of Marie-Antoinette, with whom Gustav's relations had previously been cool. Now, however, her cooperation would be indispensable for any plan he might devise for the mutual benefit of the French and Swedish monarchies.[77]

Fersen was still not happy with the situation in Sweden. Yet in view of circumstances in France he now considered even more serious, he was anxious that the king and the nobility in Sweden should conciliate their differences. If the Swedish nobles continued their "unseemly behavior," they would end by making the king a "tyrant," he wrote Taube in February 1790. "All you tell me about the situation in our country makes me shudder," Axel wrote Sophie in April 1790,

. . . alas, that of this country is no better. At least in ours one is sure of one's life and has nothing to fear from popular uprisings; there are no manor houses burned, no pillaging, no one hanged or massacred, while all these excesses have been committed here and are still being committed in the provinces and one must always fear uprisings. All the plagues at once are desolating this country and one sees it subjected to the despotism of the multitude, which is the worst of all. . . .

"God preserve our unhappy country from ever going through a revolution like this one," he wrote his father. "We would soon become a second Poland, tributary to and under the absolute domination of Russia. We have some hotheads and madmen who must be watched and kept in check." And to Sophie in December: "I wish I could lay before the eyes of the whole Swedish nobility the spectacle of all that is happening to that of France and the deplorable state of this fair kingdom to bring them to reason."[78]

Among the "hotheads" were two Swedish noblemen, Reuterholm and Silfverhielm, whom Axel saw in Paris in the summer of 1790. The former, one of Gustav III's bitterest enemies, was indeed in semi-voluntary exile, following the Riksdag of 1789, and spoke, Axel informed Sophie, of "nothing but civil war, of changes of constitution." He suspected him of "correspondence with the so-called *enragés* here or with the Propaganda Club," informed Taube he had sent Gustav III "important things . . . concerning his own safety and to prevent in Sweden what is happening here," and urged that the two be closely watched. No one could foresee that two years hence, Gustaf Adolf Reuterholm would become the most powerful man in Sweden.[79]

It appears that it was during his visit to Aachen in January 1790 that Taube gave Fersen instructions from Gustav III to remain in Paris as his special agent. He had already begun sending reports to the king; as early as 12 November 1789, he wrote Taube that he would send Gustav III information he had requested. By March 1790, Fersen obtained from Gustav unlimited leave from the Swedish army as well as his father's consent to remain in France.[80]

In February, Gustav III wrote Staël in Paris, pointedly noting that Necker's son-in-law could hardly expect to be *persona grata* as Swedish ambassador if the French monarchy recovered its power. Over a year later, on 4 April 1791, Taube advised Fersen:

The king commands me to inform you that all of Staël's dispatches are written in the revolutionary spirit; he wishes to pretend to him that he pays attention to what he tells him, but this is only to find out their [the revolutionaries'] projects and ideas. The king orders you to warn the king and queen [of France] of this so they will not be misled by it. You will assure them that the king will never waver in his sentiments and his attachment to them and that he will seek on all occasions to prove it to them. . . .[81]

6

Until the spring of 1791, Axel remained close to the royal family. His role was necessarily limited mainly to that of observer. He was kept well informed by the Comte de Saint-Priest, the most royalist of Louis XVI's ministers. who asked his opinions on political matters. A letter to Taube in April 1790, meanwhile, shows the feverish state of activity into which he now plunged:

The desire of the king will be fulfilled; he will receive the news once a week. But point out to him that being alone, not being able even to engage a secretary, and being obliged to show myself in society to avoid all suspicion, I am overloaded with things to do. The satisfaction of serving him and of being useful to the king and queen of France will let me find everything possible and if I can succeed in this, I shall be more than repaid.[82]

Fersen wrote his first long report to Gustav III from Aachen on 7 January 1790:

[The affairs] of France are distressing, and Your Majesty has grasped them in their true meaning. I believe as does Your Majesty that M. Necker is very guilty, and nothing but a war, internal or external, can reestablish France and royal authority. But how can this be brought about when the king is a prisoner in Paris? It was a false move for him to allow himself to be taken there. Now it is necessary to try to get him out, and the declaration made by the king in the month of October [1789] that he was free and that to prove it, he would visit the provinces in the spring, this declaration is a good pretext for leaving, but in the meantime the Assembly must be left to commit all its follies. If he once leaves Paris, he should be able to bring about a new order of things. If he is prevented [from leaving], his captivity will be well proven to the provinces, and in this case as well, there should be a great change. His party has already increased in the Assembly and in the provinces, and the courage, firmness, and good conduct of the queen have won many people for her. All the nobility, except certain individuals unworthy of the name, are devoted to them, the clergy the same, almost all of the good bourgeoisie, and daily the number grows. Only the rabble are still impressed by the famous words, "despotism" and "aristocrats," but a winter of experience and misery,—for everyone has made reforms, and no one spends or gives anything,—a winter will calm them and will change a great many of them. Add to this the rashness and fickleness of French spirits, incapable of consistency and as ready to seize upon the bad as the good, and a remedy for the present evil may still be hoped for.[83]

In this letter Fersen gave those ideas which had been slowly devleoping in his mind for many months and above all the fundamental materialism and skepticism of his concept of human nature. He believed the majority of men were motivated simply by material needs and desires, and that material hardship would therefore quickly quell rebellious spirits. Thus he failed utterly to understand the strength of ideas as motives for human action and self-sacrifice. All of this shows up repeatedly in his correspondence during the following years and some of these ideas deserve closer examination.

Almost all of Axel's letters, especially to Sophie, show his great admiration for the queen. This was intimately tied to his emotional attachment to her but aside from this, he regarded her as the greatest asset to the royalist cause and placed high hopes in her ability to win support. Unfortunately, as he wrote Gustav III in August 1790, "the queen is not the king," and the latter's weakness and indecision obstructed positive attempts to aid him.[84]

Meanwhile, he continuously execrated Necker—whom in 1787 he had admired—for his vanity, ambition, ignorance, abstract philosophical ideas, and the baleful influence of his imperious wife and daughter.[85]

Fersen remained convinced that the Revolution was still the work of a few determined malcontents, "persons whom hatreds, jealousies, or private vengeance have induced to behave badly toward the king and to forget the obligations they owed him, [who] no longer hoping that what they have done will be forgotten except through total subversion, ceaselessly stir up the mob with the great words, 'liberty,' 'despotism,' and 'aristocracy.' "[86]

On occasion, he was overcome with bitterness and disillusionment. The French, he wrote Taube in May 1790, were "the vilest nation I have ever known. I will be happy the day an unlimited despotism is established over them." Yet he retained a certain serene optimism. It was inconceivable that the demagogues could maintain their influence if the French people were badly enough hurt in their material interests. And since the prosperity of society depended upon the patronage and largesse of the rich and powerful, the only way to restore material well-being was to restore the old order. He repeatedly spoke of the growing misery of the artisan class, ruined by the Revolution.[87]

What then, could the king and queen do to overcome the situation? They must in the first place allow time for the Revolution to destroy itself through its excesses, an idea he had maintained since the first convening of the Estates General. "The Revolution was brought about through public opinion," he wrote Gustav III in April 1790. "It must be undone by the same means and for this it is necessary to allow time enough . . . The weak is no longer protected against the strong and the farmer trembles ceaselessly for his property. This state of affairs cannot last. . . ." "Once the discontent reaches its height," he wrote his father in November, "the new order of things will be overthrown as quickly as the old one was. This is the effect of the rashness and fickleness of French minds." The Assembly should even be protected in its operations, he advised Gustav in September; after the misery of another winter it would perish by itself, but to act precipitately could spoil everything.[88]

Fersen meanwhile placed great hopes in playing off one faction of revolutionaries against another to bring about their mutual destruction, for which any means should be legitimate. He ridiculed Necker for wanting to "remain a virtuous man among rogues," showing how utterly futile he considered this to be. Only corrupt means could have any effect in an "assembly," he wrote Gustav III in February 1790. Scoundrels must be fought with their own weapons. Louis XVI should pretend to place himself at the head of the Revolution, he wrote Gustav III in early 1790, abandon the aristocratic party "and by this means give birth to circumstances by which one might profit." Though repugnant to the king's honesty, this nevertheless "suited his character" and besides, "It is necessary to be a king before being an honest man." Early in 1790, he was much encouraged by the split between the worst of the *"enragés"* in the Assembly—"M. du Port, Barnave, de la Meth, d'Aiguillon, Mirabeau, etc."—and La Fayette and his supporters, who now hoped to form a majority for the king with the aristocratic faction, in return for acceptance of most of the changes thus far brought about by the Revolution and eventually of the new constitution. This would make it possible to destroy the extremists.[89]

By June 1790, another possibility presented itself: Mirabeau entered into a secret agreement with the king and queen to serve their interests, without the knowledge of his rival, La Fayette. Although he was a "great scoundrel" who should be closely watched, Fersen wrote to Taube, "he has quite despotic ideas" and could be very useful to the court. Unfortunately, Mirabeau needed a great deal of money to distribute, which the king could scarcely provide. But by pitting him against La Fayette, "who frightens easily," the king and queen could win time and "retain, not the same authority they formerly had, but a part of it. For this, one must exercise patience, a consistent conduct, dissimulation and above all, no violent measures at this point."[90] But more positive action would be needed if authority were to be reestablished. For this, the most important step would be to get the king and his family away from Paris, as Fersen wrote to Gustav III as early as 7 January 1790, but only under conditions that gave reasonable assurance of success. Speaking of various possibilities in his letter of 10 April 1790 to Gustav III, he wrote:

That of leaving Paris secretly and of withdrawing to Metz or to some other fortified place has been rejected as impracticable. There is in effect no means to carry it out and the weak and fainthearted behavior of the provinces does not make it possible. It is even to be feared that they might want to oppose the entry of a foreign army and that the persons of the king and his family would be endangered.[91]

In August, he developed his ideas in detail for Gustav III. Disorder and anarchy would soon reach their culmination and the time would then be right to act. "There is no remedy for so many ills except force, and force from abroad, for there is no internal force that can be relied on." Internal collapse and discontent were not sufficient in themselves to restore the situation. "The cause of the king of France is that of all kings. The example is too dangerous. It is necessary that vengeance be striking and that it frighten all those people who might wish to imitate the French." The monarchs of Austria and especially Prussia should be persuaded to intervene by "advancing their troops," using as their pretext French violations of the Treaty of Westphalia and the fiefs of German princes in France. "The king, either through necessity or through cunning, would proceed to the frontier. Here he would summon all who are loyal to him, and the number would be very great." "Your Majesty," and the kings of Sardinia and Spain could then join in his support, "the Assembly would tremble and the whole kingdom would be subjugated almost without bloodshed. . . . Here, Sire, is the plan I have worked out, the only one I believe appropriate to return to the king his authority and to reestablish things in the proper order." But this would require a great, concerted effort; no partial measures would suffice. "They must be crushed without giving them the time to breathe." The participating powers should meanwhile agree to settle the question of compensations separately. This plan, which Fersen here claims to have devised himself as early as the summer of 1790, is worthy of more than passing attention: from it developed, as will be seen, many of the features of the plan for the escape of the royal family in June 1791, the project for an armed congress of powers in late 1791 and early 1792, and finally the Brunswick Manifesto of July 1792. Meanwhile, the spread of revolution seemed only too evident. In the Austrian Netherlands, Axel wrote his father in December 1790, those "who have nothing to lose and would like to gain by a new order of things" aspired to "a total change" and independence. "It seems that the desire for revolutions is extending throughout Europe. It is as contagious as the pest and one must thus protect oneself against it."[92]

It was, however, necessary to find leadership for such enterprises and this was not easy. One would naturally look to the nobility, including both the aristocratic party in France and the émigrés abroad. Fersen, however, wrote to Gustav III in February 1790:

The aristocrats were the first instruments of the Revolution. They wished to obstruct the authority of the king to seize it for themselves. Now they are only for him because it is in their interest. They deserve everything that is happening to them and the king would have done well to abandon them from the start. There are among them the provincial nobility in general, who have always remained loyal to the king, and it is these who are to be pitied.

As for the moderates or "impartials" in the National Assembly, "Their principles are too reasonable to have any effect at this time." The émigrés Axel regarded as distinctly dangerous. He was fearful of the bold schemes of the Comte d'Artois and the Prince de Condé in Savoy in the fall of 1790, inspired by "the most determined aristocrats," who "have never been able to do anything but harm to the king."[93] The problem of finding capable leadership, acceptable at once to the royal family and to the majority of Frenchmen, was one the monarchy could never resolve.

Axel's underlying optimism during most of 1790 is meanwhile reflected in his letters to Taube and Sophie. He repeatedly assured his sister that he was in no personal danger and often spoke of Paris as being calm for the time being. "I am beginning to feel a little happier," he wrote Sophie in April, "for I am able to see my friend from time to time freely at her lodgings and this consoles us a little for all the evils she is going through. Poor woman, she is an angel in her conduct, courage, and sensibility. One has never been able to love like that. . . ." He spent most of the summer, when the royal family was at Saint-Cloud, with friends nearby. Saint-Priest relates that though La Fayette kept the royal family under close surveillance, this did not prevent Fersen from constantly visiting the queen. His letters meanwhile reflected a pleasant existence in châteaux and country houses.[94] He did not realize when he returned to Paris at the end of October that he had enjoyed the last autumn days of the old way of life.

7

Fersen was a witness to the Fête of the Federation held on the Champs-de-Mars on 14 July 1790. To its sympathizers throughout Europe, then and later, this great patriotic ceremony seemed a high point in the Revolution. To Fersen, the whole manifestation of popular emotion seemed only ridiculous. Even here, though, he saw encouragement for the royal cause. "The deputies from the provinces have behaved marvelously toward the king and queen," he reported to Taube a few days later.[95]

One cannot help feeling that as Axel was increasingly affected by his emotional attachment to Marie-Antoinette, he tended to see what he looked for, and to look for what he wanted to find. Baron Staël, meanwhile, gave a less sanguine picture of the event: "The same people who cry 'long live the king' today could bring themselves to kill him tomorrow to keep him from having any prerogative."[96]

By this time, Fersen had come to despise his old friend Staël. He disliked him for his connection with Necker and resented his forthright criticism of the queen, whose political conduct had not been beyond reproach. Yet when Staël, under instructions from Gustav III, did his best to reconcile himself with Marie-Antoinette, Fersen bitterly accused him of hypocrisy.[97] In all of this, Axel was less than fair. Staël conscientiously reported events to his government the way he saw them. His description of the Fête of the Federation as well as his other dispatches show that while Staël was a friend of reform, he was no friend of disorder and violence. Perhaps the principal difference between them was Staël's unwavering objectivity and realism, which led him to accept as political facts what neither Fersen, nor Taube, nor Gustav III could bring themselves to acknowledge.

Fersen's relations with Staël at this time show he was not above petty behavior on occasion. Nor was he above personal ambition. As early as July 1789, Staël feared Fersen might relieve him of his post since this appeared Marie-Antoinette's wish. On 15 August, Axel noted in his letter register that he had written Sophie requesting "that she speak to Our Friend about my embassy project," and again on 12 October, "spoke of the embassy." "I am much obliged, my friend, that you are occupying yourself so much with my project," he wrote on 27 November to Taube in Aachen, "we must talk together about it for there will be various arrangements to make."[98] It is thus clear that from the beginning, Axel's mission to Paris as Gustav III's secret agent was tied up with his own plan to become ambassador. From the fall of 1789 on, it was expected that Necker would resign as *premier ministre*, which he finally did in September 1790. Since Staël would probably accompany his father-in-law to his estate in Switzerland, Fersen's design was that he should be assigned to carry out Staël's duties in his absence and then, Gustav III so willing, to be appointed ambassador in his place. Indeed, it appears from a letter to Taube on 17 March 1791, that

Fersen had actually received accreditation from Gustav III which he was to hold in reserve until the right moment.[99] The plan, however, came to nothing and Axel was soon involved in activities of another kind. His ambition was only realized later—under the most ironic circumstances—when in the summer of 1792, Axel Fersen was appointed the new Swedish ambassador to France, with instructions to accompany the armies of the Duke of Brunswick into Paris.

CHAPTER V

Fersen and the Flight to Varennes, 1790–1791

1

During the fall of 1790, developments took place which would soon remove Axel Fersen from the role of passive observer and draw him deeply into the course of events. Plans were afoot to rescue the royal family from its gilded captivity in Paris.[1]

This idea was by no means new. Already in late May 1789, a secretary to the queen, Jean-Marie Augeard, had advised that the king move from Versailles to Compiègne, there establish an encampment of 30,000 men and transfer the Estates General to Soissons. On 14 July, Louis XVI considered withdrawing to Metz and henceforward proposals for a move away from Versailles and Paris became endemic. At the same time, growing popular fears of counterrevolution were closely tied to suspicions of aristocratic plots to "abduct" the king and foreign intervention against the Revolution. In September 1789, it was widely rumored the king would withdraw, surrounded by aristocratic councillors, to Metz, where, be it noted, the Marquis de Bouillé would play a leading role; at the same time, Camille Desmoulins declared that Marie-Antoinette sought to join her brother, Joseph II, who was preparing to attack France. The October days took place largely in reaction to such fears and Louis XVI was then urged by Saint-Priest and others to withdraw to Rambouillet.[2]

Thereafter, a succession of schemes were devised to get the royal family out of rebellious Paris to the supposedly loyal provinces.

Augeard gave the queen a detailed memorandum on the subject in October 1789 and the following winter the Marquis de Favras prepared a project for which he was apprehended and hanged. During the sojourn of the royal family at Saint-Cloud that summer, there was speculation over an escape, within the court and beyond, and Bouillé was again mentioned. Already in early April 1790, Fersen wrote Taube:

They are working ceaselessly to inspire confidence, but . . . there are so many people who work against this. When she is a little better established they will try to leave here. They will begin by making short trips to Saint Cloud and the project is then to go to Fontainebleau. It will have to be seen how feasible that will be.

Projects were proposed in 1790 by the Comte d'Inisdal, the Duchesse de Villeroy, a group of conspirators in Lyon, and the following spring by the Duc de Biron—the former Duc de Lauzun—and General Heymann. Throughout, the queen showed the greatest interest and was most suspected while the king remained resigned and passive.[3]

Fersen wrote Gustav III in January 1790 that order could not be restored in France unless the king were gotten out of Paris. Periodically thereafter he mentioned the possibility to Gustav III and Taube. He was consistently opposed, however, to poorly planned enterprises. Regarding the Favras Affair, he wrote Taube on 15 March, "The count [sic] spoke to me about all of these projects but I always avoided them and told him that it was folly; inform Our Man [Gustav III] of this." A year later, after the so-called *journée des poignards* of 28 February 1791, when a crowd of armed noblemen gathered at the Tuileries, Axel wrote his father, "I was not there. I have always detested useless demonstrations and bravado which do much more harm than good." Besides, such behavior offended against good taste. In March, he complained to Gustav III of French aristocratic royalists who appeared in the royal presence in frock coats, which was both "imprudent and disrespectful," and wearing pistols when "a gentleman's weapon is his sword; he has no need to carry any other."[4]

More important, meanwhile, were the speculations of the Marquis de Mirabeau. Already on 6 October 1789, the day after the king's move to Paris, he urged the Comte de La Marck to persuade the royal family to leave the capital. Soon after, he gave La Marck a lengthy memorandum, dated 15 October, which proposed that the king withdraw openly to Rouen and there appeal to the nation, promising reform of abuses and a constitution. La Marck gave this memorandum to the Comte de Provence, who deemed it useless to deliver it to the king. Marie-Antoinette had meanwhile told La Marck in September, "We shall never be so unfortunate, I think, as to be reduced to the lamentable extreme of relying on Mirabeau." It appears that Fersen knew nothing at the time of this proposal, which he first described in his diary in October 1791, and had little or no contact with its authors.

Mirabeau continued to seek contact with the court through La Marck and the Austrian ambassador, the Comte de Mercy-Argenteau. At length, the king and queen granted him a secret interview in July 1790, after which he plied them with advice in numerous and lengthy memoranda. Both Mirabeau and La Marck continually urged the royal family to leave the capital. Though the king and queen apparently remained noncommittal, Count Valentin d'Esterhazy, whose house in Auteuil Fersen occupied in August and September 1790, claimed that Louis XVI had told him of his intention to escape to Normandy at that time.[6]

This project, according to Esterhazy, fell through sometime in the fall but the king was now approached from a new quarter. The Baron de Breteuil, now in Switzerland, fearing accommodation between the king and the National Assembly, prepared a plan for the escape of the royal family. He was assisted by Monseigneur Charles d'Agoult, former bishop of Pamiers, whom he sent to Paris in October 1790 to present this project to the royal family. The queen was enthusiastic and charged Fersen with urging it upon the king. According to Count Louis de Bouillé, Breteuil's memorandum held that the king could restore order only by escaping to a safe place within the kingdom, where he should surround himself with loyal troops. Breteuil proposed that the king "assure himself of the support of the foreign powers" through "a capable person whom it seemed most convenient to choose from among those the Revolution had already forced to leave France," obviously Breteuil himself. Arrangements for the flight, including a place of asylum and loyal troops, should be entrusted to General the Marquis de Bouillé, father of the aforementioned Count Louis and commandant in the Three Bishoprics region. The general was understood to favor both reform and order, and was popular with all but the most extreme revolutionaries. It was believed in royalist circles that only he could rival in this respect his cousin, General La Fayette. Louis de

Bouillé relates that Louis XVI hesitated for several days but at last, pressed by the queen, replied: "The king has not yet considered any plan of retreat or flight but he approves the idea that has been given him and he is counting on the favorable disposition of the emperor and of Spain." He was in fact receptive. In August, he had signed despite qualms of conscience the Civil Constitution of the Clergy, which deeply disturbed him.[7]

General de Bouillé claims that he himself had already devised a plan for the emperor to advance troops to the French frontier to give him the opportunity to assemble the most dependable regular regiments, then to present petitions from the troops and the eastern departments to the National Assembly, demanding that the king himself be placed at the head of the army. D'Agoult sounded out Bouillé in Metz in late October regarding Breteuil's plan. Bouillé feared the king might hazard both himself and his crown by fleeing Paris but when d'Agoult told him the emperor and other powers demanded "his withdrawel from Paris and his complete liberty" before aiding him, the general agreed to cooperate.[8]

D'Agoult was next sent by the king to Breteuil in Solothurn with full powers, dated 20 November, to negotiate with foreign courts for the reestablishment of his legitimate authority. A week later, the National Assembly decreed an oath for all clergy to the Civil Constitution. "I would rather be king of Metz," Louis XVI complained to Fersen, "than remain king of France in such a position; but it will soon end." Late in January 1791, he wrote Bouillé that he hoped to depart Paris in March or April and accepted the general's choice of Montmédy, near Austrian Luxemburg, as goal for the flight.[9]

As early as July 1790, Mirabeau had himself suggested that the king make use of Bouillé but he remained unaware that the court had contacted him in October. His own plan meanwhile changed with circumstances. On 23 December 1790, he submitted a long and detailed memorandum on political means for the king to regain popularity and power; separately, La Marck again urged the king and queen to leave Paris. According to La Marck, Louis XVI at last accepted both parts of this program. Mirabeau realized the royal family would now have to take refuge in some well fortified place near the eastern frontier. At first he suggested the department of Le Nord, but the king objected that General Rochambeau, who commanded there, had come back from America filled with republican ideas. What Fersen now thought of his old commander is not recorded. The king preferred Bouillé's sector.[10]

In early February 1791, Mirabeau sent La Marck to Metz to sound out Bouillé. The general was secretly averted by the king. "In Mirabeau's project," he wrote, "you will perhaps find some useful things; listen to him [La Marck] without being too taken in by him and let me know your observations." Bouillé thus gave La Marck no hint of the other escape plan. He was, however, impressed with Mirabeau's project, which in his account emerges as something rather different from what La Marck described. Bouillé wrote in his memoirs that

> ...the intention of Mirabeau was to dissolve the National Assembly and to procure the freedom of the king through the force of the will of the nation itself. ... His means were to have an address presented by the departments of the kingdom for the dissolution of the Assembly, for the convocation of a new one vested with the necessary powers, and to reestablish the king in a condition of liberty and suitable authority.

By this means, the king and his family should be entrusted to Bouillé's protection at Fontainebleau or Compiègne. The plan, as Bouillé gives it, resembled in some respects his own, which also envisioned public petitions. It thus appears that La Marck and Bouillé reached a compromise.[11]

Bouillé now wrote the king that he preferred this plan to the idea of an escape to Montmédy, but in early March the latter ordered him to plan a chain of posts between Châlons and Montmédy to cover his flight. Henceforth, Mirabeau's plan was progressively thwarted, unbeknown to its proponents, by the countervailing influence of Breteuil. Meanwhile, Fersen wrote to his father in February 1791 that he enjoyed the special confidence of the French king and queen, "limited to three or four persons, of which I am the youngest," adding, "During the course of this summer, all these events should work out and be decided."[12]

What then was the basic difference between the project prepared by Mirabeau and La Marck, and that of Breteuil, d'Agoult, Marie-Antoinette, and Fersen? The crux of the matter was assistance from foreign powers. In Fersen's thinking, the flight of the royal family and foreign intervention had been connected since he first mentioned the idea to Gustav III on 7 January 1790, when he spoke of war, "external or internal." A month later, on 5 February, he complained of Louis XVI's weakness and indecision, which made it impossible to undertake anything, "even if the courts of Spain and Sardinia wished to take part." In April, as seen, he wrote that "the weak and cowardly behavior of the provinces" made flight unfeasible and his own project, which he described to Gustav III in August, was based on a simulated threat to France by a combination of powers.[13]

Fersen was clearly in close agreement with Marie-Antoinette, who already in June 1790 suggested to the Austrian ambassador, Mercy, that the emperor and king of Prussia, disapproving the treatment of their fellow monarch in France, could use the rights of German feudatories in Alsace as a pretext to address the French government "in the tone one uses when one feels oneself to be the stronger, the supporter of a good cause and provided with troops." By October, however, Leopold II told the émigrés he could do nothing for his sister and brother-in-law before they were free and safe, as d'Agoult told Bouillé. On 11 January 1791, the queen wrote Count Mercy, now in Brussels, to find out "the true intentions of the emperor and if he wishes to aid us with the forces he has in the Brabant," intimating the Sardinia, the Swiss Cantons, and hopefully Spain were disposed to give assistance. If these arrangements proved satisfactory, she would communicate "our plan" to Vienna, in order "for us to work out the time and manner of its execution." Five weeks later she wrote to Leopold himself, announcing the intention of the family to escape Paris and asking directly for support. Her frequent letters to him and to Mercy are thereafter dominated by this theme of foreign assistance.[14]

Mirabeau sought to avoid foreign intervention, putting his faith in civil war, if need be, fearing that a foreign war would discredit the king. Marie-Antoinette considered the idea of civil war "mad from one end to the other."[15]

Behind the two projects, however, lay even greater differences over ultimate aims. If Mirabeau and La Marck believed their objectives could and should be accomplished through the majority of the French people alone, they desired a constitutional monarchy that should appeal to most Frenchmen. Marie-Antoinette, Breteuil, and Fersen aspired to a restoration of Bourbon absolutism, which could not realistically be expected to command such widespread support, and thus considered outside intervention indispensable. Their views seem neatly summarized by an undated fragment of a coded message, presumably from Breteuil, deciphered in Fersen's

hand: "The revolution in France is tending to make of that kingdom a mixed republic [sic]. The king no longer counts for anything.
150,000 men."[16]

Marie-Antoinette set forth her program in her letter to Mercy
of 3–13 February 1791:

The king is at present occupying himself with gathering together all the
materials for the manifesto which he will necessarily have to make as
soon as we are out of Paris. One must first give the motives for his flight,
pardon those people who have only been misled, flatter them with expressions of love; exclude from pardon the chiefs of the factious, the city
of Paris, at least if it does not return to the old order, as well as those
persons who by a certain fixed time have not surrendered their arms;
reestablish the *parlements* as tribunals of justice only, without their ever
being able to interfere with the administration and finances. Finally,
we have decided to use as the basis of the constitution the Declaration
of 23 June [1789], with such modifications as circumstances and events
have made advisable. Religion will be one of the great points to bring
to the fore.

The queen was thus prepared to accept a constitution of a kind
and the Declaration of 23 June 1789 allowed for periodic Estates
General on the traditional pattern, based on separate orders of
society, to approve legislation and taxation. Yet the "modifications"
alluded to here obviously suggest the reduction of its future role
in favor of royal prerogative. Policy concerning the Church and
state finances are further elucidated in Fersen's letter to Breteuil
of 23 May 1791:

As for the assignats, the king thinks it necessary to return to the clergy
their property while compensating those who have purchased it, and on
condition that they [the clergy] redeem the assignats that will still be in
circulation, in silver, at their value as of the moment of his departure.
They will probably be at a 20% discount, which will reduce the value
of the total number of assignats to 900 millions; one billion could then
be demanded from the clergy. As for bankruptcy, the king thinks it
ought to be only partial while guaranteeing all life annuities to create
less discontent. This is also the opinion of several persons with whom
I have discussed it.[17]

In all, this program, incomplete as it is, points toward a benevolent
despotism. The *parlements* and Church had been tamed before in
France and the Estates General relegated to oblivion. Furthermore,
Marie-Antoinette had in Axel Fersen an adviser who could use
the example of his own country to show how a determined mon-

arch could exercise a virtual absolutism in a regime provided with both a constitution and a diet.

All this speculation was carried out in the name of the king. But what were Louis XVI's own views regarding the two projects for his deliverance? Count Esterhazy testified he had learned from the *king* of his intention to withdraw to Normandy in the summer of 1790, as advised by Mirabeau. Thereafter, it was only after a Paris crowd prevented him from visiting Saint-Cloud on 18 April 1791 to attend Easter services conducted by non-juring priests, that the king at last committed himself definitely to the project Fersen and Bouillé had worked the past several months to prepare. Fersen wrote Taube that the king would now "consent to everything."[18] One wonders, meanwhile, how many of the king's instructions to Bouillé in Metz since October 1790 had been directly inspired by Marie-Antoinette and backed by Breteuil and Fersen, all three of whom also corresponded with foreign courts. Did the king send La Marck to consult with Bouillé in February 1791 simply to mislead Mirabeau? This vacillating behavior has generally been attributed simply to Louis XVI's proverbial weakness and indecision. Yet such an explanation may be insufficient. Louis knew his English history, as Bouillé observed, and was mindful of the mistakes of Charles I and James II. More important, there seem indications, as will be seen, that Louis XVI in actuality had rather different political views from his wife. La Fayette considered the queen the real problem while both Bouillé and La Marck believed the king quite prepared to accept a constitutional monarchy. One suspects that Marie-Antoinette's unyielding insistence that the royal family either flee together or not at all was inspired in part by her fear of what might result if her husband escaped her surveillance.[19]

Fersen in any event strove to persuade Louis XVI to accept definitely the plan he and Breteuil were working out. In early January, according to Louis de Bouillé, Fersen had agreed with the king and queen that they should simply concentrate on financial and diplomatic preparations. Two months later, Fersen's views had changed. On 27 March, he wrote a memorandum for them, arguing that the constant deterioration of the king's authority, the excesses of the Jacobins, the divisions in the National Assembly, and not least of all, the determination of the émigrés to act if the king did not, all demanded prompt and vigorous action. Since Breteuil's discreet inquiries in Spain and Austria had received only vague answers and because of the problem of finding money, Fersen saw two possible courses. The first was simply to continue negotiations with the powers until a definite agreement was reached and the necessary aid in men and money promised.

The first of these courses of action is undeniably the safest; it would present fewer dangers to Your Majesties and the advantage of a success which would be less in doubt and less contested, But since it is not possible to know when this might become possible, is it not to be feared that, the ills of the state being considerably greater by that time, it might be more difficult to repair them? Might not spirits which are aroused now become calmed, might they not become reconciled to create a new order of things still disadvantageous to the king, but one which private individuals might find desirable through the peace which they would then enjoy and which they would by then prefer to the convulsions of a civil war? Might not the [émigré] princes during that time have made some attempt, and if they should succeed in it, might not they alone derive all the honor and benefit; might they not rally all the nobility, all of those discontented with the present regime, and might they not then become the masters of the kingdom and of Your Majesties?

The second possibility, according to Fersen, was to act right away, without waiting for the powers to come to an agreement first. While he admitted this would be dangerous, he wrote:

Such an act would have about it something noble, grand, impressive, and audacious, the effect of which, throughout the whole kingdom and throughout all of Europe, would be incalculable; it could win back the army and prevent its total disintegration; it could prevent the constitution and keep the factious from bringing about the changes necessary to make it bearable and to consolidate the Revolution. And, if done at this time, it could turn the movements of the princes to good advantage to the king, who, if they were to act alone and meet with defeat, would not be able at another time to serve the cause of the king again.

The choice was for Their Majesties to make and Fersen outlined the action to be taken in either case.[20]

Fear that the émigrés, led by the Comte d'Artois and the Prince de Condé, would attempt an ill-considered attack on France that would imperil not only the royal family but the counterrevolution itself, recurs constantly in Fersen's correspondence. Breteuil strove to hold Artois in check, while urging the king and queen to flee as soon as possible.[21]

The danger, however, went deeper than this. Both Fersen and

the queen repeatedly accused the émigrés of seeking to gain all the credit for saving the kingdom. Maria Theresia's daughter was no more prepared to owe her deliverance to Artois, Condé, and the émigrés than to Mirabeau, La Marck, and the constitutional monarchists, for in either case the restoration of the monarchy would be the work of a faction which would then be in a position to dominate it. Although Artois and his adviser, the former controller-general, C. A. de Calonne—Breteuil's bitter enemy—also spoke of a restoration based on the king's Declaration of 23 June 1789, the victory of their party would unquestionably mean that of the aristocratic resurgence that throughout the century had tenaciously contested the power of the crown. More than anything else, Marie-Antoinette was determined to restore her husband's full authority and to pass on to her son the crowns of France and Navarre in all their untarnished glory.[22]

On 2 April 1791, Mirabeau died following a brief illness. "He was a monstrous assemblage of vices and talents," Axel wrote his father. "He alone brought about all the evil and he alone was in a position to repair it." He ought, he added soon after, to have died either two years earlier or six months later. To Taube he wrote that Mirabeau would have been a great help to the royal family "in the execution of their project."[23] Clearly, Axel felt he should have been utilized by the court until it was strong enough to discard him. Fersen's ideas bear an unexpected similarity to Mirabeau's: both favored a strong monarchy, had little sympathy for the French aristocracy and the *parlements*, and did not scruple at using Machiavellian tactics against the National Assembly. Yet Mirabeau remained "the defender of monarchical power, *regulated by the laws,* and the apostle of liberty, *guaranteed by monarchical power,*" in his words. A letter to Gustav III from September 1791 may meanwhile show Fersen's ultimate aspirations: the powers should recognize no constitution, "not even a good one," which Louis XVI had not freely accepted. To Fersen, the most vital consideration was not reforms or constitutions *per se* but the authority from which they emanated. He was thus above all concerned with the preservation of the social bonds of discipline and subordination as the guarantees of peace, order, and secure enjoyment of livelihood, property, and rights. Like Gustav III, he was prepared to accept some measure of revolution, provided only it was revolution from above.[24]

After Mirabeau's death, Louis XVI had no alternative to the plan prepared by Breteuil and his friends. "It was Breteuil who wanted it," the king sighed as he was returned a prisoner to Paris after the flight in June.[25] Perhaps more to the point, Marie-Antoinette wanted it, and behind her, the devoted Fersen, who from at least December 1790 was entrusted with the arrangements in Paris.

It is clear the plan of escape that was adopted depended upon assistance from abroad. Yet how much help did the queen and her friends hope to get and how did they intend to use it? General de Bouillé, the queen wrote Mercy in February, "believes as we do that it would be impossible to do anything without the support of the foreign powers, which would be dangerous if we were not out of Paris." Fersen wrote a month later to Breteuil that because of the unreliability of his own men, Bouillé wanted "any number whatever of foreign troops to give them an example and to compel respect if need be." "Any enterprise would be mad if we do not obtain from the emperor at least 10 to 12 thousand men at our disposal," Bouillé informed Fersen on 18 April. Two days later, the queen wrote Mercy in Brussels, requesting that 15,000 Austrians take up positions in Luxemburg as General de Bouillé wished, to give him a plausible excuse to concentrate his own men and supplies at Montmédy. She frequently repeated this request thereafter. Louis de Bouillé maintained that the formation of this Austrian corps was "always and irrevocably" the indispensable element in his father's plan. Mercy replied cautiously that he could permit an Austrian troop movement no further than the border. If the Austrians could not serve in France as allies, Bouillé wrote Fersen on 9 May, it would be "absolutely essential" for the king to hire seven or eight thousand of them as mercenaries under his own colors. The queen meanwhile appealed directly to her brother, Leopold II, on 22 May for a corps of eight to ten thousand troops in Luxemburg, "available at our request (it being understood that this would not be made until we are safe), to enter here, as much in order to serve as an example to our troops as to contain them." Thus while the queen and her collaborators intended from the start that foreign troops should be used in France itself if required, they only gradually and indirectly revealed this side of their plan to the court of Vienna, in which they placed their greatest hopes.[26]

Fersen meanwhile sought to enlist the aid of his own monarch. It would be useless for the king of France to escape from Paris unless Spain, the Empire, and the Swiss Cantons could intervene in his favor, he wrote Gustav III on 8 March. The Northern Powers, led by Sweden, should therefore prevent the Triple Alliance of Britain, Prussia and the United Netherlands from opposing the powers friendly to the French king. To win his master's cooperation, Fersen made an appeal calculated to arouse a ready response, at the same time showing the direction of his own political thinking:

The Propaganda, that infernal abyss, has its secret agents everywhere. Already in Spain, Savoy, and Switzerland there are small movements. In Brabant, they are exciting the people to quite a considerable extent and they have even tried to win over the troops of the emperor by boasting to them of French liberty and by offering them as much as a *louis* per man. . . . All these attempts, often repeated, can finally succeed. It is a dangerous example if it remains unpunished and it should be the concern of all sovereigns to destroy in all its principles an evil which otherwise may win out and the progress of which is frightening in its rapidity. This cause is the cause of kings and not just a simple political problem. Without order there can be neither society, nor security, nor happiness. Kings are the born repositories of these things. They should conserve their authority for the maintenance of this order and for the happiness of peoples.

On 1 April, Fersen officially notified Gustav, through Taube, of the escape plan and appeal for aid from abroad. Though negotiations were still inconclusive, he claimed that the French king had the support of the emperor, Spain, Switzerland, and Sardinia. Louis, he claimed, was also prepared to buy British good-will through "advantages or reasonable sacrifices"; only if this failed would he call for support from the Northern Powers. In actuality, the French king and queen, repelled at the thought of losing any of their colonies, undertook no real negotiations with Britain. Thus by the time of their flight in June, they had no definite arrangement to prevent the hostile intervention of the Triple Alliance.[27]

Both Marie-Antoinette and Fersen took liberties in seeking support from different European courts by asserting that others had already committed themselves. The departure of the royal family from Paris, meanwhile, was delayed from May into June in awaiting some positive reply from Spain, which never came. The emperor made no very definite statement of his intentions before 6 June. What the queen and her friends counted on obtaining, however, is shown by an undated memorandum prepared by Fersen and

Quentin Craufurd a few days after the failure of the flight at Varennes, which Crauford gave William Pitt in July. Spain was to provide 14,000 troops and a loan of 6 million livres raised in Holland, Sardinia 20,000 men and the Swiss Cantons 30 to 40 thousand troops and a loan of 40 to 50 million livres, all contingent upon the successful escape of the king of France and in response to his personal request, as well as upon the participation of the emperor in the enterprise.[28]

This last, meanwhile, was the sticking point. Leopold was not unsympathetic to his sister's fate. After succeeding to the Habsburg domains in early 1790, he frequently expressed concern and desire to help, while carefully avoiding the advances of the émigés. In January 1791, he wrote he wished to give her "real and solid proofs" of his interest. When he learned of her definite plan to escape and request for his help, he expressed himself more cautiously. The appeal came at a difficult time in view of Austria's continued war with Turkey and the insurrection in the Austrian Netherlands. In March, he felt compelled to inform his sister that he presently could do nothing without support from several of the "principal courts" of Europe, for Sardinia and Switzerland alone were not sufficient. To Mercy, he meanwhile wrote that the powers could not prepare a common intervention in France until the Turkish war ended. Thereafter, Mercy sought to urge caution on Marie-Antoinette as tactfully as he could.[29]

The queen, however, would not so easily be put off. She repeatedly pressed for a positive commitment. Finally, Leopold, seeing no chance of deterring the French king and queen from their desperate venture, came through with a fairly clear assurance of help in his letters to Marie-Antoinette of 6 and 12 June. Mercy was to provide them, at their request, with "everything he can: money, troops, everything. . . ." A closer reading of this letter of 12 June shows that this assistance was conditional upon the success of the flight and cooperation of the Spaniards, Sardinians, Swiss, and princes of the Empire. It was nevertheless the best that could be expected and on 18 June, two days before the flight, Fersen noted the arrival of a "good letter from the emperor." He meanwhile assured both Mercy and Taube in May that the flight would proceed regardless of the decisions of the emperor and of Spain. When the flight itself failed at Varennes on 21 June, the conditions for all this highly hypothetical foreign support were not fulfilled and the whole project collapsed. Mercy did not even receive his instructions in time and upon reaching the Austrian Netherlands, both Fersen and Bouillé discovered that not a single Austrian soldier had been moved in preparation for the enterprise.[30]

Thus when the royal family slipped out of the Tuileries on the night of 20 June 1791, they had a plan that can be reconstructed in its broader outline. The king left in Paris a lengthy declaration, justifying his withdrawal by the indignities he had suffered and the failings of the National Assembly and its new constitution. Upon reaching Montmédy, he would have issued another manifesto, of the type that lay at the heart of all the plans of evasion for the past two years, appealing for the support of the so-called sound part of the nation. Though probably couched in conciliatory terms, stressing order, tranquility, and reform of old abuses, it would be the first step in the reconstruction of a strong royal authority. Breteuil intended to join the royal family as quickly as possible and prepared a long memorandum on his views to be given the king when he reached Montmédy. Fersen would also have joined the king and queen, very likely as Swedish ambassador.[31] With Breteuil and Fersen, Marie-Antoinette would doubtless have established an influence against which more moderate counsels would have been powerless.

These measures would be supported by Bouillé's force, soon joined by royalist volunteers and backed by 100 to 120 thousand foreign auxiliaries and considerable financial resources. Except for the emperor, who Mercy asserted in March was the only sovereign from whom "one might be sure of disinterested help," assistance would come from smaller or secondary powers not in a position to demand territorial compensation, which could presumably be bought off by promises of financial reward.[32] If, then, all worked as intended, the king could overcome his rivals for power among both the revolutionaries and the émigrés. The plan was an astute one for the hardheaded political pragmatists with no real conception of the mystique of revolution.

2

Axel Fersen's appeal to Gustav III for diplomatic support for the French king and queen reached Stockholm at an opportune time. In July 1790, after two years of uninspired campaigning on both sides, the Swedes inflicted a serious defeat on the Russian fleet at Svensksund, which opened the way to peace negotiations. Axel in Paris was much relieved and hoped this might help bring "some change in things" in France.[33] To speed the conclusion of peace, the Russians hinted at an alliance with Sweden and Gustav, on this assumption, turned his thoughts to what could be done about France. The war with Russia finally ended Russian intervention in Sweden's internal affairs but her finances were ruined and she now lacked the traditional bases of her strength: a powerful ally and a foreign subsidy. The situation in France seemed to provide the opportunity to regain both, in one way or another. Fersen's letters seemed to show that the chaos there had reached its peak, he wrote Taube in September 1790, and that a league "like that of the Greeks against Troy" should be formed "to restore order and avenge the honor of crowned heads," adding, "I should like to be the Agamemnon of that host."[34]

While peace negotiations dragged on into 1791, Gustav made his first efforts to draw his erstwhile enemy, Catherine II, into a joint action against revolutionary France. The empress, still at war with Turkey, gave only vague signs of approval until Britain and Prussia appeared ready to intervene against her. Fearful that Sweden might join them, Catherine showed a livelier interest in Gustav's French speculations and on 17 May, the Swedish king confidently offered Breteuil a Swedish-Russian force to support the king of France, in return for suitable compensation. Breteuil politely declined because of danger to the royal family while still in captivity. Gustav nonetheless continued to press the Russians for a definite commitment and in June departed for Aachen, ostensibly for his health, in reality to await the arrival of Louis XVI on the French border.

Fersen had only wanted Sweden to help assure the neutrality of Britain, hence of the Triple Alliance, and from the start showed misgivings at the idea of Gustav III's more active participation. In particular, he feared he might give away the secret of the French royal family's escape if he went to Aachen. On 11 June, he noted the departure of a M. Simiane from Paris for Aachen "to spy."[35]

There were other considerations as well, which Axel wrote to Taube on 2 May:

The secretary of Denmark [in Paris] says there is much ferment in Sweden, that it is only awaiting the departure of the king to break out and that Prince Fredrik would place himself at the head of the malcontents. The Jacobins rejoice over the king's voyage. Several of them have said he may well come to regret it, that there is much discontent in Sweden, and I know through one of their confidants that they are working to stir up insurrection there and that they have their emissaries there. I will try to find out who they are. All of this makes me greatly fear the absence of the king [of Sweden] in spite of all possible precautions. Only his presence can possibly impress them and hold to their duty the hotheads and the factious, who otherwise might rebel, and I cannot imagine without trembling all the evils to which we would be delivered. Perhaps all these considerations will induce His Majesty at least to defer his departure until such time as the king of France is at liberty. Try to persuade him to do this.[36]

This shows how anxious Fersen was to keep his king from interfering before the escape, as well as the lengths to which he was prepared to go to prevent this. Yet it contained more than an element of truth, for discontent was rife in Sweden, especially among the nobility since the diet of 1789.

Gustav arrived in Aachen in mid-June, where his enthusiasm for the French royalist cause was fired by the émigrés there. But by now, the British-Prussian threat to Russia had passed and Catherine cooled markedly toward his French ambitions, as shown by the arrival of a Russian emissary in Aachen with a lame proposal that Gustav intervene alone with 10,000 Swedes, backed by only a small Russian loan. Yet Gustav now saw his chance for a rapprochement with the Triple Alliance fade before his eyes and Russia remained his only resource until the French monarchy could be restored.

3

"It was hinted to me some months ago," wrote Quentin Craufurd in his memorandum to William Pitt in July 1791,

. . . that the Count de Fersen frequently saw the King and Queen of France in private, both at the Tuileries and St. Cloud; but the difficulty and danger seemed too great, that I scarcely gave credit to it. I have since understood from him, that, from towards the end of October, 1789, about three weeks after their Majesties were brought from Versailles to Paris, he generally saw them once or twice a week, and sometimes oftener, according as he had business with the King. The place where he constantly saw their majesties was the King's closet. He went to the Palace after it was dark, dressed in a frock, with a round hat, and was admitted to the apartments by means of one of those passes which were given to persons of the household. . . . The confidential correspondence of their Majesties, both within and without the Kingdom, was carried on by means of M. de Fersen. . . . I know him intimately, and think him a man of unquestionable honour and veracity. He is calm, resolute, and uncommonly discreet, without being reserved.[37]

In late December 1790, the Marquis de Bouillé sent his son, Count Louis, to Paris to consider plans for the escape of the royal family. As it was too dangerous for him to see the king and queen personally, d'Agoult arranged for him to meet secretly with Fersen at night at the house on the Rue de Matignon which the latter rented from Breteuil. After discussing foreign assistance, finances, the royal family's place of retreat and means of arriving there, they considered the escape from the closely guarded Tuileries palace, which the younger Bouillé considered the most difficult part of all, but "the Comte de Fersen undertook responsibility for that delicate operation. He gave me enough of the details on the interior of the palace to make me see the possibility of getting the royal family out in secrecy." Louis de Bouillé noted that "whether through negligence or excessive confidence," Fersen's comings and goings attracted little attention. Before returning to Metz, Count Louis worked out a cipher and a sure means for corresponding with Fersen in Paris. Fersen's letters were addressed to a Swedish Baron Hamilton, colonel of the Nassau regiment in Metz; letters for him were addressed either to the Russian Baroness von Korff or the Swedish embassy secretary, A. I. Silfversparre. During the half year that followed, numerous enciphered letters were exchanged between Fersen and Louis de Bouillé on his father's behalf.[38]

The house on the Rue de Matignon now became the scene of much feverish activity. Fersen wrote Taube at the end of March:

I now have so much to do and to write that I can scarcely go out, and still I must show myself in society so as not to arouse suspicions. I am entirely alone here in the city with this secret, for they have not a single person the king can rely on. God grant that it go well; I would then be amply repaid. I do not ever intend to demand anything of them. To be of some use to them and to Our Man is all I desire. . . .[39]

Already on 22 December 1790, Mme. von Korff ordered a large coach of a type called a *berline* from Jean Louis, carriage maker, on Rue de la Planche, Faubourg Saint-Germain. It was to be suitable for the journey of six persons to Russia and ready by the end of February. Meanwhile, "a certain *monsieur*" would check periodically on the work, whom M. Louis subsequently came to know to be Count Fersen. Mme. von Korff urged all haste, writing in early January that if the *berline* were not ready before March, it would be too late to use it; despite Louis's best efforts, it was not finished until the 12th of that month. The carriage maker presented his bill for 5,944 livres, not excessive, he later explained, "if one examines all the commodities of this same coach, to say nothing of its solidity." His itemized invoice shows that it was indeed very comfortably appointed. Louis de Bouillé had proposed to Fersen in December that the king travel separately from his family and in March, his father, the general, claims that he expressed to the king his misgivings over the use of a "single coach, *expressly constructed* for this purpose," which would attract attention, urging instead that the family divide and travel in two light English diligences. But it was too late; the *berline* was ordered and the king and queen held to their plan. On 3 June, Mme. von Korff had the *berline* tested by loading it with five persons and 500 pounds extra weight and having it driven to Châtillon and back. She meanwhile had Louis repair an older coach while the *berline* remained in his carriage house until further notice.[40]

Mme. von Korff and her mother, Mme. Stegelmann, applied through the Russian ambassador for passports from the French foreign ministry to leave France. On 5 June, Mme. von Korff received a pass for her to travel to Frankfurt together with two children, one woman, one valet, and three domestics. Her mother's pass meanwhile included *both* her daughter and herself, as well as a maid and two lackeys. On 17 June, the Russian ladies departed in the older coach after explaining to M. Louis that Fersen would pick up the new *berline* for the persons who would travel in it to Russia. The following day, Fersen himself secured a pass through the Swedish embassy.[41]

Fersen was meanwhile concerned with raising enough money for the enterprise. Bouillé's letters dwell constantly on this problem and Fersen assured him he was doing all he could to find adequate funds. The largest amounts would have to come through loans from foreign courts. Fersen and his collaborators hoped in due course to obtain loans of 6 million livres from Spain and 40 to 50 million livres from the Swiss cantons, as noted. Their more immediate hopes were set on a loan of 15 million livres from the emperor, 4 millions of which should be available in Luxemburg at the time of the flight.[42]

Financial aid from abroad was, however, problematic and

contingent upon the success of the escape, after which it might take time to receive. Loans from foreign courts were preferable to loans from foreign individuals to keep the project secret. Yet a few persons were entrusted with seeking additional funds privately. On 1 April, Fersen wrote Taube, asking him to try to arrange a loan from Holland through bankers in Sweden for "2 or 3 millions" in either of their names or those of others, on the pretext of buying *biens nationaux* in France. Marie-Antoinette wrote Mercy in May that the court banker, the Marquis de Laborde, "has sent my money to England with two millions of his own that are intended for me. If one could get that money to Brussels, that would at least be a resource." Her diamonds could later be used as security for further borrowing. From Brussels, Mercy made apparently fruitless inquiries about a loan from Dutch financiers or the Margrave of Hesse-Cassel. Quentin Craufurd, who was in England on unspecified business in May and June, was very likely also looking for funds.[43]

Fersen meanwhile sought to raise the greatest possible amount of ready cash in Paris, from his own and his friends' resources. He wrote Breteuil on 2 April that he hoped to obtain money through certain Dutch "patriots" and by "assembling several smaller sums." Rough notes preserved among his papers show he borrowed 93,000 livres from Mme. Stegelmann and 169,000 from Mme. von Korff, to which he added 100,000 livres of his own. He received some 300,000 livres from Eleanore Sullivan and even 3,000 from his servant, Louvet. He paid interest on all these loans for years after the flight. There may have been other personal loans as well. In 1794, Fersen claimed that he had advanced the royal family a total of 600,000 livres.[44]

How much money then did the French king and queen have available? "We have four million [livres] for immediate needs," Fersen wrote Breteuil on 16 May. He quoted the same figure to Bouillé ten days later, adding that of this, one million livres were outside of France; next day he would send Bouillé one million livres in assignats through prearranged channels. It is not clear whether he then included in his estimate the 2 million livres the king was to receive from the civil list at the beginning of June. Louis XVI later took with him in the *berline* 13,200 livres in gold and 56,000 in assignats.[45]

The expenses of the escape itself were relatively minor; the principal use for the money would be to finance the counterrevolution to follow, above all to provide prompt payment for loyal troops. As seen, the king also intended eventually to return Church properties at a profit of some 100 million livres and declare a partial bankruptcy.[46]

Marie-Antoinette busied herself with her own preparations. These included sending a large *nécessaire* with personal effects and specially constructed in 1789, according to Mme. Campan, "in case of a precipitate flight," to Brussels, ostensibly as a gift to her sister, the Archduchess Marie-Christine. Her jewelry she sent to Brussels with her hairdresser, Léonard, on the day of the flight itself.[47]

To permit escape from the royal apartments in the Tuileries, work began as early as January 1791 to provide secret doors leading from one to the other.[48] The route to be traveled to Montmédy was not decided until relatively late.[49] There remained the question of the persons to accompany the family. The queen selected, unbeknown to them, two *femmes de chambre*, Mmes. Brunier and de Neuville, to travel in a separate carriage, and the governess of the royal children, Mme. Tourzel, to ride in the *berline*. Three former members of the *gardes de corps*, dissolved in 1789, François-Melchior de Moustier, Jean-François de Malden, and François-Florent de Valory, were selected, mainly for their physical strength, as bodyguards. Bouillé claimed there should also have been a Marquis d'Agoult, but his presence was prevented when Mme. Tourzel insisted on her right to remain with the children of France, though she later denied this. As for Fersen, he wrote Bouillé on 29 May, "I will not accompany the king. He did not wish it." He intended to go to Montmédy via the Austrian Netherlands. The Duc de Lévis believed that in this hour of peril, the king did not want a foreigner to occupy a position rightly belonging to a French *grand seigneur*. Possibly Louis did not want at such a time to seem too close to a man whose name was scandalously connected with the queen's. Perhaps more important, he may have wished to avoid the appearance of foreign influence in his actions.[50]

The date of the flight was repeatedly postponed. Mme. von Korff's insistence in December that the *berline* be ready before March suggests it was first intended that the royal family should depart that month. Early in January, however, the king and queen, Fersen and Louis de Bouillé agreed that no action should be taken for three months, pending arrangements for foreign and financial support. On 22 April, Fersen wrote Breteuil, "the king is ... decided to depart during the 15 last days of May." On 26 May, he informed Bouillé the flight was delayed until the first week in June when the king was to collect 2,000,000 livres from the civil list: three days later, that the payment of this money necessitated further delay and that there was "a very democratic" *femme de chambre* attached to the dauphin until 11 June, making it impossible to get away until next day. Bouillé meanwhile wanted more time for the Austrians to concentrate across the frontier. On 7 June, Fersen told Bouillé the flight would take place on the 19th of the month but the *femme de chambre* remained until 20 June, making that evening the first opportunity to leave, as Fersen informed Bouillé on 13 June. They would depart, he wrote, at midnight.[51]

During the last days before the flight, Bouillé concentrated his forces around Montmédy, on the pretext of alleged Austrian troop movements in Luxemburg, and prepared to deploy a string of detachments between Sainte-Ménéhould and Montmédy on 21 June, ostensibly to protect a shipment of money from Paris to pay his troops.[52] Meanwhile in Paris, Fersen worked feverishly to complete the last-minute details. It has been seen that he left his diary for the period, 1780 to early 1791, in Paris where it was later destroyed; he did, however, preserve rough notes for it from the week preceding the flight which give some idea of his activities during those fatal days. On 16 June, he notes smuggling certain "effects," probably clothing, into the Tuileries and on 19 June smuggling out 800 livres and "the seals." Next day he rode out to reconnoiter Bondy and Le Bourget. He arranged the purchase of horses. On 19 June, he had the carriage maker Louis deliver the *berline* to his own courtyard, where it aroused some curiosity among passers-by until he sent it next day to Craufurd's house on the Rue Clichy. Sometime during these days, Fersen sent off a cart-load of his own possessions to the Austrian Netherlands. His diary shows also that he spent much time in the home of Quentin Craufurd, who had been in London since early May, and leaves little doubt that he there enjoyed the favors of the gentleman's mistress, Eleanore Sullivan.[53]

Not unnaturally, such lengthy and involved preparations did not fail to arouse suspicions. The actual plan, Marie-Antoinette wrote Leopold II on 22 May, was known only to Bouillé, Breteuil, and a third person—obviously Fersen—in Paris; nevertheless, a considerable number of people had to be entrusted with details and over 2,000 persons were domiciled in the Tuileries, many of them servants in the south wing occupied by the royal family. Indiscretions were committed, especially by the bodyguards selected for the flight. Preparations for a flight by the royal family were reported as early as 21 May to J.-S. Bailly, the mayor of Paris, by a Mme. Rochereuil, a woman of the queen's wardrobe, who had a liaison with La Fayette's aide, J.-B. Gouvion, to whom further denunciations were made on 12 and 17 June. Jacobin journals warned of a flight over a fortnight before it took place. In late May, the rumor circulated among former associates of Mirabeau that the queen was secretly plotting with the king of Sweden to arm the powers against France, Fersen reported to Taube. On 20 June itself, a detailed report was given to the police, describing how Count Fersen the previous evening had hired three livery horses for use that night as far as Claye.[54] That the royal family would soon attempt to leave Paris was something of an open secret abroad. The unsigned letters Fersen received in June from Mme. de Saint-Priest in London show that the matter was more or less openly discussed there, among others by the Prince of Wales, a close friend of the Duc d'Orléans, who strongly disliked Marie-Antoinette. There were rumors among the émigrés in Brussels on 18 June that the flight had taken place, two days before the event.[55]

It may be asked why amid so many rumors and denunciations those primarily responsible—Mayor Bailly and General La Fayette, who commanded the Paris National Guard—did not take effective action to prevent the escape. For one thing, Paris had for the past two years been so saturated with such rumors that it became natural to discount them, as La Fayette pointed out. For another, he did increase the security of the palace in the days before the flight and Gouvion told him confidently on the night of 20 June that not even a mouse could escape from there. That same evening, Bailly met with municipal officials to consider the danger of a flight and warned La Fayette to be on his guard.[56] Yet even before 20 June 1791, La Fayette was suspected in some quarters of secretly favoring the escape of the royal family. "M. de La Fayette knew everything," a correspondent in Paris wrote Fersen afterwards, on 16 July. "He also did not send off several couriers but only one, directly to where the king was." Suspicions of this kind of La Fayette and in some measure of both Bailly and Gouvion have persisted to the present. It would be too much to suspect that the general, a man of principle and integrity, had been bought by the court; besides, he was surely the last person the king and particularly the queen would have trusted. Yet La Fayette may have been prepared to permit an escape for his own reasons, while making an outward show of vigilance. A feasible explanation for this might be that like many other moderates, La Fayette would have been glad to remove the queen's influence over the king and was thus prepared to turn a blind eye to *her* escape, not realizing that Louis XVI himself would also leave.[57]

4

At last the day arrived, 20 June 1791.[58] A cabman later testified that he drove Fersen that morning first to a banker, then to the Swedish embassy, later to the Pont Royal, outside the Tuileries. Fersen's own fragmentary notes show that he now had a final discussion with the king and queen and that both "said they should not hesitate and that they still should go." The first part of this note is lost. If, however, there were any last-minute anxieties, it was too late to draw back. To the east, Bouillé's cavalry was preparing to deploy. At 3:00, the hairdresser, Léonard, with the queen's jewelry, set off with the Duc de Choiseul-Gouffier, who was to reconnoiter the route later to be followed by the royal party. Of his conversation with the king and queen, Fersen noted:

We agreed upon the hour, etc., etc. That if they were caught, it would be necessary to go to Brussels and have action taken on their behalf, etc., etc. In leaving me, the king said to me, "M. de Fersen, whatever may happen to me, I shall not forget all that you have done for me." The queen wept a great deal. At 6:00 I left her. She went with the children for a drive. No unusual precautions. I returned home to finish my affairs.

Fersen now sent his coachman, Baltazar Sapel, to drive the *berline*, delivered the day before, to Craufurd's, on the Rue Clichy, then to return to Fersen's stable and be ready to depart for Valenciennes with the four horses. Fersen went to Craufurd's at 7:00 and saw to the loading of the *berline* with chests, boxes, and packages.[59]

He returned home at 8:00, "wrote to the queen to change the rendezvous for the *femmes de chambre* and to have them well

instructed, [also] to be told the exact time by the bodyguards."
He delivered this note to the Tuileries, where he noticed "no
movement."[60]

Meanwhile, the bodyguards, Moustier, Malden, and Valory,
were secretly admitted to the palace by an unidentified man
around 8:30 and conferred briefly with the king and queen, who
told them Fersen would give them detailed instructions. They
were given their aliases for the voyage. Mme. Tourzel was meanwhile to travel as "Mme. de Korff," the queen as "Mme. Rochet,"
governess to the two children, "Aglaé" and "Amélie," the king
was to be the valet "Durand" and his sister, Madame Élisabeth,
a "young lady companion." The king hid Malden in a closet and
the other two bodyguards slipped out at about 8:45 to join
Fersen, who awaited them on the quay outside, bringing with
them various effects to be taken on the journey as well as a note
from the king for Fersen to give Count Mercy in Brussels in case
the escape should fail.[61]

At 9:00, a young liveryman, Pierre Lebas, arrived at Fersen's
stableyard with three horses hired for that hour. At 10:00 a person
he understood to be Count Fersen arrived with two others, had
the horses hitched to a chaise which he told Lebas to drive to the
Quai d'Orsay, across the Seine from the Tuileries, near the Pont
Royal, and there await instructions. Fersen then sent off his own
coachman, Sapel, with Moustier and Valory and the four horses
to pick up an English saddlehorse he had just bought, then to
drive the *berline* from Craufurd's to the Saint-Martin tollhouse
on the Metz road and wait there.[62]

During this time at the Tuileries, the royal children retired to
their rooms at 9:30, the king, queen, and Madame Élisabeth sat
down to dinner as usual with the Comte and Comtesse de Provence,
who themselves would flee separately to the Austrian Netherlands
at midnight. At 10:00, Marie-Antoinette slipped away to the second
floor, where she aroused the children and instructed the *femmes
de chambre*, Mmes. Brunier and de Neuville, to dress them and
be prepared to depart immediately themselves, the first these ladies
knew of the plan and their own part in it. Mme. Tourzel was
also on hand, already knowing what to expect. The queen returned
to the salon until 10:30, when she joined Mme. Tourzel and the
children in her own first-floor apartment. She then led them
through a series of rooms, using the secret doors to pass unobserved
by avoiding the long corridor outside. They emerged through a

door near its southern end, quickly stepped across into a short, dark passage leading to a door, long locked and unused, to the empty entresol apartment of the first gentleman of the bed-chamber, the Duc de Villequiers, who had emigrated a few weeks before, for which the queen had a key. From this apartment, an unguarded glass door opened to the Cour des Princes behind the south wing of the palace. In a few minutes, it opened and Fersen entered, disguised as a coachman, and led the dauphin by the hand into the court, which was brightly lit and filled with National Guards and coachmen, relaxing, talking, milling about. Madame Royale, coming after with Mme. Tourzel, glanced back, saw to her horror that her mother was following them, and was filled with dread when a National Guard brushed past. The Cour des Princes was, however, crowded with the carriages of notables who had arrived for the king's *coucher*, behind and between which the little group could pass largely unobserved. The door from Villequiers's apartment was frequently used by persons on the palace staff so that its use now was unlikely to attract much attention in the busy courtyard. Here the children and Mme. Tourzel climbed into an old two-horse chaise of a type called a *citadine*, which Fersen had had to leave in its place among the waiting carriages near the middle of the court, while the queen vanished back into the palace. Fersen drove the *citadine* around by way of the quays, the Place Louis XV and the Rue Saint-Honoré, to the Rue de l'Échelle, by the small Place du Petit-Carrousel, by the royal stables at the north end of the palace, where he and his passengers waited some forty-five minutes for the others. La Fayette passed in his carriage on his way to the *coucher*. Fersen played his part with cool nonchalance, sauntered about looking at other *équipages* with a practiced eye, and when a coachman engaged him in conversation, answered him in the true jargon of the livery stables, offering a pinch of coarse tobacco.[63]

    A few minutes before 11:00, the queen returned to her apart-ment, where Mmes. Brunier and de Neuville were waiting with the bodyguard Malden. The queen told the ladies they were to drive immediately to Claye, the second stage on the Metz road, there to await the main party. Without time to pack, change clothes or for Mme. Brunier to take leave of her family in the palace itself, they were taken out by an unknown man, across the Pont Royal to the Quai d'Orsay, where young Pierre Lebas waited with his chaise. The ladies were bundled in, their escort returned to the palace, and Lebas set off briskly before remembering to ask where his passengers were going.[64]

At 11:00, Marie-Antoinette and Madame Élisabeth went to bed, the Comte and Comtesse de Provence left and the king commenced his *coucher* in the parade bedchamber on the second floor. Soon after, Madame Élisabeth slipped from her apartment by a secret door and went through the Cour des Princes and up to the Rue de l'Échelle, where she waited quietly on a bench until Fersen recognized her. The king was detained at his *coucher* by La Fayette, who remained until 11:00. Louis now withdrew to his actual bedchamber next door, quickly changed into a simple brown suit, green frock coat, gray wig, and round hat, and though none of this disguised him very well, he was able to descend a narrow flight of steps leading to the entrance of Villequiers's apartment, from which Malden accompanied him from one courtyard to the next, the full length of the palace to the Rue de l'Échelle. When a National Guard passed too closely, the king, whose natural phlegm now served him well, calmly stooped to buckle a shoe.[65]

Some time passed before the queen could reach the others. Her servants left her in bed around 11:15, after which she put on a gray silk dress, black cape, and hat with a veil. Meanwhile, a swarm of servants had settled down for the night on mattresses, camp beds, and tables in state chambers and hallways, including some who regularly laid their mattresses in front of the doors to each of the royal apartments. Like the others, however, Marie-Antoinette avoided her normal exit by passing through adjoining rooms by secret doors, emerging opposite the passage to Villequiers's apartment. As she here opened a door to the corridor, she saw a sentry pacing outside and had to wait several anxious minutes for the chance to slip across. Reaching the empty apartment, she was met by an unknown man, perhaps the one noted earlier, who escorted her through the courtyards. La Fayette, leaving the *coucher*, suddenly passed in his coach, accompanied by tourchbearers, on a round of sentry posts, so close, according to one account, that the queen flicked at a wheel with a switch in her hand. She and her escort were, however, so startled that they became lost in the small streets off the north end of the palace and her guide had to ask a sentry the way to the Rue de l'Échelle. It was midnight when to the relief of all, Marie-Antoinette joined the others in the *citadine* and her unknown escort vanished into the night. It was nevertheless at midnight that Fersen had promised Bouillé the royal family would depart.[66]

Rather than taking the shortest route to the Porte Saint-Martin, Fersen drove first by his own house, to make sure Sapel, Moustier, Valory, and the horses were gone, then by the Rue Clichy to see that the *berline* had departed. He then drove all the way around the Boulevard, bounding Paris to the north, to the Porte Saint-Martin. The city seemed endless. At the tollhouse, they were held up by a crowd of merrymakers celebrating a wedding. Beyond it, Fersen lost a quarter hour looking for the *berline*, waiting by the road with Sapel and Moustier for some two hours, while Valory had ridden ahead to set up the first relay of horses at the post station at Bondy, some nine English miles from the center of Paris. When at last the *berline* was located, Fersen maneuvered the two coaches door-to-door, so that the occupants could move unseen from one to the other, then overturned the *citadine* with its two horses still harnessed to it in a ditch, leapt up beside Sapel and told him to drive at top speed to Bondy. "Come on Baltazar!" Fersen shouted, according to the latter. "Your horses are not in very good wind. Go faster. The horses will have the chance to rest at the regiment." They made it to Bondy in less than half an hour, arriving around 3:00 in the morning and quickly hitching up the horses Valory had ready. Fersen later told Craufurd he made one last effort to persuade the king to let him accompany him, but Louis refused: "If we should be stopped and you taken, it would probably be impossible for me to save you: besides you have a letter for the emperor, which in case of my being arrested may be of importance." He ordered him to proceed separately to Belgium, assuring him of his gratitude and friendship. As the *berline* clattered away, Fersen called out, "Adieu Madame Korff," for the benefit of the lingering post-house grooms. He was, he told Craufurd, "strongly tempted to disobey an order that was merely the effect of goodness" and to follow after, but he turned regretfully away, instructing Sapel to continue with the four coach horses to Valenciennes, and mounting the saddle-horse Valory had used, he made off by a cross road for Le Bourget on the way to Mons in the Austrian Netherlands.[67] The *berline* had meanwhile left Bondy in the direction of the first pale light of the longest day of the year. To its occupants, it was doubtless also the longest day of their lives.

5

The ride to the northeastern frontier went uneventfully for Fersen except at Le Cateau, where he had a fearful moment when the militia required him to identify himself. He arrived in Mons at 6:00 next morning, 22 June, where he found the Comte de Provence, Eleanore Sullivan, and numerous French émigrés, all in an ex- hilarated mood. A monk stopped Fersen in the street to ask if the king had reached safety. The same morning, he continued to Namur, where there was general rejoicing that the French king had been saved. Early on 23 June, he reached Arlon, across the border from Montmédy, where he found General de Bouillé, who told him the royal family had been caught at Varennes and were being returned prisoners to Paris.[68] This news crushed all Axel's hopes. It was the great tragedy of his life.

What had happened? Why had the escape failed? Various rea- sons have been adduced. It has been argued that the travel arrange- ments were needlessly lavish, that too many persons were involved or in a position to observe suspicious details. Marie-Antoinette's vanity has been much criticized. Was it essential that she have her *nécessaire,* take the children's governess, the two *femmes de chambre,* even send ahead her hairdresser? Sending her jewelry to Belgium also aroused suspicion, though there were at least practical financial reasons for doing so. "But," says Carlyle, "the whims of women and queens must be humoured."[69]

It is questionable whether the whole family should have traveled together rather than taking different routes in two light, fast carriages, as the Comte and Comtesse de Provence did and Bouillé claimed he advised in March. Perhaps more than anything, the *berline* has invited criticism and ridicule. In the popular imagina- tion, Alma Söderhjelm observed, it has become "a miniature palace, a sacrifice to monarchistic pretention and high aristocratic arro- gance." Carlyle has given the unforgettable picture of the "huge leathern vehicle:—huge Argosy, let us say, or Acapulco-Ship" with "its mountains of band-boxes and chaise behind" which "lumbers along, lurching with stress, at a snail's pace; noted of all the world." The *berline* was, however, no different from many other large traveling coaches of the time. It might still have been more prudent to use something more modest. Furthermore, though Fersen left the Rue de l'Échelle at the intended hour, the *berline* thereafter encountered repeated delays which threw off the timing of Bouillé's maneuvers from Sainte-Ménéhould on. As Msgr. Aimond has written, the king "was here to succumb in the vain search for lost time."[70]

All these factors unquestionably played a part in the failure. To them must be added the general lack of competence and initiative of most of those given responsibility in the project, particularly the three bodyguards and Bouillé's officers. Though these men were undoubtedly loyal, brave and well-intentioned, their actions on 21–22 June leave a mediocre impression. Meanwhile the troops were largely undisciplined, insubordinate and, though mostly German mercenaries, affected by revolutionary ideas. Both Bouillé and Fersen had been fearful over this situation beforehand. "The detachments did not do their duty," Fersen noted tersely in Arlon on 23 June. His relations with Bouillé thereafter remained cool while the latter scarcely mentions Fersen by name in his memoirs.[71]

Finally, public opinion was aroused by fears of an escape by the royal family, counterrevolution, and foreign intervention, as strikingly demonstrated by the speed and effectiveness with which the emergency was met, both in Paris and the small municipalities of the Argonne. To Msgr. Aimond, the whole revolutionary clash between two eras and two social castes is exemplified by the contrast between the brave but ineffectual young noble officers of Bouillé's corps and the resolute and efficient bourgeois officials and National Guards of the eastern townships.[72] The entire venture was from the beginning a desperate gamble and was only attempted because the king and especially the queen no longer saw any acceptable alternative. "It would be better to perish in seeking a means to save oneself," Marie-Antoinette had written Mercy on 7 March, "than by letting oneself be crushed entirely through complete inactivity." The queen and her friends intended to force the hands of the European monarchs through a *fait accompli* of the most striking kind.[73]

Yet the real question perhaps remains not so much why the flight ultimately failed as why it succeeded as far as it did. For this, the greatest credit must go to Axel Fersen, who carried off the most remarkable feat of the whole incredible venture: spiriting the whole royal family out of the closely guarded Tuileries palace and out of revolutionary Paris. Behind this lay an intensity of personal devotion that none of the other protagonists in the drama could match.

CHAPTER VI

Fersen, Gustav III, and the Counterrevolution, 1791–1792

1

The flight to Varennes spelled the doom of the French monarchy. Before, there was some hope that it might weather the change from an absolutistic to a constitutional regime. Now not even the desperate efforts of the *constitutionnels* could shore up the crumbling edifice. The king and queen had revealed the depth of their aversion to the Revolution, their duplicity toward the National Assembly, and their manifest readiness to turn foreign powers against their own subjects. The three-month interregnum in the summer of 1791 demonstrated that the French nation could govern itself without a king while Louis XVI's restoration in September was conditional upon his acceptance of the new constitution. Republicanism now became practical politics and the road from Varennes led inexorably to the storming of the Tuileries in 1792 and the guillotining of the king and queen in 1793.

The flight to Varennes threw Europe into an uproar. The attempt revealed the feelings of the king and queen both toward the revolutionaries and the émigrés, who presumed to speak for them in Europe. Its failure annulled any tentative projects in support of the royal cause while Louis XVI's acceptance of the constitution further hindered any international intervention in France.

During the months following Varennes, however, Marie-Antoinette and her small circle of confidants sought untiringly and through a diplomacy of exceeding complexity to win the effective support

125

of the monarchical powers for the French crown against the twin dangers posed by the revolutionaries and the émigrés. Axel Fersen was among those denounced in France for complicity in the flight and was tried *in absentia* by the provisional High Court in Orléans.[1] Unable to return to France, he continued as Gustav III's special agent for French affairs. At the same time he remained confidant and adviser to the captive Louis XVI and Marie-Antoinette, and their intermediary with foreign courts. He was at the center of all the feverish diplomacy of counterrevolution in 1791 and 1792, and through his hands passed a large part of its correspondence, much of it preserved among his papers. His diary, from late June 1791, likewise provides a valuable source on this activity. Indeed, Fersen's own story during these months is very largely that of the counterrevolution itself.

"Be reassured about us," Marie-Antoinette wrote secretly to Axel on 28 June, "we are alive." Next day she added:

I exist. . . . how I have worried about you and how I pity you for all you have suffered by not having any news of us! Heaven permit that this reach you. Do not write, it would expose us and above all, do not return here on any pretext. It is known it was you who got us out of here. We are guarded and watched day and night. It does not matter. . . . Do not worry; nothing will happen to me. The Assembly wishes to treat us leniently. Adieu . . . I cannot write more to you. . . .

Klinckowström's deletions fail to deprive this letter of its tenderness and agitation. On 4 July there arrived a note that fortunately escaped Klinckowström's scrutiny:

. . . I can only tell you that I love you and have time only for that. I am well. Do not worry about me. I wish I might know the same of you. Write to me in cipher by the post: use the address of M. Browne . . . a double envelope to M. de Gougens. Have the letters addressed by your valet. Let me know to whom I should address those I am able to write to you, for I can no longer live without that. Farewell, most loved and loving of men. I kiss you with all my heart.[2]

During the following months, Fersen's diary and correspondence give few insights into his emotions and fears for the queen and her family. Probably he sought to suppress such painful thoughts and later Baron Klinckowström piously effaced their traces.

Fersen's part in the flight of the royal family caused much excitement in France. "Colonel Fersen, whose liaisons have attracted so much attention, carried out the whole plan," wrote the *Chronique de Paris*. From Stockholm, Duchess Charlotta wrote Sophie that "our *enragés*" among the Swedish aristocracy were furious with Axel for attempting to rescue the French royal family and rejoiced that they had been recaptured, all the while "making insinuations aimed at our king." Armfelt wrote dryly to Gustav III that Fersen might have saved the king and queen had he accompanied them personally, but "was right to consider the affairs of this world with a philosophical prudence, for he is still alive and in good health, and since well-ordered charity begins at home, I suppose his papa will be well content with him. . . ." As for Axel, after visiting Gustav III in Aachen on 30 June, he noted "the boredom and remoteness I felt for Sweden" on seeing again the faces in the king's entourage.[3]

2

Leopold II reacted with unexpected vigor. Already in May he was preoccupied with a great defensive alliance to guarantee both the possessions and constitutions of the European powers. Early in July, when he received false rumors that the French royal family had successfully escaped, he immediately wrote Marie-Antoinette, putting all his resources at her disposal, and appealed to Spain and Sardinia for support. The news that the flight had failed deeply shocked but did not deter him. On 6 July, he issued from Padua a circular to the leading European powers, urging a common manifesto to the French, backed by "sufficiently respectable means," to secure the freedom of the royal family and a settlement "which saves at least the dignity of the crown and those considerations essential for the general tranquility." Thereafter, some weeks passed before Leopold received the first cautious replies.[4]

   In planning the evasion, it had been necessary to consider the possibility of failure. On the day of the flight itself, Fersen arranged with the French king and queen "that if they were arrested, it would be necessary to go to Brussels and to have action taken in their behalf." He now gave Count Mercy in Brussels the letters prepared for such an eventuality by the king and queen. Mercy forwarded the king's note to Vienna on 23 June.[5] Fersen meanwhile established secret contact with Paris. On 27 June, an adjutant assigned him from Sweden, Anders Fredrik Reutersvärd, formerly of the Royal-Suédois, arrived and was promptly sent by Fersen to Paris with letters, a mission Reutersvärd frequently carried out thereafter. Fersen's diary soon also speaks of a certain Devaux in Paris, "my man," who during the following months sent him numerous and extensive reports.[6]

Reutersvärd took to Paris a letter from Fersen to Marie-Antoinette, posing the following questions:

1. Do you wish that we should act despite all the prohibitions to do so which we will probably receive?
2. Do you wish to give full powers to Monsieur [the Comte de Provence] or to the Comte d'Artois?
3. Do you wish that he [one of the above] should employ under him the Baron de Breteuil, or do you consent to M. de Calonne, or do you wish to leave the choice to him?

He enclosed a draft for a note giving full powers to one of the king's brothers.[7]

Marie-Antoinette replied on 8 July. The king, she wrote, now felt the powers could only help through negotiation; force should be "secondary," to be employed only if the revolutionaries refused all negotiations, since it could be of "incalculable danger" not only to the royal family, but to all its supporters in France. The king declined to delegate power to one of his brothers. He desired

... that the goodwill of his relatives, friends and allies, and the other sovereigns who wish to join them should be manifested in some sort of a congress in which negotiation should be employed, well understood, of course, that there should be an imposing force to support it, but always far enough in the background that it should not provoke crime and massacre.

Breteuil should therefore join with the king's brothers to carry out the necessary negotiations.[8]

This was the program to which both Marie-Antoinette and Fersen would cling stubbornly until the war the following spring. From the start, Fersen's thinking was governed by loyalty to the persons of Marie-Antoinette and Louis XVI. After Varennes, he sought consistently to avoid any unnecessary threat to their safety, as his adherence to the queen's plan of action, his defense of her before the accusations of kings and émigrés, and his opposition to violent, ill-prepared or hasty schemes bear out.[9]

Fersen constantly feared the rashness of the émigrés. He saw both Monsieur and the Comte d'Artois in the days after Varennes. He found Monsieur "very reserved and embarrassed," though he briefly hoped he might put his confidence in Breteuil. Monsieur however, fell under the influence of his younger brother, Artois, whom Fersen feared as "frivolous and too precipitous," and the latter's confidant, Calonne, whom Fersen profoundly mistrusted. The émigrés, he noted on 27 June, were "all like madmen." His inquiry to Marie-Antoinette of that date, whether one of the princes should be given full powers, was thus probably intended to obtain in writing the expected response, that the king and queen put their trust in Breteuil alone, especially for the benefit of Gustav III, who favored the idea of making Monsieur regent of France. On 14 July, Fersen wrote in his diary:

Convinced it is absolutely necessary to exclude the princes and that all of this should be an affair to be dealt with among the foreign powers because of the intrigues in the entourages of the princes; that a congress must be formed to put an end to everything. They are talking aloud of the two parties in Coblenz: those of the queen and of Artois.[10]

Neither the émigrés nor the European monarchs showed much inclination to consult the real wishes of the king and queen of France. Separately, the emperor appealed for a common effort against the excesses in France, as seen, and the king of Spain publicly declared his indignation over them. The émigrés clamored for the immediate invasion of France under their own leadership and some even expressed "indecent joy" over the arrest of Louis XVI, as Fersen noted on 10 July.[11] Meanwhile, also acting on his own, Gustav III in Aachen began negotiations for a European grand alliance to crush the Revolution.

Gustav had given his counterrevolutionary program before Varennes through Taube, who wrote Fersen in May:

His advice . . . is that if Their Majesties can escape from Paris, to have all the *parlements* convoked and to have the National Assembly declared illegal for usurping the rights of the throne and the kingdom; to declare the individuals in it rebels and traitors to the country; to order the whole country to fall on them; to recall all the important functionaries and chiefs of the army who were forced to save themselves outside the country, as well as all the bishops; to reestablish everything as it was before the Revolution, and to restore the clergy to its ancient position; to reestablish the three orders of the state which were overthrown by a usurpation of the National Assembly, but to declare at the same time that there will be no distinction nor difference between them with regard to payment of taxes;—to have the Duc d'Orléans arrested, to have him judged and condemned by one of the *parlements* and to grant him no grace;—above all to restore discipline in the army and not to hesitate to give the most rigorous examples in order to do so;—finally, to make no accommodation with anyone whomsoever, nor to form any mixed government, but to restore royalty in its full powers;—to leave Paris forever, and to cause this den of assassins to perish through total neglect of its existence; for as long as there is a Paris in France, there will never be kings; its history proves this only too well.[12]

Shortly after Varennes, Gustav wrote Baron Stedingk, now ambassador in St. Petersburg, that though he took an interest in the French royal family, nevertheless,

... that which I take in the public cause, in the private interest of Sweden and in the cause of all kings is greater yet ... it may be all the same whether it be Louis XVI or Charles X who occupies the throne, as long as the monster of the Manège is crushed and the principles destructive to all authority are uprooted together with that infamous Assembly and the infamous lair [Paris] where it was created. The only remedy for all this is steel and cannon. It may be that at this moment the king and queen are in danger, but this danger is not as great as that to all the crowned heads that are menaced by the Revolution.

The greatest danger, Gustav felt, for France and all Europe, would be for Louis XVI to reach an accommodation with the constitutional monarchists, whose principles he considered inimical to royal authority, thus to a stable peace, the security of persons and property, and France's position as Sweden's ancient and natural ally. They were thus far more to be feared than the *"enragé democrats,"* whose follies would discredit them. By intervening, Gustav hoped not only to regain a strengthened French alliance, but also the attachment of his own rebellious aristocracy, through participation in a royalist crusade.[13]

In answer to Catherine II's suggestion for a modest intervention, Gustav proposed a grand coalition under himself and requested subsidies from Spain. He proposed that Monsieur become regent, in view of the captivity of his brother, sent Taube to negotiate with the French princes in Coblenz, and emissaries to Hesse-Cassel and Bavaria to arrange for mercenary troops.

On Fersen's suggestion, his Scottish friend, Quentin Craufurd, just arrived in Brussels, was sent back to London by Gustav III to sound out George III and Pitt over the possibility of British help and to try to raise a loan. Gustav meanwhile sent Fersen himself to Vienna to arrange for the emperor's cooperation. Though both were ostensibly representatives of the king of Sweden, their positions were complicated by conflicting interests. Both were devoted to the French queen and thus favored her policies. It was meanwhile the Archduchess Marie-Christine, co-regent of the Austrian Netherlands, who first proposed Fersen's mission. Count Mercy carefully briefed both men before departure and the Archduchess wrote her brother, Leopold II, recommending Fersen's attachment to the French royal family, wisdom, moderation, and levelheaded *sang-froid*, "such as does not exist in French veins." Thus Marie-Christine, seconded by the astute Mercy, was apparently trying to coordinate the ideas of her sister, Marie-Antoinette, with those of her brother, Leopold, using Fersen as her go-between. To complicate matters, Gustav III, with his penchant for secret diplomacy, instructed Craufurd to keep his mission secret from the Swedish minister in London; "M. de Fersen," he added, "knows why."[14]

3

On 24 July, Axel left for Vienna. According to his instructions from Gustav III, he was to request use of the port of Ostend for debarking Swedish and Russian troops, the nucleus of the coalition army. If the emperor seemed favorably inclined, Fersen should try to induce him to recognize Gustav as "head of the league, who should direct it personally" and encourage other monarchs to do likewise. If he could, Fersen was to try to borrow the Austrian siege artillery in Luxemburg. Finally, he should urge an eventual "coalition of Austria, Sweden, France, and Russia, such as existed in 1757."[15]

Next day, Fersen arrived in Coblenz, where he called on the French princes. Though Monsieur showed "some signs of sensibility," Fersen already considered him unequal to his task. Artois he regarded as frivolous and hotheaded. He spoke only of force without regard for danger and Monsieur seemed dominated by him. "After what I have seen," Fersen wrote to Gustav III, "I am still more convinced it will be necessary to act for them rather than through them." In Coblenz, Fersen also learned of the emperor's Padua Circular, sent to all the major powers except Sweden, which he felt augured poorly for his mission.[16]

Fersen arrived in Vienna on 2 August and had his first interview with Leopold II two days later. Fersen explained Gustav III's plans and requested the use of Ostend. The emperor, however, wanted replies from Spain, Britain, and Russia to his Padua proposal before committing himself; half-measures, he argued, would accomplish nothing and everything must be arranged before any action taken. Fersen noted that the emperor "speaks a great deal but listens little." Yet each was well impressed with the other.[17]

Next day, Axel presented his credentials to the vice-chancellor, Count Philip Cobenzl. "He spoke to me of the affairs of France as a frightful thing," Fersen wrote, "but difficult to change, since the whole nation was inbued with these ideas." On 6 August, he dined with Prince Kaunitz, who spoke kindly of Axel's father, and whose well-known vanity and idiosyncracies he did not fail to observe. "At dessert, he spoke very well about the affairs of France" and "said many injurious things about the French, whom he does not in general like." Two days later, the chancellor repeated at length the same reasons for delay regarding French affairs that the emperor had already explained. "All in all," Fersen wrote, "it appears to me this [affair] will last a long time and they will not put much enthusiasm into it."[18]

"According to all I can see," Axel wrote to Gustav III, ". . . the emperor seems easy to win over, but he encounters difficulties in the execution of his will on the part of his ministry, which he has neither the strength nor the means to overcome." He would request another audience to push the matter. He then introduced a new element into the negotiations on his own initiative: when Craufurd assured him Britain was not unfavorably disposed, he would propose to the emperor "the formation of a congress at Brussels or elsewhere."[19]

On 14 August, Fersen again saw Leopold II, who though still concerned over certain of the powers, especially Prussia whose desire for territorial compensation he feared, seemed "quite prepared to act."[20] Thus encouraged, Fersen sounded Cobenzl on "the king of France's idea for a congress." Cobenzl seized upon this as "the only way to come to an agreement and to achieve anything," though he felt it would take a long time to bring it about. It would be necessary to see what the new French assembly would do and what action Louis XVI would take regarding the new constitution. "If he is set free and he accepts [the constitution] freely, then we can do nothing," the vice-chancellor reflected. Fersen objected that any apparent freedom on the king's part would be illusory but further discussion proved useless. He then drew up a detailed memorandum to the emperor on the advantages of an armed congress of powers and the manner in which it should be conducted.[21]

Basically, Fersen's plan for a congress was what he wrote to Gustav III on 22 September:

> It seems to me that to simplify the French situation, there is only one thing that must be insisted on, that is the necessity for an example which will prevent the philosophers, innovators, and peoples of other countries from imitating those of France, by proving to them that the royal majesty cannot be outraged with impunity and that one cannot force one's king to change his government; that is why it is necessary to: 1) insist only upon the freedom of the king; 2) recognize no constitution, even a good one, made without this prerequisite; and 3) determine the situation in which the king must be to be recognized as free.[22]

The powers should withdraw their ambassadors from Paris to Aachen, to form a congress, backed by military contingents from each participating power, which would issue a declaration to France, demanding that the king be set free, allowed to proceed to a border locality such as Montmédy, assemble a bodyguard of his own choosing, then freely accept or reject the proposed constitution. The congress should not try to determine the form of government for France, which would "leave everyone in suspense and give hope to all," and prevent delays.[23]

The idea of an armed congress was of course that proposed by Marie-Antoinette in her letter to Fersen of 8 July and far from the intentions of Gustav, who wished to restore the monarchy through "steel and cannon." In proposing it to the Vienna cabinet, Fersen, though ostensibly the envoy of the king of Sweden, was in fact acting as the representative of Louis XVI and, more important, of Marie-Antoinette. International congresses, intervention of foreign powers, singly or in combination, in the affairs of nations torn by internal strife, the use of threatening manifestos were all well precedented devices in eighteenth-century diplomacy. As early as September 1789, it was rumored in France that "the eleven Christian monarchs of Europe" would convene a diet in Frankfurt to restore the old regime in France and the following year, Marie-Antoinette and Fersen, as seen, as well as various émigrés, conceived projects of this kind. In May 1791, the Comte d'Artois urged Leopold II to issue a "menacing manifesto," holding all public officials and "the rebellious inhabitants of Paris" collectively responsible for the royal family. Though he declined any part in such a venture emanating from the émigrés, Leopold's Padua Circular of 6 July contained virtually the same plan.[24]

By the end of the summer, Marie-Antoinette joined in secretly urging an armed congress on the emperor. The Revolution, she argued, could be destroyed by threat alone, "by the approach of war and not by war itself," at which the French would return to the king his full powers and beseech his mediation with the powers.[25] The Austrians were amenable since they themselves had already adopted a basically similar program. Yet Fersen soon suspected they favored it because it allowed procrastination and half-measures. Meanwhile, he had to admit to himself that "the king of Sweden is against the congress."[26]

Gustav III, by now having received evasive answers from Bavaria and Hesse-Cassel, and growing impatient with the emperor, saw his hopes for a European grand coalition fade. He reacted strongly against a rumor that Austria and Prussia considered "a declaration to be made in Paris to engage the French nation to modify the new constitution in such a way that Louis XVI might accept and freely sanction it." Only by destroying the National Assembly entirely could "the germ of the evil" be extirpated. His admonition was clearly aimed at the idea of an armed congress. He meanwhile set his hopes on a new plan, prepared by the Marquis de Bouillé, for a Swedish-Russian landing in Normandy.[27]

Fersen was alarmed by this and warned it would imperil the French royal family. When Gustav seemed determined to put "Bouillé's plan" into operation, Fersen besought him to postpone landings until they could be concerted with the plans of the other powers.[28]

Fearing hasty and ill-advised actions, Fersen was little pleased when the Comte d'Artois and Calonne arrived in Vienna on 19 August to exhort the emperor to violent measures. This threatened to alienate even further the court of Vienna, which disliked the émigrés, and to discourage its intervention in French affairs. Fersen warmly congratulated the emperor on his firm refusal to endorse the prince's proposals.[29]

Since the summer of 1790, the rival Germanic powers, Austria and Prussia, had been drawn together by Russian ambitions in Poland. This led to a defensive alliance in June 1791 and the emperor and king of Prussia met to discuss details at Pillnitz, in

Saxony, on 25–27 August. Followed there by Artois and Calonne, the two monarchs sought to disencumber themselves by issuing an intentionally ambiguous statement on France. Their Declaration of Pillnitz affirmed that the position of the French king was "an object of common interest" to all sovereigns, that they "hoped" this would be recognized by other courts whose assistance had been requested—a reference to Leopold's Padua Circular—and that "then and in that case" the emperor and king of Prussia were resolved "to act promptly in mutual accord with the forces necessary to attain the proposed and common goal." To this end, they would hold their troops in readiness.[30]

On learning of this meeting, Gustav III hoped Fersen had been present, but the latter, foreseeing little tangible result, had gone to Prague, where Leopold's coronation was to take place. Though his first reaction was favorable, Fersen quickly saw the Pillnitz Declaration as an Austrian trick to gain time through negotiations, lasting probably until the following spring.[31]

Meanwhile, Fersen was not very hopeful about Prussia. He met Frederick William II's favorite, Colonel H.R. Bischoffswerder, and the Prussian general Prince Hohenlohe-Ingolfingen, both of whom readily declared Prussia's willingness to join in an immediate intervention in France. But Fersen noted that Berlin opposed a congress of powers, preferring instead private negotiations with Vienna in which he rightly suspected Prussian territorial ambitions. He saw behind the Austro-Prussian alliance only the speculation of a court faction in Berlin and doubted it could last. The emperor meanwhile told him that Frederick William had warned him to put no confidence in Hohenlohe-Ingolfingen, since he had no official assignment.[32]

Fersen could at least feel relieved that Artois and Calonne had gained no real commitments from the emperor or the more impressionable king of Prussia. Yet the effect of the Pillnitz Declaration was serious enough. The French, disregarding its subtle ambiguities, were aroused by its apparent threat to the Revolution while the émigré princes issued a proclamation of their own, construing the Pillnitz Declaration to mean that Austria and Prussia were making actual preparations to attack France.[33]

Fersen's own negotiations meanwhile encountered an increasingly evasive response. On 2 September, he pressed the emperor for some reply regarding Ostend. Leopold countered that he had learned that Gustav III planned a landing in Normandy. This Fersen emphatically denied, insisting, he wrote to Gustav on 6 September, that any Swedish action would be "the result of a common plan" but that in any case a port of supply would be necessary. Gustav had in actuality never bound himself to act only under a common plan. Fersen thus took considerable liberties in interpreting his master's policy and evidently sought to hinder Gustav's plan for an immediate attack on France. Meanwhile, Fersen continued, he would do his best to bring about an armed congress and to get the emperor to permit the use of Ostend, "when Your Majesty and he have agreed upon the time and the course of action to be followed." Without this condition, it would be difficult to secure the emperor's consent. In fact, this too would help to avert Gustav's intended landing in Normandy. On 21 September, Fersen presented a draft convention which the emperor declined to accept. Probably, Fersen only did so for appearances, expecting—indeed hoping for—its rejection, which would give him an excuse to urge an armed congress on his master's behalf. Promptly the next day, he gave Cobenzl a memorandum with specific recommendations for such a congress. Yet he feared it would be long before the Austrians would act. Though he still considered the emperor well-disposed, Fersen felt unable to overcome the opposition of his ministers to an intervention in France.[34]

Since the Padua Circular of 6 July, Leopold II had in fact gradually returned to the cautious policy he had followed before Varennes. He had received evasive answers to the proposals he then made; only Sardinia, Naples, and, to a degree, Spain, showed any willingness to cooperate. The emperor was meanwhile as much concerned with Poland as with France. Under the circumstances, he could hardly consider becoming embroiled in France.

Meanwhile, developments in France itself seemed more hopeful. The *constitutionnel* majority in the National Assembly, shaken by Varennes, hoped desperately to save the monarchy as a bulwark against further disorder. Its leading "triumvirate," Antoine Barnave, Alexandre Lameth, and Adrien Duport, entered into secret negotiations with Marie-Antoinette, seeking her influence to persuade the emperor to acknowledge the new constitution when the king accepted it, encouraging other monarchs to do likewise. The queen wrote on their behalf on 30 July, describing the situation in France in optimistic terms, meanwhile admonishing the emperor and Mercy secretly to disregard this letter. In reality, she considered the constitution a monstrosity and sought to use Barnave and his friends as she had tried to use Mirabeau: as a cover to her true intentions and a means to gain time until the armed congress could be organized. Although Leopold certainly realized that his sister's letter of 30 July did not represent her real views, he was hopeful that the crisis in France was beginning to resolve itself without outside interference, which would now be unnecessary, indeed harmful. Beyond a certain point too, he tended to discount his sister's dreary tale of woe. The French Bourbons were themselves much to blame for their problems and a constitutional monarchy could bring France reforms to which he was personally not unsympathetic.[35]

By the time he received news that Louis XVI had accepted the constitution on 13 September, Fersen had concluded that it would be useless to remain in Vienna or Prague. Already a week before, he had written Gustav III that by all indications the Austrians intended only to play for time and it was thus necessary to find some way to compromise the emperor into acting. On 21 September, he suggested to Gustav that he return to Brussels and there seek to counterbalance the ministers in Vienna through the influence of the Archduchess Marie-Christine and Count Mercy. At the same time he wrote Taube, suggesting that Gustav empower him to correspond directly with Swedish diplomats in other capitals and to suggest at his own discretion "measures I might consider useful for the good of the cause and in conformity with the interests of the king." Without waiting for instructions, Fersen wrote to the Swedish envoys in St. Petersburg and Madrid, urging them to support an armed congress at these courts to "compromise" the emperor into taking action. His presence would be necessary in Brussels, he advised his father, to "prevent the follies one wishes to commit and to calm the exaggeration of French minds."[36]

On 28 September, Fersen left Prague with relief. He again visited the émigré princes in Coblenz, where he noted "diabolical intrigues," complete lack of secrecy, growing numbers of émigrés, and their formation into military units. He concluded that "the princes are no longer the masters." The émigrés were convinced after Pillnitz that sizable Austrian and Prussian forces were on the march and would scarcely believe Fersen when he assured them that this was not so. In exasperation he cut short his visit and arrived in Brussels on 6 October.[37]

4

Louis XVI's acceptance of the new constitution created a new situation and further divided the European powers over the question of intervention. Leopold II agreed with Fersen on 26 September that the French king was not free but the same evening told someone that since he had sanctioned the constitution there was nothing further to do.[38] His ministers were delighted. Austria recognized the new constitution on the basis of the king's free consent, followed by Prussia, Britain, and the United Netherlands. Leopold now felt that if the new system in France were unworkable, it would have to demonstrate its unfeasibility in practice before a genuine counterrevolution could come about, while Kaunitz counseled watching and waiting. The émigrés, the king of Sweden, and the empress of Russia were contemptuous of Louis XVI's supine acceptance of the hateful constitution. All prospects for an armed congress, however, seemed for the time being ruined.

As Coblenz was the gathering place for the French princes and the greater part of the emigration, Brussels was the center for Marie-Antoinette's faction outside France; more specifically the apartment of Quentin Craufurd and Eleanore Sullivan at the Hôtel Bellevue. Fersen was the constant intimate of the household, in more ways than one. Here also foregathered the Baron de Breteuil, Monseigneur d'Agoult, the Comte de Mercy, the Comte de La Marck, Baron Thugut, Count Franz von Metternich, court chancellor for the Austrian Netherlands, Ivan Simolin, Russian ambassador to France, who left early in 1792, Craufurd's friend, Lord Auckland, British minister to the Hague, and others. Except for Breteuil and d'Agoult, neither the hosts nor any of their regular circle were French. Fersen wrote his father that although there was much social life among the émigrés in Brussels, he had little to do with it and was "overwhelmed with work." "Since the first of January this year," he wrote, "I have always regarded myself as a foreigner in the service of France." Significantly, he did not describe himself as a Swede in the service of the king of Sweden.[39]

Upon his return from Prague, Fersen received a letter from Marie-Antoinette, dated 26 September. "For two months, I have had no news from you; no one could tell me where you were. I was on the point of writing to Sophie, if I had known her address." In July, she had sent a letter to Mercy in Brussels, to forward to

Fersen. In August, she wrote Count Esterhazy in St. Petersburg, "If you should write to him, tell HIM that many leagues and many lands can never separate hearts; I feel this truth more each day." Early in September, she sent Esterhazy a ring for Fersen. "I do not know where he is," she had written. "It is a frightful torture not to have any news and not even to know where the ones one loves are living."[40]

Concerning the constitution, Marie-Antoinette continued in her letter of 26 September:

We are in a new position since the king's acceptance. To refuse it would have been nobler, but that was impossible under the circumstances in which we find ourselves. I should have wished the acceptance had been simpler and in a shorter form, but it is our misfortune to be surrounded by nothing but scoundrels. Nevertheless I assure you this is not the least harmful project that has come about. You will judge them one day for I am keeping for you everything that . . . [deletion in Klinckow-ström's text] . . . there are papers for you. The follies of the princes and the émigrés have forced us to do what we have. It was essential, in ac-cepting, to remove all doubt that it might have been done in bad faith. I believe the best way to bring about a general disgust with all of this is to give the appearance of being entirely for it. This will soon cause them to see that it will not work at all. For the rest . . . I do not see, especially considering the Declaration of Pillnitz, that aid from abroad will be very prompt. This is perhaps fortunate, for the further we go and the more these wretches come to feel their misfortunes, the more they themselves may come to desire the foreigners. I fear that rash spirits are encouraging your king to do something that will compromise him, and in consequence, us. Much wisdom is needed. . . . You cannot know how much everything I am doing at this moment costs me. . . .

"As soon as you are in Brussels," she ended, "let me know. I will write to you quite simply, for I have a sure way always at my disposal." She added that those persons arrested in connection with the Varennes affair had now been released from prison.[41]

For Fersen, whose efforts since that unlucky episode had con-centrated upon foreign intervention in France, the queen's letter left important questions unanswered. In his reply on 10 October, he wrote that he understood that Louis XVI had had no alternative but to accept the constitution, as did many "reasonable people." However, it would now be necessary to know Their Majesties' real intentions "to moderate or to arouse the good-will of the kings of Sweden and of the other powers." Thus he inquired:

1. Do you plan to put yourself sincerely behind the Revolution and do you believe there is no other way?

2. Do you wish to be aided or do you wish that we should cease all negotiation with the courts?

3. Do you have a plan and what is it?[42]

If Fersen experienced a momentary hesitation upon receiving Marie-Antoinette's letter, he quickly overcame it. Or, in posing the above questions, he was more likely seeking support in writing for the course he was convinced was the only possible one and which he knew the queen approved. In any case, Fersen continued the same letter two days later by telling her he had persuaded Mercy to back the congress idea with the emperor, "by proving to him that some open measure should be taken to stop the princes and the assemblage which is collecting around them," which was "frightening." Since it should not appear that the congress assembled at the wish of the French king and queen, a pretext could be found in the violation of the papal territory of Avignon. Although he could not yet have received a reply to his proposal that he deal directly with Swedish envoys in the different capitals, Fersen showed his confidence in his position when he added, "I will write the king's minister in Spain in order for that court to engage the pope to call for an intervention of the powers." He advised Marie-Antoinette to try to win over the emperor. Next day, he wrote her that he was attempting to push Leopold through the other courts. He reassured her on 13 October, "Do not fear any rash undertaking on the part of the king of Sweden. I know how to stop him."[43]

Fersen was meanwhile somewhat disquieted by rumors of the queen's dealings with Barnave and the *constitutionnels*, to which she herself had alluded in her letter of 26 September. In Vienna he had even heard it whispered that the queen slept with Barnave and was completely in his power. "May your heart never go over to the *enragés*," he admonished on 13 October. "They are scoundrels who will never do anything for you. You must suspect them and use them." He must surely have understood this to be her intention and she replied to that effect on 19 October. Yet Fersen was evidently not completely advised about this situation until December, after d'Agoult went to Paris to investigate and returned with a reassuring letter from the queen. "I am saving, for the happy day when we will see each other again, a very curious volume of correspondence, so much the more curious for it must render justice to those who have participated in it," she wrote. Through the role her position obliged her to play, she was winning time, "and that is all we need." Some day, she would "prove to all those scoundrels that I was not their dupe!"[44]

At the same time, Fersen suffered chagrin from another source. Following Varennes, Ambassador Staël complained to Gustav III of "the poor wretches who involved the king and queen in such an attempt." "Staël is saying horrors about me," Fersen complained to Marie-Antoinette on 25 October. He had "corrupted" Fersen's old coachman and taken him into his service, and "seduced" many people to believe he had arranged the flight from personal ambition. His only ambition, Axel protested, was the glory of serving her. Yet Staël rightly suspected him of aspiring to his place and Fersen noted privately in his diary that the ambassador was openly accusing him of this in Paris.[45]

Marie-Antoinette sought persistently, mainly through Mercy, to persuade Leopold II to convene an armed congress, while Fersen pushed the same plan, both through Mercy and through other courts. He wrote Gustav III in early October, saying that since the emperor would surely recognize the French constitution, a congress should meet without delay, ostensibly over Avignon. Leopold would thereby be placed under pressure to cooperate for it was essential that he take part in any joint effort. Fersen added that he had already taken the liberty of writing to the Swedish ministers in Berlin and Madrid about this and urged Gustav to solicit the Tsarina's support.[46] To Taube, Fersen argued that an armed congress would so terrify the French that they would throw themselves into the arms of their monarch and implore him to mediate with the threatening powers. Until then, "all means" should be employed to inspire the French with confidence in their king. It was also important to keep the émigrés from learning of the plan, lest they act precipitately to win glory for themselves. This last the French king was anxious to avoid, as the king of Sweden "should understand better than anyone else." The princes and émigrés could, however, be useful, as Fersen wrote to Marie-Antoinette, if their actions were controlled by the congress.[47]

Gustav III had very different ideas. He still was determined to crush the Revolution by force. He profoundly mistrusted Leopold II, suspecting him of wishing to keep France weak and divided to dominate her, as Russia had dominated Sweden during the Era of Freedom, thereby depriving Sweden of her traditional ally and source of financial support. Gustav thus continued to reject a congress. He even mistrusted the king and queen of France themselves. Alarmed at their apparent cooperation with the *constitutionnels,* he feared the consolidation of a "mixed" government. If Leopold had revealed his true intention to prevent other powers from intervening, Gustav wrote Fersen in November 1791, "the shameful behavior of the king of France" which "surpassed in cowardice and dishonor anything we could have expected and which the past might show" had favored the emperor's scheme "marvelously." Both Gustav and Catherine II were incensed that the king sought to "raise obstacles" against the efforts of his fellow monarchs to help him and that the queen should prefer "subjugation" to "dependence upon her brothers, the princes, whom she appears to fear even more."[48]

Since Louis XVI's acceptance of the constitution and its recognition by several courts, Gustav put his hopes in cooperation with Russia and Spain, which likewise refused to acknowledge it. He hastened the final peace and long-awaited alliance with Russia, at last signed at Drottningholm on 19 October 1791. This convention, however, offered only a very illusory commitment from Russia, though Catherine exhorted Gustav, as well as the Austrian and Prussian monarchs, to crush the revolutionary hydra. Spain had little more than the myth of her past wealth and power, and Spanish replies to Gustav's proposals became increasingly evasive. Yet disillusionment with Russia and Spain lay in the future in October 1791, when Taube enthusiastically wrote Fersen that the empress would "contribute everything in her power" to overthrow the French constitution and that if the French king and queen had accepted it in good faith, they must be regarded as "nonentities." It was necessary to exclude "that damned Florentine," Leopold, from the intervention, to be carried out by a coalition of Sweden, Spain, Russia, Sardinia, Naples, the Swiss cantons, and the French princes, under Gustav III's supreme command.[49]

Fersen found the reactions of the king and Taube alarming. Fearing violent as well as precipitous and insufficient measures, he constantly urged a congress. He meanwhile defended the duplicity of the French king and queen in dealing with the *constitutionnel* leaders as essential for the public confidence necessary for their safety and the success of a congress.[50] He warned Marie-Antoinette of the danger from the Northern courts. "I cannot tell you how important it is for you to write as soon as possible to Sweden and Russia, confidentially, to prevent them from going over to the princes in the belief that you never intend to do anything," he advised her on 11 November. When Gustav III, following Russia, sent an envoy to the émigré "court" at Coblenz, Marie-Antoinette confided to Mercy that she feared Russian and Swedish support benefited only the émigrés, thus worsening the position of the royal family.[51]

On 26 November, Fersen wrote a long memorandum to Marie-Antoinette. Sweden, Russia, and Spain believed that the king and queen intended to do nothing and to continue under the constitution. "They sense the danger of this example and, since the reestablishment of the monarchy is important to their political interests, they will unite with the princes sooner than allow such a monstrous government to be established in France." The king of Sweden was zealous for the good cause, but "his lively and restless spirit has to be calmed," and he could not "conceive of the reasons which prevent you from delivering yourselves to the good-will of the princes." He continued:

The emperor is deceiving you. He will do nothing for you and under the specious pretext of your personal security and of fulfilling your intentions by not acting with the princes, he is abandoning you to your fate and permitting the complete ruin of the kingdom. He is delivering you to the hatred of the nobility, which he reduces to despair and which he pushes in this manner toward some desperate enterprise, as frightful for you if it should succeed, thereby making you absolutely dependent upon them, as if it should fail, thus depriving you of all means to act and perhaps exposing you all the more. . . . The emperor . . . is weak and good, and cannot resist his council, which is slow, indecisive, and fearful, which is apprehensive of compromising itself and in whose policy the abasement of France plays a part, to gain for themselves a greater preponderance in Europe.

To overcome confusion regarding their true intentions, which elsewhere in Europe encouraged both extreme and dangerous schemes, and pretexts for inaction, Fersen urged that the king and queen write directly to the various European sovereigns, clearly setting forth their views and demanding a congress of powers. In such a way it should be possible to force the emperor's hand. He described in detail the approach to take in writing to each of the monarchs, to encourage some while restraining others.[52]

In early December 1791, Louis XVI and Marie-Antoinette wrote personally to the principal sovereigns of Europe. Fersen was pleased with the letters.[53] Still, he felt something more was needed to clarify their position. Despite the risk, he himself must try to return secretly to Paris and see the king in person. He first mentioned this idea to Taube on 30 October and to Marie-Antoinette on 26 November.[54] Meanwhile, events conspired to bring about this bold venture.

In the fall of 1791, the French Legislative Assembly had become alarmed over the émigrés in the Rhineland as well as rumors of a European congress to intervene in France. On 29 November, it decreed an ultimatum to the electors of Trier and Mainz, demanding expulsion of concentrations of armed émigrés. Louis XVI sanctioned the ultimatum, hoping to force the powers, especially the emperor, to take action. Fersen's memorandum of 26 November arrived a few days later and its proposals for direct appeals to European sovereigns fitted well with the scheme for exploiting the crisis. Fersen was at first surprised by the ultimatum but quickly grasped the possibilities for intervention it provided. He wrote Gustav III that in approving it, Louis XVI wished to retain the confidence of the people but that this really gave him the chance to act. He might hope for good effects "if the electors are a bit firm in their replies and thus force the other powers to take a stand." The French ultimatum could be an excuse for a congress, which could set conditions for accession to the French demand. Or, in the event of war, if the French were quickly beaten, as was to be expected, Louis XVI could win popularity by stepping forward to "mediate" with the "enemies." If the French should possibly win, Louis would be a national hero. Fersen thus took it upon himself to write Gustav's envoy in Coblenz, to encourage the electors to stand fast.[55]

Fersen became involved in a shadowy little drama at the turn of the year. In December, he learned the Legislative Assembly was sending the Counts de Ségur and Custine on a secret mission to Berlin, which he later found was to assure Prussian neutrality in the event of war and to persuade the Duke of Brunswick to command the French armies. Fersen immediately alerted the Swedish minister in Berlin, C. E. von Carisien, who sought to counteract the French envoys. According to Gustav III, Fersen's warning was instrumental in causing Ségur to suffer a humiliating reverse.[56] In January 1792, the bishop of Autun, Talleyrand, departed for London on a similar mission, to assure British goodwill, through colonial concessions if need be, and Fersen availed himself of influential contacts there. A letter in English among his papers, signed "A.", very likely Lord Auckland, dated 9 February 1792, informs Fersen that Talleyrand was coldly received by Pitt and Lord Grenville, who refused to recognize the diplomatic nature of his visit, and that he was snubbed by the queen of England. "I am told," this correspondent added, "that though he endeavors to put a good face on all this, he is wonderfully mortified." Like Ségur, Talleyrand failed to obtain the assurances he sought.[57]

It meanwhile soon became evident to Fersen that the emperor would not back the Rhenish electors, who thus gave way to the French ultimatum.[58] Leopold was nonetheless aroused and in February concluded a closer alliance with Prussia with an eye as much to France as to Poland. From Brussels, Mercy warned of the "ferocious horde that has declared war on the human race" and in February, Marie-Antoinette sent the Russian ambassador to Paris, Simolin, as her personal envoy to impress Leopold with the seriousness of the situation.[59]

Gustav III, whose attempts to organize a Swedish-Russian-Spanish entente were increasingly frustrated, was uneasy at the thought of an Austro-Prussian intervention in France that might exclude him or reduce him to a minor role, and he turned with characteristic flexibility to fresh expedients. In December 1791, he sent Fersen a new plan for the escape of the French royal family, through Normandy to England. The family should separate and travel different routes, or better still, the king alone should flee. Fersen should persuade them to make the attempt and work out the details. He enclosed letters urging the king and queen thus to end, once and for all, the myth of their free acceptance of the constitution, which prevented the powers from aiding them. At the same time, Gustav explained to Fersen that he had opposed an armed congress in hopes the emperor could be induced to cooperate by other means but he now realized this would be the only effective way and therefore would support the idea. By taking the initiative in organizing a congress, Gustav might still keep from being excluded from an intervention in France. That he only envisioned it as a way to bring intervention through

"steel and cannon," however, was evident from his enclosed note
for Marie-Antoinette:

> ...it is only through violent remedies that violent ills may be cured....
> The king of France cannot reestablish his kingdom except by returning
> to his ancient rights. Any other remedy will be illusory. Any other terms
> will only open the door to endless discussions and will only increase
> the confusion instead of ending it. It was by the sword that the king
> was despoiled of his rights. It is with the sword that they must be re-
> conquered.[60]

Gustav was determined that leadership of the counterrevolution
should not slip from his hands. "I have been too often in the
position of conducting revolutions or of combatting them not to
know that this cannot be done unless led by a single person," he
wrote Bouillé in February. The emperor would not, however,
compromise himself through any commitment to the king of
Sweden and declined his proposal for a congress.[61]

There remained the plan for the escape of the French king
and queen. Gustav might hope for valuable advantages if he could
attach Louis XVI firmly to his "oldest ally" and the hazards of an
Austro-Prussian intervention for both France and Sweden could
thereby be forestalled. Thus it came about that in early 1792,
Axel Fersen prepared for a secret visit to Paris.[62]

5

On 15 January 1792, Ferson wrote Taube that everything was
ready for his departure. He objected, however, to Gustav III's
suggestion that the royal family separate or that Louis XVI escape
alone. This would not only threaten the queen but would leave
hostages, which would affect "the weak and irresolute spirit of
the king of France." The French would probably declare him
deposed and his son king, establish a regency and thus compel
Louis to make war on the dauphin.[63] Still, Fersen eagerly waited
to depart and no doubt intended again to interpret Gustav III's
instructions in his own way.

Fersen was to be accompanied by his adjutant, Reutersvärd.
The two were to travel through France in the guise of Swedish
envoys to the queen of Portugal, named "Captain Granfelt" and
"Lieutenant Lundberg" respectively. They prepared a diplomatic
pouch with fake letters for the Portuguese court, complete with

the royal Swedish seal and Gustav III's signature, forged by Fersen. Their departure was delayed more than once but on 11 February 1792, Fersen and his companion, well-disguised, crossed the border and took the post road to Paris.[64]

They arrived in the capital on the evening of 13 February and Fersen proceeded immediately to the Tuileries. He recorded laconically in his diary: "Went to the queen. Took my regular way. Fear of National Guards. Her lodgings marvelous. Did not see king. Stayed there."[65]

The following evening, Fersen met the king. After explaining the importance of a new flight attempt, he noted Louis XVI "does not want to leave and he cannot because of the extreme surveillance. But to tell the truth, he has scruples about this, having so often promised to stay, for he is an honest man." The most Fersen obtained was Louis' consent—grudging, one cannot but feel—to attempt a last-minute escape "through the woods," led by "smugglers," if war broke out and the allies neared Paris.

Yet Fersen evidently did not insist strongly on an escape attempt, since Louis favored the plan for an armed congress. Faced by the united strength of the powers, Fersen felt sure, the Revolution would quickly collapse and the safety of the king be assured, since the "rebels" would need him as a hostage to "obtain a capitulation" and save their skins.

Fersen urged the importance of "not allowing the establishment of a mixed government in France, of not reconciling with the rebels, but rather of reestablishing the monarchy and the royal power in all of its plenitude." The queen warmly supported this view but the king, "as a result of his weakness . . . believes it to be impossible to regain all of his authority," whereupon Fersen "proved the contrary to him . . . that this would be [accomplished] by force and that the powers wished it so." Though Louis seemed convinced, Fersen still feared that through discouragement and weakness he might later be tempted to negotiate with the rebels.[66] The king then said:

"Well now, we are alone together and we can talk. I know I am taxed with weakness and irresolution, but no one has ever been in my position. I know I missed my opportunity. That was on 14 July [1789]; I should have left then and I wanted to, but what could I do when Monsieur himself implored me not to leave and when the Marshal de Broglie, who was in command, replied, 'Yes, we can go to Metz, but what will we do when we are there?'—I let the moment pass and since then I have never recovered it. I have been abandoned by everyone." He asked me [Fersen continued his account] to inform the powers they should not be astonished at everything he was obliged to do, that he was forced and it was the result of constraint. "They must," he said, "leave me aside altogether and let me do as I may."

Marie-Antoinette told Fersen of the humiliating return from Varennes and of her dealings with the *constitutionnels*, who, she said, now felt only foreign intervention could restore order and hoped "to ingratiate themselves in advance." It was apparently now that she gave Fersen her collected correspondence with Barnave, which he thereafter preserved among his papers.[67]

On leaving the king and queen—whom he would not see again— Axel announced he would travel as far as Orléans or Tours to give the appearance of continuing on to Portugal. In reality, he went directly to the house of Quentin Craufurd and Eleanore Sullivan, who had returned from Brussels to prepare for his secret visit. Eleanore hid him, unbeknown to Craufurd, in an attic room. Here Fersen remained several days, provided with food from the master's table by the servants Josephine and Frantz, who were his confidants. It amused him that Craufurd, returning home, often dined on *his* leftovers, believing them to be Eleanore's. When Craufurd was out, Fersen enjoyed his lady's favors. When Craufurd was home, Fersen passed the time in his attic reading "4 or 5 novels" as well as "the journal of Mr. . . . , an English officer, whose crew having revolted, put him adrift in mid-ocean in a small boat with 17 men and who was fortunately able to survive," obviously Captain William Bligh's account of the *Bounty* mutiny of 1789. After a few days of this rococo masquerade, Fersen slipped out of the house and reentered, ostensibly back from Tours, for the first time revealing himself to the unsuspecting Craufurd. A few hours later, he and Reutersvärd departed Paris with Fersen's little dog, Odin, left behind at the time of Varennes. Their credentials aroused suspicion at the French border, but Reutersvärd coolly bluffed their way through. On 23 February, they arrived, half-frozen, in Brussels.[68]

If Fersen had lingering doubts about Louis XVI, he can only have been encouraged by Marie-Antoinette's determination. Thus he wrote Gustav III:

In all I found the king and queen strongly determined to endure anything rather than the state in which they now find themselves and according to the conversation I had with Their Majesties, I believe I may assure you, Sire, that they feel strongly any conciliation with the rebels would be useless and impossible, and that there is no means for reestablishing their authority other than force and help from abroad.

He again called for a congress, backed by military contingents committing the participating powers to take common action.[69]

News traveled slowly and Taube learned of his friend's desperate gamble only after it had begun. "Even if the good Lord brings you back and saves you," he wrote in alarm on 13 March, "I disapprove strongly of what you have just done. You have exposed Their Majesties and your master, and all that is most dear to you in the world. . . ."[70]

It might appear that Fersen had now gone over to Gustav III's idea of crushing the Revolution by force. Yet he had by no means reversed his views. True, he placed his hopes in the war once it began in April 1792, but by then there was no alternative. Meanwhile, he continued to urge the armed congress as strongly as ever. He repeatedly noted any indications that the mass of the French people were growing sick of the Revolution and thus could not be counted on to defend it.[71] He likewise speculated over assurances to the French to overcome their fears of foreign intervention. On 15 January, he wrote to Gustav III.

The great majority, without desiring a return to the old order in its entirety, desire a change and hope for help from the outside. They fear only bankruptcy and vengeance. By reassuring them on these two points, the task should not be too difficult, and with the aid of Your Majesty and the empress of Russia, I hope it can be accomplished.

To Taube, he wrote more gloomily the same day, "Here we have the consequences of the weakness shown at the beginning and what would have been quite simple when the revolt broke out would appear at present to be acts of despotism."[72]

Thus while Fersen wrote Gustav III that the king and queen were now "ready to endure anything rather than the state in which they find themselves," and looked to "force and help from abroad," Fersen was evidently concerned with allaying his master's anxieties about the king and queen of France, thereby encouraging him to redouble his efforts in behalf of a congress. This, rather than open warfare, was Fersen's own conception of "force and help from abroad," and it alone should cause the Revolution to collapse without unnecessary bloodshed.[73] He still saw the Revolution as supported only by unprincipled rascals who hoped to "find through pillage and disorders of all kinds a means to enrich themselves," or cowards who sought to "protect themselves from the punishment they so richly deserve."[74]

The French people are stupid and credulous [he had written in September to Leopold II]; when they hear the foreign armies are at the frontier, they will believe them to be at the gates of Paris. Fear, disunion, and perhaps risings in some of the frontier provinces will achieve the rest. ... Fear made the revolution, it is through fear that it must be defeated. ... In this manner the counterrevolution could be accomplished without it being necessary to employ more violent means. An armed congress alone would suffice. ...

He could attribute to the leaders of the Revolution neither idealism nor courage, nor could he understand the strength and appeal of their principles.[75]

At the same time, Fersen remained as implacable against the French aristocratic party as ever. He wrote his father in January 1792:

If a counterrevolution can come about, the most difficult part will still remain to be done. But French foresight does not extend that far and in destroying the sole object of all their passions, they believe they would have done everything. They do not realize that the habit of disorder they have acquired will remain with them. They do not see that the strongest democracy is perhaps that of the nobility, that there are as many plans for a new government as there are individuals, that each holds more firmly than ever to his own idea, that each believes himself to have a right to the king's recognition and favors, and that all want something. One shudders at this state of affairs.[76]

Fersen's views on the spread of revolution are meanwhile revealing. He was ever interested in any signs of international revolutionary activity. In particular, he was fascinated by the so-called *Club de la Propagande*. In June 1790, he wrote Gustav III of an assassination attempt against Count Floridablanca in Spain, allegedly by the Propaganda, "which is not, like that of Rome, for the faith; this one is for revolt and sedition." It was apparently a few days later that he warned Gustav against the Swedes, Reuterholm and Silfverhielm, then in Paris, whom he called "visionary enthusiasts," continuing,

This sect of visionaries and *illuminati* is increasing greatly in France and it is through them, but principally through the Freemasons, that the Propaganda Club is seeking to spread throughout Europe its perfidious doctrine against kings. The club is composed of all the *enragés* in the Assembly and outside the Assembly; is established to expand everywhere the same spirit of revolt and insubordination that ravages France. They hope thereby to justify all the horrors they have committed and they have their emissaries and correspondents everywhere to seduce and arouse the people. This information has been given me by a high and reliable source to communicate to Your Majesty and in order that precautions may be taken.

Fersen sought to win Gustav III's support for the French royal family before Varennes by again raising the specter of "The Propaganda," as seen. An anonymous memorandum dated 6 September 1791 on the activities of the Propaganda Club in Holland, among Fersen's papers, gives fuller details. It is here claimed that it was distinct from the Jacobin Club, its origins went back to 1786, and its purpose was international revolution. "MM. de Condorcet, de La Rochefoucauld, and the Abbé Sieyès are its prime movers: their principles are to form a philosophic society, one must be a philosopher, ambitious, discontent, or deranged." It is described as a tightly organized secret society like the infamous *Illuminati*, with strict internal discipline, two classes of brethren, "aspirants" and "initiates," and a war chest of 20 million livres, expected to increase to 30 millions by the end of the year.[77]

In July 1791, Fersen noted in his diary, "The arsenal in Amsterdam has burned, it is averred by the Propaganda. If this should not be true, it would be at least useful to spread the story." Most of his letters on the revolutionary contagion were written either to Gustav III or Taube, who were sure to be impressed, or to Swedish diplomats in European courts whom Fersen wished to influence in favor of intervention in France. "The blindness of the sovereigns is extreme," Fersen wrote the Swedish minister in Madrid; "they do not want to recognize the danger which threatens them all."[78]

Thus Fersen, though he collected much evidence of an international revolutionary movement, seems to have been interested in it largely for its practical use in stirring the royal houses of Europe to action. Still, convinced that revolutionary agitation emanated from a small clique of scoundrels in Paris, he failed to grasp its true strength or implications.

It was thus that he received, in mid-March 1792, the unexpected news of the death of Leopold II, of which he wrote in his diary, "They will say it was death by poisoning. So much the better. That will prove the necessity of exterminating the monsters in France." Although he was offended when the émigrés spoke "in the most indecent way of the dead emperor," he considered the succession of his son Francis—"a soldier at heart, more like Joseph than Leopold"—advantageous to the French monarchy.[79]

Fersen always regarded the emperor the key figure in any counterrevolutionary undertaking. Yet he never really understood Leopold II, whose sentiments and intentions regarding the French Revolution during his short reign still remain largely obscured by his natural secretiveness and temporizing, ambiguous and seemingly contradictory behavior. Fersen at first believed him well-disposed, as seen, suspecting his ministers of obstruction. Only gradually did he question the emperor's good faith. Then, like Gustav III, he suspected him of wishing to keep France weak. When during the last weeks of his life, Leopold seemed determined to act, Fersen suspected that he only wished to keep Sweden and Russia from doing so, thus to compel Louis XVI to compromise with the Assembly and accept Austrian "guardianship."[80]

What Fersen could not see was that if the emperor did not try to restore the old order in France and sought to restrain the "active and restless spirit" of Gustav III—as Fersen himself had once called it—it was because he could not undertake such a project, partly because of conditions in the Habsburg lands, partly because of his own views. Leopold's letters to Marie-Antoinette show that while he was repelled by anarchy and especially constraint or violence against the king and queen, he favored reform and the constitution. Louis XVI, he told Artois in December 1790, should solemnly disavow the Revolution while at the same time putting himself at its head. France under its new order undertook reforms similar to his own in Tuscany and his brother Joseph's in the Habsburg lands.[81]

In Prague in September 1791, Fersen observed how in society the emperor favored the bourgeoisie and common people, to the consternation of the nobility. He also noted the rising demands of the "Third Estate" in the Habsburg empire. Leopold, ascending the throne at a time of turmoil, sought to build his strength against the rebellious nobility upon the bourgeoisie and peasantry of his domains. These classes, seeing in France a continuation of the Josephine spirit, strongly opposed intervention, especially after the Declaration of Pillnitz.[82]

Leopold had at first welcomed Fersen's good sense and moderation but became disillusioned as it became evident Fersen was seeking to force his hand through other courts and was encouraging the French queen to force him into committing himself to an armed congress to restore Bourbon absolutism. As Marie-Antoinette became embittered toward her brother, he became incensed against Fersen. In March 1792, Fersen wrote Marie-Antoinette that Mercy complained to Breteuil of his activities and that the Austrians considered him "very suspicious and inconvenient." Fersen thought Mercy might even have tried to decipher his letters, but dismissed this as impossible; Mercy had in fact succeeded in doing so as early as October 1791.[83]

Leopold's death on 1 March 1792 ended the hopes of his admirers and stirred those of the reactionaries and counterrevolutionaries. While Fersen hopefully awaited developments under the new king of Hungary and Bohemia, the shattering news reached him early in April that his own king, Gustav III, had been assassinated.

CHAPTER VII

Fersen, France, and the Regency of Duke Karl, 1792–1793

1

Gustav III died in a manner in keeping with the melodramatic, indeed theatrical quality of his life. At a masquerade ball at the Stockholm Opera on the night of 16 March 1792, he was surrounded by a group of masked figures, one of whom discharged a pistol into his back. Two weeks later, he died of his wound.[1]

As in the case of Leopold II, there was much speculation about a Jacobin plot, in which Gustav himself shared before he died. Meanwhile the news was received in Paris with general rejoicing among the democrats and discouragement by their opponents.[2] What made the affair even more suspicious was that the Continent seemed alive with rumors. As early as 2 February, Fersen wrote in his diary that he had heard via Dutch sources that Gustav III had been arrested by "the guards" when he tried to leave for the Riksdag then convening in Gävle. Fersen was much concerned over this diet and was delighted when it ended without incident, as he wrote his father—who to his relief had not taken part—on 18 March, two days after the assassination.

I fear for us the influence of the French fashion and I have seen too closely all the disadvantages of that system of innovation and all the ills it has produced not to prefer to that order of things all the drawbacks and perhaps imperfections of our government. France is a sad example of the danger of the spirit of innovation. A whole people can never be set in motion with impunity and it is folly to believe its force can be stopped or modified.

154

He finally learned on 1 April that Gustav III had been shot—three days after he had died—and the next day noted that "everyone already knows of the king's murder." He still hoped at first that Gustav might survive and characteristically looked for advantage to the monarchical cause. "If, as I hope," he wrote promptly to Taube on 1 April,

... God preserves us from the misfortune that threatens us, it would be good policy to attribute this execrable attempt to the Propaganda, and this would be easy with the death of the emperor and with opinion already strongly inclined to believe it, even among the most reasonable people.

It was not until 9 April that rumor reached him that Gustav was dead and it was only by 12 and 13 April that this was confirmed.[3]

A certain Mme. Wagenfelt in Strasburg was said to have prophesied the assassination. In mid-April, Fersen and Count J.G. Oxenstierna, Swedish envoy to Coblenz, were directed to investigate. Oxenstierna made inquiries but the soothsayer refused to reveal the source of her revelation.[4]

Fersen was deeply grieved and at the same time apprehensive. The same day he received word of the assassination, he wrote Taube:

I hope the conduct of our elder has been good. I believe I know him well enough to be sure it was worthy of him, and such as I would have desired. I would be too unhappy to learn the contrary. This would be death itself to me. But still, my friend, hide nothing from me.[5]

Axel need not have worried, for his father, with most of the nobility, made his peace with the dying monarch and wrote to his son:

This unfortunate event has put an end to all resentments. Since Saturday morning, all the nobles present in Stockholm have hurried to the court, all the families have gone. Your mother went there with me.... She was called, with myself, to the king's bedside and you cannot imagine the pleasant and friendly things he said to your mother, who burst into tears.... The consternation is general and our future appears sinister and foreboding.

Taube and Sophie wrote how Gustav III during his last days constantly inquired about Axel, how he was relieved to learn of his safe return from Paris, and how he had the most brilliant plans for his future, including the embassy to France.[6]

Axel meanwhile feared for his position and the cause he represented. "What a change will this not bring about, and especially for me?" he wrote in his diary on 13 April. "I am afraid of being persecuted if I should return to Sweden and am entirely decided not to go there."[7] His correspondence with the new regent, Duke Karl of Södermanland, was amiable enough. The latter assured Fersen of his esteem and intention to continue his late brother's policies regarding France. He sent Fersen new accreditation as Swedish minister to Louis XVI with instructions to remain in Brussels, as well as the oath to the Act of Security of 1789, which Fersen did not hesitate to sign. He was relieved to learn that Taube was to remain in charge of foreign affairs on the regency council. Still, the duke's letters began by early May to hint that circumstances might compel some modification in Sweden's co-operation with the powers. The elder Fersen pressed his son to return home and Axel feared he might gain the duke's support. Even if deprived "of my small revenue," he wrote Marie-Antoinette, he would not leave; "even if I were reduced to misery. . . . I have decided nothing in the world can persuade me to abandon everything at this time."[8]

The investigation of Gustav III's assassination made such alarming progress, implicating an ever-widening circle among the nobility, that at length Duke Karl, claiming it his brother's dying wish that his assassins be pardoned, closed the inquest. Thus the episode remains largely obscured. It is no longer believed that French Jacobins directly instigated the conspiracy but it is clear that the small group of aristocratic conspirators who assassinated the king regarded their act as noble tyrannicide and were strongly inspired by the ideas of the Enlightenment and the Revolution.[9]

Immediately after he was shot, Gustav III appointed an interim government of his staunchest supporters, including Armfelt and Taube. When his end was near, he stipulated that his brother, Duke Karl, should serve as regent, at the head of this same government, until his son, Gustav IV Adolf, should reach eighteen, four and a half years hence. Duke Karl had been allowed little influence during his brother's lifetime, however, and had become the rallying point for much of the anti-royalist noble opposition. It was unlikely that he would let himself be dominated by a council of his brother's most avid supporters and no sooner was the latter dead than the principal "Gustavians" began to look to their political futures.

The duke surrounded himself with friends who had opposed royal despotism in 1789 and had welcomed the French Revolution for the limitations it placed on monarchical power. In July, Baron Gustav Adolf Reuterholm, whom Fersen had considered a dangerous fanatic in Paris in 1790, returned to Sweden where, taking only a minor post in the state financial administration, he quickly came to dominate the weak and vacillating nature of his friend, the duke-regent. It was soon understood that the "Vizier" was the real ruler of Sweden. Reuterholm had a long memory for revenge and his arrival put an end to what remained of Gustavian influence in the regency government. Taube had already resigned and Armfelt left for the Continent for a sojourn of undetermined length.[10]

Among the duke's coterie was Erik Magnus Staël von Holstein, recalled from Paris by Gustav III at the turn of the year. His opposition to Gustav's counterrevolutionary policies and support for an alliance with the new constitutional France were not unwelcome among the duke's friends.[11] Neither Duke Karl nor virtually anyone else except the faithful Taube had been enthusiastic for Gustav III's counterrevolutionary crusade.[12] Fersen himself had often felt apprehensive over the king's predilection for violent means. Sweden's delicate position was expressed some months later by Duchess Charlotta:

If the duke-regent should now enter into an alliance with France to seek to obtain a counterweight against Russian power, perhaps the mania for freedom which reigns there might also gain the upper hand in our land, which would indeed be a greater misfortune than any other. If, on the other hand, the duke continues to show himself as submissive to Russia as the late king, one might well fear that Sweden might become a new Poland.[13]

Upon the regent's choice depended the future of Fersen and his mission in Brussels.

2

In May 1792, the French government sent Raymond Verninac de Saint-Maur as its agent to Stockholm, with instructions to observe and if possible to seek an alliance. Fersen learned of his mission, warned Duke Karl on 9 May that he was "without doubt an emissary of the Propaganda," and urged that he be denied

entry into the country. The duke reassured him that he knew of
Verninac's Jacobinism and was determined not to recognize him.[14]

Staël, however, lost no time in contacting Verninac and projecting
a Franco-Swedish defensive alliance, which remained a secret
between himself, the duke, and Reuterholm; even the new
rikskansler, Fredrik Sparre, ostensibly in charge of foreign affairs,
was kept ignorant. Nevertheless, Verninac's presence in Stockholm gave rise to rumors and in the general European reaction
after 10 August 1792, it was deemed wise that he depart, with
the assurance, however, that Staël would soon come to Paris to
renew negotiations.

Fersen, though uneasy about Verninac and his contacts with
Staël, did not at the time know his actual relations with the
Swedish government.[15] As noted, his own credentials had been
renewed by Duke Karl, who, Taube wrote frequently, intended
to continue his brother's counterrevolutionary policy.[16] Still, Fersen's instructions remained vague. On 13 June, he wrote Taube
for more exact directions. The duke-regent replied on 26 June,
that Fersen was to act only if the king and queen of France should
happily be freed from their captivity, in which case he was to
assist them with his "wise counsels" and show the enthusiasm of
the Swedish court "for everything which concerns the fate of the
royal house of France." Attached, however, was a copy of a letter
to the Russian ambassador in Stockholm, explaining that Gustav
III's plans for intervention in France were based on financial
support from Spain, and that this not being forthcoming, Swedish
participation must now, for the time being, be declined. Although
to Fersen, Duke Karl wrote of "the insidious plans of the execrable
revolutionaries," Staël was at this very time conferring with
Verninac. Fersen's promotion to major general in May 1792 could
not still his anxiety over his position.[17]

The duke's instructions could only increase Fersen's apprehensions. Already on 27 April, he had written to Stedingk in St.
Petersburg that Sweden's role with regard to France would be
"less noble and less active" than if Gustav III had lived; it would
now be subordinated to that of other powers, especially Russia.
Thus, it should be to engage the Russians "to act vigorously and
to have them demand the same of us that we should direct all our
efforts."[18] Fersen continued to hope for a Russian intervention.
On 30 June, he wrote optimistically to Marie-Antoinette that Russia
would send 15,000 and Sweden 8,000 troops to the allied coalition.

Meanwhile, he came to fear that such interest as Catherine II had had in France was "created by our dear and unfortunate master and it died with him," though it was not entirely clear that Russia would not play an active part against France until the following autumn. The Swedish minister in Berlin wrote Fersen that Prussia and Austria neither expected nor wished Swedish support, since "the number of parties cooperating could impede . . . the plans for compensation that were decided in advance."[19]

Fersen summed up the situation in Sweden in his diary at the beginning of July 1792:

Letters from Sweden. Bad. The duke is inclined to take alarm at the situation in France, [but] he is completely under the influence of Bonde, who in turn is influenced by Staël, who freely associates with Verninac, that Jacobin who is the minister of France. Bonde belonged to that party which opposed the late king.[20]

3

With the death of Gustav III, Fersen evidently felt that the one sovereign capable of organizing an armed congress of powers had disappeared. On 17 April, he wrote Marie-Antoinette, "You have lost in him a firm support, a good ally, and I a protector and friend. This loss is cruel." He urged her to encourage the rebels to make a hostile move, since this now seemed the only way to move the European courts to action. On 24 April, he learned with relief of the French declaration of war against Austria. Marie-Antoinette meanwhile kept him advised on French strategic plans.[21]

Fersen and the queen developed a complex system to continue their correspondence. Henceforth, their letters were concealed in packages containing clothing, hats, biscuits, and so forth, or were written in invisible ink between the lines of fictitious business letters, written under assumed names, for the queen's part, by her secretary, Goguelat. The messages were frequently enciphered and sent via Goguelat and a Mme. Toscani, who managed Mme. Sullivan's Paris residence in her absence.[22]

If Fersen was uncertain as to his instructions from his government, he felt compelled to remain active and now undertook a project of far-reaching significance. Though a state of war now existed, he turned again to his favorite idea of crushing the Revolution by an ultimatum from the powers, backed by threat of force.

In November 1791, Fersen had mentioned in passing a certain Limon in a letter to Marie-Antoinette. The following March, he forwarded a pamphlet and letter from Limon to Gustav III. "Limon is a wretch," he wrote in his diary in May, "but we should treat him with consideration and use him, without placing our trust in him." The Marquis Geffroi de Limon had been in the employ of the Duc d'Orléans and was known as an intriguer but a skillful publicist.[23] Herein lay the beginning of Fersen's involvement in the framing of the Brunswick Manifesto.

Threatening declarations, addressed by one power to the inhabitants of another, constituted a well-precedented practice in eighteenth-century diplomacy and were part of the mentality of the times. Fersen, as a Swede, knew how the Russians had repeatedly used this device against both Sweden and Poland, while his own and others' speculations over the escape of the French royal family and an armed congress all presumed the issuing of manifestos.[24]

In March 1792 and again in May, after the outbreak of the war, the émigré princes appealed to Francis, the new king of Hungary and Bohemia, to publish a declaration, calling for the complete restoration of the old regime in France and vengeance against any who offended against the royal family. Behind this project was concealed their ambition of establishing a regency under the Comte de Provence. As this was opposed by Austria, they sought support from Catherine II of Russia.

Louis XVI and his principal advisers in Paris had reason to suspect the princes, for secrets were not closely kept in Coblenz. Louis feared the consequences of either foreign or civil war for the royal family, clergy, and aristocracy within France. His former naval minister, Bertrand de Moleville, therefore proposed to him, probably in mid-May, a project whereby both the princes and the allied monarchs should publish coordinated declarations of intention, based on a draft Louis should send them. The émigrés should also be persuaded not to intervene either in the coming campaign or in any negotiations. On 21 May, the journalist Jacques Mallet du Pan was sent to Germany via his native Geneva. To approach the émigrés, he was instructed to see the old Marshal de Castries in Cologne.

Vienna and Berlin were meanwhile aware of the princes' plan for a manifesto. Suspecting their motives, especially with regard to a regency, they revealed their intention of producing a manifesto of their own. Frederick William II discussed this with Bouillé in Magdeburg on 30 May, insisting that the allies would demand only the return of Louis XVI to his rightful power. Fersen informed Marie-Antoinette of this project a month later, when he wrote that the Duke of Brunswick would "precede his entry with a very strong manifesto in the name of the coalition powers, which will make all France and Paris in particular responsible for the royal persons. Then he will march directly on Paris."[25]

Already on 30 April, the queen had herself written to Mercy in Brussels, urging a declaration from the court of Vienna. She repeated her demand through Fersen on 4 July and a few days later Mercy replied that a threatening manifesto would certainly be forthcoming.[26]

Fersen and Mercy agreed that "one should speak of the general desire to save the king, to exclude the rebels, to say nothing about the constitution, for one must combat it without saying so, and destroy it."[27] By 18 July, Fersen could report to the queen:

We are working on the manifesto. I have had one made by M. de Limon which he has given to M. de Mercy without his knowing it came from me. It is very good and such as one would wish it to be. Nothing is promised to anyone, no party is offended, no commitment is made to anything, and Paris is made responsible for the safety of the king and his family. It is said the [military] operations will begin on 15 August.[28]

Marie-Antoinette awaited this manifesto anxiously. On 24 July she wrote Fersen of the royal family's desperate situation, imploring that it be published at once. Fersen felt the allies should not speak until their armies were ready to march but feared this might be too late to save the royal family.[29]

Meanwhile, Mallet du Pan arrived in Coblenz, where the Marshal de Castries at length arranged for him to see the princes, who received him coldly. Mallet then departed for Frankfurt, for the imperial coronation of Francis II.

Though unable to see Francis II or Frederick William II, Mallet met on 15 and 18 July with leading Austrian and Prussian statesmen, who gave every indication of approving his proposals for a manifesto, after which he left for Geneva. Final acceptance, however, lay with the emperor and king of Prussia. Limon meanwhile presented his own draft manifesto, which the monarchs accepted and the Duke of Brunswick signed.

In Brussels, Fersen learned from Limon on 26 July that his

recommendations had been at least "partly accepted." Mercy wrote further details. Two days later he received the Duke of Brunswick's manifesto, which differed only very slightly from Limon's draft. The princes and Calonne had insisted on seeing the draft but had approved it. The Austrians accepted it grudgingly, under pressure from the Prussians, who were "behaving marvelously."[30]

Behind each one of these projects for a manifesto to the French people lay different political objectives. The princes wanted a regency to assure reestablishment of the old regime and to protect French territory against Austro-Prussian designs. The men around Louis XVI in the Tuileries, on the other hand, favored cooperation with the *constitutionnels*, avoidance of foreign war, and maintenance of the constitution, though revised to provide a stronger royal authority and a bicameral legislature. A number of contemporaries were convinced that Louis XVI sincerely shared these ideas. Mallet was instructed to urge a manifesto aimed at rallying to the throne all Frenchmen, "who, without desiring the actual constitution, fear the return of great abuses."[31]

There thus seems reason to believe that Louis XVI, generally regarded as completely dominated by his wife, may have had a policy of his own which he tried to implement. Fersen himself had suspected the strength of his determination to "regain all of his authority" during his secret visit to Paris in February. The king sent Mallet to deal with the Marshal de Castries, rather than with Breteuil, the avowed representative of the queen and a man, as the Comte de Montlosier wrote, "entirely devoted" to a "despotic and absolutistic system," or to the princes' favorite, Calonne. More significantly, Louis apparently kept his project secret from Marie-Antoinette.[32]

Had she known of it, she would surely have advised Fersen. On 7 June, she warned him the *constitutionnels* were sending a certain Masson de Saint-Amand to Vienna to negotiate. Mercy should insure that the Austrians pretended to deal with him as though he were the true representative of the French king and queen, while realizing he did not express their true intentions, she wrote. Fersen suspected the *constitutionnels* of wishing for peace and their constitution in return for territorial concessions, a bargain he feared the allies, especially the Austrians, would readily accept.[33] There is no indication, however, that he knew specifically of either Mallet's mission or the princes' project for a manifesto. Doubtless, his mistrust of the *constitutionnels,* émigrés, and Austrians, as well as the allies' known intention of issuing a manifesto, prompted him to commission Limon's draft. In particular, his fears were aroused in June and July by the rumor that the *constitutionnels* intended to move the royal family to the interior of France, which would consolidate their control over them and which "only a very strong and very menacing proclamation" could prevent.[34]

Limon's draft, in any event, represented Marie-Antoinette's point of view, which Fersen probably assumed to be Louis XVI's as well. It demanded above all restoration of unlimited power to the king, unencumbered by either a constitution or an independent aristocracy. The Marquis de Bouillé recognized the manifesto to be entirely in accordance with Breteuil's principles, as Fersen wrote to Marie-Antoinette with obvious satisfaction on 26 July. In the same letter, he added that the Marshal de Castries boasted of direct communications with Louis XVI, but Fersen dismissed him as a person of little account. Clearly, he did not know what this connection was.[35]

Limon may well have been better informed. It was generally understood by contemporaries that he was the author of the Brunswick Manifesto, but they usually assumed that he was in the employ of Calonne and the princes. That Limon, however, intrigued with the émigrés on his own hook would help explain their relatively easy acceptance of his draft, since the allies would not accept a declaration from them. Fersen himself noted that Limon had been well received by the princes. Limon may furthermore have learned from them about Mallet's proposals, which would be a reason for the similarity between these and the final manifesto.[36]

Still, any influence of Mallet's draft upon Limon could only be of limited importance. The manifesto, as it appeared, agreed in all essentials with principles Fersen himself had long advocated.[37] These included a declaration by the powers, backed by force; a guarantee for the safety of the king and his family; avoidance of promises which might compromise the king's future freedom of action; and finally, assurance to the "sound part of the nation" of pardon and protection, and threat to all who offered resistance.

Considering their similarities, one nonetheless wonders why, after encouraging Mallet, the allies adopted Limon's manifesto. Mallet might easily have passed for something very much like a *constitutionnel* to the allies, as well as to the émigrés. Very likely the former only pretended to encourage him, as Marie-Antoinette had wished in the case of the *constitutionnel* Masson de Saint-Amand. In any case, the final decision rested with Francis II and Fredrick William II. It seems doubtful that Mallet's version of a manifesto, despite its somewhat more conciliatory tone, could have been more effective than Fersen's and Limon's, as sometimes averred. A comparison shows no substantial difference: both were based on what Mallet himself called a balance of "terror and confidence."[38] Mallet meanwhile had presented a lengthy memorandum while Limon astutely came with a ready-made manifesto.

The aims of the allied courts, finally, are less clear and their apparent unity covered much mutual distrust. Of the three proposals for a manifesto they received, Fersen's provided a royalist alternative to those prepared by proponents of the constitution and the aristocracy, respectively. As such, it evidently best suited the allies, especially as it was formulated broadly enough to cover their incipient differences. That the Russian envoy to the princes in Coblenz opposed Mallet at every turn further strengthened Fersen's position.[39]

Fersen was delighted with the manifesto, the fulfillment of a long desire. Imposing forces were gathering on France's frontiers, opposed by a revolutionary rabble and the remains of an army, crippled by desertion and emigration. Thus, before the test of battle, Fersen can hardly be blamed for his optimism. On 26 July, upon announcing the manifesto, he sent the king and queen a proposal from Breteuil for appointments to their new royal council. He wrote Mme. de Saint-Priest in Stockholm, offering her husband his choice of embassies to the Northern courts. On 3 August, he proposed to Marie-Antoinette that the Duke of Brunswick be lodged at the Tuileries upon arrival.[40]

In Paris, the prospect appeared less bright and Goguelat, writing for the queen, answered pointedly on 1 August that it was hardly the time to concern oneself with a choice of ministers when the slightest delay by the allies imperiled the lives of the royal family. Meanwhile, Sophie wrote on 24 August that Staël was spreading the rumor in Stockholm that Axel had written the Brunswick Manifesto, doubtless to discredit him, "for here they have considered that the manifesto is too strong and even that it will cause the people to avenge themselves against the royal family."[41]

An ominous prophecy, for news of the storming of the Tuileries on 10 August had evidently not yet reached faraway Stockholm. The consequences of the Brunswick Manifesto were, of course, the opposite of what Fersen had expected and disastrous to the cause he served, touching off the chain of events leading to the end of the monarchy and the imprisonment, trial, and execution of the king and queen. Fersen thereafter gave little indication that he comprehended his part in precipitating their downfall; if the manifesto failed, presumably it had not been backed with sufficient vigor by the allies. It was ironic but perhaps fortunate that he would remain to the end of his days secure in the belief that he— and perhaps he alone—had done everything possible to save the king and queen of France from their fate.[41a]

4

The publication of the Brunswick Manifesto represented the high point of Fersen's counterrevolutionary activity since leaving France. The months which followed were bitter with the tribulations of the French royal family, the retreat of the allies from Valmy, the French invasion of the Austrian Netherlands, the chagrin of knowing that the Swedish government no longer really supported him. In the midst of all this, his elder sister, Hedda, died of consumption in Pisa.[42]

Fersen's moment of optimism was thus short-lived. Even before the storming of the Tuileries, he cast about, in growing anxiety, for some additional means to assure the safety of the royal family. Not unnaturally, he returned to the idea of a threatening proclamation, this time suggested by Eleanore Sullivan. Fersen and Breteuil agreed to send Monseigneur d'Agoult to London to persuade the British to warn the French against any attempt upon the lives of their king and queen upon pain of "terrible retribution." Such a warning need not violate their neutrality since they would commit themselves only if the king or queen were actually harmed. D'Agoult departed on 9 August. The following day, the Tuileries palace was overwhelmed by the Paris mob.[43]

The monseigneur returned from London on 21 August. Pitt, he claimed, was much interested in French affairs but hesitated to show this publicly since the English were stirred up by swarms of "propagandists from all countries." Following the events of 10 August, Pitt recalled the British ambassador from Paris, though it is doubtful d'Agoult influenced this decision and the most the latter could obtain was the assurance that the ambassador, upon departing, would express His Britannic Majesty's "concern" over the French royal family.[44]

Fersen tried a new approach in mid-September when he persuaded Mercy to urge the idea of a British manifesto upon Lord Elgin, British envoy in Brussels, having first secured the latter's agreement. Elgin was prepared to go to Paris to handle the matter, but his government studiously avoided any real commitment, despite assurances of good-will.[45]

Hereafter, the project fell into abeyance. Following Valmy, it was rumored that the British had induced the Duke of Brunswick to retreat so as to intervene themselves the following year and establish a regime to their own liking in France. Fersen gave no credence to such rumors, for in his view, France was already weak enough to suit the British, who in turn could only stamp out the growing movement for parliamentary reform by destroying the "new principles" of the Revolution.[46] He thus remained hopeful. At the beginning of 1793, he became interested in a scheme promoted by Mirabeau's former secretary, Pellenc, for "English intelligence agents" to try to "gain through money and promises the leaders of the Orleanist party, such as Laclos, Santerre, Dumouriez. . . ." At the same time, he noted the rumor that the Prince of Wales was planning an escape attempt for the queen and her children, which briefly raised his hopes.[47]

In February 1793, after the British entered the war, Fersen gave them the plans for a landing in Normandy "which the Norman nobles sent to the former king [of Sweden] in 1791." In March, Breteuil tried to obtain six million pounds from Pitt to back the proposal of certain *constitutionnels* to secure removal of the queen and the royal children from France, but the prime minister equivocated. A certain Toustaing approached Breteuil with an undisclosed proposal from Dumouriez, whose adjutant he had been, but as the response evidently depended on Pitt, who again temporized, the matter remained unsettled. Fersen now began to suspect that the British wanted "some family other than the Bourbons" on the French throne, because of their "mistrust of everything the French do and fear of their levity," this last a sentiment with which Fersen, despite his disappointment, fully agreed.[48]

Indeed, as he became increasingly bitter against France and disillusioned with his own country, Fersen showed a growing admiration for Great Britain. His diary from August 1792 is meanwhile filled with horror and grief at events in France and disappointment with the allies. Frustration and despair turned to savage lust for revenge. "You will doubtless not forget, my dear Baron," he wrote Breteuil on 31 August, "to recommend the destruction of Varennes." The reasons should be widely publicized, for unfortunately the Brunswick Manifesto was not well known in the French provinces, "and you also know that it was through the press that the people were misled and the Revolution brought about." Localities that tried to defend themselves should be "abandoned to pillage and all the inhabitants put to the sword." The Duke of Brunswick needed encouragement in such matters, being inclined to clemency and unable to judge the situation in France as well as those who had witnessed its origins. On 12 September, Fersen complained to Breteuil that "we nowhere see that submission and eagerness to receive the allied troops we had expected," as Brunswick's conciliatory behavior only "encouraged the factious through the hope of impunity and restrains the good-will of the well-intentioned through the fear that they will again be abandoned to the cruelty of their enemies and oppressors." It was necessary to "arrest or kill all the Jacobins, or at least the most zealous leaders," which would be "easy at this moment but will be less so later on." To Taube, he showed the full measure of his despair after Valmy:

It seems there is misfortune in everything. I would have been with the Duke of Brunswick at his arrival in Paris and I would have done everything possible toward the destruction of that impious city. It is the only remedy there could be and I would still insist upon it.[49]

Fersen's papers meanwhile hint at other schemes to save the royal family. On 13 August, the very day they learned of the storming of the Tuileries, he discussed with Mercy the idea of urging La Fayette to defect to the Austrians with his army. Not long after, Fersen expressed the view that Louis XVI should never have left the Tuileries on 10 August, in which case the palace would not have surrendered and the *constitutionnels* would have gained the upper hand in the Assembly, thus at least guaranteeing Their Majesties' lives.[50] At the beginning of September, he speculated with Breteuil over a party leader in France who could take up the king's cause. None could be found among the aristocrats, Fersen felt, but among the *constitutionnels* there was a M. Acloque, a former brewer of the Faubourg Saint-Marceau, who though a "democrat," was well disposed toward the king and had rendered him services. "He has enough spirit to feel everything which has to be repaired; he has private vengeances to carry out; he has been oppressed; he feels his party has been destroyed forever; he wishes to crush that of the Jacobins." Once the allies entered Paris, such a man could be useful in seeking out the "guilty" among the more "obscure class." Not that Fersen placed any more trust in *constitutionnels* or other democrats than before:

I believe . . . once arrived in Châlons, it would be . . .[very advantageous] to seek, by all available means, the possibility of entering into discussions and negotiations with the factious and to sacrifice everything to assure the security of the king and his family, and to procure his liberty; even to slow down the march of the troops, and promise everything; to leave it until later to find pretexts for holding to only what one wishes to honor.

Meanwhile, extensive propaganda should be made to "enlighten and reassure the people," for which Limon would be well suited.[51]

Fersen's willingness to cooperate for the time being with the *constitutionnels* reveals how desperate he now realized the situation to be; it was without doubt extremely repugnant to him. Toward the *constitutionnels* he felt a particular aversion he would always keep. Though they wished to preserve the monarchy, they did so, he felt, only to protect themselves against their rivals, the Jacobins, who had simply "perfected their work." When he learned of the arrest in late August of Barnave and Charles Lameth, he hoped they would be executed, for "no one shall have deserved it more." His bitterness did not abate with time. In 1794, he attributed to them "all the blame for all the misfortunes of France and for what I have lost. I will never forgive them for what they have done to me."[52]

Fersen was scarcely less outspoken in his dislike for the émigré princes and their court, and especially their persistent plans to make Monsieur regent of France. He nevertheless admired the bravery and self-sacrifice of the émigré troops and complained bitterly of the callous treatment they received from the Austrians.[53]

After Valmy, the allied army not only retreated out of France, but was followed into Belgium and the Rhineland by the victorious armies of the new republic. Fersen was alarmed at the growth of the democratic spirit in the path of the advancing French. By 4 November, a cannonade could be heard in Brussels and all who could sought to leave. Fersen, Craufurd, Mme. Sullivan, and Ivan Simolin left together on 9 November, passing long lines of miserable émigrés, fleeing on foot. The party went first to Maestricht, then Aachen, finally Düsseldorf, where they arrived on 18 December and remained until April 1793.[54]

By now, Fersen's position vis-à-vis his own government was almost meaningless and he limited his official duties to reporting his observations, meanwhile doing what he could as a private individual. Chancellor Sparre instructed him, early in 1793, to have nothing to do with the émigrés, "on pain of being disavowed." "What a false and ignoble conduct and how horrible for me," Fersen wrote indignantly to Taube, doubtless seeing this injunction as aimed at his relationship with Breteuil.

> However, I am doing what I can on the sly, especially in England . . . . but my situation is frightful and if it were not for them [the French royal family], I would allow myself the pleasure of letting everything go to the devil and to have nothing more to do with such a base and wrong-headed policy. . . . I am working as much as I can with the Comte de Mercy to serve them. Since the death of our dear master, I have to make use of him to serve them.[55]

Because Fersen worked behind the scenes in this manner, influencing others who acted in more official capacities, his activities at this time are difficult to trace, and the few clues in his diary and private letters can only stimulate the imagination without giving any clear idea of his importance.

Fersen's influence, however, waned rapidly in late 1792 and early 1793. He was bedeviled by personal problems. In response to repeated requests for reimbursement for the expenses of his mission, the Swedish treasury in the fall of 1792 sent him, for some unaccountable reason, letters of exchange on banks in France, which, quite aside from the problem of cashing them at all, were payable in *assignats* at only half their face value. Fersen simply returned them to Stockholm. He found it distasteful to solicit and wrote Taube in January 1793 that he had hoped that the success of the allies in France would have solved his financial problems without further recourse to Sweden. By February he was compelled to renew his demands, pointing out that since Gustav III had employed him in his diplomatic post, he had received nothing for it. He had meanwhile lost his possessions in Paris while those he had saved from Valenciennes were pillaged by the French in Brussels. Only some months later did he begin to receive compensation on a somewhat regular basis.[56]

His problems were compounded by those of his secretaries, Major Carl Brelin, who served him in Brussels from July through October 1792, and A. Dalman, who succeeded him until the following spring. Both heartily disliked their assignment and wrote eloquent pleas to the *rikskansler* for transfer to more desirable, that is, more lucrative posts. Indeed, the Swedish government neglected to pay them, like their master, and only periodic loans out of the latter's pocket managed to tide them over. Their correspondence is illuminating regarding the sorry plight of diplomatic secretaries in the eighteenth century. The hapless Dalman in particular was victim of a series of misadventures. Fersen left him behind as a neutral diplomatic observer when he himself, being under sentence in France, left Brussels before the French advance in November 1792. Within a few days, Dalman deemed it prudent to leave and after a harrowing journey, rejoined Fersen in Aachen. Some months later, relieved from his post because of his tangled finances, Dalman was apprehended in Düsseldorf for passing bad checks.[57]

Fersen meanwhile feared that his secretaries had been sent from Stockholm to spy on him. By July 1792, he suspected Brelin of "democratic" sentiments. He no longer used him for confidential work and tried to discover if he corresponded secretly with Reuterholm. He likewise considered Dalman a *"mauvais sujet"* and was suspicious of his letters to *Rikskansler* Sparre. Fersen had reason to be careful. A letter expressing misgivings toward Swedish policy to his confidant, Cabinet Secretary A. I. Silfversparre, was intercepted in October 1792 by Sparre, who called for an explanation. This caused Fersen much embarrassment, warned him that his personal correspondence was not secure and increased the government's ill-will toward him. In February, he felt compelled to comment to Sparre on unspecified rumors about him in French newspapers, obviously fearful Stockholm was prepared to credit them. When Sparre pointedly forbade him further dealings with French émigrés, he stoutly denied he had any, having been charged only with what concerned Louis XVI and his family. "No one is safe from calumny," he complained to the chancellor on 5

February. In March, Taube confirmed that Brelin had indeed been spying on him.[58]

Thus, virtually powerless, on strained terms with his own government, a refugee in Düsseldorf, Fersen followed with hopeless anger the trial and execution of Louis XVI. His grief over the death of this "best and most virtuous of princes," as he described him to his father, was profound and touching, his rage bitter. "Tigers, cannibals, madmen, savages," he wrote Taube, ". . . Oh! Accursed nation! If there exists a God, this impious, sacrilegious, barbaric horde should be damned by Him. It should be annihilated, exterminated. It should find refuge nowhere. It should be overwhelmed by all evils: starvation, disease, misery."[59]

He thereafter directed his efforts, together with Mercy, to preventing the Comte de Provence from establishing a regency for his captive nephew, Louis XVII, thereby bypassing the queen. "I have proposed to that end that the powers not respond to Monsieur regarding this démarche," he wrote Taube in January 1793, now no longer holding to the idea of a threatening proclamation.

This silence of the powers is, however, still perhaps a means of saving them [the queen and her children]. For the same reason, I am opposed to any step or declaration by the emperor in favor of the queen. It would be useless with those scoundrels and it would do nothing but hasten their end.[60]

Meanwhile, Fersen watched with apprehension Staël's growing influence in Sweden. While Fersen was kept ignorant of his projects, the favor Staël enjoyed at the Swedish court contrasted painfully with the pointed neglect with which he himself was treated. Nor was he unaware that Staël had been in frequent contact with Verninac.[61] A new spirit prevailed in Stockholm. Fersen was becoming an embarrassment to the government, and it sought the first excuse to remove him from his post. This he unwittingly provided himself when he wrote Taube on 1 January 1793 that if the French republic should become "established and recognized," he could never return to "that country of cannibals," nor would he wish to return to Sweden; he would in that case prefer the post of minister to Great Britain or the Italian courts. Sophie and Taube, concerned for his health and well-being, apparently seized on this idea; to the government, it provided a convenient solution. On 13 March, Axel noted:

I got letters from Sweden which greatly disturbed me. Taube and Sophie write me the duke has awarded me the post of ambassador to London and that he intends to write me and send me letters of accreditation. This was like a stroke of lightning to me. I would be forced to leave Eleanore [Sullivan] and to go far away from Her [Marie-Antoinette] and French affairs, which give me the opportunity of serving Her and contributing to Her liberation. I was so much the more disconsolate since the duke had said to my sister that my mission here had become superfluous. I was altogether beside myself. I could not bear to think of leaving it. I decided to decline if I were not allowed to remain in Brussels.

The next day, he declined the ambassadorship, except under the obviously impossible condition that he stay on in Brussels. He then did his best to assuage Taube's ruffled feelings.[62]

The Swedish government became blunter. Chancellor Sparre informed Fersen officially on 5 April 1793 that his mission was terminated, with an indemnification of 12,000 livres. Fersen, however, gave no indication of having received Sparre's letter. He may well have ignored it at a time when the defection of General Dumouriez to the allies stirred him to a final burst of optimism before the trial and execution of Marie-Antoinette crushed forever his hopes for the woman he loved and the queen he served so faithfully.

5

Fersen's arch-rival, Staël, had meanwhile not been idle. In the fall of 1792, he prepared to resume his negotiations with Verninac. Fersen, albeit uninformed of Staël's activities, warned his government of rumors of an intended Swedish pact with the Convention, which could bring repercussions from other powers.[63] In December, scarcely a year since Gustav III had recalled him in ill-concealed disgrace, Staël set off for Paris on the pretext of personal business. Negotiating on his own authority, he concluded a secret preliminary defensive treaty with the French republic on 17 May 1793.

Events both in Sweden and abroad, however, had dampened the enthusiasm of Duke Karl and Reuterholm for a closer connection with France. In July 1792, Reuterholm had repealed Gustav III's censorship decrees and prepared a widely heralded ordinance granting freedom of the press. "If this liberty is closely watched," Fersen wrote Taube in August, "it will not present so many problems, but if the government becomes weak the dangers will be incalculable."[64] The ordinance promptly gave rise to such a rash of political pamphleteering, aimed especially against the aristocracy, that by December the government began once again to impose censorship. Reuterholm, himself considered a "Jacobin" by the "Gustavians," soon applied the same name to the growing opposition to his increasingly oppressive regime. In January 1793, the serious Ebel riot occurred in Stockholm while student unruliness and the growth of organized radicalism in the universities further alarmed the government over the spread of "Jacobinism." Meanwhile, the duke and his "Grand Vizier" were concerned over the apparent instability of the French republic ar.'. tne country as a whole was shocked by the September massacres and the execution of Louis XVI. "I am glad over what you tell me about Reuterholm's not being a Jacobin," Fersen wrote Taube in July 1793. "That is at least something, since he is where he is, but why must he give himself the appearance of being one?"[65] Meanwhile, just as Swedish sentiment had begun to turn against France, word from Fersen reached Stockholm of General Dumouriez's impending defection.

Fersen had long observed Dumouriez with interest. In October 1792, he sent his government a copy of a note from the general to the king of Prussia. The next month, he reported that Dumouriez had been negotiating with the Prussian general Manstein. "As a basis, there was proposed the freedom of the king and the royal family," he wrote, though he feared Dumouriez had only been playing for time. In December, Carl Brelin, returning to Sweden after being relieved as Fersen's secretary, had a lengthy interview with Dumouriez at Liège, in which the French general praised Sweden and its regent in the most glowing terms and warmly expressed the hope of seeing "the ancient friendship which [formerly] united two valiant and high-minded nations . . . secured in an unshakable manner."[66] It has been seen that Fersen considered Dumouriez one of the supporters of the Duc d'Orléans he hoped in early February 1793 might be won over through bribery. On 21 February, he noted in his diary that Dumouriez had arranged a private meeting with Lord Auckland when the outbreak of war with Britain intervened. This Fersen found regrettable, for he felt Dumouriez might have been persuaded at this interview "to render a great service by abandoning the army and the Orléans family as well as thereby putting an end to the war in the Netherlands." That Fersen himself subsequently played some role in bringing Dumouriez and the Austrians together is suggested by his diary for 20 March:

With my encouragement, the Baron [de Breteuil] had decided to send the Duc de Caraman to Wesel to tell Mercy about Dumouriez's proposal...he embraced the idea with warmth, said he could write to Vienna, that he would support the idea and that as much as 3 or 4 millions should be given. But considering the changed situation it would be necessary for Dumouriez to let himself be taken prisoner with both the sons of the Duc d'Orléans and that he should give up one or two important positions, that he should be given money as well as amnesty for himself and for those he should indicate and the promise of some important position by the king [of Prussia] besides.[67]

On 29 March, Fersen wrote Taube, optimistically relating the rumor that the rebels were heating up the palace of Versailles for Marie-Antoinette and her children, concluding they were "beaten everywhere." Next day, it seemed clear that Dumouriez had made some suggestions to the Prince of Coburg, the allied commander.[68] At last, on 5 April, Fersen was able to write exultantly:

An express messenger who was sent here to the Baron de Breteuil by the Duc [sic] de Caraman has brought the agreement between Dumouriez and the Prince of Coburg. I sent a messenger with the news of this to Sweden. The rejoicing was general, and I felt it doubly since I was no longer worried about the queen. I wrote Taube and asked if I should act in accordance with the orders I had received for the event the king should be freed or wait for others, and that in the latter case he should send them to me as quickly as possible, for all of this could go amazingly rapidly, and since he knows the situation better, I considered it safer to leave it to his decision than not to ask at all. In the evening, Marshal de Broglie received word that Dumouriez was marching on Paris with 50,000 men, who all wore the white cocarde and that the prince of Coburg remained at the front, ready to support him if that became necessary.[69]

"It was more than two months ago, even before entering Holland, that Dumouriez had made propositions of that kind through the Baron de Breteuil," Fersen wrote Duke Karl on 5 April.

The indecision of England whence these propositions had been communicated and suspicion, so well deserved, of Dumouriez's sincerity, had suspended and retarded their execution. It seems that it was reserved for the Prince of Coburg to end this great affair and to be the savior of the Bourbon family and of all Europe. Considering the disposition of spirits in Paris and in France, one may feel reassured about the fate of the royal family.

To Taube, he expressed himself with an optimism that reflected the repressed fears and bitterness of the past months:

I am delighted and I regard this great affair as over. There is no longer anything, according to all possible calculations, to fear for the royal family and I would not be surprised to report to you that she [the queen] has been borne in triumph through Paris.

The effect of Fersen's message in the Swedish court was striking. Armfelt's mistress, Magdalena Rudenschöld, who shared her lover's rancor toward the regency, wrote the latter on 19 April:

The good news from France has had its effect. The Swedish Jacobins have been, if not annihilated, at least intimidated. General Taube has just left me. It was through His Excellency that Fersen sent his dispatch to the duke. He went up right away to give it to His Highness. He [the duke] had the duplicity to receive this news with a demonstration of real joy. The Grand Vizier arrived, who received this blow with all the emotion of suppressed rage, grinning from ear to ear and exclaiming that this was indeed the day for surprises. The little grand chancellor [Sparre] arrived quite frightened, imploring the duke to take advantage of the circumstances by ordering Fersen to enter into negotiations. Taube, with his usual rancor, let it be understood that perhaps it was a bit late to pass the sponge over the past, but that in any case, if it were really the duke's intention to repair [it], he should not delay a moment in sending a courier to Fersen.[70]

The court chancellor, Lars von Engeström, later recounted:

... I saw the chancellor [Sparre] busily occupied with arranging a pile of papers. I asked the secretary ... what was going on. "Yesterday evening," he replied, "the news arrived that Dumouriez has gone over to the allies, and His Excellency sent for me around midnight to command me to arrange accreditation for Count Fersen as Swedish ambassador to France." I approached the chancellor and asked him why he was in such a hurry. "Dumouriez has gone over to the allies," he replied; "the Revolution is over and now Count Fersen is ruling France."—"But," I interjected, "what do you intend to do with Baron Staël, whom you yourself have recently sent to Paris?"—"He has been guillotined, I hope," was the reply.[71]

"That same evening," Magdalena Rudenschöld continued to Arm-felt, "Reutersvärd departed, provided with orders for Fersen to follow exactly the plan which the late king had outlined for him. What a triumph for the friends of The Great King!"[72]

Reutersvärd upon arrival replaced Dalman as Fersen's secretary. Fersen meanwhile lost no time in formulating policy. On 8 April, he prepared a lengthy memorandum for Marie-Antoinette, filled with political advice on the problems to be faced when she was restored to the throne. Among other things, he cautioned her that any advice the Comte de Mercy might give her would naturally reflect Austrian policies.[73] Mercy had wielded vast influence over Marie-Antoinette ever since she first arrived in France as dauphine and Fersen's warning doubtless reveals the brilliant role he en-visioned for himself at the court of the queen-regent, as a sort of latter-day, northern Mazarin.

Duke Karl must have thanked his lucky stars that he had allowed Fersen to remain at his post. Not that he had any liking for him personally.[74] The duke's letter of 16 April, however, in which he appointed Fersen ambassador to Louis XVII, breathed affability and delight at the prospect of the restoration of Sweden's ancient ally. He instructed Fersen to "profit from the earliest moments" in seeking indemnification from the French court for the large expendi-tures Gustav III had made in its behalf. It was important for Sweden's "political situation and finances" that the old alliance with the French monarchy be renewed. Fersen, for his part, strongly disapproved such petty mercenary behavior.[75]

During the Dumouriez affair, Staël in Paris was an acute em-barrassment to Duke Karl and his government. The duke ordered him to depart immediately, lest the Swedish government be com-pelled to disavow him. Staël defended his cause, stalled for time, and concluded his secret preliminary defensive treaty on 17 May. Only then did he retire to the Necker estate in Switzerland. Before he even left Paris, however, the duke had already written him that in view of changed circumstances he should stay there and press for an alliance with the republic.

The Dumouriez affair had meanwhile proven a dismal failure. On 8 April, Fersen wrote in his diary:

I was busy in the morning writing to the queen when the bishop of Pamiers came in through the door and said Dumouriez's army had risen up against him, that he had come over at Mons with his whole general staff, almost all of the fortification and artillery officers and a mass of troops of the line, [and added] as well that the remainder would follow him. National Guard stays along with cannon, ammunition, etc. . . .

Though "at first" horrified the defection had not succeeded as planned, he believed the whole French army to be in the process of dissolution and at the end of the month, urged his government to gain credit by joining in its final defeat. In mid-May, he wrote his sister, "Success will not be less sure, but it will be somewhat retarded."[76]

The defection of Dumouriez did in fact badly disorganize the French army. In the spring and summer of 1793, the allies cleared the French from the Netherlands and the Rhineland, and advanced into northeastern France. Fersen remained optimistic and his diary is filled with speculations on the restoration of the monarchy and discontent with the neutrality of his own country.

The government in Sweden was less sanguine over prospects for an allied success. Under pressure from Britain and Russia to limit its profitable trade with the French, the Swedish government pressed Staël for renewed negotiations with the republic. The behavior of the Swedish government toward Fersen after the Dumouriez affair was meanwhile painfully equivocal. On 26 April, *Rikskansler* Sparre countermanded the instructions the duke had sent only ten days earlier for the event of a speedy restoration of the French monarchy. On 30 May, the duke directed Fersen to use his diplomatic status only once Louis XVII was free and restored to the throne, but that "conjointly with the ambassadors of the emperor and king of England, you should constantly work for reestablishment of the French monarchy, without, however, compromising our neutrality." Fersen bitterly lamented the untimely loss of Gustav III.[77]

6

On 15 April, Fersen met Dumouriez, "a true Frenchman: vain, gullible, and rash, gifted with much wit but little judgment." Yet in some respects, Dumouriez's ideas were close to his own.

It had already been suggested [Fersen wrote] that the four arrested commissioners [whom Dumouriez had delivered to the Austrians] should be exchanged for the royal family. His opinion was that one should go to any lengths to arrange the exchange of the royal family, but despite recognizing the republic, we should in any case be able to continue the war. . . .[78]

The French themselves proposed to the Prince of Coburg the exchange of their war minister, P. R. de Beurnonville, and the four commissioners for Marie-Antoinette and her children, conditionally upon an armistice of indefinite length, and recognition of the republic.[79] Rescue of the queen and her family had always taken precedence in Fersen's mind, yet he now showed surprisingly little interest in this project. It would appear that he was persuaded the allies would soon win a clear-cut victory over the French and thus did not regret the Austrians' lack of enthusiasm for the idea, which ultimately caused its failure.[80] Thus passed the only project for freeing the queen and her family that the revolutionary governments of France were ever prepared seriously to carry out.

Fersen's optimism continued, with relatively few lapses, into the beginning of August. There seemed encouraging signs from Stockholm:

I received a letter from Sweden dated the 2nd [presumably of July], in which I am informed the duke has changed his views entirely and that he now hates the Jacobins with whom he formerly surrounded himself and wishes to get rid of them. . . .[81]

The allied campaign proceeded well. On 20 April, Fersen and his friends returned to Brussels, noting with satisfaction the joy of the inhabitants at being freed from the French. "I have never seen people more insolent and dirtier than these *Sons of Liberty*," Fersen's old comrade from the American war, the Duke of Zweibrücken, wrote him after the French surrender of Mainz in July. A few days later, Fersen and Reutersvärd set off for the newly conquered areas in northern France, where they witnessed the capitulation of their old garrison town, Valenciennes, on 1 August.[82]

Yet on that very day, the Convention in Paris voted to try Marie-Antoinette before the Revolutionary Tribunal and moved her to wrote him after the French surender of Mainz in July. A few days later, shattering his last illusions. In vain he struggled against overpowering despair: "I saw her destruction as unavoidable and still I sought to build up my hopes. I tried everything possible to hide my terrible sorrow."[83]

In desperation, Fersen made his final efforts to save the queen. He and the Comte de La Marck urged upon the skeptical Mercy the idea of a lightning thrust directly against the poorly defended French capital by a powerful column of cavalry; Mercy undertook to interest Vienna and the Prince of Coburg in the scheme, but to no avail. Coburg felt that this would encourage rather than prevent terrorism in Paris, but Fersen bitterly complained that he considered only "the military side of the matter" and thus covered himself with shame. "'I do not even have the strength to express what I feel," he wrote Sophie on 14 August. "I would give my life to save her, and I cannot...."

I would have had this satisfaction if cowards and rogues had not de-prived us of the best of masters. Oh! How much more strongly I now feel his loss and how much more I miss him. He alone could have saved her. His great soul would have been aroused at the recital of her woes. He would have dared all and overcome all, but he is no more and every-thing died for me with him.[84]

Fersen and his friends turned to new expedients. On 19 August, La Marck suggested that an agent be sent to Paris "to find out what is going on there, to investigate the possibilities of buying the queen's deportation with money and promises." Mercy as usual raised objections, but Fersen argued that there remained nothing else to do and that

... the [question] of the queen should be separated from all French politics to make her cause only a question of interest to the house of Austria; to try to prove to them how little use this new crime would be, how it would bring retribution down on them, and above all to tell them expressly that nothing more could hinder the advance of the allies.[85]

Even here there linger shadows of the armed congress and the Brunswick Manifesto with their threats of vengeance. A Paris banker named Ribbes was chosen to sound out Danton. Mercy remained skeptical and feared that "even if the queen should stand on the scaffold, this utmost act of cruelty could no longer hinder the powers or change their campaign plans."[86] In due course, however, Ribbes departed and was not heard of until he showed up in Brussels again on 13 September. It developed he had done no more than to write a letter to Danton, "in a manner," Fersen complained, "incomprehensible to anyone but himself."[87] Ironically, since July, well before the idea had been conceived, Danton was no longer a power to be reckoned with.

Slowly, inexorably, the queen's final hour approached. From Brus-sels, Fersen followed her trial in bitterness and despair. After years of unceasing but fruitless effort in her behalf, a strange apathy seemed to grip him. He sank deeper and deeper into melancholy broodings over his own future and bitter recriminations against the selfish interests of the allied powers and the incompetency of their generals. "I am almost always suffering without being exactly ill," he wrote Lady Elizabeth Foster at the beginning of October.[88]

At the end of the month, he was astonished by a letter from Staël, now in Switzerland, with a pamphlet by his wife. "Despite your injustices to me," Staël wrote, using the familiar *tu* that recalled happier days,

. . . despite your premeditated design of bringing about my misfortune, I cannot but send you a mark of the sentiments which I and my family have never ceased to hold toward her who is today so cruelly persecuted. The frightful misfortunes that you are suffering and which I share from the bottom of my heart have easily made me forget the chagrin you had prepared for me. I see you now only as an unfortunate friend whom I would give my life to console.

"I thank you . . . for what you wished to say regarding my misfortunes," Fersen replied frostily on 15 October, using the formal *vous*.

Those which I am experiencing and those which await me are perhaps great, but I have at least the consolation of a pure heart and of a conscience without reproach, with regard both to causes and to persons. I have fulfilled all the duties which my attachment and gratitude toward those to whom I owe all prescribe. I have only to regret that I have served them so badly and I shall always be less pitiful than those who must reproach themselves for having forgotten their benefits and having contributed to their ills.

Of Mme. de Staël's pamphlet, *Sur le procès de la reine par une femme*, Fersen observed in his diary, "There are enough good things about it but they would be still better if one did not know the author. . . . She affects great sensibility, but the constitutional spirit shows through everywhere and she tries to defend the queen by making a Jacobin of her."[89]

During this time, too, Fersen had the unhappy experience of seeing Drouet, who had warned the patriots of Varennes of the attempt of the royal family to escape in June 1791, now a commissioner of the Convention and a prisoner of the Austrians.[90]

On 20 October, the blow fell. Fersen received word of the execution of Marie-Antoinette. He was not eloquent in his grief. For weeks he had already been numb with anguish.[91] But for the rest of his life, the blow left wounds that never healed.

A few days before the execution of the queen, Fersen wrote in his diary, that if he were to lose her, "above all it must be the end of the French affair." He nevertheless requested of Duke Karl in November that he be permitted to remain at his post in Brussels and thus follow the fortunes of the war and of the French royal children. He continued to send regular bulletins on the political and military situation until the following spring. They are mainly culled from newspapers, are usually written in another's hand, and contain little of unusual interest.[92] Indeed, Fersen's personal involvement in the affairs of France ended with Marie-Antoinette's death.

CHAPTER VIII

Frankfurt, Stockholm, Vienna, 1794–1796

1

Although Axel Fersen continued for some months to report on the war, the period between the death of Marie-Antoinette in October 1793 and the Congress of Rastadt over four years later was dominated for him by personal affairs.

By the time of her death, the French queen had become largely transfigured in his mind into a hallowed martyr. During the weeks that followed, he devoted himself to piously collecting relics of her life. He charged a Belgian smuggler named Daubrus to buy in Paris portraits and cameos of the king and queen, as well as watches, rings, and other effects that had belonged to them. In January 1794, he received a long-delayed letter from the late queen's confidant, the Chevalier de Jarjayes in Turin, dated 14 June 1793, with a fragment of a letter from her. Jarjayes had left Paris in April 1793. The queen's letter to him read in part:

When you are in a safe place, I would have you give news of me to my great friend, who came last year to see me. I do not know where he is, but either M. Gog[uelat] or M. Craufurd, who I believe is in London, will be able to tell you. I dare not write but here is the imprint of my device. Say in sending it that the person to whom it belongs feels it was never more true.

"This device," Fersen wrote, "consisted of a cachet bearing a flying pigeon with the motto, *Tutto a te mi guida.* Her idea had been in time to take my arms...." In October 1795 he learned Jarjayes had hidden certain effects and papers for him at Ivry. Meanwhile, the previous March, he received from Mme. von Korff the closing line of a letter from the late queen: "Adieu, my heart is all yours." Axel was not sure how Mme. von Korff had acquired this, but was greatly moved. "It seemed to me," he wrote, "that this was a last farewell...."[1]

The long months of concern and grief had meanwhile brought Axel ever closer to Eleanore Sullivan in search of consolation. Since before the Revolution, he had been closely associated with the wealthy Scot, Quentin Craufurd, and more particularly with his mistress, Eleanore Sullivan. This pair stood out even in an age replete with colorful characters. Craufurd was born in 1743 in Kilwinning, Ayrshire, of good family, and around 1760 went to India to seek his fortune. In 1762, he accompanied the British force that took Manila and was appointed quartermaster general at an age of less than twenty years. The sobriquet the "Nabob of Manila" suggests the source of the great wealth with which he returned to Europe in 1780, after extensive travels in India, the basis of later writings, and there acquiring Eleanore. The latter's past remained largely veiled in mystery until after the Bourbon Restoration, when she provided details in a lawsuit. She was born Anna Eleanora Franchi in Lucca in 1750, the daughter of a tailor and part-time player with a traveling theatrical troupe. From the age of 13, she appeared on the stage and about two years later, married a dancer. Soon thereafter, the Duke of Würtemberg, Karl Eugen, saw her dance at a carnival in Venice and made off with her to Ludwigslust, where during the next two years she bore him a son, who died around 1793, and a daughter. Thereafter, Eleanore moved to Vienna, where she had a brief affair with Emperor Joseph II, then took up with a French diplomat in Coblenz. She soon found herself abandoned on the pavements of Paris, whence she was providentially saved by a young Irishman of gentle birth named Sullivan, who married her and took her to India. There she met the wealthy Craufurd, for whom she promptly abandoned Sullivan, and in 1783, the Scot and his mistress set up housekeeping on a lavish scale at No. 18 Rue de Clichy in Paris.[2]

Not long after, both Craufurd's and Fersen's names appear among the members of the fashionable Valois Club. Axel later observed, however, that he met Eleanore "at the most interesting moment of my life," even before he met Craufurd, which he had at first done reluctantly. Fersen's letter register shows he first began to write to Eleanore in April 1789. Their correspondence in time became enormous, especially after 1791, but her letters to him were later destroyed, as were virtually all the letters he received from women. It appears that it soon became more or less common knowledge in Paris, though unbeknown to Craufurd, that Fersen was involved with Eleanore, and the first entries in his diary, where it resumes shortly before Varennes, show he enjoyed her favors.[3] Devoted to the royal family, Craufurd and Mme. Sullivan had been Fersen's collaborators in the attempted evasion in 1791 and his secret visit to the Tuileries in 1792.

Following Varennes, Fersen lived for several years in what amounted to a *ménage à trois* with Craufurd and—only occasionally suspected by the Scot—their common mistress. Not that either of the men was happy with the situation. Although he gives the impression of having been astonishingly naive and good-hearted, rumors occasionally reached Craufurd from the servants' quarters. These gave rise to periodic scenes, which Fersen with the tired tolerance characteristic of both his age and his individual outlook, regarded as unnecessary and undignified, and which he sought through small subterfuges to avoid. Fersen, who had started Craufurd in a modest political role by recommending him to Gustav III in 1791, felt Craufurd owed him more gratitude and deference than he showed. Yet for all its petty intrigues and scenes, in which a whole crowd of lesser figures eventually became involved, this stormy relationship would continue, with relatively short interruptions, until 1799.[4]

Craufurd's biographer, Émile Dard, holds that the affair began when Fersen sought to divert attention from his dealings with Marie-Antoinette early in the Revolution and that the queen knew and encouraged this. Even if Fersen's relationship with the queen were platonic, as Dard maintains, this seems doubtful, considering Marie-Antoinette's very human love for him. Had Axel used Eleanore as a decoy, he would probably have told Sophie, to forestall disquieting rumors. As it was, Sophie, who idealized the French queen, wrote Axel in alarm in December 1791 that he was said to be "greatly enamored" of "an Englishwoman named Krabens" or something similar, and warned such rumors would cause "*Her*" a "mortal pain." Fersen thereafter gradually accustomed his sister to the idea of the other woman in his life, apparently revealing all only when he returned home in October 1794. "I often curse the moment I left Sweden," he meanwhile wrote Sophie in February 1793,

> . . . that I have known anything but our rocks and pines. I would not, it is true, have had so much joy, but I have now paid well for it and I would have avoided much pain. I weep very often alone, my dear Sophie, and together with E. when we are able. But she is herself too afflicted by what has happened and by fears for the future to be able to console me. But at least I have the consolation of weeping together with someone. This good woman is excessively attached to them [the French royal family]; she has made many sacrifices for them and has even exposed herself and it is that which makes me love her.

The following September he revealed his emotional dependence on Eleanore in contemplating the approaching fate of the queen: "I will then have lost three sovereigns, my benefactors and friends . . . there only remains for me one woman, whom I love and who loves me, but her character is very different from my own and she belongs to another; she cannot follow me and I cannot always follow her."[5]

Already by the fall of 1793, Axel was thinking of how best to entice her away from Craufurd. A stranger match could scarcely be imagined: the melancholy and introverted Swedish aristocrat and the hot-blooded daughter of a strolling Italian comedian. The Swedish diplomat Lars von Engeström, who met her in Frankfurt in 1796, praised her beauty, but added:

> Mme. Sullivan did not have a pleasant manner. Her gaiety was of the loud Italian kind; she shrieked when she should have spoken and laughed a full-throated laugh. As long as Count Fersen was with her, she was nevertheless silent and lost in observation like him. When Craufurd was home, things also proceeded decently; but when both these gentlemen were away, there were games and forfeits, kisses were bestowed and there was enormous hilarity. . . .[6]

It is not surprising that it was long before Axel considered marriage, preferring the idea of voluntary cohabitation. Yet his dependence on Eleanore became such that he continued to endure the increasing frustration of a three-cornered relationship, while brooding endlessly over schemes to escape with her from the cares of the world. Eleanore, while at first seemingly favorable to the idea, put Axel off on various pretexts.[7]

Axel's relationship with Eleanore Sullivan was clearly quite different from his love for Marie-Antoinette. "Eleanore will not replace her in my heart," he wrote in his diary in November 1793.

> What sweetness, what tenderness, what kindness, what solicitude, what a loving and sensitive and delicate heart. The other does not have all of that but nevertheless I love her, I regard her as my only consolation and without her I would be too unhappy. But I must find again the kindness of her character and her feeling behind the thousand brusque acts and the thousand slights that afflict me and to which I find it hard to reconcile myself.[8]

His reminiscences of Marie-Antoinette and of the past throughout his later years show that she retained her unique place in his emotions. Nevertheless, his life between 1793 and 1799 was largely dominated by his affair with Eleanore and his hopes of winning her away from Quentin Craufurd.

As time passed, Fersen became increasingly concerned with his finances. He had provided considerable sums for projects in behalf of the French royal family, particularly the flight to Varennes. He also contributed generously to help numerous poor émigrés. He estimated to Taube in February 1794 that he had dispensed "15 or 18 thousand livres" for this purpose and was then having shirts made by a woman from "one of the first houses of France." He also bought up at generous prices various small treasures his émigré friends had saved from France and his account book notes constant gifts to needy refugees.[9]

Still, Fersen felt that to compete with Craufurd over Eleanore, he needed substantial resources. He could, of course, have supported himself decently in the service of his country, but his desire to participate in public affairs was lukewarm at best, especially under the regency, and he had no wish to return to Sweden to stay.[10]

On 8 January 1794, however, Fersen wrote Taube, asking him to seek for him the post of minister to the Italian courts, then occupied by Baron Armfelt, who was at odds with the government. Among his reasons was the following:

> I have financial interests for myself and for others to take care of. I have close to a hundred thousand *écus* to repay to Mme. Korff, which she loaned to the late king of France; it is almost her entire fortune. If I leave [the Continent], God knows when she will be repaid. As for myself, Their late Majesties bequeathed to me 1,500,000 livres which they

had gotten out of France in 1791 at the time of their departure, about which the world knows nothing, and which are in the hands of Count Mercy. I have their note, which I have not yet presented to him, since I am awaiting news from a man who is in Turin who left Paris in April [1793] and who has informed me that he is charged with something for me which I would like to know about before claiming anything.[11]

Fersen thus made his first reference to a strange and mysterious affair.

On 21 February, Fersen showed Mercy the note he had mentioned to Taube. It was dated 20 June 1791, the day of the escape from Paris, and was signed by both Louis XVI and Marie-Antoinette. It read:

We request that Count Mercy remit to Count Fersen all of our money which is in his possession, about 1,500,000 livres, and we request of Count Fersen that he accept this as a sincere mark of our recognition and as an indemnification for everything he has lost.[17]

This caught Mercy by surprise. He had indeed received a considerable sum in money and valuables from the royal family, but had turned it over to the Archduchess Marie-Christine. He complained of formal irregularities in the note and was surprised that Fersen had not presented it when he first came to Brussels. Fersen replied that his delicacy of feeling concerning the tragedy of the royal family had prevented him from mentioning the matter earlier. Mercy recognized the letter to be entirely in Marie-Antoinette's hand and noted the signatures of the king and herself. He therefore undertook to advise the archduchess of the situation.[13]

The money had meanwhile been transferred to Vienna. In April 1794, when Francis II visited Brussels, Mercy advised Fersen to approach his favorite, Count Colloredo, on the matter, but the latter wrote that since the emperor was only holding the money in deposit, he had no right to dispose of it. Fersen found Colloredo's reply "quite idiotic" and "written in bad French" besides, and objected that he asked no more than disposition of the money according to the wishes of the depositors.[14]

Fersen's correspondence with Vienna dragged on for over a year. Throughout, he showed repugnance toward the matter, and sisted, to others and in his diary, that were it not for Mmes. von Korff and Stegelmann, who had lent almost all they owned for the escape of the royal family, and also for Eleanore, he would give up the attempt, satisfying his dignity with "a very proud letter" to Vienna. Meanwhile, he considered appealing to the sentiments of Catherine II, "if she has any," since Mmes. von Korff and her mother were her subjects, and even to Monsieur. At length, it became apparent he would have to go to Vienna himself to seek satisfaction.[15] This, however, was delayed for almost a year by new developments.

2

For some time, the old Count Fredrik Axel von Fersen had been declining, aggrieved that despite frequent entreaties, his eldest son remained far away on the Continent. Axel, though fearing his father's end was near, could not bring himself to leave while Marie-Antoinette lived, or later to tear himself away from Eleanore.[16]

On 12 May 1794, Axel learned of his father's death. A few days later, he at last decided to visit Sweden to tend to his affairs. He nonetheless procrastinated throughout the summer. With Craufurd and Mme. Sullivan, he again left Brussels before the advancing French in June and settled in Frankfurt. His efforts regarding both the money in Vienna and Eleanore continued without result, while Craufurd did his best to exclude him from his home. Finally, on 30 September, Fersen departed for Sweden.[17]

On 19 October, after a violent storm on the Sound, Fersen returned to Swedish soil for the first time since 1788. "The country, with everything that is being done here and all the changes that have been made, is offensive to me," he complained and a postmistress warned him that in Stockholm there were many who "thought and spoke in an unsuitable manner."[18]

The Sweden to which Fersen returned seethed with discontent after two and a half years under the duke-regent and his favorites, though Gustav III had not been universally popular and Duke Karl had been at first well enough received by a country exhausted by war and internal strife.[19] Fersen, however, with most of the late king's stalwarts, had from the start mistrusted the new regime and with time became increasingly disillusioned.

The short liberal period at the beginning of the regency drew to a hasty close by the end of 1792 as the duke and Reuterholm took alarm at the spread of "Jacobin" radicalism. Throughout 1793, opposition on both the right and the left became increasingly vociferous, but it soon became evident that the bitterest rivalry lay between the new regime, headed by Reuterholm, and the Gustavians, centered around Armfelt. In December 1793, Reuterholm revealed a Gustavian "plot" against the government and during the following months brought to trial alleged participants in this so-called "Armfelt conspiracy." In the fall of 1794, Fersen returned to Sweden to find himself attainted by his Gustavian associations and sentiments.

Baron Armfelt had been on the regency government that Gustav III had appointed on his deathbed, but had soon lost patience and departed for an indefinite stay on the Continent. To his correspondents in Sweden—particularly his mistress, Magdalena Rudenschöld, at the court itself—he wrote bitter criticisms of the new regime.

In October 1792, Armfelt visited Fersen in Brussels. Relations between them had always been cool, but recent developments now drew them, at least temporarily, closer together. Armfelt wrote:

Just how cold and careful Count Fersen is . . . [I have] indicated elsewhere. Still, together we shed tears over the memory of Gustav III and he could not conceal that he felt that the intentions of the duke-regent and his councillor [Reuterholm] were, if not entirely bad, at least in many respects ill advised. But then he did not know as well as I did, those who would show themselves on the scene and therefore he still hoped that time and experience would bring improvement.

Fersen was alarmed by what Armfelt told him, especially that the duke sought to isolate the young king "from all those persons who were devoted to the late king," thus assuring his own future domination after the end of his regency. Fersen saw Armfelt a few more times, who continued to "speak very bitterly about events in Sweden, and very openly," before continuing to Vienna.[20]

The regency government now appointed Armfelt minister to the Italian courts, which released him from all other responsibilities and in effect exiled him. Enraged, he and his associates speculated over insurrection in Sweden. The immediate impetus was the rumor in the summer of 1792 that the regency government would convene a Riksdag, in defiance of Gustav III's testament, which Armfelt feared would precipitate revolution, as had the meeting of the Estates General in France. Accordingly, he himself drew up a "plan of revolution," whereby the "royalists," that is to say the Gustavians, should pretend to come to an agreement with the "Feuillants," or "monarchicals," that is, the old opposition of 1789, to destroy the "Jacobins": Reuterholm, Staël, and their friends. At this point, the Russian empress should issue a manifesto, guaranteeing Gustav III's testament and the original regency council. The "royalists" would them disassociate themselves from the "Feuillants" and establish themselves in power.[21]

During 1793, prospects for a coup diminished. The estates were never convened. The government proved as anti-Jacobin as the Gustavians themselves and Catherine II showed increasing goodwill toward the Swedish regime. Armfelt apparently resigned himself to waiting out the regency. Reuterholm meanwhile began to intercept his correspondence with Sweden, which contained abusive remarks both about the "Vizier" and his shadow, *Rikskansler* Sparre. By December 1793, Reuterholm fancied he had enough evidence to prosecute Armfelt and his closest associates, several of whom, including Magdalena Rudenschöld, were arrested while a warship was dispatched to Naples to seize Armfelt himself. The government announced the discovery of a plot to assassinate the duke and overthrow the regime. Armfelt's friends were forewarned, thus able to destroy incriminating evidence, while Armfelt escaped, aided by the Neapolitan royal family, to Russia. The trial thus proved embarrassing to the government until Reuterholm's agent, the engraver Francesco Piranesi, managed to purloin Armfelt's papers from the safekeeping of the British minister to Florence, bringing to light Armfelt's plan of revolution. The charges were changed against his accomplices, who after a parody of a trial were given sentences that in severity contrasted unfavorably with the leniency shown most of Gustav III's assassins. Meanwhile others, not previously suspected, now found themselves implicated.

Fersen, in Brussels, followed the trial closely. On 6 January 1794, word of the arrest of the conspirators reached him. He despaired that they had adopted "means suitable for no one except Jacobins" and suspected Armfelt, since he was a *"frondeur"* by nature. Still, it was hard, as he wrote Sophie, to believe that Armfelt could be such an "imbecile" as to try to direct such a conspiracy from 600 leagues away and he had written to sound him out on this, while making his own disapproval clear. Soon after, he received a reply from Armfelt, who made no mention of the plot, which in Fersen's view proved his guilt.[22]

Fersen was distressed by the conspiracy and felt no sympathy for its protagonists. He hastened to congratulate Duke Karl on its discovery:

Its purpose does not appear to me to be in doubt. It is the fruit of the contagion of the principles of the French Revolution, founded upon forgetfulness of the most sacred obligations. This monster menaces all Europe with total subversion and this new example is one more proof of the necessity of stifling a doctrine, the foundations of which are the overthrow of all thrones, the destruction of all authority and the legal establishment of anarchy and disorders of every kind. In offering Your Highness the expression of my joy at the good fortune of stopping this horrible plot, I pray also that Your Royal Highness also accept that of my deep pain at seeing Swedes guilty of such an execrable attempt.

The duke too, in describing the episode to Catherine II, branded the conspirators as "Jacobins." The irony of this need hardly be emphasized, since in plotting their coup, Armfelt and his friends intended to crush "Jacobinism" in Sweden.[23] Privately, Fersen also criticized the government's handling of the trial, though characteristically because of its effects on public opinion, particularly abroad, rather than the injustice of the proceedings, while his fear of Jacobin influence among the conspirators soon subsided.[24]

An increasing number of important figures were compromised through the trial. Fersen noted uneasily that they were "all the late king's men; it is that which hurts me," though he was relieved that neither he nor Taube had the least thing to do with the affair.[25]

Armfelt's correspondence, however, soon drew both of them into the net; on the day he learned of his father's death, he noted bitterly:

This sorrow was meanwhile not enough. It is believed now that I was involved in Baron Armfelt's affair through my letters which were found among his papers and in which I express my disfavor toward policy, for which I throw the blame on the shoulders of the duke's entourage. They sent me selections from these letters and at the same time a dispatch to tell me I was no longer needed. This disturbed me greatly. First I was unhappy over not being employed any longer and besides at being involved in such a base affair, but when I looked at the matter more closely and [considered] that all this would not receive any publicity, that the cause furthermore was not at all dishonorable and that finally it would only be two years to wait [until the end of the regency], I was able to console myself. . . . What wounded me the most was to have had the least thing to do with the whole affair. I was also aroused over this sort of inquisition and pressure exerted upon freedom of opinion of the individual, and I determined to write the duke himself about it.[26]

Fersen's letters to Armfelt during 1793 had been concerned mainly with the general European situation, but a few comments showed his distaste for the regency. Of Staël's suspected negotiations with the French, he wrote:

Despite the millions this could mean for us, I feel it would be selling one's honor at a cheap price and, for the sake of interests of the moment, sacrificing perhaps those of several centuries. Our relatives in Sweden are mad, my dear Baron, but I hope we will one day have the pleasure of proving it to them.

The duke's entourage was unworthy of the name of Swedes, he insinuated in June, and in August he said, "I will not speak of our unfortunate fatherland, nor of the role we are playing. I should like to be able to stop thinking about it, for the thought is altogether too painful for me."[27]

By mid-June 1794, Fersen learned he had been included by Armfelt in his plans for a new "royalist" government. To be sure Armfelt had not considered giving his old rival any very weighty assignment. According to one plan, Fersen was to be "general adjutant with baton," in another, "commandant in Stockholm."[28]

On 13 May, Fersen wrote Duke Karl that he had never been close to Armfelt and had often disapproved of his conduct. The views expressed in his private letters to him had not been intended for other eyes and had not been written in any special sense. He ended with assurances of loyalty and respect, doubtless made in good faith; however bitterly he had criticized the regime, he had never cast blame on the duke himself, except to deplore in the privacy of his diary his weakness of character, which subjected him to the influence of his entourage, especially Reuterholm and Staël.[29]

Duke Karl was less well disposed toward Fersen, who had been one of his brother's favorites, had advocated a hard counter-revolutionary policy, and had once been romantically involved with his wife, Duchess Charlotta. Both Sophie and Taube now did their best to intercede in Axel's favor, with little result. Reuterholm seemed more amiable and Taube recommended that Axel write him, which he did reluctantly in July, out of consideration for his friend.[30] Of Reuterholm's reply, received shortly before he left for Sweden in September, Fersen noted, "It was not very edifying reading. It breathed self-importance and I regretted I had ever written to him. Fortunately, I can do without all of them, for I demand and desire nothing and would not accept anything even if they offered it to me."[31]

Fersen clung as long as he could to the idea that the duke was well-disposed toward him and that it was his councillors who led him astray. Taube and Sophie often praised him and when Axel arrived at the family estate of Lövstad in October 1794, "all agreed in speaking well of the duke." In Stockholm, Fersen was welcomed affably by Reuterholm, Sparre, and even Staël. The duke, however, treated him with studied coldness, which Fersen suspected was "inspired by someone in his entourage." He later particularly suspected Chancellor Sparre, "since he knew the former king intended to give me that position. . . ."[32]

On 11 November, Fersen finally had an audience with the duke, against his natural inclinations, "for I do not like explanations." Duke Karl seemed little moved by what he had to say but made a somewhat unconvincing show of reconciliation. Relations between them remained cool throughout Fersen's stay in Sweden.[33]

Reuterholm was friendly, however, and Fersen surmised that he might be considering him for an official position. In December, Fersen noted a rumor that he might be appointed chancellor. He was immediately suspicious:

Everything indicates they have gotten this idea and it would not surprise me if they, to get themselves out of all the complications which have arisen, should wish to remove Sparre and give me his place. But nothing in the world could persuade me to accept it right now and it will depend to the greatest extent upon circumstances whether I will ever accept it.[34]

He later feared that the duke and his advisers, to escape responsibility for the state of affairs they had created, intended to turn the government over to the young king to cope with as best he could, and he remained anxious to avoid the embarrassment of himself being offered a position.[35] His continued mistrustfulness is expressed in a letter to Taube in December 1795, after his return to the Continent:

If it is true, my dear friend, as you suspect, that they are still going to the trouble of opening our letters, they will be quite surprised to find nothing in them and they will be little repaid for the pains they take. One is only too happy not to have to involve oneself with public affairs and the turn these are presently taking is not agreeable enough to tempt one to make it the subject of a friendly correspondence.[36]

As seen, Fersen's main criticism of the duke-regent was his weakness. On 23 March, he wrote about the trial of the Armfelt conspirators:

God, what abominations and maladroit actions they [his advisers] are persuading the duke to commit, and how criminal it is when people let themselves be led only by their own personal desire for revenge. . . . What a frightful century we live in and how fearsome for all courts, especially those which have a weak ruler. That is the worst disaster that can befall a kingdom; a tyrant would be a thousand times better.[37]

Fersen meanwhile put his hopes for a better future in the young king, who was to reach majority on 1 November 1796. In November 1793, Fersen had written enthusiastically:

I received letters from Sweden. What pleased me most was the understanding they seem to have of the king's independence. That is a very important quality in a sovereign. He can do nothing without it and becomes a plaything in the hands of all intriguers. We see a sad example in the king of Prussia and the emperor, and it was that which overthrew the unfortunate and altogether too good Louis XVI.[38]

Gustav IV Adolf became in time widely unpopular and has remained a highly controversial figure. Thus Fersen's observations, written at this time by one sympathetic to him, are of particular interest. He conveys the impression of a serious, polite, well-intentioned youth, yet an enigmatic personality. After observing the young king at a dinner, Fersen noted:

. . . the king hardly speaks at all, but one notes that nothing escapes him. He avoids most scrupulously showing that he prefers anyone, whomsoever it might be, or giving the appearance of complaining of anything, and it is perhaps this which makes him so taciturn and reserved. For the rest, it is impossible to form any definite conception of his disposition. No one knows him, but from what one can see one must conclude he is very determined, has sound judgment, is exact to the extreme, strict and very orderly.[39]

On another occasion:

He is very serious, vain, easily offended and loves attention, despite the fact that it embarrasses him. At supper parties he goes around alone, stands, looks around, listens, but seldom sits down and speaks even more rarely. . . . I believe the cause for this behavior, so strange for his age, is to be found in a shyness which is to a large extent natural, as well as in the difficulty of his position, which he himself is very conscious of. He broods a great deal and when he speaks, everything he says is right. He is a completely honorable man and cannot bear those who are not. He is also very virtuous and very economical, and we will certainly receive many blessings from his reign. But he will never be amiable and his court will never be pleasant.[40]

Undemonstrative as he was, Gustav IV Adolf was particularly well-disposed toward Fersen, as both the latter and others did not fail to notice.[41]

When Axel returned to Sweden in October 1794, French arms were successful on all fronts and Revolution seemed to threaten all lands. "God knows what may happen to us in a few years," he wrote on the day he landed. "Under the best of circumstances, we will be reduced to the same condition as the French émigrés. . . ." Even in Sweden he saw, or fancied he saw, danger signs. Shortly after reaching Stockholm, he spoke with "M. Adelsvärd, my cousin, who is a very strong democrat," who told him that a deputation from the province of Västergötland, consisting of two clergymen, two burghers, and two peasants, was on its way to the capital to "thank the regent for his zeal in upholding peace both within and without." Fersen felt "such deputations are a great danger to the government, for today they come to thank, tomorrow to complain and find fault, and the day after to threaten or to constitute themselves an assembly." The following day he commented:

I find this way of acting most dangerous in the century in which we live. One should instead, as much as possible, now exclude everyone from government, not permit, and even less encourage, them to favor or complain; one should work only to make it [the government] respected, to be just, to raise oneself above the murmurings of the people, to which one should not pay the least attention.[43]

A few days later, Fersen noted that another deputation, from Östergötland, had finished its business in the capital, but there was now one from Södermanland, "and the other provinces will no doubt follow suit." He expressed the same apprehension in January 1795:

Last Sunday, a proclamation by the king was read in all the churches, which deplored the fact that the poor in the city had been taxed altogether too highly, together with an order to the governor of the city to correct this situation. Nothing could be more ill-considered and better suited to stir up the lower people and rabble. Never has one yet seen a ruler complain for the people when they themselves have not complained. This is to point out to them the way to insurrection against their authorities and it is certainly the height of ignorance.[44]

Fersen observed with misgivings Duke Karl's apparent preference for the Stockholm bourgeoisie over the aristocracy. The duke was reputed to have told his wife that "all resistance and uproar" came from the nobility, "that it was a group it was impossible to lead and that one should make an alliance with the mob and make mincemeat of them." Duke Karl was no Jacobin, but Fersen was evidently impressed with this story, an ominous portent of his own tragic end, sixteen years later.[45]

Not only did Fersen perceive a more "democratic" spirit, even under the repressive regency, but also a lowering of tone and elegence in court and social life. At Drottningholm, he spent an evening

. . . in the same salon where I had so often seen the late king sitting and drawing. This memory tormented me. I found there nothing of the old [days], I felt as though I were in a new world. Everything was different, faces and conduct, and I could not have felt myself more foreign had I been in Madrid.[46]

His diary is filled with complaints of the monotony of court functions. Of a dinner given by Duchess Charlotta:

These suppers are deadly boring. Everyone plays [cards], and with those who do not, it is impossible to strike up a conversation. The late king understood how to start and keep up a conversation. Now it is all over with everything. Nothing remains, and especially among the younger men there exists neither politeness nor fine manners. Social life has been totally destroyed. Hardly has one gotten up from the table when everyone goes his way, although it is hardly 12 o'clock. The duke comes in for a moment, the rest of the time he spends at home with his friends. Reuterholm is always there and Staël almost always. . . .[47]

To Fersen, the growing informality of court life represented an insidious danger to the established order. "Lord God, how little royal persons understand their own interests," he wrote, "when they do not uphold the prestige which imposes a distance between them and ourselves."[48]

Axel's father had been a charter member of the Swedish

Academy, founded by Gustav III in 1786. Following his death, the poet Axel Gabriel Silfverstolpe was elected to his place, and in March 1795 he gave a memorial address on his illustrious predecessor. Axel, who attended, considered the speech "simple, powerful, and beautiful," not noting its thinly veiled attacks on the regency. The duke became aroused not only against Silfverstolpe but the Academy itself, which he considered a hotbed of opposition and which he now took the opportunity to close. It was not reopened until the end of his regime.[49]

Opinion was greatly aroused. Yet Fersen himself showed no sentimental attachment to the Academy and evidently regarded its closing as a prudent political move. He wrote contemptuously that "the *frondeurs* have set up a hue and cry," and later,

... supper at the duchess's. They spoke only of the Academy affair. They are turning this insignificant matter into something of enormous importance. It has, however, an unfortunate consequence; namely, that it accustoms people to find fault with the government and to oppose its measures.[50]

Fersen was never a friend of unbridled freedom of expression, nor did he hold its defenders, philosophers and scribblers, in high repute. Still, the duke's behavior in this instance brought forth a bitter commentary which showed how disillusioned Fersen had become with the regent since his return:

This prince's whole manner of behaving is a rare proof of his inconsistency: he attacks the Jacobins and he actually hates and detests them, and all of his nature inclines him to this, but he does not see he is forced to behave in such a way that he himself appears to all Europe to be one, for he has not been satisfied with being neutral, but has protected them as well. Look at the empress [of Russia]. She has done no more than we, but she has maintained a good appearance. Baron Reuterholm is no more a Jacobin than the duke, indeed less of one, but I am beginning to believe both of them are being duped by I know not whom, but it could be Staël....[51]

Once again Staël. Fersen's dissatisfaction with the regency did not evidently stem from the repressive internal regime; if anything, Fersen even feared that a somewhat too democratic tone prevailed. Its principal cause still lay in foreign affairs, where Staël predominated.

Staël's preliminary defensive alliance with France of May 1793 was never ratified on either side, due principally to Danton's fall from power, and Swedish diplomatic relations with the republic fell into abeyance during the Terror. Staël turned to organizing a Danish-Swedish armed neutrality to protect commerce with France against British and Russian threats, which functioned well in 1794–95. Early in 1795, he returned to France, where he negotiated a Swedish-French defensive alliance, signed on 14 September 1795.

Fersen naturally opposed his country's neutrality in the struggle against revolutionary France. He likewise resented Sweden's trade with the French and did not object to Russian efforts to stop it. In April 1794, he noted, "The English have confiscated a merchant convoy of 150 Danish and Swedish ships which were carrying war material and provisions to France. It is unpleasant for me to have to see Swedes mixed up in such a base undertaking." "What a shame for us," he complained of the armed neutrality with Denmark, "and what baseness on Staël's part." In August 1794, he even feared Denmark might go to war with Britain, involving Sweden as well: ". . . this would be the height of the horror if we should declare ourselves for the regicides . . ."[52]

Yet Fersen's fears were soon realized. In February 1795, he learned that France would appoint a minister to Stockholm. "I find it hard to believe this news and that we should openly declare ourselves to have reached the point where we recognize the republic would be to drive rather too far our underhanded and miserable policies." On 21 March, Louis-Marc Rivals arrived in Stockholm. He was not at first officially received, but created an immediate stir. "The whole day there was nothing but talk of him," Fersen wrote on 28 March. "They found him very amiable, talkative, polite, and ingratiating. He gave the appearance of not being a Jacobin, of abhorring Robespierre and all the crimes and horrors that have been committed." All this he found hard to believe and he was gratified that the young king strongly opposed receiving the French envoy. News soon came, however, that Staël had been presented to the Convention, thereby recognizing the French republic on his government's behalf.[53]

What Fersen saw in store for his own country seemed borne out by the Dutch alliance with France in May 1795, which virtually reduced Holland to a French province. "This development should . . . open the eyes of the democrats in other countries who are not fanatical Jacobins or *sans-culottes*, to what they can expect from the French republic, and make them conscious of the secret schemes of certain intriguers." He feared contact with republican France could create troubles in Sweden by force of example. Indeed, Rivals, disgruntled at the Swedish government's evasiveness in receiving him, did in fact toy with schemes of revolution in Sweden.[54]

Fersen's presence in Stockholm aroused much excitement and curiosity, as he himself observed with a certain vanity. "I noticed this stir especially at the opera," he confided to his diary in November 1794. "When I entered the amphitheater, all the parterre and loges turned toward me." He created a lively sensation among the ladies in his new Guards uniform and reflected that he could easily have his pick of them. He was amused by the eagerness of the mothers of marriageable daughters. But he felt little attraction for the social whirl, which he regretted now centered almost entirely around the court, at the expense of the more intimate and exclusive society of the great private households in former days. Being in the capital, Fersen was required to serve part of the time at court as captain of the Guards, but found the duty tiresome and sought the first opportunity to establish his nephew, Count Charles Piper, as his successor in this post. "I was delighted to be free," he wrote in May 1795, when released from his duties at court. "I felt so relieved . . . no longer to be dependent upon anyone but myself. I am no longer accustomed to that kind of life and I am astonished how much one's taste can change with the years. I remember very well when that sort of life comprised my happiness."[55]

Another situation proved more difficult to avoid. On 7 November 1794, he observed:

For some time it appears my brother was paying court to *la petite,* and the husband did not seem to pay any attention. Since my return, it has been noted that she treats him less well and seems to want to take up with me again. I have also noticed this, but since I do not intend to follow it up, I have paid no attention to it. But it appears that the husband has noticed, that he is having me spied on, and that this is in part the cause of the dissension that is going on between them. . . .

The lady in question was clearly Duchess Hedvig Elisabeth Charlotta, wife of the duke-regent, who at this time was commonly understood to have a liaison with Fabian Fersen and who was Sophie Piper's bosom friend. It is evident she had been involved with Axel before, very likely during his visit to Sweden in 1786–87. His letter register shows he began to correspond with *"la petite"* in May 1787 and continued at fairly frequent intervals until March 1791. Shortly after this, the duchess revealed to Sophie, in a letter of 21 July 1791, her heartbreak for the past two years at the thought that Axel did not really love her. In November 1794, following Fersen's return to Stockholm, Duke Karl treated his wife with much suspicion and ill-will.[56] During the months that followed, *"la petite"* doggedly pursued Fersen, seeking in every way to renew the affair. She sought him out at every gathering, visited Sophie constantly, wrote him secret notes beseeching him for rendez-vous, reminded him of "past times and their delights," pressed her knee against his under the table, looked eagerly for signs of love from him, and offered him her all. Axel felt alternately amused, bored, and sympathetic. He was alarmed by her lack of caution and the attention her behavior aroused, yet sometimes tempted to take advantage of so willing a conquest. Still, when the time came, he found excuses to avoid it, feeling qualms of conscience toward Eleanore, Fabian, and *"la petite"* herself.[57]

During his nine months in Sweden in 1794–95, Axel constantly criticized his countrymen, often with surprising asperity. He attacked their lack of esthetic taste, their extremes of suspicion or enthusiasm for foreign innovations, their pettiness in social matters, their lack of refinement and manners. He deplored their gluttony and drunkenness, the dowdy and overweight women, even the language, which he complained was unsuitable for the stage.[58] "I wish I had been born an Englishman," he exclaimed with exasperation on Christmas Day, 1794. "That is the land where one can live the best. In this [country], they concern themselves only with the doings of others and there is no society."[59] While some of his comments are astute, many are undeniably petty and his diary for this period produces on the whole a dreary and lugubrious impression, not least of the commentator himself.

Modern Swedish critics have taken Fersen to task for his carping and faultfinding during this sojourn, deriving from it the picture of a cold egotist, a tired and bloodless representative of a decadent *ancien régime*, a symbol of all a more vigorous and passionate generation rebelled against.[60] To do so, however, is to take this period and part of his diary out of context and to distort the man into a caricature. Axel's marked irritability, anxiety, vanity, indolence, and brooding self-preoccupation, as well as his pathetic dependence on Eleanore Sullivan at this time, all unquestionably derived largely from the inhuman burden of emotional strain, fatigue, grief, and disappointment he had borne so long. His diary would in later years reveal a more tranquil, fair-minded, and sympathetic character. Furthermore, much had changed in Sweden since his last visit in 1788, which a man of his background and tastes could not but regret. Had Fersen been more attuned to intellectual matters and the new cultural impulses of the time, which no longer centered around the court, he would have seen a very different Sweden, one filled with vitality. But the rococo world of decorum and of playful fantasy, the world of Gustav III, was now beyond recall.

Still, not all of his impressions were negative. He was deeply drawn to his native countryside and felt great satisfaction in visiting the family estates. Steninge had been neglected under his late uncle, Carl von Fersen, but Axel was moved at the thought that the manor house had been built in the late seventeenth century by Count Karl Gyllenstierna, with help from Karl XI's queen, Ulrika Eleonora, whose lover he had been. "The analogy," he wrote, "made me even more attached to it." He enjoyed the quiet life at Lövstad and was delighted by the excellent condition in which he found Ljung, where he wrote,

... I took pleasure in my property. I felt strongly when I saw all of this the love for one's own soil and how attached one can become to it, and I was sorry I had ever traveled away and felt another sentiment that drew me away from my home, where I thrive so well and enjoy greater esteem than in any other land. We drove out in the evening, the countryside is delightful. . . .

Along the roadways he arranged to plant trees, which still stand, and he dreamed of laying out extensive English gardens. "I was in church," he wrote at Ljung on a Sunday in July, "and I enjoyed playing the role of lord of the manor and being able to say to myself that all these were my peasants." Later that day, when guests had departed, "we again sank into our solitude, which suited me excellently and with which I was completely happy and satisfied."[61] He was very pleased to see Stockholm again, foresaw he would leave there "with nostalgia," and was "grieved" to do so on 19 June 1795. On his way back to the Continent, he spent an idyllic day with Evert Taube and Sophie, whose husband,

Count Adolf Piper, had died in May, at the spa at Medevi, where Axel recalled happy memories from "eighteen years ago." "When I saw the happy relationship between Sophie and Taube," he wrote, "I envied their lot. It must be delightful."[62]

On one occasion, he observed somewhat wistfully, "Those Swedes who travel abroad cannot long remain away from their land; that is their misfortune." And when his sojourn came to an end, he wrote, "At my departure, I was filled with emotion which made me see how true it is that for persons of birth, the fatherland is dear."[63]

3

When Count Fredrik Axel von Fersen died on 24 April 1794, he left his heirs one of Sweden's greatest fortunes. Axel, as eldest son, received the largest share, including the Fersen palace in Stockholm, the entailed estates of Steninge, near Sigtuna, and Ljung, near Linköping. As personal property, he also received the smaller Finnåker in Östergötland and the extensive Wuojoki manor with its dependencies, near Björneborg in Finland. Attached to Ljung and Finnåker were ironworks while Finnåker also included a flour mill. Axel's share likewise included half the stock his father, a leading figure in the Swedish East India Company, had acquired in that enterprise, though this had now depreciated to half its original value. Fabian received Mälsåker manor on Lake Mälaren while their mother retained the estate at Lövstad, entailed in her family, which after her death in 1800 went to Sophie.[64]

Much of Axel's inherited wealth was in fixed entails, both real and movable, while income from his lands was relatively inflexible due to established tenancies. There were also debts and obligations connected with his father's estate, for which Axel assumed the greatest responsibility. He was meanwhile concerned for Sophie, whose husband died in May 1795, leaving most of his property entailed to his children.[65] Axel's inheritance, nevertheless, at last provided him with a stable economic establishment of his own, compensating for the loss of his regiment in France and freeing him from dependence on employment or sinecures from the Swedish court at the very time he fell into disfavor.

For the time being, Fersen continued to lease Steninge as his father had done, keeping his other properties under his own control. He rightly gave full confidence to Eric Nortun, for many years business manager for the entire Fersen family, and to his estate manager at Ljung. Following his permanent return to Stockholm in 1799, he lived in a princely fashion by Swedish standards and when he died in 1810, he left an estate apparently greater than his father's in 1794.[66]

Having become a landowner in Sweden, Fersen soon also became a plantation owner in the West Indies. Since boyhood, he had been closely associated with the Baron de Breteuil, who had done him many favors, especially by helping him finance the purchase of his regiment in 1783–84. Most likely Axel still owed him money when he emigrated in 1789. Thereafter, Fersen did what he could to help Breteuil and his daughter. In February 1792, he purchased the contents and furnishings of a library in Paris, decorated by the sculptor and *ébeniste* André-Charles Boule (1642–1732) from the baron for 58,000 livres in *assignats*. These effects were doubtless seized as émigré property in September 1792, together with those Fersen had left in Paris the year before. He protested to the French foreign minister that he was a foreign subject, no longer in French service, but to no avail. Ultimately, Fersen was able to preserve very little, despite occasional efforts to that end.[67]

In April 1795, he learned from Breteuil's daughter, Mme. de Matignon, that her father had been ruined financially. Axel was much distressed at his friend's plight. In August 1795, he arranged to purchase Breteuil's plantation in the Grande Anse district, Jérémie parish, on Santo Domingo, for 800,000 livres Tournois, according to terms arranged privately with the Baron. In April 1796, he executed an agreement, renouncing disposition of the property in favor of Breteuil and his heirs, to use as their own in Count Fersen's name.[68] Though the British now occupied the island, the fortunes of war could change; the plantation might hopefully be saved from confiscation in case the French returned if owned officially by a neutral subject.

It would be interesting to know if Fersen himself ever saw the property. He spent about a fortnight on Santo Domingo on his return from the American war in 1783 and very likely visited his friend Breteuil's plantation. This normally provided the baron with 60,000 livres annually and included a sugar mill as well as facilities for roasting coffee and distilling rum. A letter from Fersen's factor, Génin, in 1799, mentions 209 "cultivators."[69] Since he expected to turn the income over to Breteuil, this doubtless constituted formal payment for the purchase, for Fersen's accounts show no other. In the event of a French restoration, he probably intended to transfer the property back to the baron.

The plantation proved, however, a constant source of trouble. The British confiscated slaves for an auxiliary corps to fight the French, denying compensation to absentee landowners not in British or allied service. Fersen wrote the Duke of Portland in early 1797, seeking recompense for "a considerable number of Negroes." A year later, he besought Lady Elizabeth Foster to use her influence with the duke to prevent the loss of his property. Meanwhile, the French drove out the British and confiscated the plantation. Fersen sought diplomatic support from his government vis-à-vis both Spain and France, and made repeated representations to Talleyrand, now French foreign minister, who finally arranged the return of the property following the Peace of Amiens. In 1803, Fersen wrote his old comrade-in-arms, General the Vicomte de Rochambeau, son of his commander in America, then in Santo Domingo, asking protection for his factor, Génin, and his plantation.[70] Thereafter, nothing further is heard of it but it was of course lost, with all other European properties, in the Haitian revolution after 1804. Breteuil, after living quietly in Hamburg, returned in 1802 to France, where he received a pension from Bonaparte, and died in 1807.

4

Following his sojourn in Sweden, Fersen set off for Frankfurt to take up the matter of the 1,500,000 livres bequeathed him by the French king and queen. In Hamburg, he received a letter from Count Colloredo, "as commonplace and stupid" as all the others. Here his attention was diverted by serious rioting against French émigrés, which ended with troops firing into the crowd. To Fersen, this was one more proof of the dangerous growth on every side of the "spirit of revolt." By early August he was back in Frankfurt. He spent the next five months there and in nearby Wilhelmsbad, occupied with observing the war and his tangled relationship with the Craufurd-Sullivan *ménage*.[71]

Since before his journey to Sweden, Fersen had considered going to Vienna to press his claim. He now watched with interest a development which could affect its outcome. In the summer of 1795, the French government proposed to release Princess

Marie-Thérèse-Charlotte—Madame-Royale—in return for the commissioners abducted by Dumouriez: a return on a reduced scale to the plan the French had raised with the Prince of Coburg two years before. In December, Madame-Royale arrived in Vienna and the following month, Fersen left for the Austrian capital.[72]

Once in Vienna, Fersen looked for ways to present his claims. Opportunities were not easy to discover and as the days passed, his activities were largely limited to observing the Viennese scene. He was soon disappointed to learn Madame was retiring and seldom saw anyone. In actuality, the princess was closely watched by her Habsburg hosts. Francis II and Chancellor Thugut were anxious to secure her prestige and wealth by marrying her to a Habsburg archduke. The pretended Louis XVIII was equally anxious to wed her to his nephew, the Duc d'Angoulême. In both cases, the money Fersen regarded as rightly his own was a factor.[73]

On 14 February, Fersen spoke with Baron Thugut of his affair. Thugut was evasive and suggested that Fersen bring the matter up with the emperor. Fersen began to doubt his eventual success. As early as March 1795, he had written Catherine II about Mmes. von Korff and Stegelmann, urging that her ambassador in Vienna seek to obtain their money for them. He now wrote again to St. Petersburg for support.[74]

On 24 February, Fersen at last obtained an audience with Francis II. The emperor already knew of the matter and protested he could do nothing: the money belonged to the princess and only she could dispose of it when she came of age. Fersen decided to concentrate on seeing Madame-Royale and appealing to her sensibilities on behalf of Mmes. von Korff and Stegelmann, hoping she might then prevail on the emperor to help them.[75]

It was difficult to see the princess. Meanwhile, his hopes tended to produce a highly idealized picture of her in his mind. Finally, on 27 March he was allowed an audience, but only with several others, thus given no chance to speak privately with her. A few days later, Fersen wrote her of his affair and a fortnight after, met her principal lady-in-waiting, Mme. de Chanclos. Still the matter dragged on. It became apparent that no private meeting with Madame-Royale could be obtained.[76]

Despite a flattering letter from Catherine II, Fersen found the Russian ambassador, Count Andrei Razumovsky, who had at first encouraged him, increasingly evasive until he finally declared he could not handle the affair as a diplomatic matter. Thugut at length lost patience and asked what Fersen thought the Austrian government should do about all the other destitute pleaders who besieged it with their claims. Finally Mme. de Chanclos dealt the hardest blow by revealing that the chief obstacle was Madame-Royale herself. The princess, she said, was very parsimonious and felt that if the debt were to be paid at all, it should be taken care of by her uncle, Louis XVIII. Mme. de Chanclos related other things which made the princess suddenly appear very hard and cold.[77] "After all this, I understood she was neither openhearted nor magnanimous, that her character was arrogant and vain, and little sensitive to friendliness, everything I had heard her mother say."[78]

The results of Fersen's efforts were disappointing. Finally, through the Comte de Saint-Priest, now representing Louis XVIII, Madame-Royale was persuaded to write to the emperor, who granted 1,000 ducats to Mmes. von Korff and Stegelmann. Further efforts through the émigré bishop of Nancy, to obtain at least recognition of the debt, came to nothing and by 8 June, Fersen concluded, "without sorrow, that everything was over."[79]

The situation was highly frustrating and Axel reacted strongly against it. It showed, he wrote Taube in March, "how monarchs make little of the attachment one shows their colleagues," and in May he added, "often I am not so surprised that people become democrats." With mixed feelings of bitterness and relief, he departed Vienna on 9 June 1796 and returned to Frankfurt.[80]

The whole episode of the 1,500,000 livres is a perplexing one. In the first place, where did all this money come from? A considerable sum had been amassed outside France in preparation for the flight of the royal family in 1791. Craufurd informed Pitt that the Abbé de Montesquiou was employed from February 1791 on to take money abroad. In May 1791, Marie-Antoinette had written Mercy that her banker, Laborde, had sent her money to England with two million livres of his own, intended for her, which the queen wanted transferred to Brussels. Mercy wrote Kaunitz on 21 June 1791 that he had just received from the French queen a box and several sacks of money which he had not yet had time to count but which he estimated at about 20,000 louis (or 480,000 livres), together with letters of exchange for an additional 600–700,000 francs (livres), in all, between 1,080,000 and 1,180,000 livres. Fersen himself made the arrangements to send the queen's jewelry to Mercy at the time of the flight and when the French advanced on Brussels in November 1792, he was particularly solicitous that Mercy should remove it to safety. Meanwhile, following Varennes, Fersen said "nothing about the money or other things" to the Comte d'Artois, as he noted in his diary for 28 June 1791. In October of that year he reported to Marie-Antoinette that the Marquis de Bouillé had turned over the balance of the money Louis XVI had sent him in the spring to the émigré princes, a sum of 700,000 livres, but asked the queen what she wished done with the money she had in Holland. On 11 September 1793, he wrote in his diary, "The Abbé de Montesquiou came to see me.... He told me that M. de Mercy should have received from the queen 15 hundred thousand francs [*sic*] which he, the abbé, had removed [from France]."[81]

One cannot but wonder why Fersen, possessing a note deeding him the money, dated 20 June 1791, waited until 8 January 1794 before revealing its existence to anyone, in this case Taube, and only thereafter attempted to use it. Why did he not try to obtain this money when he was seeking to bribe certain revolutionary leaders, notably Dumouriez and Danton, to release Marie-Antoinette and her children, in February and August 1793? It is possible the note was antedated and smuggled out to Fersen at a later time. He had, for instance, dealings with the Chevalier de Jarjayes, who escaped from France to Turin in April 1793.[82] More likely, Fersen had the note since June 1791, but other considerations kept him from using it. The note was doubtless intended only as a last resort, if the king and queen were unable ever to reclaim the money themselves. If Fersen did not try to use it for tenuous schemes for the release of Marie-Antoinette and her children through bribery, he might have done so if ever convinced entirely that these provided the only alternative, stood any real chance of success, and could not be financed by the allied governments instead. It had probably been agreed beforehand that the money should provide the royal family with an independent resource *after* their escape and that only if this failed, should it be used to compensate Fersen and his friends. Marie-Antoinette instructed Jarjayes, presumably in April 1793, to find out from Mercy what had become of her "treasures, both in jewelry and in paper," for the time when "the great eclipse shall have passed"; if Mercy were difficult to locate, "M. de F ... will be able to give you exact information." Fersen wrote the same month to Taube, "I am continuing constantly to concern myself with the money in case we will have need of it." That he did not present his note until some months after the queen's death was explained by Fersen himself when he told Mercy on 22 February 1794 that "my sense of delicacy had prevented me from using it and consequently of speaking of it."[83]

Finally, one is impressed with the great sum involved. Still, if obtained, it would serve mainly to recoup losses incurred by Fersen and others in connection with the flight to Varennes. Fersen wrote Thugut in August 1794 that 600,000 livres of the total constituted repayment for his own personal loans, for which he had documentary proof. Notes among his accounts show he borrowed 169,000 livres from Mme. de Korff and 93,000 livres from Mme. Stegelmann, to which he added 100,000 of his own. A receipt dated 1 June 1791 shows that he borrowed 300,000 livres from Eleanore Sullivan, for which he obligated himself to pay 6 percent interest, or 18,000 livres, annually. He also borrowed 3,000 livres from his concierge, Louvet, and very likely raised other smaller sums elsewhere. This, then, amounts to at least 665,000 livres of his own money and that of others for which he was responsible. In addition, Fersen told Thugut that he had lost 40,000 livres in interest in France as a result of his loans.[84] Presumably he meant loss of income from profitable investments during the past three years. This left out the question of the loss of his 100,000-livre investment in the Royal-Suédois regiment or of all the personal property he had lost in France. Fersen meanwhile paid interest out of his own pocket on his loans from Mmes. von Korff, Stegelmann, and Sullivan, and from Louvet, which over a period of years amounted to considerable sums. On 25 September 1794, before leaving Frankfurt for Sweden, Fersen notarized a document recognizing his debt and interest to Eleanore, against the security of all his property, so that she would recover her fortune in the event of his death. It was her situation which most directly affected him in this affair. Upon its outcome depended the means for a dowry for her daughter by the Duke of Württemberg, Eleanore de Franquement—"Quella"—upon whose marriage Eleanore's financial independence from Craufurd would depend.[85]

It is difficult to conceive how much money 1,500,000 livres amounted to at that time. It was in any case less than the 2,000,000 Louis XVI received from the National Assembly in June 1791 as his quarterly payment on the civil list and not much more than the 1,344,000 livres granted Craufurd by the Restoration monarchy in 1815 for the losses sustained by himself and his wife, the former Mme. Sullivan, and their loans to the royal family.[86]

Although he possessed a cool head for business matters, Fersen had a patrician distaste for financial transactions. He continually lamented the necessity of taking any action whatsoever regarding the bequest and were it not for the others involved, he would have preferred to let the whole matter drop. He procrastinated for months at a time and when he at last set off for Vienna, he complained, "I detest the role of a solicitor." In this capacity, he performed with notable lack of success, obtaining only 1,000 ducats for Mmes. von Korff and Stegelmann. The next year, he tried to persuade Francis II to grant them an annual pension of that amount, "which would not even pay the interest on their money," and decried to his sister "the barbarity and indignity" of not supporting two such deserving gentlewomen. Similar attempts in the spring of 1798 to obtain aid for them from Louis XVIII proved equally fruitless.[87]

Was it not naive of Fersen to present such an enormous claim under such circumstances?[88] The money was in the hands of the emperor, who was perennially in financial straits and engaged in a costly war with France. Furthermore, the sole surviving member of the French royal family was now free to claim the remnants of her family fortune. Whatever happened to the money, it was unlikely that Francis II, Madame-Royale, or Louis XVIII would feel any obligation to give it to the Swedish count.

Fersen could, however, only claim the amount specified on the note, in hopes of receiving as much of it as possible. In actuality, he was never very optimistic about obtaining any, let alone all of it. As early as August 1794, he was willing to give 700,000 livres of the total to the Austrian government as a "patriotic contribution, reimbursable without interest at the end of the war." Later, he reduced his demands to repayment to Mmes. von Korff and Stegelmann of their loan, or even the interest on it for the time being. Still, even in the face of such obstacles, Fersen can hardly be blamed for making the attempt or be considered naive for doing so.[89]

It is with some relief that one turns to Fersen's observations in the Austrian capital. In Vienna and Prague in 1791, he had been occupied with his diplomatic mission and had had little opportunity to take note of life around him. During the first half of 1796, however, time hung heavy on his hands. He wrote Taube in February that he was caught up in a strenuous social whirl, "and I have almost had my head turned by a way of life so little suited to my tastes and habits."[90]

He complained of life among the first rank of the nobility, composed mainly of women, "cold by nature or design," who cared little for men, nor "life, either with their own husbands or with others." Their own men keep away from their gatherings, he observed, and "either keep bad company" or associate with the lower nobility, where "one enjoys oneself the most, where there are the most beautiful women and the best social life and gallantry." Men and women now kept largely to themselves in society and only the Russian ambassador, Count Razumovsky, still kept an "open table," where persons of quality could dine every evening without invitation.[91] In Vienna as in Stockholm, Fersen could perceive a decline of elegance and good tone which suggested overtones of democracy.

He naturally attributed much of the blame to the poor example of the imperial court. At the theater, which he did not find good, he saw the emperor and empress alone in their loge, looking like "a couple of bourgeois." "How undiplomatic it is of them at a time when that sort of people should try to impress," he complained indignantly. In the Prater, the emperor's carriage was like that of a "greengrocer" compared with the magnificent equipages of the nobility. Of the archdukes, "all five of them had no bearing, no manners, no talent for conversation." Characteristically, at Kinsky's ball, the small archdukes, sons of the emperor, were dressed worse than anyone else. The whole court, meanwhile, was shot through with intrigue.[92]

On 20 March, Fersen

. . . was at Mme. Zois's concert, which was held at 12:00 o'clock, at which quartets by Haydn were played. Delightful, especially the sixth. He himself was there and performed on the violin. He is small, thin, and seems very shy. He is not a good violinist, but an excellent composer. He is still in the service of Prince Eszterhazy. During [Eszterhazy's] . . . father's time, he served at table as a servant; now he no longer waits table, but still eats with the servants.[93]

Fersen was meanwhile a great social success. By mid-March, he was practically living in Razumovsky's home, where he met the leading lights of Viennese society. The ambassador's wife showed a marked weakness for him; he wrote Sophie that she was affected by that air of mystery and melancholy his life had bestowed on his features. By the end of April, Fersen was increasingly anxious to make a graceful departure, for by then a Baroness von Specht was also madly in love with him.[94]

Among Fersen's friends in Brussels had been Baron Franz Maria von Thugut, now chancellor and the real power in the Habsburg state. Upon arrival in Vienna, Fersen was "especially satisfied" with him. Thugut was a determined, if not fanatical, opponent of the French Revolution, while he thoroughly detested the émigrés.[95] He was, however, a man of common origin, on bad terms with the nobility. Later, after he dropped all pretense of favoring Fersen's cause regarding the money, relations between them became embittered. By the end of April, Fersen wrote:

Thugut's plan, to try to remove the high nobility from the government and replace them with his own supporters, points toward democracy, but it is not. His motive is the retention and strengthening of his influence, which he could not do with the high nobility, who regard him as an upstart. He never meets them and is seen nowhere. He does not own his own house, has no servants, visits no one and never invites anyone to dinner. No one even knows where he lives. He is in the state chancellery from 7:00 to 3:00 o'clock and from 6:00 to 10:00; there he works and receives visits. . . .[96]

Fersen was much bothered by the "happy insouciance" of the Viennese toward the struggle against the French. "The whole day I had heard nothing but talk of balls, celebrations, and divertissements," he wrote soon after his arrival, "and I was struck by how little they think of and are concerned with the war." Returning to Frankfurt in July, he contrasted that city, where everyone talked of politics and war, to Vienna, where they seldom did.[97]

Fersen was admittedly not one to describe his opponents in entirely unprejudiced terms when his own interests were at stake. Yet his diary gives interesting insights into the atmosphere of the Austrian capital in this period, with its staid and dowdy court, its frivolous society, its intrigues and hidden struggles for power. It was against this tired dynastic state that the armies of the Directory were scoring their most brilliant victories. More than anything else, the last stage of the War of the First Coalition between the new French republic and the ancient Habsburg monarchy exemplified the conflict between the new forces and the old; between what was all too often conviction, drive, and efficiency on the one hand, and apathy, cynicism, and frivolity on the other. Never again would the expiring eighteenth century and the new era then replacing it stand in such striking relief. Seen through the eyes of a determined defender of the old order, this contrast can only appear the more impressive.

CHAPTER IX

Reflections on War, Peace, and Politics, 1793–1797

1

When Axel Fersen returned to Frankfurt in July 1796, nearly three years had passed since Marie-Antoinette's death had ended his active role in affairs. Much of this time had been occupied with personal concerns. The year that followed was perhaps the most uneventful of all for him. He had by now lost faith in the surviving Bourbons: he had only contempt for the pretended Louis XVIII and his émigré following, while his experience in Vienna disillusioned him with Madame-Royale. His association with Eleanore had long kept alive nostalgic memories of the old Versailles, but now this relationship was gradually breaking up. And in November 1796, when the regency in Sweden ended, a new era in his fortunes became imminent.

During this period, Fersen's diary became more voluminous than ever as he observed events around him. Before the execution of Marie-Antoinette, he had been deeply involved in the projects and politics of counterrevolution. Thus his thoughts had tended to be practical, concerned with specific tactics. From the fall of 1793 on, however, his diary and letters reveal a broader, more abstract view, a greater tendency to see the Revolution as a whole, and following his return from Sweden in 1795, increasing resignation, detachment, and objectivity. The picture they provide is of interest, not least for what it tells of the observer himself.

213

Fersen long considered Robespierre a man of order and reason. As early as September 1792, he wrote Breteuil that Robespierre appeared less a rogue than formerly, that he had a large following among the Jacobins and that the counterrevolution might perhaps exploit the split thus caused. A few days later, he noted in his diary:

Robespierre is triumphing and strives for a dictatorship; the Assembly is still enslaved. I hope this will come about. Robespierre has revealed less cruel sentiments, spoken with respect for royal authority, and left the presidency of the Court of Blood. In a word, he has less crimes, it will be easier for him to accept a new system to repair his own [sins]; but whether he will remains to be seen.[1]

Fersen's partiality towards Robespierre continued even into the Terror.

It seems it is Robespierre who has the most influence, [he wrote in December 1793], but it appears that he will not be able to keep it, for he and his partisans wish to uphold order in the government and build a dam before the flood of murder. But they will fail in this, as all others have before them.[2]

"The gazettes from Paris...are most interesting," he reported in his dispatch of 16 March 1794,

The heads of the government are dividing and two parties are forming in Paris. Robespierre is at the head of one; this one appears to wish to become moderate and desires to reestablish order to maintain authority. Hébert, Collot d'Herbois, and Danton are at the head of the other and cannot get ahead save by the continuation of crimes and anarchy.[3]

The coup of 9 Thermidor, however, confirmed Fersen's belief that usurped power must inevitably succumb to fresh upheavals. On 8 August, he observed that "both the brothers Robespierre, Couthon, Saint-Just, and others were arrested, and that this was by the party of Collot d'Herbois. If this is true, then it will be even crueler and bloodier than Robespierre's party." A few days later, almost regretfully:

In the *Journal général de Cologne* there is a report on the executions which came about as a result of the fall of Robespierre. These are proof of the lack of political wisdom, cowardice, and baseness of the French character and of the members of the government. Today, the worst crime is to have received a post from Robespierre; yesterday, it was a crime not to admire him.[4]

Why this curious partiality toward the man later generations regarded as the very Revolution incarnate? Fersen no doubt recalled Robespierre as the opponent of the war in 1791–92. Later, Danton, Hébert, and Marat had led the attack on the Girondins while Robespierre himself had intervened against the excesses of the dechristianizers, all of which might suggest a certain moderation on the latter's part.[5] But it would seem that there was a more fundamental reason for Fersen's attitude: Robespierre's apparently authoritarian views. Fersen had little sympathy for those earlier revolutionaries who had sought to end the Revolution, such as Mirabeau or Barnave, persons surely more moderate than Robespierre. Fersen himself became increasingly authoritarian in his views as the revolutionary era advanced. To him, the Revolution represented above all the tragedy of weak and divided leadership. Robespierre, it might well seem to an outsider, had no use for constitutions, elected assemblies, or toadying favorites, while he got things done with astonishing dispatch. This, in Fersen's innermost thoughts, might well be the man Louis XVI and his brother monarchs should by right have been.

The Thermidorian coup of July 1794 ended the autocratic regime of the Committee of Public Safety and reestablished government by constitution and elected assembly. Fersen's criticisms of the Revolution descend once again to their accustomed level of disdain.[6]

Meanwhile, there was the war. The French, through bold and imaginative measures, met the challenge far more effectively than the coalition powers. Prussia, Holland, and Spain one by one made terms with France. Fersen especially decried Prussia's "shameless" separate Peace of Basel in March 1795.[7]

Traveling through Germany in July 1795, Fersen noted, "Everywhere I passed, I found a single, common longing for peace. Everyone wished for it, and I was welcomed, for they believed I was on my way to Basel to work for it." But his next comment gives pause for thought. "This is explainable for everything has gone up in price in the most alarming way, especially grain and fodder. . . ."[8] He could deplore the "barbarity and indignity" of the emperor in not providing for two improverished Russian gentlewomen, yet dismiss the longings of the common people of Germany as simply the result of high prices. He here reveals something of the prejudices of birth of his time, seeming to believe that only gentlefolk were really capable of unselfish valor, devotion to principle, or true suffering.

With Prussia, Holland, and Spain out of the war, it appeared that Austria and Britain must follow suit. In August 1794, Fersen learned with deep regret of the death of the Comte de Mercy-Argenteau. Though Mercy had sometimes been too cautious, Fersen commented, he had held enormous influence, on several occasions declining Kaunitz's position as foreign minister. It seemed, too, that Mercy alone had kept Austria in the war against France, despite growing sentiment for peace. Many thus seemed to rejoice over his death; "they do not know that we will have to begin the war all over again and that peace is incompatible with the program of the regicides."[9]

If the emperor followed Prussia in making peace, Fersen felt that the British would have no choice but to do likewise, unless they succeeded in backing the rebels in the Vendée.[10]

Following the Peace of Basel, Frankfurt was just inside the neutral zone of northern Germany dominated by Prussia. On various pretexts, French officers and soldiers frequently passed through the city. Nearby to the south, the war continued between France and Austria. Thus Fersen now had opportunities to observe the French at close range. As a military man and their opponent, he showed a lively interest in their armies and generals.

His attitude was in this regard ambivalent. As a former officer of the old French army, he was naturally familiar with those qualities and traditions that had caused it to be considered, almost axiomatically, Europe's finest. But as an aristocratic officer of the old regime, he also tended to equate excellence in troops with precision in drill and smartness in appearance. Thus he commented with distaste on the slovenly French soldiery he saw, considering it humiliating and disgraceful to be beaten by such men. He regarded them much as he had the ragged American troops in the War of Independence. Their victories were difficult to comprehend, seeming to contradict all he had learned of the art and science of war. Of French advances in Piedmont in the spring of 1796, he commented:

... their victories are incomprehensible and frightening, and one ends by believing they have Providence on their side, for never before has there been a country, torn by revolutions and inner turmoil which has stood against all the great powers of Europe, which united to combat it, and at the same time carried the war on all fronts home to the enemy. This is a trial of strength which shows the greatness and resources of France.[11]

Fersen was, however, enough of a professional to recognize some of the better qualities of the French troops: they were generally well behaved and disciplined, they fought bravely and their artillery, as always, was very good.[12] In particular, he was impressed with the republican generals. Yet here again, old prejudices reappear when he writes that Generals "Marceau and Bonnard, who are almost good, are certainly, to judge by their conduct, disguised noblemen." When Marceau was wounded and taken prisoner, "everyone here was very distressed by that, for his conduct had been unusually fine when he was here and he had prevented much evil." Two days later: "Marceau has died of his wounds. Everyone here mourns him as a man."[13]

Fersen was, however, above all concerned about the inadequacies of the allied war effort and tended to seek here the real causes for French successes. He constantly decried the incompetence of the allied generals and lack of cooperation among the powers. When the Austrians failed to use their advantage in Flanders and the British surrendered Toulon in the fall of 1793, Fersen wrote:

This reverse is a terrible blow, and one feels at times like abandoning all hope, because of the lack of talent, of military capacity, of determination in action and daring which prevails in the armies. There has not been a single splendid operation, not a single bold attack, not a troop movement; and this against people who are completely ignorant of what they are doing, without weapons, without clothes, undisciplined; among whom half are dissatisfied and are there because they are forced to be; led by generals who are merchants, painters, doctors. It is terrible to think about.[14]

Some two months later:

In this way the French republic will never be crushed. One may aver, not without fear and indignation, that almost all the powers allied against France, divided by mutual partisan conflicts, indeed, almost mutual warfare, could not succeed in weakening that land; but it is because none of these powers yet understands the danger that threatens them all. Each hopes to have nothing to fear for its own part, and to derive advantage from this situation, and to dupe the others in order to weaken them.[15]

Fersen, after his experiences with Gustav III and Louis XVI respectively, was deeply impressed with the values of a strong leader and the dangers of a weak one.

What a misfortune it is, [he wrote in February 1794], to see on the thrones of Europe, as for example, those of Vienna, Berlin, Madrid, Portugal, Holland, Turin, Sweden, Denmark, only weak rulers or those in a state of decay like the empress [of Russia]. England's is bound by the constitution and must always follow his ministers. The princes of Italy do not comprise any great power, and those of Naples and Tuscany are as weak as the others. Only the pope has shown himself worthy to reign, and alone among all, has refused to bow down before the French when all Italy trembled . . .

And in August of that year, "It seems that it is only the French to whom the gift of initiative has been granted. They alone make use of all possible means. . . . But it is our naiveté and lethargy which cause them to win."[16]

2

How could the coalition powers overcome their failings and destroy the Revolution? Many of the answers were most succinctly expressed by Jacques Mallet du Pan, whose *Considérations sur la Révolution française* was published in Brussels in August 1793 and who thereafter corresponded regularly with Fersen's associates, Lord Elgin and Count Mercy.[17] Fersen's diary shows how impressed he became by early 1794 with Mallet's ideas. He strongly approved his view that unless the allies attacked France in sufficient force—with armies considerably larger than those now in the field—the war was actually beneficial to the revolutionary regime by providing occupation for the army and the unemployed, thus keeping them out of politics at home.[18]

In April 1794, Fersen saw a writing in which Mallet maintained the republic could not be defeated by outside force alone, but that "one must use against the Jacobins the same severe forceful measures which they themselves use," that the allies should promise to punish the ringleaders of the Revolution but to pardon the mass of the people, that "fanaticism" must be stirred up "for the good cause," that a counterrevolutionary party in France itself must be formed, that all the émigrés should be placed in the vanguard of the allied armies to rally all enemies of the Convention in France and organize them into an effective force. The war would then lose the character of one between powers and would take on the nature of a civil conflict. Fersen considered Mallet's memorandum "wise and well-written," and concluded that "it would be fortunate if it were followed to the letter."[19]

Mallet's *Considérations* created a sensation in Europe and appears to have had a strong impact on the thinking of allied statesmen, especially Pitt and Mercy.[20] Fersen does not seem to have been in personal contact with Mallet, thought the latter was in Brussels in 1793. The two had different ideas as to the final outcome of the counterrevolution, Mallet recognizing the necessity for fundamental changes to the *ancien régime,* Fersen holding out for the unqualified restoration of royal authority. Mallet's ideas on how to combat the Revolution were, however, close to those Fersen himself had long since formulated.

Fersen and Mallet, it will be recalled, had both been involved in the background to the Brunswick Manifesto in 1792. The idea of such a declaration was not a new one with Fersen at the time and even afterwards was one to which he continually returned. Similarly, the idea of proclaiming the intentions of the allies was always central to Mallet's thinking. Fersen, like Mallet, regarded the war as a conflict of principle, of vital concern to all the thrones and nations of Europe, to which all other interests must be subordinated.

All the counterrevolutionary forces must be mobilized under a single, unified leadership. Mallet proposed a striking expedient: the allies must have their own "Committee of Public Safety." To Mercy and Elgin, he argued:

To will, command, and be obeyed, are to the Committee of Public Safety the work of an instant. It acts with the speed of lightning while the allies deliberate; all authorities are subject to it; it is able to constrain consent, or do without it; while ministers, separated from each other by two or three hundred leagues, all alike distant from the scene of war, have need of discussions, explanations, endless couriers, before they can adopt unanimously any one measure. So long as the allies have not, after the fashion of the French, their Committee of Public Safety, that is, a congress of plenipotentiaries, furnished with general and positive instructions posted in the vicinity of the troops, diligent in collecting information, and in daily ascertaining indisputable facts, authorized to set forward operations with a promptitude corresponding to the circumstances, you will lose the result of your most costly efforts.[21]

Fersen took to this recommendation with enthusiasm. Already on 28 February 1794, he wrote:

The powers have still not seen the necessity of a Committee of Public Safety. . . . Such [a committee] would be valuable in expediting operations and resolving unforeseen and difficult questions. If one had existed during the last campaign, I am convinced the armies would now be on the Somme . . .

Some two weeks later, "If we do not get a Committee of Public Safety on the model of that in Paris, everything will fail."[22]

The idea of a congress of powers, directing concerted measures against the French had of course long been central to Fersen's thinking. In March 1793, he wrote Duke Karl in Sweden, that it appeared a congress would be convened to concert war operations, regulate exchanges and compensations, and decide a form of government for France. He hoped, he confided to Taube, to be appointed Swedish envoy, thus committing Sweden to the common effort and putting himself in the best position to help the French royal family. Fersen here doubtless had in mind the meeting of allied representatives in Antwerp in April 1793, which was concerned mainly with the eventual partition of French territories rather than with coordination of the war effort. He nevertheless continued to speculate over a congress into the summer of 1793 and again in the winter of 1794, fortified by Mallet's arguments.[23]

In April 1794, Fersen noted with anticipation the arrival of Emperor Francis II in Brussels to take command of the allied armies. The experiment soon proved disappointing and the emperor departed a scant month later for Vienna, to the dismay of Fersen and many others. "What hope can there be for a cause deserted by its chiefs?" complained one of Mallet's correspondents.[24]

Fersen meanwhile speculated on other expedients. He considered the intended *levée en masse* of 1793 in France a typically French "folly." A year later he spoke of a scheme for arming the populace of the Rhineland against the French with some interest, though he doubted the allies could organize such a mobilization. Shortly after, in August 1794, he criticized the Elector of Cologne for failing to put himself at the head of "the voluntary mobilization," which would have made him "the savior of Germany"; because of this, the people of the region showed little enthusiasm for arming and thus exposing themselves. The thought of the resources in men and materiel available if only Germany could unite under a single leadership, was tantalizing to Fersen, as it had been alarming to the French statesmen of the past. In July 1796, Fersen wondered why the emperor did not acquiesce in dividing Germany with Prussia, which he could not prevent after the Peace of Basel, then fall on the French and drive them out. This would mean the "end of the republic," at least as a power in Europe.[25]

Ever mindful of the force of public opinion, Fersen was naturally interested in ways to turn it to account. In November 1792, he criticized the Austrians to Duke Karl for not granting the traditional liberties of Brabant under the *Joyeuse Entrée*, which would be "not too unjust." The Austrian Netherlands would then have provided enough troops and money to repel the enemy, "for the Brabançon democrats do not desire the French regime; they have seen from too close its disadvantages and misfortunes for them not to fear it." In time he considered more daring expedients. By 1796, he was not only enthusiastic at the prospect of a *levée en masse* in Swabia and Franconia, but also over the use of popular insurrection against the French in occupied areas. This idea derived above all from actual uprisings in 1796–97: in southwestern Germany, Piedmont, Belgium, the Tyrol. Popular movements—even if directed against French democrats—were not however easy for an aristocratic officer of the old regime to accept and Fersen's attitude remained equivocal. On 8 October 1796, he wrote Taube:

The rallying of the peasantry [in the Black Forest] is continuing. They have even made proclamations to call their confreres to the common defense. This was good for the moment, but I do not like that these gatherings should be prolonged or that any importance should be attached to them. They could in that case just as easily become harmful if an ambitious man seized control of them. They have even had portraits of their leaders engraved. All this serves no purpose.[26]

The dangers inherent in popular initiatives seemed reconfirmed by the British naval mutinies the following spring. "You doubtless know of the English sailors' petition," he wrote Taube in May 1797.

Their demands are just but their manner [of presenting them], though moderate, is for that very reason all the more dangerous. They surely have a chief or hidden adviser whom it would be most useful to discover to bring him to justice and deliver him to the hatred of the public. It is felt that it will be necessary to accede to almost all their demands. Lord

Howe is very much at fault for not having given the government the opportunity to anticipate these demands by bringing them to the king's attention in time.

Fersen suspected Fox and his faction, whose behavior in Parliament was "criminal," to be "the real factious" who had encouraged the revolt. He sympathized with the seamen and conceded that the English people, accustomed to "speak and reason about affairs of government have, by the same token, greater reasonableness and cool-headedness." But leniency to the mutineers would only encourage revolt among others: the "workers," the dissenters, the Irish. The situation in Britain seemed to him critical in the extreme.[27]

The kind of voluntary support Fersen naturally preferred is shown in a letter to Taube in November 1796:

You doubtless know of the generous devotion of the Hungarians, who are giving the emperor 80,000 men, three million florins in money, and an equal amount in supplies. Prince Eszterhazy alone is giving 1,000 men, fully equipped, and is providing their maintenance for the entire war. One is fortunate to be in a position thus to demonstrate one's attachment to one's master.[28]

If the European monarchs feared their subjects almost as much as their enemies, the situation was different when it came to exploiting the most promising of popular insurrections, that of the enemies of the Revolution in France itself. After the execution of the king and queen, Mallet became the leading exponent of changing the war into a civil conflict, uniting all enemies of the Revolution, in the emigration and in France itself, against the common enemy, aided though not dominated by the European coalition. Fersen came increasingly to share this view. From the start, he believed the Revolution must eventually destroy itself, as he reiterated to Taube in January 1797:

It appears as though in moments of crisis Providence always helps those scoundrels and preserves them from total ruin; she wishes, perhaps, for the sake of example, to leave to them the task of their own destruction and to cause them to perish at each others' hands through the excess of their crimes. This will come about, without doubt, but it will take too long.[29]

Fersen was thus highly interested in the civil war in the Vendée and with allied projects to support it. The Vendéeans, he felt in the spring of 1794, caused the republic more difficulties than the external war. In August 1795, when most of the coalition seemed about to make peace, Fersen still hoped the rebels with British assistance might ultimately succeed in restoring the monarchy. The defeat of the combined British-émigré expedition at Quibéron in the summer of 1795 was a deep disappointment, "the consequence of England's poor system of always doing things a little at a time; it was thus they lost America." Preparations for new British landings later that year came to nothing.[30]

In his emphasis on a tightly coordinated coalition, under unified leadership, professing a common, stated set of objectives, in his belief in a war of principle, affecting all countries and governments, in his presentiments about the importance of public opinion and of national feeling, the arming of peoples and the central importance of Germany, Fersen was in many respects looking ahead to the Fourth Coalition and final defeat of France, some twenty years later, which he himself did not live to see.

3

Should the allies ultimately succeed, what sort of monarchy, in Fersen's view, should be restored in France? During the first half of 1793, a coalition victory seemed imminent, in which case a regency government under Marie-Antoinette would surely have been established.[31] As Swedish ambassador to her court, Fersen would doubtless have wielded great influence in the reconstruction of the French state. But Fersen's thoughts were then understandably preoccupied with the war, thus he left only a few scattered references from which to gather his views.[32]

Most important, in his opinion, was that absolute power be returned to the monarch, uncontested by either constitutions or elected assemblies. He realized, however, that this could not be accomplished all at once if fresh disorders were to be avoided. In conversations with Mercy, he agreed that the constitution must be destroyed, "the monarchy and the three estates must be restored," the monarch must resume "all of his authority," and the old order should be restored gradually, over a period of 10 to 15 years. One wonders to what extent Fersen realized that the *ancien régime* could not be completely reestablished; whether he did not see, with Mallet du Pan, that "new interests have been developed by these vicissitudes" which could not be ignored. Fersen seems to have concerned himself relatively little with specific reforms. In April 1793, he felt no new constitution should be drawn up, which would start people thinking about "the new ideas" again, but that any necessary changes should be made within the framework of the old system. Considering all of Fersen's projects since the beginning of the Revolution, this seems to summarize his attitude very well: he was not opposed to reform as such, as his criticisms of the old regimes in France, Austria, and his own native Sweden show, but to him the criterion by which it should be judged was the authority from which it emanated.[33]

As it appeared evident that the Revolution could only be defeated with the support of a sizable part of the French people themselves, Fersen speculated over how specific the coalition powers should be in announcing their political intentions. Because of mutual differences, the allies at first made no statements on this subject at all. Fersen in the beginning approved of this official silence, as it might encourage the hopes of all factions in France and avoid offending any of them. Breteuil, however, felt that this would make the French suspicious that the powers only wanted French territory, arousing their national passions. La Marck discounted such nationalist sentiments, feeling that "it was only feelings of misfortune and dissatisfaction which affected the people," and approved the allies' silence. Fersen was soon won over by Breteuil, "for instead of winning us supporters, this uncertainty had inspired all parties with such mistrust and fear that no party would support the powers for fear of possibly playing into the hands of one of the others." Discontent in France, he added, must meanwhile be actively encouraged by "enlightening and reassuring the people."[34]

Fersen thus turned again to the idea of a proclamation, calling for restoration of the monarchy, punishment of specified revolutionaries, and amnesty to the people as a whole.

... This would divide interests and reassure those who took part in the conflict only out of fear of retribution and persuade those who doubt that we desire anything but conquest. This would be the only way to gain support in France, which the powers do not now have because of the silence they have kept regarding their intentions.[35]

There was, of course, the danger that the powers might declare themselves for a less positive restoration of royal power in France than Fersen wished. He was fearful that both the Vendéeans and the British might settle for a limited monarchy, though he welcomed the latters' proclamation in October 1793, calling on all Frenchmen to follow the example of Toulon and cooperate in reestablishing a royal government, since this was the first allied statement definitely calling for a monarchy, of whatever kind. Following Thermidor, there seemed signs that the Revolution had run its course, though its final result still seemed to be an established constitutional system. In January 1795, Fersen observed, with obviously ambivalent feelings:

The news from France reveals to what a great extent the moderate regime is becoming fatal to the existence of the Revolution, through the freedom of utterance and of the press, and it shows that minds and attitudes have changed. One might be able to predict that they may return to the constitution of 1791, and that the powers will be delighted to accept it with modifications.[36]

Indications seemed to be increasing that a majority of the French desired a return to monarchy in some form. By the fall of 1797, Fersen was prepared to believe that the current rulers of France were not actually "Jacobins," but only wished to appear as such to keep themselves in power.[37]

The problem was meanwhile complicated by the question of whom to place on the throne. The succession fell to the Comte de Provence, who proclaimed himself King Louis XVIII on the news of the dauphin's death in June 1795 and issued from Verona a manifesto, promising chastisement of the revolutionaries and reestablishment of the old order in all its details. Fersen had never been on good terms with the pretender and considered this Verona proclamation "more like a bishop's pastoral letter," which "invites ridicule with the exaggerated expressions which appear almost constantly in it." In actuality, it was instrumental in dividing the royalists within France and driving the constitutional monarchists into the arms of the Thermidorians. If Fersen had long been zealous in the service of the house of Bourbon, he had no desire to serve its latest representative; when approached with such a suggestion, he complained in his diary that "this would accomplish nothing but to make oneself extremely ludicrous." In all the pretender did, he observed in May 1795, one saw "the quasi-learned phrase-maker and theater-king. It is distressing."[38]

Fersen thus reached the point of actually abandoning his strictly legitimitist attitude toward the restoration. In April 1796, he learned there was much talk in the French army of peace, over-throw of the Directory, and reestablishment of a king. The soldiers preferred, however, the young Duc d'Orléans—the son of "Philippe Égalité" and future Louis-Philippe—and on no account wanted a Bourbon for fear of retribution. Fersen now felt that Louis XVIII should abdicate his claim in favor of the Duc d'Angoulême, son of the Comte d'Artois, as the only means of preserving the crown in the Bourbon line.

His father and uncle have too much behind them; and the king [Louis XVIII], through his manifesto, has committed an error which can never be repaired. The Duc d'Angoulême, however, is a young man who has not yet had the opportunity to take a position, and thus could take one which was better suited to the circumstances.

Angoulême should marry his cousin, Madame-Royale, to strengthen his dynastic position. Civil war might thus be avoided between legitimists and Orleanists, which might ensue if the Duc d'Orléans were placed on the throne. Still, Fersen was skeptical that Louis XVIII would agree to such an arrangement and suspected the revolutionaries would fear retribution even under Angoulême. The "court" of Louis XVIII in Verona, Fersen meanwhile reflected, was "a Versailles in miniature," with "the same intrigues, the same jealousies. . . . All of this is a sorry situation and such a king would be a new misfortune for France."[39]

It has been seen that Fersen genuinely admired certain of the French generals. This also had its political aspects, for despite the Dumouriez debacle of 1793, the defection of the French army under its generals always seemed an intriguing possibility. Signs were not lacking that the temper of the army had greatly changed under the Directory. "Generally speaking," Fersen noted opti-mistically in August 1796, "the whole army is the declared enemy of the Jacobins."[40]

Fersen now placed high hopes in the generals. He showed par-ticular interest in Marceau and it was with real disappointment that he noted in September 1796,

Marceau had died of his wounds . . . he was a great loss, for he had been won over. Baron Leickham had persuaded him to speak openly and he had promised to leave the army, together with a number of other gen-erals, and go to Paris to set himself at the head of a party there, which is already in existence, to overthrow the Directory and force it to make peace on the basis of acceptable and reasonable terms. He had, however, always refused to have anything to do with treason or to accept any economic inducement. Baron Leickham had, through stubbornness and prejudice against the French, in the meantime refused him the meeting he had requested in Frankfurt, so that they could undertake to make preparations and so that he could explain certain things. How shall he [Leickham] not regret this, especially since he does not know this general's connections nor to whom he should turn to replace him? It is not through such prejudices that politics are conducted.[41]

At the same time, another French general attracted Fersen's attention. In July 1796, he observed, "Buonaparte is a young man, filled with fire and ambition, and with whom it would be possible to deal. His victories have made him a fanatic, but he would be easy to win over." Fersen, however, came closer to the mark the following month: "I find it hard to believe Buonaparte is [a Jacobin], and I believe he has the secret intention of attempting to use the army he has at his disposal to set up a monarchical form of government, within which he himself would presumably play a large role."[42]

By the spring of 1797, only Austria remained in the field against the land forces of the republic and was no match for France. Fersen could not but resign himself to the inevitable end of the war on the Continent. On 4 April 1797, he wrote:

Prince Rosenberg, the major general, arrived from Vienna. He said that everyone except the emperor and Thugut were for peace, that the latter had said that even if the enemy stood outside Vienna, they should not accept ... but rather move on to another location. Vienna is not the same thing as the empire. With a prince like the great Frederick, this would have made no difference, but with a weak master like the emperor, that could be very dangerous and Austria's situation is critical in the highest degree.[43]

The Austrians, he saw, had no alternative but peace on the best terms possible, yet it was a bitter experience to see the war finally end thus. The terms ultimately proved even more severe than he anticipated. To Taube, he wrote indignantly on 12 May 1797:

... is there anything more shameful and could there be anything worse even if the French were the masters of Vienna? Ought one not, faced with such proposals, have made yet one last effort, which promised favorable results owing to the critical position Buonaparte was in with the Austrians on his flanks and at his rear. It is true they were not there in force but they would have been aided by general insurrection in the Venetian states and *levées en masse* and other [help] from Hungary and all the hereditary lands would have furnished great resources. Ought they not have tried once again and accepted such hard conditions only at the last extremity? The empire, the allies, the security and tranquility of Europe, the glory of the emperor, everything has been abandoned and this peace contains within it the germs of continual wars and of the overthrow of Europe through the example of peoples in revolt against their sovereigns and always protected and supported in their insurrection. . . . This peace is worthy of a war so badly conducted. It provides no consolation for what we have seen and experienced for nine years. . . . The sovereigns have themselves lost their cause . . .[44]

The dangers of peace with revolutionary Frence were quickly apparent.

The constitution of Venice has been completely changed [he wrote on 21 May]. Verona, Vicenza, Padua, and the whole Terra Firma have already risen up and constituted themselves a republic. After having used every possible pretext for a conflict with the republic [of Venice], Buonaparte surrounded the city by land and sea, and made a number of representations. The council finally agreed to everything, the doge has handed in his resignation, and this republic is going to be transformed from an extremely aristocratic despotism into, without a doubt, an only slightly democratic democracy. If it were not for the inconvenient times and the consequences, that is to say, the influence this example will have on the rest of Italy, this change would be a good thing. But Italy is lost. . . . Thieves, murderers, and rascals will rule there . . . and sooner or later, Florence, Rome, and Naples will suffer the same fate as Venice. It is impossible to watch cold-bloodedly everything we must experience and to think of the consequences which all this will bring with it, and how easily it all could have been prevented.[45]

Soon after, he noted the French were agitating in the Rhineland, "to stir up the people to overthrow the yoke of their sovereigns and form a republic under French protection, on the model of Italy. . . ."

It is strange that the example of France has not made people more sensible. Everyone hopes that things will go better for him. But the same causes bring about the same effects everywhere and when a people once sets itself in motion, nothing can stop it.[46]

4

Only a few months after Fersen returned to Frankfurt from Sweden, Baron Staël, as noted, finally attained the defensive alliance with

France he had so long striven for, on 14 September 1795. According to its terms, Sweden was to receive a subsidy from France and maintain her neutral shipping rights at sea.

Reuterholm and Duke Karl now turned to the perplexing task of finding a queen for the young Gustav IV Adolf. Considering the European conflict, any match would draw Sweden closer to one of the great powers, creating complications with the others. In late 1795, Reuterholm made a pact for the hand of a Mecklenburg princess, satisfactory to France, with which Staël had just concluded his alliance. This proved offensive to Russia, not least because Catherine II had long hoped to marry one of her own granddaughters to the Swedish king. The Russians made threatening gestures while France showed a studied indifference to the situation. At length, the regency gave way, broke the Mecklenburg match and negotiated a Russian one, which was only prevented at the last moment by the young king's reaction to certain of Catherine's demands. The empress was deeply mortified and a paralytic stroke ended her life a few weeks later.[47]

While all this was taking place, Fersen was in Frankfurt and Vienna. News of the Swedish-French treaty of September 1795, being supposedly secret, reached him only gradually and he laconically noted its details. The reception of the new French ambassador, L.G. Le Hoc, in Stockholm in November 1795, however, provoked a display of bitterness at seeing his own government enter into close relations with the "regicides":

They sent me from Sweden the speech Ambassador Le Hoc held at his audience. It was outrageous. When one receives an envoy from those villains, one deserves that. I am only sorry that this falls upon the king, who does not deserve it, since he has no part in it.

The reception, he wrote Taube, aroused in him a feeling of "horror at the human race and at a century in which such events could take place."[48]

Fersen naturally disapproved of the "idiotic" Mecklenburg match, as an obvious adjunct to the French alliance, and in April 1796 feared that it might lead to a war with Russia in which he himself would feel disinclined to serve the regency.[49] He was, however, no more enthusiastic over a Russian match. When Taube told him in April 1797, after Catherine's death, that there was still hope for this in some quarters, Fersen feared, "The Russian power is an especially sensitive structure and it rests on loose sand. The hand that held it all together is no more. Its successor, I believe, does not have the strength to do so." Fersen himself preferred a match with an English princess, but Taube feared this might encourage "English principles" in Sweden and someone intimated to Gustav IV Adolf that the English princesses had dubious morals.[50] These speculations were resolved in May 1797 when Taube departed for Germany on a secret mission. Visiting Fersen in Hanau, he confided he was to consider the princesses of Baden. Taube soon concluded a contract for the hand of Princess Frederike, sister-in-law to Grand Duke, later Tsar, Alexander of Russia. In October, she was married to Gustav IV Adolf by proxy in Stralsund, with Evert Taube standing in his monarch's place.[51]

In the meantime, a new era had commenced on 1 November 1796, when Gustav IV Adolf attained his eighteenth year, ending the regency. "This day," Fersen wrote, "will determine for a long time to come the happiness or unhappiness of Sweden and my own political existence."[52]

CHAPTER X

Fersen and the Congress of Rastadt, 1797–1798

1

The personal reign of Gustav IV Adolf began seemingly under most favorable auspices. Reuterholm was dismissed and Duke Karl withdrew into private life until events called him to the scene more than a decade later as King Karl XIII. The young monarch seemed to have a strong will and to be determined to avoid a rule through favorites such as had aroused opposition under both his father and his uncle. "All these details," Fersen wrote in November 1796,

... made me very happy and I felt pleased at seeing all that clique struck down and the king's firmness against them. I felt a great satisfaction at seeing that the king has determination and character. God grant that he may keep this; it is the most important thing for a ruler and so rare in our century ...[1]

The new reign nonetheless faced serious difficulties. The negotiations for Gustav IV Adolf's marriage had caused friction with Russia, the French alliance of 1795 had proved disappointing, and Sweden was at odds with Britain over the rights of neutral shipping. Internally too, things were far from ideal. Gustav III had left a legacy of class strife. The Austrian chargé d'affaires reported in April 1797 that "the new French doctrine" was making such alarming progress among the "Third Estate" in Sweden, "that it is to be feared that that sort of Jacobinism, already fomented by the late

231

king against the nobility might declare itself in our times both against that order and against the throne."[2]

In the face of these problems, the young king set about his tasks. He was particularly interested in foreign affairs and instructed his diplomats abroad to report directly to himself. Despite his dislike for favoritism, which won wide approval, Gustav Adolf from the beginning sought counsel from certain secret advisers. He was anxious to return to the policies of his father's last years, abandoned during the regency, and thus turned first of all to their foremost proponent, Baron Taube. These principles included staunch opposition to revolutionary France, cooperation with Russia, and hostility toward Denmark, based on the design of uniting Norway with Sweden to form a powerful Scandinavian state. In internal policy, they above all opposed the convening of the estates.[3]

Gustav Adolf's natural reserve nonethless kept him from throwing himself wholeheartedly into the arms of any single faction. Thus the purge of state officials, so eagerly awaited by the Gustavians, never came about and most of Reuterholm's men kept their posts. These included important figures in the chancellery and diplomatic service, such as Staël and Lars von Engeström, who desired neutrality and cooperation with France, while mistrusting Russia, and sought to counteract Taube and the Gustavians as best they could.

Taube's influence was doubtless based largely on his ability to play on the young king's natural prejudices. Since childhood, Gustav Adolf had feared and hated the French revolutionaries, who he believed had been behind his father's assassination. He also inherited Gustav III's distaste for representative assemblies, in his own country or elsewhere. These attitudes Taube had taken pains to foster during the king's minority. Axel Fersen had meanwhile sought through his friend to counteract the influence of the regency. In February 1793, he wrote Taube in cipher:

Give my thanks to our young master, my friend. Tell him of my respect, of my love for his late father. . . . As soon as the new arrangements I have made to be informed of what is going on in Paris . . . are in order, I will not fail to satisfy our master's wish, but it will be through you, my friend, for fear that a correspondence with him might arouse suspicions. Give him to understand, if you consider it appropriate, that this is the only reason that prevents me from following my desire to report on affairs; but this will always be through you. The sensibility he has shown is worthy of the son of Gustav . . .

Much in Fersen's lengthy, detailed, often encoded letters to Taube was thus intended for the young king's ear. Following dismissal from his diplomatic post in 1794, he continued to provide Taube with the same kind of material. Fersen's good relations with Gustav IV Adolf in Sweden in 1794–95 have been noted. By late 1796, his correspondence with Taube shows a turn from resignation and detachment toward a growing spirit of engagement as the regency came to an end. On occasion, he sent direct messages or requests to the king through Taube. His letters meanwhile express his satisfaction at Gustav Adolf's apparent strength and dignity, his veneration for his father's memory, and compassion for the French royal family. At length in January 1798, some months after again assuming diplomatic responsibilities, Fersen wrote Taube, "Henceforward I will send [messages] directly to the king. If I have followed another method, it is because I believed he would prefer it and also to prevent certain [things] from passing by way of the chancellery."[4]

Nevertheless, an age prone to seek influence behind every royal decision tended to overlook the fact that ultimately Gustav IV Adolf himself chose his advisers. He was not above seeking rapprochement with France or convening a Riksdag for reasons of expediency in the early years of his reign and knew how to profit from the struggle between Taube and his opponents. Like his father, he showed a marked predilection for secret diplomacy, frequently conducted through Taube and other special envoys, unbeknown to the *kanslikollegium*. All this led to apparent inconsistencies in his earlier foreign policy, which makes it especially tortuous to follow.[5]

Since the beginning of Gustav Adolf's personal reign, Fersen was considered to replace *Rikskansler* Fredrik Sparre, as Taube apparently preferred the role of Gray Eminence. As early as 20 October 1796, even before the king took power, Fersen was aware he was considered for the post.[6]

That he did not receive it was doubtless due partly to his own protestations. He did not seek the position and would turn it down if offered, he commented in October. Yet his feelings were ambivalent, for his vanity was aroused by the rumor that Stedingk might get the appointment instead. In response to Taube's inquiries, Fersen requested that he not be given any assignment for at least a year; later, that he be given a ministerial post, preferably in London, for two years before being considered for chancellor.[7]

Fersen made various rationalizations. He wished to enjoy his freedom "and first see what our young ruler's position is and how much or how little character he has." He was bothered by gout. The thought of leaving Eleanore disturbed him, though he fancied her ardor had cooled.

... I fought a hard battle between my ambition and my personal inclinations [he wrote in January 1797]. My ambition could well be flattered, but I felt the strongest aversion toward burying myself in Sweden, taking a position, after which I could neither receive nor desire any other, and renouncing other lands, my friends, and acquaintances. I would be delighted if the king did not consider me at all for this position.

Perhaps most of all, he feared being unequal to the task and detested decisions, as he confided to his diary in March.[8]

In January 1797, Fersen was apparently considered for ambassador to St. Petersburg and in April heard the king had promised him the embassy in London if it should fall vacant. In August, Taube again mentioned the chancellor's post. By now, ambition began to gain the upper hand, for Fersen no longer felt he could categorically refuse. Thus, "as things now stand, I would accept the position for at least a few years and then my health might serve as a pretext for resigning if I should not wish to remain a longer time."[9]

The prospect would have to wait—Taube expected for only a few months—for meanwhile Fersen received another assignment from the king. On 18 July, there arrived "to my great surprise," a royal appointment as plenipotentiary commissioner "to the congress which will be held to settle the peace of the Empire," stipulated in the Preliminaries of Leoben of April 1797 between France and Austria.

I was at first very flattered, especially that the king had remembered me and also that I would be able to play a role at this [congress]. But when I found out the king had not received any invitation to send a minister there, [and thought] of my ignorance and limited ability for taking part effectively in discussions over rights, for which one must at least be well-grounded in history, I hestitated to accept the offer and waited until the following day to think about the matter.

It would, however, be ungrateful to decline the king's first assignment to him, an honorable one which would allow him to return to Sweden with some accomplishment to his credit. "The unpleasantness of having to deal with the French must also be taken into account," he wrote, "but since I would only have to oppose and protest along with all the others, this will not be so great...." He wrote his acceptance next day, inquiring about Sweden's relations with Russia and Prussia, and asking that the Swedish legation secretary at Regensburg, Carl Schörbing, be assigned to him because of his exceptional knowledge of German affairs.[10]

That Taube was influential in obtaining this appointment seems obvious and was generally assumed.[11] After more than four years of political inactivity, Fersen had once again been given a role in his nation's affairs. Despite his initial hesitations, the situation he faced did not at first seem unpromising.

2

In concluding their armistice in April 1797, the French and Austrians had agreed that a "congress" should be held, "to negotiate and conclude the definitive peace between the two powers on the basis of the integrity of the Empire." Secret territorial agreements made it nonetheless problematical that this integrity could be maintained. "The preliminaries will lend themselves at the definitive peace to all the modifications you might desire....," General Bonaparte wrote the Directory; because of Austria's interest in Venetian territory, he was confident France might obtain the left bank of the Rhine.[12]

Territorial changes were to be expected and as usual the Germanic body would be the prime object of attention. Since the Thirty Years' War, Sweden had a particular interest in Germany, as possessor of ducal Pomerania and co-guarantor, with France, of the Treaty of Westphalia. Both Swedish Pomerania and the guarantorship seemed threatened by the peace negotiations.[13]

Gustav IV Adolf was naturally alarmed. It accorded with both his interests and sentiments to defend the integrity of the Empire. He thus needed effective representation at the congress.[14]

The charge has been made in older Swedish historical writing, hostile to Gustav IV Adolf, that he sought at the Congress of Rastadt to maintain an impossible position as unilateral guarantor of the Peace of Westphalia and the integrity of the Empire, in the face of three great Continental powers, intent on territorial revision.[15] The accusation is unfair. The king and his advisers realized that Sweden must cooperate with at least one of these powers.

The Austrian, like the Swedish government, feared a Prussian-French entente at the coming peace, and as early as August 1795, persuaded the Germanic diet to appoint a nine-man *Reichsdeputation* to negotiate with France, which included an Austrian but not a Prussian representative. Following the armistice of April 1797, Chancellor Thugut placed his hopes in the forthcoming congress and his ability to persuade the German princes to defend the integrity of the Empire, while internal dissension would sap the strength of the French republic or a new anti-French coalition might be formed. A strong Swedish representation at the congress, committed to German integrity, would thus be an important asset to Austria.[16]

In addition to the *Reichsdeputation,* the other Germanic states were permitted to send representatives to watch and advise. Some ninety responded when the congress convened. As duke of Pomerania, the king of Sweden could also send such an envoy, but he considered this inadequate to protect his interests. There was, however, a way for him to gain an influential voice: he could send a special envoy as guarantor of the Treaty of Westphalia. Neither the Swedish nor the Austrian governments was slow to realize this.[17]

Contemporaries and earlier historians have regarded the Swedish mission to the congress as singularly unfortunate and the choice of Fersen as its head as remarkably ill advised. Yet at the time of his appointment, he was eminently suited to serve the policy Gustav IV Adolf then intended to follow. No more determined opponent of France could be found and no Swede knew the Revolution there more intimately. His consistency and loyalty were beyond question and his political experience considerable. He was familiar with Germany and well known in Vienna. The dangers inherent in his assignment did not pass unnoticed. Yet assuming strong Austrian resistance to French pretensions and close cooperation with Sweden, he could justifiably be expected to play an effective and influential role.[18]

Fersen's appointment was in any event a declaration of Gustav IV Adolf's policy and a direct challenge to France.[19] Taube had the double pleasure of securing Sweden's representation at this critical juncture by his closest friend and of undercutting his pro-French rivals in the chancellery.

Circumstances soon changed, however. The coup d'état of 18 Fructador in September 1797 brought a more intransigent faction to power in Paris. Fersen wrote Gustav IV Adolf that the coup showed "a great resemblance to the Revolution of 1789; it is presently the Directory that is revolting against its sovereign, the Council of Five Hundred, as the Assembly did then against the king."[20] Thugut now concluded it would be unrealistic to put faith in French weakness or moderation, while no new coalition seemed imminent. Austria came to terms with France in the Peace of Campo Formio of 17 October. Unable to exclude the French from Germany, Thugut sought as large a compensation in Italy as possible, through cooperation with rather than resistance to France. The final territorial arrangements remained intentionally vague. The congress to settle the final peace with the Empire was to meet at Rastadt in Baden, seat of an earlier peace conference between France and the Empire in 1714. There both Thugut and the Directors hoped to manipulate the minor German princes to their own advantage.

One problem threatened the designs of both Austria and France: the anxiety of other large powers to intervene in the congress and influence the smaller German courts. Prussia had obvious interests in the reorganization of the Empire. Russia, through the Treaty of Teschen of 1779, was a guarantor of its integrity. When Paul I learned of the king of Sweden's intention to be represented as a guarantor, his jealousy was aroused.

Because of this, Fersen was able to change his title from plenipotentiary commissioner to ambassador. In September, he wrote Gustav IV Adolf, prompted by Knut Bildt, Swedish envoy to the diet of Regensburg, that since Russia was understood to have appointed both an ambassador and a minister to the congress, Sweden should do likewise. To his delight, the king followed this suggestion. Bildt was designated minister and Schörbing embassy secretary. The ambassador's title nevertheless proved a false triumph: Russia never sent anyone to the congress and Fersen eventually found himself the highest-ranking diplomat present under anomalous, even humiliating circumstances.[21]

Article 10 of the Treaty of Campo Formio, meanwhile, limited

participation in the congress to the principalities of the Holy
Roman Empire and the French republic. The Austrians wished to
bar Prussia from the negotiations and compensation within the
Empire; the French opposed any Russian participation.

Once the peace was signed, both powers were anxious to hold
the congress as quickly as possible to push through their programs
before other powers could intervene. On 7 November, Fersen
learned that the congress was to convene almost immediately.[22]

Sweden's position was now profoundly changed, as confirmed
in Thugut's instructions to Count Ludwig von Cobenzl for the
congress, dated 20 November. The appointment of Count Fersen
could not be agreeable to France and was contrary to the emperor's
interests; "far from preventing the French plenipotentiaries from
getting rid of the Swedish representative, it would be much more
expedient to encourage them in this, while remaining, however,
as much in the background as possible and letting the opprobrium
which will result in Stockholm fall on them." If, contrary to
expectation, the French accepted the Swedish envoy, then Austria
should demand admission of a Russian one.[23]

Ironically, the French position toward Fersen would be less
categorical.

News of Fersen's appointment was greeted in France with indignant
and often scandalous journalistic commentary. Interest and curiosity
were aroused in other parts of Europe, where newspaper comments
were often culled from the Paris journals. This has been seen as a
plot by the Directory to ruin Fersen's reputation before the
congress.[24] Fersen was, however, notorious enough already to arouse
public interest. Already some months before his appointment he
wrote his sister in March 1797;

You will no doubt have believed as I did, my dear Sophie, that I had
been forgotten in Paris. Well now, we are completely mistaken, for my
name is in all the Paris papers as being charged with following interests
and affairs here against the republic and with working in concert with
the English. They speak of the couriers I receive and send off, &c, &c.
I am charmed that they believe me constant in my principles, but I
would prefer that they did not speak of me.

In October, an English newspaper, commenting on his appointment, stated that Count Fersen "is not a very decided partisan of

republics!" "I was not sorry about this article," he remarked with obvious satisfaction.[25]

Paradoxically, there was a reason why the new French foreign minister, Talleyrand, should prefer not to frighten Fersen away from the congress. Talleyrand had received his post in the summer of 1797 largely through the influence of Baron Staël and his illustrious wife. Soon thereafter, Stockholm was advised that the republic was prepared to restore normal relations, which had broken down with the collapse of the alliance of 1795, provided Staël were reappointed Swedish ambassador to Paris. Talleyrand was evidently anxious to return a favor.

Gustav IV Adolf strongly opposed employing Staël in Paris again. He had never approved the pro-French policies of the regency, for which Staël had always been the most consistent proponent. Fersen's position at Rastadt, however, gave Talleyrand a basis for bargaining. His instructions to the French envoys to the congress were noncommittal on this point and contained virtually nothing concerning Sweden.

On 12 September, Lars von Engeström, former Swedish minister to Warsaw and London, arrived in Frankfurt. In May, he had himself requested the post to which Fersen had now been appointed but stood for a very different policy. It would be vain, he felt, to try to impede changes in the Empire; Sweden should instead cooperate with France to increase her territory and prestige there. Prussia too would be interested in such arrangements, he told Fersen. "What a miserable policy!" the latter complained. "The princes are bringing about their own misfortune and are sowing the seeds of long wars...." The following month, Engeström showed Fersen an elaborate exchange plan he had prepared to counter those of Prussia,

... according to which, Sweden should receive Bornholm from Denmark and the island of Ösel outside Wismar from the bishop of Eutin, and eventually perhaps a strip of coast between that city and Pomerania, all of this against compensation to be provided by the ecclesiastical territories in Westphalia.

Fersen strongly disapproved of "such immoral and impolitic plans."[26]

Engeström meanwhile became increasingly concerned over the

probable outcome of the Swedish mission to Rastadt. In his memoirs, he later claimed that he told Fersen he would not be accepted at the congress and advised him to present himself as minister for Swedish Pomerania, while after Fersen departed, he sent Schörbing after him in a last attempt to persuade him "not to hazard the king's dignity," but that Fersen, "determined to be an ambassador," disregarded his warnings.[27]

On 28 December 1797, Engeström wrote Gustav IV Adolf, criticizing the mission and expounding his own views at length. Sweden, he held, was now faced with the alternatives of having to defend the Westphalia settlement, which was clearly impossible, or of backing down, which would be humiliating. Sweden should be represented at Rastadt by a more modest mission for Pomerania only and cooperate with France to gain real advantages. But this would be impossible as long as Fersen was Sweden's envoy. In his private correspondence, Engeström bitterly attacked those who abused the young king's confidence "to further private ends" but who still considered themselves "the pillars of the throne," including both Taube and Fersen.[28]

Engeström's derogatory and rather ridiculous picture of Sweden's and Fersen's role at Rastadt was unfortunately taken all too seriously by older Swedish historians and has only more recently been challenged.[29] Engeström was undoubtedly disappointed at not getting Fersen's position. Though he noted that Engeström was reputed to hold "democratic" views and regarded him as something of an arriviste, Fersen seems to have been on amiable enough terms with him. Indeed, when the court of Vienna had refused to accept Engeström as Swedish minister in 1796, on grounds of his alleged connections with "Jacobins" and Polish revolutionaries—he had long lived in Poland and had a Polish wife—Fersen had done his best to intercede for him with Thugut.[30]

Engeström was in any event distressed over Sweden's position at Rastadt. His memoirs, written years after these events and after later developments had poisoned his relationship with the Fersen family, are misleading, though it might be too much to accuse him of deliberate falsification.[31] Fersen did not lack vanity, but he had not sought his appointment, nor do his papers confirm Engeström's alleged warnings. More important still, he did not need Engeström to worry for him. His diary and dispatches show how attentively he followed events in the summer and fall of 1797 and sought to divine their effects on the coming peace settlement. Engeström himself noted that Fersen sent off couriers "night and day." Fersen's dispatches show that he constantly requested information on Sweden's policy and relations with other powers.[32] It is hardly realistic to suggest, as Engeström did, that Fersen simply could have refused the mission. He had already accepted it when it had not appeared infeasible. To abandon it would mean a serious loss of prestige both to Sweden and himself. Fersen also believed firmly in the policy he had been appointed to uphold.

On 4 November, he wrote a long dispatch, clearly setting forth his views. The integrity of the Empire could be regarded from two aspects: in relation to neighboring powers and to its component states. If the Austrian Netherlands were removed and the left bank of the Rhine "republicanized," its external integrity would be violated, while its internal integrity would be destroyed through the territorial exchanges and secularizations which would follow. He believed Austria now desired changes, but that for this very reason Prussia would adopt the opposite course. A union of all the German princes supported by Britain and the "Northern Powers" would be the only means to prevent dissolution of the Empire and the spread of French principles which leveled all social bonds. Such a union could drive the French beyond their own borders if only the powers would subordinate all other interests. He pointedly expressed pride at serving to support the integrity of the Empire and inquired how far the king would go with regard to an armed alliance, threatening démarches, hostile demonstrations, and in the last analysis, war. Though he discreetly asked what territorial compensations Stockholm might contemplate if such a "false and iniquitous policy" became unavoidable, he probably only wanted complete instructions for every eventuality and, more important, to discover if the views of Engeström and his friends were gaining ground.[33]

Such apprehensions were not unfounded. *Rikskansler* Sparre quietly sounded out Berlin regarding cooperation in a territorial reorganization of the Empire in November. The new Prussian king, Frederick William III, however, had no wish to commit himself to any set course of action with Sweden, a rival power in northern Germany. At this point, Engeström was right: only an appeal to France might save the situation. But by then, the Congress of Rastadt was already convened and the fate of the Swedish mission to it decided.

3

Fersen departed for Rastadt on 13 November 1797. Two days later, he met Schörbing, who caught up with him in Karlsruhe.

M. Bildt had sent him to prepare me for the difficulties which would arise concerning my reception at the congress, according to Article 20 of the peace treaty, and to inform me that the [imperial] commissioner [to the diet at Regensburg], Baron Hügel, had said to him that he feared I could not be accepted since the Empire had not requested the king's guarantee. All this disturbed me a little.[35]

Arriving in Rastadt, he installed himself in a manner suitable to his position. In view of the outcome of his mission, contemporaries conceived exaggerated ideas of the incongruous splendor of his establishment. In actuality, he complained to Sophie of the expense of living, "without wishing to be magnificent" but "as befits an ambassador of the king," and as usual had trouble obtaining from Stockholm the compensation awarded him, which amounted to less for Fersen—the only diplomat with ambassador's rank at the congress—than the envoys of, for example, Saxony, Würtzburg, or Bremen.[36]

Fersen meanwhile set about planning his strategy:

While I was discussing with Schörbing, who is quite familiar with German politics and history, I decided to adopt the same behavior as Count Oldenburg, the Danish ambassador at the Peace of Nijmegen, who, to avoid problems of protocol between the emperor and the English, decided to remain incognito, while at the same time he lived and acted as an ambassador. He did not proclaim his position publicly and did not mount the arms of his country on his house until the day he departed. I think in this case, I will not seek to be accredited, and to exercise a necessary and direct influence upon affairs, I have suggested to the king that M. Schörbing be appointed resident for Pomerania, for the king is in any case obliged to have a representative in this capacity. At the conclusion of the congress, I will then protest against all the decisions that have been arrived at, and that I was not accepted.[37]

The situation did not seem promising. The ministers of Baden and Mainz, Barons Edelsheim and Albini, anticipated trouble and encouraged Fersen to keep in the background. Meanwhile, his own government remained strangely silent and he complained vainly, "were it not for Taube, I should have no idea about anything."[38]

On 25 November, General Bonaparte arrived to head the French delegation. Fersen sent Schörbing to pay an informal call and convey the Swedish ambassador's greetings, making conspicuous use of that title to test his reactions. Bonaparte was polite but avoided any inference that he recognized Fersen's status at Rastadt. If, Fersen commented, "one could assume a knowledge of diplomatic usage and customs on Buonaparte's part and the ability to weigh his words, one would have reason to fear difficulties...." The following day, Baron Edelsheim called on Bonaparte, who asked "whether there were not a minister...from Sweden. There was both an ambassador and a minister," Edelsheim answered, "but Buonaparte made no reply to this." He added, however, "Yes, Sweden and the republic are very good friends now. The small discords which existed previously have now been eliminated and there is really nothing to talk about."[39]

On 28 November, Fersen, accompanied by Bildt, went to make his own call on Bonaparte, "in a remarkably fine coach," according to Schörbing, "drawn by six white horses and surrounded by his servants." Bonaparte was attended by General Berthier and two adjutants, one of whom announced Fersen as the Swedish ambassador. There was at first polite conversation on indifferent subjects, but Bonaparte avoided addressing Fersen as ambassador. At length, Bonaparte inquired politely whether he was in Baden in connection with the king of Sweden's marriage. No, Fersen replied, "I have been sent here in the capacity of ambassador of the king to the congress." Bonaparte affected not to notice but soon asked, almost innocently, "Do you have a chargé d'affaires at present in Paris?" The answer was, of course, known to him, and Fersen could only reply that due to recent but insignificant misunderstandings, there was none at present. However, taking his cue from Bonaparte's conversation with Edelsheim the previous day, he pointed out that these difficulties were now apparently resolved and that diplomatic relations would now surely be renewed. Bonaparte pressed his advantage. "Yes," he replied,

... it seems to have been disagreeable to have to recognize the superiority of a republic, but I don't understand how Sweden can have such a poor understanding of her interests and does not see that she ought to enter into a treaty with the French republic. Since this latter always acts in a straightforward manner, it does not tolerate that lack of respect should be shown toward it and that persons should be sent to it who are repugnant because of the political role they have played, exactly as the king of Sweden would refuse to accept a person, whom one might wish to send to him, if he had taken part in a political movement directed against the king, and I hereby declare to the king of Sweden that the republic shall know how to uphold its dignity and that it will not tolerate that persons should be sent to it who perhaps are included on the list of émigrés and who directly took part in politics. All of this was much longer and more circumstantial, and was expressed slowly . . . like a lesson learned by heart, which he had mastered beforehand.

"I felt offended and upset by this declaration," Fersen continued, "which clearly referred to me." Bildt tried to fill the embarrassing silence that followed by saying something about the common interests of the two countries, then Fersen, adding he was sure his monarch would seek to maintain good relations with France, rose to leave.[40]

Bonaparte had not minced his words. He did not, however, even by his own testimony, definitely exclude the Swedish mission, or even Fersen personally, from the congress. In his official report to Gustav IV Adolf, Fersen played down Bonaparte's personal inferences, concluding:

Your Majesty will no doubt feel it is impossible on the basis of the details I have had the honor of placing before your eyes to conclude anything, and all I have seen cannot enlighten me any further whether this is due to lack of knowledge of the forms and usages, or if the failure to use the title of ambassador was intentional. The arrival of Count Metternich will resolve this doubt, and he is expected in three or four days.[41]

Bonaparte's version of the interview, in his report to Talleyrand of 30 November, showed considerable truculence:

The king of Sweden has sent the Baron [sic] de Fersen as his ambassador to the congress. The king of Sweden hopes to take part in the congress as a guarantor of the Peace of Westphalia. You will see he is looking a bit far back. If one were to authorize the king of Sweden, this would also authorize the emperor of Russia to intervene here as the guarantor of the Peace of Teschen. The Baron de Fersen came to see me, displaying all the fatuities of a courtier of the Œil-de-Bœuf. After the customary compliments, made by both but listened to by neither, I asked him who was the minister of H.M. the king of Sweden in Paris. He told me that for the time being there was none, but that this was the result of one of those little misunderstandings which can easily be worked out, and that already the petty dispute which had existed between the two powers had been settled. I then addressed him in these terms: The French nation and the house of Sweden have been joined together for several centuries; they have aided each other to destroy the pretentions of that arrogant house which in past centuries aimed, not without some prospect, at universal monarchy. A power, more dangerous to Sweden because it is closer, makes it no less imperative for her to reach an understanding with the French republic and unite geographically the political systems of the two powers. How can one then explain the conduct of the court of Sweden, which seems to make a point of seizing on opportunities to send—either to Paris or to French plenipotentiaries—agents, ministers, or ambassadors, whose persons are basically disagreeable to all French citizens? The king of Sweden would doubtless not regard with indifference a minister who had sought to stir up the people of Stockholm. No, Sir, the French republic will not tolerate that men who are too well known to it because of their connections with the former court of France, included, perhaps on the list of émigrés, should flaunt themselves before the ministers of the first people of the world. The French people, before considering its interests and its policies, will always first consider its dignity. During this discourse, the Baron de Fersen changed from one color to the next; he behaved in the manner of a courtier; he replied that His Majesty would take into consideration what I had said, and departed. I accompanied him, naturally, with the usual ceremonial. The Baron de Fersen was accompanied by the minister of the king of Sweden to Regensburg, who appeared to understand perfectly how the discourse I had held should serve as a guide for the conduct of the court of Stockholm.[42]

Bonaparte exhibited a similiar attitude the following day. He told Baron Albini he could not understand in what capacity Fersen was in Rastadt and could only regard him as an émigré. The same day, Edelsheim visited Bonaparte, who, according to Fersen,

. . . also spoke to him about me and said to him that it would be impossible, and that he would betray the Directory if he dealt [with me], that I had been in the French service and that I had been the leader of that party which had been the most violently opposed to the Revolution. The Baron, with whom I had spoken yesterday, said he knew it to be a fact that I had been in [French] service, but believed he had heard I had been released and had left the service in '89 or '90. Buonaparte said to him that he did not know everything: that I had slept with the queen. Edelsheim answered laughingly that he thought these epochs of ancient history had already been forgotten. Buonaparte repeated what he had already said before, and added that I had always acted against the republic, that they could not deal with me, and that besides, Sweden could not have ministers here, for if they were accepted, then Russia and other [powers] would also have [them], and upon Edelsheim's interjection that there had been no question of that, he replied that it was never too late.

Later in the day, Bonaparte told Albini he could not receive missions from any foreign power and that the Swedes could do what they wished, though he hoped they would not make themselves unpleasant to the French or seek to impede the peace settlement.[43]

What lay behind Bonaparte's behavior toward Fersen and his mission? In his instructions, Talleyrand had directed him to use all the resources of diplomacy, including intimidation. According to Ludovic Sciout, Bonaparte adopted from the start "the manners of an absolute monarch" at Rastadt and gave the Germans to understand that he contemplated the complete overthrow of the constitution of the Empire. "He strove," Sciout continues, "to terrify the plenipotentiaries to make them quickly accept all his proposals. The violent scene he made before Count Fersen could well have been premeditated toward this end." Bonaparte wanted "to distinguish himself by a stroke of brilliance and, scarcely having arrived, to play the part of the thundering Jupiter." In this respect, he evidently scored at least an initial success. "All the ministers are in despair," Fersen noted on 30 November, "and see everything in the blackest black." He considered seeking accreditation from the imperial minister and the *Reichsdeputation*, then having nothing further to do with the French; he foresaw, however, that fear would drive the Germans to refuse. "I see that all are gripped with terror," he wrote, "though they will still gain nothing by it." In the end, however, Bonaparte's threatening behavior did not bring the congress to a speedy conclusion. It dragged on for some seventeen months until the renewed war put an end to its long since futile existence.[44]

Bonaparte's conduct nonetheless showed certain ambiguities. He had not closed the door completely on the Swedish ambassador. Fersen brought himself to call on Bonaparte's two civilian associates, Bonnier, who was absent, and Treilhard, who was polite though noncommittal. He meanwhile wrote his king that only the arrival of the Austrian delegation would finally resolve his situation.[45]

If Bonaparte did not at first unconditionally exclude Fersen, it was probably in deference to his friend Talleyrand's designs for securing Staël's appointment to Paris. Bonaparte can, however, have seen little advantage in keeping the Swedish ambassador at Rastadt while circumstances made it possible to use him in the most striking manner to intimidate the German princes. Furthermore, by eliminating him, Sweden would be prevented from backing either Austria or Prussia against France at the congress, and most important, Russia would have no pretext for representation.[46]

If Bonaparte still hesitated, however, the matter was definitely resolved with the arrival of the Austrian delegates, Lehrbach, Cobenzl, and Metternich. On 29 November, he met with Ludwig von Cobenzl and, wrongly suspecting Fersen to be a protégé of the Austrians, emphasized his stern treatment of him. The Austrians, of course, now wanted Fersen excluded altogether and Cobenzl reminded Bonaparte that to accept him would violate the Treaty of Campo Formio. If, despite this, he were accredited, Austria would demand Russian representation. Bonaparte thereupon agreed no outside powers should be admitted, as he stressed later the same day to both Edelsheim and Albini, and in his report to Talleyrand on his interview with Fersen.[47]

The importance of Fersen himself to the manner in which his delegation was received has been much discussed. It was formerly assumed that French animosity toward him personally was a major, if not decisive factor in its rejection. Fersen himself expressed such fears to Taube in December 1797.[48] Later studies have, however, demonstrated the overriding importance of political factors.[49] Fersen's personal importance derived partly from the program he was known to represent, partly from his international reputation, which together with Sweden's diplomatic isolation permitted Bonaparte to make an example of him with telling effect and without fear of reprisal.

This naturally caused a sensation. Count Lavalette, one of Bonaparte's two adjutants present at their interview, called it the one remarkable event of the general's short stay at Rastadt.[50] Its effect on the German delegates has been seen. In Paris, the *Moniteur,* after a truculent description of the meeting, based almost word for word on Bonaparte's report to Talleyrand, concluded triumphantly, "We are informed that M. de Fersen retired somewhat taken aback... and one is tempted to laugh at the figure which one of the heroes of the former court was obliged to cut in the presence of the hero of the republic." From Rastadt and Paris, the news spread throughout Europe. *The Times* of London, for instance, made a number of comments on the incident and expressed apprehension over "the known principles of the new Diplomatic Revolutionary System." Fersen, who read *The Times* regularly, took exception to these notices, which he felt were not entirely accurate, and "they speak of me and the unfortunate queen, which offended me."[51]

To the surprise of all, Bonaparte departed Rastadt after only five days, on 2 December 1797. Though his absence was announced as only temporary, speculation was soon rife. It was rumored he was on bad terms with Treilhard and Bonnier, who intrigued to remove him. Fersen quickly suspected deeper reasons:

Perhaps also—and this seems most likely to me—it is the Directory which uses the excuse of pressing business, while their reason is actually to be able to keep inside France a man who seems dangerous to them and whose repute arouses their jealousy and envy; so much the more as they live in a republic. However it may be, this man is moving, sooner or later, toward his fall, if he returns to France. But he is a Frenchman and gullible, for they learn nothing from example. Anyway, after seeing how petty this supposedly great man is in his behavior, I will say amen to anything that may happen to him.

Fersen's personal bitterness, characteristically repressed, is evident. "This famous general," he wrote the day before, "in his manner and conduct is an absolute upstart who thinks it distinguished to be insolent and worthy to be arrogant." He rightly concluded that Bonaparte would not return and continued to suspect the sincerity of his republicanism. When in the spring of 1798, Bonaparte was sent to Brest to command the Army of England, Fersen concluded this was simply to get him out of Paris. It seemed to confirm the end of his active career, for, Fersen noted, the semi-official *Rédacteur* was now urging that it was in India that Britain should be attacked. The French expedition which had meanwhile begun to form in Toulon gave rise to some fantastic speculation. One possibility, Fersen shrewdly wrote his government on 25 April, was that the French intended "to seize Egypt and to move from there against India." This idea was not as impractical as it seemed; Vergennes had considered it during the American war. The Indian potentates might be stirred up against the British. But this depended on naval superiority in the Mediterranean, and "without the cooperation of the Turks, the operation would become impossible because of the ease with which provisions could be removed and the country through which this armed corps would have to pass could be ravaged." Fersen thus looked for more likely objectives; the most probable seemed to him that suggested by the Prussian diplomat, Baron Jacobi, on 15 May: that the French expedition "was destined for the Crimea in order to support Poland and to revolutionize Europe by stealing in the back door in this way."[52]

Meanwhile, Fersen sought to learn Austria's attitude toward his mission. On 5 December, he called on his friend, Baron Franz von Metternich. Sweden, he argued, could not be considered a "foreign power," as "possessionary within the Empire and guarantor," and

. . . I assumed that, whatever the result of this negotiation [with France] might be, this naturally would not influence the imperial ministers and the Empire, since the king [of Sweden] in his double role had the right, even the duty, to be represented and to take part in a congress convened to deal with and watch over the maintenance of the Empire and its constitution . . .

Metternich took refuge in evasiveness, claiming that only the *Reichsdeputation* could decide the question, but urged him to postpone his request for recognition. Lacking definite instructions from Stockholm, Fersen felt constrained to do so.[53]

The attitude of the Austrian government was emphasized by the coolness with which Fersen was treated socially by its representatives, especially Cobenzl. The delegates of the petty German principalities hastened to follow suit and Fersen found himself largely ostracized, a new and disagreeable experience for one lionized all his life. In private, Lehrbach, whom Bonaparte dismissed as the "Tyrolese Don Quixote," was amiable enough and Metternich was distressed by the role he was obliged to play in public.[54]

As early as May 1797, Fersen wrote his sister of the rumor that the Austrians were prepared to sacrifice the Austrian Netherlands to France for compensation in Italy. From that time on, he was apprehensive of an understanding between the Austrians and the French at the expense of the Empire. He observed French efforts to "republicanize" the left bank of the Rhine with much anxiety, seeing in them the prelude to annexation, while by the end of November he understood Austrian policy to be "diametrically opposed to the obligations of the emperor as head of the Empire." By this time, the other envoys to the congress were no less worried.

The denouement came on 9 December, when Lehrbach announced the withdrawal of Austrian troops west of the Rhine; the following day the French advanced on Mainz. The furor that followed quickly spread throughout Europe. Abandoned by their emperor, the smaller German princes struggled to survive the territorial reorganization as best they could. The Treaty of Westphalia was now a dead letter. "Everyone is sacrificing his neighbor to preserve himself and to indemnify himself at the latter's expense," Fersen wrote his government on 30 December 1797. By early January, Mainz capitulated. The futile bargaining with the French began, in which the Germans were forced back, step by step, to the Rhine. On 20 January, the Directory demanded the cession of the entire left bank. "You cannot imagine what passions prevail against the emperor," Fersen wrote Taube on 26 December, ". . . worse treachery and falseness have surely never been seen before." Fersen meanwhile perceived French policy within Germany to consist of strengthening the smaller principalities along the Rhine and attaching them to France through fear, self-interest or gratitude, to counterbalance the great Germanic powers.[55] The idea was a venerable one in French diplomacy and would come to fruition with the Confederation of the Rhine in 1806.

There remained little Fersen could do. He sent Bildt to the diet at Regensburg to vote on behalf of Swedish Pomerania for the integrity of the Empire.[56] According to Schörbing, Fersen "lived as befitted an ambassador, often saw a crowd of German envoys to the congress at his table, . . . frequently attended the public gatherings. . . ." Meanwhile, he could only speculate and write his recommendations to Stockholm. He realized the title of ambassador was now a liability and suggested to Taube on 20 December his reappointment as minister. A week later, he wrote that if the rejection of his mission were a matter of his person, he was prepared to give his place to someone else, painful as that would be. Already on 16 November, he recommended that Schörbing be separately appointed envoy for the duchy of Pomerania; by early January, he proposed that his own mission represent Pomerania only. Finally, on 21 February, on Taube's suggestion, he recommended that he divide his time between Rastadt and Karlsruhe, letting Bildt represent Sweden as minister for Pomerania, without himself renouncing his appointment, allowing him thus to continue to follow affairs.[57]

4

In Stockholm, the news from Rastadt caused considerable alarm and the young king seemed sunk in dejection. The Swedish government sent Fersen vague and useless instructions, and often none at all. Before long, however, there were signs of a change.

On 19 December, *Rikskansler* Sparre resigned and the management of foreign affairs was confided to Fredrik Wilhelm von Ehrenheim, formerly minister to Denmark, in the subordinate office of *hovkansler*. Eventually then, a new *rikskansler* could be installed; perhaps Gustav IV Adolf still wanted Fersen when circumstances permitted. Ehrenheim's appointment nonetheless marked a new direction in Swedish policy. On 29 December, Staël was at last appointed envoy to Paris with instructions to improve Franco-Swedish relations. In March 1798, Lars von Engeström was made minister to Berlin.

Ehrenheim directed Staël to seek Fersen's accreditation at Rastadt. Staël went through the motions with a certain lack of zeal and readily accepted Talleyrand's reply: "after the astonishment this choice has caused in Europe and the commotion that followed it, how can one keep insisting?"[58]

Staël's appointment to Paris represented a remarkable *volte-face*. If the choice of Fersen in the summer of 1797 showed Sweden's intention of opposing France, that of Staël at the end of the year clearly demonstrated the desire for rapprochement. Various factors worked in favor of such a change, including Sweden's diplomatic isolation and stiffening French policy toward neutral shipping.

The real reason for the new policy, however, was revealed gradually in Ehrenheim's correspondence with Staël. Sweden would not oppose changes in Germany, despite the Treaty of Westphalia, but would seek to protect Swedish possessions and obtain compensations with French assistance. On 20 January 1798, he revealed his concrete plan: a great project of territorial exchanges through which Sweden would acquire Norway from Denmark. Pomerania would be ceded to Prussia, which would compensate Denmark in north Germany. The king was prepared to offer concessions for French support, though he would not go to war in France's behalf and he declined to use force against Denmark.[59]

The acquisition of Norway was no new idea. Gustav III had been particularly taken with it, encouraged by Creutz and Taube, and it was of course eventually to be realized in 1814. Taube cannot have failed to impress its importance on the young king. Given Sweden's difficult diplomatic position, the idea of profiting from the reorganization of Germany to acquire Norway naturally suggested itself.

The king must have feared Taube would disapprove of acquiring Norway if this meant cooperation with France, for he showed an increasing coolness toward him by the turn of the year. Given the objective, however, even Taube, it appears, temporarily overcame his animosity toward France. As early as 15 December 1797, he urged Fersen that it was "entirely necessary," despite the slights to which he might be exposed, that he maintain the greatest courtesy toward the French, "for the sake of the good cause." Fersen repeatedly assured his friend that unpleasant as it was, he was making every effort, though the French remained hostile.[60]

Fersen was not slow in recognizing the signs of change from Stockholm. He quickly surmised that Taube was losing influence with the king and feared that which Ehrenheim might exert in his stead. Both he and Taube were alarmed and indignant to discover signs that their private correspondence was being opened and read by unknown persons, whom Taube presumed to be acting on behalf of Staël and his friends. Fersen was greatly upset upon learning of his old antagonist's appointment to Paris, while the thought that his own recognition at Rastadt might be arranged in return for this filled him with chagrin. All these signs pointed toward the thing he was most strongly set against: an entente with the French republic. He continued to oppose territorial acquisitions as both unethical and impolitic, and strongly disapproved of the Norwegian exchange plan when he finally learned of it, for "I do not favor changes in general just now and especially making any use whatsoever of the mediation of the French," and Norway could only be obtained through humiliating or compromising concessions.[61]

Fersen wrote his own views regarding France and the peace settlement to Gustav IV Adolf on 31 January 1798. He recommended a plan which had come to his attention to prevent the French from obtaining German territory,

... and asked him whether he wished me to support this, as well as to demand that he and Russia should be mediators, and whether he in such a case would not wish to abstain from demanding any territorial gains, which would make his voice more effective and [himself] better able to play his role as mediator. It seemed to me it was important to present this perspective to prevent him from committing himself too much or concluding an alliance with the French; and I recommended to Taube in the most energetic terms that such a treaty be prevented with so unreliable and unstable a government, which would only leave us exposed.

The *Reichsdeputation* should make peace as quickly as possible with France, leaving details of compensation and exchange, which were an "internal affair," to be worked out later, with Russia and Sweden as guarantors, and even France, if this could not be avoided, but only on condition that French troops be withdrawn from the Empire. "Your Majesty will without doubt feel this course would be the wisest for the Empire," he wrote.

It will hasten the conclusion of the peace which is in my opinion the only remaining way to save Europe, to destroy the power of the republic and to put an end to projects destructive of all monarchies; for once their armies have returned to France and no longer have anything to occupy them except internal affairs, civil war cannot fail to break out, and because of the spirit of hatred, jealousy, vengeance, and egotism that reigns there, it will surely be terrible. The republic will then no longer be in a position to intervene in external matters and this would be the only time to force it to give up its conquests and to stop the propagation of its revolutionary principles.[62]

What seemed most striking to Fersen about France was not strength—which in his eyes derived mainly from disunity among her opponents—but rather weakness. The answer to the European crisis lay in that union of the German courts with the Northern powers that he had proposed to his king on 4 November 1797, before the congress had convened. In frequent dispatches during the winter of 1797–98, Fersen strove to impress these considerations upon his monarch.[63]

Opposed by France and abandoned by Austria, Fersen now focused his interest on Prussia. Upon the influence of that power at Rastadt would depend the chances of a union of the German princes to stem the tide of French expansion. Before the congress, Fersen had been concerned over rumors of Prussian plans of aggrandizement. When Austria sought territorial changes in concert with France, however, he assumed Prussia would take the opposite course and seek to persuade the German delegates at Rastadt to uphold the integrity of the Empire.[64]

Barons Görtz and Jacobi, representing the Prussian king as elector of Brandenburg, arrived in Rastadt in mid-December. Fersen was soon on good terms with them and Jacobi undertook to reason with Treilhard, now chief of the French delegation, concerning Fersen's accreditation, though without result. It was upon recommendation of the Prussian envoys that Fersen proposed to relinquish his ambassador's title for that of minister, later that the Swedish mission be "patterned after that of Prussia," that is, ostensibly to represent Pomerania only, and finally, that the Swedish Pomeranian mission work in concert with that of Prussian Brandenburg. Before long, however, Fersen's hopes gave way to disillusionment. Berlin was too cautious to declare itself unequivocally either for or against territorial changes and as relations between France and Austria deteriorated, took the lead among the smaller German courts in a temporizing and ambiguous policy toward both sides.[65]

To *Hovkansler* Ehrenheim in Stockholm, Fersen was not only an obstacle to rapprochement with France, but obviously the wrong man to represent a policy of territorial compensation and exchange. Gustav IV Adolf was gradually obliged to concede on this point. Meanwhile, Ehrenheim privately instructed Bildt in Rastadt on 19 and 29 December to inform the French envoys of the king's desire for friendly relations with their government. In mid-January, Treilhard showed himself favorable toward a Swedish representative for Pomerania and well-disposed toward Bildt personally.[66]

Step by step the Swedish government retreated at Rastadt. On 24 January 1798, Fersen was sent new accreditation as minister; he was to seek representation for Pomerania if it could not be obtained for Sweden, as he himself had suggested. On 13 February, he was directed to sign documents only as major-general and three days later, to withdraw to nearby Karlsruhe, using as a pretext the exchange of the Swedish marriage contract with that court. On 22 February, Bildt was instructed to take over the mission and was received as minister for Pomerania by Treilhard. On 29 March, Fersen departed for Karlsruhe.[67]

Despite the reproaches of older historians, Fersen carried out his assignment as well as could be hoped for under the most difficult of conditions. Originally appointed to represent a hard anti-French policy at the congress in conjunction with the Austrians, he found himself abandoned by them. He then made every effort to secure recognition for his mission through unofficial representations, seeking to avoid the humiliation to his government of a formal refusal. He sought support first from Austria, then from Prussia. Aware of his country's isolation, he also tried to come to good terms with the French delegation. Throughout, he remained true to his own principles and defended them to his government despite its shifting policy. He could hardly have done more and he could write with a certain satisfaction on 2 April, how Gustav Adolf had told Taube, "that he could not praise highly enough my wise behavior, my courtesy and self-forgetfulness in the advancement of his interests."[68]

The Norwegian exchange plan quickly fell through. Staël in Paris made only halfhearted soundings in its behalf while Engeström in Berlin constantly opposed the sacrifice of Sweden's German territories. By the end of March 1798, Ehrenheim informed Staël that the exchange was no longer feasible; it was evident that the three-way agreement between France, Austria, and Prussia, upon which it was predicated, would not now come about and a new European conflict seemed in the offing.

Considering this project in retrospect, one is impressed by its manifest impracticality. Gustav IV Adolf entertained the most sanguine hopes for it but one cannot but wonder whether Ehrenheim, with his close acquaintance with Denmark, could sincerely have believed in it. A more probable explanation seems to be that he used it as a means to induce the king to abandon the untenable position he sought to maintain at Rastadt, to avoid overdependence on Russia and to restore normal relations with France, thereby assuring Sweden's neutrality and security. By the time the plan was jettisoned, these ends had been at least temporarily attained. The likeminded Staël and Engeström had been installed in vital posts in Paris and Berlin, where they then apparently helped Ehrenheim to bury the project to which they owed their appointments. Taube lost influence and Fersen was dismissed from Rastadt. Speaking of diplomacy, Engeström had complained in December 1797, "Our vocation is like a violin, a difficult instrument, yet all still play upon it." On 5 April 1798, Ehrenheim was able to write to him that foreign affairs "are now handled in such a way that no one is likely to look into them except those who should and can be trusted."[69]

CHAPTER XI

Karlsruhe, Berlin, and Karlsbad, 1798–1799

1

Fersen departed with mixed feelings. The experience at Rastadt had been a bitter one. He had nonetheless hoped to remain there to avoid the appearance of submission to the French and "to follow all the intrigues, happenings and persons" from the scene itself. The order to leave "is furthermore a superfluous measure, since the French did not even think of it." They were still glad to see him go, as Talleyrand assured Staël.[1]

The exchange of marriage contracts at the court of Karlsruhe involved only a few simple formalities. Fersen, however, remained there for nearly a year, as long as the congress continued in Rastadt, only six hours away. According to older accounts, his activities were now limited to giving good dinners. Clearly the presence of a diplomat of high rank and international reputation at the modest court of Baden implied more than this. Gustav IV Adolf instructed him to follow events and assist Bildt with advice.[2]

From Karlsruhe, Fersen wrote constant and detailed dispatches. He sent news from a wide variety of sources of the continued progress of the congress, internal developments in France, Bonaparte's Egyptian campaign, the spread of revolutionary activity in Switzerland, Germany, and Italy, the tyranny of the French in the regions they occupied, the rivalry between Austria and Prussia, and the steady drift toward a new war.[3] These were doubtless of great value to his government at a time when news consisted

256

so largely of rumor. Fersen's diary and dispatches do not suggest that he gave Bildt much in the way of advice. Little could now be expected from the congress or Bildt's participation. If the situation had changed, Fersen might yet have played a significant part. Meanwhile, his position was discouraging. Neither he nor Bildt was kept well informed by their government. "I recalled continuously that day seven years ago," he mused on 19 June 1798. "It was the day before the departure [for Varennes]. . . . What a difference in my position! I was then the friend and confidant of three sovereigns, at the head of a great enterprise. This failed, and the three princes are dead."[4]

In his dispatchs, Fersen consistently maintained the viewpoint he had upheld at Rastadt. He continued to oppose annexations, exchanges, or any commitments toward France. His ideal remained the great coalition of German and Northern powers against the republic, for which he urged that Sweden be prepared to abandon her neutrality. Any accommodations with the French would lead to fresh encroachments. They could only be halted by determined opposition.[5]

Fersen's ideas seemed vindicated by events during the remainder of 1798. The congress soon became stalemated: Austria began to look for allies in a new coalition, while the smaller German princes, fearful both of war and the spread of revolutionary principles, played for time. The Revolution advanced rapidly in Italy and Switzerland, where satellite republics were established, and seemed to threaten all of southern Germany.[6]

Fersen's anxiety over the revolutionary threat now seemed to reach its peak, becoming greater than during the Terror itself. The Revolution then seemed on the point of destroying itself, a hope Fersen was loathe to give up. As long as the war continued, even when the French were most successful, monarchical Europe was at least capable of resistance. Now that peace had come, the Directory could employ "more treacherous means" to "revolutionize" Europe. "The intention of the French," he wrote in January 1798, "is clearly to turn all Europe into republics, and through their ignominious behavior and lack of unity, the [European] rulers are destroying each other mutually."[7]

It was not France as a power he feared; the weaknesses of the Directory were obvious. He felt only contempt for the German princes who cringed and toadied to the French at Rastadt and deplored their "blindness" to their real, common interest. The

Directory exploited their avarice and encouraged them to intrigue against each other.[8] By submerging their differences, Fersen was confident that the united powers could defeat France, even in a single campaign. The French were not blind to their predicament and despite their bluff at Rastadt were anxious to avoid war. For this very reason, they should be attacked without delay.[9]

The real danger, in Fersen's eyes, was that France was the center of Jacobinism and "new ideas" which threatened the "total dissolution" of all organized society. Indeed, the Directory itself, no less than other European governments, seemed menaced by them. After the coup of 18 Fructador, the moderates, having used the Jacobins to purge their royalist opponents, appeared increasingly threatened by their former allies to the left.[10]

In April 1798, the French envoy to Vienna, General J.-B. Bernadotte, provoked a riot there by flying the tricolor flag from his balcony. Bernadotte, Fersen wrote of the future king of Sweden, was "one of the raging Jacobins," and he suspected him of staging the affair to embarrass the Directory and influence elections in favor of the extreme faction.[11]

With the approach of a renewed war, Fersen wrote in November, the Directory feared that the Jacobins might gain the upper hand.

Meanwhile, the exaggerated demands of the Austrians will presumably drive them to war; for put in the position of having to choose between two evils, between being driven out [of power] and accused of treason for having proposed an ignominious peace, or reconciling themselves with the Jacobins under the hardest terms, they will surely choose the latter. One sees on the basis of all these details that the Directory is disconcerted and that this would be a favorable time to attack it with a strong coalition.[12]

The Directory could not suppress Jacobinism, which must therefore be accomplished by crushing the Directory. Only then would France cease to be a center of contagion. As seen, Fersen believed once the French armies were driven within their own frontiers, a civil war would develop which would hasten the final collapse of the Revolution.

If Jacobinism continued to exist, this seemed to him less the fault of the hapless Directory than of the European monarchs in whose power it lay to destroy it. Everything depended on their ability to unite. As 1798 wore on, the powers moved toward a new coalition and a new war seemed imminent. Symptomatic was the new affability Count Cobenzl, recently so uncivil, showed toward Fersen by the spring of 1798.[13]

By fall, preparations proceeded rapidly on both sides. There was unrest in the Rhineland, Alsace, and the Vendée; the Netherlands and Switzerland were in open revolt. The Turks declared war on the invaders of Egypt and the Neapolitans invaded the Roman republic. When Russian troops passed through Austria on their way to Italy, the Directory sent its ultimatum to Vienna.[14]

Even after Austria entered the war, the French maintained their mission in Rastadt to seek to prevent the smaller German states from joining the coalition. The emperor withdrew his delegation and notified the congress that he no longer regarded Rastadt as neutral ground. This was emphasized by the appearance nearby of wild Szekler hussars. Most of the German delegates departed forthwith. When the three French ministers attempted to leave on 28 April 1799, however, they were mysteriously ambushed and killed by a band of Szeklers.[15]

Thus ended the Congress of Rastadt. The assassination of the French delegates caused a sensation throughout Europe. The Austrian government denied responsibility but could not dispel rumors that highly placed persons were involved. Characteristically, Fersen suspected provocation by the French themselves. "It justifies all the lies which the French can spread," he wrote indignantly on 7 May, "and can be dangerous for all ministers."[16]

2

Fersen's presence in Karlsruhe did not pass unnoticed in counterrevolutionary circles. In Rastadt, he had scrupulously avoided contact with émigrés, seeking to deny the French pretexts to refuse his mission.[17] Now he was under no such constraint.

Mallet du Pan, driven from his native Switzerland by revolution, passed through Karlsruhe where he visited an émigré named Saint-Génié, who lived in Fersen's *Gasthaus*. Mallet also called on Fersen before continuing on his way. Saint-Génié then introduced himself, thereby opening a curious and interesting episode. On 15 July, Fersen noted:

M. de Génié came to see me and confided he was at the head of the society for counteracting the Jacobins which was mentioned in an article in the Frankfurt newspaper. . . . He is working in the greatest secrecy to get this underway. He showed me his plan which is based on the idea that there should be a center, from which everything should emanate, but that to prevent treachery, this center should consist of only four persons, and all the other members should have to deal with only two persons, selected by certain others who should be directed and for whom meetings should be arranged in a suitable manner. This could well be useful, but to be so, it is necessary that it should really be kept secret, that there should be other writers, a printing shop, and that sufficient care be taken that it not degenerate into acts of cruelty like the secret tribunal in Germany. He told me it would be necessary to have a leader or protector and appeared to wish this should be the king of Sweden. I would not hear of this. I know very well the late king would have been ideal for this, but I do not know the present one well enough to know whether he would be interested in proposals of this kind.[18]

Though Fersen's first reaction was characteristically cautious, the basic idea could not but impress him. It appealed to fundamental principles in his own thinking: his belief that Jacobinism could only be fought effectively with its own weapons, that the anti-Jacobin forces should unite under a central leadership—a "Committee of Public Safety"—and that public opinion must be prepared in France for a successful military invasion. Thereafter, Saint-Génié frequently visited Fersen, in whose diary there emerge the rough outlines of an anti-Jacobin league. Its hierarchical organization was clearly based on the secret lodges which throve so luxuriantly in the last years of the old regime. The identity of its highest council, which was to include Fersen, would not be divulged to less exalted members and elaborate provisions were made for secret rendezvous. Lest monarchs fear the formation of a state within their states, they might be invited to participate. The purposes of the society were to be several: to disseminate anti-Jacobin propaganda, to spy on the Jacobins to discover their intentions, to plan strategy against specific Jacobin projects in different areas, to gain influence in European courts and advise monarchs of these threats, of measures to counteract them, and the identity of Jacobin sympathizers within their own territories and governments. Measures were apparently also considered for direct action against suspect individuals where considered necessary.[19]

Saint-Génié himself seems a character out of a romantic novel. He was, Fersen commented, "a man no one really knows."

He says he is Spanish by birth, that he had a fortune in France and was descended from the royal family. He has been used by Louis XVIII to win supporters and influence elections [in France], has had dealings with Mr. Wickham in Switzerland, has been in England, has been employed by the old regime in Turkey, &c., &c. He has been everywhere and has kept his connections with the Jacobins in France.

Little more is known of him, for the émigré literature scarcely mentions him. That he was an adventurer and an accomplished intriguer is clear. He had mysterious dealings with a variety of people, including the French chargé d'affaires in Karlsruhe, though Fersen, after initial suspicions, seems to have been satisfied that his anti-Jacobinism was genuine enough. Saint-Génié later acquired much influence over Margrave Karl Friedrich of Baden, to the dismay of his principal minister, Baron Edelsheim, who favored cooperation with France. He was later suspected of influencing Gustav IV Adolf to join the Third Coalition in 1804. Saint-Génié was finally expelled from Baden in 1805 and apparently made his way to the Russian army.[20]

Through Saint-Génié, Fersen met the no less colorful Auguste Danican, a former republican general who had fought against the Vendéeans but was suspected of intriguing with them, later commanded the royalist *sectionnaires* in Paris on 13 Vendemaire, but escaped to become a vociferous counterrevolutionary pamphleteer. He now offered to go to Berlin, Fersen wrote, "to discover the Jacobins who are scattered throughout the army and bureaucracy."[21]

The Prussian envoy at Rastadt, Baron von Görtz, upon whom Fersen urged Danican's proposal, was understandably unenthusiastic and it was dropped. Fersen was, however, impressed with Danican's zeal in uncovering Jacobin plots and skill as a propagandist. The local authorities frequently observed the two together. In July 1798, Danican published his best-known pamphlet, *Cassandra*, calling for the assassination of the Directory. He was therefore later suspected of complicity in the murder of the French envoys to Rastadt in the spring of 1799. The point is debatable and has nothing to do with Fersen, who strongly disapproved of the deed. Danican meanwhile supplied him with a steady stream of disturbing reports on the growing Jacobin menace throughout Europe. For a time these apparently formed the substance of much in Fersen's own dispatches to Stockholm. Danican also continued his pamphleteering, with financial assistance from Fersen.[22]

Fersen, Saint-Génié, and Danican strove to influence various German courts and impress them with the danger threatening them all. On 29 October, Fersen visited the Austrian envoy, Count von Lehrbach, in Rastadt,

> ... to whom I told the details I had gotten from General Danican, of which he demanded a summary. I also spoke with him about the plan for an [anti-Jacobin] association and he was completely in favor of it. He said such [an association] had been under consideration for a long time and that he, with this in mind, had recommended to his government that the Jesuit order be reestablished.[23]

The parallel is striking. A week later, Fersen sent Lehrbach a plan that Danican had prepared for countering Jacobin plots in Württemberg, then considered the center of revolutionary ferment in Germany. The project, which reveals the level of its author's political sophistication, begins with a grandiose description of alleged French ambitions to spread revolution, first in south Germany, then beyond. It was their strategy to "revolutionize" the region between the Rhine and the Danube, clearing the road to Vienna and encouraging insurrection in Bohemia and Hungary. "Let us observe," the author warned, "that Pasawan Oglou [sic] still exists and that his situation is not desperate." The rest of the Empire would be like "a city blockaded between two towns already taken," while "the total ruin of the Directory will not prevent it from ruining its neighbors."[24]

French machinations must thus be met with "counter-machinations." The Jacobins in Stuttgart without question planned disturbances to compel the duke of Württemberg to repress them. The insurgents would then raise the cry of "tyranny" and call on the French to intervene in "the plaintive accents of good citizens demanding their liberty." The writer therefore proposed to stage a little scene between a pretended "Jacobin" and a "moderate," who would "meet by chance" at an inn, where they would fall to arguing loudly and publicly about politics, the "Jacobin" making preposterous and frightening statements. The "moderate" would threaten to report him. The "Jacobin" would leave and disappear without a trace. An "agent of the police" would arrive and searching the "Jacobin's" room, find a box, in which

> ... there is discovered a quantity of notes, letters, plans, some of which are written in an enigmatic fashion and others in sympathetic ink. Great pains are taken to put into these notes everything that might alarm the peasants. There is mention of all the resources to be found in the country

in horses and provisions of all kinds. A connection between the revolutionizing of Württemberg and that of Bavaria must not be forgotten. Two or three national cocardes and some civil and military passports from the French republic are found in the small trunk. (We have all of this.)

The shocking discovery would be announced to the public and the duke would be justified in taking repressive measures. The Stuttgart Jacobins would be "petrified" and "honest men would gain the upper hand." At the same time, pro-monarchical propaganda would "rally subjects to their prince." The author offered his own services for this "counter-intrigue," which would require only a fortnight, plus naturally the necessary funds.[25]

Saint-Génié and Fersen meanwhile attempted to win over the margrave of Baden, but the amiable and elderly Karl Friedrich wavered between fear of Jacobinism and the pro-French opportunism of Baron Edelsheim. Danican went to Württemberg to warn its ruler of his impending fate. Meanwhile, Saint-Génié visited Brunswick. "He was delighted with the duke," Fersen noted, "who spoke of me with respect and good will, and sent greetings to me." The old field marshal of 1792 favored their cause, adding his prestige to it, and turned his influence in Berlin against the peace party of Prince Henry. That the anti-Jacobin league developed beyond the imaginations of its authors seems verified by a letter from a Baron von Berckheim in Baden, which Fersen received in May 1799. People were no longer armed as in the days of the *Vehmgerichte*, the baron commented; police were more efficient and rulers feared secret organizations. Nevertheless, the movement was catching on and there were more recruits than could be utilized.[26]

In time, Danican's sensationalism became too much even for Fersen. After receiving one of his alarming reports in November, Fersen observed, "I believe he is right, but I doubt it will go as fast as he seemed to believe." "I received a new letter from General Danican," he wrote a few weeks later. "He is really altogether too alarmed and sees far too many Jacobins, though it is evident such exist and that the danger is at hand." Fersen thereafter apparently lost interest in him. Perhaps his ironic comments in March 1799 about an English soldier of fortune named Morgan, formerly in French service, and now in contact with the exiled Carnot and Pichegru, reflect his disenchantment with Danican and his type.

Saint-Génié, who had pretentions to gentility, was no doubt more to his taste and they continued to correspond for a time after Fersen left Karlsruhe.[27]

With his two associates, Fersen had striven to establish the anti-Jacobin League and to fulfill some of its functions. Their actions as individuals could not, however, bring great results and they were only one of many competing anti-revolutionary cabals. When Berckheim wrote of the progress of the movement in his area, Fersen commented, "I fear such associations will spread regardless of the rulers if they do not join them." Fersen knew how impotent such groups could be against the forces of the Revolution and was too much a royalist to approve their existence independently of, or even in competition with, legitimate monarchs. To be effective, the league would have to be sanctioned by the monarchical powers, which could best be achieved if it were headed by an important royal person. One of Fersen's first acts when he returned to Stockholm in October 1799 was thus to describe the whole ambitious project to Gustav IV Adolf and to offer him its direction.[28]

3

Fersen was no stranger to Karlsruhe. In the fall of 1797, he met Gustav IV Adolf's intended bride and her family, and while in Rastadt he not infrequently visited their court. He soon became the close confidant of Crown Princess Amalia Frederike, mother of the young Swedish queen, who showed a marked weakness for him. He was thus kept informed of the most intimate details of her daughter's marriage, shared her concern over its unpromising beginning and her relief when, as Fersen expressed it delicately, the young couple "found the key to solve the great mystery." Indeed, before long it seemed the king was too preoccupied with his young consort, to the neglect of state matters.[29]

Fersen's diary gives an interesting picture of life at a small German court in this period, with its pretentions to grandeur on a modest scale, its miniature Versailles, its favorites, its scandals. "I saw," Fersen mused, "that there was no court too small to carry on the same intrigues as a large one."[30]

Fersen's stay in Karlsruhe was not overly eventful and he frequently complained of boredom. "I felt doubly," he wrote in June, "how dreary it is to have to live alone and abandoned to one's servants, for no matter how unusual they are, one can never enjoy their company." His health remained indifferent. Though he avoided Rastadt for a few months, later he often visited the city while the congress continued, noted of course by the French. On such occasions, he delighted in political and social gossip, and keenly regretted that circumstances kept him from the center of things. Nevertheless, when the time came, he left Karlsruhe with a certain poignant sadness: "... it felt as though I had left my own family, so well had I been received and so much had I already become accustomed to being here."[31]

On 25 December 1798, Fersen learned from Ehrenheim that the king would shortly terminate his mission, though he regretted losing Fersen's "enlightening correspondence." Because of information Fersen could obtain but Bildt in Rastadt could not, events in this critical period may have given Gustav Adolf second thoughts, for Fersen's orders failed to arrive week after week. When hostilities in the area became imminent, Fersen finally departed Karlsruhe without them on 3 March 1799.[32]

4

Fersen might have returned to his former existence. Indeed, it was rumored in Sweden that he would remain a permanent expatriate.[33] Shortly before he left Karlsruhe, however, his relationship with Eleanore Sullivan finally broke up. Eleanore had long assured Axel she was not happy with Craufurd and wished to be his alone. For about a year, in 1796–97, she even separated from Craufurd, though for propriety she would not live with Axel and was circumspect about seeing him. The situation thus remained frustrating. "As for marriage," Axel wrote Sophie in April 1797,

... she has never spoken to me about it out of delicacy but she would be far from refusing it if I should insist.... but I, my dear friend, prefer to live with a person free in choice and will, and to be assured that there is nothing forced or constrained in our pleasures or the proofs of attachment she gives me. I would love her and would treat her as my wife, and perhaps I would end by marrying her, but I do not wish to start with this. I would not cease to fear she would be with me only because of that and from then on I could no longer be happy ...

"The marriage day is the tomb of love," he wrote in his diary in January 1799. There meanwhile remained the problem of Eleanore's daughter, Quella, whom Axel could not abide and for whom he neither could nor would assume responsibility. Repeated negotiations for the girl's marriage failed, to Fersen's chagrin, because of her shameless coquetry with all and sundry, or her lack of a sufficient dowry to outweigh her obvious faults of character. Axel and Eleanore thus awaited an end to the war, which would permit Craufurd and her to return to Paris to straighten out their finances, so that Eleanore could provide for Quella and make a decent break with Craufurd. This last was important. Both Axel and Eleanore were by nature discreet and careful about appearances, while despite their awkward relationship, Fersen and Craufurd remained friends. Thus while Fersen dreaded the approaching peace for political reasons, he awaited it eagerly to resolve his personal problem. Eleanore repeatedly promised "in the strongest and most solemn manner" to leave Craufurd when circumstances permitted. Fersen's diplomatic appointments in Rastadt and Karlsruhe intervened, and during 1798 he saw Eleanore only once, in August. He meanwhile suspected that despite her good intentions, she was too soft-hearted and weak to break with Craufurd. On occasion he felt her ardor was cooling and he was himself more prepared to contemplate a future without her. She no longer possessed her great beauty and her disposition sometimes seemed to have changed for the worse. He was apprehensive how she might react to life in Sweden and be received there. With the accession of Gustav IV Adolf to personal power, Fersen's thoughts were increasingly drawn to his future in public life. The brief peace of 1797, meanwhile, did not give a chance for Eleanore and Craufurd to settle their affairs.[34]

The long stalemate was finally broken in tragicomic fashion. Ivan Simolin, the former Russian ambassador to Paris—now ninety years old—had lived with the Craufurd-Sullivan *ménage* since 1792. He was himself warmly attached to Eleanore, to whom he willed his fortune at his death in September 1799. Meanwhile "*Il Vecchio*," as they affectionately called him, served as intermediary between Axel and Eleanore. In January 1799, he mixed up letters Eleanore had given him to mail to Fersen and Craufurd. Craufurd now learned all and was enraged, Fersen was deeply embarrassed, and poor Simolin suffered a shock from which he apparently never recovered. Eleanore again promised to leave Craufurd after a decent interval; though Fersen saw her briefly in January, he agreed not to return to Frankfurt. He saw her again in July 1799, when she renewed her assurances. But Fersen no longer believed her and understood the affair was over, though he continued to correspond with her occasionally as late as 1806.[35]

In time, Craufurd recovered his customary equanimity. The pair returned to Paris in 1802, after the Peace of Amiens, and were at last married in Roman Catholic, Anglican, and civil ceremonies. Craufurd thereafter devoted himself to literary pursuits and to building a notable art collection. He was on excellent terms with Napoleon, Josephine, Talleyrand, and, after the Restoration, with Louis XVIII. Quella married Count Albert Grimod d'Orsay and Eleanore lived to see her grandchildren marry into the highest ranks of the French nobility.[36]

Thus ended the second great love of Fersen's life, so different from the first, yet perhaps no less important in his life. The principal obstacle to his return to Sweden and the service of his king had now at last disappeared. Developments in his homeland meanwhile seemed to improve his chances of playing an important role.

The failure of the Norwegian exchange scheme largely disillusioned Gustav IV Adolf with Ehrenheim and the pro-French faction, and he quickly reverted to his natural gallophobia. When in exchange for Staël's appointment to Paris, the former *conventionnel* and regicide, François Lamarque, was designated French ambassador to Sweden, the king announced—with obvious reference to Bonaparte's interview with Fersen—that he would not receive an envoy who had made himself known in the history of the Revolution. His correspondence with Staël shows how fearful Gustav Adolf was over the spread of Jacobinism, especially in view of recent events in Switzerland, Italy, and Germany, as well as Sweden's own internal turbulence during the past half century. Fruitless negotiations over Lamarque's acceptance dragged on until the end of the year when, in the face of a new Continental war, the king recalled Staël from Paris. "He is now unemployed for the third time, which delights me," Fersen exulted, and he congratulated Gustav Adolf on his firmness, which impressed the Germans at Rastadt.[37]

Fersen's dispatches from Rastadt and Karlsruhe doubtless strongly influenced the king at this time. In December 1798, he had the satisfaction of becoming a Commander with the Grand Cross of the Order of the Sword, a distinction which he had long coveted, and the rumor again circulated in Stockholm that he would take over the direction of foreign affairs from Ehrenheim.[38]

At the same time, Taube regained influence at court and in September 1798 he was sent to Berlin on a confidential mission. Neither Ehrenheim nor Minister von Engeström in Berlin were advised of its real purpose nor held the key to Taube's cipher. When Engeström years later discovered Taube's dispatches to the king, he found he had used the opportunity to cast aspersions on both his own and Ehrenheim's political reliability. It was at this time too, that Taube wrote Fersen that Ehrenheim was "a bit of a Jacobin deep down," which much distressed Fersen, for "this attitude generally does not change, but rather as a rule becomes more and more pronounced."[39]

Taube was accompanied to Berlin by Sophie Piper. Upon leaving Karlsruhe, Axel naturally went to join them. In his progress across Germany, he visited, among other places, Weimar, where he noted the confidant of the duke was a "Professor Goethe," an outstanding man, "not given to the new ideas." On 4 April, Fersen arrived in Berlin where he found Taube and Sophie, as well as Baron Armfelt, who was then living there, awaiting pardon for the conspiracy of 1793. Fersen here received instructions to persuade the new elector of Bavaria, his old friend the former duke of Zweibrücken, to lend the large fortune he was believed to have inherited to the Swedish treasury, but Fersen, knowing the Bavarian coffers to be empty, found other occupation. He and Taube were invited to dinner by Frederick William III at Potsdam, where Fersen, apprizing the various court factions, concluded that Prussia would take no part in a new war against France.[40]

Ostensibly, Taube had been sent to Berlin to discuss a possible sale of Swedish Pomerania. In actuality, Gustav IV Adolf was now strongly interested in joining the new coalition, thus anxious to find out Prussia's intentions. Taube's dispatches were well calculated to encourage this idea and it was soon rumored in Stockholm that Taube was secretly managing foreign affairs from Berlin. There Taube came in close contact with the Russian minister. If Gustav IV Adolf remained hesitant, it would appear that a letter from Taube, dated 2 April 1799, hinting that with Russian support some sort of exchange might be arranged, presumably Pomerania for Norway, finally determined him to join the coalition. Fersen's diary for 27 April gives the contents of Gustav Adolf's reply, the original of which has not been preserved:

The king wrote Taube in the most definite manner concerning matters of policy, and that he had expressed himself very openly with regard to these [matters] with the Russian ambassador, Budberg, to whom he had said that for his part, he was tired of the role of neutral and was quite decided to act and to enter into the coalition; and that he had 7,000 men and vessels all ready, if he were provided with some money. He permitted Budberg to explain this to the emperor [of Russia] and authorized Taube to communicate this to Berlin. He told Budberg to address himself directly to him alone if there should be important matters to communicate. His letter is perfect and astonishing for a young man of twenty years. He knew about Ehrenheim and suspected him.[41]

Secret negotiations with St. Petersburg ensued during the next several months.

Fersen was at this time much concerned over Swedes suspected of Jacobin sympathies and zealously sought to expose them. In June 1798, a letter from a young Swedish Baron d'Albedyhl to Bonaparte, entreating him to initiate an international law code, came to Fersen's attention.

This letter would have been fully worthy of some young republican who wanted to make his way by burning incense at the feet of him he believes the man of the hour. It was completely in the style of the Carmagnoles. From beginning to end it spoke only of peoples and nations, but not a single word about sovereigns. . . . Baron d'Albedyhl may have been seized by some sort of a mental disturbance, for he is otherwise an intelligent boy and capable in his work . . .

Not long after: "I told the king about Baron d'Albedyhl's letter. . . . I felt it my duty to let him know what sort of man he is, in case he should think of using him."[42]

He noted that Engeström and his legation secretary, S.N. Casström, who had been in Poland with him, were not well regarded in Berlin: "Both are considered democrats. They are connected with the Abbé Sieyès and the Poles who hold the wrong views and are also frequently seen with the princes, Henry and Ferdinand, who are known for their democratic ideas." In May 1799, Fersen arranged for Saxon officials to seize a Swede named Gyllenstorm, "greatly suspected of democracy," on the Austrian border and to forward any papers discovered on him. This man, Fersen believed, was connected with "the whole democratic league" in Sweden, even including Duke Karl, the "intermediary for letters to him." But Gyllenstorm evaded the Saxons and was only lightly searched by the Austrians, who, Fersen complained, were so clumsy that "they pursue honest émigrés but let Jacobins through," and he thereafter disappeared.[43]

Late in May, Fersen with his sister and Taube left Berlin for Karlsbad, the favorite *Kurort* for the wealthy and fashionable since the war had driven them from Spa and Aachen. Long lines of Russian troops along the roads reminded of distant hostilities. Nonetheless a brilliant assembly foregathered at Karlsbad, including Russians of untold wealth as well as Duke Karl, Duchess Charlotta, and their suite from Sweden, who departed in time to avoid an embarrassing encounter with Armfelt in June.[44]

Baron Taube was not well. During their stay in Karlsbad his condition worsened and on 15 August he died. The blow was grievous to both Sophie and Axel. He was buried in the local Protestant cemetery. "I was the clergyman," Fersen wrote, "and carried out the ceremony and offered prayers, but my voice trembled." Among the small group of Swedes at the graveside was Armfelt, once Taube's greatest rival for Gustav III's favor, who now wrote his wife, "Our young king now has one less true servant, and since the number is small, the loss is serious." In Stockholm, Gustav IV Adolf deeply mourned the death of his adviser and friend.[45]

An unfortunate sequel followed. Rumors spread that Taube had been poisoned and that Lars von Engeström was implicated, and these were traced to Fersen's sister, Sophie. The idea apparently originated with Taube himself during his final illness. His health, however, had long been failing and his death was attributed to protracted jaundice. It did not escape notice that Taube willed his fortune to Sophie Piper, naming Axel Fersen his executor, thus bypassing several needy relatives. The fateful connection between Sophie Piper's name and suspicions of poisoning was thereby established, which would in time lead to tragic consequences.[46]

On 19 August, Axel and his sister left Karlsbad to return to Sweden. They passed through Saxony, where Fersen admired the general prosperity, and Brunswick, where he relived memories of his student days. He also dined with the duke, of whom he wrote,

He was extremely friendly toward me and spoke for a long time. . . . He disapproved the behavior of the king of Prussia and did not know the reason for it. He wished the king of Sweden might send a man who enjoyed his confidence to the king of Prussia to speak to him, for he knew that the example of the former meant something to him. He has also often been held up as an example to him.[47]

In Hamburg, they were amazed by the luxury they saw and visited the Baron de Breteuil. On 13 October, they reached Stockholm.[48]

As Taube lay dying, Gustav IV Adolf seemed to be moving toward the consummation of his father's plans, and Taube's: open intervention against revolutionary France in conjunction with Russia and acquisition of Norway. In late April, he sent a declaration for Bildt to read before the Germanic diet in Regensburg, urging defense of the Empire against France. Fersen was delighted. It would be "glorious," he wrote the king, thus to have "provoked in all the princes of the Empire the true sentiment of their honor and interest," adding in his diary, "One may be sure Ehrenheim was not consulted about this; the thought of this made me glad." Ehrenheim, who knew nothing in advance, was aghast and his assurances that Gustav Adolf had acted here as duke of Pomerania, not as king of Sweden, were scarcely convincing to Paris. The Prussians were embarrassed, the Austrians delighted. Lehrbach saw in the manifesto Fersen's "excellent views." "See how cheaply one may win honor!" Axel commented. "In any case, I was flattered by the idea." In Stockholm, too, it was rumored that the declaration had emanated from Fersen in Berlin.[49]

These developments raised again the question of an exchange of ambassadors between Stockholm and Vienna, in abeyance since the imperial court had refused Engeström in 1796. Fersen was considered for the post but suspected in this an intrigue to keep him away from the king.[50]

Gustav IV Adolf's Regensburg Manifesto encouraged Paul I to bring Sweden into the new coalition. Negotiations to this end broke down, however, when it became evident that the allies planned a campaign in Holland rather than in northern Germany, which would allow territorial readjustments that could give Norway to Sweden. A separate Russo-Swedish pact was nonetheless concluded at Gatchina on 29 October 1799, ostensibly a defensive alliance but which secretly provided for an auxiliary corps of 8,000 Swedes to join the Russians against France, in return for subsidies and suitable compensation at the peace, meaning no doubt Norway.[51]

The War of the Second Coalition at first seemed quite different from that of the First. From Italy, Germany, and Switzerland came news of an almost unbroken series of resounding allied victories. From the republic came word of fresh dissensions. After a decade of turmoil and war, the collapse of France and the destruction of the Revolution seemed imminent. At this crucial hour, Gustav III's son committed Sweden to join in the final assault and Axel Fersen returned to Stockholm to his monarch's side.

CHAPTER II

Fersen and Gustav IV Adolf: The Fight against the Swedish Radicals, 1799–1801

1

Axel Fersen's return to Stockholm created a considerable stir. Gustav IV Adolf could not wait to see him and supplied missing parts of his Guards uniform so that he might immediately present himself at court. They conversed long and earnestly on international affairs in the following weeks. On 16 November, Fersen was made *"En av rikets herrar"*—literally, "One of the Lords of the Realm"— with the title of Excellency.[1]

Fersen lost no time in laying before the king the project for an international anti-Jacobin league and in urging that he place himself at its head. Gustav IV Adolf seemed interested and flattered. Their discussions meanwhile give some further insight into some of the more ominous details of the project:

He favored the idea of the league and seemed to wish to take it upon himself to be its chief. He did not wish to permit that anyone other than himself should have the right to pronounce the death sentence and proposed that the lower authorities should have the power to mark persons by branding them in order to prevent misdeeds.[2]

On leaving his first interview with Gustav Adolf on 15 October, Fersen met *Hovkansler* Ehrenheim, "who appeared little pleased to see me come from seeing the king with a portfolio under my arm." As noted, it was rumored that the count would shortly take over the chancellery. Fersen found himself treated with special consideration by courtiers, bureaucrats, and favor-seekers. In early November, Duchess Charlotta congratulated him as "premier minister." Others were less sanguine. "If Count Fersen's headship of the chancellery will cause Ehrenheim's work to cease," the disgruntled Engeström wrote in December, "abilities will be lost which Count Fersen cannot replace." Fersen persistently denied these rumors, and reacted to them with characteristic ambivalence. He suspected in them the work of persons in fact anxious to prevent him from becoming *kanslipresident,* such as Ehrenheim or Duke Karl. The latter Fersen even suspected of wishing to have him appointed governor of Stockholm to ruin his political future, believing "that I will make myself impossible in this position, since I had no idea of what was needed for it and that the townspeople, who cannot abide me, will know how to get rid of me." This last is grimly ironic in view of his death in that city a decade later. Besides, Fersen felt self-doubts and admitted to himself, "I would be very uncomfortable over accepting this position" of chancellor.[3]

After the first welcome, meanwhile, he noted that Gustav Adolf was friendly and considerate, "but what a difference from his father's way of acting." "It is strange," he observed soon after, "what a high opinion everyone has of the favor and confidence I enjoy with the king"; actually it was nothing significant because of the latter's fear of "showing confidence in anyone, or to be more exact, to come under anyone's influence."[4]

Fersen did, however, try to exert influence with regard to the political reliability of Swedish diplomats abroad, many of whom he suspected. To point out ideologically suspect persons in government service was of course an important function of the anti-Jacobin league. Above all, he now mistrusted Lars von Engeström. Though he discounted the rumor that he had poisoned Taube, which his sister had spread and which the king appeared to believe, he strongly urged Engeström's recall. When the king hesitated for lack of a pretext, Fersen insisted that the minister's "opinions and ideas" were reason enough. Engeström, however, remained in Berlin until 1806.[5]

2

Gustav IV Adolf was in fact most receptive to Fersen's views. He was convinced that the disorders of his time—the upheaval in France, his father's assassination—were the results of "philosopical" innovations, toward which he grew increasingly apprehensive. Everywhere, Jacobinism seemed to rear its ugly head. The Austrian chargé d'affaires had noted in 1797 the partiality of the "Swedish nation" for France and "French ideas," considering it "always restless and revolutionary." By 1799, economic distress heightened discontent. That fall, Bonaparte's return from Egypt was warmly welcomed in many circles. In Stockholm, a mixed company of Frenchmen and Swedish "Jacobins" celebrated the event, to the accompaniment of Swedish, French, and "republican" cheers. Fersen, whose nephew observed the festivities from outside the house, was of course outraged and wrote the king of his apprehensions. The affair was considered serious by the Swedish government and the Russian ambassador.[6]

To an autocrat of Gustav IV Adolf's anti-intellectual bias, the universities, which throughout the 1790s had been centers of radicalism, were a prime object of suspicion. In October 1799, at the time of Fersen's return to Sweden, the prominent Uppsala radical, Hans Hierta, created a sensation with his satire, *Some Thoughts on the Means to Reestablish and Secure the Ancient French Monarchy*, which facetiously proposed to set up in France a full-fledged "Bureau for Opinion" under trustworthy civil servants, since "the *littérateurs* should never be left on their own," which would prevent writers like Rousseau, Helvétius, or the "frightful" Voltaire from attacking "all that was sacred and lofty and noble." Hierta's pamphlet, obviously aimed more at Sweden than at France, was quickly suppressed. It seems meanwhile to have had a direct connection with Fersen's return and supposed influence with Gustav IV Adolf; Hierta evidently suspected Fersen's project for an anti-Jacobin league and directed his writing specifically against the latter's political views.[7]

The so-called "new philosophy" of Immanuel Kant enjoyed a great vogue in academic circles but was regarded by the conservatives as practically synonymous with Jacobinism, threatening grave moral consequences. At the universities too, the news of French victories and Bonaparte's return produced demonstrations which further deepened the king's mistrust. At Uppsala, the students sang an indecent parody of the hymn, *"En jungfru födde ett barn i dag"* ("A Virgin Gave Birth to a Child Today"), casting obvious aspersions on the paternity of the newly born crown prince, which quickly spread to the capital. The king, who since childhood was chancellor of the university, took the opportunity to act.

He summoned Axel Fersen and explained his dissatisfaction with "Uppsala Academy" because of "the principles of the professors and the manner of instruction." In Fersen's words:

He intended to go up there . . . call them [the professors] together and declare to them that he was dissatisfied with the university . . . and to command them to convene and in accordance with their rights, to choose someone immediately who would be worthy of his trust. He thought of letting them know that this ought to be me, and then have me immediately . . . installed.

The king explained that the chancellorship would not take much time nor prevent other employment. He assured Fersen "that it was not necessary to be a learned person to be chancellor" and that he had all the abilities, and more, than were needed. What he wanted was "a man, firm in character, with proper attitudes, who could keep watch over the education of the youth, which was a very important matter." Fersen could hardly refuse, "and said yes very unwillingly, for I know nothing about that academy and its care." The king told him about the parody of the hymn and other scandalous songs made up by the Uppsala students and in fact repeated them all from memory.[8]

Fersen discussed the matter with Count Carl Axel Wachtmeister, chancellor of justice and also of Lund University.

His view is, and I approve of it, that one should seek to prevent too many from attempting to follow the path of learning and striving for positions in the civil service, by making this path long and hard, and thereby frightening them off, so that they remain farmers and craftsmen. This whole crowd of petty scribblers, advocates, notaries, is a scourge to the country and a center of infection. Thus, for example, a complete knowledge of Latin should be required of those who study jurisprudence, before they are permitted to take their examinations.[9]

A week later, Gustav Adolf, with Fersen in his suite, traveled to Uppsala. The king made a speech before the academic consistory, which according to Fersen was very fine and "completely dumbfounded" the professors, reading in part as follows:

. . . nor can I conceal on this occasion with what displeasure I have found an attitude to prevail among a part of the youth studying here, neither suitable nor creditable for young persons who are supposed to be here to be educated as true subjects, capable officials, and honorable citizens. Meanwhile I fear with good cause that a part of this growing youth is often beguiled into accepting new and harmful principles which through a perverted instruction allow one to view according to one's own convictions and with little respect those objects which for all right-thinking people ought to be most sacred, and since this respect and reverence is declining, my thoughts concerning the future of this youth cannot be reassuring. From this it appears that it is only a matter of the purity of the instruction and the principles which the students receive from their teachers here, and it is thus upon their strictest responsibility that I enjoin that the principles which are disseminated by all of you without exception shall be in accordance with our established religion and social order. . . .[10]

The king instructed the consistory to withdraw and elect a new chancellor. "He had had the rector come in beforehand," Fersen continued, "to confide to him his intentions and instruct him to propose me for this post. Instead of 1:00 o'clock, they returned at 12:00; I have been elected by acclamation." Gustav IV Adolf thereupon installed him and delivered "a very fine harangue." Fersen then spoke a few words, which caused him no little embarrassment, since he found it hard to write in Swedish and in his nervousness his memory failed him.[11]

The following day, the king strolled about the town, "followed by almost all the students," while Fersen surveyed his new domain. He was not greatly impressed. "The library is small and arranged without taste. There are not many rare books. . . . The coin collection is not much to speak of, neither is the riding hall, and the armory is nothing at all, where the youth are instructed without elegance, and that is a mistake." The natural history building from Gustav III's reign he meanwhile found attractive. Fersen was never to feel much attachment to the town or university of Uppsala. His diary occasionally reveals the boredom and aversion they inspired in him. Thus, about a year later, he complains, "one must do something to last out a day in Uppsala," or in 1803 he remarks that one must truly be a slave of habit to live in such a place and pities its inhabitants with all his heart.[12]

Fersen nevertheless took his duties seriously, the foremost being the suppression of "Jacobinism" and disorder. The morning after his installation, the new chancellor noted, "The patrols I had sent out during the evening and at night had not met a single student in the streets of Uppsala, a phenomenon that had not occurred in fifty years. . . ." "In the town the greatest order prevailed and the king's speech made the best possible impression," he wrote next day. "The majority were visibly affected and spoke with me about it with tears in their eyes, but there were also several hardened Jacobins." These, however, kept their views to themselves; since Fersen became chancellor at Uppsala, Duchess Charlotta wrote in December, "neither teachers nor students have given any cause for complaint."[13]

It was as the king had assured Fersen: his duties in connection with Uppsala University did not take much of his time. Purely academic matters remained the domain of the rector and the consistory. The chancellor was concerned with occasional questions affecting appointments, promotions, dismissals, salaries, facilities, finances and, of course, discipline. He was provided with a secretary, Gabriel Eurén, who did most of the work, succeeded after his death in 1806 by J. J. Beckmark. Fersen's diary does not often mention university affairs and he did not visit Uppsala more than once or twice a year, for a few days at most. All in all, he was a conscientious and well-intentioned chancellor, but he firmly denied unbridled academic freedom, in accordance with both his monarch's and his own views. He was generally regarded the most determined anti-Jacobin in Sweden; in G. G. Adlerbeth's words, "a declared *French royalist*" had been made "the Swedish Jacobins' schoolmaster."[14]

In his memoirs, Count Hans Gabriel Trolle-Wachtmeister, then a student at Uppsala, later described the reaction as follows:

The election of this enforced candidate for chancellor aroused the greatest unrest among the students. Fersen's earlier experiences and all his sympathies made him appear in the eyes of all more as a French émigré than as a Swedish citizen. This, together with his chivalrous devotion to the Bourbon house and his unsuccessful mission in Rastadt made him at that time the object of the most unfavorable attention, and the order that he be elected chancellor was regarded as a deliberate insult to the academy, just as it was believed that the same inference might be found against the current hero, Bonaparte, in Fersen's appointment as Swedish plenipotentiary to the congress. In addition, there was that which was repugnant to us in his manner, which was altogether that of a *grand seigneur* of the Versailles of bygone times, which in its deliberate, cold pride was never guilty of any insult or any discourtesy toward the person he saw, but on the other hand, which pretended not to see most of those persons he met. No form of hauteur is as offensive and as irritating as this kind of negative insult, especially among us, who are not used to it. And Fersen had to pay for it some years later with his life.

Young Trolle-Wachtmeister complained to his father, chancellor of justice and of Lund University, of Fersen's strictness and presumed plans to dismiss teachers and forbid instruction in certain subjects, insisting that "learning under all circumstances requires freedom." Fersen noted with sober satisfaction that the father "found it natural that I should forbid one or another doctrine and dismiss those who did not accommodate themselves to this."[15]

The academic most directly concerned at this point was the Kantian philosopher Benjamin Höijer, to whom the king denied a chair in theoretical philosophy in December. When Höijer departed for the Continent the following spring, a crowd of Uppsala students staged an obstreperous celebration in his honor. In reaction, Fersen wrote a stern warning to the consistory, expressing his "greatest displeasure" over this "noisy and indecent disturbance." He declined to mete out the punishment the offenders so richly deserved and "the maintenance of peace and order demand." The students were nonetheless to be warned of their chancellor's displeasure and admonished against "excesses of whatever type they might be, which, most culpable at a general seat of learning, should never take place without stern punishment to those who cause and take part in them." For the sake of their families and themselves, the students should work hard and behave themselves. Fersen again denied Höijer appointment in 1806 and when the following year the philosopher sought to lecture on philosophy and the history of the fine arts, the chancellor sustained the consistory's ruling that he might not receive pay or examine students. Only after the coup d'état of 1809 did Höijer receive his long-awaited chair, shortly before his death.[16]

Another noted Uppsala personality, the historian and publicist Gustav Abraham Silferstolpe, received permission from the *Kanslikollegium* to open a bookstore in the spring of 1800 in Norrköping, where a Riksdag was to be held. Fersen countered by forbidding this "known Jacobin" to absent himself from his duties as preceptor at Uppsala. When Silfverstolpe's influential father came with his son, "that very ugly fish," to urge Fersen to let the young man take his seat in the noble estate at the diet, Fersen refused outright and gained the king's backing.[17]

The irrascible Silfverstolpe doubtless sought revenge through an incident in April. When the university celebrated Gustav Adolf's coronation in Norrköping, Silfverstolpe, who was in the academic orchestra, tricked its elderly director into preparing a piece containing passages from the *Marseillaise*. When the embarrassed director then tried to substitute a Haydn symphony, Silfverstolpe and his friends refused to play. For this lark, the offenders were dealt with sternly. In September, Fersen noted, "I concluded the affair of the preceptors Silfverstolpe, Wallenberg, and Hultin, and confirmed the judgment of the consistory, which banishes the first forever, the second for one year, and gives the third fifteen days in jail. I pardoned the music director, Leijel, because of age and poverty." That this might appear "petty and ridiculous" did not escape Fersen. He took the consistory to task for not reporting the incident promptly, since swiftness in punishment determined its effectiveness, especially in discouraging "further insolence." That this ludicrous affair should be taken seriously and that Fersen should consider the sentences just and proper, is a telling indication of the temper of the times and the policy he had been chosen to represent.[18]

The so-called "Music Trial" was the deathblow to political radicalism at Uppsala. Thereafter the university remained quiet enough during Fersen's chancellorship. Little is heard of unrest or unorthodoxy. In September 1800, Fersen "admonished the physician [Pehr] Afzelius to be careful about his political views." The warning was apparently taken to heart. A. F. Skjöldebrand called Fersen's chancellorship the "Iron Age" of the university and this sobriquet is often applied to Swedish culture as a whole in the first decade of the nineteenth century. However, Fersen alone was hardly responsible for the intellectual reaction. He was only one—even if the most conspicuous—of the representatives of a conservatism enjoying wide approval within the academic world itself. Bernhard von Beskow, who then studied at Uppsala, later wrote that "in general, Fersen was considered more tolerant than the other guardians of learning at that time." His material contributions to the university, meanwhile, were greatly appreciated, especially the improvement of academic salaries. In July 1801, Fersen presented a delegation of professors, who thanked the king for this increase, after which "they ate dinner with me and were quite delightful." Fersen gave careful attention to faculty appointments and seems to have given special help to deserving academics. The Linnaean natural history museum was completed in 1807, in commemoration of which a medal bearing Fersen's profile was designed by J. T. Sergel in 1805 and finally cast in 1835. He arranged for special funds to purchase important private libraries. In 1801, he donated a collection of Russian copper medals, inherited from his father, and in 1803, acquired the remainder of Queen Lovisa Ulrika's mineral cabinet from Drottningholm. Ever conscientious in financial matters, Fersen was apparently a good steward; much of his official work concerned the leasing to tenant cultivators of those properties throughout Sweden that provided most of the university's economic support. In 1809, he was much concerned with a great fire in Uppsala in June.[19]

Fersen was not averse to practical curricular or procedural changes. In 1804, he approved certain new texts and in 1808 the replacement of statistics for the study of the constitution of the Holy Roman Empire. In 1809, he requested that the king increase the number of *magister* degrees conferred by the faculty of philosophy to 75 per year in view of the increasing number of qualified candidates. In this connection, he mentioned that Uppsala University now had some 600 students, in contrast to Lund and Åbo, each of which had less than 300. The same year, he approved the theological faculty's request that candidates under 15 years of age no longer be admitted to the *examen theologicum*. Finally, Fersen's refusal in 1804 to protect a young Baron Rudbeck from well-deserved punishment for obstreperous behavior in class, despite vigorous representations from the boy's father, shows a commendable firmness in backing the authority of his faculty even in the face of aristocratic pressure.[20]

Fersen was not unaware of the incongruity of his academic position. In September 1800,

...the rector and the consistory came and I held an audience for all of those who needed to speak with me until 8:00 o'clock. I felt like the parody of a king, for I held court for the consistory and, exactly like a king, I spoke with each one. I was only sorry I did not have anyone with whom I could have laughed at the whole business.

Yet on another occasion in 1803, in a more sober mood, he expressed the dilemma which all in such positions know only too well:

Many departments need new quarters since the present ones are too old or in poor condition. All asked for improvements from me and as is customary, each regarded his own specialty as the most important and wanted advantages at the expense of the others. What is hard about this business is how to be fair in the distribution of means.[21]

It speaks well for his services that the eminent naturalist and theologian Samuel Ödmann, himself no reactionary, should comment in January 1803, when Fersen was returning from Italy, "Count Fersen is expected home any day. It is a general wish that he should assume the chancellorship again." He remained chancellor until his death in 1810 and his official correspondence shows that the university absorbed ever more of his time and concern; it was never more voluminous than in the last year of his life. He was always most interested in the natural sciences and subjects of practical applicability. When elected a member of the Scientific Society of Uppsala in 1804, he warmly appreciated the honor. Lars von Engeström, while no friend of his, was prepared to admit that Fersen "had all the education a man of normal intelligence cannot help acquiring when he lives only in good society." The learned Beskow went further: "Those who considered him unsuitable as the chancellor of an academy apparently did not know that he was more thoroughly educated than perhaps any chancellor in later times...." Among other things, Beskow was impressed that until the end of his life, Fersen could correspond in Latin.[22]

Fersen's position involved him, *ex officio,* in other cultural or educational matters. He was, for instance, on a committee for the Christianizing and civilizing of the Lapps, though his diary gives no details and it apparently met only rarely.[23] Its responsibilities were given to a new organ, the *Kanslersgille* or Chancellor's Committee, established in 1801 when the old *Kanslikollegium* was dissolved and its varied functions given to new governmental bodies. The *Kanslersgille* was charged with education and distinguished by both a greater control over the whole educational system and a more laic character than ever before. Fersen likewise served on this board. In October 1801, the *Kanslersgille* was directed to prepare a new school ordinance, "suited to the present time." Swedish education was still mostly controlled by the Church and prepared mainly for ecclesiastical careers. It was thus suited neither for government officials nor for persons in commerce or manufacture, and came under increasing attack.[24]

The task of actually preparing the new ordinance was given to a working committee that did not include the university chancellors themselves. The full *Kanslersgille* met only rarely to approve the resolutions of the subcommittee. Fersen's diary makes only occasional mention of the *Kanslersgille*. The school ordinance was at last promulgated in 1807, providing a modest beginning in the instruction of physical sciences, modern languages, and even physical education. It was the first of a long series of reforms through which Swedish education evolved toward secularism and practical utilitarianism.[25]

In the working committee, the real contest lay between Canon Eric Waller of Västerås, an intransigent reactionary who sought to freeze instruction in the forms of a century before to stem the tide of "philosophy," and the broadly cultivated moderate Göran Gudmund Adlerbeth, who labored to bring about such reforms as seemed necessary yet possible within an atmosphere of political and cultural reaction. Fersen rallied to Adlerbeth's defense. Canon Waller, he wrote in May 1807,

... caused a thousand difficulties and insisted on an article concerning the precautions which should be taken against Jacobinism. We were all against this, for one should not in this way point out any sect or anticipate crimes. The regulation should establish controls to prevent the development of dangers of all kinds. This Waller is a real Jesuit, a former member of the clerical estate in the diet and a terrible intriguer.

Fersen apparently played a role of some importance in securing acceptance for Adlerbeth's proposals, the substance of the ordinance as adopted.[26]

This should serve to modify the usual image of Fersen as the determined opponent of innovation, or perhaps more correctly, to show that his conservatism was more subtle and complex than might always be evident. It did not rest on any religious or metaphysical base and he was ever contemptuous of ignorance or superstition. It was rather in part the product of ingrained habit; ultimately he never seems to have questioned the basic rightness of the social order in which he was born and raised. But his views on society and government were also pragmatic; his experience seemed constantly to bear out that human welfare was best served by the preservation of order, balance, and harmony in the existing social structure, and by an authoritarian monarchy, able to govern in the interests of all. Thus Fersen could oppose the clerical obscurantism of a Canon Waller and approve reforms in education which prepared youth for useful functions in government and the economy, as long as they did not threaten the bases of social order: propriety, respect, obedience, sense of duty. Alma Söderhjelm has characterized Fersen as "a strange mixture" of liberalism and a conservatism that revealed itself only when it came to the spread of Jacobin ideas. Fersen's interest in good government and a variety of practical problems and improvements during the final decade of his life in Sweden seems largely to bear out this appraisal.[27]

3

Unrest was not limited to the universities. During the winter of 1799–1800, there was serious rioting in a number of provincial towns which contemporaries attributed mainly to economic problems: especially a series of poor harvests, the dislocation of foreign trade by the European war and the chaotic state of the Swedish monetary system.[28]

Fersen was concerned about these problems and saw how they could provide grounds for unrest. He nonetheless deplored the indulgence and ineptitude of the authorities. Though people might have understandable grievances, "whatever the cause may be, all disorderly movements must be severely punished at their inceptions." Characteristically, he perceived a concerted conspiracy. On 11 January 1800, after learning of a riot in Linköping, he explained to Duke Karl that

... the food shortages they complain about are only a pretext; they begin by agitating against the bourgeois, to stir them up against the nobility and the king. ... The duke was surprised it was quiet in Stockholm. But this is because everything emanates from here. The other [disturbances] are only preparatory moves, on the one hand, to arouse spirits, and on the other, to accustom them to the idea of revolt in the event the government should show itself to be weak. They are only feeling the pulse a bit.

When the king received anonymous threatening letters in January, this seemed to Fersen to confirm his apprehensions. One such letter

... began with very strong reproaches against him for neglecting state affairs out of indolence, squandering his time traveling back and forth between Haga and Stockholm, with prophecies that it will end with his being seized during one of these trips, that the plan for a revolution with this in mind has been prepared in Stockholm at a gathering of over fifty persons, among whom the author was also present. The anonymous [letter] ended with a testimonial of zeal and devotion.[29]

The most difficult economic problem confronting Sweden was the state of her currency. Since 1789, there had been two types of money in circulation: bank currency and so-called *riksgäldssedlar*, unbacked credit or national debt notes, issued in large numbers by the National Debt Office to finance Gustav III's Russian war, officially as government bonds for small amounts. The results for credit transactions, foreign trade, and government finance were ruinous. The agio or differential between the two types of currency widened by 1799 to as much as 60 percent while bank notes and metallic coin all but disappeared. During the first two years of his personal reign, Gustav IV Adolf had tried to meet the problem of government finances through strict economies, but poor harvests and declining foreign trade undermined his efforts. If the state were not to go bankrupt, the currency would have to be reformed without delay.[30]

Constitutionally, such a measure required a Riksdag. The king had thus far avoided calling one. He lacked parliamentary experience and his father's eloquence and dramatic flair. More important, it was to be feared that a Riksdag might lead, in Adlerbeth's words, to "possible outbreaks of the spirit of liberty."[31] Certain of Gustav Adolf's advisers nonetheless convinced him that he had no alternative.

Fersen resolutely opposed convening the estates. However difficult it might be, he felt some other expedient must be found, for a Riksdag would be calamitous. Not only recent rioting in Sweden but the French Estates General in 1789 doubtless came to mind in mid-January, when he wrote,

Everyone is concerned over the present situation, the condition of the finances causes special anxiety and many can discover no cure other than a diet. But how may one hope for anything but fatal consequences if the king calls together the estates with empty hands and as a last resource? That would be the same as to deliver oneself completely into their hands, and can one attribute to them so much morality and honor that they would not misuse their power and wish to concern themselves with everything, reform the whole administration, dismiss officials, etc., etc.? And who, given the spirit that now prevails, can guarantee that there will not be a general upheaval? This would be an unfortunate expedient, but something must be done about the finances, which receive too little attention. If only we had the late king; we are now sorely in need of his genius and strength.[32]

And soon after:

I should prefer any other possible way, for an assembly of this sort, at a time when spirits are worked up to this extent by the new ideas, can bring incalculable results. If one adds to this the king's youth, inexperience, impulsiveness, and inflexibility, the perspective becomes even gloomier.[33]

Fersen did his best to warn the king, who now seemed little inclined to listen or even to grant Fersen an audience. When he got his chance on 6 February,

The king seemed to have been lulled into a feeling of the greatest security, which I, however, could not share. I did not hide this. I raised for him some of the objections, for instance, that they would grant subsidies only in return for concessions, for example, for a limited period which would necessitate the calling of the diet at regular intervals, changes in the constitution, the repeal of the Act of Union and Security, control over the expenditure of revenues, etc. The king reassured himself [with the idea] that such concessions would be illegal and that he had the right to dissolve the diet. Yes, but what would be your position then? I finished by pointing out to him how important it would be to have a plan completely ready to present to prevent the estates from presenting one, also that one should be prepared for the most unpleasant eventualities, so that one would not then be caught off guard and so that one would be ready with the answers. I fear they have given him too much confidence and that he puts too much trust in his honest intentions.

Thereafter, it was more difficult than ever to see the king. "I understand that just now he does not wish to speak with those he believes opposed to calling the estates."[34] Gustav Adolf's careful avoidance of contrary argument once his mind was made up was a characteristic Fersen would encounter repeatedly in the future.

The tsar's ambassador, Baron Andrei von Budberg, likewise found it difficult to approach the king. His government knew from long experience how turbulent Swedish diets could be and feared the spread of Jacobinism in the North. On 4 February 1800, Budberg told Fersen, with whom he was on close terms, that he had just received Paul I's offer of "the strongest support" for Gustav IV Adolf if only he would avoid a Riksdag. But by now it was too late, the diet had been announced. "It is terribly aggravating that this assistance did not come earlier," Fersen complained. "It could have affected his decision." The tsar continued to warn the Swedish king of dire perils and even offered to put an army corps at the disposal of the Swedish ambassador,

Stedingk, in St. Petersburg, to occupy Finland. Though Gustav Adolf tactfully declined, he apparently counted on his alliance with the tsar to help overawe any prospective opposition.[35]

On 15 January, the estates were summoned to meet on 10 March in Norrköping, to avoid outside pressures from both the Stockholm populace and the foreign diplomatic corps. Though Fersen, like many others, complained of the location, he later admitted that "indecent behavior" during the diet might have been even worse in the capital.[36]

4

Elections were now held for the estates of the clergy, the burghers, and the peasants; the *Riddarhus,* or House of the Nobility, consisted of the heads of each noble family or their deputies. The clergy were as usual strongly pro-government. The peasants, too, sent an overwhelmingly royalist house, as expected. Among the burghers, the elections were more hotly contested. Fersen was struck by the activity of this class, especially of those with "Jacobin views," and spoke of a Stockholm tailor called Lindgren who campaigned for limitation of all unearned incomes to 1,000 *riksdaler* and distribution of surpluses to the people. "One may not be sure that more such crazy ideas may not arise." On 7 February, however, he was relieved that the elections of the Stockholm burghers had come off smoothly and with good results. Though all three lower estates returned royalist majorities, Fersen felt it was naive and foolhardy of the government not to have brought pressure to bear to influence the elections; "Louis XVI did exactly the same thing on the advice of M. Necker."[37]

The nobility did not attend in force, with representatives of less than half the noble families usually in attendance. Many in civil or military service were unable to come, others were put off by the inconveniences of Norrköping, while Gustav III's later despotism and the Revolution in France left much of the aristocracy demoralized, resigned, or cynical. Expecting the lower estates in any case to override any noble opposition, many old moderates stayed home, abdicating the field to a majority of declared royalists and a minority of zealous but inexperienced young radicals. Fersen, however, by no means sure of a government victory, criticized the nobles. "This indifference is criminal," he wrote on 22 February; "I said this to several of them. I am far from sharing their calm and I hold no illusions that they will not attack the authority of the king by forcing periodic convocations of the estates."[38]

The first order of business was the election of speakers for each estate. There was much speculation over who would be *lantmarskalk* or speaker in the House of the Nobility.

Some guess it will be Count Axel von Fersen. [Hedvig Elisabeth Charlotta wrote] He would be the least suitable. To be sure, his firm character and royalist attitude leave nothing to be desired, but since he has lived mostly in France, he is all too unfamiliar with our laws and what is required for such a position.

It seems doubtful Fersen would have wanted it. Instead, Count Magnus Fredrik Brahe was elected, an honest and well-intentioned man, though lacking in leadership ability.[39]

The estates now elected members to the various joint committees to prepare legislation. The most important was the Secret Committee, under the chairmanship of the king himself, concerned with matters adjudged confidential in the national interest. Here a proposal would be prepared to solve the monetary problem.

According to Fersen's diary, he played a lively part in the royalist caucuses though he himself was not anxious for a committee appointment, as his rank and seniority would almost automatically make him chairman. In the end, he did not serve on any committee. Meanwhile, he strongly disapproved of the government's failure to exert pressure to secure reliable committeemen, leaving this to "chance" and "good will... which under present conditions is ruinous."[40]

Clearly, Fersen was not bothered by any constitutional scruples, faced with what appeared to him a dangerous threat to royal power and a frightening reappearance of the circumstances surrounding the outbreak of revolution in France in 1789. He was prepared to condone any feasible expedient to restrain or overawe the opposition. He did his best to persuade the king to invite the foreign diplomatic corps to Norrköping, since the situation was no longer as it had been "in the days of the old partisan struggles," hoping that Baron Budberg's presence would be more impressive there than in Stockholm. He complained sharply that the government had no previously devised strategy, no effective leaders in the *Riddarhus*, no money to hand out. He was disgruntled that certain of the king's staunchest supporters—including without doubt himself—were not invited into his confidence. "The king is unusually honorable and expects that all others are just as completely so."[41]

The diet, which officially opened on 15 March, nonetheless got off to a promising start, marked by a general optimism and determination to deal with the nation's problems.

On 3 April, Gustav IV Adolf and his queen were crowned in Norrköping cathedral. By all accounts, the ceremony was unimpressive and frugal. Fersen bore the great "Banner of the Realm" and confided to his diary his disappointment over the inept and undignified arrangements. It was gratifying to the royalists, however, that the nobility appeared in fair numbers and made no difficulties about swearing allegiance to the crown and the Act of Union and Security.[42]

The Secret Committee had meanwhile begun to consider the monetary and financial problem, at length producing a plan to redeem two thirds of the 15 million *riksdaler* in national debt notes in bank currency at a discount of one sixth of face value, through a special levy of 2 percent of the total national wealth; the remaining third would be replaced by a new type of credit notes, *courantsedlar*, to be redeemed over fifteen years through regular taxation. The plan represented a compromise and though completely satisfactory to no one, seemed the only solution that could win the approval of the estates. The king privately told Fersen that he hoped the government could in time find pretexts to revise it as needed.[43]

Though Fersen too had misgivings, he was anxious that the measure should pass for political reasons, which for him were by far the most important. Like Mirabeau in 1789, the opposition considered the government's financial distress its greatest asset. Fersen did not permit himself any real optimism and amid the general goodwill perceived "many hardened hearts" within the noble estate.[44]

The estates of the clergy, burghers, and peasants gave the government little cause for alarm. Most of the nobles were also reliable, including not only a core of old royalists but many from the old opposition of Gustav III's time. Meanwhile, there was also a vocal minority, called by its opponents the "Jacobins" or "'The Mountain." It was characteristic of what passed for "Jacobinism" in Sweden at that time that it should be represented most strongly at the diet within the noble order itself. These were mostly younger men without previous parliamentary experience. Fersen noted "a crowd of poor noblemen and most shabby individuals, belonging to be sure to our very oldest families, but who might be suspected of coming to the diet, paid by others and with bad intentions." He soon perceived a split within his estate between "the lower nobility and the propertied."[45] Though suspected by their opponents of being no more than fortune-seekers, the young opposition was genuinely inspired by the ideas of the day, especially that of diminishing corporate privilege. Fersen noted, for instance, that some of them spread the idea among the peasants that the clergy should no longer be represented. Otherwise, their aims were rather indefinite, due mainly to lack of experienced leadership, despite Fersen's conviction that they were "well organized" and "led by persons who wish to remain anonymous."[46] Between the royalists and the "Jacobins," avowed moderates were few.

The first dispute arose on 19 March when the radicals proposed that the deliberations on the Bank and Secret Committees be made public. The *lantmarskalk*, Count Brahe, quashed the motion and was sustained by the king. This, according to Fersen, caused great consternation within "The Clique,"

... which is less concerned with the National Debt Office than with making a breach in the constitution. These gentlemen promised to have their revenge when it came to the question of the grant and to refuse to agree to one. Fortunately, they do not have much influence and the other estates will always set themselves in opposition, if only out of hatred for the nobility, and in that way the king can, if he sacrifices the nobility, make himself master of the situation.

Anti-aristocratic sentiment was very much alive among the lower estates. Fersen noted that there were many among the peasants who wished to abolish both the clerical estate and the remaining privileges of the nobility. He could himself consider with equanimity that the king could "sacrifice" the nobility to win support from the other three estates, as Gustav III had done in 1789. After his experiences in France, he unhesitatingly placed the interests of the crown above those of his peers.[47]

The so-called "Publicity Controversy" was only a trial of strength and a foretaste of things to come. It was nonetheless of great significance for the remainder of the diet and even the future of the reign. Henceforward, the estates had no real role in formulating financial policy and could only vote on the proposals of the Secret Committee, dominated by the government. Count Brahe largely discredited himself. Gustav IV Adolf, badly shaken by this eruption of dissension and radicalism, threw himself into the arms of ultra-royalist advisers. The government now resorted to devious and questionable expedients to override the opposition: packing the noble estate with its supporters, barring certain proposals from consideration, instituting legal proceedings against members of the diet and, apparently, falsifying protocols.

Fersen, it seems clear, though doing his best for the royalist cause, did not belong to the inner circle of the king's confidants. The other old Gustavians regarded him as a "foreigner" and a dangerous rival. Since Taube's death, he had no close connections. Meanwhile, he made only occasional and noncommittal references to the royalist leaders, for the most part aggressive careerists of generally modest origins, thus not persons to whom he felt naturally attached. His terse remarks about one of their number, Count Samuel af Ugglas, in November 1799, reveals something of his attitude: "He has the proper views. He has made a rapid career. He is the son of a very poor clergyman. It was the late king who fifteen years ago raised him up from nothing." He thus generally maintained a tactful silence concerning them.[48]

After the first few weeks, the estates subsided into relative inactivity while the committees prepared their proposals. Although the play of intrigue remained intense, many members of the estates left Norrköping to attend to personal affairs. A new sickness, "influenza," had appeared, reaching epidemic proportions in Stockholm. Axel and Fabian hastened home to their mother's deathbed. A fortnight later, Fabian's youngest son, aged five months, succumbed. Sophie was so ill that Axel despaired at the prospect of life without her. It was only by 24 May, after a month's absence, that Fersen returned to Norrköping.[49]

The estates now reconvened to consider the currency conversion plan submitted by the Secret Committee. The three lower estates quickly adopted it. Among the nobility, the majority favored the project or saw no feasible alternative. The "Jacobins," however, opposed it, since they hoped to compel the king to call periodic diets, despite his prerogative of convening the estates at his pleasure. They thus sought to separate the question of monetary conversion from that of the grant. Here they were on weak ground, however, for the success of the redemption plan depended on an adequate grant to run uninterrupted for at least fifteen years. The government meanwhile packed the noble house with officers from the Stockholm garrison to assure passage of the finance plan; Fersen encountered many along the way on his return to Norrköping, where they were given proxies to represent absent noble families.[50]

On 26 May, the plan came up for debate in the House of the Nobility, where it occasioned long and bitter controversy. The Left vigorously urged limiting the duration of the grant.

The meeting [Fersen wrote] was noisy and was marked on both sides by neither distinction, dignity, nor any knowledge of the subject. It is scandalous and pitiful: a crowd of young men who had no idea about anything and who only caused an uproar, and some older persons who only sat dumbfounded.

At last after some twelve hours of heated debate, the *lantmarskalk* formally called for a vote. Upon a question from the floor, Count Brahe stated it was "self-evident" that the vote would apply only to the conversion plan and not the grant, after which the measure passed.[51]

Two days later, discussion of a statute on employment of agricultural laborers permitted the Left to ventilate its social views, to the indignation of the majority of the nobles. The king refused to allow the protocol of the session to be published. The young radicals, according to Fersen, sought to outdo each other in outrageous schemes, and

. . . to spew out and spread Jacobin ideas and attitudes among the public . . . I have noticed among all . . . the new philosophical spirit concerning the rights of the people and the concessions which should be made to them, making itself felt to a greater or lesser degree. These attitudes which are destructive of all authority and which have plunged France into ruin will in the same way lead all other kingdoms to their destruction.[52]

Among their proposals at this and other sessions was renunciation by the nobility of the exclusive right to own manors, establishment of the special levy for the conversion plan on a progressive scale based on wealth or income, representation of persons not legally members of any of the four estates on the assessment committees for the levy, or even organization of these committees without reference to social status.

On 29 May, the protocol for the meeting of the 26th was presented to the noble house for ratification. It was found to contain no reference to the question whether the vote had pertained only to the monetary conversion, not the grant, and Count Brahe refused to add this reservation to the protocol. It was then shrewdly proposed that the personal word of the *lantmarskalk*, that the separation of the two questions was "self-evident," be considered a sufficient guarantee. Brahe was compelled to admit this had been only an expression of personal opinion. Excitement had risen steadily and now pandemonium broke loose. The opposition was convinced it had been tricked, that the government had taken advantage of their naiveté to sidestep the issue. Members climbed on their benches, shouting at their opponents. One young radical drew his sword and had to be restrained by his comrades. In the midst of the uproar, five young noblemen, including Hans Hierta, renounced their noble status and dramatically left the hall, followed by seven others who refused to participate any longer in the current Riksdag. As a number of others filed out, the *lantmarskalk* adjourned the session. When, during the days that followed, the moderates tried to protest to the king of the government's irregularities, they were coldly rebuffed, to Fersen's great satisfaction.[53]

The renunciation of noble status by the five young "Jacobins" caused much excitement, as indeed it was intended to do, but the radicals thus virtually abdicated the field to their opponents. Duchess Charlotta complained that the nobility had behaved like a "rabble" at Norrköping and that "One must have really lowminded Jacobinical views to wish to renounce one's nobility and change one's name." Fersen's feelings may be imagined.[54]

The king ordered the trial of six of the most outspoken radicals, following the Riksdag, for offenses against the dignity of the *lantmarskalk*. Several of those so arraigned thereupon published statements, presenting themselves as martyrs of liberty. Hierta—who now respelled his name Järta—in particular turned the trial into a farce. In 1801, one defendant was acquitted while five received only token punishments. The following year, Gustav Adolf forbade further renunciations of noble status on pain of loss of citizenship, hoping to strike another blow against democratic tendencies.

The remainder of the Riksdag passed relatively smoothly. The conversion plan was considered passed by the three lower estates and the crown was granted revenues to continue until the next diet, that is, for an indefinite period. Thereafter, much legislative business was accomplished before the diet dissolved with appropriate ceremony on 15 June.

"The king was on the whole very satisfied with the results of the diet," wrote Duchess Charlotta, "and he had every reason to be. He had won even greater power than his father had had." The Riksdag has been called the greatest government victory of the entire Gustavian period.[55] Yet the king's aversion to diets had been so strengthened by the opposition he encountered that nine years later, when his last chance to save the throne—if not for himself at least for his dynasty—lay in calling the estates, he steadfastly refused to consider this expedient.

The conversion plan ultimately failed to solve the monetary problem. The collection of the special levy, which had to be raised by 20 percent, proceeded slowly until 1802, when the government changed the plan without recourse to the estates. In the end, the bank did redeem the designated 15 million *riksdaler* in national debt notes but Sweden's war with Russia in 1808 brought fresh issues of credit notes which again undermined the currency.

The Riksdag of 1800 was an important event in Fersen's life. In contrast to his father's long and active parliamentary career, this was Axel's only diet. It was a landmark in the growth both of the Gustavian autocracy and of the new liberalism which was to triumph in 1809. It was furthermore both better documented than any previous Riksdag and highly illustrative of political and ideological conflict in Sweden and Europe at this critical time. Among the accounts, Fersen's diary is of unique value in depicting the Riksdag from the royalist side, since literature on the subject generally reflects the viewpoint of the more articulate and prolific radical writers. He thus shows the aspirations and fears of the government and its supporters. He also reveals how his own experience in France caused him to regard the situation surrounding the convening of the Swedish estates in the darkest light. Though Fersen did not play a prominent part in committee, open debate, or the inner circle of the king's advisers, he was apparently as active behind the scenes—playing a role he naturally preferred—as circumstances would permit, and if the king did not often seek his advice, it was not because he was not ready to give it. Gustav IV Adolf nevertheless seems to have valued his contributions, for among the honors conferred at the end of the diet, Fersen was made a knight of the Order of the Seraphim.[56]

Alma Söderhjelm has written that Fersen "would not have denied the right of the estates to participate in government" and that "in all of his diary there is no remark to indicate he would have favored the absolutistic form of government."[57] Considering no more than his reactions to the Norrköping Riksdag, this is quite untenable. He showed neither attachment to parliamentary forms nor scruple in dealing with an opposition he considered inspired by ideals destructive of all social order. It may meanwhile be assumed that the diet of 1800 further strengthened his aversion toward the estates.

As a sequel to the Riksdag, Fersen served on one of the assessment committees for the special levy, consisting of two members from each estate, in Stockholm. He was tempted to refuse this duty, but "as I am generally called The Foreigner and it is believed I am unfamiliar with the affairs of my country, I decided to accept, however dull and unpleasant it may be to tax the possessions of others." The task indeed proved disagreeable. At the Riksdag, Fersen had been much chagrined by his own noble estate. Now fresh disillusionment followed. Everywhere noblemen brazenly perjured themselves to avoid taxation, while people of other classes generally showed remarkable honesty. He complained indignantly that military officers, "as though by common agreement quite simply declare that they own nothing." Even if literally true, they ought out of decency to contribute something, "especially as the poor wretches who do not own more than 50 *riksdaler* are forced to declare it." This caused Fersen much embarrassment before his fellow committee members from other estates, who made their assessments effectively. With undoubted relief he greeted the last meeting of the group on 15 January 1801.[58]

Probably out of the same sense of *noblesse oblige*, Fersen became a director of the Stockholm Fire and Insurance Office, the first institution of its kind in Sweden, founded in 1746, which his father had also served in a like capacity.[59]

In the midst of such occupations, Axel Fersen ended his first year back in Sweden. After years of idleness, frustration, and apathy, his diary shows him reanimated by his return to his native land and to the world of practical affairs, capable and conscientious in the fulfillment of his assigned duties, including those for which he felt little inclination.[60] Meanwhile, developments in foreign affairs conspired to bring him again to the fore.

CHAPTER XIII

Fersen at Home and Abroad, 1801–1805

1

In the fall of 1799, the collapse of France through invasion and insurrection seemed imminent. Yet even then the tide had begun to turn: by September the French went on the offensive and in November General Bonaparte established the Consulate. Tsar Paul, disillusioned with Austria and Britain, recalled his forces. Sweden, committed by the Gatchina pact to the war against France, was not required to take part because of the tsar's quarrel with his allies. The prospect seemed a gloomy one to Fersen as peace with Russia saved the revolutionary "hydra" in France, allowing French armies to carry the war abroad rather than to overthrow the regime at home, perpetuating the danger of ever-renewed conflicts.[1]

Fersen's intransigence against France doubtless explains Gustav IV Adolf's coolness toward him in the fall of 1800. As Tsar Paul drew closer to France, the king saw his opportunity to settle grievances with the British over neutral shipping rights, especially since they had seized two large Swedish convoys in 1798. During the summer of 1800, Paul, encouraged by Sweden and Denmark, proposed to reestablish the League of Armed Neutrality of 1780. In November, Gustav Adolf announced he would travel to St. Petersburg to negotiate personally with the tsar, a form of diplomacy of which Fersen remarked,

For my part, I cannot but disapprove of this journey, as in general of all journeys which that sort of persons make to meet each other. Such meetings bring no advantages and cause a good many inconveniences.

It would be far better if they did not know each other and were ignorant of each others' merits and weaknesses.[2]

Considering Gustav Adolf's policy, it seemed surprising that he appointed Fersen to the interim government to manage affairs in his absence. On 29 November, Fersen conferred privately with the king, which some interpreted as a sign of special confidence, particularly when Fersen emerged with a packet of papers, which in truth contained only Fersen's project for an anti-Jacobin league, which the king now returned. This episode may demonstrate the tendency noted in Gustav IV Adolf's earlier reign, to separate his internal policy, which was rigidly and consistently conservative, from his foreign policy, which was often opportunistic to the point of favoring France, directly or indirectly. In this instance, Fersen could serve as a reliable instrument in the former area but not for the time being in the latter.[3]

The interim government consisted of seven members headed by the chancellor of justice. Its activities were many and varied while the king was in St. Petersburg in December 1800. Stockholm and other cities had to be provisioned through import and sale at controlled prices of foreign grain. Measures were taken against a yellow fever epidemic from Spain. Order was maintained in the capital and a food riot suppressed near Malmö. When a case of suspect political journalism arose, Fersen demanded strong and prompt measures, considering it the king's intention to erode away the remaining freedom of the press, "as it is not suitable considering the spirit which now prevails." The interim government was well regarded, as Fersen was pleased to note.[4]

In St. Petersburg, a League of Armed Neutrality was established, with provisions for armed convoys. The British retaliated by embargo and by seizing the Danish Virgin Islands and Swedish St. Barthélemy in the West Indies.[5]

Gustav IV Adolf was of course right that Fersen would oppose the armed neutrality. Fersen foresaw the total destruction of Swedish commerce and feared involvement at an inopportune time in the European war. Worst of all, Sweden was in effect "allied with that monstrous republic."[6] A further disappointment was the Peace of Lunéville of February 1801, "an eternal shame for all the sovereigns of Europe."[7]

On 14 January 1801, the king nevertheless appointed Fersen to a committee for reorganizing the *Kanslikollegium*, one consequence

of which was the creation of the *Kanslersgille* or educational council on which Fersen himself served, as seen. The principal concern of the chancellery was, however, foreign affairs and Fersen's
appointment to the special committee of six was taken, by himself
and others, to mean that he would soon become *kanslipresident*, or
foreign minister.[8]

On 23 January, Gustav IV Adolf called Fersen and confirmed this
intention. As previously, Fersen was torn between vanity, ambition,
and self-doubt. "I do not have confidence in my ability," he wrote
on 14 January, "and I am afraid I could not justify the good opinion
people have of me"; and on 23 January, "I was afraid of every meeting with the king because of the proposal I am expecting and which
I would do everything in the world to avoid, at least for a year."
Duchess Charlotta too, had misgivings: though Fersen would
doubtless be a good counselor to the king, " I believe, however,
that he loves his comfort too much to be able to handle a task
that demands much time and application. His markedly French
manner and behavior would perhaps furthermore be unsuitable
here." Finally, Sweden's relationship to France could make his
appointment awkward.[9]

Fersen nonetheless accepted the offer on 24 January, to Gustav
Adolf's apparent joy. Aware of Sweden's foreign situation, however,
he urged the king not to hesitate to dismiss him if circumstances
should require.

I also pointed out to him that it should be carefully considered whether
this appointment might not prove harmful to the relations the king
might enter into with France; that my views in this regard were altogether too well known; that without the greatest care my person might
have caused great harm at Rastadt; that the republicans hated me as
much as I detested them; that I was ignorant of what the king's relationship to France was and what his intentions were in this regard; but I
bade him consider what inconveniences my appointment might bring
about, and in such a case, not to make it. He answered that everything
had been carefully considered; that he did not have any relations with
France; that he wished to have as few as possible; that besides Buonaparte seemed to be adopting a different attitude and that he believed
the hatred for me would then disappear, but in any case he could do
what he wanted in his own country.[10]

The final appointment was delayed, though on the strength of
rumor several people congratulated Fersen, which was embarrassing: "It was very unpleasant to have to deny such a completely

decided matter." On 20 February, the king left for southern Sweden to attend the military preparations, after again constituting an interim government of five, including Fersen.[11]

2

The Armed Neutrality died a sudden death. The British attacked the Danish fleet in Copenhagen Roads on 2 April 1800, forcing Denmark to abandon the league, then appeared off the Swedish naval base at Karlskrona. News now arrived of the assassination of Tsar Paul. Gustav IV Adolf, while acting in a bellicose manner, was not unprepared to parlay.

Fersen in Stockholm followed these events closely. The death of Paul he considered advantageous to Sweden, bringing an end to dangerous complications, though a fatal example in an era of revolution. The tsar's mistake, he felt, had been to fill the Senate with "dissatisfied men," as this body "actually represented the legislative power in this truly aristocratic government." "On the basis of this state of affairs," he observed, "one may predict a decadence within that colossus which only through Catherine was able to derive strength and cohesion." The king's warlike behavior in Karlskrona seriously alarmed him, taking it, as he did, at face value. Despite grain shortages, merchants would not send ships to Russia for fear of the British fleet. "Public opinion becomes worse each day. The language being used is frightful. . . ." A British naval attack against Stockholm itself was feared. The interim government, evidently under Fersen's own direction, made hasty defensive preparations, though plagued by lack of troops, provisions, and munitions.[12]

Fortunately, these dispositions were not put to the test. The new tsar, Alexander, made terms with the British, whose fleet departed the Baltic. Though the collapse of the Armed Neutrality prevented the satisfaction of Swedish maritime grievances, Gustav IV Adolf and his principal confidant at this time, the young cabinet secretary Gustaf Lagerbjelke, now turned to reconciliation with France, hoping to serve an even greater Swedish interest: the acquisition of Norway. Already in February 1801, the king told Fersen that he felt obliged to send an ambassador to Paris as the tsar intended to do so.[13] That spring, Sweden renewed diplomatic relations with France, following the Peace of Lunéville.

This shift in policy obviously made Fersen's appointment as

chancellor impolitic. On 30 April, Fersen received a suggestion from Lagerbjelke that he now undertake a projected journey to the Continent. Fersen replied that he felt no need to go on his travels yet and remained confident of the king's promise. He further warned against any agreements with France. But it soon became evident that Sweden was to "have more intimate relations with France, which is against my principles, and the welfare and advantage of Sweden, for we cannot receive any protection against our neighbors or any support from a government which is upheld by a single man, and one whose policies are so treacherous and base." "Everyone spoke of my appointment as foreign minister," he wrote on 17 May, "and was surprised it had not yet been made."[14]

Gustav IV Adolf returned from the south on 9 May, affecting the dress and appearance of Karl XII, and dissolved the provisional government. On 18 May the blow fell. The king told Fersen as tactfully as he could that he would not now appoint him chancellor. He reminded Fersen of considerations he himself had raised concerning the effects of his appointment on relations with France. The king assured him of his esteem and asked his opinion on various aspects of foreign policy. Finally, he offered him, clearly as a consolation prize, the position of *riksmarskalk* or grand marshal, a prestigious but politically insignificant post charged with supervision of the court and royal household. Fersen, badly shaken, asked leave to consider and on departing suffered the secret humiliation of being congratulated as *kanslipresident* by those waiting in the antechamber. "They could least of all imagine what had really taken place."[15]

The offer of the position of *riksmarskalk* was particularly galling. When Count Brahe, the unfortunate marshal of the nobility at the Norrköping Riksdag, had declined the same post in November 1800, Fersen had observed, "it is really the only occupation suitable for his talents." His first impulse was likewise to refuse. He nonetheless did not wish to appear offended at not receiving a post he had not sought or "to depreciate a position of honor which was the second or third in precedence in the realm."

I am satisfied to have done my duty by giving the king a sign of my zeal, by not having refused him my services and at the same time, not to have to take part in foreign affairs just at this time, when I should risk the good opinion which is now held of me; but my self-esteem is offended by the king's changeability and because I am getting such an insignificant post as that of grand marshal after everyone had me picked out as chancellor.

Fersen told Chancellor of Justice C. A. Wachtmeister that he considered this new position "as an honorable retreat and myself as out of service...," though the latter assured him the king wished to keep him on in the government and have him attend all council meetings. Furthermore, the duties of the grand marshal under new court regulations were greater than before, including,

... everything concerning the court, the menus, the housekeeping, the storerooms for the household supplies, the palace, the stables, [household] justice, all of this comes under him. This increases the importance of this office which previously was without interest and importance.

On 23 May, Fersen accepted the position, resolving to leave as soon as possible on an extended journey to the Continent.[16]

The birth of a princess provided the occasion for a number of appointments. Ehrenheim was kept in charge of foreign affairs and promoted to *kanslipresident*. Fersen was made *riksmarskalk*. It was generally understood that the king had broken a promise to Fersen, though most would probably have agreed with Adlerbeth that the nation had gained thereby. No one was meanwhile more surprised than Ehrenheim, who had dismissed his servants in anticipation of retirement. He told Fersen that the foreign ministry "would in all ways have been better placed in my hands. Everyone says the same, and this general opinion flatters me more than the position itself would have done."[17]

The sequel to Gustav IV Adolf's change of system helps explain why Ehrenheim was retained rather than Fersen. The king and Lagerbjelke entered into secret negotiations with France and Prussia, of which the *kanslipresident* was not even advised, in hopes of acquiring Norway through a far-reaching exchange of territories. Though Fersen knew nothing of this, the king and his secretary could well imagine his reaction and Lars von Engeström indeed suggested that Fersen's appointment as chancellor had been blocked by Lagerbjelke's intrigues.[18]

3

The eighteen months following Fersen's return to Sweden in the fall of 1799 were filled with disappointment over events at home and abroad, culminating in the loss of the post of foreign minister just as, after years of anticipation, it had seemed to lie in his grasp. Characteristically, he gave vent to no extravagant expressions of chagrin; his bitterness emerges in a more roundabout way, through the intensity of his criticisms of the king and his court in his diary in 1801, from May onward.

With his usual cool objectivity, he had, of course, observed the royal family since his return. He thus speaks of Gustav Adolf's indolence, lack of interest in routine work, inclination toward suspicion and jealousy. The king was determined not to be influenced by others, which was commendable but led to lack of unity in the regime since he did not work hard enough to hold together the various departments. Fersen describes him as generally maladroit socially and in matters of protocol. He was excessively thrifty for one in his position; on one occasion Fersen was surprised that for dinner the royal table provided only eight courses and four desserts! He considered the queen pretty, amiable, and intelligent, though lacking in grace, brilliance, and ambition.[19]

In May 1801 and thereafter, his criticisms became more frequent and sharper in tone. The king now appeared downright rude, particularly to the burgher class and the foreign diplomatic corps. His personality weighed heavily upon his court; at a *cercle*, for instance, "the king spoke with everyone but as usual about nothing. He is terribly dull and has a hard time finding amenities to say and cannot generally converse at all. He did not say four words during the afternoon to either the queen or the duchess but only sat and stared." The king "takes stiffness and constraint for dignity." At an army encampment:

The king was there the whole afternoon and evening, and presumably did nothing but what he does in the city: walk around, look at himself in the mirror and brood without thinking about anything or deciding anything, for these are his daily occupations in Stockholm when he is not holding audiences on state matters.

Duchess Charlotta described this tendency perceptively two years later:

Ambition is a counterweight to his indolence and if he did not respect the particularly praiseworthy principle of giving precedence to duty, he would certainly rather sit with his hands folded than work with his ministers. His devotion to duty often expresses itself in a certain pedantry, which prevents him from diverging in the least degree from established practices. Everything must proceed according to the old forms and only very seldom can he persuade himself to permit any change.[20]

Gustav Adolf was indecisive in state matters and thus fell under the influence of others, despite his intentions. Fersen perceived the growing influence of the queen, who had both character and intelligence. On the whole, however, those who seemed to enjoy the king's greatest confidence were persons Fersen suspected, especially Lagerbjelke with his opportunistic attitude toward France. Thus: "I see the king wishes to have in his service only persons who blindly follow his ideas. This agrees at the same time with his taste for organizing and his mental laziness and his inability to reason things out." Or again: "... he does not know people, does not understand which ones he can employ and does not distinguish them [from those who] serve him unselfishly out of zeal and devotion." Particularly alarming was what seemed a certain lack of good faith and a perplexing inconsistency in Gustav Adolf's attitudes and actions. In September 1801, Fersen wrote in a more thoughtful vein:

This prince distinguishes himself through a mixture of strictness and indulgence, of hardness and good-heartedness, of strength and weakness, which is remarkable and which can derive only from his frivolousness in regard to matters of state and lack of familiarity and ability for such. He likes order and shows it, but still permits disorder; he is precise only in details, while what is important always escapes him.

Finally, he suspected the king's temper was changing in unfortunate ways:

The king lets himself be influenced in the strangest way; this prince is in all respects greatly transformed. His love of truth, his word of honor, and the inclination he showed to use wise people have completely disappeared, and the state secretaries [i.e. Lagerbjelke] lead him because of his lack of foresight, experience, industriousness, and interest in state affairs.[21]

Granted Fersen's remarks in the spring and summer of 1801 are those of a disappointed man, they nonetheless come from one whose belief in legitimate, autocratic monarchy and personal attachment to the Vasa dynasty were beyond question. Already then the king enjoyed little popularity. No one, however, wished more devoutly than Fersen to love and respect his sovereign. Thus his comments are particularly revealing. They already now give the impression of an increasingly erratic and unstable character on the throne of Sweden.[22]

4

For some time, Fersen had been anxious to travel on the Continent. Sophie had been in delicate health since the influenza epidemic of April 1800. But there were other reasons. Fersen still could not feel at home in Sweden. The drabness of the court and the vulgarity of the social tone made him dream of other times and places. Since his return, he had associated mostly with foreign diplomats, especially the Russian ambassador, Baron Andrei von Budberg, and the ministers of Denmark and Spain, Edmund Bourke and Jerónimo La Grua y Salamanca. In particular, he was interested in La Grua's wife, Marianne, with whom he had a brief but intense affair, behind the backs of both her husband and her recognized lover, early in 1800, before the Spanish minister was transferred to Parma. Upon becoming *riksmarskalk*, Fersen obtained permission from the king to leave on his travels, together with the promise of four months leave each year.[23]

Fersen and his sister departed Stockholm in September 1801, accompanied by Sophie's daughter, Hedvig, and son-in-law, Otto Reinhold Möllersvärd. The party made its way through Germany to Italy, enjoying the hospitality of various small courts and noble estates. Italy was much changed by war and revolution since Axel had last been there in 1783 and provided his first and only direct experience of the new order in Europe that the French Revolution had brought about.[24]

In December, the travelers arrived in Parma, where they were warmly welcomed by Duke Ferdinand and Duchess Marie-Amélie, a sister of Marie-Antoinette. Here Fersen found Marianne La Grua, who had meanwhile been involved with other men, though this did not prevent a revival of their affair. Fersen's interest soon waned, for in March 1802 he met in Florence a woman of greater fascination, Princess Yekaterina Nikolaevna Menshikova, a former mistress of Armfelt, a *grande dame* and a full-blown woman, with whom he quickly became involved. "Ketty," as he called her, returned to Russia in April and Fersen learned to his dismay soon after that she was pregnant, though this ended prematurely. Fersen continued to think of Ketty with real nostalgia. In February 1803, she urged him to join her in Dresden. He was sorely tempted: "I have always had to be separated from the objects of my devotion and it is written in the stars that I shall never be happy."[25]

The group next proceeded to Bologna, then in the midst of the carnival. Here, the local French commander called on Fersen, offering him a military escort to Florence.

. . . I did not feel I could decline this honor. I had not expected it and it felt strange that I should be escorted by Frenchmen. M. de La Salindière then reminded me he had seen me at Cap [in Santo Domingo during the American war], where he had been serving in the Armagnac Regiment. He was very polite and said very wise things to me about the former and present regimes.[26]

Fersen's carriage thus arrived in Florence, capital of the newly created kingdom of Etruria, in February 1802, escorted by two French dragoons. He was presented to the king and queen, and the French minister, General Clarke, invited him to dinner. The general, he noted,

. . . is a fine-looking man, but all the others looked like upstarts. He was very polite toward us, but I do not feel comfortable with that sort of people and could not but find it strange to be in the home of one of them in such a friendly manner.[27]

Fersen's courteous reception by French officials in Italy did not pass unnoticed. Duchess Charlotta observed in April:

It is actually true that Bonaparte treats with distinction all those persons who were close to Louis XVI and who made sacrifices for him. I could give many proofs of this. The most striking is that Axel Fersen is received, indeed even sought after by all the Frenchmen in high positions in Italy. They always tell him that this is in accordance with the orders of the First Consul. . . . You will perhaps reply that this is done for the sake of the king and that Fersen is treated with such distinction thanks to his high rank. It is possible, but I know for sure that he sometimes corresponds with Bonaparte and occasionally mediates for émigrés. They are then always protected and helped and Bonaparte himself sees to it that they receive positions . . .

This contains a liberal dose of imagination; there is no evidence that Fersen ever corresponded with Bonaparte on this or any other subject. It is quite likely, however, that Fersen was shown special consideration on orders from Paris to gain Swedish goodwill.[28]

In Florence, the travelers were joined by Baron von Budberg and Bourke. Following the collapse of the Armed Neutrality, Budberg had resigned his Stockholm embassy, offended, among other things, by his friend Fersen's exclusion from the foreign ministry.[29]

In Rome in April, though they were received by Pope Pius VII, their welcome was less cordial. Since the French minister did not associate with them, the Roman aristocracy was afraid to do so. Fersen was contemptuous of their servility. In northern Italy, he had encountered a more outspoken dislike for the French. For instance, among those Fersen had frequently seen in Florence was the Countess of Albany, widow of Prince Charles Edward Stuart, and her lover, the poet Count Vittorio Alfieri, whose early enthusiasm for the French Revolution had turned to the deep disillusionment of his *Misogallo.* Only as a special favor would the poet, "who no longer wishes either to read or to speak French," converse in that language with his foreign guests. Though northern Italy appeared prosperous, Fersen criticized the duke of Pàrma for gross sensuality combined with superstitious religiosity—qualities he generally found objectionable in the Italians—and noted how the Tuscans missed their former Habsburg archdukes.[30]

By mid-May, Fersen and his party continued on to Naples, where they remained until August, in the villa in Belvedere once occupied by Princess Menshikova, visiting Pompeii and the grotto at Posillipo, climbing Vesuvius.[31]

Naples was still deeply affected by the turbulent events of 1798–99; the French invasion, the short-lived Parthenopean Republic and its destruction by Admiral Nelson and the royalist-Catholic crusade of Cardinal Ruffo's *sanfedisti.*[32] Fersen arrived just as the city was expecting the return of Ferdinand IV from Palermo. "At one o'clock the king's ship was sighted from Ischia and a cannon fired at San Elmo fortress," he wrote on 26 June: "The joy of the people was tremendous; all, including the children, went down to the shore shouting *il re, il re.*" The following day he witnessed the king's entry:

He was preceded by three or four bands of *lazzaroni,* or rather rascals, who shouted and made a tremendous commotion to show their joy. Such cries always give me a terrible feeling; I recall that I have heard the same thing to express entirely the opposite kind of sentiment. These memories saddened me at the same time as I was moved by the joy which the king's return seemed to arouse.[33]

There was no such welcome from the upper classes, which had provided the *giacobini* of the preceding decade and had suffered at the hands of the royalist counterrevolutionaries. "I was at the Teatro Nuovo," Fersen wrote on 30 June:

The king came there. They were very indifferent and no demonstrations of joy took place. Among the majority of the people an indifference, even a dissatisfaction, exists toward the government and the royal persons, especially among the nobility, who at the same time complain of the impudence of the people. This attitude has always existed among the nobility and perhaps it has been increased by the fact that they were ruled by foreigners, but after the horrors of the revolution and the injustices which followed, it has grown.[34]

Fersen showed much tolerance toward those aristocrats who had served the republic; ". . . the unfortunates who were abandoned here by their monarch and could not get away were really forced to accept offices to save their lives."[35] It would seem that despite all, he still found it hard to believe a noble could be a convinced Jacobin. In Naples, the greater onus of violence and rapine evidently lay with the other side. As Count Trolle-Wachtmeister wrote after visiting Naples in 1805,

Those who regard the outrages committed during the French Revolution as solely the consequences of the successful efforts of the Enlightenment to remove the bonds of religion from the masses—ought to journey to Naples and find out about the atrocities which the Neapolitan rabble and the Calabrians committed while they most diligently praised God, for whom they considered themselves to be fighting at the same time as for their king, whose palace they nevertheless plundered. . . . these . . . unenlightened Calabrians and *lazzaroni* committed, in proportion to the time available, their numbers, and the scope of the theater for their massacre, much greater atrocities than the Jacobins of France . . .[36]

To Fersen, the questions of right and wrong in this instance were probably more perplexing. For the most part he remained silent on such matters, though his diary for Naples conveys a rather depressing atmosphere. That he was a staunch royalist and anti-revolutionary doubtless explains the special consideration he received from Ferdinand IV and his principal minister, J. E. Acton, which aroused the suspicions of the French minister, as well as the little attention he and his companions received from the Neapolitan aristocracy. They associated mostly with the foreign colony, particularly the Russians. The group departed on 10 August, shortly before Queen Marie-Caroline's return from Vienna.[37]

They traveled to Rome, thereafter with an escort of dragoons to Livorno, where tragedy overtook them. Sophie's health was so poor that Axel feared for her life. Misfortune, however, struck from another direction. Budberg had become involved in a lively flirtation with Sophie's daughter, Hedvig, causing her husband, Möllersvärd, much grief. In Livorno, the latter contracted a fever and died on 12 September. He was buried beside Axel's elder sister, Hedda Klinckowström, who was buried there in 1792. Within a week, Hedvig Möllersvärd talked of marrying Budberg. Though this never came about and she eventually married the afore-mentioned Count Trolle-Wachtmeister, Fersen's friendship for the Russian was at an end.[38]

Fersen and the ladies now returned to Parma at the time of the duke's death, amidst general lamentations, "for three quarters of the town lives on the charity of the court." At the request of Duchess Marie-Amélie, he remained for a time to comfort and advise her as a friend. On 10 October, he arranged out of curiosity to see the French general, J. V. Moreau, on the pretext of applying for a pass. The general "spoke boastfully," claiming the region rightfully belonged to France and expressing contempt for the Italians. In late October, the group visited Venice, where the Austrian commander sent an honor guard of a corporal and six men to Fersen's lodgings. On the return voyage through Germany, Fersen was welcomed at the court of Karlsruhe, relived memories in Rastadt and Frankfurt, and at Itzehöhe, near Hamburg, visited the aging Mme. von Korff. After spending most of January in Copenhagen, where Fersen was struck by the general opulence, the party crossed the Sound with great difficulty because of ice-floes, arriving in Sweden on 29 January 1803.[39]

5

Following his travels, Fersen devoted himself to his official duties. He now assumed the varied responsibilities of the grand marshal. In addition, there was the university chancellorship and special committees and appointments. Though his regular positions were not of a political nature, Fersen was nevertheless in a position to influence the formation of policy, though by its very nature such influence would be difficult to appraise. Fersen participated in the king's councils and presided over the interim government of 1803–1805. Furthermore, Gustav IV Adolf frequently bypassed the regular organs of government, relying instead on persons in subordinate or unrelated positions. This was particularly true in foreign affairs; thus the titular head of the foreign ministry was little more than a chief clerk and not always cognizant of the king's designs, a situation to which Ehrenheim, but doubtless not Fersen, could resign himself. Gustav Adolf also preferred to fill important positions with careerists from the lower aristocracy. An influential member of the old high nobility in a position of responsibility, particularly one with strong and fixed ideas of his own in an area of policy the king was determined to reserve to himself, could prove awkward. Both the French minister, J. F. de Bourgoing, and the envoy of Baden, Count Lodren-Lateran, reporting on Gustav Adolf's advisers in 1803, considered Fersen a person of little influence. Bourgoing claimed that Fersen had himself declined appointment as *kanslipresident,* "more out of indolence than modesty," while Lodren-Lateran called "his abilities very limited, his activity null, his character weak and indecisive," maintaining that he showed little enthusiasm for the service of his king. Fersen, however, was not demonstrative by nature and was temperamentally best suited to less direct forms of influence. His part in policy-making was unquestionably greater than his official positions would suggest and surely far more important than Bourgoing or Lodren-Lateran realized.[40]

The position of *riksmarskalk* kept Fersen in constant, close association with the royal family. Following his return from the Continent, the king treated him with special amiability as did the queen and queen mother. Fersen's diary thus provides one of the most valuable sources concerning Gustav IV Adolf, his family and court at this time.[41]

Fersen's observations are now on the whole quite favorable; the sharply critical tone of his diary two years earlier is absent. In his descriptions, Gustav Adolf was steadier, more sensible, relaxed and friendly. The queen now showed more spirit and exercised an unobtrusive yet growing influence over her husband. Even the court seemed less dreary.[42]

Nevertheless, there were disquieting signs. The king occasionally revealed a strongly suspicious nature. He persisted in the belief that Baron Taube had been poisoned and that Sophie Piper's ill health derived from the same cause. An entry in Fersen's diary in May 1803 is more revealing:

For two days the king has been in a terrible humor. When these out-breaks of temperament come upon him, all those around him must bear the brunt. He lashes out against everyone and seeks out every possible pretext to become aroused. He became so when he heard a page coughing and spitting in the vestibule and wanted to send him to jail. He said later that the company was so miserable and the conversation so in-consequential that there was nothing to do but go to bed, which he did. . . . I found him in better spirits and it was said that it was my visit that did it . . .[43]

Certain events in the spring of 1803 show something of the king's manner. At the time of Fersen's return, Gustav Adolf was visited by Prince William of Gloucester, a young nephew of George III. The king, hoping to solve the problem of the confiscated Swedish convoys of 1798, warmly welcomed the prince until it became evident that this did not achieve the desired results. He thereupon became insufferably rude and drafted a sharp message to the king of England which he only thought better of sending after Gloucester made its contents common knowledge. All this only strengthened Fersen's belief that royal persons should not deal with each other personally.[44]

The prince, who by now had considerably overstayed his welcome, meanwhile became embroiled in a most curious episode, the so-called Boheman affair. In February, the king was alarmed by a secret warning that the royal palace in Stockholm harbored a nest of "Illuminati." This led to the arrest of one Karl Adolf Boheman, an adept in occult arts and grand master of a secret lodge, frequented by persons of the highest society, including Duke Karl, who in Fersen's words was, "always enthusiastic and gullible when it was a matter of superstition," and Duchess Charlotta, who had set up a kind of mystic temple in their apartment in the palace. The investigation proved that Boheman had perpetrated numerous hoaxes and was deeply humiliating to the duke and duchess, whose papers were seized and searched. Gustav Adolf took the affair in deadly earnest, perceiving a far-reaching web of con-spiracy against the state and society, and was fearful that the "Illuminati" were trying to poison him. The scandal hastened the departure of the prince of Gloucester, then on the point of becoming an initiate. Boheman was deported to avoid the embarrassment of a public trial.[45]

Though the government kept the proceedings secret, Fersen was well-informed and his diary provides one of the best sources for the episode. It was falsely rumored that Fersen himself knew Boheman, had used him in the past and had supplied the information leading to his arrest. Boheman's surprising wealth caused much speculation; according to one story, he had been Fersen's valet in France and had absconded with the queen of France's jewels, left in Fersen's safekeeping.[46] Axel's own views toward the episode were ambivalent. At first he thought it no more than "an inopportune and harmless Freemasons' correspondence," all rather ridiculous, but as the investigation proceeded, he became more fearful that it involved principles "in conflict with all religion and all government, a means for making fanatics, who could later be used, in a word, true Illuminati. . . ." Throughout, he found it hard to understand how intelligent people could thus allow themselves to be duped. The Boheman affair nonetheless was a phenomenon characteristic of its time: a widespread fascination with the occult and esoteric secret societies, combined with exaggerated fears that such things were a covert threat to existing society. Furthermore, secret lodges flourished with particular luxuriance in Sweden; at the time of Boheman's arrest, according to Fersen, Stockholm "swarmed" with "minor orders."[47]

This affair was soon overshadowed by a far more serious crisis when Sweden came close to war with Russia in April 1803. The immediate cause was a rather ridiculous detail: the painting of the bridge at Aborrfors to the disputed island of Germundsö, on the Swedish-Russian frontier in Finland. When Gustav Adolf ordered it painted in the Swedish colors, he inadvertently provided St. Petersburg with a welcome opening, for behind the bridge loomed European conjunctures of far greater import. France and Britain were drifting toward a new war while Franco-Russian relations were cooling. The possibility that Russia might become involved in the forthcoming conflict raised once again the strategic problem of St. Petersburg, dangerously exposed if Sweden should join Russia's enemies. As Sweden was diplomatically isolated in the spring of 1803, the situation was favorable for a sudden attack and the extension of the Russian frontier to the Gulf of Bothnia.[48]

Gustav Adolf's orders for repainting the bridge called forth a

Russian ultimatum to desist, while Russian forces concentrated on the Finnish border. That the Russians nearly provoked the war they sought is shown by Fersen's diary for 10 April. The king was determined to stand fast. Fersen remonstrated.

It is after all this clear that the bridge was only an expedient and that the king's behavior toward the [Russian] emperor has finally angered him, since the king after Paul's death has rejected all the emperor's attempts at rapprochement and done this in a cold and patronizing manner. This was difficult to say to him. I contented myself with representing to him that the affair over the bridge was only an excuse, that there most certainly were other causes, and that, if one were to insist on a new commission to regulate the frontier . . . one could at least win a respite and gain time for negotiation. I emphasized the danger for us of a war at the present time with our poor finances, with the [monetary] conversion under way, discontent in the country, and the consequences which the total ruin of our finances would bring by making the king entirely dependent upon the estates or some foreign power. He saw all of this and was ambivalent in his feelings.

At dinner, the king's bearing "was exemplary,"

. . . and one could not have noticed that he was very much concerned over this; and without allies as we are, and with cool relations with all other powers, there is truly reasons to be so. He understood this and noted himself that simply to rearm—regardless of how the war might go—would be a misfortune for us.[49]

Gustav Adolf nonetheless had not yet decided to give way. Chancellor Ehrenheim and the Russian chargé d'affaires, David Alopaeus, himself of Finnish origin and well-disposed toward Sweden, tried their best to urge moderation.

. . . but we still have not succeeded in persuading him to choose this course. . . . It is Baron Lagerbjelke who hinders this, for in order to insinuate himself into the king's favor, he always adopts his views. All the dangers a war would bring to Sweden have been strongly pointed out to him: the situation of our finances; the position of the country, if through the changing fortunes of a war we should be unfortunate enough to lose the same; the queen, his children, etc., etc. But he lets himself be led by his false conceptions of honor.[50]

By 14 April, however, Gustav Adolf decided to compromise. Baron Stedingk, in Stockholm on leave, provided a face-saving formula for the review of outstanding border disputes which was accepted by St. Petersburg. Dissension had arisen in the cabinet there and the British made every effort to keep peace in the Baltic. Tsar Alexander himself felt ambivalent about a war with his brother-in-law. The affair was soon forgotten; already by 20 April, Fersen noted that no one spoke of it any longer. "On the whole, it aroused less of a sensation than it should have, considering its importance."[51]

The outbreak of war between Britain and France in May 1803 soon improved Sweden's situation, bringing a favorable settlement of long-standing Anglo-Swedish maritime disputes.

6

Gustav IV Adolf had long wished to visit his wife's family in Karlsruhe. As early as May 1800, he had mentioned this to Fersen. In May 1803, Fersen, as grand marshal, was charged with the travel arrangements. On 3 July, he was made head of an *ad hoc* committee to expedite state business before the king's departure, and on 25 July Gustav Adolf appointed an interim government of nine, over which Fersen was to preside. Fersen opposed the journey, thus the king resorted to subterfuge, claiming he intended only a brief visit to Swedish Pomerania, after which he would consider whether to go further; "But I understood he will do this [i.e., continue to Karlsruhe] without regard for anything and that he had been encouraged still more by the queen's even greater desire to journey there." On 26 July, the royal family sailed from Stockholm.[52]

The interim government was charged with greater powers than formerly in such cases. On 29 July, Fersen observed that most of Stockholm society had left the city after the king's departure; "This taste or mania for going out to the country is so general that during the summer affairs are left to the state secretaries and to subordinates. We are only three in the government instead of nine. . . ." Nevertheless, his duties cannot have been too arduous, for academic and courtly functions absented him also at times and he speaks of the government only occasionally and briefly.[53]

Duchess Charlotta is in some ways more informative. In September, she commented that on the interim government, "there are not two who have the same views or are good friends. What one maintains is always opposed by one of the others." In February 1804, although the government was divided by personal rivalries,

"Fersen has succeeded in gaining respect and they often seem to follow his advice."[54]

In connection with the interim government, the duchess wrote a description of Axel Fersen in September 1803 which is worth citing in full. This was, she noted,

> . . . a task for which I ought to be competent, since I have known him since his earliest youth. He is honest and the most steadfast friend to his friends. A true royalist, he is prepared to do anything for his king, has made it his law to serve him diligently, was warmly devoted to Gustav III, holds the same feelings toward his son and the whole royal family. Fersen has suffered hard trials, he sought to save his benefactor, Louis XVI, but failed and grieved deeply over this. He is altogether too proud to intrigue; when opportunity arises, he expresses his opinion uprightly and fearlessly. Although he does not always favor the measures of the government, he observes here, if possible, even greater discretion and consideration than otherwise; he suffers in silence—a word of slander or criticism never crosses his lips. In his company, government and politics are never discussed. How truly tactful he is, is shown by deeds as well as his demeanor. The public unjustly blames him for not being a good Swede. Many years' sojourn abroad has naturally prevented his following the course of events here, but he has since his return worked to familiarize himself with conditions and to learn what is necessary to fill properly the post he holds and to fulfill the tasks the king entrusts him with. Those who only know Fersen superficially consider him haughty, but he is no more so than is necessary to command respect. He has a steadfast character and wishes to maintain order. If sometimes his behavior appears condescending, he knows well how to soften this impression.[55]

Meanwhile, Fersen also busied himself with his duties as grand marshal. There were tours of inspection of the royal palaces in the Stockholm region and details regarding the attached farms and stables.[56] There were court ceremonials to be arranged.[57] There was the inspection of Duke Karl's regiment.[58] He took part in the direction of the Academy of Painting in Stockholm and was concerned over a collection of 535 paintings the king's agent had purchased in Italy from "that rascal" Francesco Piranesi—notorious for his part in the Armfelt conspiracy—and which Fersen considered a swindle.[59] He was involved in the upbringing of the four-year-old Crown Prince Gustav and with the personal problems of various courtiers.[60] When the king's uncle, Duke Fredrik of Östergötland, died after a long illness in Montpellier, Fersen arranged for the return of the body, a funeral in fitting style and pensions for his two former mistresses.[61]

The period of the king's absence was thus not very eventful in Sweden. Perhaps most interesting for Fersen was the visit of the Bourbon princes to Kalmar in October 1804. In the spring of 1803, the self-styled Louis XVIII in Warsaw, seeking a new place of refuge, had asked to settle in Swedish Pomerania, as Gustav III had once suggested, through the Comte de Saint-Priest in Stockholm. Gustav Adolf, according to Fersen, was moved to tears by the request, which he granted, but the pretender established himself in Mitau, under Alexander I's protection, instead. In July 1804, however, he proposed to meet in Sweden with his brother, the Comte d'Artois, then in Britain, if the tsar would not allow them to do so in Vilna. Fersen was not at all enthusiastic; a meeting of this sort could attract international attention and compromise Sweden's neutrality. "The whole business is terribly unpleasant," he felt; Saint-Priest likewise found it embarrassing. Gustav Adolf, however, sent permission from Germany for the Bourbon princes to meet in Kalmar, referring to the Comte de Provence as "the king of France." Fersen was instructed to arrange their reception and to attend them personally during their stay.[62]

Fersen meanwhile learned that the princes intended to issue a manifesto from Kalmar, condemning all that had taken place in France since 1789. The Russian government for this reason forbade the meeting on its territory. Fersen and Saint-Priest agreed that the proclamation could cause difficulties and Fersen was determined to prevent it.[63]

Arriving in Kalmar on 13 October, he was received by the civil and military authorities and called immediately on the Comte d'Artois and his son, the Duc d'Angoulême, who were delighted to see him again and revived his nostalgia for the past. Thereafter, he was in constant attendance on the princes, who here, for the first time since Provence's "accession" in 1795, were received with royal honors. "They are very polite to those who come to visit them and speak with everyone," Fersen noted, "although most cannot answer, since they cannot speak a word of French." The princes greatly appreciated the courtesy shown them and naturally caused great excitement in the small provincial town.[64]

Fersen meanwhile consulted with the princes about the projected manifesto. The British had tried to prevent the meeting and opposed public representations at that point. Fersen rightly surmised that Britain and Russia agreed on this matter. "I suggested that the proclamation be dated on the high seas, which would compromise no one and also that its announcement be postponed until it was agreed to by both powers." The princes accepted these arguments; Provence had in fact by now already assured Gustav IV Adolf that he would make no pronouncements from Sweden. "I also reached an agreement with the king [i.e. Provence]," Fersen noted,

> ... that in the drafting of this [proclamation], any expression of the illegality of what had been done should be avoided so as not to take from the people involved in the Revolution and those who derived benefit from it all hope, which always has a bad effect.

This comment echoes a recurrent theme in Fersen's thinking in 1791–92.[65]

The princes had been separated since 1792. Something of their recent activities was revealed when Artois read for Fersen "in its entirety the account of the latest conspiracy with Pichegru and Moreau," the so-called Cadoudal plot of the previous winter, "for which the whole plan had been prepared by himself." Fersen, who had previously mistrusted Artois's recklessness and irresponsibility, was now well impressed with him. "He reasoned justly and moderately," he wrote, "and I am sorry it is not he who is Louis XVIII." As for the latter, "This prince has great learning and besides an especially good memory and wit, but he has no sense of politics and his weak character makes him still less suited for the role he must play." Fersen, of course, did not live to witness the actual reigns of Louis XVIII and Charles X. The Duc d'Angoulême he considered "pitiful morally as well as physically." Fersen left for Stockholm on 21 October; the princes and their entourages went their several ways soon after. The Bourbon manifesto, when it finally appeared as a modest pamphlet in Germany in December 1804, created little stir.[66]

7

With Fersen's return from Italy in early 1803, a new, more tranquil period of his life had begun. His diary begins to show him reconciled to his own and his country's situation. He was no longer anxious to travel abroad. His journey to the Continent would seem to have laid to rest that debilitating nostalgia for the old Europe that had so long kept him from finding his place in his own land.

More and more as time passed, he became absorbed in his official duties.

His relationship with his sister was a constant source of comfort and satisfaction. When Sophie's younger daughter, a maid of honor at court, was found to be pregnant in the fall of 1804, Fersen showed his hidden warmth for those closest to him by arranging her marriage to her lover—despite Sophie's worldly misgivings that "marriages of love rarely succeed"—providing a suitable economic "establishment" and a handsome wedding.[67] At the same time, he was much absorbed with the family estates at Lövstad, Ljung, Mälsåker, and Steninge.[68]

Fersen's official and social positions, as well as his own tastes, called for lavish entertainments and a certain display of magnificence, arousing admiration and envy, both gratifying to his vanity. He often speaks of the stir caused by his handsome equipages and splendid supper parties. In November 1803, he describes a *souper* he gave for sixty persons, which created "a great effect and was tremendously admired." Following another for a hundred guests a year later, "everywhere" there was talk of nothing else; "I did not deserve this, but it was fortunate for me that everyone had either not seen or had forgotten the old France." In February 1804, he invited the entire foreign diplomatic corps and many others to dinner; "The French legation were also there; I would never have believed the day would come when I would have to invite those people." At a ball at the Bourse in March, "That I stayed so long . . . and that I danced was the great news in town. This was a great event."[69]

The letters of Fersen's *chef de cuisine* during this period, Félix Berger, give further insight into his master's social activity. "I have every day for dinner and supper," Berger wrote in March 1803 to his brother, a *curé* in Provence, "at least 15 dishes to serve, sometimes 20, other times 30 or 40, but at least 15; I assure you that I have enough work for me alone to do with three kitchen maids who are not capable of assisting me. They do only the rough work. . . ." His complaint in October 1804 gives a picture of the lively bustle of the great noble establishment:

. . . I am in the midst of enormous activities since the first of June. I am *maître d'hôtel*; ours left for Paris. Since that time, I have been responsible for the entire household until another is found . . . I have the kitchen, the office, the wine cellar, the linen, the silver, the wardrobe, everyone to pay: valets, domestics, postillion, coachman, groom, laundresses, and everyone else, down to the tradesmen. . . ."[70]

Since his return, Fersen continued to regard his own country and people with a keenly critical eye. He often noted the shabby appearance of things compared to other times and places, particularly the court and its functions. The army seemed neither smart in appearance nor well prepared. Many of the officers seemed "mere children" and after reviewing the Göta Guards in June 1804, "what a difference from our regiments in France . . . what a pleasure it would have been for me to show the Royal-Suédois regiment and how amazed they would have been over it." The theater, opera, and art exhibitions were generally poor, in his opinion. In April 1805, he saw *Dido*; "But what a difference from *Dido* in Paris! Luckily there was no one there who could make comparisons. What painful memories and what longings did not fill my heart when I saw this piece!" The Swedes did not dress well and their equipages were generally unattractive. Social functions were often tiresome. "Since everyone in this country likes to go home early," he noted after dinner at an inn near Stockholm, "we left at 11:00 o'clock. This is what makes all the women fat, wrinkled, and old before their time." "Here they gossip enormously," he complained in December 1807, "and all ladies over a certain age are gossips. They generally know neither what it means to love or to live and it is impossible to establish a proper love affair in Stockholm." At a new type of gathering called a "dance-picnic" in 1803, he mused on how little the Swedes understood the art of conversation and how low social life had sunk; the men all gathered around the buffet table, leaving the ladies sitting around the walls of the dance floor, while even those who danced "looked as though they were going about their daily work." Table manners left much to be desired. Yet the social whirl was increasing. The number of people who held open table was by 1804 much greater than four or five years previously; there were now five or six *soupers* in top society each evening, "and often there is none at my place." "One must invite six or seven days in advance to be sure of one's guests, and still all complain of their poverty." Then too, there were new forms of entertainment, not only the "dance-picnic," but an evening affair called a "tea," at which one gathered at 6:00, played cards and was served bouillon, pastries, ham, cold cuts, and so forth at 9:00, but Fersen was skeptical, since "people want supper. And where shall one go after 11:00 o'clock?"[71]

Occasionally his criticisms were more serious and bear out the opinion of posterity that this period was a low point in Swedish morality, public and private. He notes how army officers were arrested for counterfeiting and organized burglary, how murders had doubled in the past ten years, and how "a certain unnatural inclination" had become "quite common here." His explanation for all this was characteristic for his age: "Luxury, which has greatly increased, has in the same degree increased immorality and ruined morals."[72]

The conditions of the social classes and the relationships between them were always of great importance to Fersen. He often took noblemen to task for undignified or irresponsible behavior. He could not condone offenses on their part that he would condemn in other classes. At the same time, the increase in prosperity and spread of new ideas often encouraged behavior by his social inferiors which Fersen found surprising or unsuitable. In the midst of a snowstorm in 1800, he had dinner at the farm of a peasant *Riksdagsman,* whose wealth astonished him. Shortly before, he had dined with a certain Arfwedson, a rich Stockholm merchant, "But without ostentation and with the proper restraint, as befits them." The great dinner a certain Herr Lorich gave in April 1804, however, made the host appear "the typical *bourgeois gentilhomme.*" When the rich merchant J. D. Wahrendorff died in 1803, Fersen was amazed that forty-two persons of "our finest families" went into mourning. On New Year's Day, 1804, a festivity was held at the Bourse, at which nobles were to appear in court dress, which meant,

. . . that there were fewer people than usual, for the burghers are offended by the difference in dress and do not go and others stay away so as not to have to take the trouble to dress, which nowadays is considered a nuisance. Now they only like to go in uniform and one cannot tell the difference between a nobleman and a shoemaker.

He noted, however, that the burghers now apparently enjoyed a gayer social life than the nobility. That important appointments in government and court rightly belonged to persons of birth was beyond question in his view. Thus he complained, for instance, in 1800 of the influence of the merchants in government and of the casual manner in which lower officials were recruited, discouraging application by "all distinguished persons" and leaving appointments "in the hands of the Third Estate, whose attitudes are in general more or less ruined."[73]

Still, after his return from Italy in 1803, Fersen's criticisms are no longer the bitter reactions of the expatriate by choice and show increasingly the personal engagement of the insider. He was now much more prepared to recognize what was unique and praiseworthy in Sweden. He speaks of its natural beauty. Sometimes even he will admit that a dramatic or musical performance or social event was in fact not at all bad.[74]

Alma Söderhjelm has called the period between 1803 and about 1806 probably the happiest of Fersen's mature years. Yet socially and culturally he tended increasingly to lose touch with his milieu. His associations were ever more limited to the royal family and, to some extent, the foreign diplomatic corps. Thus, while he himself felt more and more at home in the land of his birth, he appeared increasingly to others as a survivor from, indeed the symbol for, the age now past recall.[75]

At last, after eighteen months, Gustav IV Adolf and his queen returned from Germany in February 1805. The king was amiable and confidential with his grand marshal. As a special sign of favor, Fersen, though a bachelor, was invited to witness the birth of Princess Amalia Maria Charlotta on 22 February. Gustav Adolf now seemed more relaxed and generally in better spirits. Yet a constant undertone of anxiety is now perceptible in Fersen's comments on the king. His indolence was as exasperating as ever. "I saw the king to take care of various matters, but not at all, as he was impatient to quit," Fersen wrote in March. "It sometimes seems as though it were one's own affairs one comes with, and not his."[76]

Gustav Adolf's tendency to make much of small matters was shown, for instance, by his dismissal of the French theatrical troupe in Stockholm in 1805 because of what he considered the frivolity and impropriety of its repertory. Fersen had already noted in April 1795, when visiting Sweden:

The king does not like the theater. He almost always finds it boring there. He told me this himself and also gave me the reason, namely that he had been compelled to go so often to the theater when he was a child. During his reign, the opera will surely be abolished. And it is indeed also as expensive as it is bad.[77]

This prophecy proved a shrewd one. In 1806, Gustav IV Adolf dismissed the company and commanded that the Stockholm opera house be razed to the ground. The authorities stalled for time until estimates for the expense of demolition turned his thoughts to more pressing matters. Fersen was, of course, appalled by such arbitrary willfulness.[78]

By that time, it was evident that Gustav Adolf felt a growing aversion to his own capital. From early 1806, Fersen had ample opportunity to observe this alarming obsession and was convinced that the king positively wished harm upon the city. By the end of his reign, the king's ill-will seems to have spread to all of his Swedish nation.[79]

Gustav Adolf's maneuverings in the field of foreign affairs while in Germany in the meantime gave Sweden more substantial reasons for concern.

CHAPTER XIV

Fersen, Gustav IV Adolf, and the War of the Third Coalition, 1803–1807

1

Although Gustav IV Adolf had departed for Germany in the summer of 1803 because his queen longed for her family and childhood home in Baden, he had political interests as well and it was rumored that he wished to encourage the formation of an anti-French coalition. Before this, he had of course periodically shown interest in joining the struggle, yet throughout 1803, he held to neutrality and a watchful opportunism. If he mixed with émigrés and counterrevolutionaries who sought his support, he also carried on obscure negotiations with French diplomats in Germany over a possible alliance with a view to acquiring Norway, and even sent Fersen's old associate, Saint-Génié, to Paris on a secret mission. By the end of the year, however, the king became increasingly mistrustful toward both France and Prussia.[1]

It was Bonaparte's abduction of the Duc d'Enghien from Baden in March 1804 which gave Gustav Adolf the final impetus to join the anti-French camp. He immediately instructed his minister in Paris to protest vigorously and to plead for the consideration to which the duke's birth entitled him. "This action on the part of the king was beautiful, noble, and high-minded," commented Fersen, to whom Gustav Adolf had written at length of his actions. But he felt little optimism.

The king expressed to me in his letter to what a great degree he was aroused over the deed and that he hoped the reigning princes would react against the insult in a worthy manner. I answered him that I was convinced of the opposite. I believe the démarche will be only a spark in the water. The émigrés through their usual weakness for gossip have themselves given cause for this event, for they had gathered in crowds along the Rhine and recklessly spread the rumor that there was a revolution in Paris and that the First Consul would be murdered.

The Duc d'Enghien was executed on 21 March to the horror of all Europe. When Gustav Adolf protested through the Regensburg diet, Fersen felt this did him honor, but

... it will be no use, for no one will follow his example. Meanwhile, I am in the depths of my soul very pleased, although this can cause great inconveniences for us and my hope remains that we can avoid war. All is lost if we go to war and do so without help or cooperation from abroad. Neither the government nor anyone else had any idea of this measure.[2]

Gustav IV Adolf and Tsar Alexander I were, however, not prepared to stop at protests. By the end of March 1804, each had sounded the other out about an alliance. In April, both refused to recognize Bonaparte's new imperial title and Gustav Adolf recalled his minister from Paris, which filled Fersen with foreboding. "The honorable démarche Your Majesty is taking," he wrote tactfully to the king on 18 April, would

... doubtless indispose the First Consul by offending his pride. The consequences of this are impossible to foresee and Your Majesty will without doubt give thought in Your wisdom to what Your Majesty might wish to do to combine the dignity of Your person and crown with the interests of Your country, its internal situation and the limited resources it can provide.

By May, it seemed clear to Fersen that the Russians were in earnest, though Prussia acknowledged the self-proclaimed emperor, increasing Gustav Adolf's suspicions of that power, as did Austria.[3]

Paris now exerted pressure on Karlsruhe to encourage Gustav Adolf's departure. The king, however, bided his time, to the consternation of the margrave of Baden and of Fersen, whose letters to Lagerbjelke show much anxiety; at last he departed in July to visit various German courts.[4]

The king was meanwhile subjected to scurrilous attacks, at home and abroad. In March 1804, an anonymous pamphlet, *Lettre du*

Baron G. au Comte B. Francfort, was mailed to influential people in Sweden, which was, Fersen commented, "a hidden satire against the king in the guise of praise. I also received a copy; it is poorly written and the historical facts are wrong." It was generally believed to be the work of Baron Reuterholm in Frankfurt, though G. G. Adlerbeth believed the Fersen family sought to blame Lars von Engeström, who at this time was recalled from Berlin. There is no evidence for this from Fersen's side and Engeström wrote that following his final return to Sweden in 1806, "the greatest courtesy" prevailed between himself and the *riksmarskalk.* "About him I had nothing to complain," he added, though he naturally remain suspicious of Sophie Piper, who had insinuated that he had poisoned Baron Taube.[5]

A more serious attack appeared in the *Moniteur* in Paris on 14 August 1804, depicting Gustav Adolf as a vain and childish fool, the misfortune of the "loyal and brave" Swedish nation. Fersen noted that it was immediately translated and spread about Stockholm. Gustav Adolf indignantly severed his last links with Paris. Fersen conveyed to the interim government the king's order forbidding Swedes any contact with persons in French service.[6] The import of new French books and journals was forbidden as was any mention in the Swedish press of events in France; the French head of state was henceforth to be referred to simply as "M. Bonaparte."

Gustav Adolf meanwhile entered into negotiations with Britain and remained in Stralsund in Swedish Pomerania through the fall, supervising defensive preparations. Fersen was again skeptical. "The wisest thing to do if the French came would be to abandon everything, for resistance would be impossible; but it is to be feared that the example of Karl XII, which the king has constantly before his eyes, will drive him to take certain ill-advised measures. . . ."[7]

The principal threat at this point seemed Prussia, rather than France, for the Berlin cabinet sought to guarantee the neutrality of northern Germany as a Prussian sphere of influence, which Swedish involvement in a war against France could upset. It therefore made thinly veiled threats to occupy Swedish Pomerania, which evoked counter-threats from St. Petersburg.

Thus by the time he returned to Sweden in February 1805, Gustav Adolf had embroiled Sweden with both France and Prussia, and had sought alliances with Russia and Britain. The decisions were his own; though many of his counselors were anti-French, none, not even Fersen, favored commitment of Sweden's slender resources to a conflict of the great powers.

A sequel occurred not long after; as Fersen described it on 3 May 1805:

The king has taken a step which is bound to pain all his good servants. He has returned the Order of the Black Eagle to the king of Prussia, since he no longer wishes to wear it because the king of Prussia has accepted the Legion of Honor. . . . It is impossible to calculate the consequences of this insult, which is altogether an open criticism of all the sovereigns who have accepted [the Legion of Honor], and it will be regarded with disfavor by all. The English minister has expressed himself in this sense and that of Russia has spoken in the same terms with President Ehrenheim about it . . . [who] replied that since this was an entirely personal matter, it could not have any influence on the political situation. It is not impossible that this line of reasoning will be put to shame.[8]

The king showed Fersen his letter to Frederick William, doubtless expecting approval. The count replied with measured words:

I told him—and it was true—that it was remarkably well written and as polite as the subject allowed. . . . The king saw himself unhappily forced to return a sign of friendship, the great value of which he realized. He did not wish to enter into explanations painful to them both but he could not consider Bonaparte and his like otherwise than as unworthy to be knights. This was in the main its contents. I repeated that the letter was very polite but that the action was blunt and could not but give offense. The king admitted this but added that it was in accordance with his views and ways of seeing things, that he did not recognize Bonaparte, that he does not believe himself to be sufficiently influential to set a precedent, but besides acting according to his principles he hoped at least through his conduct to arouse some reflection in the sovereigns who have not yet made up their minds. He said he would not be surprised if the king of Prussia returned the Order of the Seraphim to him, but that it was inconceivable that he could be so offended that this could affect his political behavior. . . . This matter once having taken place, it was unnecessary to dwell on what was good or bad about it. I limited myself to repeating that the measure was a sharp one and that I hoped it would not bring about any great inconvenience. In the depths of my heart, I could not help finding the sentiment that dictated his behavior beautiful and honorable, and this made me glad. The king is the only sovereign who has maintained a sense of his position and who has self-respect, and he has in carrying out [his measures] observed all possible consideration not to give offense. But from a political point of view, it is impossible to favor what he is doing.[9]

The consequences were just what Gustav Adolf had regarded as "inconceivable": Prussia broke diplomatic relations, thus seriously compromising Sweden's participation in the War of the Third Coalition half a year later. The French press heaped abuse upon the young Swedish monarch and began to question his very sanity.[10]

2

The king's return gave Axel Fersen the chance to visit Princess Menshikova in Dresden. On 3 June 1805, he departed Stockholm, together with Sophie, Hedvig Möllersvärd and her five-year-old daughter. In Stralsund, Fersen met the governor general of Swedish Pomerania, Baron Hans Henrik von Essen, and Baron Armfelt, now commanding the military forces there, who further impressed him with the seriousness of Sweden's situation.[11]

The travelers continued to Berlin, where "the situation is not favorable for a Swede to show himself at court . . . ," thence to Dresden, where they stayed until late September. Ketty was undeniably a disappointment. She had grown "enormously fat," perhaps because of her uncompleted pregnancy in 1802, and had a French émigré lover. Though Fersen corresponded with her sporadically in later years, the affair was clearly over. He meanwhile found in Dresden society some fragments of the old Europe, as yet largely undisturbed by revolution or war. The court was almost as he remembered it thirty years earlier. Here, too, was assembled an illustrious company of the old cosmopolitan high aristocracy, including threadbare former courtiers from Versailles and Russians who entertained on a princely scale.[12]

Yet even here Fersen could not avoid political developments. His order, *Pour le mérite militaire,* received from Louis XVI for service in the American war, evoked a protest from the French chargé d'affaires to the Saxon government. The foreign minister and the Swedish chargé d'affaires tried tactfully to persuade Fersen not to wear it, which aroused both his indignation and his apprehension over his own monarch's reaction, well knowing Gustav Adolf's meticulousess concerning orders and decorations. The best plan seemed to avoid the Saxon court, but as might be expected, Gustav Adolf ordered Fersen to appear there in full regalia, seeing in the affair "an irrefutable sign of the dictatorship France seeks to establish over the various states of Europe." The matter was embarrassing. As he was just on the point of departing for Leipzig, Fersen pretended he had received the order too late to carry it out. But it was no use. Upon his return, he found instructions to resume the affair, which he now simply disregarded, a striking sign of his declining faith in his monarch's competence. In late September, Fersen and his companions departed Dresden to return home.[13]

3

Negotiations proceeded slowly over Sweden's entry into an anti-French coalition. After the first flush of excitement, Gustav IV Adolf proved a shrewd bargainer. Though Sweden's own resources were small, her position on the Sound and the Baltic, as well as her bridgehead in Pomerania, were important strategic assets, to be exchanged for sufficient subsidies to avoid the need for a Riksdag. Furthermore, Gustav Adolf insisted that the allies undertake to restore the Bourbons in France, which met with an evasive response from London and St. Petersburg. The visit of the Bourbon princes to Kalmar in October 1804 gave point to his demand, as did his reception of the Comte de Saint-Priest into the Stockholm diplomatic corps and employment of the émigré Duc de Piennes as his personal adjutant under the title of *premier gentilhomme de chambre* to King Louis XVIII of France. Gradually, however, alliances were formed with Russia and Britain by October 1805. There were in Swedish Pomerania in November, a month after the war began, some 12,000 Swedish troops, about one fifth of Sweden's total military strength.[14]

The king was meanwhile impatient of delay. Coming events, he wrote Fersen in Dresden, would show whether the man of violence would realize his ambitions or would fall victim to a just retribution. Fersen, returning from the Continent, visited Gustav Adolf at his headquarters at Beckaskog in Skåne in October:

The king received me in a charming manner and with emotion, and after he had spoken at some length with me about political matters, he said he was rather perplexed and in need of my advice concerning whom he should take with him [to Pomerania], who could always be together with the foreign diplomats and confer with them. He did not want, he said, to take the *kanslipresident*, as he was needed in Stockholm, where the diplomatic corps was located, but he had thought if my health and home affairs permitted, he would propose me and would be extremely happy if I would accept; that my knowledge of other lands and the prestige I enjoyed would be most useful to him and that it would be most reassuring to him to have by his side a person whose devotion to him and whose views were known and also inspire respect. He bade me reflect on this and repeated that I would make him very glad.

Fersen was "in despair," seeing that this would not suit him "from all points of view," but the king countered all his objections and "made it quite impossible to refuse."[15]

Gustav Adolf, in offering Fersen this position, clearly believed that of all his counselors he was the most uncompromising enemy of revolutionary France and of Bonaparte, and the most steadfast supporter of the Bourbon cause. Up to this point, he was most likely correct, but he hardly realized how much more moderate and cautious Fersen had become since his return to Sweden in 1799. As in that year, when conflict with France seemed imminent, Gustav Adolf now again turned to Axel Fersen, hoping to find in him consistent and unquestioning support. In this respect, he was before long disappointed.[16]

Fersen's comments on France after 1800 are remarkably dispassionate. At first he speculated on the instability of the Consulate, dependent upon the First Consul, whom "death, a dagger, or a revolution" could carry away; but when Bonaparte became "emperor of the Gauls" and created a new imperial court, it seemed evident that "the old titles and even the old institutions will return." His main concern was now no longer to try to undo the work of the Revolution in France or Europe, but rather to assure the welfare and security of his own native Sweden.[17]

The following day Fersen reluctantly accepted Gustav Adolf's request. He was permitted to take Sophie Piper with him to see to his delicate health and to put his affairs in order in Stockholm before joining the king.[18]

On 31 October, Sweden declared war on France and Gustav Adolf assumed overall command of the allied forces in northern Germany, including 17,000 Russians in Swedish Pomerania and a British corps which in November landed at the mouth of the Elbe.

Fersen and his sister left Stockholm on 2 November. At Lövstad manor, "I deeply regretted not being able to stay here, which I should greatly have preferred to what now lies ahead of me." They soon learned of a great French victory over the Austrians near Ulm, which made problematical any further operations in northern

Germany. Soon after, they had a sad meeting with Queen Fredrika, traveling home to Stockholm from Skåne. "She cried a great deal," Fersen wrote, "entrusted the king to my care and bade me watch over him."[19]

4

The campaign in the north should have been pressed with all dispatch against the French flank, but Gustav Adolf was restrained by his mistrust of Prussia, which he feared might attack him from the rear and which now began to occupy Hanover as the French withdrew. Prussia meanwhile negotiated secretly with Russia over joining the coalition. Gustav Adolf, uncertain of the intentions of Berlin, sent Count Gustaf Löwenhielm with a letter to Frederick William III, brusquely demanding clarification. The count arrived during a visit by Tsar Alexander and was thus virtually ignored, allowing no opportunity to deliver his letter. Gustav Adolf recalled him indignantly and was deeply offended by the tsar's apparently greater consideration for the Prussian king than for himself.

Such was the situation when Fersen arrived in Stralsund on 11 November 1805 to assume the unpromising position of the king's "acting foreign minister," as Duchess Charlotta styled it. Barons von Essen, Lagerbjelke, and Armfelt briefed him and hoped his arrival would produce "good results." "I was flattered," he wrote, "but at the same time quite depressed, knowing well how very little power one can have over the king as soon as he has made up his mind about something and already announced it." Fersen went to see Gustav Adolf and during the next two hours managed to calm his ill temper. The king agreed to send his letter once more to Berlin as "a way out of the dilemma he has gotten himself into," and Fersen tried to arrange for Russian pressure on Frederick William to accept it.[20]

The matter seemed cleared up and the British and Russian ministers were well pleased. But they still could not persuade Gustav Adolf to advance his troops with the Russians to the west. Fersen feared he could not influence the king on this point since he could not answer for Prussia's intentions. Besides, Gustav Adolf's indignation kept welling up to obstruct any rational solutions, spurred by rumors of the ridicule to which he was subjected in Berlin. On 13 November, Fersen wrote,

In all my conversations I found him furious against Prussia and over the insult he received from that quarter. He wanted only satisfaction and was not at all concerned with important matters because of this private affair, which he meanwhile regarded from his own point of view and wanted to make into a common cause which he even thought the allies should take up. He does not understand that [international] politics do not include matters of knightly honor. I grieved greatly at having been compelled to come here.[21]

The British minister, Henry Pierrepont, was beside himself with chagrin. Fersen did his best to calm him and to urge Gustav Adolf to let his troops march. The king appeared to understand, but procrastinated. The following day,

I found . . . the king had changed entirely and was more determined than ever to wait for an answer from Berlin. He even became quite vehement and said he preferred not to have any allies at all rather than those who were not concerned with him and did not feel themselves offended by the offense that had been done him. I understood that beneath all of this lay a jealousy toward Prussia and over the consideration with which the others treated that power. In order not to arouse him to any more violent action, I said nothing.[22]

Such indirect answers as were forthcoming from Berlin were not however to Gustav Adolf's liking and British assurances that Prussia had no designs on Swedish Pomerania failed to satisfy him.[23] On 30 November, Pierrepont told Fersen that Britain saw little immediate prospect for conciliation from the Prussian side, even with British encouragement. Fersen feared that this would put the king in a rage, but the British minister tactfully suggested that while Gustav Adolf's hesitation had not thus far affected the campaign, the Swedish force ought now to advance.

I decided to make use of all this and to give the king's actions the appearance of policy and that all his demands in Berlin had only been a subterfuge to disguise his real reason. This succeeded wonderfully and after quite a long pause which followed my exposition, which I made as politely as possible, I presented my views. The king accepted my viewpoint and even said that this had always been his thought. I then continued and suggested to him that he himself as well as his army should move across the Elbe and announce to his allies that although he had not received from Berlin the information he had requested, he was willing nevertheless to give proof of his zeal and interest in the good cause by moving to the other side of the Elbe, except that the unsure situation had forced him to remain until he saw how it developed. The king was satisfied with this suggestion, saying this would be the best way to get out of the situation.

Gustav Adolf thereupon drafted a statement, blaming Prussia for his delay, but Fersen persuaded him to limit himself to generalities, since "one would have the advantage of being able to use and explain it as one wished and besides offend no one." "I was very glad to have succeeded so well," he concluded, "much beyond my own expectations."[24]

Next day, the king was in good spirits. He had just received an encouraging letter from the tsar in Olmütz. A dispatch from a Swedish liaison officer there contained less heartening details about the Austrian and Russian armies. "All these details were terrible," Fersen commented, "and it was grievous to think that Europe rests just now in the hands of the Prussians, whose short-sighted and servile policy cannot clearly be comprehended." On 2 December, the Austrians and Russians were crushed by Napoleon at Austerlitz. The following day, Gustav Adolf finally gave the command for the Swedish army to join its allies in Hanover. On 6 December, he officially notified the foreign envoys at his head-quarters that Count Fersen would deal with them in his behalf and that all communications should pass through him.[25]

5

Gustav IV Adolf did not himself leave Stralsund without further delay. He now often seemed tired of his position and policy. "He is not so wrong," Fersen observed, "and the best thing he could do would be to leave the whole thing himself; his character is not nearly flexible enough for a personal coalition." But the arrival of fresh British subsidies cheered the king considerably, since, as Fersen noted, the war chest had been empty for nearly a week. Gustav Adolf left to join the army on 8 December, followed shortly by Fersen and his entire household, consisting of "18 persons, 6 carriages, 17 horses of my own, and 13 post horses."[26]

Meanwhile, the Prussian foreign minister, Prince Hardenberg, tactfully urged the Swedish king through the Russian minister, Alopaeus, to send a conciliatory letter through someone in his confidence to Frederick William, in which case the foreign minister promised to try to bring the Prussian forces under Gustav Adolf's overall command when Prussia joined the coalition. "Nothing could be more flattering to the king," Fersen felt. But Gustav Adolf insisted that the king of Prussia must take the first step toward rapprochement personally, which roused Fersen to an outburst of despair:

> It is shameful that the king will not accommodate himself to this attempt at conciliation for the sake both of his own land and of the common situation, for if this can be in any way saved, it can only be through Prussia, and this land alone will be responsible for the fate of Europe. If it joins France, all Europe will be tyrannized.[27]

News of Austerlitz arrived on 13 December, immediately overshadowing all else. Fersen was mortified and now believed,

> . . . more than ever that this enterprise is lost and peace is near at hand. It will be an unfortunate one. I felt the deepest distress over this. It is terrible to see how many crimes remain unpunished and it is hard to admit that cohesion and effectiveness are only to be found on the wrong side. This is the disadvantage of coalitions.

"Sovereigns," he added ruefully, "ought never to mix themselves in with such matters except at a distance. They have other duties to fulfill, especially if it is not a matter of directly defending their crowns."[28]

Ten days later he advised Gustav Adolf that the French would now turn toward the north while Prussia would not now join the allies. He counseled that the Swedes advance no further, adding that prudence would only make the Swedish king greater in the eyes of Europe. On 27 December, he urged Gustav Adolf to suspend further operations and return to Sweden. "Necessity, Sire, is a hard law," he wrote, "and the emperor of Germany and even of Russia feel it in a painful manner at this moment; and the king of Prussia with 300,0000 men must be pained to have to sacrifice his resentment to necessity and the fear of even greater evils." Gustav Adolf, Fersen noted when he saw him on 18 December, "considered all was lost and hoped we would be able to preserve the status quo until spring and then go home"; but his cheerful attitude seemed to belie his words, as later developments would show.[29]

There ensued a kind of *drôle de guerre* as the allies awaited the outcome of confused developments to the south. As a last attempt to bring Prussia into the sagging coalition, Britain and Russia offered to replace Gustav IV Adolf with Frederick William III as supreme allied commander in the north. The Swedish king was of course outraged. He had no intention, he wrote proudly to Fersen on 8 January 1806, of putting his forces under the king of Prussia:

My sentiments toward my allies are too well known for me to repeat them here. Abandoned by almost all, I could consider myself in a situation in which I were freed from all obligation with regard to military operations, since circumstances have changed in such a singular manner. But faithful to my principles, I have demonstrated up to the present how much I take to heart the good of the common cause. I shall hold to the same conduct in the future, while at the same time giving to my peoples and my army all the consideration that I owe them and which is compatible with the general interest.[30]

The order of priorities in the last sentence is worthy of note.

It was too late. On 15 December, Prussia made an alliance with France, allowing for a Prussian occupation of Hanover. Austria made peace at Pressburg. The Russians and British began to withdraw from northern Germany. On 10 January 1806, Fersen urged Gustav Adolf to follow suit. "Prudence and wisdom united with courage characterize the hero," he wrote tactfully. "... It is no longer a question of war, Sire ... negotiations have taken the place of military operations: efforts are being made only to obtain peace." The king should not allow himself to be left out.[31]

Gustav Adolf, however, established headquarters at Boitzenburg, on the right bank of the Elbe. Though he too withdrew from Hanover proper, he announced he would occupy the small Hanoverian territory of Lauenburg, north of the Elbe, on behalf of its master, the king of England, and not evacuate it unless formally requested to do so by London. Gustav Adolf's motives were evidently both emotional and calculating. He wished to spite the Prussians, hold the British to payment of their subsidies and if possible drag them into his quarrel with Berlin. Fersen believed the king was embarrassed at thus far having accomplished nothing and actually wanted a brush with the Prussians, "so that he like the others might have smelled gunsmoke," little realizing the seriousness of the consequences.[32]

Fersen urged strongly that the Swedes withdraw entirely from Hanoverian territory. The British, he wrote Gustav Adolf on 25

January, tacitly accepted the occupation of the electorate by withdrawing their troops while the Russians were also recalling theirs. On 31 January, the king announced he would move his headquarters to Ratzeburg, in the center of Lauenburg; when the *Hamburger Zeitung* published Frederick William's proclamation of his occupation of Hanover until the peace, no one dared show it to Gustav Adolf for fear, Fersen wrote, "that he might countermand his orders to his troops, who had not yet moved very far . . . for it is better that they should reach their destination before he sees this in the newspaper." Pierrepont's assurances that Britain did not expect Sweden to endanger her forces in Lauenburg and entreaties to withdraw were without effect, as was the plea of the Hanoverian state minister in mid-February to leave so as to spare the civil population needless suffering. The king insisted on a formal statement from London. Such an explicit acceptance of the Prussian occupation, Fersen wrote him on 15 February, could hardly be expected since the king of England would avoid prejudicing his future claim to his hereditary lands. The British and Russians, however, now seemed less interested in Hanover than in making peace; thus Sweden should not count on their help in a showdown with Prussia. To this, the king replied that he had still received no "clear and satisfactory explanation" from London, that he sought to act on his principles and if these should provoke the king of Prussia, then "I believe I should run the risk and I would be honored by it." He still considered Britain and Russia obliged to help him.[33]

Pierrepont received instructions from London on 24 February to express George III's desire that the Swedes leave Lauenburg. "The wishes of the king of England," Fersen wrote Gustav Adolf, ". . . appear to be clearly enunciated here." But the king did not consider this an acceptable reply. By mid-March, Gustav Adolf decided to consider an attack on Lauenburg tantamount to an attack on Sweden itself. Fersen did his best to warn of the consequences. The British, he wrote Gustav Adolf on 16 March, had never spoken of ceding Hanover, whereas the stand contemplated by the king would be "a veritable conquest" and could appear to Prussia "a declaration of war," since that power, "which has indeed shown by its patience that it wishes to avoid everything which might seem to provoke one," might be forced into hostilities with Sweden by France.

With only a handful of men, does Your Majesty not think that when his ally declares himself and invites him to withdraw, Your Majesty has not done all that is necessary for his glory? . . . . The struggle would be too uneven, courage would become foolhardiness and it is also glorious to cede in time to circumstances, especially when one has not yet been compromised.

The king should therefore withdraw with all possible forces to Sweden.[34]

A yet more succinct British request for withdrawal arrived the next day, but, Fersen commented dryly, this would probably have no greater effect, "for there are not many arguments which affect the king's political or military ideas. He mixes personal honor with the interests of the state." Indeed, considering the Treaty of Paris of 15 February, by which Prussia annexed Hanover and closed its North Sea ports to Britain, Gustav Adolf was sure the British must already have changed their minds. In the confusion that followed, there seemed encouraging signs from both London and St. Petersburg. Though Gustav Adolf withdrew in late March to Swedish Pomerania, he left a token detachment of some 300 cavalrymen in Lauenburg to assert his presence. The line was drawn. Under the circumstances, the Prussians could hardly fail to cross it.[35]

Fersen's position was not a pleasant one. Since early December, he had generally been quartered at some distance from the king, whom he seldom saw. When he did, Gustav Adolf now avoided political discussions. He was clearly disillusioned with Fersen, the apostle of international counterrevolution. "This stubbornness," Fersen brooded on 3 March,

. . . in defending a land which has been abandoned by its proprietor is beginning to invite ridicule. I no longer spoke with him about either staying or leaving. I had already had enough of that; it was unnecessary, since the king knows what I think. Besides, when I am here and he is there, he certainly has no need of my advice. It becomes superfluous and although I personally am happier to be far away, I am not satisfied with my position, which is not what it ought to be. M. Pierrepont is there and the king confers directly with him. . . . I would as gladly have stayed in Sweden.

Pierrepont's frustration was certainly as great: "God only knows what he wants. When there was an enemy, it was impossible to get him to advance; when there is none, one cannot get him to retreat." He would not be unhappy, Fersen complained in February, "to fight with anyone at all."[36]

As these events transpired, the king's staff amused themselves in Lauenburg as best they could. Gustav Adolf busied himself with phrenology under the tutelage of its originator, the renowned Dr. Franz Josef Gall, prompting Armfelt to quip, "This study of heads does not seem to have served any purpose other than to turn a wooden head into a head of lead lined with pig iron." Fersen was characteristically more sober. "His lectures," he wrote of Dr. Gall, "are interesting as curiosities but upon weak souls they could have a dangerous influence."[37]

More serious was the king's readiness to lend an ear to French royalist conspirators. In December 1805, Fersen was contacted by Louis Fauche-Borel, who complacently observed that his name would not be unknown because of his part in the Pichegru conspiracy and who wished to convey "some details which might be of infinite interest to you under the circumstances." On 15 January 1806, Fersen wrote Gustav Adolf of the arrival in Lauenburg of a certain M. de La Coudraye, of whom Fauche-Borel had spoken to the king, with a letter from the Comte de Moustier in Berlin. He had once seen La Coudraye at Breteuil's home near Hamburg, Fersen continued; he had had good principles then and perhaps did still, but his numerous connections with Bonaparte's entourage made it appear that "he is a man who behaves somewhat according to the circumstances ... Your Majesty will see that he is a real hothead ... who wishes for results without calculating well the means to them." He advised the king to be on his guard. In his diary, he was more direct: La Coudraye was "a madcap, highly exalted, a typical Frenchman and *marseillais,* a tiresome prattler and difficult to understand." He was meanwhile apprehensive about Gustav Adolf; "He listens to everyone who talks big and presents big plans." La Coudraye "had the most extreme views" and "his exaggerated praise for the king's conduct will make it even harder to persuade him to be careful in his actions."[38]

La Coudraye returned from his interview with Gustav Adolf in high spirits, claiming they had agreed that Louis XVIII should join the king of Sweden and the tsar, gather 50,000 men and get financial support from Britain. "God only knows," Fersen complained in his diary,

All that he said and hoped. It was easy for him to hope for and believe in success. . . . the king has a very strong desire to undertake some action. . . . I was much grieved by this conversation. I had already foreseen that it would result in our being dragged into fantastic projects, impossible to realize, which will make the carrying out of reasonable measures difficult.

The nature of the scheme discussed is further clarified by a letter from Cabinet Secretary Gustav af Wetterstedt to Fersen of 9 March, nearly two months later:

The king has not yet returned to me the letter from Louis XVIII as well as the memorandum that accompanied it. It is a question of a new coalition in which the king of France would be an integral, and above all, an active partner. A hundred thousand Russians and Swedes would embark on the coasts of France with Louis XVIII at their head. But to achieve this, the court of Great Britain would have to call His Most Christian Majesty to England as soon as possible; and it is in this that he requests the intervention of the king [of Sweden] . . .

Besides this plan, reminiscent of Gustav III's project in 1791, Fersen's letter to Gustav Adolf of 15 January, announcing La Coudraye's arrival, already speaks of another idea: that La Coudraye himself go to Paris to organize Bonaparte's assassination. "If he does indeed hold the right principles," Fersen mused, "I believe that in this connection he would be a suitable tool." But shortly after he was again alarmed at the thought of any involvement with La Coudraye and his friends. He had spoken to Pierrepont, as directed, about these matters, he wrote the king on 20 January:

Mr. Pierrepont seemed to feel how desirable and useful [its] success would be for the repose and tranquility of Europe but he felt that the court [of St. James], which had already so often been disappointed, either by traitors whose assurances had been at least as positive [as La Coudraye's] or by well-intentioned persons who, giving less consideration to their means than to their desires, had given hopes not subsequently realized or justified by the successes that had been promised, would hesitate to adopt any measure before receiving the most positive assurances. In effect, Sire, when one recalls the negotiations of the same sort of Messrs. Wickham, Spencer Smith and Drake, and how these ministers have been misled by the appearance of a false zeal or by the appearance of an enthusiasm that circumstances quenched, one has reason to be apprehensive and I cannot avoid those fears that this man arouses in me. It seems to be extraordinary that a man of so violent a nature could moderate his behavior to the extent that he could remain in Paris and that he should be so little suspect that he should be free to leave and return [there].

When the former French foreign minister and general, Dumouriez, sought out the king in Stralsund in April, Fersen was again suspicious and fearful.[39]

The episode illustrates strikingly the change in Fersen's own attitude. In 1799, at which time he had probably first met La Coudraye, he had himself been deeply involved with French royalist intriguers of the same type in forming far-reaching plans for a great international anti-Jacobin league, at the head of which was to stand the king of Sweden himself.

6

Gustav Adolf now set up headquarters in Greifswald. Fersen established himself in Stralsund, where he and his sister became the center of a little coterie of relatives. On 10 May, Sophie's son, Axel Piper, married a daughter of Baron Armfelt, in honor of which Fersen gave a ball for three hundred persons. In the same month, in accordance with Napoleon's wishes, the heir apparent to the margrave of Baden and Gustav IV Adolf's brother-in-law, was engaged to a cousin of Josephine. The emperor of the French created kingdoms and principalities. "It is terrible to think," Fersen wrote on 16 April, "that the weak and idiotic policy of the European powers has brought them to a situation which makes it impossible for them to prevent such unexampled changes."[40]

Gustav IV Adolf's occupation of Lauenburg placed Berlin in a difficult quandary. It hesitated to expel the Swedes for fear of the Russians. Napoleon meanwhile warned that if the Prussians did not occupy Lauenburg, the French would do so themselves. Berlin thus determined to seize the territory after tactfully warning both Sweden and Russia. Though Fersen found Gustav Adolf little concerned over the growing concentration of Prussian troops on the Pomeranian frontier, the indirect warning from Berlin put him in a foul temper. He entrusted himself to Providence, he said, and to the justice of his cause. He spoke to Armfelt of attacking Prussia and to Fersen of "attacking and destroying" Prussian commerce. Fersen was reluctant to argue, but Gustav Adolf "practically forced me into a discussion and I then told him everything

I thought": all the considerations he had already raised in his letters. The fate of Europe, he reiterated, depended on Prussia; to be at odds with her could force her into the arms of France, with dire consequences for the North. Despite Prussia's behavior, "as unwise as it was unreliable," one must regard that country

... in the same way as a child and try to help it mend its ways. He said to me that it must be punished and that he would punish it and that he would set it as low as it deserved to be. He became greatly agitated and I said nothing more. When I had finished my report and what I had to say, he calmed himself and returned again to the same subject without becoming upset.[41]

The king thereafter avoided discussing the situation with Fersen. On 18 April, the Prussians marched into Lauenburg. The small Swedish force, greatly outnumbered, withdrew after a token resistance.

In retaliation, Gustav Adolf proclaimed an embargo on Prussian vessels in Swedish ports. Fersen greatly disapproved of this but nonetheless was obliged to sign the king's manifesto proclaiming it. He saw serious consequences for Sweden's economy, and indeed more Swedish ships were seized by the Prussians in reprisal than vice versa. On 28 April, Fersen wrote a long remonstrance, which he scarcely expected to be heeded. He held that though Berlin had done everything to avoid provocation, a Prussian invasion of Swedish Pomerania now seemed imminent, which neither the British nor the Russians would prevent. Furthermore, both these allies might at any time make peace with France. England's policy had always been "egotistical" and she was ever prepared to abandon allies when advantageous to her. Fersen thus counseled withdrawing to Sweden all troops not needed for the defense of Stralsund itself.[42]

Gustav Adolf, however, prepared to meet any attack. He proclaimed a levy of his Pomeranian subjects to form a *Landwehr,* thus being the first European monarch to adopt the revolutionary principle of conscription.

"It is impossible to understand the purpose of all he undertakes," Fersen wrote on 3 May. On 30 April, Gustav Adolf sent "a very well-drafted dispatch" to St. Petersburg, urging unity among the Northern courts. But at the same time, he ordered a blockade of Prussia's Baltic ports. "It is such things that the king intentionally hides from one," he commented bitterly; "it is no pleasure to serve him." Next day, Gustav Adolf spoke to Fersen about his last letter, "but he never discusses and cannot be reasoned with." The king said that Prussia ought to be partitioned and Austria the only great Germanic power. "He also believes in the effectiveness of coalitions," Fersen observed; "I mentioned to him as an example to the contrary the present coalition and all that he himself had done in complete contradiction to the wishes of his allies," to which the king simply replied, "That cannot be helped."[43]

St. Petersburg, hoping Prussia might still join the anti-French camp, became increasingly impatient of the Swedish-Prussian imbroglio and in May sought to mollify Gustav Adolf. Fersen implored the king to take advantage of this opportunity. On 12 May, an envoy arrived with a letter from Frederick William III urging an end to the dispute. Fersen besought Gustav Adolf not to reject this attempt at reconciliation which ought to satisfy his dignity and could encourage a Prussian change of system. The king would thus have "moderated his courage and sacrificed his aversion for the general good." But Gustav Adolf insisted on the restitution of Lauenburg. Fersen protested:

I pointed out to him that if everyone wished to act on his own account without regard for and without agreement with his allies, the common cause would suffer thereby and that it was in just such a way that Europe had been plunged into ruin.

The only alternative the king would consider was the opening of the Elbe to British commerce, which was equally impossible. The king had furthermore just ordered the Swedish blockading squadron to put Prussian ports under forced contribution on pain of bombardment. Fersen was aghast and protested so strongly that at length the king wrote a counter-order, which he later simply neglected to send off. Fersen now considered a Prussian attack unavoidable but Gustav Adolf "wanted to end this in-between situation that was neither war nor peace."[44]

Thwarted in their attempts to influence the king, Fersen, together with Armfelt, Wetterstedt, and the former Swedish minister to Berlin, C.G. Brinkman, made an attempt at personal diplomacy in late May. The envoy of Mecklenburg-Schwerin in Berlin undertook to suggest that the Swedish-Prussian dispute be turned over to special negotiators appointed by the two kings. Frederick William seemed interested but Gustav Adolf now announced he would accept no further indirect approaches, only direct communications from the king of Prussia. Fersen and his friends felt compelled to reveal what they had done, which Brinkman did so skillfully that the king's ire was, in appearance at least, avoided. The attempt had at least still helped delay a Prussian attack until Berlin was diverted by other problems.[45]

In the meantime, Fersen was released from his duties in Germany. On 28 May, the king asked him to accompany the queen from Stockholm to her summer residence at Beckaskog in Skåne. This task hardly required the *riksmarskalk* himself: "I understood very well this was only an honorable way of dismissing me." Nevertheless: "I was delighted to be able to go my way and to leave politics, for it is terrible and one cannot in any way avoid hanging one's head in shame for all that is being done, or at least being suspected of doing so." Word soon spread and many expressed regret, not least of all Henry Pierrepont.[46]

Fersen took leave of Gustav Adolf on 4 June and sailed from Stralsund two days later, though not without one parting effort to argue his views. The tsar had sent an envoy to Berlin with a comprehensive project for settlement of the Swedish-Prussian dispute. Fersen implored the king to seize this opportunity, lest Russia abandon Sweden for Prussia, facing the Swedes with a possible "war in Germany, Finland, and the sea." "Nothing, Sire, would appear grander and nobler," he wrote, "than to have joined so much wisdom and prudence to the courage and steadfastness for which Your Majesty is known by withdrawing intact from so unequal and dangerous a conflict."[47]

7

Returning to Stockholm, Fersen accompanied Queen Fredrika to Beckaskog, where he remained a week. He might well have stayed longer; he enjoyed the countryside and the queen was "greatly moved" at his departure. But Fersen feared he might be recalled to Pomerania and hastened home to Stockholm. From time to time thereafter, he was apprehensive of this and pointedly informed the king of the pressing demands of his academic duties, private affairs, and delicate health, determined to refuse if asked.[48]

There was in fact little chance of this. It was generally understood that he had fallen from favor, giving rise to rumors. It was claimed that Gustav Adolf, whose tastes were Spartan, had resented the size and luxury of Fersen's household in Germany; others held that he now felt a strong dislike for Countess Piper, whom he considered a "real devil." Duchess Charlotta, however, rightly perceived the real reasons for Fersen's fall from grace when she wrote in June 1806,

At first, Fersen was entrusted with all diplomatic negotiations and in this connection always expressed his opinions openly, which were probably unwelcome. In accordance with his convictions, he favored neutrality and said quite honestly that even if he had been chosen to come along on the basis of his abhorrence for Bonaparte, this personal sentiment must give way when it was a question of the good of the fatherland; this must come before all else. The king remained silent, as always when he is contradicted, simply followed his own ideas and no longer conferred with Fersen, not even about the manifesto that was issued with his signature. . . . Fersen's comportment must be described as particularly judicious. When it was impossible for him to serve his country's interests through diplomacy, it was wisest to withdraw and thereby escape public criticism. But he is altogether too loyal to complain, to show dissatisfaction or find fault; his whole conduct is distinguished rather by the greatest discretion. Although promised that he would continue to be advised on political questions, he receives communications but seldom.[49]

The duchess here calls to mind Fersen's own comments to Gustav Lagerbjelke in July 1804, when the latter had struggled to maintain Sweden's neutrality:

Be well assured . . . my dear Baron . . . that I sympathize with your position and if you will recall, I had the honor of speaking with you about it at the time of your departure. I am aware of all the difficulties and I foresaw them. One cannot without injustice hold you responsible for the will of another and when one has fulfilled one's duty as an honest man and has not disguised the truth when it was demanded of one, one no longer has anything with which to reproach oneself and then the testimony of conscience and the approbation of reasonable men should suffice to console one for the injustice of the public, which is often guided by envy and jealousy.[50]

H.G. Trolle-Wachtmeister—who married Fersen's niece, Hedvig Möllersvärd, in 1806—revealed something of Gustav IV Adolf's feelings toward Fersen and his family:

I recall a remark by the king during the Lauenburg campaign . . . that he would gladly avoid having *distinguished persons* (that is, persons of good family) in his service, for if he became dissatisfied and wanted to get rid . . . of someone of that sort, there was immediately an uproar in the whole clan. Likewise, he is supposed once to have expressed himself just as unfavorably toward the rich—"who," he said, "are always impudent." In his hatred for independence and other supposed greatness aside from that which is fully dependent upon the whims of the monarch, one may find a parallel with Louis XIV, such as he was portrayed by Saint-Simon. The hatred for Paris and the hatred for Stockholm increases the likeness.[51]

The well informed Trolle-Wachtmeister noted in his diary that the Fersens' correspondence between Pomerania and Sweden had been opened by the police, who in April 1807 planted a spy in their household in Stockholm. The king was especially suspicious of Duchess Charlotta's almost daily visits to Sophie Piper. "He constantly expresses hatred for the house of Fersen and no excuse to manifest his ill-will escapes him; one would believe his intention is to compel Axel Fersen to leave his post through humiliation." The king was only barely dissuaded by the chancellor of justice from reprimanding Fersen formally over some minor changes in the royal palace. He flew into a rage in December when Fersen sent sleds rather than carriages to bring him and his suite to Stockholm.[52]

The situation in Germany continued for a time as before. By August, however, Prussia, faced with the prospect of war with France, withdrew its troops from Lauenburg, which Gustav Adolf promptly reoccupied. The Swedish king could finally enjoy what Armfelt called "the triumph of obstinacy" and the whole dispute with Prussia vanished almost miraculously.[53] In October, France disastrously defeated the Prussians at Jena and Auerstädt, the Swedish force in Lauenburg was trapped, and the French advanced to the borders of Pomerania.

The French did not attack until early 1807, being concerned with the Russian-Prussian forces in Poland and East Prussia. Since Swedish Pomerania exposed his flank, especially to British landings, Napoleon sent peace feelers to Gustav Adolf, who summarily rejected them while making furious efforts to gather a force of 30,000 men, frustrated by constitutional limits to his raising of revenue. In desperation, he confiscated 375,000 pounds in British subsidies that happened to be crossing Sweden on the way to Russia, claiming the Russians owed him this amount. Fersen observed astutely, "if present circumstances prevent this action from having unfortunate consequences, it will in any case leave a seed of discord which cannot but cause us trouble in the future, for we will never be so strong that we need not show consideration to our neighbors." It has been suggested that Alexander collected on the debt in Finland the following year.[54]

The French invaded Swedish Pomerania in January 1807 but after a short, hard-fought campaign, signed an armistice in April when their forces were needed in the east. Gustav Adolf meanwhile arranged for increased British subsidies and support from British and Prussian troops.

The king arrived in Stralsund in mid-May 1807, burning with enthusiasm. "It is believed," Fersen wrote,

. . . that the English and Prussians are going to undertake a great operation in Germany—one may possibly believe this when it comes to the English, but the Prussians can accomplish nothing. . . . under all conditions the king's presence there, even aside from the risks he runs, is useless, for we will never be strong enough to be able to play a role there. The other powers will constantly destroy his plans; he will then consider himself offended and the result will be nothing but imbroglios. I doubt if anyone will entrust him with the command of his troops. . . . It seems as though the king will go to Germany only to try to lure away Frenchmen to desert from the army to form a new army for Louis XVIII . . .[55]

Gustav Adolf did in fact attempt to raise a corps of French émigrés and deserters under the Duc de Piennes, grandiloquently entitled the *Régiment du Roi,* which arrived in Stralsund in May mustering a total of 19 men. It never during the year that followed numbered over a hundred. The king met with the French Marshal Brune, ostensibly over the armistice, and tried to persuade him to return to his "rightful king," Louis XVIII. The latter was invited to head the émigré force. Before he could arrive, however, it was already too late; the pretender passed through Sweden in October on his way from Mitau to England.

The Swedish king was in an exalted frame of mind by the summer of 1807. Always seriously religious with strong pietistic and mystical leanings, he began to identify Napoleon as the Beast of the Apocalypse as interpreted by the German mystic Johann

Heinrich Jung-Stilling, and feared that by negotiating with him he would condemn himself to both temporal and eternal woe. There was now speculation, at home and abroad, over his sanity, a question that still perplexes historians.

Reinforced with Prussian and British troops and Pomeranian *Landwehr*, Gustav Adolf had hopes of fielding 36,000 men and on 3 July announced that he would terminate the armistice after the stipulated two weeks. Meanwhile, the situation changed radically. The Russians, defeated at Friedland, concluded both peace and an alliance with Napoleon at Tilsit on 7–9 July. Prussia made peace and recalled her troops from Pomerania. Shortly after landing, the British withdrew to attack Copenhagen, thereby driving Denmark-Norway into the Franco-Russian alliance. The French attacked in overwhelming force. Stralsund quickly surrendered and the king, too ill to command, returned to Sweden. The last Swedish troops evacuated Rügen in late September. In all, some 10,000 returned, leaving behind at least 6,000 killled or imprisoned.

Thus ended Sweden's ill-starred campaign in Germany. In retrospect, it seems a reckless and poorly conceived venture. Yet in 1805, there had been much to recommend it. Napoleon was a menace to the peace and stability of all Europe while Sweden and Finland were secure against attack as long as Britain and Russia were allies and Denmark-Norway neutral. Sweden could offer important strategic advantages to the coalition and expect valuable compensations through a victorious peace. Until the summer of 1807, Gustav Adolf avoided risks and limited his actions to his means. Even his quarrel with Frederick William III was not entirely his fault, there being good reasons to mistrust Prussia. Meanwhile, he was plagued with misfortune: Austerlitz ended his first attempt to go on the offensive, Friedland his second.

Yet Gustav IV Adolf lacked those qualities his difficult situation demanded, while possessing others that under the circumstances were dangerous. The price Sweden paid for her failure and that of her allies by the end of 1807 was not excessive in material terms; even Swedish Pomerania could be and eventually was regained through the fortunes of war. Sweden's greatest sacrifice was loss of confidence in the sovereign by both his allies and his own subjects. When greater problems overwhelmed him in the months that followed, he no longer found the support he needed until in March 1809 he was overthrown by insurrection.

The reasons for this crisis of confidence emerge clearly enough through the reluctant testimony of Fersen's diary, a document probably without equal for just this period.[56] From his hesitant admiration in 1804–1805 for Gustav Adolf's outspoken integrity in matters of principle concerning the Duc d'Enghien and the Prussian Order of the Black Eagle, he became increasingly concerned over his monarch's behavior until his experiences in the campaign of 1805–1806 ended in his complete disillusionment.

Fersen was chosen by the king to accompany him as an internationally recognized symbol of counterrevolution, and was so understood at home and abroad. When Napoleon announced to the Grand Army on 26 December 1805 that "the queen of Naples has ceased to reign," he added, "may she go to London to augment the number of intriguers ... she might call there, if she sees fit, Baron Armfelt, MM. de Fersen, d'Antraigues, and the monk Morus." In July 1806, *L'Abeille du Nord* of Altona, in attacking Sweden, singled out Fersen and Armfelt in particular as "spies and murderers." Yet Fersen opposed from the start Sweden's participation in the war and was probably Gustav IV Adolf's most forthright critic. "Today we have gotten out Count Fersen's correspondence with the former king," wrote the poet C. C. af Leopold to Nils Rosén von Rosenstein on 6 September 1810, the date on which—two and a half months after Fersen's death—P. A. Wallmark published the first installment of it in his *Journalen för Litteratur och Theater,* and added, "one would scarcely have believed him capable of such a style or way of thinking." In his memoirs, A.F. Skjöldebrand wrote, "When Gustav Adolf in Pomerania began his follies, Fersen wrote letters to him that would do honor to the greatest statesman and patriot."[57] In consequence, he quickly lost whatever influence he might have possessed and was sent home in disfavor.

Gustav IV Adolf's foreign policy provides one of the classic problems of Swedish historiography. Traditionally, it has been strongly criticized as impractical, incompetent, and headstrong, though certain more recent historians have sought to challenge this view.[58] Ironically, the diary and letters of that steadfast royalist, Axel Fersen, give impressive support to the traditionalist critique of Gustav Adolf's reign.

CHAPTER XV

Fersen's Last Years and Death, 1806–1810

1

During the last four years of his life, Axel Fersen was concerned mainly with personal affairs. He lived lavishly by Swedish standards of the time. Well could his *chef de cuisine*, Berger, boast in 1802 that he served "the greatest seigneur in Sweden." Lars von Engeström called his household "the first in Stockholm." Taxation and census records for 1809 and 1810 describe the silk and gilded furnishings of his town house and a collection of no less than fourteen carriages and sleighs. When in September 1807, Fersen, his sister, their guests, and household moved from Lövstad to Ljung, they needed 26 horses, plus another 6 for the servants. The latter formed a numerous retinue. By 1810, Fersen kept a staff of some twenty persons in his Stockholm house, to which must be added Sophie's four personal servants. By all accounts, Fersen was a good master to his household and the numerous tenantry on his estates. He is described as stern, yet just, solicitous, and kindly with his people, who seem to have been warmly attached to him. Perhaps Fersen may be imagined as practicing, on the scale permitted him, that kind of paternalistic and enlightened absolutism that formed his political ideal.[1]

He now spent more time on his estates at Steninge and Ljung, and especially at Sophie's Lövstad, than had been his custom before. The life of a country gentleman suited him well. "In such a way people change their tastes according to their state of mind

348

and circumstances," he wrote in October 1807; "Not long ago I would not have believed I would thrive so well there."[2]

During the summer of 1806, his diary reveals the beginnings of his last love, with Emelie Aurora De Geer of Finspång manor, near Lövstad and Ljung. When her mother, a renowned beauty, died in 1806, Emelie, then 26 years old, gave up her position as lady-in-waiting at court to devote herself to the family estate. Fersen, it would appear, admired her determination and helped with her affairs. Through sparse in detail, his diary shows they saw each other frequently in the country and in Stockholm in 1807–1808, while his letter register shows a lively correspondence between them when separated. This source refers on 9 September 1806 to a letter in which Fersen discussed "the manner of living," evidently containing some kind of proposal. Very likely Fersen was still wary of the bonds of marriage while Emelie, despite the permissive atmosphere of the time, would consider nothing less. Fersen complained in December 1807 that it was impossible to establish a proper love affair in Stockholm. After that month, he no longer recorded his letters to Emelie and his diary ends three months later. After his death, his brother Fabian returned Emelie's letters. Yet his account books mention presents to her in 1808–10. When Emelie's father died in January 1809, Fersen was one of his trustees and guardians of his children. According to family legend, he was engaged to Emelie at the time of his death.[3]

His official duties following his return from Germany were not numerous. There were occasional meetings of the boards of the Stockholm Fire Insurance Company and the Academy of Painting, troop inspections, and visits to Uppsala. The *Kanslersgille* held its final meetings on the new school ordinance in May 1807. Fersen attended shareholders' meetings of the East India Company and as a director spent six weeks at Göteborg in the spring of 1808 investigating its tangled affairs. "Aside from that little time occupied with official duties and the management of his estates," A. F. Skjöldebrand recalled, "he busied himself with entertaining, seeing how his horses were looked after, sometimes himself driving an excellent team, sometimes riding."[4]

Fersen's relative inactivity reflects the disfavor into which he had fallen with Gustav IV Adolf. Trolle-Wachtmeister noted how the king flew into a rage over Fersen's handling of details when he at last returned to Stockholm in December 1807. Fersen himself found Gustav Adolf fairly amiable, though anxious to avoid his officials and any discussion of policy. The king established a *kunglig beredning* or royal committee to expedite state business and avoid regular council meetings. When Fersen received a letter from him concerning the royal stables in January 1808, it was the first time in two years Gustav Adolf had written to him. His duties as grand marshal were not demanding. The king reduced his court establishment and Fersen even noted without comment a rumor that his own office would be abolished. On 8 March 1808, he spoke of a rumor that he had been arrested. Behind such notions lie intimations that Gustav Adolf's attitude toward Fersen was far less amiable than he gave him to believe. When Chancellor of Justice Count Wachtmeister tried to secure the grand marshal's appointment to the new Royal Committee in January 1808, Gustav Adolf refused emphatically, calling Fersen incompetent and his sister "a devil in human form." During the king's absence on Åland during the Finnish war later that year, Fersen nonetheless served on the interim government, though previously assigned duties as grand marshal kept him largely absent from Stockholm. In February 1809, the Duc de Piennes, who had commanded the émigré *Régiment du Roi* in Pomerania, rather mysteriously fell into the king's disfavor. Fersen did his best to defend the unfortunate duke and took him into his house. His courageous defense of his friend evidently intensified Gustav Adolf's ill will.[5]

Fersen noted in the winter of 1807–1808 that Gustav Adolf was weary, apathetic, suffered from periods of "melancholy and hypochondria," and was on bad terms with the queen. He avoided Stockholm and secluded himself at Gripsholm castle. Yet Fersen witnessed the popular enthusiasm for the king at the unveiling of Sergel's statue of Gustav III before the Stockholm palace in January 1808, on what may have been the last really happy day of Gustav Adolf's life.[6]

Soon after, on 31 March 1808, Fersen's diary terminates. Documents from Fersen himself are extremely scarce for the last two years of his life. His biographer is compelled to rely mainly on the testimony of others and at times on conjecture. The diary, if continued, could have told much about this period, in which Fersen himself played a significant part, one of the most eventful and decisive in Sweden's history. Its absence is scarcely less regrettable than the loss of the part for 1779-91.

It is not clear why the diary ends here. Fabian wrote Sophie following their brother's death that Axel's diary was lacking after March 1808 and that Axel had burned "a number of papers" after the coup d'état a year later. Yet it seems doubtful that these included any part of the diary. It ends in mid-page, as does his letter register in the same month, carefully kept since 1783, while his later account books remain in rough draft. More significantly, his interest in the diary seems to have tapered off over nearly two years, since his return from Pomerania; the notations become progressively briefer and, on the whole, less interesting. Most likely he simply stopped writing it, though with characteristic fastidiousness, on the last day of the month.[7]

One explanation might be the growing cautiousness of Fersen's later years, apparent in the extreme brevity and discretion of his diary entries concerning Emelie, which was likewise noted by contemporaries.[8] More important would seem indications of ill health and a growing tiredness, discouragement, and fatalism, of a progressive narrowing of emotional involvement to his family, a few old friends, his comforts and the accumulated habits of a lifetime: tendencies to which he had long been prone. "My friend," he had once written Evert Taube in 1794, "I persist in believing we have lived too long. . . . I only wish to live tranquilly for myself and my friends." The Danish Prince Christian Frederik—later King Christian VIII—who met him in Copenhagen in 1803, wrote of Fersen already then: "Sorrow and misfortune have aged him so that he looks twenty years older than he is." His niece's husband, Count Trolle-Wachtmeister, later wrote unkindly of the "theatrical haughtiness and inaccessibility" with which Fersen in his later years "covered his inner emptiness."[9]

2

In the Treaty of Tilsit of July 1807, France and Russia agreed to force Britain to make peace by closing the remaining gaps in the Continental System. Denmark-Norway joined the Franco-Russian system and Alexander I made diplomatic efforts to persuade his brother-in-law, Gustav IV Adolf, to abandon his British alliance. In February 1808, the Russians suddenly attacked Finland. Denmark declared war in March and behind the Danes stood the French under Marshal Bernadotte in northern Germany.[10] The situation was grave but not hopeless. The Finnish army, cut off by the frozen Gulf of Bothnia from reinforcement from Sweden, retreated to the northwest, according to plan, but the Russian force was at first not much larger, due to terrain and climate. Meanwhile, British sea power shielded Sweden proper.

But the holding action in Finland was weaker than anticipated. General Moritz Klingspor's field army withdrew too rapidly and the great coastal fortress of Sveaborg, covering its southern flank, surrendered ignominiously. Although during the summer of 1808, the Finns, thanks largely to Klingspor's new adjutant, Colonel Carl Johan Adlercreutz, regained ground, by the end of the year the Russians had conquered all of Finland and advanced into northern Sweden.

Though Gustav Adolf was largely the victim of circumstances, he was undeniably a poor commander and worse still, a poor inspirer of men: moody, impetuous, inconsistent, absorbed in petty detail. He dismissed generals, countermanded his own orders, degraded the entire Guards brigade. "He wants to be a general," wrote Duchess Charlotta, "and is really only a corporal."[11]

Despite these reverses, Gustav Adolf hoped to reconquer Finland the following year, though faced with formidable logistic and, above all, financial problems. His only source of support remained Britain, but his willful, erratic behavior increasingly strained relations with his ally. In May 1808, Sir John Moore arrived with 10,000 troops in Göteborg to take part in the operations. Fersen was in that city on the business of the East India Company, attended a reception for General Moore and Admiral Saumarez, and visited the flagship, Nelson's Victory.[12] Unfortunately, Moore and the Swedish king could not agree on how the British were to be employed until they sailed away for Spain, leaving Anglo-Swedish relations further embittered.

Sweden was thus thrown back on her own resources. Despite the urging of his advisers, notably Count Wachtmeister, the king refused to summon a Riksdag but in January 1809 decreed on his own authority a war levy equal to five times the annual taxation granted by the estates in 1800, to the horror of his counselors and the dismay of the nation.

Under these conditions, the frustrations accumulated during the thirteen years of Gustav IV Adolf's personal absolutism, and more important still, those engendered by military failure, heavy taxation, the degradation of the Guards, disillusionment with Britain, fear and admiration for France, all broke to the surface. On 13 March 1809, Gustav Adolf was deposed by a revolution that proved almost bloodless. Yet it too would in time claim its sacrifice: Count Axel Fersen.

3

The revolt had been brewing since the previous summer among disgruntled Guards officers and former radicals of the diet of 1800. At the same time, there was much talk in upper bureaucratic circles of a kind of general strike to force the king to convene the estates. While the various oppositional groups more or less neutralized each other in Stockholm, Lieutenant Colonel Georg Adlersparre, one of the radicals of 1800, raised the standard of revolt on the western front. Arranging, in effect, a private armistice with the Danish commander in southern Norway, Prince Christian August of Augustenburg, he issued a manifesto on 7 March, calling for peace, a Riksdag, and a "change of system," and began a march on Stockholm at the head of some 3,000 insurgent troops.[13]

Gustav Adolf was slow in apprizing the danger. On 12 March, however, he suddenly decided to act and left his summer residence at Haga to return to the palace in Stockholm, some three miles away. Axel Fersel was at Haga to celebrate the queen's birthday. The king requested that he remain with her until his return. There was no room available and the grand marshal was seen early the following morning sitting alone with his thoughts before a fireplace in his red and black court dress. What might he have known, what rumors might have reached him? Probably little more than he had learned that day. That the atmosphere was heavy with opposition to the king was clear; but Fersen probably was neither told nor wished to hear anything more specific.[14]

Around 2:00 A.M. on 13 March, Gustav Adolf decided to leave the capital with his family, court, and Stockholm garrison for royalist Skåne, there to rally his forces against the insurgents. He summoned Fabian Fersen, chairman of the State Bank Commission and demanded 2 million *riksdaler*. Fabian protested that he could not release funds as the commission was responsible to the estates, then played for time by gaining permission to consult the whole commission that evening. He meanwhile helped prepare for the king's departure. Gustav Adolf sent word to Haga for the queen, her children, and household to prepare to leave. The ladies-in-waiting were frightened that the king might flee the country, forcing them into exile, but Fersen reassured them that in such a case they need only accompany the royal family as far as the border.[15]

The king summoned General Klingspor, who arrived at the palace around 8:00 A.M., accompanied by Adlercreutz, himself now a general, and several other officers. In a private audience, Klingspor urged Gustav Adolf not to leave and to call a diet, "the Western Army's only wish." When the king angrily refused, Adlercreutz and the others burst into the room and arrested him. This palace revolution had been hastily organized to forestall both civil war and the intervention of Sweden's enemies, as well as the uncertain dangers of social revolution the triumphant Adlersparre was feared to bring with him from the west.[16]

News of the coup reached Haga as preparations were still in progress. Fersen had the difficult task of informing the queen. She was beside herself with despair and feared the king had been killed until General Suremain arrived around noon with a note from Gustav Adolf that he was alive and well. Fersen was avid for details and asked if he should remain at Haga, to which Suremain replied that in such circumstances a man like Fersen could only give good counsel to the queen.[17]

The generals now prevailed on Duke Karl to become provisional head of state. He immediately appointed a new council to replace Gustav Adolf's Royal Committee, including most of that body, plus four others, including Generals Adlercreutz and Klingspor, and the grand marshal, Axel Fersen.

Fersen's inclusion on what was essentially a revolutionary council seems at first glance surprising, yet he was in many respects well qualified. As *riksmarskalk*, he was second in precedence among royal officials; failure to include him would have appeared arbitrary. His courageous opposition to the king's policies in the Pomeranian campaign was well known as was his cool relationship with Gustav Adolf since then. Most important, Fersen's presence could reassure wide circles of conservative and aristocratic opinion. The appointment was furthermore surely one Fersen's sense of duty would scarcely let him refuse at this critical time.[18]

The following day, the new government called a Riksdag for 1 May in Stockholm, repealed the special war levy, reestablished the Guards regiments, and sent peace feelers to Sweden's enemies. During April, press censorship was eased, resulting in a spate of fiercely partisan journalistic activity. The new council contained much talent, but lacking unity and leadership, was referred to, rather unkindly, as "Noah's Ark."

Its most difficult problem was the succession to the throne. Adlercreutz, Klingspor, and their friends intended only to take power from a monarch they felt could not manage it, naturally assuming he would be succeeded by the nine-year-old Crown Prince Gustav. Duke Karl wished only to serve as regent for his grand-nephew, who was strongly supported by the duchess, most of the court, the majority of councillors—including both generals and of course Fersen—as well as by broad strata of public opinion.

On 22 March, however, Georg Adlersparre made his triumphal entry into the capital, where he established a headquarters and issued orders to his troops, independently of the city commandant. With two of his supporters, he was added to the council. Though a man of considerable talents, Adlersparre was fearful and suspicious by nature, obsessed with securing himself against future retribution by excluding from the throne both Gustav IV Adolf and his heirs. He intimated that he would stop at nothing to accomplish this. The problem could be solved temporarily by raising Duke Karl to the throne, but he was already sixty years old, in poor health, and without heirs of his own. Even if Prince Gustav should eventually succeed him, a long regency might intervene, the uncertainties of which neither Adlersparre nor anyone else wished to contemplate. A new elected successor of mature years and proven ability would remove this danger. By the end of March, Adlersparre succeeded in winning much support, but his arrogant and mistrustful behavior also stimulated in many quarters a growing reaction in favor of the old dynasty.[19]

Colonel Isaac Lars Silfversparre, a participant in the coup of 13 March, was appointed the king's warden at Gripsholm castle and urged him to abdicate. Gustav Adolf accepted with surprising ease and had in fact himself long considered abdication. On 27

March, Silfversparre arrived in Stockholm with the message that the king would give up his throne in favor of his son.

Duke Karl and the "Gustavians" on the council were delighted to accept. Count Wachtmeister, however, in agreement with Adlersparre, arranged a meeting of the council in his home that same evening, attended by Fersen, Klingspor, Adlercreutz, Adlersparre's confidant, H. H. von Essen, Count Wachtmeister and his son, H. G. Trolle-Wachtmeister, who described the occasion. Wachtmeister protested that abdication by a prisoner could be considered invalid and that the succession should take into account the views of Napoleon, now Sweden's only possible support against Russia. All conceded. He then dictated a memorandum to the duke advising that he did not have authority to accept the abdication without consulting the estates. All signed, though apparently Fersen and Adlercreutz did so reluctantly. The duke therefore declined the king's offer.[20]

Adlersparre and his friends had thus parried the immediate threat. It seems unlikely that Duke Karl, Fersen, or the generals realized how they had been led into compromising their cause. The Adlersparre faction now sought to entice the king into abdicating in such a manner that the duke might become his immediate successor while allowing the duke to accept without having directly to repudiate Prince Gustav. Once the duke committed himself, the crown prince would be debarred from succeeding him.

Significantly, neither Fersen nor the other Gustavian members were present at the next council, held secretly two days later. The duke had finally agreed to accept the throne. The council discussed a mission to Napoleon to request mediation with Sweden's enemies and his views on the succession. The crown prince was to be represented in an unfavorable light and the emperor's suggestion sought for a successor who might restore what Sweden had lost in the war or secure her obvious compensation, meaning of course Norway. Thereafter, Prince Gustav's chances were almost hopeless. When the council again discussed the succession in early April, only the Adlersparre faction was present. At the end of the month, Gustav Adolf was persuaded to abdicate unconditionally, subject to confirmation by the estates, but he steadfastly refused to mention the rights of his heirs.

It meanwhile seemed clear that a diet would bring a general attack on the existing constitution of 1772 and the Act of Security of 1789. To keep the initiative, a subcommittee of the council, including among others Adlersparre, Adlercreutz, Klingspor, and as grand marshal, Fersen, undertook to prepare a new draft constitution. Before long, however, both Fersen and Klingspor were excluded: the former, in Trolle-Wachtmeister's words, because he was "unqualified," the latter because he was "not needed." One senses behind this the influence of Adlersparre, with whose most sensitive concern Fersen's support for the crown prince naturally collided. According to Trolle-Wachtmeister, Adlersparre "considers an enthusiasm unequal to his own as the same as personal enmity—and he never forgives an enemy."[21]

The Riksdag opened on 1 May. Axel did not take part; Fabian represented the family in the noble estate but was notably inconspicuous.[22] On 2 May, Axel was, however, present at a meeting of several councillors with leading representatives of the estates, in Wachtmeister's home, to consider Gustav Adolf's abdication, just arrived from Gripsholm. Adlersparre strongly urged exclusion of Gustav Adolf and all his heirs, according to Bernhard von Schinkel, on the following grounds:

1.) The former king had, through his godless and indefensible regime, broken his oath, for which reason the nation should immediately consider itself free from its oath; 2.) fatal persecutions of those who had participated in the revolution could not be prevented except through the deposition of the *entire* old dynasty, to which must be added 3.) the importance of avoiding a regency for a minor heir, and 4.) the hope of new territorial acquisitions if a new reigning family were elected.

Schinkel continues:

Against these considerations, which were supported by several speakers, first Fersen and thereafter Adlercreutz and [Carl] Lagerbring took the floor and objected on the basis of rather weak arguments; but since the majority appeared to adhere to Adlersparre's view, these speakers gave way and joined the rest.

It remained to pick someone to propose deposition of the Vasa house to the estates. The matter was apparently decided by the constitutional committee, to which Fersen no longer belonged, together with leading *riksdagsmän*, on 4 May. The choice fell on Baron Lars Augustin Mannerheim. The following day, Duke Karl, Klingspor, and Adlercreutz seemed to waver over the exclusion of the crown prince, but were brought back into line by the furious Wachtmeister. "The time, thank God, is past," his son wrote, "when states and peoples were considered the private property of an individual and existed not for *their* sakes but only for *his.*"[23]

"Several unexpected features appear in this picture," Bernhard von Beskow later commented:

At the preparatory consultation, at which the change of dynasty was decided, Axel Fersen was present and concurred. After this pledge to the new situation, one would not have expected that he would be designated as the sacrifice on 20 June [1810] as head of the Gustavian party, especially as his honorable and upright character was commonly known.

He further noted that several prominent Gustavians, including Klingspor and Stedingk, were not present. The question Beskow raises is perplexing: why did Fersen, whose life had so largely been devoted to the cause of legitimacy, ultimately vote to exclude the rightful heir from the Swedish throne? Fersen himself left no explanation. Some insight may be provided by Duchess Charlotta, who wrote how in April the council had gradually come to oppose Prince Gustav's succession. Fersen, however,

. . . did not consider that there was any danger in letting the crown prince succeed to the throne, for it should be possible to raise him so that he would not hold feelings of revenge but rather the warmest gratitude toward those who saved his father's throne for him. But misgivings concerning a regency government Fersen found justified; only this consideration persuaded him to vote with the majority.

It still seems that dislike for a regency—well based as this might be in Fersen's own experience—is not a sufficient explanation. One suspects, as the Adlersparre faction soon did, that his vote on 2 May was a tactical concession, not an unequivocal endorsement for the expulsion of the Vasas. Such was clearly the case with Adlercreutz, who with Fersen had opposed the proposition. The general was anxious for the king to abdicate even his son's rights to prevent the anti-legitimist faction from "imitating the French Jacobins" by demanding a public inquest into his reign and even reviving an old slander that Gustav Adolf was not the legitimate son of Gustav III, thus that he and his descendants were not rightful heirs to the throne. Adlercreutz was anxious to save the king and his family from ruinous calumny while believing Gustav Adolf could not in any case legally renounce his son's rights. Thus he joined the majority on 2 May, feeling that "at this point one must flow with the stream," but his letters thereafter show that he did not consider the case closed and hoped to work in other ways for the eventual restitution of the crown prince.[24] Though there is no evidence that Fersen and Adlercreutz concerted their efforts, Fersen's calculations were probably similar. He must certainly have wished Prince Gustav might yet ascend the throne of his fathers. Still, the observations of the duchess and of Beskow remain significant. Fersen's thoughts and actions, particularly in recent years, had revealed that ultimately he too would agree with Count Trolle-Wachtmeister, that the state was not the private property of any individual, and that even above the claims of legitimacy he placed the values of social order and tranquility.

On 6 May, the Swedish envoy returned from his mission to Napoleon, who had declined either to mediate with Alexander or to commit himself on a successor. On 7 May, the acting foreign minister, Gustaf Lagerbjelke, in close touch with Adlersparre, called a meeting of the speakers and leading members of the estates, at which he apparently took the liberty of intimating that Napoleon would accept Duke Karl only if neither Gustaf Adolf nor any of his heirs should ever succeed him. This meeting evidently had considerable effect.

On 10 May, the estates met in *plenum plenorum*. Gustav Adolf's abdication was presented, and Baron Mannerheim proposed that he and his descendants be barred permanently from the throne. This was met with a great shout of assent, followed by a profound silence. No voice was raised for the crown prince. The Gustavians feared both for themselves and for the royal family. An act of deposition was drawn up but it was not forgotten in the future that passage of a resolution by acclaim was not legally valid in Riksdag proceedings.

The estates rejected the draft constitution and demanded that a committee of their own prepare another for Duke Karl, to accept as the condition of his election to the throne. The constitution then prepared, largely by A. G. Silfverstolpe, G. G. Adlerbeth, and the committee's secretary, Hans Järta, contained a number of complexities and compromises, yet has remained Sweden's fundamental law to the present. While reconfirming the estates' control of taxation, it extended their right to initiate legislation and established a measure of ministerial responsibility. It was ready by the beginning of June and passed on the 27th of the month.

The duke was elected King Karl XIII on 6 June and crowned on the 29th amid traditional ceremonies in which the grand marshal played his part. The new monarch bestowed honors and distinctions, including Fersen's promotion to general. It was noted that the king here passed over the senior lieutenant general and that Fersen had not seen active service with the Swedish army since 1788. The distinction was, however, simply a consolation prize, for the grand marshal was not included on the *statsråd* or permanent state council established on 9 June. Queen Hedvig Elisabeth Charlotta wrote it was generally understood that Adlersparre and Lagerbjelke had influenced the appointments and that they considered Fersen "altogether too strong a royalist."[25]

There are few indications as to Fersen's activities during the remainder of 1809. He evidently spent much time at Lövstad, Ljung, and Finspång. As grand marshal, he was much occupied by an inventory of the possessions of the Vasa family. Meanwhile, he seems to have done what he could, officially and privately, to ease the ordeal of Queen Fredrika and her children.[26]

4

Adlersparre lost little time in proposing his candidate for successor to Karl XIII: none other than Prince Christian August of Augustenburg, the enemy commander in southern Norway. The prince was widely popular with the Norwegians and Adlersparre raised hopes he might bring Norway with him into a union with Sweden. On 18 July 1809, all four estates elected Christian August crown prince, though he refused to come to Sweden before peace was concluded or to have anything to do with a Norwegian revolt against Denmark.

Since Napoleon declined to mediate, Sweden was forced to negotiate directly with Russia for peace, at length concluded at Fredrikshamn in September, at the cost of a third of her territory and a quarter of her population: all of Finland and the Åland Islands were lost. It was not the least ruinous of the settlements of the Napoleonic period and the most permanent of them. Sweden thereafter made peace with Denmark on the basis of the *status quo ante bellum* in December and with France in January 1810, as a result of which she was compelled to enter the Continental System.[27] The Gustavians, meanwhile, by no means gave up. During the summer of 1809, they emerged as a vigorous party in the Riksdag, led by Counts Jacob De la Gardie and Eric Ruuth, which sought to disconcert and discredit the government party at every turn. The air was thick with rumors of Gustavian conspiracies, many of doubtful authenticity. De la Gardie, Ruuth, and Adlercreutz did, however, attempt, with some apparent success for a time, secretly to persuade Karl XIII to dissolve the Riksdag and decree a new, more strongly monarchical constitution, which among other things would invalidate the existing succession settlement. The government party countered by organizing the so-called Mannerheim Club to concert strategy and engaged the embittered former civil servant and skillful polemicist Carl August Grevesmöhlen to organize their own secret police to keep watch over the Gustavians and propagandize against them. In November, the government quietly sent Gustav Adolf and his family into exile abroad.[28]

The prince of Augustenburg at last departed Norway in January 1810, accompanied by Adlersparre. At Göteborg, he was officially welcomed by Fabian Fersen and at Drottningholm by Axel. Arriving in Stockholm on 21 January, he was officially adopted by Karl XIII as Crown Prince Karl August, as Christian sounded offensively Danish. Though unprepossessing in appearance and modest in manner, he became enormously popular with all classes in Sweden. He repelled Adlersparre's more obvious attempts to dominate him and sought with remarkable success to conciliate all political factions. In Gustavian circles it was intimated that the bachelor Karl August would eventually adopt Prince Gustav as his own heir. Ruuth and De la Gardie were well satisfied and Karl XIII became warmly attached to the prince. The nation was hard pressed after years of crisis and peril. "Our diet is still going on," Fersen wrote Lady Elizabeth Foster in April, ". . . we are hoping, however, that in a fortnight the king will send them all home. They may flatter themselves with the thought that they will not be missed." The dissolution of the Riksdag in May evoked both relief and disillusionment, after the failure of the high hopes of 1809. In this situation, Karl August alone seemed to hold out hope to all groups within the nation.[29]

So much the greater then was the general despair when the new crown prince suddenly died on 28 May. In the wake of this tragic event, the rumor arose that he had been poisoned by an aristocratic conspiracy, centering around Count Axel Fersen.

5

That such a story should gain credence was the result of a complex interaction of several factors. It was rumored during the summer of 1809 that the "aristocrats," Ruuth, De la Gardie, Ugglas, Armfelt, and the others, had formed a "counterrevolutionary club" in which they spun their intrigues and which by fall met regularly in the Fersen home. Counts Axel and Fabian, and especially their sister, Countess Piper, were said to be actively involved and the new queen was also suspected. Such ideas were encouraged by Grevesmöhlen and his secret police. That there ever was such a "club," that the Fersens engaged in political intrigue or were even socially influential was emphatically denied by H. G. Trolle-Wachtmeister, who though attached to the government party had family connections but little affection for the Fersens. Neither Axel nor Fabian held important positions in government. They and their dull little circle of old courtiers preferred to while away their time playing *patience*, Trolle-Wachtmeister commented dryly, and were "completely innocent as well with respect to politics as to everything else that required thought or its implementation." This picture is obviously overdrawn. Jacob De la Gardie's letters to his wife in December 1809 frequently speak of seeing the Fersens—though more often Fabian and Sophie than Axel—and on the same occasions some of his own political associates. Yet even if these contacts were only social, Fersen could still be worrisome to the government party, for in the event of a Gustavian coup, he doubtless would be included in a new government or regency council for prestige or symbolic value.[30]

It was widely rumored that the Fersens were on bad terms with the new crown prince and regarded him with contempt. Fabian was said to have treated him coldly in Göteborg and to have objected haughtily when he wished to place his secretary, a man of modest birth, at his own table. Fabian secured the appointment of Josef Rossi, who was of Italian descent and attended the Fersen family, as the prince's physician. "But is there no honest Swede to send to the prince?" Grevesmöhlen asked slyly; "Italian and poisoner, it amounts to the same thing." When Karl August left for Skåne in May 1810, Fabian is supposed to have upbraided him for not taking all the accouterments appertaining to his status. When shortly after, Karl August took ill, it was Fabian who sent Rossi to care for him.[31]

There were fewer rumors about Axel and no good reason to believe he ever had any dispute with the prince. Schinkel recounts that when he received Karl August at Drottningholm, Fersen addressed him "in an elegant and fluent French," with a dignity bordering on coldness, at which the prince replied that he knew the count's mother tongue and should prefer to use it, after which the conversation "did not leave the bounds of a forced politeness." When Karl August made his formal entry into Stockholm, the grand marshal was said to draw unseeming attention to himself by the magnificent equipage with which he led the procession. In the official festivities that followed, Fersen seems to have caused resentment among members of the non-noble estates over arrangements for their attendance and exchanged heated words with the speaker of the burghers' estate.[32]

What is clear is that Karl August was simple and unaffected in his ways, with no taste for court etiquette, while the Fersens, particularly Axel, were the foremost representatives of the old school. Their formality and reserve seemed an inexcusable coldness, arrogance, and cynicism to a more impetuous, earnest, and romantic generation. It was rumored that Karl August was called the "prince of the mob" in high aristocratic circles. Schinkel alleges that the prince could never feel close to the Fersens, whose manner he considered "a survival from a bygone era, refined on the surface although fundamentally barbaric and unchristian."[33]

There is little evidence of what Karl August himself felt about the Fersens. His Danish adjutant, J. H. von Holst, wrote the prince's brother that Fabian Fersen seemed "devoted" to Karl August and described the *riksmarskalk* as rather ordinary, though "very vain." Karl August wrote in an undated letter to his brother:

The principal factions are actually 2. At the head of the one there stands, as is known, Adlersparre, etc. At the head of the other, la Gardie, Ruuth, Armfeldt. This latter group is for the most part composed of well-known persons, ... affects, when it dares to, attachment to the former dynasty and works through the Counts Fersen and their sister, a certain Countess Piper, who is notorious and surely known to you, upon the queen, and through her ... although seldom and with little success, upon the king ...[34]

After Karl August's death, Fabian Fersen wrote to Adlersparre and Sophie Piper to Trolle-Wachtmeister in early June, expressing their sorrow. This may have been mainly intended simply to clear the family of suspicion. Yet Axel and his family undoubtedly regretted sincerely enough Karl August's death, for it again threatened Sweden with grave uncertainties.[35]

The idea that the prince had died of poisoning had even longer antecedents. It was characteristic of the times to suspect such foul play when important political or princely persons died untimely deaths. De la Gardie had suspected the anti-Gustavians of plotting to poison Gustav IV Adolf in the spring of 1809 and when a leading peasant *riksdagsman* died in December, an autopsy was necessary to still suspicion. Such rumors surrounded Karl August long before his death. Karl XIII had feared the Danes intended to poison him before he could come to Sweden. On 13 January, after a particularly effective Gustavian parliamentary maneuver, Grevesmöhlen "revealed" to the Mannerheim Club a Gustavian plot to poison the prince of Augustenburg before he could reach Stockholm and the estates swear fealty to him. Adlersparre, then accompanying the prince from Norway, was informed of this by letter and, being ever suspicious, did not question its veracity. The story was obviously a fabrication, apparently intended to counteract the Gustavians' parliamentary tactics.[36]

Karl August had been in poor health since well before coming to Sweden. Thereafter, his periodic indispositions fed persistent rumors of attempts to poison him, directed chiefly against Ruuth, De la Gardie, Ugglas, and Armfelt, who were also accused of secret intrigues with the new Russian ambassador, Count Peter van Suchtelen. This campaign of abuse reached new heights in March and April, when the Mannerheim faction suspected Karl August's interest in Prince Gustav and the scheme for a royal coup to change the constitution, both of which were evidently effectively scotched. Thereafter, both the king and the crown prince turned progressively against the Gustavians.[37]

The Fersens were first attacked by this insidious campaign in April and Sophie Piper was singled out for particular attention. She was widely regarded as a woman who, as Schinkel put it, "stood high on the lists of intrigue and gallantry." Trolle-Wachtmeister maintained that her enemies did too much honor to "her limited intellect, suited only for small courtly and large amorous intrigues." She was nevertheless believed to exercise great but concealed influence, especially through her lifelong, intimate friendship with Queen Charlotta, in which the older Sophie was apparently the dominating personality. Indeed, as one reads Hedvig Elisabeth Charlotta's voluminous diary, one wonders how many of her ideas derived directly from Sophie, thus perhaps indirectly from Axel Fersen. Countess Piper meanwhile had long been suspected as a poisoner. She was held responsible for the rumor that Lars von Engeström had poisoned Baron Taube in 1799; that Taube bequeathed a considerable fortune to her, however, caused some to suspect that she herself had been the poisoner. This whole episode presumably caused Gustav IV Adolf's strong dislike for her, which apparently affected Axel as well. The death of her husband, Count Adolf Ludvig Piper, in 1795 now seemed suspicious to her enemies and when her niece, Hedda Trolle-Wachtmeister, died of consumption in the spring of 1810, it was whispered that this was her work, an allegation Count Trolle-Wachtmeister himself contemptuously rejected. It was even rumored in June that one of Sophie's maids had discovered her mistress's secret and had been poisoned to keep her from revealing it; in July the woman turned up alive and well, claiming that in fifteen years' service she never had the least reason to be suspicious. Fabian too had made enemies with his hasty temper, and it was understood that "in his capacity as a man" he was even closer to the queen than his sister.[38]

Such was the atmosphere by 28 May, when Crown Prince Karl August, in the midst of cavalry maneuvers at Kvidinge in Skåne, fell senseless from his saddle and died within half an hour. Two days later, Rossi performed an autopsy, believing he could not preserve the body long enough to seek instructions from Stockholm, witnessed by three medical professors from Lund University. News of the death reached Stockholm on 31 May, where the effect was devastating. Rossi had doubtless been anxious to perform an autopsy because of suspicions to which he was already subject. The day the news arrived, the council in Stockholm sent off to Kvidinge the physician Magnus Pontin and the chemist Jöns Jacob Berzelius to determine, in the words of Lars von Engeström, now foreign minister, whether "the crown prince had died of poison." Since the leading Gustavians—Ruuth, De la Gardie, Armfelt—were no longer in Stockholm, suspicion concentrated on the Fersen family. Their connection with Rossi immediately came to mind. Already on 31 May, hostile crowds gathered outside the Fersen palace on Blasieholmen. The queen, herself suspected, sought to warn Sophie but realized to her sorrow that the Fersens would not condescend to listen to scandalous and menacing rumors. Axel and his sister meanwhile visited Lövstad, Ljung, and Finspång during most of June and were absent from the capital while sentiment against them gathered force.[39]

Those most directly affected by Karl August's death were the Men of 1809, who were thus deprived of the barrier they had so painstakingly contrived against a Vasa restoration. It was necessary to convene the estates again to elect a new successor and on 1 June a Riksdag was announced for 23 July in Stockholm. Prince Gustav's name immediately reappeared. Adlersparre lost no time in securing the endorsement of the king and council for the dead crown prince's brother, Duke Frederik Christian of Augustenburg. Though the Mannerheim Club had disbanded with the end of the diet in May, Baron Mannerheim and his friends quickly formed a new organization called the Opinion Club, apparently including mainly members of the earlier club in or near Stockholm. The flood of scandalous rumors and writings that now circulated throughout the country, aimed at the Gustavians and particularly the Fersens, was commonly understood to emanate from the Opinion Club.

Surviving examples of handwritten and printed leaflets, pamphlets, and broadsides show the vehemence of the political passions involved. On 8 June, a leaflet addressed to "The People, August's Avenger" appeared in the streets, calling for a general uprising two days later, in which "blood must flow," with clear references to the grand marshal and his sister. Another called for revenge against "the highly distinguished monstrosities on Blasieholmen." Such ideas were encouraged by the autopsy on the dead prince. Rossi's report was received by the Collegium Medicum, which announced the cause of death to be an apoplectic stroke. Pontin and Berzelius, however, objected to the carelessness of the autopsy, especially as it was too late for another, and questioned Rossi's legal competence to perform it in view of his personal connection with the case. Thus although they concurred that the prince had died of natural causes, their criticisms, imprudently made public, were misconstrued as confirmation that he had been poisoned.[40]

The effects of all this were attested by J. A. Ehrenström, who was told by a seaman as early as about 10 June that the populace in Stockholm were aroused

... against those they believe had poisoned the crown prince and they have decided to murder Count Fersen just at the time of the prince's funeral, and will then tear down Count Ugglas's house, do in Councillor Ramel and many other distinguished persons who it is claimed did not love the prince.

The seaman had heard this "everywhere among the crowds at the southern sluice-gate [Slussen], in the fishing harbor, and in many places where I was, and out loud too." Though shaken, Ehrenström did not believe such threats could be carried out.[41]

The most devastating blow was struck by the new radical journal, *Nya Posten*, which on 14 June published an anonymous allegory in verse entitled "The Foxes," which by the best evidence was written by a struggling young journalist named Bengt Johan Törneblad. The fable related how according to an ancient manuscript, after an unworthy king had been deposed in "The Animals' wide Kingdom ... many hundreds of years ago," "a Riksdag" was called to decide what was needed. "*A King!*—So cried all together, who *nota bene*, knew the danger of having none—But those who knew not this, (namely the fox party) and who themselves would rather rule, they cried: *Several Kings! Several!*" However a "crown prince" was elected, and "every honest beast was agreed, that such a lion-prince never had been seen," who wished "equal justice for both high and low." All should now have been satisfied. "But history decreed otherwise." The foxes were now wild with rage and fear.

What serves us then—(shrieked one of them)—
What serves us then our cunning, gold and decorations,
If he be Regent who, we see, will not govern at our whim? . . .
Who sees in each and every beast his brother
And makes not differences of person, be he great or small?
Then all our credit will go to Blazes!
And the nation's eyes will open soon—they cannot fail to do so—
To all the foxy tricks that we have played to date since centuries ago—
Then the Devil will surely take us, that I can see plainly now.
"But softly, softly, *mon ami* (thus there spoke a tall *marquis*
Of that treacherous *parti*),
"*Parbleu!* It seems un *peu abominable!*
But fate can well be *variable* . . .
And before the Devil us shall take, which surely would be *execrable*—

Let us find a way—let's see—a way"—*Aha!*
"I've found one that is extremely good, mon cher!
(There now cried out a female fox)—*"And it is practicable*; But—"

At this point the "manuscript" becomes "somewhat faded," but "some pages further on it says, plainly to be understood, that the Lion-Prince was *stone dead...*." The story ends when another lion prince, "(whose name the manuscript does not reveal)... from a distant land arrived," built a great pyre where he "burned the whole pack of foxes...to dust and ashes," and thereafter ruled justly over the "whole four-footed Kingdom." Fox fables were a venerable part of folk tradition and allusions to "foxes" in radical journals during the preceding months had found a ready response. The poem was soon widely known throughout Sweden and made the fortunes of the struggling *Nya Posten.*[42]

Recent studies show how widely the Fersens and the high aristocracy in general were considered implicated in the crown prince's death throughout the country, above all in Stockholm, and among all social classes except the court nobility itself. In the province of Uppland, adjoining the capital, where Fersen owned Steninge manor and was chancellor of Uppsala University, both of which he seldom visited, opinion was distinctly hostile to him and notably among the younger academics. According to an anonymous account in the Moscow archives, it was feared in Stockholm that "a great party of peasants had demanded permission to take part in Karl August's funeral, and this was said in such a manner as to arouse the suspicion that the peasants intended to enter the city by force." One region which appears to have been inclined in his favor was, significantly, Östergötland, where he spent much time in his last years—including early June 1810—at Lövstad, Ljung, and Finspång. In these places Fersen enjoyed real popularity.[43]

Suspicion extended into the royal palace itself. Though the queen never questioned her friends' innocence, Karl XIII had never shared her enthusiasm for the Fersens. In recent months he had turned against the Gustavians and had fallen increasingly under the influence of their opponents on the state council. Of her husband, Queen Charlotta wrote that he

...has both talents and abilities. But he has unfortunately too little confidence in his own ability, thus hesitates when he has to make decisions, lets himself be influenced by his advisers, who often abuse his trust. ... he is always too easily impressed by those around him, can thus be brought by intriguers to unfavorable attitudes toward those who are truly devoted to him but who lack the opportunity to see him daily and in their actions to prove the falsity of the slander. At times, it has been possible to arouse him against them to the point that he absolutely refuses to listen to an explanation. Consequently it is important that his advisers always be right-thinking and honorable, so that his pure and good intentions will be properly brought to bear. That is my warmest wish!

Karl August's death was a bitter blow to the old monarch. Several of his councillors were convinced of the Fersens' guilt, some quite openly. The king's correspondence with Foreign Minister von Engström shows he too believed in the poisoning plot. According to the queen, Karl considered the so-called Opinion Club "beneficial."[44]

Preparations were meanwhile made for the reception of the crown prince's body in the capital on 20 June. The king appointed Major General I. L. Silfversparre acting general adjutant for Stockholm for that day. On 17 June, Karl XIII approved Silfversparre's projected general orders for the cortege to the royal palace. On 19 June, the council officially charged Silfversparre with the security of the capital and that evening the king gave him final verbal instructions. Silfversparre knew disturbances could be expected. Yet the troops were neither given instructions for such an eventuality nor live ammunition. In case of trouble, ambiguities and discrepancies in the standing and special orders affecting Silfversparre's assignment required that he relinquish command to either the regular general adjutant of the army, General Adlercreutz, or the governor of Stockholm, Field Marshal Klingspor.[45]

On 19 June, Axel Fersen returned to the capital to take his place as grand marshal in the cortege next day. Warnings had already reached him in the country. The queen wrote that he had there visited "a lady he counted among his friends"—doubtless Emelie De Geer—"but disregarded her warnings when she bade him not to return to Stockholm but rather plead illness." Once back in the capital, it is related that the former *riksmarskalk*, the poet J. G. Oxenstierna, urged Fersen to stay home on the morrow and offered to take his place, but that Fersen did not wish to confirm the suspicions against him and was sure adequate measures would be taken to maintain order. It was still probably the desire to reassure himself on this score which brought him out to Haga palace at about 6:00 that evening. According to his friend, Marianne

Ehrenström, who recounted the scene, Fersen asked a courtier to announce him to the king but received the reply that the latter did not have time to receive him. He asked the courtier to return, explaining that he wished "some more detailed instructions in connection with the arrival of the prince's cortege." After a quarter of an hour, the courtier returned and in a troubled tone said, "His Majesty has so much to do that it is impossible for him to see Your Excellency." "What," rejoined Fersen, "the king cannot see his grand marshal when he requests His Majesty's further orders for tomorrow?" He then bowed deeply to the ladies present and conversed pleasantly to cover the embarrassment of the situation before returning to Stockholm.[46]

Karl XIII may at that very time have been discussing final arrangements for the next day with Silfversparre. What was said will never be known, though it probably would not have given Fersen much reassurance. The king had recently remarked to General Suremain, "If I were in the Fersens' position, I would have myself arrested and demand to be judged. That would stop the mouths of that whole pack. But these are measures I cannot advise; they must be resorted to of one's own volition." To Silfversparre, the monarch is supposed to have said, "It would not hurt if that haughty lord were given a lesson."[47]

That evening the Fersens gave a splendid *souper*. "Everything proceeded there just as at court," a lady later recalled, "... Not a word was uttered during the entire evening that in any way suggested the possibility of a riot the following day. Fersen was calm and amiable as always, a representative of the old school." The effect of the brightly lit Fersen palace on the eve of the prince's cortege on many Stockholmers may be imagined. Meanwhile in the city, leaflets were being passed out, calling for a "fox hunt" next day.[48]

6

On the morning of 20 June 1810, the hearse bearing the body of the crown prince and its escort arrived at Horn Tollhouse at Stockholm's southwestern limit.[49] As Fersen prepared to set forth, his old coachman implored him not to go, but when he proved immovable, loyally fulfilled his duty. An anonymous letter was later found in Fersen's wallet, presumably given him that morning, which read in part:

To Axel Fersen. Wretch. Read this letter and tremble. Do you and your league believe that 2 million people will let some aristocrats commit unpunished whatever horror they wish and let themselves be trampled by conspiring traitors, shall this unhappy land remain eternally under the oppression of audacious men of violence . . . the hour of retribution will come! even though your abominable father the proud aristocrat succeeded in his game . . . even though your long neck . . . escaped the guillotine in France . . . a nation in frenzy and despair is frightful. . . . Shall this ancient Realm gradually lose its independence and its existence among the Nations of Europe through the faithlessness, infamy, and treason of its nobles? . . . Despicable creature, when you come into the city in all your presumed greatness and pomp, know that the lowest peasant spits on you and feels himself to be a greater and a better man than you, arrogant wretch! . . . know that this letter is the voice of the public. . . . Karl August shall be avenged.

In the margin was written in large letters, "Copies of this letter are in many hands." Fersen breakfasted at the royal palace with General Suremain, who noted that "He showed the calm of a man whose conscience is pure and who is disturbed by no fears." They rode out together to Hornstull.[50] Meanwhile in the city, taverns were dispensing free beer and schnapps, brewers' carts were renewing the supply, and money was distributed to some of the poorer and rougher inhabitants. According to Colonel Salomon Brelin, a citizen later stood in "the square," openly boasting the day had cost him a thousand *riksdaler*.[51]

At noon, the procession set forth to the ringing of church bells and the firing of cannon. At its head role General Silfversparre and a half squadron of Horseguardsmen, thereafter a group of mounted adjutants and the carriages of various officials, among them Fabian Fersen. Then came the *riksmarskalk*, Axel Fersen, in his coach, followed by the hearse, beside which four mounted generals bore the corners of its canopy, and a lieutenant and 24 Guardsmen marched. These were followed by a corporal and six Guardsmen, mounted, then another long line of carriages, in one of which was the physician Rossi. At the end rode the cavalry escort that had accompanied the coffin from Skåne. On all the squares and open places along the route detachments of troops were drawn up. However, no members of the royal family were present and Karl XIII just then held a meeting of the full council at Haga. The Stockholm civil guard did not take part and the police were notable by their absence or inactivity.[52]

According to General Skjöldebrand, Fersen rode

... in his own equipage, a magnificent old-fashioned state coach drawn by six white horses with red morocco harnesses, richly ornamented with gilded bronze. On either side of the coach walked three lackeys in white liveries with broad, multicolored bands along all of the seams. He himself sat in the coach dressed in mourning with the grand marshal's staff in his hand and after him came the hearse covered with a simple black canopy, dusty after the journey and without ornament ... the splendor in which the grand marshal rode made an unpleasant contrast to the simplicity of the hearse ... he looked like a triumphant conqueror dragging behind him a defeated foe.

Though Fersen only followed prescribed court ritual, the effect may easily be imagined following the agitation of the past three weeks.[53]

Along most of the route, through the southern part of Stockholm, the crowd was sullen and hostile. However, as the cortege crossed the sluice-bridge to the Old City and entered Kornhamn Square, it neared its destination, the royal palace, and Suremain, one of the generals beside the hearse, began to breathe more freely. At this point, however, the crowd grew more menacing. An outrider asked Fersen if he should go after help, then rode off to find the commanding general adjutant. At the entrance to Stora Nygatan from the square, a large crowd was waiting with a ready supply of rocks with which, as though at a given signal, they began to pelt the coach as soon as it entered the street. Here Fersen was caught in a trap. Stora Nygatan, some 400 yards long between Kornhamn and Riddarhus Squares, was only about a dozen yards wide, wall-to-wall, laterally accessible only through narrow alleys, and crowded with people along the sides. The troops at either end of the procession neither knew what was happening to the grand marshal nor could come to his aid. The small detachment around the hearse did not and probably could not do much in such a situation. The barrage of rocks smashed the carriage windows and stunned the coachman. From a window, the visiting Professor Rasmus Nyerup from Copenhagen heard the approaching commotion and saw Fersen, "sitting pale as death in the most frightful fear and distress." He was soon forced to the floorboards with his cape over his head, while the crowd roared.[54]

Outside the present No. 1 Stora Nygatan, a few steps from Riddarhus Square, several Finnish-speaking men in seamen's garb stopped the carriage. Georg Bartholin, a Danish-born former non-commissioned officer, waiting in the doorway in uniform, opened the carriage door and urged the grand marshal to take refuge within. Fersen doubtless hoped to run the gauntlet to its end and get out of Stora Nygatan, which would probably have saved him, but he now had no choice. Bartholin led him to the second floor, where the owner of the house, Jonas Hultgren, a minor court functionary, kept a tavern, where a number of people were gathered. Fersen gained a few minutes respite in a back room. A goldsmith who lived in the house offered to show him a back way from which he could escape to the palace nearby, but Fersen preferred to wait for "the watch" to come to his aid. The wait proved long and trying. The procession continued on its way. The crowd grew in Hultgren's tavern; the inquest later identified no less than 120 persons who had been there at the time, mostly of the middle classes. A mob assembled outside while the windows of the house opposite were filled with people, among them a notorious police spy, according to Brelin, who later claimed he knew nothing and recognized no one. The crowd in the tavern pushed into the back room, taunting Fersen with the epithets "fox" and "tall Marquis." A German-born merchant, J. G. Lexow, and an actor of French parentage, J. A. Lambert, took the lead. They accused him of causing the French Revolution and wishing to provoke a similar upheaval in Sweden by murdering the crown prince. J. P. Häggman heard that some in the crowd even accused him of complicity in the murder of Gustav III and the deposition of Gustav IV Adolf. Someone shouted he should no longer be called count but simply "*Herr* Fersen." Lexow replied he was still a count but that the law would strip him of his title, to which Fersen assented, "Let the law judge me." Lambert, Lexow, and others tore off his decorations, coat and sword, which were thrown out the window to the crowd below.[55]

The outrider from Kornhamnstorg finally found General Silfversparre at the palace, where the procession was straggling in, including Fersen's coach, which General Skjöldebrand noted to be almost demolished. As Fabian Fersen and Rossi dismounted from their carriages, they were recognized by the crowd and forced to take refuge in the palace. The commander of the cavalry escort requested permission to break up the crowd around the Hultgren house, but Silfversparre refused; when the officer later dispatched a platoon in that direction, they were turned back at the general adjutant's orders. Neither of the authorities to whom Silfversparre was responsible in case of disorder was immediately available: Klingspor was too feeble to mount his horse and inaccessible most of the day in the palace, while Adlercreutz was at the council session at Haga. Silfversparre set off for the Hultgren house with only an adjutant and four Horseguardsmen, explaining that the crowd would break up if he spoke to them. The general was enthusiastically acclaimed in the street and himself joined in the cheering, waved his hat, and shook many hands, including that of a seaman, the déclassé Finnish nobleman. Otto Johan Tandefelt, who said, "He shall be done in." "My friends," Silfversparre cried, "I have a heart as well as you, we all think alike. . . . I will wager my life for you, my friends, you should not make me unhappy." According to Skjöldebrand, he said, "Yes, you are right, my friends, you are right, but just be reasonable." General Suremain, a French émigré in Swedish service who vividly recalled similar scenes in his own country, vainly urged Silfversparre to use force, but the latter assured him nothing would happen and entered the house to the cheers of the crowd. Suremain set forth posthaste for Haga to report to the king while Skjöldebrand tried to get a nearby battalion to intervene. But its commander had "no orders" and it soon marched away.[56]

Inside Hultgren's tavern, Silfversparre asked what the people's intention was of Lambert, who replied that Fersen should be arrested. Silfversparre offered to conduct him to the palace but the crowd, including Lexow and Tandefelt, protested he would then simply be released and insisted that he be taken to the city hall on Riddarhus Square or the notorious criminal prison at Smedjegården. After some show of objection, Silfversparre agreed to take Fersen to the city hall if the crowd would promise not to molest him. Those inside accepted, provided Silfversparre first sent away the four Horseguardsmen at the entrance, who in any case had been instructed not to use force. On Lambert's advice, Silfversparre announced the agreement from the window to the crowd below, from which voices protested that Fersen would never be brought to justice and demanded that he be thrown out the window. Silfversparre and Lambert escorted Fersen out of the back room, at which the people in the tavern promptly broke their promise by further insulting him and striking him with canes and umbrellas. Someone said to him, "You shall die, and before 12:00 o'clock tonight, the Piper woman, Ugglas, and two others shall die." As they descended to the street, Fersen said, "I see that it will soon be my last hour."[57]

Adlercreutz now arrived from Haga, having missed Suremain, in time to see Fersen emerge from the Hultgren house supported by Silfversparre and Lambert, and was heard to comment, "Now they have it the way they want it." The crowd cheered, Adlercreutz waved his hat and joined in, and someone persuaded him that if he rode away the crowd would break up and follow him. He set off down Stora Nygatan to Kornhamnstorg, accompanied by part of the crowd, which he proceeded to harangue.[58]

Once in the street, Lambert and Silfversparre were quickly separated from Fersen. The general was admonished "not to interfere in the people's affair" and was told that the crowd had no quarrel with him but only with "the traitor to the kingdom and regicide who wanted to make Sweden as unfortunate as he made France." Silfversparre went off to the palace to look for his horse, absenting himself at this critical moment. Fersen struggled into Riddarhus Square, where all this time a battalion of Svea Guards had stood immobile. At the corner, he sought shelter between General E. E. G. von Vegesack's horse and the wall, but the animal, frightened, shied away. Fersen was rushed across the square amid a compact mass of people. Some junior officers and soldiers in the formation attempted to protect him but were ordered by their commanding officers to stand fast. According to Schinkel, Silfversparre now reappeared and said to some of those involved, "I command you not to leave your posts, since the least movement by the military would be the signal for a bloodbath." Three young officers off duty—A. Ehrengranat, A. G. von Düben, and D. Schultz—courageously defended Fersen and got him into the guard room of the city hall, barring the door behind them. The officer commanding the civil guards on duty there asked what he should do when the regular troops did nothing. Fersen pleaded with the guards to protect him, promising handsome rewards.[59]

Fersen had thus gone to the city hall as Silfversparre had promised, but did not long find shelter there. Until this time, the crowd had seemed to consist mainly of middle-class people but now it evidently became poorer and rougher, and included a conspicuous number of persons in seamen's dress. This mob soon broke into the guard room, dragged Fersen outside and there stripped, beat, kicked, and trampled him to death. The coup-de-grâce was evidently given by Tandefelt, who jumped on his ribcage and crushed it.[60]

Even after Fersen was dead, the crowd in its fury continued to kick and desecrate the naked corpse. Only then did Silfversparre ride forward and the crowd begin to scatter, bearing with them their bloody trophies. Bits and pieces of Fersen's hair and clothing in the days immediately following turned up in far corners of Sweden. But one young man, who proudly identified himself as a master mason and citizen of the city, returned Fersen's gold watch to Silfversparre, explaining, "We are not thieves but only the avengers of Karl August's death."[61]

7

Only after Fersen was dead did Silfversparre report to the king at Haga and request instructions. Suremain had meanwhile obtained orders from Karl XIII for Silfversparre to use all necessary means to restore order. Returning, Suremain found Fersen lying dead in Riddarhustorget, the situation confused and Silfversparre "quite beside himself." Adlercreutz too was badly shaken. Silfversparre did not consider the king's order explicit enough, so Suremain again returned to Haga. This time, Karl came into the capital, arriving around 4:00, replacing Klingspor with General Skjölde-brand as governor of Stockholm, and according to the Danish minister, "showed more firmness than all the others together."[62]

When Silfversparre wished to remove Fersen's body from the square, there were protests from the crowd that it should be hauled away to the Gallows Hill on the executioner's cart. Only later in the afternoon was it taken into a police watch room by the city hall and dumped into a rough wooden coffin. Crowds of curiosity seekers pushed in to see the count's naked and mangled remains until finally cleared out toward evening. Early next morning, the estate manager from Steninge arrived by boat to claim the body.[63]

The day did not pass without further disorder and bloodshed. Around 4:00 p.m., live ammunition was issued to the troops, the guard around the palace was reinforced and detachments posted at bridges, squares, and other key positions. That evening, the crowd tried to attack the Fersen house of Blasieholmen, but were forced back. They stoned Count af Ugglas's house and were only prevented from dragging out the count himself by the timely arrival of a troop of cavalry. Around the palace, heavy crowds insulted and stoned the military until shooting broke out and the cavalry charged with sabers. At this the crowd scattered, leaving or dragging away an unknown number of casualties. Heavy rain around 10:00 p.m. finally helped to clear the streets. Those who took part in the evening's disturbances were noted to be from the lower social classes, in Brelin's words, "journeymen, apprentices, working people, and petty bourgeois."[64]

Unrest continued until after Karl August was finally buried in Riddarholm Church on 13 July. Inflammatory writings continued to appear, there were attempts at arson and to incite the troops to mutiny. General Skjöldebrand dealt with the situation with a firm hand. Military reinforcements were called in, something like a state of siege established.

Axel Fersen was not the only one whose life was threatened on 20 June. Fabian Fersen and the surgeon Rossi, though not generally recognized by the crowd, were forced to flee into the palace, as noted. Sophie Piper was offered asylum in the foreign minister's residence by her neighbor—Baroness von Engeström—but fled, disguised as a peasant woman and accompanied by her nephew, Baron Axel Klinckowström, and the faithful Duc de Piennes, to Vaxholm fortress, where she gave herself into protective custody and remained the next several months. Count af Ugglas's narrow escape has been related. Fortunately, Armfelt, De la Gardie, and Ruuth were absent from Stockholm. The queen herself remained the object of suspicion because of her close ties with the Fersens and for a time was prepared to flee from Haga.[65]

Finally, in the later afternoon of 20 June, Foreign Minister von Engeström and General Adlercreutz called on Fabian Fersen at the palace, where they found him in a state of shock. What was said is not known but shortly after, Fabian's wife sent a hastily scribbled note to Engeström saying, "[Fabian] Fersen has asked me to ask you to request that the king graciously send the chancellor of justice to seal the papers of my unfortunate brother-in-law." A formal request by Fabian Fersen for the immediate confiscation and search of his brother's papers was then appended to the minutes of the council for 20 June. Sophie Piper wrote from Vaxholm on 28 June, requesting that her papers also be examined to prove her innocence. On 5 July, the chancellor of justice announced that the investigation had been completed, revealing no incriminating evidence whatsoever.[66]

CHAPTER XVI

Epilogue

1

Already on the evening of 20 June, the vice-governor of Stockholm opened an investigation of the events of that day. A week later, on 26 June, a special tribunal convened for an inquest that lasted nine months. Some 900 persons were interrogated by the police, many of whom were also investigated by the tribunal. The Collegium Medicum upheld its pronouncement that Karl August had died a natural death and later medical studies have concurred. Nothing incriminating was found among Fersen's papers, as seen, and on 5 November 1810, the special tribunal formally absolved Fabian Fersen and Sophie Piper of any responsibility in the death of the crown prince. Josef Rossi, however, was tried for incompetence in connection with the autopsy and ended his days abroad.[1]

Chief Master of Ceremonies for the Court, L. von Hausswolff, wrote a friend on 25 June:

That His Excellency Fersen was innocent, I am convinced, and for several reasons. *Primo.* He was a good and honest man. *Secundo.* He was too proud and haughty to enter into such a plan, which would disgrace himself and his entire family. *Tertio.* He was too lazy ever to think of anything that might change his way of living. This man was thus the victim of something the future will reveal.

Axel Fersen's innocence was soon generally acknowledged, though the radical press continued through 1810 to allude darkly to "foxes" and Fersens. Sophie Piper's sinister reputation long survived her and in some circles she and her brothers remained suspect years later. In 1838, a Danish traveler was assured by an official in Stockholm that Axel Fersen and his sister were "not free of guilt" in the death of the crown prince. Even those who came to accept the Fersens' innocence, could continue to believe Karl August had been poisoned, as did Georg Adlersparre's son, Carl, who suspected Danish agents. Armfelt suspected that Adlersparre and his clique had themselves poisoned the prince when they could not make him their tool. As late as 1894, Elof Tegnér polemicized against the "Adlersparre school" of history, for which the poisoning still remained "an article of faith."[2]

At Steninge, Fersen's body was subjected to autopsy on 28 June, showing no one injury had killed him but rather all combined. It was embalmed and placed in a small garden pavilion. Several months passed before it could be buried. L. F. Norstedt wrote his brother on 10 July:

In Sigtuna there is supposed to be a burial vault for the owners of Steninge manor, thus it was intended that Fersen should be interred there. They were ready to permit this burial to take place without ceremony when two persons arrived from Stockholm and said: God forbid that you should have anything to do with this, for in Stockholm the body is regarded as stolen, and since the public on Riddarhus Square loudly condemned it to the gallows hill, whence the wretch was to have been hauled on an open cart accompanied by this same public, watch out, it may go badly with you. . . . This kind of warning made it so that no one would touch the coffin, much less carry it.

The king wished to send troops to assist with the burial. But as they recovered their nerve later in the summer, Fabian Fersen and his sister insisted that Karl XIII bury their brother in the capital with the full ceremonial due a grand marshal and knight of the Seraphim, to acknowledge his innocence. They were supported by the queen, who enlisted the aid of the new crown prince—elected by the Riksdag in August—Karl Johan, the former French Marshal Bernadotte, whom Fersen in 1798 had regarded as "one of the raging Jacobins." This alliance at length overcame the fears of the king and several of his advisers of fresh disorders. Strong security measures were taken under the watchful eye of the former Jacobin marshal and on 4 December 1810, Axel Fersen was laid to rest in the Wachtmeister vault in Riddarholm Church, amid time-honored pageantry and without disturbance. He was later reburied beside his father in Ljung Church. The pavilion at Steninge was converted into a little brick chapel in Gothic-romantic style, bearing a medallion by the sculptor E. G. Göthe, and the inscription by the poet, Johan Olof Wallin:

Here were kept for four months the mortal remains of Count AXEL VON FERSEN, Grand Marshal of the Kingdom of Sweden, while the power that ended his days refused to let him rest in the tomb of his ancestors. May Truth recalled by Time protect in History his memory and render justice to his virtue . . .

Sophie Piper raised a simple monument with a medallion by Sergel in the English park at Lövstad. There is no memorial in Ljung Church. "So, dear friend, ends this world's greatness," wrote Fabian to his sister after the funeral, "For us there remains nothing but the sense of loss; for him, silence."[3]

Altogether different was the epitaph proposed in an anonymous poem entitled "The Fersiad," evidently written by a student at Uppsala in protest against the memorial service held by the faculty there for the late chancellor in March 1811:

I hate the praise of fools and hypocrisy's honeyed poison
An urn I justly would begrudge his grave:
Here A--l F--'s bones a final resting place have found,
Since on Riddarhus Square he reached his earthly goal.
Citizen! Whoe'er upon this stone may gaze
Upon it shed a tear of fearful sorrow!
Weep not for desire's slave—weep o'er the nation's degradation
That in its bosom others like him yet must hold.—
Here behold an example of noble arrogance,
Nurture in thy breast the wish that here might stand,
Beside the name of this mighty lord, his sister's, many others', written,
That for the same intrigues they might too in such a death have paled.

There follows a description of Fersen's career which summarizes neatly the principal slanders against him during his lifetime:

That he enjoyed his manhood, no honest person will deny,
Also that he general, and decorated was,
Pour le mérite, of course, then in its silver glory,
Antoinette herself with laurels crowns his brow
For all the hours of bliss that in his arms she found.

But after the flight to Varennes:

Now like a man of honor he flees the evil wrath
And to be sure takes with him his royal patrons' wealth.

At Uppsala:

And later he was Chancellor—Though it is said in reprimand
That both in science and in art he scarcely A.B.C. did understand.
. . . .

Like a prince he then did live, forgetting what had happened,
Remained always just like himself and was the haughtiest Excellency
That the North did ever see.
. . . .

That he deserved the death he died, I need not demonstrate
Since with the praise of millions his slayers are now hailed.
. . . .

No, fury's hidden poison and murder's open blade
Shall be for thee with blood avenged, Oh! Svea's folk.
. . . .

What serves the social order when birth gives right and law
And gilded vice preferment gains and day by day advances?
Sweden regains of her renown of old
Scarce more than that each king a hasty end does meet,
Who equal to his task dares with the Hydra fight
And well-born power with mighty blows to smite.
No less than four bright stars sunk in the sea of eternity
And once again a Regent have they sent into his grave.
Freely may the professors make offerings to Fersen's name!
Which in the annals of time shall bring to them eternal shame.[4]

2

The events of 20 June 1810 sent a wave of horror throughout
Sweden, indeed throughout Europe. In his eulogy at Fersen's
funeral, Bishop Gustaf Murray said:

The 20th of June was the unhappy day upon which this man, deserving
of respect for his way of thinking, his official positions and his gray hairs
alike—during the most solemn fulfillment of his duty, in a well-ordered
society, in a guarded capital—became in the frightful manner described
the undeserving victim of the bloodthirsty frenzy of a misled public . . .

The bishop's words gave voice to thoughts many had already expressed in private. Armfelt, visiting St. Petersburg, Stedingk, again Swedish ambassador there, and Lagerbjelke, now minister in Paris, felt the full brunt of the reaction abroad.[5]

What had happened on 20 June? There were various reactions. The most natural and immediate one among the propertied classes was to regard the events of that day as simply a frightful outburst of mob violence, with alarming overtones of Jacobinism. Incendiary leaflets found in the streets of Stockholm scarcely allayed such fears. One of these, dated 21 June, read:

God Almighty has commanded, you true, brave and noble Swedish subjects of the Third and Fourth class, that you should avenge yourselves over the death of the late regretted Royal Highness the Crown Prince. What harm did he do you, asks the noble-minded soul.—The first act has been carried out. Four acts remain. Now is the time to save the unhappy nation. Consider to yourself how untold many years you have been trampled under the feet of the nobility. *Unite now,* clear away the rank growth, the time has come, for King Karl the 11th's vision is now at hand. Spare none who took part in the damnable murder. The second act will begin with a Ruuth, an Ugglas, a Fabian Fersen, a physician Raussie [sic], a Countess Piper, who with her accursed claws prepared to order the medications, and it was practicable, she said. The formulas are still kept by her. *All shall be killed without pardon.* In the other acts, which shall quickly come about, all of the blue *cordons* and stars together, whose stars did not agree with our Gracious Crown Prince during his lifetime, will be caught. The remainder of the bloodsuckers, by which I mean the above-named class, will be designated at a later time. Courage, valor, and disgust over the many cabals that have been the work within Sweden's boundaries of fawning courtiers to oppress the poor public, you may be happy when despots are no more,—*command us, Brothers, to seek revenge.*

A postscript to the above read, "Do not fear the military, there are many in the group." On the same day, Professor Nyerup observed:

But what a sudden change of spirit! Even sensible and thoughtful men during yesterday's tumult were as though caught up in a Maelstrom, and to the point where they saw the manifestation as a patriotic deed and a sacrifice to propitiate the shade of the man who fell at Kvidinge. ... Today, however, they regard the affair with different eyes. They were indignant that the officer in command, instead of doing his duty, parleyed with the mob ...[6]

For the politically aware, meanwhile, it seemed evident that behind the seeming spontaneity of the riot lay a cunningly devised conspiracy, not only to propagandize but to prepare and direct the violence itself. The notable activity of middle-class persons on 20 June suggested to aristocratic observers that the plot originated within bourgeois circles dissatisfied with the social results of the revolution of 1809. General Skjöldebrand, for instance, wrote that

... the wild, murderous crowd consisted largely of a kind of middle class, which more than the rabble envied the great and thus willingly believed them guilty, for which reason they seized with pleasure the opportunity to take out their resentment against one of them.

The Danish and Russian ministers in their dispatches likewise stressed bourgeois hatred for the aristocracy.[7]

A more sinister interpretation soon appeared: that the plot had emanated from highly placed persons within the government and that even the elderly monarch was involved. Already on 12 June, the French chargé d'affaires suspected that members of the government derived satisfaction from the growing agitation. Later, Napoleon asked Lagerbjelke about "the assassination of the Comte de Fersen, committed with the acquiescence—what do I know?— with the assent of your government." The emperor went on to describe the Swiss avalanches that carry all before them. "Such is Jacobinism," he warned. "Be on your guard! I desire a strong government, a central government. *Adieu, monsieur!*"[8]

Each of these three interpretations unquestionably contains its element of truth. Times were hard for the poorer classes in Stockholm, which since the 1760s had suffered economic decline, aggravated by the recent war years. Misery was widespread, creating an undercurrent of frustration and discontent as the lower classes became increasingly literate and politically aware. Both Sophie Piper and the queen stressed the unsettling influence of the large domestic servant class: what Sophie called the "lackey proletariat." The generally inarticulate political attitudes of the poorer classes might be summarized as a combination of suspicion and latent hatred for the rich and powerful in general, with a kind of basic popular royalism containing much loyalty to the old dynasty. They generally believed, with the middle classes, that as in 1788 and 1792, the aristocracy had betrayed the nation in an hour of peril. Though individuals of the poorer classes were often on more amiable terms with the higher nobility than with the commercial bourgeoisie, the poor as a class were highly susceptible to anti-aristocratic agitation. "Among those who murdered the grand mashal," J. A. Ehrenström wrote to a friend in August,

... were surely many who with sheep-like stupidity imagined that in him they avenged, besides the poisoning of the crown prince, Gustav III's assassination, the deposition of his son, the exclusion of the latter's family from its hereditary rights and even the abandonment of Sveaborg and the loss of Finland. It was necessary to put such ideas into circulation to set the masses in motion.[9]

There could meanwhile be no mistaking the prominent part played by persons from the middle classes. The economic stagnation of the capital bore heavily on much of the city's lower bourgeoisie; one of those indicted in the Fersen case, J. G. Lexow, was reputed bankrupt. As a whole, the Swedish and especially the Stockholm bourgeoisie had long been strongly anti-aristocratic and showed greater enthusiasm for strong monarchy and less for parliamentary government as such than did the nobility. Indeed, much middle-class hostility was evidently directed against the oligarchs of the new constitutional regime, deriving principally from the lower nobility, a situation De la Gardie's party had shrewdly exploited. The anonymous Moscow report, interpreting the Swedish revolution of 1809 as an aristocratic reaction against royal autocracy, said of the situation in June 1810, "It was no longer only the death of the crown prince which would trouble the peace of the country; it was evidently the mortal hatred toward the Fersens and their party, if not the desire to overthrow entirely the whole order that had recently been reestablished in the country," adding that the leaders of the "revolutionary party" seemed to be "certain bourgeois." It was recalled that Fredrik Axel von Fersen had been the most prominent of the aristocratic "Hats" in the 1750s and 1760s. Axel's own attitude toward the bourgeois had been distant and reserved, and he himself had noted their ill-will toward him since his return to Stockholm in 1799.[10]

The middle classes clearly put great faith in Karl August. The Danish minister wrote on 26 June:

They comforted themselves with the hope that the crown prince after ascending the throne would diminish the preferences of birth. His popularity, his great freedom from affectation and the dislike he was believed to feel toward the nobility joined in encouraging the hope that during his reign they would be put down. When this hope was destroyed through his death, they wished to take advantage of this to attain their goal: to accuse the higher nobility of having poisoned the prince.

Popular sentiment, he continued, had turned against the whole noble class and ambitious persons hoped, by showing the strength of the masses, to strip the nobility of its remaining privileges at the next Riksdag and to "introduce a complete equality within society."[11]

A prominent part in the political life of the capital was played by middle-class elements—in the wider sense—particularly prone to frustration and particularly vocal: minor officials or would-be officials, discharged subalternate or non-commissioned officers, journalists, unenfranchised persons of property or education, derogated noblemen, refugees from Finland, persons of foreign origins, and *déracinés* in general. Rune Hedman, in his recent, careful statistical study of the crowd in the Fersen riot, has stressed the central role of elements with relatively high social but relatively low economic status, and vice versa. *Nya Posten* and the other radical publications were written primarily for such a clientele. To such categories may be reckoned Hultgren, Lambert, Lexow and Tandefelt, Törneblad and other journalists: indeed, virtually every person positively identified as having played an active role in humiliating and injuring Fersen.[12]

Some aspects of 20 June, finally, could evidently only be explained by the involvement, active or passive, of highly placed persons within the government itself: the absence of police, inadequacy of military preparations, inactivity of the troops, absence of responsible officials. All important positions of command in Stockholm that day were in the hands of Men of 1809; Adlercreutz, Klingspor, and Silfversparre had been the leading figures in the arrest of Gustav IV Adolf. The new regime was based on that revolution. The sudden death of Karl August exposed its authors, who controlled the government, to the danger that Prince Gustav might be reinstated as successor. Were Karl XIII to die, there would probably be a regency council—certainly including Fersen—and a change of constitution. In any event, it raised the specter of eventual retribution when Prince Gustav came of age.[13]

The legal proceedings following 20 June provided a great deal of information—much of it contradictory—about the events of the day itself, but did not reveal the conspiracy behind them or the identity of its instigators. The special tribunal concluded its inquest on 20 March 1811, after holding some 150 sessions, interrogating about 700 witnesses and accumulating 3,456 pages of testimony. A dozen or so persons were indicted before the regional superior court in Stockholm, which passed judgment on 20 August 1811. Its proceedings were in part reviewed by the supreme court of appeal, which gave its verdict on 21 November 1811. Lambert, Lexow, Tandefelt, and one or two others received prison sentences. They had obviously been only pawns in the intrigue. Further attempts by the chancellor of justice to reopen the case led to no result. As Hedvig Elisabeth Charlotta wrote in July 1811:

It emerged clearly that the police wished to avoid the necessity of having to punish high officials who had taken an active part in the revolution of 1809. In order to protect them, the deed itself was forgotten. The investigation was not completed, leaving only suspicions.[14]

Certain tentative conclusions may nevertheless be drawn about the events of 20 June. It would appear, first of all, that they resulted from the rather loose interaction of various levels of complicity and responsibility. Contemporaries generally agreed that the basic plan had been to humiliate Fersen, not kill him. Incitement of demonstrations against prominent representatives of rival factions was a common political tactic at the time and is not unknown today. In Sweden, Gustav III himself had first utilized the crowd against his aristocratic opponents during the military-constitutional crisis of 1788–89.[15] In June 1810, a plot of this kind was possibly conceived in official circles, or more likely, by someone in contact with them, with their approval, explicit or implicit.

There were a number of probable motives for the existing government to favor such a manifestation. The view most commonly expressed has been that the Men of 1809 intended to frighten the Gustavians out of supporting Prince Gustav at the coming Riksdag, as apparently happened. The prince did not emerge as a contender despite much sympathy for him.[16]

It seems natural that the new men wished to destroy the presumed power and influence of the Fersens and others of the high nobility, whom as a group they envied and mistrusted. "Guilty or

innocent," Schinkel wrote, "the grand marshal's person was undeniably the most convenient one that could be designated as a
sacrifice to partisan calculations." J. A. Ehrenström considered the
attack on the Fersens aimed principally at the queen, who was
protected by her position.[17]

To Trolle-Wachtmeister, a pretext for moving the forthcoming
diet to the provinces was sufficient to explain the conspiracy. In
Stockholm, the estates would be exposed to pressures from foreign diplomats and popular disturbances. The government was
surely aware of latent Gustavianism among the lower classes in
the capital. After the Fersen assassination, Karl XIII announced
the Riksdag would be postponed until 23 July and held in Örebro.[18]

These objectives could best be attained by proving Fersen guilty
in the death of the crown prince, which Karl XIII and several of
his councillors clearly suspected. Thus his comment to Suremain—
that if he were Fersen, he would demand his own arrest and
trial—might help explain the curious behavior of Bartholin, Lambert, and Lexow in the Hultgren house, who according to the
inquest had alternately insulted, threatened, and protected Fersen,
all of which could have been staged to provide Silfversparre with
the opportunity to take him into custody. This would permit investigation of Fersen's papers, one of the government's first actions
following his assassination, though it did not produce the expected results.[19]

Finally, Karl XIII evidently remained dissatisfied with his powers
under the new constitution, as did some of his closest advisers.
On 10 July 1810, Gustaf Lagerbjelke wrote the king from Paris:

I concur with H.E. Baron Engeström's view, that Providence perhaps
permitted this deplorable event only to give a government, as firm as
it is enlightened, the *opportunity* and *justification* for developing that
power, authority, and indeed that salutary severity that the general
good unfailingly demands.[20]

Disaffected middle-class elements in the city apparently had very
different reasons for humiliating Fersen. Rather than humble one
aristocratic faction and prevent a Vasa restoration, *per se*, they
would seek to strike a devastating blow against the entire nobility,
including the oligarchs of 1809. These elements were doubtless in
touch with official circles through persons with contacts in both
groups. Most of the detailed planning and preparation for 20 June

appears the work of middle-class conspirators, including journalistic activity and the dispensing of money and alcohol. Within the bourgeois plot itself were probably various levels of knowledge and activity. Some may from the beginning have been prepared to murder Fersen. In any case, the government officials involved were most likely unaware of all the preparations and intentions of the middle-class conspirators. The latter could count, meanwhile, on the inactivity of the police and the army, and the anti-aristocratic sentiments of the Stockholm bourgeoisie as a whole, cultivated through intensive propaganda, as borne out by its prominence in the crowds and among the souvenir hunters of 20 June.

Still, to give mass and impact to the demonstration, it was necessary to call upon the poorer classes, also aroused by the crown prince's death and the recent rumors, and provided with real incentives in money and liquor. But the poor were inclined not so much against aristocracy as such as against all who possessed wealth or authority. The crowd therefore apparently got out of hand, while the inactivity of the military made it appear that their actions were tacitly favored by the government itself.[21] In killing Fersen, they must surely have gone beyond the calculations of the official circles involved, and at least most of the middle-class intriguers as well. The military, meanwhile, was not prepared to act promptly and was alarmed at the size of the crowd.[22] By evening, the rioting showed ugly signs of class warfare, distressing to officialdom, nobility, and bourgeoisie alike. Those arrested that evening or identified among the casualties were all from the poorer classes. Thereafter, the poor remained strongly hostile to the authorities, the military, and the wealthy in general. Many prosperous burghers found it expedient to withdraw for the time being to their country houses.[23]

It remains to be asked whether responsibility may be attributed to any specific persons. Obviously not with any great certainty. However, a number of suspects deserve at least brief consideration.

The greatest criticism has concentrated on the military commanders and, particularly since his death, the king. The former, especially Silfversparre and Adlercreutz, have generally been charged with simple incompetence and with losing their heads.[24] Karl XIII has been criticized mainly for his callous indifference to the prospect of Fersen's humiliation and his failure to prevent it.[26] The king and the generals must thus be held accountable for not taking action that lay within their power and responsibility. More serious suspicions have also been expressed. In 1850, C. A. Adlersparre, son of the revolutionary of 1809, accused the "cowardly and intriguing monarch" of prime responsibility in Fersen's murder. Recent investigation has shown that Silfversparre and Adlercreutz had contact with persons implicated in the events of 20 June. The circumstantial connection between developments in the Hultgren house and Silfversparre's proposal to arrest Fersen has been noted. Finally, the conscientious efforts of the various courts to solve the mystery of 20 June were frustrated by the persistent refusal of both Karl XIII and Crown Prince Karl Johan to permit investigation of the military commanders involved.[26]

It nonetheless seems doubtful that the generals could initially have conceived the plot. Adlercreutz was considered well-meaning and honorable, though politically naive, thus easily manipulated. Silfversparre was generally regarded as inexperienced, inept, and of mediocre intelligence.[27] In any event, contemporaries blamed the king and the generals mainly for sins of omission. Their suspicions concerning active promotion of the crime most often turned to the so-called Opinion Club and its presumed leader, Baron L. A. Mannerheim, widely regarded as the real instigator. According to several sources, the baron was among the spectators on 20 June, though after Fersen was dead, he was reputed to say, "No, that went too far."[28] The club was generally considered the center from which the slander circulated against Fersen. If it cannot be proved that it originated there, one may doubtless accept Queen Charlotta's verdict that it played a leading part in spreading it.[29]

Among persons believed associated with the club, certain ones attracted particular attention. Armfelt suspected, among others, Gustaf Abraham Silfverstolpe, one of De la Gardie's bitterest opponents in the diet of 1809–10, who had scores to settle with Fersen since the Riksdag and so-called Music Trial of 1800. G. A. Silfverstolpe's brother, Axel Gabriel, also one of the more notable Men of 1809 in the recent diet, likewise apparently had a grievance: when he incurred the disfavor of Duke Karl and Reuterholm through his eulogy for Fredrik Axel von Fersen in the Swedish Academy in 1795, he had implored protection from Axel, if he should "come to stand at the head of affairs," who had contemptuously rebuffed him. J. M. Crusenstolpe considered A. G. Silfverstolpe—"half Jacobin and half aristocrat"—the "political oracle" of the government party and the Opinion Club, claiming that through "arithmetical calculations" he coolly reasoned it to be in the public interest "to sacrifice one or another harmful member of society."[30] Among the "most fanatical" members of the club, Queen Charlotta included Chancellery Councillor Eric Bergstedt, Swedish chargé d'affaires in Paris in 1791–92, whom Fersen had then considered a dangerous Jacobin.[31] Another was B. B. von Platen, a state councillor particularly vocal in his belief in the poisoning of Karl August and the Fersens' guilt. Indeed, as far as the council is concerned, suspicion is reflected in one way or another against so many of its members that it is hard not to conclude that all had at least some foreknowledge of what awaited Fersen. Lars von Engeström's role seems most ambivalent. Though his wife offered Sophie Piper asylum on 20 June, remarks in his unpublished papers seem to belie his protestations of magnanimity toward the Fersens in his published memoirs. Marianne Ehrenström later recounted how after she gave Queen Charlotta details in June 1810 on the late Karl August's poor health long before he came to Sweden, Engeström reprimanded her angrily for "great indiscretion." "Did they wish," she wrote, "to give credibility to the rumor that the crown prince had been poisoned," thus to suppress the exonerating information she offered?[32] In any event, the dismay some of these councillors later expressed over Fersen's horrible death must be taken with due reserve: one could conceivably favor a demonstration against the grand marshal for personal or political reasons, yet be frightened and indignant at his assassination.[33]

Von Platen was closely associated with Georg Adlersparre, as were, according to the queen, various others in the Opinion Club. Adlersparre himself was immediately suspected of complicity in the events of 20 June. The anonymous Moscow account claims he was "the most redoubtable enemy of the Fersen party" and sought to "arouse the populace still more" against it. Häggman noted the rumor that at the news of Karl August's death, Adlersparre "broke out into bitter accusations against the grand marshal and let fall the words: 'this will cost one of us his life.'" Schinkel later intimated that he expressed warm satisfaction over Fersen's assassination. Armfelt suspected that he was "the hidden but principal instigator." Adlersparre's son, Carl, protested in 1854, against Schinkel's insinuations, that his father had left Stockholm a fortnight before the assassination and had been indignant on learning of it. Both Adlersparres continued to believe Karl August had been poisoned, though they later suggested that Danish agents had been behind the deed. Nonetheless, Georg Adlersparre was always the most determined and consistent opponent to the succession of Prince Gustav. He hinted in 1809 that he was prepared to go to any lengths to prevent it and in early June 1810 he had gained the council's endorsement for Karl August's brother as the next crown prince. In his private correspondence at the time and later, he intimated that he could reveal what could not otherwise be known. Years later, his letters show that he continued to consider Fersen one of the principal intriguers who in 1809 had sought to persuade Karl XIII to adopt Prince Gustav and against whom Adlersparre felt he had struggled almost single-handedly. In 1834, he wrote that if Karl XIII had died in the fall of 1809, when he had been quite ill, Queen Charlotta would have ruled as regent with Jacob De la Gardie and Axel Fersen "at her right side and her left." Adlersparre was an intriguer of consummate skill and it is difficult to believe that he did not consider, with like-minded persons, a crippling blow against the Gustavians in the person of the grand marshal.[34]

Hans Järta, then state councillor, has been revered for his contributions to the constitution of 1809 and has not been suspected in the Fersen case. Yet he was one of the most important Men of 1809, an astute politician not above opportunism. Engeström says he was one of those on the council most anxious on 31 May to send Pontin and Berzelius to ascertain whether "the crown prince had died of poison." After Fersen's murder, Trolle-Wachtmeister met a Colonel Schönström, formerly an adherent of the Adlersparre faction, who had tried to warn the Opinion Club that if the populace were stirred up they could not be controlled. "I said this to Järta," Schönström related, "I said this to all of them." But none would listen. "Well fine! and so it went as it did. Now they go around deflated and long in the face." Järta proposed the council meeting at Haga just when Karl August's cortege was to enter Stockholm, where he brought up financial matters of minor importance. Järta also had connections with persons involved in the events of the day in Stockholm and later tried unsuccessfully to get his hands on the minutes of the police investigation.[35]

Still, even if *all* these persons were in some way connected with the plot—which seems doubtful—and even if the initial idea of humiliating Fersen originated among them, the logic of the situation would make it improbable that any of them could have been the prime instigator. Their positions in government, politics, and society would have made it too hazardous to immerse themselves too deeply in compromising details and though all were experienced intriguers or at least not overly scrupulous politicians, it is questionable whether any of them at this time had close enough contacts with the Stockholm middle and lower classes to coordinate an overall plan which depended primarily upon these groups. Logically, the person best fitted to mastermind such a conspiracy would be someone from the Stockholm bourgeois milieu itself, of proven acumen in politics, agitation, and intrigue, and with widespread and influential contacts within both official and bourgeois circles. There seems at this time to have been only one person ideally fitted in all ways for the task: Carl August Grevesmöhlen, erstwhile head of the Mannerheim Club's secret police during the diet of 1809–10.

Grevesmöhlen was at his country house near Sigtuna during most of late May and June 1810, thus little suspicion focused on him at the time. Schinkel's *Minnen,* however, singled him out in 1854 as the most suspicious figure in the affair: "probably the wildest demagogue that the recent annals of Sweden have to show, . . . a kind of Marat in miniature." He was evidently instigator of the first rumor of a Gustavian plot to assassinate Karl August, in January 1810, and à propos Rossi's appointment as the prince's physician, made the remark about Italians and poisoners. Ambassador van Suchtelen reported to St. Petersburg in June 1810 that Grevesmöhlen was at the center of a group of Stockholm malcontents, particularly aroused over the alleged poisoning of the crown prince, with a rallying point in the country. From here, Grevesmöhlen need not have visited Stockholm often, if at all, to make contacts and arrangements. Though his whereabouts on 20 June are not known for sure, his son was present during the rioting against Fersen, together with a secretary in the general adjutant's office and a man later sentenced to prison for violence against Fersen's person. Count af Ugglas, obviously an intended victim, was known as Grevesmöhlen's particular personal enemy. Finally, an anonymous leaflet in April, warning that "certain high and distinguished persons" intended to poison the crown prince, presumably the first in which "the haughty Count Fersen" and his "unscrupulous" sister are clearly identified, ends by praising "the honorably minded Grevesmöhlen," who "wishes to root out the oppressors of the nation."[36]

If then, the lines of conspiracy appear to converge on C. A. Grevesmöhlen, what was his relationship to the centers of power? It has recently been suggested that there is no need to assume a concerted plan to explain the passivity of the military and civil authorities on 20 June, who were simply paralyzed at the prospect that rioting might turn into revolution, and that the instigators were not the Men of 1809, but rather their enemies to the left: men who wished to transform society according to Jacobin ideals.[37]

It would, however, seem too much to abandon the idea of complicity in official circles, in the face of so much evidence. That Grevesmöhlen and his friends were working toward very different ends than the officials, however, seems altogether plausible. Grevesmöhlen warmly admired Robespierre and the French Jacobins, and with several others mentioned in van Suchtelen's dispatches in June 1810, perhaps most notably the wealthy brewer Isak Westman, as well as the strongly French-oriented General Gustaf Wilhelm af Tibell, played an important part—in his own view, the leading role—in securing the election of the French marshal, Bernadotte, as crown prince at the Örebro Riksdag in August. Tibell appears to have begun working for Bernadotte's candidature immediately following Karl August's death; the idea was proposed to the marshal soon after in Paris by Tibell's close associate, Lieutenant Count Gustaf Mörner. Grevesmöhlen and his friends were exultant over Bernadotte's election. An article in *Nya Posten*, probably by Grevesmöhlen, in October 1810, suggested that this was "in actuality a greater revolution than that which took place on 13 March 1809" and would end "*aristocratic* oppression, which of all forms is that which the Swedish people can least endure and which in many periods has brought to Sweden her worst misfortunes." The day after the election, a contemporary wrote, "some recall the allegory in *Nya Posten* and presume that since the *lion-prince* has now been provided, the *fox-byre* should not be far off either." In this context, the insurrection of 20 June 1810 could first eliminate the Gustavians as opponents to Bernadotte, then demonstrate the need for a strong man of action, such as the marshal, in preference to the mild-mannered Duke Fredrik Christian of Augustenburg, preferred candidate of Adlersparre and the government party. In the end, however, Bernadotte, the old Jacobin, turned out a disappointment to the radical activists of the summer of 1810; though rewarded with places and pensions, neither they nor their ideas thereafter proved influential. Grevesmöhlen ended his days an exile in Norway.[38]

Perhaps this summary consideration of motives and responsibilities for 20 June should end with the comments of two contemporaries. A foreign diplomat wrote on 12 June that in Sweden, "everything is intrigue"; ironically, he was the chargé d'affaires of France. And on 28 June, L. von Hausswolff mused, "In a word, one becomes lost in speculations."[39]

3

The Fersen murder was one of the great political assassinations of the revolutionary and Napoleonic age, producing important consequences in Sweden and beyond.

Doubtless the most important is the most difficult to assess. On 12 June 1810, the French chargé d'affaires had reported on the agitation against the Fersen family but had added, "Those persons who know the Swedish temperament do not worry about these symptoms of unrest."[40] The Fersen assassination proved such things *could* happen in Sweden as elsewhere. The nation was deeply shaken and if it has since gained a well-deserved reputation as a law-abiding and orderly society, the Fersen murder doubtless played its part. The event has been called the nadir of Sweden's degradation: the point of departure for the regeneration of the nation's morale and energies in the years that followed.[41]

A much more immediate result of 20 June was the wave of fear it produced that Sweden stood on the brink of violent revolution, the eruption of Jacobinism in all its horror, the dissolution of society itself. On 29 June, Court Accountant L. F. Norstedt wrote from Stockholm to his brother in Norrköping:

The state of fright in which the inhabitants of the capital find themselves must necessarily lead thoughts hither and yon. People see imaginary ghosts and are frightened by almost every possible thing that happens. Just as they fear the arrival of the peasantry in masses, they believe they already see the avant-garde of an approaching Russian army, without being sure the English will remain passive, who are so close to our coasts. . . . When one sees with what great effort order has been restored here, by such a large armed force with the aid of the greatest possible activity by the police, what disorders may not be feared in the countryside if the people see cause to avenge the prince, for naturally they are strengthened in the belief that the prince was poisoned when they have been able here to kill such a mighty lord as Fersen for complicity.[42]

Rumors of Russian intervention seemed scarcely less alarming than fears of social upheaval. Häggman claimed that Russia offered the Swedish government 40,000 troops, "with which to suppress disorders." The anonymous Moscow account reports the rumor in Sweden that St. Petersburg plotted to install a Russian crown prince and was sending an army to Stockholm "to aid the grandees." According to the same source, it was rumored

. . . that if the nation only wished to support its liberty worthily, General Adlersparre should place himself at the head of ten thousand Norwegians and come at the moment the diet assembled, and that at the same time the peasants would revolt in the Swedish provinces; that French, Austrian, Prussian, and Polish troops were already on the move to attack Russia, and that the Finns awaited with impatience only the right moment to throw off the odious yoke.[43]

The Danish minister reported on 26 June:

The crime committed has opened the eyes of those thoughtless men who give encouragement to a dangerous delusion but who are far from wishing the overthrow of the social order. They have drawn closer than ever to the government.

Such apprehensions were influential in producing a pronounced swing to the right in Swedish political life, a rapprochement between the constitutional and royalist factions in the estates, a general demand for stronger, more efficient government, for an able and vigorous successor to the throne. After 1809–10, Swedish parliamentary life long remained relatively stagnant, the Riksdag generally acceding with little resistance to the demands of the government and indeed retaining its organization in four estates as late as 1866. Perhaps the influence of the Fersen assassination is most evident in the unconstitutional limitation of freedom of the press in 1812. Political reaction after 1810 had its counterpart in intellectual and cultural life and the Fersen murder may well have had some imponderable influence on the predominantly conservative nature of Swedish romanticism.[44] The liberals of the 1830s and 1840s nonetheless also used the Fersen murder to criticize Karl XIII, who died in 1818, and by implication, the existing regime in general.[45]

Fersen's death doubtless helped secure Marshal Bernadotte's election as crown prince in August 1810. Prince Gustav's last hopes were destroyed. Many were attracted to the French soldier as a man of order, as indeed he turned out to be. Trolle-Wachtmeister claims discipline was restored to Swedish society only after his arrival and that "It may be said that Fersen, who was always a knight-errant of monarchy, may have the eternal satisfaction of knowing that with his blood he held together the monarchy in his own fatherland."[46] Fersen's fate also seems to have influenced the future of the lost portion of the kingdom, Finland, by being instrumental in persuading G. M. Armfelt to leave Sweden and become a subject of the tsar in 1811, after which he took the lead in securing Finnish autonomy under Russian overlordship.[47]

Finally, one other judgment by Count Trolle-Wachtmeister deserves consideration:

Fersen's shade can also rejoice at having, through his death, opened the way to the throne of France for the Bourbons, to whose cause he was so devoted. Those familiar with events and especially circumstances in 1812 and 1813 . . . know that Napoleon would not have fallen if the crown prince [Karl Johan] had not cooperated—and this crown prince would not have been here if the murder of 20 June had not occurred.[48]

Here one enters the realm of imponderables. Yet there is undeniably an element of truth in Trolle-Wachtmeister's assertion. Ironically, no one except the former French marshal could apparently have led Sweden back into the war against Napoleon, thus contributing to the final result Fersen had so long and avidly desired.

The return of the Bourbons did not prove lasting nor did it restore the world of Axel Fersen's youth. Most of his own generation, meanwhile, did not long survive him. Armfelt died in 1814 in Tsarskoe Selo, followed two years later by Sophie Piper at Lövstad. In 1818, it was the turn of Karl XIII, Hedvig Elisabeth Charlotta, and Fabian Fersen. The latter's second son, Gustaf Hans, the last male member of the house of Fersen, died in 1839. Meanwhile, Emelie De Geer, who in 1817 married Sophie's son, Count Charles Piper, died at Lövstad in 1828. Stedingk died in 1836, in the same year as Charles X, the last Bourbon king of France, who died in exile in Prague, followed by Gustav IV Adolf, who passed away obscurely in St. Gallen in 1837. His son, the unfortunate

Prince Gustav of Vasa, died an Austrian field marshal in 1877, but his great-granddaughter, Princess Victoria of Baden, married Gustav V, great-grandson of Marshal Bernadotte, in 1881, making the present king of Sweden, Carl XVI Gustaf, the descendant equally of both the old and the new dynasties.

4

It was Axel Fersen's fate to become a legend in his own time and since his death to appear under the guise of various stereotypes. Gustav IV Adolf, Napoleon, and much of Europe considered him a paladin of counterrevolution and so he has been remembered in the history of the revolutionary era. Meanwhile, he distinguished himself as Marie-Antoinette's devoted knight-errant and in this role has since become the object of a kind of pious cult of chivalry. Gouverneur Morris, on the other hand, asserted that "the Queen's lover" had "the Air of a Man exhausted"; for many in his time, Axel Fersen seemed to embody those characteristics they most disliked in what they regarded as a decadent old order.[49] This was especially true in his native Sweden, where he was ultimately massacred as a hated symbol of the past and where later commentary has served to perpetuate this view. As the object of all this legend-making, Fersen appears as simply "the bearer of a destiny," in Olle Holmberg's words, who "experienced a love" and "came to experience a death."[50]

Each of these stereotypes contains, of course, its element of truth, the more so since Fersen, though caught up in the cataclysmic events of his age, was not one of its great creative personalities. For that very reason, he is "more typical than if he had been a genius," as Albert Guérard says of La Fayette.[51] As with La Fayette, many of the most influential forces of the time are combined in a striking manner in his life experience. Still, each of these symbolic roles has served to obscure the real Axel Fersen.

That he was a leading figure in the international counterrevolution is clear enough; indeed he was more important than heretofore believed. Yet his political thinking was neither static nor lacking in perception and subtlety. Like his revolutionary opponents, he too was a product of the intellectual currents of his age. On no account can he be dismissed as simply a blind and self-centered reactionary.

The eighteenth century has often been seen as an era of classic diplomacy and classic warfare; perhaps more than any other, it was also an age of classic politics. Questions of the allocation of sovereign power and the political functions of each recognized order of society were then subjects of as intense a concern and as keen a debate as matters of faith in an earlier period and those of the socioeconomic structure in a later one.

In the Europe in which Axel Fersen grew to maturity, only two political forms were considered feasible for the governing of states: on the one hand, aristocratic oligarchy, on the other, royal absolutism. In his youth, he was torn between these two ideals. The recent past in Sweden and elsewhere had shown the pitfalls of oligarchic rule and on various occasions he voiced his mistrust of "aristocratic" government, as in America in 1780–83 and France in 1787–88. Still, his experience with Gustav III's autocracy was frequently disillusioning and by early 1789, relations with his king had reached a low point. Only when the Revolution advanced a third ideology, democracy, based on popular sovereignty and civic equality, inimical to both the status of the aristocrat and the authority of the monarch, did Fersen accept unreservedly the ideal of royal absolutism.

He thus underwent earlier than most of his class that metamorphosis from aristocratic and constitutional, to royalist and absolutist political views which the European nobility as a whole experienced during the revolutionary period, transforming them by the time of the Restoration from determined opponents to zealous defenders of royal power. His bitterness toward the French princes and their émigré following shows not only his personal attachment to Marie-Antoinette but his reaction to the aristocratic Fronde of 1787–88, which remained alive within the Emigration.

Axel Fersen was thus in agreement with Gustav III by the time the latter wrote the Marquis de Bouillé in early 1792, concerning the Swedish nobility: "We are trying to make them understand that in the eighteenth century it is necessary that this first order of the state be sustained by the stability of the throne and by its protection, and not by seeking to fight against their sovereign."[52] Fersen himself perhaps best expressed his royalist faith when he had written to Gustav III of events in France almost a year earlier:

This is the cause of kings and not just a simple political problem. Without order, there can be neither society, nor security, nor happiness. Kings are the born repositories of these things. They should conserve their authority for the maintenance of this order and for the happiness of peoples.[53]

The antithesis of this order was "the despotism of the multitude," in which he had by then come to see the worst tyranny of all. The thought of the uncontrolled mob never failed to arouse a chill of horror in him. "What a frightful century we live in and how fearsome for all courts," he commented in March 1794, "especially those that have a weak ruler. That is the worst disaster that can befall a kingdom; a tyrant would be a thousand times better." In November that year, he wrote that one should "as much as possible exclude everyone from the government, not permit and even less encourage them to favor or complain; one should strive only to make it respected, to be just, to raise oneself above the murmurings of the people, to whom one should not pay the least attention." With Spinoza, Fersen would hold that it was not wisdom but authority that made laws. He was thus a firm proponent of enlightened despotism at a time when, for all its shortcomings—which no one knew better than Fersen himself—it still offered the most feasible means for most of Europe to just and effective government. Even the French themselves were prepared by 1799 to welcome an autocrat and by 1814, a restored Bourbon monarch.[54]

Despite his determined opposition to aristocratic political pretensions, Alex Fersen held to the principle of a hereditary nobility, justified by service to and defense of royal authority. This did not imply servility. "He bore his head highest," wrote M. G. Crusenstolpe, "in the presence of princes and their entourages." In November 1797, Fersen wrote to Gustav IV Adolf, "I regard with horror that maxim, so generally accepted, that one ought to serve princes in spite of themselves. Experience has proved to me how badly they are served in this way." His public career nevertheless shows he often interpreted his monarch's instructions at his own discretion and in so doing served them well, for beyond the crown lay an even higher concern. "Ought one to serve the king? Ought one to serve the state?" Thus he had written to his father during the troubles in Sweden in early 1789.[55] He did not then provide an answer, but his subsequent career shows how he regarded monarchs as ultimately the means to the all-important goal of the common welfare.

In the writings of the Men of 1809 in Sweden, Fersen often appeared the most unbending champion of the old order and a powerful influence behind the anti-French and reactionary policies of Gustav III and Gustav IV Adolf. Torsten Fogelqvist has more recently applied to him the old cliché about the French émigrés: that he apparently neither learned nor forgot anything[56] A closer examination of Fersen's career shows that on the contrary he served as a primarily stabilizing and moderating force with monarchs more extreme in their views than he. He strove consistently in 1791–92 to bring about foreign intervention in France through diplomatic means and to prevent Gustav III from resorting to armed invasion. Despite his emotional attachment to Marie-Antoinette, his advice to her is generally characterized by a cool-headed realism while his close association with the Baron de Breteuil suggests that the restoration of complete royal authority in France— the focus of all his activity—he envisioned as the basis for practical reforms through a revivified and enlightened autocracy, similar to Gustav III's ideal for Sweden. Thus, like most of the leading figures in the counterrevolutionary camp, he did not strive simply to reestablish the old order that had existed before 1789. At Rastadt in 1797–98, he did his best to prevent Gustav IV Adolf's anti-French policy from leading to a disastrous confrontation with the victorious republic, then sought to hold Sweden to her basically anti-revolutionary principles when the king and his advisers swung over to an opportunistic pro-French policy in hopes of acquiring Norway. He was from the start deeply skeptical of Gustav IV Adolf's plans to join the Third Coalition and more courageously than anyone else strove to counteract his irresponsible behavior during the war that followed. In internal policy, Fersen was by no means opposed to pragmatic reforms affecting administration or economy. Although his name is connected with an oppressive period in Swedish intellectual and cultural life, he was a discriminating patron of the arts, a better university chancellor than he has been given credit for and a good deal more open-minded in such matters than Gustav IV Adolf and a number of other leading figures of the time.[57]

But an autocratic regime gives only limited scope and credit to individual servants of the crown, as shown for instance by the protocols of royal councils and interim governments, which scarcely mention the parts played by their various members. Fersen fulfilled his duties conscientiously but considered it beneath his dignity to advertise himself or seek popular approval. The full extent and nature of his public role can therefore never be known. Fersen's moderating influence was thus generally forgotten after 1809–10. Ironically, his very moderation may have helped prolong the unpopular regime of Gustav IV Adolf, in the end increasing the violence that claimed Fersen himself as its victim.

A study of the whole of Axel Fersen's eventful and many-sided life should make it clear that his greatest historic significance lies in the political sphere. Yet he has always been and will doubtless be remembered first and foremost for his relationship with Marie-Antoinette, the exact nature of which he veiled with characteristic discretion. That Fersen and the French queen loved each other, that this was the greatest emotional experience of their lives and profoundly affected their behavior, is beyond doubt. Ironically, however, if he was indeed a queen's lover in the full sense, he left more evidence that the lady in question was Hedvig Elisabeth Charlotta, later queen of Sweden. Marie-Antoinette was by no means the only woman in his life; among others, the colorful Eleanore Sullivan occupied a place scarcely less important. Yet it was Marie-Antoinette who inspired him to his greatest feats of selflessness, courage, and activity. No other was as unwaveringly devoted to her through all her vicissitudes. In this sense, he deserves to be remembered as the queen's knight, as he conceived himself. M. J. Crusenstolpe later wrote, "Their relationship to each other was surely not *sans reproche,* but Fersen's chivalry *sans peur."*[58] The first assertion remains problematical; the second must surely stand.

During his later years, Fersen became the object of resentment and ill-will as Sweden's most prominent representative of the old high aristocracy, while since then the overromanticized legend of the White Knight from the North has produced its natural reaction. That Fersen could have been involved in worldly relationships with a number of women proved disillusioning to many while the neurotic self-centeredness, vanity, and idleness revealed in his papers from his unhappy middle years produce an impression as unattractive to twentieth-century minds as to the younger spirits of his own time. Olle Holmberg has dismissed him as "a quite insignificant person" in comparison with his father, a typical representative of the second generation, while Erik Lönnroth has seen him as a figure distinguished primarily by the magnitude of his failures. "When one has become acquainted with Fersen's type—

for he is more of a type than an individual—such as he appears in this [middle] phase of his life," Torsten Fogelqvist wrote of him, "one understands the Revolution and Romanticism." Fersen was himself sometimes aware of a disparity between him and his era. "We live in an evil century," he wrote Taube in 1797, "and we would, I think, have been very happy to have been in this world fifty years earlier or to have entered it fifty years later."[59]

Yet all of this points up the truth that goes beyond all facile generalization: that more than the paladin of counterrevolution, the queen's knight, the proud symbol of the old regime, Axel Fersen was a man, with all the complexities this implies. His was a withdrawn, complex, and elusive personality. He could be haughty, though those who understood him best realized that this derived from a time when, as A. F. Skjöldebrand observed, there were still magnates in Sweden who enjoyed the consideration due to princes. M. J. Crusenstolpe recalled from his childhood that Fersen in his later years was proud in the presence of the high and mighty, but relaxed and amiable with others, especially young people. Bernhard von Beskow considered that at a time when Swedish society was distinguished by many great personalities, Axel Fersen was widely considered "the most chivalrous and noble of them all."[60] At the same time, his diary and letters candidly reveal that he was often weak, self-indulgent, inert, sickly, vain, and morose. He was inclined toward secretiveness and on occasion toward devious means to attain desired ends. Less frequently, he was petty and unjust.

If Fersen's failings generally seem aristocratic, however, his strengths were likewise. He was refined in taste and sensibility, tactful and discreet. He was admirably loyal to ideals and to persons. He was independent in judgment. He was inspired by a profound sense of obligation as a nobleman to serve his king, country, and dependents, to protect the weak and aid the helpless. He was ever conscientious and capable in the service of royal masters and the management of his affairs.[61] At heart, he was fair-minded and humane. He maintained a lofty stoicism in the face of good and evil fortune alike. Above all, he was superbly courageous, physically and morally. "With his cold expression, he possesses a very sensitive spirit and great honesty," G. M. Armfelt, who had not always been on the best of terms with Fersen, wrote in 1799. "The more one gets to know him the more highly one thinks of him. He is one of those rare and dependable human beings, whom our era but seldom brings forth."[62] At Steninge, sheltered by a great oak, Axel Fersen's weathered epitaph remains: "May Truth, recalled by Time, protect in History his memory and render justice to his virtue. . . ."

Notes and References

CHAPTER I

1. On the Fersen family, see article, "von Fersen" in *Svenskt biografiskt lexikon* (Stockholm) [hereafter abbreviated *SBL*], XV (1956), 644–51, and articles on early members of the family, *ibid.*, 652–79; F. von Versen, *Geschichte des Geschlechtes von Versen und von Fersen*, 2 vol. (Berlin, 1885, Stettin, 1909); F. F. Flach, *Grefve Hans Axel von Fersen. Minnesteckning jemte utdrag ur hans dagbok och brefvexling* (Stockholm, 1896), 1–2; cf. "Anteckningar rörande ätten von Fersen och Riksmarskalken grefve Axel von Fersen," Lars von Engeströms arkiv, Biogr. F., no. I.f.8, Kungliga biblioteket [henceforth abbreviated *KB*]; "Anteckningar rörande friherrliga och grefliga ätterna Fersen," an anonymous geneological account from the early 19th century, H.f.1., *KB*. Branches of the family remained in Germany, the Baltic Provinces and Russia, and there are members of these branches alive today, including in the United States. On Fredrik Axel von Fersen, see Olof Jägerskiöld, "Fredrik Axel von Fersen," *SBL*, XV, 686–708; Alma Söderhjelm, "Å ömse sidor om strömmen," in *Gustaf III:s syskon* (Stockholm, 1945), 5–66.

2. See Bengt Hildebrand, "Eva Sophie von Fersen," *SBL* XV, 750–54, and "Fabian Reinhold von Fersen," *ibid.*, 754–58. In keeping with common Swedish practice, Axel himself omitted the *von* from his signature; he is thus most frequently called simply Axel Fersen.

3. Alma Söderhjelm, *Fersen et Marie-Antoinette* (Paris, 1930) [henceforth abbreviated *FMA*], 16–18; Bengt Hildebrand, "Carl Reinhold von Fersen," *SBL* XV, 680–86.

4. *Hedvig Elisabeth Charlottas dagbok*, ed. C. C. Bonde & Cecelia af Klercker, née Lewenhaupt, 9 vol. (Stockholm, 1902–42) [hereafter abbreviated *HEC*], I, 43–46, 446–49; VII, 270; R. M. Klinckowström, ed., *Riksrådet och fält-marskalken m. m. Fredrik Axel von Fersens historiska skrifter*, 8 vol. (Stockholm, 1867–72), III, 196 [hereafter abbreviated *FAF*, *HS*]. F. A. von Fersen gives his somewhat unenthusiastic views of Count Piper in a letter to Jacob Forslund dated 5 October 1773, in a private collection of his letters to the latter graciously put at my

405

disposal by *Ingeniör* Arne Forslund, Stockholm. Previously, F. A. von Fersen had prevented an engagement between his niece, Ulla Fersen, and the Duke. Söderhjelm, *Gustaf III:s syskon*, 77–80.

5. F. A. von Fersen to J. Forslund, 26 June 1770, 18 Oct. 1773, Forslund letters. Cf. Bernhard von Beskow, *Lefnadsminnen* (Stockholm, 1870), 40.

6. On the use of French in Sweden, see Ferdinand Brunot, *Histoire de la langue française*, VIII:1 (Paris, 1934), 423–44; Gunnar von Proschwitz, *Gustave III de Suède et la langue française* (Göteborg & Paris, 1962). I cannot agree with Alma Söderhjelm, *FMA*, 15–16, who claims it is "easy to perceive the mental translation" behind F.'s writing of French; rather, such mental translation seems evident in his less frequent use of Swedish. As early as 1770, he complained that he wrote with "infinite difficulty" in Swedish. F. A. von Fersen to J. Forslund, 8 Oct. 1770, Forslund letters.

7. Hildebrand, *SBL* XV, 708.

8. On Bolemany's career, see F. to Gustav IV Adolf, 3 Oct. 1797, Diplomatica: Allmänna fredskongresser, LXVII, RA; and in Skölde-brevssamlingen: Ansökningar om adelskap, B, RA.

9. F.'s diary for his grand tour is contained in the first two of three notebooks in Stafsundssamlingen, Hans Axel von Fersens arkiv IV, RA [hereafter abbreviated *F. arkiv IV:1* and *2*]. It has not been published *in extenso*, but Söderhjelm in *FMA*, 23–50; in the introduction to *Axel von Fersens dagbok*, ed., Alma Söderhjelm, 4 vol. (Stockholm, 1925–36) [henceforth abbreviated *Dagbok*], I, 15–36; and in her "Les débuts de Fersen d'après son journal intime," *Bibliothèque universelle et Revue de Genève* (May 1929), 556–68, summarizes and gives extensive quotations from the diary for this period. R. M. Klinckowström, ed., *Le comte de Fersen et la cour de France*, 2 vol. (Paris, 1877–78) [henceforth abbreviated as simply Klinckowström], I, xi–xxxiv, also gives selections.

10. F. A. von Fersen to J. Forslund, 26 June 1770, Forslund letters.

11. Söderhjelm, *FMA*, 23–25; *Dagbok* I, 17–22.

12. F. arkiv IV:1, 49–85, RA; F. to father, 22 June 1771, Stafsundssamlingen, Fredrik Axel von Fersens arkiv, RA [henceforth abbreviated *FAF arkiv*] VIII; Söderhjelm, *FMA*, 25–26.

13. F. arkiv IV:1, RA, 88–103; F. to father, 28 Oct. 1771, FAF arkiv VIII, RA; Söderhjelm, *FMA*, 26–27.

14. F. arkiv IV:1, RA, 106–108, 172; F. to Sophie, 23 Dec. 1771, 21 Jan. 1773, Lövstads arkiv VII; F. to father, 15 Aug., 20 Oct. 1772, FAF arkiv VIII, RA Söderhjelm, *FMA*, 28–29.

15. F. arkiv IV:1, RA, 172–76; rough notes inserted into *ibid.*, VI:2; Söderhjelm, *FMA*, 29–30. On Breteuil's acquaintance with the Fersens, FAF, *HS* V, 222; F. A. von Fersen to Forslund, 18 Oct. 1773, Forslund letters.

15a. F. arkiv IV:2, RA, 1–91, and rough notes; Söderhjelm, *FMA*, 30–42.

16. Auguste Geffroy, *Gustave III et la cour de France*, 2 vol. (Paris, 1867), I, 359.

17. F. arkiv IV:2, RA, 96–128; Söderhjelm, *FMA*, 46–47.

18. F. arkiv IV:2, RA, 105; Söderhjelm, *FMA*, 30–31, 48–49.

19. Hildebrand, *SBL* XV, 708.

20. Cf. *HEC* I, *passim.*; FAF, *HS* III, 217–19, 240–41; F. to Sophie, Gripsholm, (?) Jan. (year?), and undated. Lövstad arkiv VIII.

21. Söderhjelm, *FMA*, 52. Cf. Gustaf Johan Ehrensvärd, *Dagboksanteckningar förda vid Gustaf III:s hof*, 2 vol. (Stockholm, 1877–78), I, *passim.*; Stig Stenström, "Gustaf III:s divertismenter och de sista gustavianska riddarspelen," *Livrustkammaren*, 1946, 99–120; Beth Hennings, *Gustav III* (Stockholm, 1957), 144–46. F. to Sophie, Lövstad, 6 July (year?), Lövstad arkiv VII.

22. Ehrensvärd, *Dagboksantechningar*, I, 86–88; Söderhjelm, *FMA*, 52; FAF, *HS* III, 240–43; *HEC* I, 70–72.

23. Ehrensvärd, *Dagboksanteckningar*, I, 16; *HEC* I, 40; F. arkiv IV:2, RA, 195; F. to father, 4 May 1778, FAF arkiv VIII, RA; FAF, *HS* V, 306–307.

24. Söderhjelm, *FMA*, 52–54; Flach, *Fersen*, 36–37. According to one unverified account, efforts were made from F.'s childhood to betroth him to his cousin, Eva Helena von Fersen, who in 1774 married Count Erik Göran Adelswärd. See Princess Schahovskoy-Strechneff, *Le comte de Fersen, Charles Gustave de Lilienfeld, la princesse Zélmire* (Paris, 1910), 20–21, 23, 26–28.

25. F. arkiv IV:2, RA, 195–266; F. to father, 24 May, 2 June, 7 Aug. 1778, FAF arkiv VIII, RA; Söderhjelm, *FMA*, 54–56.

26. F. arkiv IV:3, RA, 37; F. to Sophie, 27 January 1773, Lövstad arkiv VII; F. to father, 30 Apr., 2 June, 21 July 1779, FAF arkiv VIII, RA.

27. F. U. Wrangel, *Origines et débuts du Royal-Suédois actuellement 89e du ligne* (Paris, 1914), 115–44; Hildebrand, *SBL* XV, 680, 708; Jägerskiöld, *ibid.*, 689–90.

28. F. arkiv IV:2, RA, 237–42, 261–64; *ibid.*, IV:3, 5–26; F. to father, 24 May, 7, 17, 26 Aug., 8 Sept., 21 Oct., 19 Nov., 15 Dec. 1778, 20 Jan. 1779, FAF arkiv VIII, RA; Söderhjelm, *FMA*, 66–67; H. L. von Dardel, *Fältmarskalken von Stedingks tidigare levnadsöden skildrade efter brev till överståthållaren Carl Sparre* (Örebro, 1922), 70.

29. F. to father, 26 Aug., 8 Sept., 19 Nov. 1778, 13 June 1779, FAF arkiv VIII, RA.

30. F. to father, 26 Aug., 1 Oct., 19 Nov. 1778, *ibid.*; Klinckowström I, xxiii–iv. Cf. *HEC* I, 99–102.

31. F. arkiv IV:3, RA, 6–36; Klinckowström I, xxiii–ix; F. to father, 1, 21 Oct. 1778, FAF arkiv VIII, RA; Dardel, *Stedingks tidigare levnadsöden*. On Mesnil-Durand, see J. R. Western in *New Cambridge Modern History*, VIII (Cambridge, 1965), 198.

32. F. arkiv IV:3, RA, 3; cf. Söderhjelm in *Dagbok* I, 43–44. On Mme. von Korff, see Louis Hastier, "Une amie de Marie-Antoinette—la

baronne de Korff," *Revue des Deux Mondes*, 15 Aug. 1961, 524–44, which contains, however, certain inaccuracies.

33. F. arkiv IV:3, RA, 90–92; F. to father, 20 Jan., 21, 30 Mar., 30 Apr., 24 May, 5, 13 June, 18 Sept. 1779; FAF arkiv VIII, RA. On Stedingk in the American war, see Dardel, *Stedingks tidigare levnadsöden*, 5–116; Adolf B. Benson, *Sweden and the American Revolution* (New Haven, 1926), 147–55.

34. F. arkiv IV:3, RA, 90–92; F. to father, 1 Oct 1778, 21, 30 March, 30 April, 24 May, 2, 5, 13, 21, 29 June, 1 July 1779, FAF arkiv VIII, RA. Cf. Söderhjelm *FMA*, 67–68; Klinckowström I, xxxiii–iv.

35. F. to father, 4, 16 July, 6, 16, 25 Aug., 18 Sept., 6, 15 Oct., 10, 26 Nov., 14 Dec. 1779, FAF arkiv VIII, RA; F. to Sophie, 18 Sept. 1779, Lövstad arkiv VII. Cf. Söderhjelm, *FMA*, 70–71. See also A. Temple Patterson, *The Other Armada* (Manchester, 1960).

36. F. to father, 13 June, 1 July, 28 Sept. 1778, FAF arkiv VIII, RA; same to same, 5 Jan., 3, 23 Feb., 2, 15 Mar. 1780 F. U. Wrangel, ed., *Les lettres d'Axel de Fersen à son père pendant la Guerre de l'indépendance d'Amérique* (Paris, 1929), 45–59; Dardel, *Stedingks tidigare levnadsöden*, 85.

37. Most of the existing portraits of F., as well as other members of his family, have been reproduced, some in color, in the four volumes of his *Dagbok*, ed. Söderhjelm. Cf. Sixten Strömbom ed , *Index över svenska porträtt 1500–1850*, 3 vol. (Stockholm, 1933–43), I, 270–71. Bernhard von Beskow claimed that none of F.'s portraits did full justice to him. *Lefnadsminnen*, 34.

38. Cf. Lydia Wahlström, "A Queen's Cavalier," *American-Scandinavian Review* (1931), 748–55; Olle Holmberg, "Riddaren av det förgångna," *Dagens nyheter*, 16 Mar. 1952, 4.

39. Duc de Lévis, *Souvenirs et portraits, 1780–1789* (Paris, 1813), 130; Comte Alexandre de Tilly, *Mémoires du comte Alexandre de Tilly*, 3 vol. (2nd ed., Paris, 1828), II, 118–19.

40. F. arkiv X: Brevregister, RA; Eugène Bimbinet, *La Fuite de Louis XVI à Varennes*, 2 vol. (2nd ed., Paris, 1858), II, 140.

41. F. arkiv IV:1 and 2, *passim.*, esp. IV:1, 12, 14, 68–77; IV:2, 23; Söderhjelm, *FMA*, 20–21, 23, 26, 30–39. Many of F.'s belongings are preserved at Lövstad. See [Agneta Furumark], *Från Axel von Fersens tid. Skatter från Lövstad* (exhibition catalog, Norrköpings museum, March 1967); E. Nordenfalk, *Axel von Fersen. Ett 200-års minne* (pamphlet, Norrköping, 1955). Many of F.'s belongings are also included in the entailed property held by the Barons Klinckowström at Stafsund.

42. Klinckowström I, xviii.

43. F. arkiv IV:2, RA, 165, 237; IV:3, 2.

44. *Ibid.*, IV:2, 124–26.

45. Söderhjelm, *FMA*, 22. I am indebted for information on the library at Lövstad to *Amanuens* Frans Carlsson and *Fil. dr.* Nils Gobom, who catalogued it. F. to E. Taube, 2 June 1797, Stafsundssamlingen, Evert Taubes arkiv III, RA.

46. Söderhjelm, in *FMA*, 22, states that the only summary of a book

he ever made was a work on military history, which is not true. F.'s collections of documents on the Swedish-Russian war of 1788–90, the French Revolution, Gustav IV Adolf's German travels and Pomeranian campaign, 1803–1807, are most valuable for their respective subjects. F. arkiv XVI–XIX, RA. F.'s diary comprises F. arkiv IV–IX. See also F. arkiv X: letter register.

47. F. to father, 15 Dec. 1778, 30 Mar. 1779, FAF arkiv VIII, RA; Wrangel, *Lettres*, 149; F. to Taube, 15 June 1796, 9 Sept. 1797, Taube arkiv III, RA; F. to Sophie, 30 Apr. 1796, Lövstad arkiv VIII; F. to Gustav IV Adolf, 3 October 1797, Allmänna fredskongr., LCVII, RA.

48. Cf. Hennings, *Gustav III.* See also my "Gustav III of Sweden and the Enlightenment," *Eighteenth-Century Studies*, VI (1972), 1–34.

49. Cf. Gunnar Castrén, *Gustav Philip Creutz* (Stockholm, 1917).

50. F. attributes this work to "Mirabeau"; it was published the same year under the *nom de plume* "Mirabaud." F. arkiv IV:1, RA, 8.

51. *Ibid.*, 42–43; cf. Söderhjelm, *FMA*, 24.

52. F. arkiv IV:1, RA, 66–67.

53. *Ibid.*, 102; cf. Söderhjelm, *FMA*, 27.

54. Söderhjelm, *FMA*, 35.

55. *Ibid.*, 30–32, 57; F. arkiv IV:3, RA, 3–4.

56. Ehrensvärd, *Minnesanteckningar*, I, 17.

57. F. to father, 30 Apr., 2, 21 June 1779, FAF arkiv VIII, RA; F. to Sophie, 11 Apr. 1797, Lövstad arkiv VII; Wrangel, *Lettres*, 75–76, 140; *Dagbok* I, 181; Söderhjelm, *FMA*, 32.

58. Klinckowström I, xlix, 80. As late as 6 May 1791, however, F. criticized the "philosophic spirit" and the "spirit of Systems," together with ignorance and bad faith, rather than philosophy as such, deploring that "applications" had not been made, "less false and more useful to a great empire." FAF arkiv IX, RA.

59. F. arkiv IV:1, RA, 88–103.

60. *Ibid.*, IV:3, 39–42; Wrangel, *Lettres*, 73–74. Cf. Abbé Raynal, *Histoire des établissements des européens dans les deux Indes* (2nd ed., 1774), V.

61. F. arkiv IV:2, RA, 109–10, 110–16.

62. *Ibid.*, 251–62.

63. *Ibid.*, 223; cf. *Dagbok* I, 43.

64. F. arkiv IV:2, RA, 250–51.

65. *Ibid.*, 195; F. to father, 4 May 1778, 10 Nov. 1779, FAF arkiv VIII, RA. Cf. FAF, *HS* IV, 164–66.

66. F. arkiv IV:2, RA, 261–62; F. to father, 7, 17 Aug. 1778, FAF arkiv VIII, RA.

67. FAF, *HS* IV, 139, 206.

68. *Dagbok* I, 22; F. arkiv IV:2, RA, 183; Klinckowström I, xxix–xxxii; FAF, *HS* IV, 137–39; V, 313. Cf. Hildebrand, *SBL* XV, 731.

69. Söderhjelm, *FMA*, 27.

70. Cf. F.'s comments in favor of freedom of trade in Wrangel, *Lettres*, 174. FAF, *HS*, V, 21. Alma Söderhjelm in *Dagbok* IV, 571, maintains that F. was brought up on the ideas of the "Economists," which

"surely left a stronger impression on him that those of the men of the Enlightenment properly speaking."

71. F. arkiv IV:2, RA, 168, 205–208, 215; IV:3, 6, 8, 27–28.
72. Söderhjelm, *FMA*, 45.
73. F. arkiv IV:1, RA, 172; IV:2, 173, 208–209.
74. Söderhjelm, *FMA*, 39–42; F. arkiv IV:2, RA, 97–98, 245.
75. F. to father, 10 Nov. 1779, FAF arkiv VIII, RA; F. arkiv IV:2, RA 170–72, 212.
76. F. arkiv IV:2, RA, 251.
77. Beskow, *Lefnadsminnen*, 40.
78. F. arkiv IV:3, RA, 39–43.

CHAPTER II

1. Geffroy, *Gustave III et la cour de France*, I. 360-61. Most older works have accepted Creutz's evidence without further question concerning F.'s motives for participating in the American war. Cf. Paul Gaulot, *Un ami de la reine* (Paris, 1892), which represents it as a purely chivalrous move, an idea widely repeated in other works.

2. Wrangel, *Lettres*, 18–19, 53; cf. Beskow, *Lefnadsminnen*, 40. See also Katherine Prescott Wormeley, ed., *The Diary and Correspondence of Count Axel Fersen* (London, 1902), 19–20. Although Miss Wormeley's collection contains many of the same materials as Klinckowström and Wrangel, her translations from the original French are undependable and I have preferred to make my own. Georgina Holmes, trans., "The French Army in the Revolutionary War. Count de Fersen's Private Letters to his Father, 1780–81," *Magazine of American History*, XXV (1891), 55–70, 156–73, is also poorly translated and has not been used here.

3. See Amandus Johnson, *Swedish Contributions to American Freedom, 1776–1783*, 2 vol. (Philadelphia, 1953–57), I, 147–53, 189–201; II, 429–30; cf. Aurélien Vivie, ed., *Letters de Gustave III à la comtesse de Boufflers et de la comtesse au roi de 1771 à 1791* (Bordeaux, 1898), 101–102. For a general discussion of the subject, see my "Sweden and the War of American Independence," *William and Mary Quarterly*, 3rd ser., XXIII (1966), 408–30.

4. Harald Elovson, *Amerika i svensk litteratur 1750–1820* (Lund, 1930), 98–125.

5. F. arkiv IV:2, RA, 237–41.

6. Cf. my "Sweden and the War of American Independence," 428–29; cf. Elovson, *Amerika i svensk litteratur*, 131–35.

7. My "Sweden and the War of American Independence," 412–16.

8. F. to father, 14, 28 Dec. 1779, FAF arkiv VIII, RA; Wrangel, *Lettres*, 94.

9. Dardel, *Stedingks tidigare levnadsöden*, 93.

10. My "Sweden and the War of American Independence," 312–19; cf. Elovson, *Amerika i svensk litteratur*, 86–87; and the same author's, "De svenska officerarna i nordamerikanska frihetskriget," *Scandia*, II (1929), 316–17.

11. Bernhard von Beskow, *Om Gustaf den tredje såsom konung och menniska*, 5 parts (Stockholm, 1860–69: *Svenska akademiens handlingar ifrån 1796*, vols. 32, 34, 37, 42 and 44), III, 131–35, 160–61; cf. C. T. Odhner, *Sveriges politiska historia under konung Gustaf III:s regering*, 3 vol. (Stockholm, 1885–1905), I, 529–30.

12. Wrangel, *Lettres*, 55, 75, 132; cf. Ingegerd Hildebrand, *Den svenska kolonin S:t Barthélemy och Västindiska kompaniet fram till 1796* (Lund, 1951), 2–5, 12n.; Harald Elovson, "Kolonialintresset i Sverige under slutet av 1700-talet," *Samlaren*, ny följd, IX (1928), 207–11.

13. Klinckowström I, v–vi; cf. *Dagbok* II, 298; Söderhjelm, *FMA*, 334. G. Lenotre, in *Le drame de Varennes* (Paris, 1908), 9n., makes a surprising assertion that seems to have passed unnoticed: he speaks of a certain "Baron A.F., 'sole descendent of Count Axel [Fersen]' and possessor of the greater part of his papers, notably 'of the part of his diary between 1780 and 1791, the part which Fersen himself believed to be lost'. . ." It seems most probable that "Baron A.F." was the great-great-grandson of F.'s cousin, Eva Helena von Fersen, the French socialite and *littérateur*, Baron Jacques Adelsward-Fersen (1880–1927), of whose life Roger Peyrefitte has given a popularized account in his *Exile of Capri* (London, 1961). Lenotre probably used the Baron's initials only since the latter had been publicly disgraced in a homosexual scandal in Paris a few years before, when the press had limited itself to using the initials only of those involved. The Baron was captivated by the memory of Axel Fersen, whose family name he added to his own, and apparently imagined some highly fanciful things about him, even conceiving F. himself to have been homosexual! *Ibid.*, *passim.*, esp. 11, 13, 86, 190, 195. That Adelsward-"Fersen" was the "sole descendant" of F. or that he could have been "possessor of the greater part of his papers" are patently false claims. M. Peyrefitte has privately assured the author that neither he nor surviving relatives of Adelsward-Fersen, with whom he checked on the author's behalf, have ever found any evidence that Adelsward-Fersen could have possessed the lost portion of F.'s diary.

14. Wrangel, *Lettres*, 70–71. Diaries kept by two fellow members of Rochambeau's staff throughout the American campaign throw much light on episodes in which F. was involved but which he did not describe in his own letters. See Count Mathieu Dumas, *Memoirs of His Own Time*, 2 vol. (London, 1839), I, 16–114; and esp. Evelyn M. Alcomb, ed., *The Revolutionary Journal of Baron Ludwig von Closen* (Chapel Hill, 1958). See also Howard C. Rice, Jr. and Anne S. K. Brown, trans, and eds., *The American Campaigns of Rochambeau's Army, 1780–83*, 2 vol. (Princeton, 1972).

15. Benson, *Sweden and the American Revolution*, 132.

16. Wrangel, *Lettres*, 72–77; F. to Sophie, 6 Aug., 8, 14 Sept., 13 Nov., 7 Dec. 1780, Lövstad arkiv VII; cf. Söderhjelm, *FMA*, 72–73. See Duc de Lauzun, *Mémoires* (Paris, 1929), 190, 214, for additional details on the Hunter family.

17. Wrangel, *Lettres*, 123–24.

18. *Ibid.*, 57, 75.

COUNT HANS AXEL VON FERSEN

19. *Ibid.*, 82, 101, 113, 125–32; Closen, *Journal*, 88, 107; Benson, *Sweden and the American Revolution*, 137. Cf. Bernice Krumhansl, "Side by Side with Washington," *American Swedish Monthly*, November 1966, 26–27, a brief account of Fersen's activities in the American war.

20. Benson, *Sweden and the American Revolution*, 133–34. Also Wrangel, *Lettres*, 125–32. Cf. the letter from an anonymous Swedish naval officer with de Grasse's fleet, in *Stockholms-Posten*, No. 299, 27 Dec. 1781, according to which F. was supposed to have served with distinction at Yorktown and to be "generally loved and respected" in Rochambeau's army.

21. Wrangel, *Lettres*, 121.

22. *Ibid.*, 132–36; cf. F. to Sophie, 25 March 1782, Lövstad arkiv VII. See also Closen, *Journal*, 177–89.

23. Wrangel, *Lettres*, 150–51; Closen, *Journal*, 197, 214.

24. Wrangel, *Lettres*, 87–91.

25. *Ibid.*, 145, 181; Söderhjelm, *FMA*, 73–74; Closen, *Journal*, 222.

26. Wrangel, *Lettres*, 157; Closen, *Journal*, 242.

27. Closen, *Journal*, 297–98, 298n.

28. Wrangel, *Lettres*, 161–83; F. to Sophie, (?) March 1783, Lövstad arkiv VII; Söderhjelm, *FMA*, 46; Closen, *Journal*, xxvii, 276–336; Dumas, *Memoirs*, I, 107–12.

29. Klinckowström I, xxiv–xxviii; F. to father, 1, 21 Oct. 1778, FAF arkiv VIII, RA; Dardel, *Stedingks tidigare levnadsöden*, 71–73.

30. F. to father, 21 June, 4 July, 14 Oct. 1779, FAF arkiv VIII, RA; Wrangel, *Lettres*, 57–68.

31. Wrangel, *Lettres*, 73, 115–16.

32. *Ibid.*, 45–47, 57–58, 76–77, 85–86, 102, 125.

33. *Ibid.*, 123–24, 143; F. to Sophie 25 Apr. 1782, Lövstad arkiv VII.

34. Wrangel, *Lettres*, 54, 113–14, 122–23, 163, 165; cf. Closen, *Journal*, xxv–xxvi, 264, 271, 274–75, 285; Dumas, *Memoirs*, I, 94.

35. Durand Echeverria, *Mirage in the West: A History of the French Image of American Society to 1815* (Princeton, 1957), 97.

36. Wrangel, *Lettres*, 161–62; Benson, *Sweden and the American Revolution*, 132; Baron Axel Leonhard Klinckowström, *Baron Klinckowström's America*, ed. and trans. Franklin D. Scott (Evanston, 1952), 36–37.

37. Wrangel, *Lettres*, 73–74; cf. F. to Sophie, 8 Sept. 1780, Lövstad arkiv VII.

38. Wrangel, *Lettres*, 82; cf. Closen, *Journal*, 62, 64, 102, 251, 257; *Writings of George Washington*, ed. John C. Fitzpatrick, XXI (Washington, 1937), 226.

39. Wrangel, *Lettres*, 78, 91, 97, 109.

40. F. arkiv IV:2, RA, 261–62; F. to father, 7, 17 Aug. 1778, FAF arkiv VIII, RA; Wrangel, *Lettres*, 85, 89, 108, 171.

41. Wrangel, *Lettres*, 171.

42. *Ibid.* 81, 94, 98–99, 165–66. This was a common complaint among European officers in America. See Echeverria, *Mirage in the West*, 83–85, 92–93; Closen, *Journal*, 128–29, 198–99, 229, 257–59, 267.

43. Wrangel *Lettres* 74.
44. *Ibid.* 98–99.
45. FAF, *HS* III, 84–85, 113, 116–17, 121.
46. Wrangel, *Lettres*, 117, 133–34; cf. Benson, *Sweden and the American Revolution*, 164; Dumas, *Memoirs*, I, 102–103. Other foreigners also noted the "aristocratic" character of the Virginians. See Echeverria, *Mirage in the West*, 99; Closen, *Journal*, 187.
47. Wrangel, *Lettres*, 157–58.

CHAPTER III

1. Hildebrand, *SBL* XV, 708.
2. Söderhjelm, *FMA*, 75–76; cf. F. to father, 19 Aug. 1783, FAF arkiv VIII, RA.
3. Wrangel, *Lettres*, 176–80; Söderhjelm, *FMA*, 74–75, 79–80; cf. J. Christopher Herold, *Mistress to an Age: A Life of Mme de Staël* (Charter ed., New York, 1962), 57–60.
4. Wrangel, *Lettres*, 82–83, 85–87, 91, 145, 158, 165, 176, 181; F. to father, 11, 31 July, 10 Aug. 1783, FAF arkiv VIII, RA; cf. F. to Gustav III, 16 Oct. 1780, *ibid.* On Gérmaine Necker's interest in F., see Söderhjelm, *FMA*, 80; Henry Vallotton, *Marie-Antoinette et Fersen* (Paris, 1952), 190–91; and Schahovskoy-Stretchneff, *Le comte de Fersen*, 47–51.
5. See Wrangel, *Origines du Royal-Suédois*; Gunnar W. Lundberg and F. E. F. Desfeuilles, "Les comtes de Sparre et le comte de Fersen, colonels du Royal-Suédois," *Révue internationale militaire comparée*, 1939, 33–62. During the French Revolution, Alexandre Sparre wrote the Convention that born into a caste he had always "detested," he offered his sabre as a patriotic gesture to someone who might use it in the defense of the fatherland. F.'s bulletin, 16 Apr. 1794, Diplomatica: Gallica, Vol. 500, RA.
6. Wrangel, *Lettres*, 180–89; F. to father, 11, 21, 28, 31 July, 10, 19 Aug., 7, 14, 20 Sept. 1783, FAF arkiv VIII, RA; F. to Gustaf III, 27 June, 21 Aug., 14 Sept. 1783, F. arkiv I, RA; cf. Söderhjelm, *FMA*, 77–78, 88–90.
7. F. A. von Fersen to F., undated fragment, F. arkiv XIII, RA; cf. Söderhjelm, *FMA*, 84–86.
8. Wrangel, *Lettres*, 180–82; F. to father, 11, 21, 28 July, 10 Aug., 7 Sept. 1783, FAF arkiv VIII, RA; F. to Gustav III, 27 June, 21 Aug., 14 Sept. 1783, F. arkiv I, RA; cf. Söderhjelm, 77–79, 81–83, 88; Gustav III to Taube, 25 July 1783, FAF, *HS* V, 286.
9. F. to father 10, 19 Aug., 7, 14, 20 Sept. 1783, FAF arkiv VIII, RA; cf. Söderhjelm, *FMA*, 86–91; Wrangel, *Lettres*, 187; Geffroy, *Gustave III*, I, 362–64, 408; Dardel, *Stedingks tidigare levnadsöden*, 106.
10. Söderhjelm, *FMA*, 91–92; Wrangel, *Lettres*, 188; FAF, *HS* V, 174–75.
11. This and further discussions of Sweden's political position under Gustav III are based principally upon the following works: Ludvig Stavenow, *Gustavianska tiden* (Stockholm, 1925); Odhner, *Gustav III:s*

regering; Hennings, *Gustav III*; Olof Jägerskiöld, *Den svenska utrikes-politikens historia*, Vol. II: 2, *1721–1792* (Stockholm, 1957); and Sten Carlsson, *Svensk historia II: Tiden efter 1718* (Stockholm, 1961). In English, there are good brief accounts in Ingvar Andersson, *A History of Sweden* (London, 1956); and R. Svanström and C. F. Palmstierna, *A Short History of Sweden* (Oxford, 1934). R. Nisbet Bain, *Gustavus III and his Contemporaries*, 2 vol. (London, 1894), is badly outdated and must be used with caution.

12. FAF. *HS* III, 84–85, 113, 116–17, 121, 130–31; cf. Ehrensvärd, *Dagboksanteckningar*, I, 113–14.

13. F. to father, 20 Oct. 1772, FAF arkiv VIII, RA.

14. The constitution is given in English in William Coxe, *Travels into Poland, Russia, Sweden and Denmark*, 4 vol. (London, 1787), IV, 429–47. Coxe gives an interesting analysis of it in this volume. See also my "Gustav III and the Enlightenment."

15. FAF, *HS* III, 444–45; Coxe, *Travels*, IV, 446.

16. Hennings, *Gustav III*, 59, 285; Stig Boberg, *Gustav III och tryck-friheten 1774–1786* (Göteborg, 1951), 51–62, 75–76, 343; Vivie, *Lettres*, 65–74; Nils Staf, *Polisväsendet i Stockholm 1776–1850* (Uppsala, 1950), 1–69.

17. FAF, *HS* I, xxii.

18. FAF, *HS* IV, 56–58, 91–98; *HEC* I, 153; F. to father, 20 Jan. 1779, FAF arkiv VIII, RA.

19. On Gustav III's journey to the Continent, see Henning Stålhane, *Gustav III:s resa till Italien och Frankrike* (Stockholm, 1953); Henrik Schück, ed., *Gustaf III:s resa i Italien. Anteckningar af Gudm. Göran Adlerbeth* (Stockholm, 1902); Elof Tegnér, *Gustaf Mauritz Armfelt. Studier ur Armfelts efterlämnade papper samt andra handskrifvna och tryckta källor*, 3 vol. (Stockholm, 1883–87), I, 74–132; Beth Hennings, ed. *Ögonvittnen: Gustav III* (Stockholm, 1960), 194–230.

20. F. to father, 29 Oct., 8 Nov. 1783, FAF arkiv VIII, RA; Söderhjelm, *FMA*, 92–94; E. G. Geijer, ed., *Konung Gustaf III:s efter-lemnade och femtio år efter hans död öppnade papper* (2nd ed.: *Erik Gustaf Geijers samlade skrifter*, supplement I, Stockholm, 1876), 367–68; Tegnér, *Armfelt*, I, 77.

21. H. Schück, ed., *Rutger Fredrik Hochschilds memoarer*, 3 vol. (Stockholm, 1908–1909), I, 64–65; Geijer, *Gustaf III:s efterlemnade papper*, 372.

22. F. to father, 29 Oct. 1783, FAF arkiv VIII, RA; cf. Wrangel, *Lettres*, 103.

23. FAF, *HS* V, 302–304; Tegnér, *Armfelt*, I, 82, 87–90; Schück, *Gustaf III:s resa*, 38–58; Geijer, *Gustaf III:s efterlemnade papper*, 373–78; F. arkiv X:1 (letter register). Though Gustav was well impressed with Leopold of Tuscany, neither he nor his brother, Joseph II, was favorably impressed with him. See Alfred, Ritter von Arneth, ed., *Joseph II und Leopold von Toscana. Ihr Briefwechsel von 1781 bis 1790*, 2 vol. (Vienna, 1872), I, 177–79, 191–92.

24. FAF, *HS* V, 304; Stålhane, *Gustav III:s resa*, 105; Tegnér, *Armfelt* I, 96n.; Schück, *Gustaf III:s resa*, 74–75, 184.

25. FAF, *HS* V, 304–305; cf. Tegnér, *Armfelt* I, 102. For description and pictures of Gustav III's "Swedish dress," see Coxe, *Travels* IV, 24–25.

26. FAF, *HS* V, 306–307.

27. Tegnér, *Armfelt* I, 94n.; Elis Schröderheim, *Skrifter till konung Gustaf III:s historia jemte urval ur Schröderheims brefväxling*, ed., Elof Tegnér (Stockholm, 1892), 212; Söderhjelm, *FMA*, 96; Arneth, *Joseph II und Leopold von Toscana* I, 179, 192; Geijer, *Gustaf III:s efterlemnade papper*, 383n.

28. Tegnér, *Armfelt* I, 106–10; FAF, *HS* V, 308–11; F. to Sophie, 10 Feb. 1784, Lövstad arkiv VII; Dorothy Margaret Stuart, *Dearest Bess. The Life and Times of Lady Elizabeth Foster* (London, 1955), 18–21, 26, 29.

29. F. arkiv X:1, RA; FAF, *HS* V, 206–207, 309–10; M. F. F. Biörnstierna, ed., *Mémoires posthumes du feld-maréchal comte de Stedingk, rédigés sur des lettres, dépêches et autres pièces authentiques*, 2 vol. (Paris, I, 72–73); cf. Beskow, *Gustaf den tredje* III, 162–64; Geijer, *Gustaf III:s efterlemnade papper*, 417n., 418n.; Benson, *Sweden and the American Revolution*, 158, 160.

30. F. to father, 27 Apr. 1784, FAF arkiv IX, RA; cf. FAF, *HS*, 312–13; F. arkiv X:1. It is my understanding that F.'s Order of the Cincinnati is presently in the possession of Countess Greta Gyldenstolpe, Stockholm.

31. FAF, *HS* V, 313–16; Tegnér, *Armfelt* I, 116–17.

32. FAF, *HS* V, 317.

33. On Gustav III's activities in Paris, see Geffroy, *Gustave III*, II, 21–50. On his relations to the French royal family, see G. A. Crüwell, *Die Beziehungen König Gustafs III. von Schweden zur Königin Marie Antoinette von Frankreich* (Berlin, 1897); also Schröderheim, *Skrifter*, 102; FAF, *HS* V, 217–18, 227–30. Joseph II had written ahead to Marie-Antoinette, n.d., describing Gustav III as "false, petty, miserable, a fop at his looking glass. . . . I recommend him to you in advance." Vallotton, *Marie-Antoinette et Fersen*, 130.

34. F. to father, 1 July 1784, FAF arkiv IX, RA. See also Geijer, *Gustaf III:s efterlemnade papper*, 172n. It would appear that Louis XVI undertook to pay the 100,000 livres; that F. arranged to repay this through a loan from Breteuil, which he would repay from his pension and/or other income. Cf. F. to father, 19 Aug. 1788, FAF arkiv IX, RA. According to his letter register, F. wrote Breteuil and Marie-Antoinette on 15 Apr. 1785, "that my affairs with my father have ended well." F. arkiv X:1, RA; cf. Söderhjelm, *FMA*, 104. See also F.'s military service record from the French Ministry of War, in Vallotton, *Marie-Antoinette et Fersen*, 418–19.

35. F. to father, 29 Oct., 8, 30 Nov., 19 Dec. 1783, 3 Jan., 3 Feb., 8 June, 1 July 1784, FAF arkiv VIII, RA.

36. N.d., Charles Kunstler, *Fersen et son secret* (Paris, 1947), 119.

37. F. arkiv X (letter register); *ibid.*, XXIII (accounts, 1784–94); F.

to father, 8 Nov. 1784, FAF arkiv IX, RA; Söderhjelm, *FMA*, 102–103.
38. FAF, *HS* VI, 171–72; Söderhjelm, *FMA*, 103–104.
39. F. to father, 24 Aug., 10 Oct., 30 Nov. 1785, 10 March 1786, FAF arkiv IX, RA; Vallotton, *Marie-Antoinette et Fersen*, 124; Geijer, *Gustaf III:s efterlemnade papper*, 438; Beskow, *Lefnadsminnen*, 40; Hochschild, *Memoarer* I, 83, 86; Hennings, *Gustav III*, 257.
40. Söderhjelm, *FMA*, 109; Herold, *Mistress to an Age*, 61–62, 76; Stuart, *Dear Bess*, 21; Hildebrand, *SBL* XV, 708; Hochschild, *Memoarer* I, 118; Gustaf Murray, *Personalier öfver . . . Herr Grefve Hans Axel von Fersen, upläste vid Dess Jordfästning i Riddarholms-Kyrkan den 4 December 1810* (Stockholm, 1811), 8–9; F. to Sophie, 14 June, 12 July 1787, Lövstad arkiv VIII; F. to father, 10 Mar. 1786, 12 July, 28 Dec. 1787, 30 Jan., 27 Feb. 1788, FAF arkiv IX, RA; F. to Gustav III, 20 July 1786, Handskriftsavdelningen F 501, Uppsala universitets bibliotek [hereafter abbreviated UUB]. In his letter to his father of 30 January 1788, F. gives details on the pensions for his Swedish posts.
41. FAF, *HS* V, 230–31, 242; Hochschild, *Memoarer* I, 29, 51, 66–70; Hennings, *Gustav III*, 149; *HEC* II, 37–38, 43, 56.
42. See Sten Carlsson, *Ståndssamhälle och ståndspersoner 1700–1865* (Lund, 1949), 247–66; also Michael Roberts on Sweden in A. Goodwin, ed., *The European Nobility in the Eighteenth Century* (London, 1953).
43. F. to father, 30 Jan., 27 Feb., 7 June 1788, FAF arkiv IX, RA; *HEC* II, 146; cf. F. to Sophie, 12 July 1787, Lövstad arkiv VII. A police-spy report for early March 1787 shows that F. and Fabian were frequent visitors to Count Magnus Fredrik Brahe, one of the leaders of the opposition at the diet of 1786. Staf, *Polisväsendet*, 118.
44. Odhner, *Gustaf III:s regering* II, 353–54, 448; Hennings, *Gustav III*, 260.
45. F. to father, 3, 28 Dec. 1787, FAF arkiv IX, RA. Vallotton, *Marie-Antoinette et Fersen*, 133–34.
46. F. to father, 28 Dec. 1787, 27 Feb., 17 June 1788, FAF arkiv IX, RA; F. to Sophie, 14 April 1788, Lövstad arkiv VII; Söderhjelm, *FMA*, 116–17; Stavenow, *Gustavianska tiden*, 155–56.
47. FAF, *HS* VII, 151–53; cf. F. to Sophie, 14 July 1788, Lövstad arkiv VII. F. arkiv XVI, RA, contains much material of great interest on the campaign, including a General Order Book for 7–21 July 1788.
48. Elof Tegnér, ed., *Konung Gustaf III:s bref till friherre G. M. Armfelt*, Historiska handlingar XII:3 (Stockholm, 1883), 35; F. to Sophie, 5 Aug. 1788, Lövstad arkiv VII. Cf. France. Commission des archives diplomatiques, *Recueil des instructions données aux ambassadeurs et ministres de France depuis les traités de Westphalie jusqu'à la Révolution française*, 25 vol. (Paris, 1884–1929), II, 471–76.
49. See A. R. Cederberg, *Anjalan liiton historialliset lähteet. Lähdekriitillinen tutkielma* (Helsinki, 1931), 233–326, for texts of the documents of the officers' mutiny of 1788, in the original Swedish and French; the work includes a German summary. The "Liikala note" is also in F. arkiv XVI, RA. See also Bruno Lesch, *Jan Anders Jägerhorn* (Helsingfors, 1941).

50. FAF, *HS* VII, 157, 160–62.
51. For the Anjala declaration, see *HEC* II, 315; cf. F. arkiv XVI, RA.
52. FAF, *HS* VII, 160–62; cf. Hennings, *Ögonvittnen* 273–76. The Empress Elizabeth had offered the Finns autonomy under Russia in 1742.
53. F. arkiv XVI, RA, contains a number of such writings.
54. FAF, *HS* VII, 164–65.
55. *Ibid.*, 54–56, 163–65; Carlsson, *Svensk historia* II, 233; Staf, *Polisväsendet*, 131; Schröderheim, *Skrifter*, 273; *Dnevnik A. V. Khrapovitskago*, ed. N. Varsukov (Moscow, 1901), 86; FAF arkiv XXXIV (F. A. von Fersen's and his wife's testament), RA, 79; Sten Carlsson, "Hans Gabriel Wachtmeisters dagbok 1807–1809," *Vetenskaps-Societeten i Lund, Årsbok 1943* (Lund, 1944), 55, 57.
56. Biörnstierna, *Mémoires posthumes* I, 121, 132–33; FAF, *HS* VII, 162.
57. F. to Sophie, 23 [Aug. 1788], Lövstad arkiv VII.
58. FAF, *HS* VII, 57, 59; *HEC* II, 286–87; Staf, *Polisväsendet*, 132–38.
59. Tegnér, *Bref till Armfelt*, 51; Elof Tegnér, "Folkväpningen i Sverige 1788," *Historisk tidskrift* (1881), 240; cf. *HEC* II, 354–55, 395–96, 403–404, 430.
60. *HEC* II, 339, 350–51, 354–55; Hochschild, *Memoarer* I, 153–54; Schröderheim, *Skrifter*, 260–61, 266, 272; Tegnér, "Folkväpningen," 235; Staf, *Polisväsendet*, 138–43.
61. FAF, *HS* VII, 167–68.
62. Söderhjelm, *FMA*, 120.
63. FAF, *HS* VII, 168–69.
64. F. to father, 19 Aug. 1788, FAF arkiv IX, RA; F. to Gustav III, 1 Oct. [1788], F. arkiv I, RA; cf. Klinckowström I, xliii.
65. FAF, *HS* VII, 14, 116.
66. Lars von Engeström, *Minnen och anteckningar*, ed. Elof Tegnér, 2 vol. (Stockholm, 1876), I, 64; Armfeltska samlingen XII (Handlinger rörande Erik Ludvig Armfelt), RA; F. to Taube, 24 May 1790, Taube arkiv II, RA; F. to Gustav III, 28 June 1790, Autografsamlingen: Brev från Generalen Hans Axel von Fersen, KB; same to same, 1 May 1789, F. arkiv I, RA; F. to F. Sparre, 5 Feb. 1793, Diplomatica: Gallica 500, RA.
67. FAF, *HS* VII, 170–72; *HEC* II, 421; III, 16; Staf, *Polisväsendet*, 143.
68. Carlsson, *Ståndssamhälle och ståndspersoner*, 247–66, 346–51; Hennings, *Gustav III*, 284–93. On Forslund, see F. to Gustav III, 21 Aug. 1784, F. arkiv I, RA; Hochschild, *Memoarer* I, 168.
69. Carlsson, *Ståndssamhälle och ståndspersoner*, 254–55. For this and other historiographic questions concerning Gustav III, see Georg Landberg, *Gustav III i eftervärldens dom* (Stockholm, 1945).
70. Hennings, *Gustav III*, 285.

CHAPTER IV

1. Söderhjelm, *FMA*, 119, 121.

418

2. Paul Gaulot, *Un ami de la reine* (Paris, 1892), 217–18; Klinckow-ström.

3. Hildebrand, *SBL* XV, 744; Söderhjelm, *FMA*, 377–78; Alma Söderhjelm, "Marie-Antoinettes brev till Fersen," in her *Kärlek och politik* (Stockholm, 1933), 175–79; A. Mathiez, "Les papiers de Fersen," *Annales historiques de la Révolution française* VII (1930), 557–59; J. M. Thompson, "The Fersen Papers and Their Editors," *English Historical Review* XLVII (1932), 73–85. It should be pointed out that in all respects except for F.'s relationship with Marie-Antoinette, Klinckow-ström is reliable, as can be verified from existing documents, and has long comprised a major source on the French Revolution.

4. F. arkiv X, RA; Hildebrand, *SBL* XV, 744–45, which gives a year-by-year breakdown of the numbers of letters sent to *"Reine"* or *"Reine de France,"* and to *"Josephine."* Söderhjelm, *FMA*, 384–86, and Hilde-brand, *loc. cit.*, have shown that in all but a few cases the name "Jo-sephine" meant Marie-Antoinette, but on occasion meant a maid in the home of F.'s friends, Quentin Craufurd and Eleanore Sullivan, who may have served as a go-between in delivering his letters to the queen.

5. Vallotton, *Marie-Antoinette et Fersen*, 11–12n.; cf. André Castelot, *Queen of France* (New York, 1957), 180–81; Auguste Geffroy, "Studio sopra Maria Antonietta e Fersen," *Accademia dei Lincei, Roma, Atti,* ser. 3 (1878–79), 99; cf. Maxime de La Rocheterie & Marquis de Beau-court, *Lettres de Marie-Antoinette* (Paris, 1896).

6. See M. de Lescure, "Le comte de Fersen et Marie-Antoinette d'après des documents nouveaux," *Le Correspondant,* CX (1878), 5–31, 238–52, 404–29; and M. de La Rocheterie, "Le comte de Fersen et la cour de France," *Revue des questions historiques* XXV (1879), 201–13. Both these works are based entirely on Klinckowström. Cf. Maxime de La Rocheterie, *The Life of Marie-Antoinette,* 2 vol. (London, 1893), I, 163.

7. See, for instance, Flach, *Fersen*; Gaulot, *Ami de la reine*; O. G. de Heidenstam, "Fersen et Marie-Antoinette," *Revue de Paris* III (1912), 492–94, and the same author's *Marie-Antoinette, Fersen et Barnave. Leur correspondance* (Paris, 1913); Mildred Carnegy, *A Queen's Knight: The Life of Count Axel de Fersen* (London, 1911); Schahovs-koy-Stretchneff, *Le comte de Fersen*; Bimbinet, *Fuite,* I, xxii–xxviii; Henry Bordeaux, *Châteaux en Suède* (Paris, 1928), 191–246; and many others. Also Vallotton, *Marie-Antoinette et Fersen,* which has more re-cently held a basically similar position with considerable persuasiveness.

8. Kunstler, *Ferson et son secret* (1947); in his historical novel, *Fersen et Marie-Antoinette* (Paris, 1961), Kunstler still holds to this view, see esp. 12; Marjorie Coryn, *Marie Antoinette and Axel de Fersen* (London, 1938); Castelot, *Queen of France* (1957). Castelot, in his earlier *Varennes, le roi trahi* (Paris, 1951), 20, considered it "puerile" to deny that F. had been the queen's lover.

9. Söderhjelm, *FMA,* esp. Ch. VIII, 370–90; Hildebrand, *SBL* XV, 713–14; Stefan Zweig, *Marie-Antoinette: The Portrait of an Average Woman* (New York, 1933); Stanley Loomis, *The Fatal Friendship*

(New York, 1972); Kjell Strömberg, *Mänskligt högvilt i närbild* (Stockholm, 1973) and "Fersen, la reine et ... Louis XVII," *Nouvelle Revue des Deux Mondes* (Jan. 1974), 100–13.

10. Roger Sorg, "Le vrai visage d'Axel Fersen," *Revue de France* XIII (1933), 525–40.

11. Söderhjelm, *FMA*, 57–64; Comte de Saint-Priest, *Mémoires des règnes de Louis XV et Louis XVI*, ed. Baron de Barante, 2 vol. (Paris, 1929), II, 67–68. Saint-Priest wrongly dates this incident to 1779. See also Dardel, *Stedingks tidigare levnadsöden*, 85; Pierre de Nolhac, *Le Trianon de Marie-Antoinette* (Paris, 1924).

12. Wrangel, *Lettres*, 51–59; Söderhjelm, *FMA*, 62–69; Geffroy, *Gustave III* I, 359–61; Vallotton, *Marie-Antoinette et Fersen*, 103. On 8 March 1783, Creutz wrote Gustav III that Marie-Antoinette's zeal in promoting Staël's marriage to Gérmaine Necker was perhaps motivated by her jealousy of the latter with regard to F., then still in America. Vallotton, *Marie-Antoinette et Fersen*, 190–91.

13. F. to Sophie, 18 Sept. 1779, 18 Sept. 1780, 25 Apr. 1782, Lövstad arkiv VII; Söderhjelm, *FMA*, 71, 74–76. Frequent references then and later in his letters might suggest that a Countess Ribbing was the "charming countess" in question.

14. Söderhjelm, *FMA*, 81–82; Comtesse de Boigne, *Mémoires de la comtesse de Boigne*, ed. Charles Nicoulland, 2 vol. (Paris, 1907), I, 32.

15. Söderhjelm, *FMA*, 101–102. Cf. note 4, above.

16. Söderhjelm, *FMA*, 104–105; F. to father, 23 Oct. 1785, FAF arkiv IX, RA; M. de Lescure, ed. *Correspondance secrète inédite sur Louis XVI, Marie-Antoinette, la cour et la ville, 1777 à 1792*, 2 vol. (Paris, 1866), II, 37.

17. Saint-Priest, *Mémoires* II, 80.

18. *Ibid.*, 67–68; Tilly, *Mémoires* II, 117n.; Söderhjelm, *FMA*, 113–14; cf. M. A. de Bacourt, ed. *Correspondance entre le comte de Mirabeau et le comte de La Marck pendant les années 1789, 1790 et 1791*, 3 vol. (Paris, 1851), I, 41, 56–57. By the end of 1787, F. noted that the Polignac circle was losing its influence and the Comte de La Marck observed that F. carefully avoided it, despite its efforts to win him over. *Ibid.*, 56–57; Söderhjelm, *FMA*, 113–14.

19. Söderhjelm, *FMA*, 117, 119, 121.

20. See Vallotton, *Marie-Antoinette et Fersen*, 393; Castelot, *Queen of France*, 181. F. to Taube, n.d. [1789], Taube arkiv II, RA, ends, for instance, "Farewell my friend. I embrace you and love you with all my heart." Söderhjelm, *FMA*, 204; Hildebrand, *SBL* XV, 714; Bordeaux, *Châteaux en Suède*, 192–93. The note in question was discovered by Lucien Maury. See his "Staël et Fersen," *Revue bleue*, vol. 114 (1932), 372–74.

21. Geffroy, *Gustave III*, I, 361; cf. Tilly, *Mémoires* II, 118–19; Saint-Priest, *Mémoires*, II, 80; Söderhjelm, *Kärlek och politik*, 175–79.

22. Bimbinet, *Fuite de Louis XVI à Varennes*, II, 131–43, which gives a suite of love letters from an unidentified woman, clearly Mme. de Saint-Priest, which F. left in France in 1791; cf. *ibid.*, note 50. There are 16

known surviving letters from Marie-Antoinette to F., of which 6 are in the queen's hand, the rest having been written presumably by her secretary, Goguelat. Two of the latter exist only in facsimile in Klinckowström. Hildebrand, SBL XV, 744; Vallotton, Marie-Antoinette et Fersen, 9n.; Klinckowström II, 289n.

23. Söderhjelm, FMA, 241–42, 247–48; Vallotton, Marie-Antoinette et Fersen, 386–89; Castelot, Queen of France, 182–84; Henri Hauser, review of Söderhjelm, FMA, Revue historique v. 164 (1930), 178; cf. photographs of the famous "resté là" passage, in Vallotton, Marie-Antoinette et Fersen, facing p. 384.

24. Saint-Priest, Mémoires II, 67–68, 72, 80, 84, 90–92; cf. Söderhjelm, FMA, 170–71; Richard Henry Fox, Lord Holland, Foreign Reminiscences, ed. Henry Edward, Lord Holland (2nd ed., London, 1851), 18–19; Castelot, Queen of France, 183–84. Bacourt, in Correspondance entre Mirabeau et La Marck I, 119n., 294n., demonstrates: 1) that Mme. Campan was not in Versailles on the night of 5–6 October 1789, and 2) that her husband and others were in the queen's apartment to guard it until at least 1:00 A.M. Cf. Jeanne Louise Henriette Campan, Mémoires sur la vie particulière de Marie-Antoinette, 3 vol. (Paris, 1822). La Marck, in Bacourt, op. cit., 294n., indicates Talleyrand as the "acquaintance" of Mme. Campan who told Lord Holland this story. Cf. G. Lacour-Gayet, Talleyrand, 1754–1838, 4 vol. (Paris, 1933–34), IV, 21, 181. Elizabeth (Vassall) Fox, Lady Holland, The Journal of Elizabeth, Lady Holland (1791–1811), ed. Earl of Ilchester, 2 vol. (London, 1908), I, 87; Gouverneur Morris, A Diary of the French Revolution, ed. Beatrix Cary Davenport, 2 vol. (Cambridge, Mass., 1939), I, 271; Söderhjelm, FMA, 363–64. For Louis XVI's testament, see Castelot, Queen of France, 323; cf. Vallotton, Marie-Antoinette et Fersen, 422–25. For a general discussion of the remarks by Saint-Priest, Talleyrand, Lord and Lady Holland, and Napoleon, see Söderhjelm, op. cit., 382–83; Kunstler, Fersen et son secret, 6–9; Coryn, Marie Antoinette and Axel de Fersen, 10–13; Zweig, Marie-Antoinette, 238–40.

25. Hildebrand, SBL XV, 714; Hastier, "Baronne de Korff," 530; James Hutton, ed., Selections from the Letters and Correspondence of Sir James Bland Burges, Bart. (London, 1885), 364n.; Hochschild, Memoarer I, 83; Dagbok I, 286; see Strömberg's circumstantial case for F.'s paternity of the second dauphin in Mänskligt högvilt, 42–47, and in "Fersen, la reine et . . . Louis XVII," 107–12.

26. Söderhjelm, FMA, 370–90, esp. 379, 386–89. See also Arthur Nordén, "Var Fersen drottningens älskare?", Stockholms-Tidningen Stockholms-Dagblad (17 January 1932). Olle Holmberg wrote somewhat ironically in "Riddare av det förgångna," 14, of Alma Söderhjelm as "the lady professor, the last of those who fell offer to the 'beau Fersen's' legendary power over the feminine heart." Hildebrand, SBL XV, 714. The late Professor Hildebrand assured the present author in 1962 that there was really "no doubt" that F. was Marie-Antoinette's lover. Zweig, Marie-Antoinette, 237–47; Loomis, Fatal Friendship, 88–97, 335–37; Strömberg, "Fersen la reine et . . . Louis XVII," 107–13.

Notes and References   421

27. Kunstler, *Fersen et son secret*; Coryn, *Marie-Antoinette and Axel de Fersen*, esp. 9–23; Vallotton, *Marie-Antoinette et Fersen*, esp. 402; Castelot, *Queen of France*, esp. 184–85.

28. Saint-Priest, *Mémoires*, II, 80, 84, 91–92; cf. Castelot, *Queen of France*, 182–83; Söderhjelm, *FMA*, 138. Miss Coryn in particular makes much of the queen's lack of privacy. *Marie-Antoinette and Axel de Fersen*, 17–18.

29. Söderhjelm, *FMA*, 241–47.

30. Zweig, *Marie-Antoinette*, 243–44, 246–47; Söderhjelm, *FMA*, 229.

31. See, for instance, Georges Girard, ed. *Correspondance entre Marie-Thérèse et Marie-Antoinette* (Paris, 1933); Castelot, *Queen of France*, 154–56; Coryn, *Marie-Antoinette and Axel de Fersen*, 13–15.

32. Söderhjelm, *FMA*, 389; Tilly, *Mémoires* II, 118–19; Campan, *Mémoires* I, 101–102.

33. Hastier, "Baronne de Korff," 329–31; cf. Söderhjelm, *FMA*, 180–81, 183–84, 198. Cf. Wahlström, "A Queen's Cavalier"; Holmberg, "Riddaren av det förgångna"; Hauser in *Revue historique* (1930).

34. F. arkiv X:1, RA; Söderhjelm, *FMA*, 97–98; F. to Sophie, 7 Sept. 1785, Lövstad arkiv VII; cf. Geijer, *Gustaf III:s efterlemnade papper*, 378.

35. On the duchess, see Söderhjelm, *Gustaf III:s syskon*, 28–29. F. later refers to her as "*la petite*"; his letter register shows fairly frequent letters under this name between May 1787 and March 1791, although in later years, he used "*la petite*" for other women. It seems most likely that F.'s affair with her took place during his sojourn in Sweden, July 1786–May 1787. See F. arkiv X:1, RA. Cf. F.'s greetings to "*la petite*" in letter to Sophie, 3 July 1788, Lövstad arkiv VII.

36. Söderhjelm, *FMA*, 147–48; F. to Sophie, 15 Oct. [1790], Lövstad arkiv VII; cf. Bimbinet, *Fuite* II, 131–43; Saint-Priest, *Mémoires*; note 22, above.

37. F. to Sophie, 10 Feb. 1784, Lövstad arkiv VII; Stuart, *Dear Bess*, 19–21, 26, 29; F. arkiv X:1, RA; *Dagbok* I, 390–91; II, 54; Auguste Geffroy, "Lettres du comte Axel de Fersen à Milady Elizabeth Foster, Devonshire House à Londres (collection d'autographes à La Haye)," *Revue d'histoire diplomatique* II (April 1888), 90–99.

38. Söderhjelm, *FMA*, 140–41, 161–62; F. to Sophie, Mälsåker, n.d. [1788], Lövstad arkiv VII.

39. Söderhjelm, *FMA*, 152–54, 161–62.

40. Vallotton, *Marie-Antoinette et Fersen*, 399; cf. *ibid.*, 398–402.

41. *Ibid.*, 402.

42. F. to Gustav III, 26 May 1785, F. arkiv I, RA; Gustav III to F., 7 June 1785, F. arkiv XI, RA; Geijer, *Gustaf III:s efterlemnade papper*, 428–31; Odhner, *Gustaf III:s regering* II, 339.

43. Söderhjelm, *FMA*, 107; F. to father, 24 Aug. 1785, 10 Mar. 1786, FAF arkiv IX, RA; Gustav III to F., 30 Sept. 1785, F. arkiv XI, RA.

44. Klinckowström I, xli-xlii.

45. Söderhjelm, *FMA*, 198; Alma Söderhjelm, *Den stora revolutionen*, 2 vol. (Stockholm, 1927–29), I, 130.

46. F. to Gustav III, 4 Jan. 1788, F. arkiv I, RA; same to father, 3, 28 Dec. 1787, FAF arkiv IX, RA, according to which he planned to make the Royal-Suédois a completely Swedish regiment, with its officer billets subject to the king of Sweden's nomination, a privilege unlike any granted to any of the other so-called "German" regiments, and to recruit soldiers in Sweden for 8 years' service. F. to Sophie, 15 Jan., 27 Feb. 1788, Lövstad arkiv VII.

47. F. to Sophie, n.d. [1788], Lövstad arkiv VII; cf. Söderhjelm, *FMA*, 118; Vallotton, *Marie-Antoinette et Fersen*, 174.

48. F. to father, 15 June 1787, FAF arkiv IX, RA; cf. Klinckowström I, xlii; cf. same to Taube, 10 Apr. 1787,Taube arkiv II, RA.

49. F. to father, 30 June, 12 July, 6, 20 Aug., 20 Sept., 12 Oct., 3 Dec. 1787, FAF arkiv IX, RA.

50. John Trumbull, *The Autobiography of Colonel John Trumbull, Patriot-Artist, 1757–1843*, ed. Theodore Sizer (New Haven, 1953), 152; F. is the fifth mounted figure from the left in Trumbull's painting.

51. F. to Gustav III, 27 Dec. 1787, F. arkiv I, RA; Söderhjelm, *FMA*, 113–14, gives a small extract.

52. F. to father, 6, 20 Aug., 3, 28 Dec. 1787, 30 Jan. 1788, FAF arkiv IX, RA.

53. Söderhjelm, *FMA*, 120; Klinckowström I, xliv–xlv; cf. F. to Taube, 10 Dec. 1788, Taube arkiv II, RA.

54. Klinckowström I, xlv–xlvi; F. to father, 10 Jan., 8 Mar. 1789, FAF arkiv IX, RA.

55. Söderhjelm, *FMA*, 123–24; F. to father, 10 Apr. 1789, FAF arkiv IX, RA.

56. F. to father, 8 Mar. 1789, FAF arkiv IX, RA; FAF, *HS* VII, 116, 130; Hennings, *Gustav III*, 290–91; Staf *Polisväsendet*, 147–52.

57. Söderhjelm, *FMA*, 126.

58. *Ibid.*, 128–29; F. to father, 18 Mar., 10, 27 Apr., 25 May, 8 June, 22 July, 15 Aug. 1789, FAF arkiv IX, RA; F. to Taube, 15 Aug. 1789, Taube arkiv II, RA; Hochschild, *Memoarer* I, 185–86; Söderhjelm, *Gustav III:s syskon*, 40–43; FAF, *HS* VII, 176; F. A. von Fersen to F., 22 Feb. 1789, F. arkiv XIII, RA.

59. FAF, *HS* VII, 118–19; cf. *ibid.*, 135–36.

60. F. to father, 25 May, 8 June 1789, FAF arkiv IX, RA. It would appear that F. went so far as to send his resignation to the king. In a letter to an unidentified general, dated 11 July 1789, Fredrik Axel claims Axel was carried away by public opinion in France but is sure he will reconsider; "In that hope, I pray you return to me his letter for the king. ..." F. arkiv XIII, RA.

61. F. to father, 22 July, 15 Aug. 1789, FAF arkiv IX, RA; F. to Taube, 15 Aug. 1789, Taube arkiv II, RA; Vallotton, *Marie-Antoinette et Fersen*, 174; Söderhjelm, *FMA*, 129; F. to Sophie, "ce 22" (?) [1789], Lövstad arkiv VII.

62. F. to Taube, 29 May 1789, n.d. [1789], Taube arkiv II, RA; cf. Gustav III to Taube, 22 Jan., 24 July 1790, Taube arkiv I, RA; Schröderheim, *Skrifter*, 304; Söderhjelm, *Gustav III:s syskon*, 37. Ac-

cording to Hochschild, *Memoarer* I, 243–44, the "patriots" in Sweden accused the elder Fersen of having forbidden his children to resign from state service out of avarice over the pensions they received.

63. Tegnér, *Bref till Armfelt*, 196.

64. F. to father, 8 May 1789, FAF arkiv IX, RA; cf. same to same, 25 May, 8 June 1789, *ibid.*; L. Léouzon le Duc, ed., *Correspondance diplomatique du baron de Staël-Holstein et du baron Brinkman* (Paris, 1881), 99; cf. Vallotton, *Marie-Antoinette et Fersen*, 161–62; Klinckowström I, xlvi–xlvii.

65. Klinckowström I, xlvii–xlviii; cf. F. to father, 27 Aug. 1789, FAF arkiv IX, RA. On the disorders in Valenciennes, see *Mémoires du comte d'Esterhazy*, ed. Ernest Daudet (Paris, 1905), 236–50.

66. Klinckowström I, xlviii–l; F. to father, 27 Aug., 3, 14, 30 Sept. 1789, FAF arkiv IX, RA; Bacourt, *Correspondance entre Mirabeau et La Marck* I, 79; Söderhjelm, *FMA*, 134.

67. Klinckowström I, li; Söderhjelm, *FMA*, 134–36, 147; Lady Holland, *Journal* I, 87; Lord Holland, *Foreign Reminiscences*, 18n.; Bacourt, *Correspondance entre Mirabeau et La Marck* I, 119n.; Tilly, *Mémoires* II, 117–18n.; Friedrich Bülau, "Graf Axel Fersen," in *Geheime Geschichten und rätselhafte Menschen*, VIII (Leipzig, 1857), 371; Saint-Priest, *Mémoires* II, 22, 86–87, 90.

68. Klinckowström I, li; Söderhjelm, *FMA*, 135.

69. Saint-Priest, *Mémoires* II, 91–92.

70. Söderhjelm, *FMA*, 137; cf. F. to Taube, 27 Nov. [1789], Taube arkiv II, RA; same to father, 2 Mar., 28 June 1790, 16 Jan. 1791, FAF arkiv IX, RA, on question of the dissolution of the "German" regiments of the French army.

71. On Gustav III's concern over the French Revolution, see the following especially: Tegnér, *Bref till Armfelt*; Biörnstierna, *Mémoires posthumes* I; Léouzon le Duc, *Correspondance diplomatique*; Vivie, *Lettres;* Geffroy, *Gustave III*, II; Alma Söderhjelm, *Sverige och den franska revolutionen*, 2 vol. (Stockholm, 1920–24) [henceforward abbreviated Söderhjelm, SOFR], I; Erland Hjärne, "Gustav III och franska revolutionen," *Svensk tidskrift* XIX (1929), 502–22.

72. FAF, *HS* VII, 186–87; cf. Söderhjelm, *SOFR* I, 218.

73. Tegnér, *Bref till Armfelt*, 95; Söderhjelm, *FMA*, 132.

74. See, for instance, Léouzon le Duc, *Correspondance politique*, 107–108, 115–25, 137–46, 150; also Geffroy, *Gustave III* II, 88–93; cf. Herold, *Mistress to an Age*, esp. 96–97, on Staël's situation; Söderhjelm, *SOFR* I, 201–10; cf. F. to Taube, 14 Feb. 1790, Taube arkiv II, RA, on Mme. de Staël.

75. Léouzon le Duc, *Correspondance diplomatique*, 107; F. to Taube, 12, 20, 27 Nov. 1789, Taube arkiv II, RA.

76. Söderhjelm, *SOFR* I, 223–25; cf. F. to father, 11 Jan. 1790, FAF arkiv IX, RA; Gustav III to Taube, 22 Jan., 24 July 1790, Taube arkiv I, RA.

77. Cf. Crüwell, *Beziehungen König Gustafs III. von Schweden zur Königin Marie-Antoinette von Frankreich.*

424   COUNT HANS AXEL VON FERSEN

78. F. to Sophie, 7, 31 May, 19 Dec. 1790, Lövstad arkiv VII; same to father, 12 Sept. 1790, FAF arkiv IX, RA; Söderhjelm, FMA, 52; to Taube, 4 Feb., 24 May, 24 June, n.d. 1790, Taube arkiv II, RA. These passages, like most dealing with politics in F.'s letters to Taube in 1790–91, are in Swedish.

79. F. to Sophie, 31 May 1790, Lövstad arkiv VII; same to Taube, 1, 16 July 1790, Taube arkiv II, RA; F. to Gustav III, n.d. [c. July 1790], Autografsamlingen F, KB. In G.A. Reuterholm samling, RA, there are a number of notes from F. to Reuterholm, most undated but two dated "September," dealing with social activities they attended in Paris, at which time F. was probably trying to get information on him. On Silfverhielm's mysticism, see Dagbok II, 256–58.

80. Klinckowström I, 74–75; F. to Taube, 12 Nov. 1789, 24 Mar. [1790], Taube arkiv II, RA; cf. Söderhjelm, FMA, 143; Gustav III to Taube, 22 Dec. 1789, Taube arkiv I, RA.

81. Vallotton, Marie-Antoinette et Fersen, 193–94; F. to Taube, 4 Apr. [1791], Taube arkiv II, RA.

82. Söderhjelm, FMA, 149.

83. Klinckowström I, 74–75.

84. Söderhjelm, FMA, 150–54; F. to Gustav III, 5 Feb., 9 Aug. 1790, Autografsamlingen F, KB.

85. Klinckowström I, lii–lv; cf. F. to Gustav III, 5 Feb. 1790, Autografsamlingen F, KB, which is almost identical; Söderhjelm, FMA, 156; cf. F. to Taube, 15, 24 Mar., 9 June, 5 Sept. 1790, Taube arkiv II, RA.

86. F. to Gustav III, 5 Feb. 1790, Autografsamlingen F, KB; cf. Klinckowström I, liii, 80–81; F. to father, 31 May 1790, FAF arkiv IX, RA.

87. Klinckowström I, lii–liii, lv; F. to father, 6 Dec. 1790, FAF arkiv IX, RA; F. to Gustav III, 5 Feb., 9 Aug. 1790, Autografsamlingen F, KB; Söderhjelm, FMA, 153–54. On the prevalence of the idea of the importance of the rich to the economy, see Jacques Godechot, La Contre-révolution: doctrine et action (1789–1804) (Paris, 1961), 42.

88. F. to Gustav III, 5 Feb., 10 Apr., 9 Aug. 1790, Autografsamlingen F, KB; Klinckowström I, lviii, 81; F. to father, 8 May 1789, 11 Jan. 1790, FAF arkiv IX, RA; Söderhjelm FMA, 156, 158; F. to Taube, 4 Feb., 17 Sept. 1790, Taube arkiv II, RA. Cf. Gustav III to Staël, (?) Feb. 1790, Vallotton, Marie-Antoinette et Fersen, 194, which expresses the same idea, possibly deriving from F.'s reports.

89. F. to Gustav III, 5 Feb., 10 Apr. 1790, Autografsamlingen F, KB; cf. F. to Taube, 5 Feb. 1790, Taube arkiv II, RA; same to same, I Apr. [1790], Handskriftssamlingen F 520, UUB.

90. Söderhjelm, FMA, 146–47; F. to Gustav III, 9 Aug. 1790, Autografsamlingen F, KB; Klinckowström I, 80.

91. F. to Gustav III, 5 Feb., 10 Apr. 1790, Autografsamlingen F, KB; Klinckowström I, 74–75; F. to Taube, 4 Feb., 24 Mar. 1790, Taube arkiv II, RA.

92. F. to Gustav III, 9 Aug., n.d. 1790 (incomplete), Autografsamlingen F, KB; F. to father, 3, 11 Jan., 27 Dec. 1790, FAF arkiv IX, RA;

F. to Taube, 16 July 1790, Taube arkiv II, RA. See also Marie-Antoinette to the Comte de Mercy-Argenteau, 12 June 1790, in Alfred, Ritter von Arneth, ed., *Marie-Antoinette, Joseph II und Leopold II. Ihr Brief-wechsel* (Leipzig, 1866), [henceforth abbreviated *MAJL*], 130, where she mentions the possibility of a threatening gesture by Prussia and Austria.

93. F. to Gustav III, 27 July, 9 Aug., 5 Sept. 1790, Autografsamlingen F, KB; Klinckowström I, 81; F. to Taube, 24 Mar. [1790], Taube arkiv II, RA; same to same, 5 Apr. [1790], Handskriftssamlingen F 520, UUB; Söderhjelm, *FMA*, 155. Vallotton, *Marie-Antoinette et Fersen*, 239, shows Marie-Antoinette's fear of the émigrés.

94. Söderhjelm, *FMA*, 151–59; F. to father, 22 Oct. 1789, FAF arkiv IX, RA; Klinckowström I, lvii; Saint-Priest, *Mémoires* II, 92.

95. Klinckowström I, lvi–lvii, 77–78.

96. Léouzon le Duc, *Correspondance diplomatique*, 166.

97. Vallotton, *Marie-Antoinette et Fersen*, 194; F. to Taube, 17 Sept. 1790, 14 Feb. 1791, Taube arkiv II, RA; Söderhjelm, *FMA*, 156, 159.

98. Léouzon le Duc, *Correspondance diplomatique*, 107; F. arkiv X:1, RA; F. to Taube, 12, 27 Nov. 1789, 7, 15, 24 Mar., 9 June, 17, 30 Sept. 1790, Taube arkiv II, RA. In 1783 Taube had expected the appointment to the Paris embassy that went to Staël. See Vivie, *Lettres*, 294.

99. F. to Taube, 12 Nov. 1789, 9 June [1790], 17 Mar. 1791, Taube arkiv II, RA; Söderhjelm, *FMA*, 156–57; cf. F. to Sophie, 15 Oct. [1790], Lövstad arkiv VII; Söderhjelm, *SOFR* I, 224–25; Vallotton, *Marie-Antoinette et Fersen*, 194.

CHAPTER V

1. There is a large literature on the flight to Varennes; note particularly: Victor Fournel, *L'événement de Varennes* (Paris, 1890); and the same author's "La fuite de Louis XVI," *Revue des questions historiques* V (1868), 107–88, 426–84; Charles Aimond, *L'énigme de Varennes* (Paris, 1936); Bimbinet, *Fuite de Louis XVI à Varennes*; G. Lenotre [G. Gosselin], *Le drame de Varennes* (Paris, 1908); Max Lenz, "Marie Antoinette im Kampf mit der Revolution," *Preussische Jahrbücher*, LXXVIII (1894), 1–28, 255–311, esp. the first part. On F.'s role, see also Kunstler, *Fersen et son secret*; Söderhjelm, *FMA*; and Vallotton, *Marie-Antoinette et Fersen*.

2. Fournel, *L'événement*, 13–20; Aimond, *L'énigme*, 1–14; Godechot, *La Contre-révolution*, 163; Saint-Priest, *Mémoires*, II, 86–87. On the idea of withdrawing to Metz on 14 July 1789, cf. Klinckowström II, 7.

3. Fournel, *L'événement*, 23–37, 59; François-Claude Amour, Marquis de Bouillé, *Mémoires du marquis de Bouillé*, ed. M. F. Barrrière (Paris, 1859), 232, 248; F. to Taube, 4 Apr. 1790, Handskriftsavdelningen F 520., UUB; Jeanne Arnaud-Bouteloup, *Le rôle politique de Marie-Antoinette* (Paris, 1924), 213; Klinckowström I, 115–16.

4. Klinckowström I, 74–75, 88; cf. F. to Gustav III, 5 Feb., 10 Apr., 9 Aug. 1790, Autografsamlingen F, KB; same to Taube, 24 Mar. 1790,

Taube arkiv II, RA; Söderhjelm, *FMA*, 146; F. to father, 7 Mar. 1791, FAF arkiv IX, RA.

5. Bacourt, *Correspondance* I, 106–107, 113, 120–25, 130–31, 139, 365–82; Fournel, *L'événement*, 39; Söderhjelm, 221.

6. Bacourt, *Correspondance* I, 193, 200; II, 103–109, 113–19, 244–45; Fournel, *L'événement*, 39–41; Esterhazy, *Mémoires*, 282–89. In Lövstad arkiv XX are a number of anonymous memoranda concerning France ca. 1790–91, including one attributed, in a notation by Taube, to "Pellin": presumably Mirabeau's secretary, Jean-Joachim Pellenc. On Marie-Antoinette's relations with Mirabeau and La Marck, see Max Lenz, "Die Vorbereitungen der Flucht Ludwigs XVI. (Oktober 1790 bis Juni 1791.) Ein Beitrag zur Kritik der französischen Memoirenliteratur," *Historische Zeitschrift* LXXII (1894), 31–33n.; F. S. Feuillet de Conches, ed., *Louis XVI, Marie-Antoinette et Madame Élisabeth: lettres et documents inédits*, 8 vol. (Paris, 1864–73) [hereafter abbreviated Feuillet de Conches], I, 447–48.

7. Esterhazy, *Mémoires*, 289; Arnaud-Bouteloup, *Rôle politique*, 213–27; Fournel, *L'événement*, 31n., 42–43, 47–50; Louis J. A., Marquis de Bouillé, *Mémoires du marquis de Bouillé (comte Louis), lieutenant-général, sur le départ de Louis XVI au mois de juin 1791*, in S. A. de Berville & M. F. Barrière, ed., *Collection des mémoires relatifs à la Révolution française* XLI (Paris, 1823), 17–20; [Marquis de] Bouillé, *Mémoires*, 215–16, 228. Of these accounts of the Varennes affair by the two Bouillés, Count Louis's is the more concise and reliable. For an evaluation of these and other sources, strongly critical of the Marquis de Bouillé's memoirs, see Lenz, "Vorbereitungen," 5, 31–33, 41, 229–33. This valuable study seems almost unknown among French historians.

8. Bouillé, *Mémoires*, 213–16, 219–20; Louis de Bouillé, *Mémoire sur le départ*, 20–22.

9. Feuillet de Conches I, 370. A number of the letters attributed to Marie-Antoinette in this collection, especially in Vol. I, are apocryphal, thus this work must be used with caution. On this and other editions of the queen's correspondence, see introductions to La Rocheterie & Beaucourt, *Lettres de Marie-Antoinette* I, *passim.*, esp. xix–xx; II, vii–x; Girard, *Correspondance entre Marie-Thérèse et Marie-Antoinette*, 8–9; Zweig, *Marie-Antoinette*, 466–68. My own procedure has been to use only those letters allegedly by Marie-Antoinette in Feuillet de Conches accepted by La Rocheterie and Beaucourt, or cited by Arnaud-Bouteloup, who relied on verifications by Alfred, Ritter von Arneth, and Jules Flammermont. See Arnaud-Bouteloup, *Rôle politique*, 368n. On d'Agoult and the king's accreditation of Breteuil, see also Louis de Bouillé, *Mémoire sur le départ*, 20–21; on the choice of Montmédy, *ibid.*, 22, 37–39, 50–52; Bouillé, *Mémoires*, 219–20; Lenz, "Vorbereitungen," 13.

10. Bacourt, *Correspondance* I, 235–38; II, 414–504.

11. *Ibid.*, I, 238–44; Fournel, *L'événement*, 45–46; Louis de Bouillé, *Mémoire sur le départ*, 55–56; Bouillé, *Mémoires*, 226–29. On Bouillé's political views, see *ibid.*, 233, 245–46, 239–60, 416–19. Lenz, in "Vor-

bereitungen," 229–33, shows that Bouillé's professed liberal political views must be taken with skepticism.

12. Bouillé, *Mémoires*, 228–29; Fournel, *L'événement*, 47–50. The original of F.'s letter to his father, FAF arkiv IX, RA, is dated simply "Paris, janvier"; Klinckowström I, lviii–lix, dates it "Paris, février 1791," while Söderhjelm, *FMA*, dates it February 1790. The correct date is surely sometime in January 1791.

13. Klinckowström I, 74; F. to Gustav III, 5 Feb., 10 Apr., 9 Aug. 1790, Autografsamlingen F, KB; Gustav III to Taube, 22 Dec. 1789, Taube arkiv I, RA. Godechot in *Contre-révolution*, 3, has shown that the appeal for foreign intervention was characteristic of counterrevolutionary action from at least 1768 on.

14. Arneth, *MAJL*, 130, 146–79; Feuillet de Conches I, 396–97. Hanns Schlitter, ed., *Briefe der Erzherzogin Marie Christine Statthalterin der Niederlande an Leopold II. nebst einer Einleitung: Zur Geschichte der französischen Politik Leopolds II.*, Fontes Rerum Austriacarum: Diplomataria et Acta, XLVIII, Teil 1 (Vienna, 1896), xvi. The former controller-general, Calonne, proposed foreign diplomatic pressure to free the French royal family to Joseph II in late 1789 or early 1790. Godechot, *Contre-révolution*, 162–63. Louis de Bouillé, *Mémoire sur le départ*, 18–19, 22–23, 26, 34–36, suggests that the Tuileries and Breteuil had already carried on much negotiation with foreign courts between October and the end of December 1790.

15. Bacourt, *Correspondance* I, 199–200; Arneth, *MAJL*, 134.

16. Facsimile, n.d., Bimbinet, *Fuite* II, following 152; Schlitter, *Briefe*, xxxiii–xxxv n.; cf. Feuillet de Conches II, 43–49.

17. Feuillet de Conches I, 446–47; Klinckowström I, 128, 131; cf. J. H. Clapham, *The Causes of the War of 1792* (Cambridge, 1899), 45–46; Lenz, "Marie Antoinette im Kampf," 255–57. In October 1789, Louis XVI wrote the Spanish ambassador, protesting all acts contrary to royal authority imposed on him by force since July and stating his intention of fulfilling the promises of his Declaration of 23 June. J. M. Thompson, *The French Revolution* (Oxford, 1944), 199; cf. F. to Breteuil, "2 April" 1791, Klinckowström I, 96n. According to Lenz, "Vorbereitungen," 25n., this letter should be dated 22 April 1791. Jacqueline Chaumié, *Les relations diplomatiques entre l'Espagne et la France de Varennes à la mort de Louis XVI* (Bordeaux, 1957), 8, 18–21, 69.

18. Söderhjelm, *FMA*, 164; Klinckowström I, 103–106, 108. On the importance of this incident, see Bouillé, *Mémoires*, 242; Bacourt, *Correspondance* I, 265.

19. Bouillé, *Mémoires*, 216–17, 223; Louis de Bouillé, *Mémoire sur le départ*, 18, 23, 31–32, 39–40; Bacourt, *Correspondance* I, 6–7. Cf. Bimbinet, *Fuite* I, 174–75, 242–43; Fournel, *L'événement*, 63–64; Arnaud-Bouteloup, *Rôle politique*, 229.

20. Louis de Bouillé, *Mémoire sur le départ*, 36–37, 40–42; Klinckowström I, 91–93.

21. Klinckowström I, 112, 120, 125, 133–35.

22. Feuillet de Conches I, 220; II, 16, 34; Arneth, *MAJL*, 172;

Klinckowström I, 96, 112, 133–35; Arnaud-Bouteloup, *Rôle politique*, 245–50. On the anti-royalist aristocratism of most of the Emigration, see Jacqueline Chaumié, *Le réseau d'Antraigues et la Contre-révolution, 1791–1793* (Paris, 1965), 23–43.

23. F. to father, 4, 12 Apr. 1791, FAF arkiv IX, RA; Söderhjelm, *FMA*, 163; Klinckowström I, 86; Bouillé, *Mémoires*, 224–25, 245–46; Fournel, *L'événement*, 60.

24. Bacourt, *Correspondance* I, 199–200, 205, 213; Feuillet de Conches IV, 113.

25. Aimond, *L'énigme*, 6.

26. Feuillet de Conches I, 445; II, 37; Arneth, *MAJL*, 147, 156, 160–61, 165, 169, 172, 175; Klinckowström I, 95, 107, 109, 111, 122, 124–27, 129–32, 134, 138; Bouillé, *Mémoires*, 241, 245; Louis de Bouillé, *Mémoire sur le départ*, 36, 44–46, 50. Although Klinckowström attributes letters to the Marquis de Bouillé, Louis de Bouillé, in *ibid.*, 43–44, states that he handled all the enciphered correspondence with F. on his father's behalf.

27. Klinckowström I, 87–90, 97–98; Schlitter, *Briefe*, xxviii–xxix, xxxiv n.; Arneth, *MAJL*, 148; Lenz, "Vorbereitungen," 25–26.

28. Arneth, *MAJL*, 147; Klinckowström I, 87, 96–97, 109–10, 114, 121, 123; Hutton, *Bland Burges Correspondence*, 374–76. Cf. Pitt to George III, 20 Aug. 1791 (copy), F. arkiv XVII, RA; Chaumié, *L'Espagne et la France*, 21. Vallotton, *Marie-Antoinette et Fersen*, 218, states he could not find any evidence of Breteuil's negotiations with the Cantons in Swiss archives.

29. Arnaud-Bouteloup, *Rôle politique*, 231, 234–36; Clapham, *Causes*, 28–31; Schlitter, *Briefe*, v–xxxv; Adam Wandruszka, *Leopold II*, 2 vol. (Vienna, 1963–65), II, 353–59; Arneth, *MAJL*, 131–32, 145, 147–81; Feuillet de Conches II, 52–58; Lenz "Vorbereitungen," 213–15. Cf. Louis de Bouillé's suspicions of the emperor's motives vis-à-vis France, in *Mémoire sur le départ*, 34–36, 52–54.

30. Feuillet de Conches I, 36–37; II, 43–45, 48; Schlitter, *Briefe*, xxxiii–xxxv n., xliv–xlvi; Klinckowström I, 95, 109, 113–15, 122, 129–31, 138; Arneth, *MAJL*, 173, 177–78; Hutton, *Bland Burges Correspondence*, 374–75; F. to Taube, 16 May 1791, Taube arkiv II, RA; Söderhjelm, *FMA*, 184; Bouillé, *Mémoires*, 302; Louis de Bouillé, *Mémoire sur le départ*, 71.

31. "Déclaration du roi . . . ," in Feuillet de Conches II, 95–119; Klinckowström I, lx, 110, 122–23, 125, 129–31, 137–38; Hutton, *Bland Burges Correspondence*, 366n.; Lenz, "Marie Antoinette im Kampf," 301–302. Breteuil's memorandum has unfortunately not been found.

32. Arneth, *MAJL*, 149. See also Bimbinet, *Fuite* I, 66–67, 101; Fournel, *L'événement*, 72–75; Bouillé, *Mémoires*, 223–24; Hutton, *Bland Burges Correspondence*, 376, according to which the Comte d'Artois was to "assemble and direct" the royalists in the Midi and to direct there "the operations of the Spanish and Sardinian armies." Cf. Klinckowström I, 123. An undated, anonymous fragment of a deciphered message

in F. arkiv XVII, RA, speaks of sending Condé to the Midi for the same purpose.

33. F. to Sophie, 31 July, 8 Aug. 1790, Lövstad arkiv VII; same to father, 31 July, 8 Aug., 12, 30 Sept. 1790, FAF arkiv IX, RA; same to Taube, 16 July 1790, Taube arkiv II, RA. Cf. Ch. IV note 71, above.

34. Gustav III to Taube, 3 Sept. 1790, Taube arkiv I, RA.

35. Klinckowström I, 1, 84–85. On 18 June 1791, Mme. de Saint-Priest wrote F. from London that it was rumored among émigrés there that he was in constant correspondence with Gustav III and that it was F. who "led" the Swedish king. Bimbinet, *Fuite* II, 140.

36. Klinckowström I, 112–13. Already on 17 March 1791, F. wrote Taube that he feared "restless spirits" in Sweden might take advantage of Gustav III's absence. Taube arkiv II, RA. Cf. *HEC* III, 343–44, 362–63, 375–76.

37. Hutton, *Bland Burges Correspondence*, 364–65.

38. Louis de Bouillé, *Mémoire sur le départ*, 23–46; Lenz, "Vorbereitungen," 6, 12. Cf. Söderhjelm, *FMA*, 162–63. A key for the cipher used by Bouillé is given in facsimile in Bimbinet, *Fuite* II, facing 152; see also *ibid.*, I, 45–53. On F.'s house, formerly 17 Rue de Matignon, torn down in 1927, see W. Legran [F. U. Wrangel], *Ur arkivens gömmor* (Stockholm, 1912), 154–69; Albert Vauflart, "La maison du comte de Fersen, rue Matignon," in *Extrait des mélanges Émile Le Senne* (Paris, 1916), 283–317. There is an engraving of the house in Lenotre, *Drame*, 19.

39. F. to Taube, 28 Mar., 13 May 1791, Taube arkiv II, RA; Bimbinet, *Fuite* II, 129–30, 144, 148–49. Aimond, *L'énigme*, 20, mistakenly claims that F. during this period visited "the émigrés" in Aachen, Mercy in Brussels, and Bouillé in Metz twice. F. caused his lieutenant colonel, Baron K. L. von Fürstenwärther, some anxiety by neglecting his regiment in Valenciennes. Bimbinet, *Fuite* II, 129–30 (where he is called "Furstenwarten"). Cf. Closen *Journal*, 349.

40. Bimbinet, *Fuite* I, 18–20; II, 51–55; Alma Söderhjelm, "Berlineraren var en svensk herrskapsvagn," in her *Spel och verklighet* (Stockholm, 1941), 43–59; Hastier, "Baronne de Korff," 526–28; Louis de Bouillé, *Mémoire sur le départ*, 39–40; Bouillé, *Mémoires*, 240–41. Cf. Feuillet de Conches I, 445–46. Lenotre, *Drame*, 59, gives an engraving of the *berline*; it was later used as a diligence between Paris and Dijon until destroyed by fire. Söderhjelm, *Spel och verklighet*, 59.

41. Bimbinet, *Fuite* I, 33–37, 54; II, 151–52, also facsimiles facing 150, 152; Hastier, "Baronne de Korff," 533–37; Söderhjelm, *FMA*, 180; Fournel, *L'événement*, 69–70.

42. Klinckowström I, 95–98, 107, 109, 111, 114, 120, 122–23, 130; Feuillet de Conches II, 15; Schlitter, *Briefe*, xxxiii n., xxxvii–xxxviii, xliv–xlv.

43. Söderhjelm, *FMA*, 166; Feuillet de Conches II, 15, 39; Schlitter, *Briefe*, xxxiii n.; Hutton, *Bland Burges Correspondence*, 366; Lenz, "Vorbereitungen," 31. On 22 April 1791, Taube replied to F. that it was impossible to raise the loans F. wished in Sweden, for if he

used F.'s name with Swedish merchants, F.'s father would immediately learn of it and fear his son intended to ruin his inheritance, while, Taube added, it would also be impossible to gain credit "on my own and my friends' physiognomies.'" F. arkiv XIV, RA.

44. Söderhjelm, *FMA*, 165–66, 170; Söderhjelm in *Dagbok* II, 356, 469n.; Hastier, "Baronne de Korff," 540; Klinckowström I, 97; O. Karmin, "Le trésor de Marie-Antoinette et le comte de Fersen," *Revue historique de la Révolution française* XV (1923), 141–43. F. arkiv XVII, RA, contains rough notes on F.'s loans. F. arkiv XXII, RA, shows his interest payments and his note for Eleanore Sullivan, as well as numerous small expenses connected with the flight in winter-spring 1791. In July 1798, F. complains of having lost the receipts for Mme. von Korff's and Mme. Stegelmann's loans. *Dagbok* III, 251.

45. Klinckowström I, 111, 123, 130. For a somewhat higher estimate of the total funds, see Thompson, *French Revolution*, 203; Aimond, *L'énigme*, 11. The king sent 993,000 livres in *assignats* to Bouillé at the end of April, of which Bouillé later deposited 600,000 with Frankfurt bankers. Klinckowström I, 143; Vallotton, *Marie-Antoinette et Fersen*, 366–67. On the 2 million livres from the king's civil list, cf. Klinckowström I, 130.

46. F. to Breteuil, 23 May 1791, Klinckowström I, 128 (here mistakenly attributed to Breteuil); cf. *ibid.*, 123, 131.

47. Campan, *Mémoires* II, 140–43, 319–23; Arneth, *MAJL*, 170; Aimond, *L'énigme*, 56; F. to Taube, 15 Mar. 1794, Taube arkiv III, RA. Cf. Lenz's criticism of Mme. Campan's *Mémoires* regarding Varennes, in "Vorbereitungen," 226–28.

48. Fournel, *L'événement*, 76; Bimbinet, *Fuite* I, 26–28; II, 17–18, 34–35, 43–44, 49–50, 55–56; Charles-Nicholas Gabriel, *Louis XVI, le marquis de Bouillé et Varennes* (Paris, 1874), 97.

49. Bouillé, *Mémoires*, 222–23, 240; Louis de Bouillé, *Mémoire sur le départ*, 37–38, 42, 46–49; Fournel, *L'événement*, 45–47; Klinckowström I, 118, 121.

50. Bouillé, *Mémoires*, 241, 254–55; Louis de Bouillé, *Mémoire sur le départ*, 40; Lenz, "Vorbereitungen," 41–43; Aimond, *L'énigme*, 17; Lévis, *Souvenirs et portraits*, 130–31; Klinckowström I, 132, 138.

51. Klinckowström I, 96, 107–108, 119, 132–33, 136–38; Söderhjelm, *FMA*, 180; Louis de Bouillé, *Mémoire sur le départ*, 37, 70–71.

52. Aimond, *L'énigme*, 14; Bimbinet, *Fuite* I, 54–66, 69–73; II, facsimile facing 160.

53. Söderhjelm *FMA*, 180–81. Cf. Klinckowström I, 1; Hastier, "Baronne de Korff," 529–31; Bimbinet, *Fuite* I, 20–22, 42–44, 74; II, 28–30, 54–55, 57–58.

54. Arneth, *MAJL*, 165; Bimbinet, *Fuite* I, 13–16, 23–25; II, 64, 149–51; Campan, *Mémoires* II, 311–15; Fournel, *L'événement*, 77–92; Aimond, *L'énigme*, 51–53; Klinckowström I, 127; Jean Palou, "Autour de la fuite du roi," *Annales historiques de la Révolution française*, XXXIII (1961), 189–90.

55. Bimbinet, *Fuite* I, 5–13; II, 131–43; Fournel, *L'événement*, 92. Cf. Saint-Priest, *Mémoires* II, 100–103.

56. Fournel, *L'événement*, 92–94, 102–103; Aimond, *L'énigme*, 53; Bimbinet, *Fuite* I, 23; Klinckowström I, 1.

57. Fournel, *L'événement*, 92–103. Cf. Aimond, *L'énigme*, 53; Arnaud-Bouteloup, *Rôle politique*, 240; Schlitter, *Briefe*, xx n.; Louis de Bouillé, *Mémoire sur le départ*, 90–91; *Dagbok* I, 75. Palou, in "Autour de la fuite du roi," 190–92, reports finding testimony which he claims demonstrates definitively that both La Fayette and Bailly were implicated in the escape plot; he furthermore states his intention in a future article of proving that La Fayette "is the main link in that chain of royal evasion [schemes] which extends . . . from July 1789 to February 1792." *Ibid.*, 192. On Gouvion, see Lenotre, *Drame*, 39n., 42n.

58. The account of the escape is based principally on Bimbinet, *Fuite* I, 78–87; II, 7–10, 57–62, 98; Fournel, *L'événement*, 103, 112–24; Aimond, *L'énigme*, 56–60; Castelot, *Queen of France*, 263–67; Söderhjelm, *FMA*, 178–80; Lenotre, *Drame*, 26–55. Lenotre's plan of the royal apartments in the Tuileries and map of the surroundings of the palace, *ibid.*, 28, 41, are useful. See also Loomis's gripping account in *The Fatal Friendship*, 125–83.

59. Lenotre, *Drame*, 21–24; Bimbinet, *Fuite* II, 28–30, 57–58; Fournel, *L'événement*, 113–14; Söderhjelm, *FMA*, 181.

60. Söderhjelm, *FMA*, 181.

61. *Ibid.*, 180–81; Lenotre, *Drame*, 31–34, 57.

62. Bimbinet, *Fuite* II, 7–10, 58.

63. Lenotre, *Drame*, 34–42, 48–50; Fournel, *L'événement*, 114–16, 119–20; Gabriel, *Varennes*, 97; Castelot, *Queen of France*, 263–65; Bimbinet, *Fuite* II, 65–68, 74–77.

64. Lenotre, *Drame*, 42–44; Bimbinet, *Fuite* II, 10, 68–70, 77–79.

65. Lenotre, *Drame*, 26–30, 44–51; Bimbinet *Fuite* II, 16–19, 33–35.

66. Bimbinet, *Fuite* II, 45–46, 51–52; Castelot, *Queen of France*, 265–66; Fournel, *L'événement*, 117–18; Gabriel, *Varennes*, 100; Söderhjelm, *FMA*, 179. The unknown man who accompanied the queen is mentioned in F.'s diary, 14 Feb. 1792, Klinckowström II, 7–8, as simply "M. de . . ."

67. Lenotre, *Drame*, 52–55; Bimbinet, *Fuite* II, 59–62; Söderhjelm, *FMA*, 180; Hutton, *Bland Burges Correspondence*, 366; Louis de Bouillé, *Mémoire sur le départ*, 92; Fournel, *L'événement*, 123–24. Fournel, *ibid.*, 124, and Aimond, *L'énigme*, 59, state that F. returned to Paris and took a turn around the Place de l'Hôtel de Ville and La Fayette's residence to make sure nothing was afoot before departing for Mons. F.'s diary notes for the night of 20–21 June 1971, Söderhjelm, *FMA*, 181, however, read: "moi la traverse à 3 h au Bourget et parti."

68. Söderhjelm, *FMA*, 181–83; Klinckowström I, 139–40.

69. Aimond, *L'énigme*, 8–9, 51; Thomas Carlyle, *The French Revolution, a History* (Modern Library Edition, New York, 1934), 353; Campan, *Mémoires* II, 139–43, 311–15. See also Lenotre, *Drame*, Ch. IX, "Le cas de M. Léonard," 270–91.

70. Bouillé, *Mémoires*, 240; Louis de Bouillé, *Mémoire sur le départ*, 39–40, 93–94; Söderhjelm, *Spel och verklighet*, 58–59; Carlyle, *French Revolution*, 204; Aimond, *L'énigme*, 7–9, 14, 47.

71. Bouillé, *Mémoires*, 241, 245–46; Bacourt, *Correspondance* I, 241; Klinckowström I, 118, 122, 130, 136; Söderhjelm, *FMA*, 169, 183, 328; Bimbinet, *Fuite* I, 67, 69, 273–76; Aimond, *L'énigme*, 17–18, 22–30.

72. Aimond, *L'énigme*, 25–26, 31–36.

73. Feuillet de Conches II, 16; Klinckowström I, 92, 95, 109.

CHAPTER VI

1. Bouillé, *Mémoires*, 267–69; Louis de Bouillé, *Mémoire sur le départ*, 141–43.

2. Klinckowström I, 142, 152; Söderhjelm, *FMA*, 204. Cf. Maury, "Staël et Fersen," 373. Also Ch. IV, note 20, above.

3. Söderhjelm, *FMA*, 184–89; Vallotton, *Marie-Antoinette et Fersen*, 225–26; also *ibid.*, 225, for quotation from *Chronique de Paris*.

4. On the diplomacy of the counterrevolution, summer 1791 to spring 1792, see especially: Albert, Sorel, *L'Europe et la Révolution française*, 8 vol. (Paris, 1885–1904), II; the same author's "La fuite de Louis XVI et les essais d'intervention en 1791: Varennes et Pillnitz," *Revue des Deux Mondes III* (1886), 314–46; Clapham, *Causes*; Arnaud-Bouteloup, *Rôle politique*; Lenz, "Marie Antoinette im Kampf," 255–311. Leopold II's Padua Circular of 6 July 1791, in Alfred, Ritter von Vivenot, ed., *Quellen zur Geschichte der deutschen Kaiserpolitik Österreichs während der französischen Revolutionskriege, 1790–1801*, 5 vol. (Vienna, 1873–93), I, 185–87. Cf. *ibid.*, 208–11, 213–16; Schlitter, *Briefe*, xlviii–liv.

5. Söderhjelm, *FMA*, 181; Feuillet de Conches II, 91; Louis XVI's note is given in Arneth, *MAJL*, 184–85, wrongly dated July 1791. Cf. Schlitter, *Briefe*, xlvi, 129, 311; Lenz, "Vorbereitungen," 225n.

6. *Dagbok* I, 74n., 84, 88, 90; Lennart Norrlin, *Anders Fredrik Reutersvärd* (Karlskrona, 1953, 31 pp.). F. arkiv XII, RA, contains 57 unsigned letters attributed to a Devaux-Germain in Paris as well as another 14 attributed to his brother, all from 1791. Excerpts from Devaux's reports between 21 June and 16 July 1791 are given in *Dagbok*, 71–75.

7. Klinckowström I, 141. Cf. Hutton, *Bland Burges Correspondence*, 368.

8. Klinckowström I, 147–48. Cf. Feuillet de Conches II, 169–70; Hutton, *Bland Burges Correspondence*, 374.

9. Klinckowström I, 157.

10. F. to Gustav III, 3 [July 1791], F. arkiv I, RA; Söderhjelm, *FMA*, 183–84; Klinckowström I, 6. Concerning the schism between the party of the princes and Calonne, and the so-called "party of the Tuileries" and Breteuil, see Chaumié, *Le réseau d'Antraigues*, 23–45; Arnaud de Lestapis, "Royalistes et monarchiens," *Revue des Deux Mondes* (1960), 271–78, 501–13.

11. Klinckowström I, 1, 3, 4, 7; Ernest Daudet, *L'Histoire de l'émi-*

gration pendant la Révolution, 3 vol. (Paris, 1905–1907), II, 73–76; Geffroy, *Gustave III*, II, 166–67. F. arkiv XVII, RA, contains a copy of a "Déclaration du Roi d'Espagne au mois de juillet [1791]."

12. Klinckowström I, 117.

13. Geffroy, *Gustave III*, II, 164–65, 174–75; Söderhjelm, *SOFR* I, 257–60; Feuillet de Conches III, 356. Cf. Nils Åkeson, *Gustaf III:s förhållande till den franska revolutionen* (Lund, 1887), 83.

14. Klinckowström I, 3–4, 6; Schlitter, *Briefe*, lv n., 129–30, 134, 138, 151; Wandruszka, *Leopold II*, II, 361; Hutton, *Bland Burges Correspondence*, 367–73; Pitt to George III, 20 Aug. 1790 (copy), F. arkiv XVII, RA; Åkeson, *Gustaf III:s förhållande*, 74–81, 90–101. On Craufurd, see also Émile Dard, *Un rival de Fersen, Quentin Craufurd* (Paris, 1947).

15. Klinckowström I, 148–50; accreditation (in Latin), 21 July 1791, F. arkiv XI, RA.

16. Feuillet de Conches III, 431–32; Klinckowström I, 4, 150–51; Gustav III to F., 19 Aug. 1791, F. arkiv XI, RA. Cf. Godechot, *Contrerévolution*, 170.

17. Feuillet de Conches III, 427–28, 430–31; IV, 86; V, 29; Klinckowström I, 9–11. On Leopold's position, see Arnaud-Bouteloup, *Rôle politique*, 265; Clapham, *Causes*, 73–74, 79–80; Schlitter, *Briefe*, lv–lix.

18. F. to Gustav III, 10 Aug. 1791, Ericsbergsarkivet: Brevskrivare, RA; F. to father, 20 Aug. 1791, FAF arkiv IX, RA; Klinckowström I, 11–14. On Kaunitz's views, see Clapham, *Causes*, 81–82.

19. Klinckowström I, 156, 186–87.

20. *Ibid.*, 14–15. Cf. Schlitter, *Briefe*, lx–lxi.

21. Klinckowström I, 16–17; Feuillet de Conches IV, 87–95, 117–24.

22. Feuillet de Conches IV, 113, 117–30; Arnaud-Bouteloup, *Rôle politique*, 260.

23. Feuillet de Conches IV, 87–95, 104–14, 117–24; Klinckowström I, 21, 23, 187–91.

24. See my article, "The Origins of the Brunswick Manifesto," *French Historical Studies* V (1967), 146–51. In her letter to Mercy of 12 June 1790, Arneth, *MAJL*, 130, Marie-Antoinette attributes to "M . . ." the idea of foreign diplomatic pressure backed by force. Clapham, *Causes*, 47, and Arnaud-Bouteloup, *Rôle politique*, 219n., believe this to have been Mirabeau but this is unsubstantiated in Mirabeau's papers and contradicts his known views on counterrevolution. It seems more reasonable that "M . . ." was the foreign minister, the Comte de Montmorin, as indirectly suggested by Gouverneur Morris, *Diary* II, 174–75.

25. Arnaud-Bouteloup, *Rôle politique*, 258–62; Schlitter, *Briefe*, lxxiv, lxxxi–lxxxii; Feuillet de Conches II, 208–309, 383–86.

26. Feuillet de Conches IV, 87–95, 104–10; Klinckowström I, 23; cf. Bouillé, *Mémoires*, 299–300.

27. Gustav III to F., 9 Aug. 1791, F. arkiv XI, RA; Klinckowström I, 180–83; II, 186–93; Åkeson, *Gustaf III:s förhållande*, 128–33. F. arkiv XVII, RA, contains undated "Notes instructives sur le point le plus commode et le plus utile pour la déscente que l'on se propose d'effectuer sur

434 COUNT HANS AXEL VON FERSEN

la côte de la Basse Normandie." On Buillé's service under Gustav III, see Bouillé, *Mémoires*, 280, 283.

28. Klinckowström I, 21, 187–91; Feuillet de Conches IV, 70, 90–91, 107–108; Gustav III to F., 2 Sept. 1791, F. arkiv XI, RA. Cf. Bouillé's "Observations sur différents points de débarquement sur les côtes de France," dated 3 Mar. 1792, including a recommendation for a landing at Quibéron Bay, with description of that place. F. arkiv XVII, RA.

29. Klinckowström I, 19, 22–23, 161–64, 166–67; Schlitter, *Briefe*, lxi–lxiv.

30. Vivenot, *Quellen* I, 234; Schlitter, *Briefe*, lv–lvii, lxi, lxxi–lxxii; Sorel, *L'Eur. et la Rév. franç.* II, 231–64; Sorel, "La fuite."

31. Gustav III to F., 2 Sept. 1791, F. arkiv XI, RA; F. to Taube, 1 Sept. 1791, Taube arkiv II, RA; Feuillet de Conches IV, 87–90; *Dagbok* I, 118.

32. Feuillet de Conches IV, 89, 94–95; Klinckowström I, 13, 14, 16, 29–30; *Dagbok* I, 129. Cf. Schlitter, *Briefe*, xxiv, lvi–lviii.

33. Schlitter, *Briefe*, lxviii–lxix; Wandruszka, *Leopold II*, II, 367–68; Feuillet de Conches II, 228–36, 364–65; *Dagbok* I, 118; Klinckowström I, 30.

34. Feuillet de Conches IV, 87–95, 103–33; Klinckowström I, 186–87, 191; Schlitter, *Briefe*, lxxi.

35. Arnaud-Bouteloup, *Rôle politique*, 296–300; Schlitter, *Briefe*, lix–lxi, lxix; Wandruszka, *Leopold II*, II, 366; Klinckowström I, 14; II, 134; Arneth, *MAJL*, 187–98, 206–208; Vivenot, *Quellen* I, 242. On Marie-Antoinette's relations with Barnave, A. Lameth, and Duport, see Alma Söderhjelm, ed., *Marie-Antoinette et Barnave. Correspondance secrète (juillet 1791–janvier 1792)* (Paris, 1934), and her *Marie-Antoinettes stora hemlighet* (Stockholm, 1934), based on the above. The older work by O. G. de Heidenstam, *Marie-Antoinette, Fersen et Barnave. Leur correspondance* (Paris, 1913), is unreliable. Cf. Alma Söderhjelm, "Heidenstam, Barnave och Marie-Antoinette," in her *Kärlek och politik*, 183–210.

36. Feuillet de Conches IV, 91, 108, 114; Klinckowström I, 190; F. to C. A. Ehrensvärd, 25 Sept. 1791, F. arkiv III, RA. F. to father, 15 Sept. 1791, FAF arkiv IX, RA. F. arkiv XII, XIII, XIV, RA, contain from this point on numerous letters from Swedish diplomats, containing valuable information on the Revolution and the policies of the European courts in 1791–94, mostly in French.

37. Klinckowström I, 31. Cf. Arnaud-Bouteloup, *Rôle politique*, 286–88.

38. Klinckowström I, 30. Cf. Wandruszka, *Leopold II*, II, 367–69. Sophie wrote F. on 16 Oct. 1791, that Mme. de Saint-Priest, now in Stockholm, blamed Louis XVI's weakness in accepting the constitution on Marie-Antoinette, but Sophie believed this derived from her jealousy of the queen over F. F. arkiv XIII, RA.

39. Söderhjelm, *FMA*, 195–98, 210; Alma Söderhjelm, "En politisk salong i Bryssel," in her *Revolutionärer och emigranter* (Stockholm,

1918), 155–237; F. to father, 12 Oct., 4, 26 Dec. 1791, 22 Jan. 1792, FAF arkiv IX, RA.

40. Klinckowström I, 192; Arneth, *MAJL*, 187, 192, 193n., 210–11; Esterhazy, *Mémoires*, xxxiii–xxxv. Cf. Vallotton, *Marie-Antoinette et Fersen*, 249–50; Geffroy, *Gustave III*, II, 458.

41. Klinckowström I, 192–93. Marie-Antoinette seems to allude in this letter of 26 Sept. 1791, though vaguely, to the *constitutionnels*; the "papers" she mentions were probably her correspondence with Barnave, which F. acquired, evidently during his secret visit to Paris in February 1792, and which Alma Söderhjelm has published in *Marie-Antoinette et Barnave* and *Marie-Antoinettes stora hemlighet*. Cf. Arnaud-Bouteloup, *Rôle politique*, 278–79, 283. On F.'s secret correspondence with Marie-Antoinette, see Söderhjelm, *FMA*, 217; Klinckowström I, 257; II, 220. On 11 Apr. 1798, F. wrote Gustav IV Adolf for permission for the former *garde du corps*, Moustier, to settle in Sweden. Handskriftsavdelningen F. 657 b., UUB.

42. Klinckowström I, 193–95.

43. *Ibid.*, 31–32, 193–96, 202; Feuillet de Conches II, 419; Söderhjelm, *FMA*, 208; Arnaud-Bouteloup, *Rôle politique*, 268–71, 321.

44. Klinckowström I, 196, 198–200, 213, 265–70; Söderhjelm, *FMA*, 225–31; *Dagbok* I, 151.

45. Vallotton, *Marie-Antoinette et Fersen*, 225; Klinckowström I, 202; Söderhjelm, *FMA*, 221.

46. F. to Gustav III [(?) Oct.] 1791, Klinckowström I, 197–98, where it is dated "30 June 1791," an obvious mistake. F. arkiv XVII, RA, contains three copies of an anonymous, undated "Projets de déclaration commune," based on the non-validity of Louis XVI's acceptance of the constitution and following on the whole F.'s often-expressed ideas for the congress. One copy is annotated with "les changements de l'Espagne."

47. Klinckowström I, 216–17, 244; cf. F. to Taube, 18 Oct., 22, 27 Nov., 4 Dec. 1791, 1 Jan. 1792 (misdated "1793"), Taube arkive II, RA. Taube, chagrined that the opportunity had been lost to take direct action against France before the onset of winter, due to the emperor's delays and lack of funds, was prepared by late September to accept the congress as the only recourse, though Gustav III remained opposed; by late November, Taube turned against the idea, since he no longer believed it could force the emperor to act. Taube to F., 27 Sept., 18, 25 Nov. 1791, F. arkiv XIV, RA.

48. Klinckowström I, 223–25, 263, 274–75; II, 133–34; Åkeson, *Gustaf III:s förhållande*, 232. Cf. Arnaud-Bouteloup, *Rôle politique*, 319.

49. Klinckowström I, 200–201, 227.

50. *Ibid.* I, 216–17, 259–62; II, 113, 134–35, 211–15; Feuillet de Conches IV, 368; Söderhjelm, *FMA*, 254–55.

51. Klinckowström I, 222; cf. *Dagbok* I, 147. The idea that F. urge Marie-Antoinette and Louis XVI to write to Gustav III and Catherine II to keep them from abandoning them in favor of the princes was sug-

gested by Taube in his letters to F. of 18, 25 Oct., 6, 16 Dec. 1791, F. arkiv XIV, RA. Cf. Arneth, *MAJL*, 226.

52. Klinckowström I, 233–59.

53. Feuillet de Conches IV, 269–81, 290–92; Klinckowström I, 265, 271, 273; Carisien to F., 14 Jan. 1792, F. arkiv XII, RA; Arnaud-Bouteloup, *Rôle politique*, 311; Clapham, *Causes*, 124–25; Schlitter, *Briefe*, lxxxvii–xciv. F. arkiv XVII, RA, contains a copy of the letter from Louis XVI to "Sa Majesté catholique," dated 3 Dec. 1791. Lenz, in "Marie Antoinette im Kampf," 282n., points out that this is the letter wrongly addressed to "Gustav III" in Feuillet de Conches, IV, 271.

54. Klinckowström I, 206, 258.

55. *Ibid.*, 271, 308–12; Geffroy, *Gustave III*, II, 209–14; Feuillet de Conches IV, 296–303; Arneth, *MAJL*, 231–35; Arnaud-Bouteloup, *Rôle politique*, 308–10, 314–16; Clapham, *Causes*, 114–15; Schlitter, *Briefe*, lxxxvii–lxxxviii.

56. Klinckowström I, 310–12; II, 109–10, 134, 151; Feuillet de Conches IV, 375, 379–82; Åkeson, *Gustaf III:s förhållande*, 242–43; F. to Carisien, 25, 27 Dec. 1791, F. arkiv III, RA; Carisien to F., 14 Jan., 17 Feb., 10 Mar. 1792, F. arkiv XII, RA; Sorel, *L'Eur. et la Rév. franç.* II, 338–42. According to Taube, Gustav III while in Aachen in June 1791 considered proposing to Louis XVI and Marie-Antoinette that they take the Duke of Brunswick as their *premier ministre* for a few years, "for a native [Frenchman] . . . would never have the power to restore them to their former power and would be deflected by too many private interests. . . ." Taube himself approved this idea and suggested it to F. during Brunswick's invasion of France in the fall of 1792. Taube to F., 5 Oct., 9 Nov. 1792, F. arkiv XIV, RA.

57. Klinckowström II, 132; "A." to F., 9 Feb. [1792], F. arkiv XVII, RA. Cf. *Dagbok* I, 88; Åkeson, *Gustaf III:s förhållande*, 199; Engeström, *Minnen* I, 178; Feuillet de Conches V, 339–42. The basic work on this episode is G. Pallain, ed., *La mission de Talleyrand à Londres en 1792. Correspondance inédite* (Paris, 1889), which does not mention F. or Lord Auckland.

58. Klinckowström II, 1, 114–15.

59. Schlitter, *Briefe*, lxxvii–lxxviii, lxxxvii–cvii, 344; Klinckowström II, 157–58; Arneth, *MAJL*, 243–45; Feuillet de Conches V, 165–73; Söderhjelm, *FMA*, 240. Simolin had served in the 1770s as Russian minister to Stockholm, where he was notorious for his intrigues in Swedish internal affairs. Cf. Ehrensvärd, *Dagboksanteckningar* I, 21–25.

60. Klinckowström I, 274–75, 278–303; Taube to F., 20, 21–22 Dec. 1791, F. arkiv XIV, RA. Cf. Fournel, *L'événement*, 263–308, section entitled "Les projets d'évasion du roi après l'événement de Varennes." F. to C. E. Ehrensvärd, 12 Jan. 1792, F. arkiv III, RA.

61. Bouillé, *Mémoires*, 314; Klinckowström II, 146–49, 159–60.

62. Hjärne, "Gustaf III och franska revolutionen," 520–21; Söderhjelm, *FMA*, 225, 231–32.

63. Söderhjelm, *FMA*, 236.

64. Klinckowström II, 3–5. Cf. Åkeson, *Gustaf III:s förhållande*, 217.

Notes and References

As seen, F. first notified Taube of his scheme on 30 Oct. 1791; already on 18 Nov., Taube replied that a courier would be sent to F. with "the two passports" and a letter of recommendation to the queen of Portugal. F. arkiv XIV, RA.

65. Söderjhelm, *FMA*, 241–42; 247. Cf. Ch. IV, note 23 above.
66. Söderhjelm, *FMA*, 242–44; Klinckowström II, 179–83.
67. Söderhjelm, *FMA*, 242–44. On the correspondence between the queen and Barnave, see *ibid.*, 250–51; Klinckowström I, 268.
68. Söderhjelm, *FMA*, 244–47; *Dagbok* I, 167–70.
69. Klinckowström II, 179–83.
70. Söderhjelm, *FMA*, 249.
71. *Dagbok* I, 155–56; Klinckowström III, 131–32, 202–204, 211–17.
72. Klinckowström I, 27, 128; II, 2, 132; F. to Taube, 15 Jan. 1792, Taube arkiv II, RA.
73. Klinckowström I, 215–17. Cf. annex to F.'s dispatch to Gustav III, 29 Feb. 1792, "Mémoire sur les différentes manières d'opération pour le congrès," Gallica 499, RA.
74. Klinckowström I, 264; II, 211–17; *Dagbok* I, 145, 156.
75. Feuillet de Conches IV, 119, 121, 122. On the prevalence in Europe of the myth of the basic cowardice of the revolutionaries in France, see André Fugier, *La Révolution française et l'Empire napoléonien* (Paris, 1954), 41.
76. F. to father, 22 Jan. 1792, FAF arkiv IX, RA. Cf. same to C. Bildt (Vienna), 28 Mar. 1792, F. arkiv III, RA; also F. A. von Fersen to F., 30 Dec. 1791–3 Jan. 1792, F. arkiv XIII, RA.
77. F. to Gustav III, 28 June, n.d., 1790, Autografsamlingen F, KB. The second of these two letters may be dated sometime in the first half of July 1790 through F.'s letter to Taube of 16 July 1790, Taube arkiv II, RA. Klinckowström I, 84. Anonymous memorandum, "Notions secrètes sur la Propagande de Hollande," dated 6 Sept. 1791, F. arkiv XVII, RA, evidently deriving from the same anonymous source as the similar report, dated The Hague, 30 Apr. 1791, in Great Britain, Historical Manuscripts Commission, *The Manuscripts of J. B. Fortescue Preserved at Dropmore*, 10 vol. (London, 1892–1927) [henceforth abbreviated *Dropmore Papers*], II, 69–70. Cf. Clapham, *Causes*, 36–37. Marie-Antoinette similarly played heavily on the theme of the spread of revolutionary propaganda in attempts to gain support from Leopold II. See Arnaud-Bouteloup, *Rôle politique*, 236–37.
78. *Dagbok* I, 88; Klinckowström II, 116–17, 135, 144, 160, 210–11.
79. *Dagbok* I, 181–82; Klinckowström II, 202, 204–205. Cf. Carisien to F., 10 March 1792, F. arkiv XII, RA, on reactions in Berlin to Leopold's death, including rumors of poisoning.
80. Klinckowström I, 8, 213–14, 262; II, 185, 198–201; *Dagbok* I, 160; F. to Taube, 23 Nov. 1791, 25 Jan., 7 Mar., 1 Apr. 1792, Taube arkiv II, RA.
81. See Arneth, *MAJL*, 198–203, 242, 282–87; Feuillet de Conches III, 248–49; Schlitter, *Briefe*, xviii–xix, xcvii–xcviii; Arnaud-Bouteloup, *Rôle politique*, 297–99; Wandruszka, *Leopold II*, II, 360–62, 367–69.

82. *Dagbok* I, 120–21, 127–28. Cf. Wandruszka, *Leopold II*, II, 371–81; Ernst Wangermann, *From Joseph II to the Jacobin Trials* (Oxford, 1959), 56–105.

83. Klinckowström II, 197–98; Feuillet de Conches V, 281–82; Schlitter, *Briefe*, ci–cv, 245, 251, 270–71, 344–45. See G. Bellissent, "Le comte de Fersen, créancier du roi," *Revue historique de la Révolution française* XV (1923), 363–66, on the cracking of F.'s cipher.

CHAPTER VII

1. On the assassination of Gustav III, see especially Hennings, *Gustav III*, 303–29; Lolo Krusius-Ahrenberg, *Tyrannmördaren C. F. Ehrensvärd* (Stockholm, 1947); R. Nisbet Bain, "The Assassination of Gustavus III of Sweden," *English Historical Review*, 1887, 543–52.

2. Taube to F., 4 May 1792, F. arkiv XIV, RA; Söderhjelms, *SOFR*, II, 14, 25–29.

3. *Dagbok* I, 159–60, 182–84, 188–91; F. A. von Fersen to F., 20, 27, 30 Mar. 1792, F. arkiv XIII, RA; Taube to F., 20, 29 Mar. 1792, F. arkiv XIV; F. to father, 22 Jan., 18 Mar. 1792, FAF arkiv IX, RA; same to Taube, 25 Jan., 18 Mar., 1, 8, 10 Apr. 1792, Taube arkiv II, RA.

4. Duke Karl of Södermanland to F. (and Oxenstierna), 10 Apr. 1792, F. arkiv III, RA; Klinckowström II, 251; C. G. Oxenstierna to F., F. arkiv XIII, RA; Söderhjelm, *SOFR* II, 21–22.

5. Söderhjelm, *FMA*, 225.

6. Vallotton, *Marie-Antoinette et Fersen*, 279; Taube to F., 23, 29 Mar., 3 Apr. 1792, F. arkiv XIV, RA; Sophie to F., 3 Apr. 1792, F. arkiv XIII, RA.

7. *Dagbok* I, 190; cf. Söderhjelm, *FMA*, 257. Already in his letter of 20 Mar. 1792, describing the assassination, F. A. von Fersen feels F.'s "present role" would soon end and inquires about his future plans. Vallotton, *Marie-Antoinette et Fersen*, 279.

8. F. to Duke Karl, 18, 22 Apr. 1792, Gallica 499, RA; same to same, 6, 20 May 1792, F. arkiv I, RA; Duke Karl to F., 3 Apr., 1, 4, 18, 21, 26 May 1792, F. arkiv XI, RA; F.'s accreditation as Swedish minister to Louis XVI, dated 29 Mar. 1792, Lövstad arkiv XII; F. to father, 20 May 1792, FAF arkiv IX, RA; same to Taube, 22 Apr., 2, 6 May 1792, Taube arkiv II, RA; Klinckowström II, 242–43; *Dagbok* I, 191, 205. Taube and Sophie also informed F. of the Duke's assurances of good-will. Sophie to F., 10 Apr. 1792, F. arkiv XIII, RA; Taube to F., 3 Apr., 4, 11 May, 1 June 1792, F. arkiv XIV, RA. On 25 July 1792, however, Taube wrote that "one must walk softly with him and not show him any discontent or [ill] humor. . . ." *Ibid.*

9. See Staf, *Polisväsendet*, 181–97; Krusius-Ahrenberg, *C. F. Ehrensvärd*; Stig Jägerskiöld, "Tyrannmord och motståndsrätt," *Scandia* (1962), 113–66.

10. Taube wished to retire because of poor health, discouragement, and because "I see too many regicides in the world I live in to be able

to get along well there." Taube to F., 29 Mar., 3, 17, 27 Apr., 1, 11, 22 May 1792, F. arkiv XIV, RA. Cf. Söderhjelm *SOFR* II, 66–68.

11. F. to Taube, 25 Jan. 1792, Taube arkiv II, RA; *Dropmore Papers* V, 518–21. On 18 Oct. 1791, Taube wrote F., "I have just obtained Staël's recall, at first through a leave of three months." F. arkiv XIV, RA. On 18 Nov. 1791, Taube claimed that Staël had several times proposed to Gustav III "subsidies from the [National] Assembly." *Ibid.*

12. *HEC* III, 333–34, 362–63, 375–78, 392, 485–87; Söderhjelm, *SOFR* I, 301; II, 64–65; Söderhjelm, *FMA*, 248; F. A. von Fersen to F., 5 Oct., 30 Dec. 1791–3 Jan. 1792, n.d. 1792, F. arkiv XIII, RA; Sophie to F., 15 Dec. 1791, *ibid.*; Taube to F., 27 Sept. 1791, 18 July 1792, F. arkiv XIV, RA.

13. *HEC* IV, 6–7.

14. F. to Duke Karl, 9 May 1792, Gallica 499, RA; F. to Taube, 9 May 1792, Taube arkiv II, RA; Taube to F., 15, 25 May, 12 July 1792, F. arkiv XIV, RA; Duke Karl to F., 18, 25 May 1792, F. arkiv I, RA; Söderhjelm, *SOFR* II, 29–31, 41–42. Cf. S. J. Boëthius, "Gustaf IV Adolfs förmyndareregering och den franska revolutionen," parts I–II, *Historisk tidskrift* (1888) and III–IV, *ibid.*, (1889), I, 102, 104; Sten Carlsson, *Den svenska utrikespolitikens historia*, III:1, *1792–1810* (Stockholm, 1954), 25–26.

15. Taube to F., 15 May, 11 July 1792, F. arkiv XIV, RA; F. to Taube, 1 July 1792, Taube arkiv II, RA; F. to Sophie, 22 July, Lövstad arkiv VII.

16. Söderhjelm, *SOFR* II, 66–68.

17. Duke Karl to F., 1 May, 26 June 1792, F. arkiv XI, RA; Duke Karl to J. G. Oxenstierna (Coblenz), 26 June 1792, F. arkiv XVII, RA; F. to Duke Karl, 15 July 1792, Gallica 499, RA; Taube to F., 13, 17, 27 Apr. 25, 29 May, 1, 5, 22, 26, June, 12, 18 July 1792, F. arkiv XIV, RA; F. to Taube, 30 May, 1 July 1792, Taube arkiv II, RA; F. to A. I. Silfversparre, 5 Sept. 1792, F. arkiv III, RA; Klinckowström II, 290–92, 310–13; *Dagbok* I, 203. On the position of Spain, see Chaumié, *L'Espagne et la France*, 77, 91–95.

18. Klinckowström II, 246–47, 324.

19. *Ibid.*, 174–75, 265–69, 280, 284, 286, 296–98, 300–302, 305, 314–15, 328, 334–35, 375, 380, 382–84. Cf. F.'s dispatch, 10 June 1792, Gallica 499, RA; F. to Taube, 24 June 1792, Taube arkiv II, RA.

20. *Dagbok* I, 210. Sophie speaks of the close connection between Bonde, Reuterholm, L. von Engeström, and Staël in her letter to F. on 14 Aug. 1792. F. arkiv XIII, RA. Taube warns of the same clique, and behind them, the young king's governor, Nils Rosén von Rosenstein. Taube to F., 18 Nov. 1791, 1, 8 Aug., 9 Nov. 1792, F. arkiv XIV, RA. In a fragmentary letter dated 17 Apr., presumably 1793, Taube considers Engeström and Rosenstein the "chiefs" of the "Jacobins" in Sweden and the protectors of the "cowardly and traitorous Azor [Staël]," and that it is necessary "that these three monsters be gotten rid of and even destroyed for the tranquility of this country. . . ." *Ibid.*

21. Klinckowström II, 220–21, 230–32, 242–43.

22. *Ibid.*, 220, 231. Cf. Söderhjelm, *FMA*, 259–60.

23. Klinckowström I, 258; F. to Gustav III, 14 Mar. 1792, with enclosure, Limon to Gustav III, 5 Mar. 1792, Gallica 499, RA; *Dagbok* I, 200. For sources on Limon, see my "Origins of the Brunswick Manifesto," 159n.

24. On the use of threatening manifestos in the eighteenth century and for general sources for the following discussion, see my "Origins of the Brunswick Manifesto," 146–51; also Ch. VI, Section 3, above.

25. Daudet, *Histoire de l'émigration* I, 190–92; Klinckowström II, 315; *Dagbok* I, 213–14. On Austrian and Prussian policy, my "Origins of the Brunswick Manifesto" makes use of unpublished documents from the Haus-, Hof- und Staatsarchiv in Vienna and the Prussian Geheimes Staatsarchiv, presently at the Deutsches Zentralarchiv, Abteilung Merseburg (East Germany).

26. Arneth, *MAJL*, 263–65; Klinckowström II, 377; Feuillet de Conches VI, 191, 205–206.

27. Klinckowström II, 21–22.

28. *Ibid.*, 329. Some mistrust still remained between F. and Mercy, who believed F. to be behind Marie-Antoinette's bitterness toward Leopold II. Cf. Jules Flammermont, *Négotiations secrètes de Louis XVI et du baron de Breteuil avec la cour de Berlin, décembre 1791–juillet 1792* (Paris, 1885), 20. F. meanwhile rightly suspected Mercy of favoring a "dismemberment" of France. See F. to Taube, 23 May 1792, Taube arkiv II, RA; my "Origins of the Brunswick Manifesto," 166.

29. F.'s dispatch, 21 June 1792, Gallica 499, RA; Klinckowström II, 21, 316–17, 332–33; F. to Taube, 13 June 1792, Taube arkiv II, RA.

30. Klinckowström II, 24–25, 336–39; *Dagbok* I, 216n. Regarding F.'s suspicions of Austrian lack of enthusiasm for the counterrevolution as opposed to Prussian zeal for it, see Carisien to F., 24 Mar., 3, 19 Apr., 23 June 1792, F. arkiv XII, RA; F.'s dispatches, 10, 24 June, 29 July 1792, Gallica 499, RA; F. to Taube, 10 June 1792, Taube arkive II, RA; same to A. I. Silfversparre, 24 July 1792, F. arkiv III, RA; same to Carisien, 2 Aug. 1792, *ibid.* It appears that Carisien in Berlin was largely responsible for encouraging these suspicions, and that he in turn reflected those of Count Friedrich von der Schulenburg, the Prussian foreign minister.

31. See my "Origins of the Brunswick Manifesto," 162–64. On Mallet du Pan's political philosophy, see Godechot, *Contre-révolution*, 75–92.

32. Klinckowström II, 6; F. to A. I. Silfversparre, 27 July 1792, F. arkiv III, RA. Cf. Vivenot, *Quellen* I, 432; Comte de Montlosier, *Souvenirs d'un émigré, 1791–98*, ed., Comte de Larouzière-Montlosier & Ernest d'Hauterive (Paris, 1951), 54.

33. Klinckowström II, 275–76, 295, 300–303, 305–306; F. to Taube, 23 May 1792, Taube arkiv II, RA; *Dagbok* I, 213–14. Cf. my "Origins of the Brunswick Manifesto," 164.

34. F. as well as the émigrés was fearful that the *constitutionnels* might persuade the allies, especially the Austrians, to accept a negotiated peace, which would permit them to remove the royal family to the

Midi. Klinckowström II, 24, 298–99. 315, 321, 323, 326–28, 330–31. On 18 July 1792, F. did, however, write to Marie-Antoinette that the émigré princes were spreading the "false" rumor that the king of France, "misled" by the "*constitutionnels*," was seeking a negotiated peace. *Ibid.*, 328. Cf. F.'s dispatches, 9 May, 21, 24 June 1792, Gallica 499, RA; F. to Stedingk, 16 July 1792, F. arkiv III, RA; "Note des Princes envoyée à toutes les puissances," 10 July 1792, F. arkiv XVII, RA. Cf. Daudet, *Histoire de l'émigration* I, 198–99.

35. Klinckowström II, 336–37.

36. Montlosier, *Souvenirs*, 90; Daudet, *Histoire de l'émigration* I, 199; Klinckowström II, 341; F. to Taube, 1 Aug. 1792, Taube arkiv II, RA. A. Sorel, in *L'Eur. et le Rév. franç.*, II, 509, mistakenly assumed that F. and Calonne together had charged Limon with his task "in conformity with their common views." Godechot, *Contre-révolution*, 176–77, claims that Limon worked for the émigrés and that he was assisted by Mirabeau's former secretary, Pellenc.

37. For the Brunswick Manifesto, see, for instance, J. M. Thompson, *French Revolutionary Documents 1789–94* (Oxford, 1933). Regarding a number of other declarations to the French from various parties which accompanied or followed the Brunswick Manifesto, see my "Origins of the Brunswick Manifesto," 154–56, 160–61.

38. My "Origins of the Brunswick Manifesto," 164–65.

39. *Ibid.*, 165–69.

40. Klinckowström II, 336–37, 342; F.'s dispatch, 29 July, Gallica 499, RA; F. to father, 29 July 1792, FAF arkiv IX, RA; F. arkiv X:1, RA; Saint-Priest, *Mémoires* II, 143–44.

41. Klinckowström II, 341; Sophie to F., 24 Aug. 1792, F. arkiv XIII, RA.

41a. Cf. Lenz, "Marie Antoinette im Kampf," 301–302.

42. Cf. F. to father, 19 Sept., 14 Oct., 8, 22 Nov., 24 Dec. 1792, FAF arkiv IX, RA; F. arkiv X, RA.

43. *Dagbok* I, 219–20; cf. Klinckowström II, 27–29, 344–45, 349–51. For F.'s reaction to the storming of the Tuileries, see Söderhjelm, *FMA*, 269.

44. Klinckowström II, 31, 350–52.

45. *Ibid.*, 34–37; F. to Sparre, 30 Sept. 1792, Gallica 499, RA.

46. Klinckowström II, 48–49, 391.

47. *Dagbok* I, 268, 278–79, 283, 286; Klinckowström II, 403–404; F. to Taube, 19 Mar. 1793, Taube arkiv III, RA.

48. *Dagbok* I, 294, 301–302; cf. Klinckowström II, 64–65.

49. F. to Breteuil, 31 Aug., 12 Sept. 1792, F. arkiv III, RA; Söderhjelm, *FMA*, 271, 279–80, 300; cf. Klinckowström II, 267–68.

50. Klinckowström II, 29–30, 32–33.

51. *Ibid.*, 358–60, 368–69. Acloque commanded a division of the Paris National Guard, which La Fayette in June 1792 had hoped to use against the Jacobins. See A. Mathiez, *La Révolution française*, 3 vol. (Paris, 1922–27), I, 208.

442   COUNT HANS AXEL VON FERSEN

52. Klinckowström II, 24, 43, 321, 323, 326, 336, 357; *Dagbok* II, 60.

53. *Dagbok* I, 224–25, 235–36, 237, 286–88, 290–91; Klinckowström II, 18, 302, 323, 365, 378–79.

54. *Dagbok* I, 250–52, 255–57, 264–65, 266, 276, 319; Klinckowström II, 51–55, 391–95; F. to Taube, 10 Oct. 1792, Taube arkiv II, RA; same to Sparre, 10 Oct. 1792, Gallica 499, RA.

55. F. to Taube, 22 Jan. 1793, Taube arkiv III, RA. Sparre's instruction was dated 27 Nov. 1792. Cf. F. to Sparre, 5 Feb. 1793, Gallica 500, RA.

56. F. to Taube, 6 June 1792, Taube arkiv II, RA; same to same, 8 Jan. 1793, *ibid.* III; same to same, 12 Feb. 1793, F. arkiv I, RA; F. to Sparre, 16 Sept. 1792, F. arkiv III, RA; same to same, 12 Feb. 1793, F. arkiv I, RA; same to same, 15 Dec. 1793, Gallica 500, RA; same to Duke Karl, 12 Feb. 1793, F. arkiv I, RA; note, same to same, 6 Apr. 1793, Gallica 500, RA. Cf. letters to unidentified persons dated 16, 24 Dec. 1792, relative to reimbursement of expenses, Ericsbergsarkivet. Brevskrivare: Fersen, Hans Axel von, RA.

57. F. to Sparre, 5 Feb., 15 Mar. 1793, Gallica 500, RA; same to same, 15 May, 16 June, 7 July 1793, F. arkiv III, RA; *Dagbok* I, 303; Taube to F., 18 Oct. 1791, 8 Aug. 1792, F. arkiv XIV, RA; Carl Brelin's dispatches, 1792, Gallica 499, RA; A. Dalman's dispatches, 1792, *ibid.*; same for 1793, Gallica 500, RA; C. F. Reutersvärd's dispatches, 1793–94, *ibid.*

58. F. to Taube, 15 July, 12 Aug., 1 Nov. 1792, Taube arkiv II, RA; same to same, 15 Mar. 1793, Taube arkiv III, RA; F. to Sparre, 31 Oct. 1792, 12 Apr. 1793, F. arkiv III, RA; same to same, 5 Feb. 1793 (2 letters), Gallica 500, RA; F. to Duke Karl, 31 Oct. 1792, Gallica 499, RA; Sophie to F., 23 Nov. 1792, F. arkiv XIII, RA; Taube to F., 28 Nov. 1792, F. arkiv XIV, RA. F.'s incriminating letter to Silfversparre has not been located, but it apparently suggested that F. and his friends were seeking to bypass the *rikskansler* and deal directly with the duke. Cf. Taube to F., 8 Aug. 1792, *ibid.*; F. to Taube, 1 Nov. 1792, Taube arkiv II, RA.

59. Söderhjelm, *FMA*, 271, 274–83; F. to father, 27 Jan. 1793, FAF arkiv IX, RA.

60. F. to Taube, 22 Jan. 1793, Taube arkiv III, RA; Klinckowström II, 364–65.

61. Klinckowström II, 223; Söderhjelm, *SOFR* II, 56–57.

62. F. to Taube, 1 Jan., 14, 15, 19, 22 Mar. 1793, Taube arkiv III, RA; same to Duke Karl, 14 Mar. 1793, F. arkiv I, RA; *Dagbok* I, 303–304. Sweden then had a minister in London; Duke Karl apparently considered giving F. the rank of ambassador.

63. Söderhjelm, *SOFR* II, 98; F. to Taube, 15 July 1792, Taube arkiv II, RA; F. to A. I. Silfversparre, 15, 27 July, 5 Aug. 1792, F. arkiv III, RA; same to same, 9 Aug. 1792, Gallica 499, RA; F.'s dispatch 28 July 1793, Gallica 500, RA. In about April 1793, Taube wrote in an undated fragment to F., that he wished F. could arrange to have the papers of

"that traitor"—obviously Staël—seized, which would certainly contain "the treaty which he and Verninac proposed," and which Taube hoped Staël could be forced to deny publicly. F. arkiv XIV, RA.

64. F. to Taube, 12 Aug. 1792, Taube arkiv II, RA.

65. F. to Taube, 7 July 1793, Taube arkiv III, RA.

66. "Mémoire de Mr. Dumourier [sic] au Roi de Prusse," annex to F.'s dispatch, 17 Oct. 1792, Gallica 499, RA. A copy in F. arkiv XVII, RA, is dated in F.'s hand, 16 Oct. 1792. F.'s dispatch, 7 Nov. 1792, Gallica 499, RA; Brelin to Duke Karl, 12 Dec. 1792, *ibid.* In this letter, Brelin confirms F.'s suspicions of his political views, when he tells the duke that in his view, France offers "the only, the most effective means" for Sweden to acquire subsidies.

67. Klinckowström II, 63, 66. Cf. F. to Taube, 22 Mar. 1792, Taube arkiv III, RA.

68. *Dagbok* I, 310, 313; cf. Klinckowström II, 66–67.

69. Klinckowström II, 67.

70. F. to Duke Karl, 5 Apr. 1793, Gallica 500, RA; cf. F.'s bulletins, 2, 9 Apr. 1793, *ibid.*; Söderhjelm, *FMA*, 289; Ernest Daudet, "Un drame d'amour à la cour de Suède, 1784–95," *Revue des Deux Mondes* X (1912), 690–91. Cf. Klinckowström II, 415–16.

71. Engeström, *Minnen* I, 206.

72. F. to Sparre, 29 Apr. 1793, Gallica 500, RA; Daudet, "Drame d'amour," 691. Cf. Söderhjelm, *SOFR* II, 301.

73. F. to Marie-Antoinette, 8 April 1793, Klinckowström II, 408–10. Marie-Antoinette naturally never received this letter. Cf. *ibid.*, 67.

74. Cf. Daudet, "Drame d'amour," 679.

75. Klinckowström II, 412–14, 418–20; F. to Duke Karl, 29 Apr. 1793, Gallica 500, RA.

76. Klinckowström II, 67–68, 416–17; F.'s bulletin, 9 Apr. 1793, Gallica 500, RA; F. to Sparre, 29 Apr. 1793, *ibid.*; F. to Taube, 29, 30 Apr., 12, 19 May 1793, Taube arkiv III, RA; Söderhjelm, *FMA*, 291.

77. Duke Karl to F., 28 May 1793, F. arkiv XI, RA; Klinckowström II, 422; F. to Sparre, 12 May, 26 June 1793, Gallica 500, RA; F. to Duke Karl, 21 July 1793, *ibid.*; *Dagbok* I, 343; F. to G. M. Armfelt, 19 July 1793, Armfeltska samlingen III, RA. Cf. Carlsson, *SUPH* II:2, 32.

78. *Dagbok* I, 317–18; cf. F. to Taube, 23 Apr. 1793, Taube arkiv III, RA.

79. Klinckowström II, 71, 417.

80. Cf. Diary, 9 Oct. 1793, Söderhjelm, *FMA*, 306, according to which the captured French commissioner, Drouet, assured Baron Franz von Metternich that "if it had been proposed in time, they would have given up the queen and her family for the 4 commissioners delivered by Dumouriez; that that was decided. . . ." Cf. *ibid.*, 294; Kunstler, *Fersen et son secret*, 279–81, 289; Gaulot, *Ami de la reine*, 342, 344.

81. *Dagbok* I, 351–52.

82. *Ibid.*, 353–59; cf. Klinckowström II, 77–81, 425; F. to Taube, 23 Apr. 1793, Taube arkiv III, RA; same to Armfelt, 6 Aug. 1793, Armfeltska samlingen III, RA.

83. Söderhjelm, *FMA*, 297. F. arkiv XVII, RA, contains a copy of the "Acte d'accusation et interrogation de Marie-Antoinette d'Autriche, ci-devant reine de France." For F.'s fears and anguish over the royal family, see Söderhjelm, *FMA*, 277–78, 281–82, 296–98, 299, 303.

84. Söderhjelm, *FMA*, 297–99; *Dagbok* I, 365; cf. F. to Armfelt, 16 Aug. [1793], Armfeltska samlingen III, RA; F. to Taube, 17 Nov. 1793, Taube arkiv III, RA. Cf. Mercy's correspondence with Coburg and Thugut on this idea. Vallotton, *Marie-Antoinette et Fersen*, 347–50.

85. Klinckowström II, 86–87.

86. *Dagbok* I, 367, 371–73; cf. Klinckowström II, 87–91. It is possible that "Ribbes," who is not more closely identified, was Raimond Ribes, a former deputy in the Legislative Assembly, who had had secret dealings with Louis XVI in 1792, or someone related to him. Cf. Saul K. Padover, *The Life and Death of Louis XVI* (New York, 1963), 257–58.

87. *Dagbok* I, 391, 397; Söderhjelm, *FMA*, 303.

88. *Dagbok* I, 397, 407–409, 413–15; F. to Taube, 31 Oct. 1793, Taube arkiv III, RA; Geffroy, "Lettres," 96–97.

89. Söderhjelm, *FMA*, 307, 312. After all the bitterness of their relationship during the revolutionary years, F.'s feelings for Staël still remained curiously ambivalent. "I have never seen a man more generally hated and despised," he wrote Sophie on 30 Mar. 1794. "I pity him, for he was basically good and honest, but he is weak and has been spoiled by those around him and by his wife, who has involved him in actions that do him little honor. Weakness is the worst of all faults, and he has all of them." Lövstad arkiv VII.

90. *Dagbok* I, 401–406; cf. Söderhjelm, *FMA*, 303–306.

91. Söderhjelm, *FMA*, 309–14.

92. *Dagbok* I, 409; F. to Duke Karl, 24 Nov. 1793, F. arkiv I, RA; F. to Taube, 15 Nov. 1793, Taube arkiv III, RA. F.'s last official bulletin was dated 18 Aug. 1794, though none had been sent before that since 11 May 1794. Gallica 500, RA.

CHAPTER VIII

1. Söderhjelm, *FMA*, 314, 322–23, 326–27, 335, 340; F. to Taube, 24 [doubtless Jan. 1794], Taube arkiv II, RA. Cf. Château de Versailles, *Marie-Antoinette, archiduchesse, dauphine et reine* [exhibition catalog], 16 mai–2 novembre 1955 (Paris, 1955), 274.

2. On Craufurd and Sullivan, see Dard, *Rival de Fersen*, 13–30; Armand Praviel, "La maîtresse de Fersen: variété inédite," *Les œuvres libres*, vol. 166 (1935), 207–60; Hastier, "Baronne de Korff," 629–30.

3. Söderhjelm, *FMA*, 180–81, 196–98; *Dagbok* I, 435; III, 300, 321. Dard's details on Craufurd and Sullivan before 1783, in *Rival de Fersen*, are preferable to Söderhjelm's, in *FMA*, 195–98, which differ somewhat. F.'s letter register, F. arkiv X, RA, lists hundreds of letters to Eleanore, many in response to letters from her, which he cites by date. Söderhjelm, *ibid.*, 198, states that her letters to him were long preserved privately in Sweden but were finally burned "out of respect for Fersen's memory."

Considering her delicate situation with Craufurd, Eleanore probably destroyed most of F.'s letters to her without delay. Strömberg, in *Mänskligt högvilt*, 41, claims to have located a portrait of Eleanore at the Duc de Gramont's chateau of Mortefontaine.

4. The whole long course of this relationship is given in detail, from June 1791 on, in F.'s diary, *Dagbok* I–III, *passim*. Cf. Söderhjelm, *FMA*; Kunstler, *Fersen et son secret*; Vallotton, *Marie-Antoinette et Fersen*; and Dard, *Rival de Fersen*. It is also summarized in Söderhjelm, *Revolutionärer och emigranter*, 155–237. Cf. Craufurd to F., 13 Aug. 1795, F. arkiv XII, RA.

5. Dard, *Rival de Fersen*, 6–8, 27, 30, 32–36; Söderhejlm, *FMA*, 232, 282, 303; *Dagbok* II, 204. In later years, F. continued to lament the loss of Marie-Antoinette and of Gustav III, who he remained convinced could have saved her. Cf. F. to Taube, 20 June 1792, Taube arkiv II, RA; same to same, 17 Nov. 1793, 16 Oct. 1795, Taube arkiv III, RA; same to Sophie, 24 Oct. 1797, Lövstad arkiv VIII.

6. Söderhjelm, *FMA*, 174, 308–309; Bimbinet, *Fuite* II, 136; Engeström, *Minnen*, II, 21–22.

7. See for instance *Dagbok* I, 241–42, 277, 282–83, 303, 359–60, 398, 409, 415–16, 424, 435; II, 19, 57–58, 144, 181; Söderhjelm, *FMA*, 323–24.

8. Söderhjelm, *FMA*, 315; cf. *Dagbok* I, 433.

9. F. to Taube, 24 Feb. 1794, Taube arkiv III, RA; *Dagbok* II, 40–41, 356; F.'s accounts, 1792–94, F. arkiv XXII, RA.

10. Söderhjelm, *FMA*, 308–309, 316–17; *Dagbok* I, 439; II, 19, 38.

11. *Dagbok* II, 16; F. to Taube, 8 Jan. 1794, Taube arkiv III, RA. Söderhjelm's translation of this letter, *Dagbok* II, 16n., is poor; she gives the figure of *300,000 écus*, which F. had to repay Mme. von Korff. One *écu* equaled 3 *livres*. Cf. Thompson, *French Revolution*, viii. Mme. von Korff and her mother had lent close to 300,000 *livres*.

12. Karmin, "Trésor," 122; Söderhjelm, *FMA*, 325–26.

13. Söderhjelm, *FMA*, 325–26; Karmin, "Trésor," 123–26. Cf. Hastier, "Baronne de Korff," 538–39.

14. *Dagbok* II, 55, 62, 71, 74; cf. Söderhjelm, *FMA*, 328; F. to Taube, 15 Mar., n.d. [18 June] 1794, Taube arkiv III, RA.

15. *Dagbok* II, 98, 103–106, 110–11, 144, 164, 171, 206, 294, 321.

16. Söderhjelm, *FMA*, 316–17.

17. *Dagbok* II, 74, 78, 90, 114, 123, 127, 144, 177, 181; F. to Sophie, 5 Apr., 27 [Apr.], 11, 14 [May 1794], Lövstad arkiv VII.

18. *Dagbok* II, 191–92.

19. Söderhjelm, *SOFR* II, 216–17. On 24 July 1792, *Rikskansler* Fredrik Sparre had written to F., "After the many hard blows the fatherland has suffered, there is now H.R.H. the Duke of Södermanland's daily care to heal its wounds, introduce order, and through an exact justice to return unity to the divided spirits." *Ibid.*, 217–18.

20. Tegnér, *Armfelt* II, 84; *Dagbok* I, 246–50, 255, 268; F. to Taube, 1 Nov. 1792, Taube arkiv II, RA. Cf. Söderhjelm, *Gustaf III:s syskon*, 52–53.

446 COUNT HANS AXEL VON FERSEN

21. On the Armfelt Conspiracy, see especially Tegnér, *Armfelt* II; J. A. Ehrenström, *Statsrådet Johan Albert Ehrenströms efterlemnade historiska anteckningar*, ed. S. J. Boëthius, 2 vol. (Stockholm, 1883), I–II; Staf, *Polisväsendet*, 243–64. On 26 Jan. 1794, F. wrote Taube that Duke Karl would be "lost" if he were weak enough to allow the convening of the estates. Taube arkiv III, RA. While the Gustavians feared a Riksdag would usher in a revolution, many of their opponents hoped it might turn into a constituent body. See Martin Nylund, *G. A. Reuterholm under förmyndaretiden 1792–1796* (Stockholm, 1917), 31.

22. *Dagbok* II, 16, 19, 25–26, 34; F. to Sophie, 2 Feb. 1794, Lövstad arkiv VII; F. to Taube, 29 Jan. 1794, Taube arkiv III, RA. Cf. Armfelt to F., 4 Mar. 1794, F. arkiv XII, RA, in which Armfelt protests his "horror" for "all that may be called conspiracy." Cf. Tegnér, in *Armfelt* II, 246, who takes F.'s letter to Armfelt to show that F. was convinced of Armfelt's innocence.

23. F. to Duke Karl, 21 Jan. 1794, Gallica 500, RA; cf. *Dagbok* II, 16n.; F. to Taube, 8, 26, 29 Jan. 1794, Taube arkiv III, RA; Söderhjelm, *SOFR* II, 214; Ehrenström, *Hist. anteckn.*, I, 450–52, 467–71, 487–94; II, 146–47.

24. *Dagbok* II, 53–55; F. to Sophie, 2 Feb. 1794, Lövstad arkiv VII. F. to Sparre, 20, 23 Mar. 1794, Gallica 500, RA, in which F. reports preparing and publishing in Brussels journals the Swedish government decrees against the Armfelt conspirators.

25. *Dagbok* II, 68, 71.

26. *Ibid.*, 78; cf. F. to Sparre, 18 May 1794, Gallica 500, RA.

27. F. to Armfelt, 17 May, 14 June, 19 July, 16 Aug. 1793, Armfeltska samlingen III, RA; cf. Handskriftsavdelningen F 647 e., UUB. Tegnér, *Armfelt* II, 218, gives Reuterholm samlingen, vol. 57 [RA] as its source for this correspondence. Cf. *Dagbok* I, 305, 337, 369, 429, 434, 439.

28. *Dagbok* II, 114; Tegnér, *Armfelt* II, 197; *HEC* IV, 142–43.

29. Tegnér, *Armfelt* II, 297; cf. F. to Sparre, 18 May, 18 Aug. 1794, Gallica 500 RA; *Dagbok* I, 332, 434, 439; II, 55–56, 114; Söderhjelm, *Gustaf III:s syskon*, 51–52.

30. F. to Taube, n.d., Taube arkiv III, RA (according to F. arkiv X, RA, apparently dated 22 June 1794); same to same, 6 July 1794, *ibid.*; F. to Reuterholm, 9 July 1794, Reuterholm samlingen VIII, RA; F. to Sparre, 9 July 1794, F. arkiv III, RA; same to same, 18 Aug. 1794, Gallica 500, RA; F. to Sophie, 11 Aug. 1794, Lövstad arkiv VII; Sophie to F., 20 June 1794, F. arkiv XIII, RA; *Dagbok* II, 118–19, 142.

31. *Dagbok* II, 176; F. to Taube, n.d. [Presumably 15 Sept. 1794], Taube arkiv III, RA.

32. *Dagbok* II, 119, 204, 206, 208, 209, 218–19.

33. *Ibid.*, 218–19.

34. *Ibid.*, 229, 236.

35. *Ibid.*, 239, 385.

36. F. to Taube, 15 Dec. 1795, Taube arkiv III, RA. Cf. same to same, 22 Nov. 1796, *ibid.*, in which F. speaks of having requested further leave from Swedish service for reasons of health and personal affairs.

Copies of many of F.'s and Taube's letters to each other are preserved in Reuterholm samlingen, RA.

37. *Dagbok* II, 56.

38. *Dagbok* I, 426; cf. F. to Sophie, 12 Mar. 1793, Lövstad arkiv VII.

39. *Dagbok* II, 214; cf. *ibid.*, 228.

40. *Ibid.*, 263–64.

41. *Ibid.*, 207, 236, 273, 321–22; F. to Taube, 9 Dec. 1795, Taube arkiv III, RA. Cf. Gustav IV Adolf to F., 17 June 1792, F. arkiv XI, RA, in which the young king assures F. that if he has lost a friend and protector in Gustav III, he will find another in his son.

42. *Dagbok* II, 191.

43. *Ibid.*, 212–13.

44. *Ibid.*, 218, 254.

45. *Ibid.*, 234.

46. *Ibid.*, 207, 210.

47. *Ibid.*, 210; cf. *ibid.*, 211, 213, 225.

48. *Ibid.*, 324.

49. *Ibid.*, 277–78; cf. Söderhjelm, *SOFR* II, 268–73. Fredrik Axel was himself somewhat skeptical over his appointment to the Academy and wrote of Gustav III's reign, "Sweden had never been so rich in academies and so poor in educated men." FAF, *HS* VI, 67–68.

50. *Dagbok* II, 283, 285; cf. *ibid.*, 278–87.

51. *Ibid.*, 281.

52. *Ibid.*, 60–61, 64–65, 68, 69, 165.

53. *Ibid.*, 261, 290, 293, 303, 322, 332.

54. *Ibid.*, 282, 329; Boëthius, "Förmyndareregering," III, 31–33.

55. Söderhjelm, *FMA*, 332–34; *Dagbok* II, 218, 232, 256, 262–63, 266, 270–71, 295–96, 298–300, 304–305, 308, 312–16, 318.

56. Söderhjelm, *FMA*, 191, 332; Söderhjelm in *Dagbok* II, 207n., 212n.; F. arkiv X, RA; *HEC* IV, 272–77. The duchess makes no allusion to this affair in her diary.

57. *Dagbok* II, 207, 212, 223–25, 265, 275–76, 286, 288, 293, 305, 313, 318–19, 322–23, 338–40; cf. Söderhjelm, *FMA*, 335; Söderhjelm, *Gustaf III:s syskon*, 27–29, 51, 116, 130–31.

58. *Dagbok* II, 203–351, *passim.*; see for instance, 209–10, 213, 225, 227, 231, 233, 237, 251, 287–88, 304, 327; cf. Söderhjelm, *FMA*, 330–38.

59. Söderhjelm, *FMA*, 333.

60. Cf. Torsten Fogelqvist, "Drottningens vän" in his *Typer och tänkesätt* (Stockholm, 197), 244–54; Holmberg, "Riddare av det förgångna"; Wahlström, "A Queen's Cavalier."

61. *Dagbok* II, 204, 333, 340, 342–46; F. to Sophie, 23 Aug. 1796, Lövstad arkiv VIII; same to Taube, 13 Aug. 1796, Taube arkiv III, RA; cf. Söderhjelm, *FMA*, 337–38.

62. *Dagbok* II, 205, 323–24, 326, 340, 346–48; cf. Söderhjelm, *FMA*, 338.

63. *Dagbok* II, 227, 340.

64. F. A. von Fersen's testament, FAF arkiv XXXIV, RA, 749 pp.,

448 COUNT HANS AXEL VON FERSEN

giving a complete and detailed inventory of all fixed and movable property, income from all tenancy leases, both in specie and in kind, etc., etc.; F.'s estate inventory, 1810, F. arkiv XXI, RA; F. to Sophie, 15 June 1794, Lövstad arkiv VII, in which F. considers his father's legacy "judicious and well distributed." On the Fersen palace in Stockholm, see F. U. Wrangel, *Blasieholmen och dess inbyggare* (2nd. ed., Stockholm, 1914), 66–72; Flach, *Fersen*, 128n.; on Steninge, Gustaf Upmark, "Steninge," in *Svenska slott och herresäten: Uppland IV* (Stockholm, 1909), 55–64; on Ljung, Axel L. Romdahl in *ibid.: Östergötland* (Stockholm, 1909), 45–52; on Lovstad, Anders Lindblom, *Lövstad i Östergötland* (Stockholm, 1961, pamphlet); on Wuojoki, Wilhelm Gabriel Lagus, *Underforskningar om finska adelns gods och ätter* (Helsingfors, 1860), 60.

65. F. A. von Fersen's estate included debts and obligations totaling 32,525 *rdr.*, FAF arkiv XXXIV, RA, 212–13. F. increased his share in order to relieve his mother and sister. *Dagbok* II, 242. On Sophie's circumstances, see *ibid.*, 326.

66. F. to Taube, 6 July, 11 Aug. 1794, Taube arkiv III, RA; *Dagbok* II, 344, 346. F.'s annual account books, F. arkiv XXV–XXXVII, RA, prepared by Nortun, balance, for instance, as follows: in 1787–88, at 4,025 *rdr.*; in 1796–97, 24,254 *rdr.*; in 1799–1800, at 79,463 *rdr.*; in 1804–1805, 67,413 *rdr.*; in 1806–1807, 73,808 *rdr.* F.'s estate inventory, dated 13 Nov. 1810, F. arkiv XXI, RA, gives a total evaluation of 230,-896 *rdr.*, with debts and obligations of 71,197 *rdr.* A second inventory in *ibid.* shows bequests to F.'s heirs totaling 158,698 *rdr.*, not counting Wuojoki manor in Finland, now under Russian rule, separately valued at 90,720 *rdr.* on 24 Aug. 1810. The above figures do not take into account changing monetary values; it still appears Axel's estate at his death was larger than his father's, valued at 191,945 *rdr.* with 32,525 *rdr.* in debts and obligations. FAF arkiv XXXIV, RA, 212–13.

67. F.'s accounts, F. arkiv XXII, RA, including memorandum on the sale, dated 30 Feb. 1792, and inventory of art works in two "corps de bibliothèques . . . de Boule" in Paris; *Dagbok* II, 228–29; F. to unidentified member of the Section du Roule, Paris, 6 Sept. 1792, F. arkiv III, RA; F. to Foreign Minister Le Brun, 24 Sept. 1792, *ibid.*; F. to Taube, 24 Nov. 1795, 2 June 1797, Taube arkiv III, RA.

68. *Dagbok* II, 300; "Projet de procuration pour Mrss. Thelusson frères & comp., négociants de Londres. " sent to Mme. de Matignon, 22 Aug. 1795, F. arkiv III, RA; agreement, dated Vienna, 22 Apr. 1796, F. arkiv XX, RA.

69. F. to Taube, 29 Jan. 1794, Taube arkiv III, RA; "Projet de procuration," F. arkiv III, RA; Génin to F., 1 May 1799, F. arkiv XX, RA.

70. F. to Taube, 17 Sept., 30 Dec. 1796, F. arkiv XX, RA; same to [Taube?], 30 Dec. 1796, *ibid.*; same to Barthélemy (Basel), 22 June 1797, *ibid.*; same to Duke of Portland, 15 Feb. 1797, *ibid.*; same to Sparre, 17 Feb. 1797, *ibid.*; Génin to F., 1 May 1799, *ibid.*; F. to "Ministre des relations exterieures," 6 Apr. 1800, *ibid.*; same to Talleyrand, 6 May, 10 June 1800, 22 Dec. 1801, *ibid.*; F. to "Ministre de la

marine," 10 June 1800, *ibid.*; F. to C. A. Ehrensvärd (Paris), 18 Dec. 1801, *ibid.*; F. to Gustav IV Adolf, 18 Dec. 1801, Handskriftsavdelningen F 657b., UUB; F. to Vicomte de Rochambeau, 25 Mar. 1803, F. arkiv XX, RA; F. to Sophie, 20 Sept. 1796, Lövstad arkiv VIII; Geffroy, "Lettres," 98.

71. *Dagbok* II, 361–64. On the situation with Eleanore and Craufurd, see *ibid.*, 253, 261, 343, 362–402, *passim.*, 409–10, 422, 426–27, 454–55, 469, 471–72, 513.

72. *Ibid.*, 373, 412, 428, 455; Söderhjelm, *FMA*, 341–42; F. to Sophie, 15 Jan. 1796, Lövstad arkiv VIII.

73. See Söderhjelm in *Dagbok* II, 430–47; also *ibid.*, 459.

74. *Ibid.*, 459, 467, 469–70; Schahovskoy-Stretchneff, *Comte de Fersen*, 95–100; cf. Hastier, "Baronne de Korff," 540–41; F. to Taube, [18 June 1794], 17 Feb. 1796, Taube arkiv III, RA.

75. *Dagbok* II, 477–78.

76. *Ibid.*, 487, 489, 494–95, 497–98, 500–503. Lars von Engeström, in Vienna at this time, later wrote in *Minnen*, I, 65, that F. came to return to Madame-Royal the "jewel box" he had gotten from Marie-Antoinette and to seek compensation "from the Austrian government" for his expenses in connection with the flight of the royal family.

77. *Dagbok* II, 495, 497–98, 504–509, 518–21, 528–29; Schahovskoy-Stretchneff, *Comte de Fersen*, 100; cf. Hastier, "Baronne de Korff," 541; F. to Sophie, 9 Mar., 23 Apr., 28 May 1796, Lövstad arkiv VIII; F. to Taube, 27 Apr., 11 May 1796, Taube arkiv III, RA.

78. *Dagbok* II, 519.

79. *Ibid.*, 526–28, 531–36; Söderhjelm, *FMA*, 354–55, 358; Bellissent, "Fersen, créancier du roi," 353–66; Hastier, "Baronne de Korff," 542.

80. Söderhjelm, *FMA*, 344, 348, 350, 352, 355; F. to Sophie, 21 May 1796, Lövstad arkiv VIII.

81. Hutton, *Bland Burges Correspondence*, 365n.; Schlitter, *Briefe*, xxxiv n.; Vallotton, *Marie-Antoinette et Fersen*, 366–67; Klinckowström I, 143, 203; Aimond, *L'énigme*, 10–11; Söderhjelm, *FMA*, 184, 272; Diary, 11 Sept. 1793, F. arkiv V, RA. *Dagbok* I, 391, for this entry wrongly gives the figure "15 million." Dard, *Rival de Fersen*, 42, maintains Craufurd took a sum of money to England for Louis XVI in June 1791. Roger Sorg, who so strongly attacked F.'s relationship with Marie-Antoinette in his "Le vrai visage d'Axel Fersen," here also accuses F. of cynical opportunism in seeking to gain the 1,500,000 livres for himself through fraud, on the basis of circumstantial evidence interpreted in the least favorable light. *Ibid.*, 525–40. He gives particular importance to F.'s diary entry of 11 Sept. 1793, above, maintaining that this was the first F. knew of the money. That such could not have been true should be clear from the above discussion. It is also clear from F.'s diary and letters that his primary reason for claiming the money was to repay Mmes. von Korff and Stegelmann, and Eleanore Sullivan. Sorg's theory that the note from Louis XVI and Marie-Antoinette, deeding the money to F., which Mercy himself recognized as authentic, was a clever forgery to which F. attached blank signatures from the French royal

couple previously sent him for other purposes, is highly implausible, quite aside from the incongruence of such a maneuver with F.'s whole character, as revealed throughout his lifetime.

82. F. to Taube, 8 Jan. 1794, Taube arkiv III, RA; Söderhjelm, *FMA*, 314, 322–23.

83. Marie-Antoinette's note to Jarjayes of May 1793, is copied in F.'s diary for 25 Mar. 1794, *Dagbok* II, 56–57; cf. Söderhjelm *FMA*, 302, 326–27; F. to Taube, 23 May 1793, Taube arkiv III, RA.

84. Karmin, "Trésor," 141–43; cf. Bellissent, "Fersen, créancier du roi," 358; F. to Taube, n.d. [18 June 1794], 24 Feb. 1796, Taube arkiv III, RA; note, 4 June [1791] and note, n.d. [1791], F. arkiv XVII, RA; copy of receipt to Eleanore Sullivan, 1 June 1791, F. arkiv XX, RA, with annotations showing renewal in Sept. 1794 and June 1796; Söderhjelm, *FMA*, 166, 344; Söderhjelm in *Dagbok* II, 356, 469n. In his diary for 6 July 1798, F. complains of having lost the receipts for Mmes. von Korff's and Stegelmann's loans. *Dagbok* III, 251.

85. F. arkiv XXII, RA, and F. arkiv X, RA, show he sent Mme. von Korff 1,000 livres on 3 July 1792, 15,720 on 16 Aug. 1792, 15,720 on 15 Aug. 1793, 3,000 on 27 May 1794, 3,000 on 2 Sept. 1794 and 200 *riksdaler, Hamburger banco,* on 14 Jan. 1798; they also show regular small interest payments to his servants, Louvet and wife, and "John," as well as to Eleanore's maid, Josephine. Cf. Diary, 25 Sept. 1794, Söderhjelm, *FMA*, 329, according to which F. recognizes a debt to Eleanore Sullivan of "400,000 livres" at 6 percent interest. On the problem of the burdensome Quella, see *Dagbok* II, 231, 233, 253–54, 261, 290, 301, 361, 367, 374, 387, 418, 422–28, *passim.*, 450, 454–55, 490; F. to Sophie, 26 Mar., 12 May, 4 June 1796, Lövstad arkiv VIII; Dard, *Rival de Fersen,* 47, 57–58, 91–92.

86. Klinckowström I, 128; Dard, *Rival de Fersen,* 30, 100; Thompson in *French Revolution,* viii–ix, reckoned in 1944 that one livre around the outbreak of the Revolution equaled about $.33, though its purchasing power was about four times as great as its modern equivalent. Changing monetary values are not taken into account in the above.

87. *Dagbok* II, 455; III, 65, 237, 248, 251; F. to Taube, 17 Feb. 1796, 24 Mar. 1797, Taube arkiv III, RA; Söderhjelm, *FMA*, 344, 348, 350, 361; F. to Sophie, 9, 19, 26 Mar., 2 Apr., 28 May 1796, 22 Mar. 1797, Lövstad arkiv VIII.

88. Söderhjelm in *Dagbok* II, 358–59.

89. Karmin, "Trésor," 142; F. to Taube, [18 June 1794], 22 Dec. 1795, 4, 17, 24 Feb. 1796, Taube arkiv III, RA; *Dagbok* II, 495, 502–503, 509.

90. F. to Taube, 4 Feb. 1796, Taube arkiv III, RA. Cf. Marcel Brion, *Daily Life in the Vienna of Mozart and Schubert* (New York, 1962).

91. *Dagbok* II, 485–86.

92. *Ibid.*, 461, 464–67, 475, 488. By the fall of the next year, however, F. greatly admired the Archduke Charles's military skill and bravery. F. to Sophie, 25 Oct. 1797, Lövstad arkiv VIII.

93. *Dagbok* II, 489.

94. *Ibid.*, 476–77, 487–88, 513, 529–30, 535; F. to Sophie, 9, 19 Mar. 1796, Lövstad arkiv VIII. Count Razumovsky had been ambassador to Stockholm in 1786–88, where he had been on amiable terms with the Fersen family. Cf. *Dagbok* II, 264.

95. *Dagbok* II, 463, 469; Söderhjelm in *ibid.*, 432–38.

96. *Ibid.*, 514, 523.

97. *Ibid.*, 460; *ibid.* III, 16; F. to Taube, 16 Mar. 1796, Taube arkiv III, RA.

CHAPTER IX

1. Klinckowström II, 361; *Dagbok* I, 233.

2. *Dagbok* I, 440; cf. Klinckowström II, 410–11. The idea that Robespierre was the man of order who would put an end to revolutionary anarchy was evidently widespread. See Sorel, *L'Eur. et la Rév. franç.*, IV, 74, who writes that Europe "persisted in seeing the image of Cromwell in him who was not even the caricature of Torquemada."

3. F.'s bulletin, 16 Mar. 1794, Gallica 500, RA.

4. *Dagbok* II, 159, 163; F. to Taube, 14 Aug. 1794, Taube arkiv III, RA.

5. Cf. Söderhjelm in *Dagbok* I, 374.

6. See, for instance, *Dagbok* II, 246; III, 108–109. Cf. Chaumié, *Réseau d'Antraigues*, 39–43, who speaks of a certain "terrain d'entente" between Breteuil and the supporters of enlightened absolutism, and the *montagnards* in the Convention, on the one hand, and between the anti-royalist aristocrats and the Girondins, on the other.

7. *Dagbok* II, 261, 263, 270, 305, 311, 313, 326.

8. *Ibid.*, 365.

9. *Ibid.*, 169–70; cf. Söderhjelm, *FMA*, 329.

10. *Dagbok* II, 326, 367.

11. *Ibid.*, 391, 516; F. to Taube, 13 Jan. 1797, Taube arkiv III, RA.

12. *Dagbok* I, 330; III, 24, 26, 69; F. to Taube, 23 June, 5 Aug. 1796, Taube arkiv III, RA.

13. *Dagbok* II, 449–50; III, 26, 34, 42, 45, 49. Énnemond Bonnard was a former sergeant while François-Séverin Marceau-Desgraviers was a lawyer's son.

14. *Dagbok* I, 413.

15. *Ibid.*, 419, 444; II, 31–32, 36–37, 38, 171; cf. F. to Taube, 15 Jan. 1794, 23 June 1796, Taube arkiv III, RA; F. to Sparre, 9 June 1793, Gallica 500, RA.

16. *Dagbok* II, 35, 163, 277; Söderhjelm, *FMA*, 300; F. to Taube, 20 Apr. 1796, Taube arkiv III, RA.

17. For Mallet's political correspondence, see *Correspondance inédite de Mallet du Pan avec la cour de Vienne (1795–1798)*, ed. André Michel, 2 vol. (Paris, 1884). On Mallet's political thought, and its European influence, see Godechot, *Contre-révolution*, 75–92; also Frances Alcomb, *Mallet du Pan (1749–1800): A Career in Political Journalism* (Durham, N.C., 1973). A lengthy "mémoire," dated 30 June 1793, unsigned but

apparently in Reutersvärd's hand, in F. arkiv XVII, RA, expresses many ideas strongly suggestive of Mallet's.

18. *Dagbok* II, 45–46.

19. *Ibid.*, 65–66; cf. Mallet's memoranda to Elgin and Mercy of 20 Nov. 1793 and esp. 5 Mar. 1794, the latter probably the "writing" to which F. here referred. A. Sayous, ed., *Mémoires et correspondance de Mallet du Pan*, 2 vol. (Paris, 1851), I, 394–419; II, 70–78. Cf. Godechot, *Contre-révolution*, 87.

20. Bernard Mallet, *Mallet du Pan and the French Revolution* (London, 1902), 164; *Dagbok* II, 35, 168–69. On 5 Dec. 1798, F. sent a work by Mallet on the destruction of the Swiss republic to Gustav IV Adolf, adding that it should be "translated into all languages to serve as a lesson to the peoples." F. arkiv II, RA.

21. Sayous, *Mémoires de Mallet du Pan* II, 77. Cf. Sorel, *L'Eur. et la Rév. franç.* IV, 4–5.

22. *Dagbok* II, 46, 51.

23. Klinckowström II, 406–407; F. to Taube, 15, 19, 22 Mar., 17, 30 Apr., 12 May, 3 July 1793, 2, 15 Mar. 1794, Taube arkiv III, RA; *Dagbok* I, 310, 312, 347, 353; cf. Georges Lefebvre, *La Révolution française* (Paris, 1951), 295–97, 304; Sorel, *L'Eur. et la Rév. franç.* III, 320–24, 366–67.

24. Sayous, *Mémoires de Mallet du Pan* II, 84–85; *Dagbok* II, 36–38, 59, 70, 98–101, 104. Cf. Sorel, *L'Eur. et la Rév. franç.* IV, 47, 75, 84–85.

25. *Dagbok* I, 392; II, 163, 167; III, 30.

26. Klinckowström II, 394–95; F. to Taube, 1 June, 3, 24 Sept., 1, 8 Oct., 11, 22 Nov. 1796, 13 Jan., 21 Apr., 12 May 1797, Taube arkiv III, RA; F. to Gustav IV Adolf, 17 Oct. 1797, Diplomatica: Almänna fredskongresser, LXVII, RA [hereafter abbreviated Allm. fredskongr.]; Sorel, *L'Eur. et la Rév. franç.* IV, 5. Godechot, in *Contre-révolution*, 4, holds that of all the tactics of the counterrevolution, only large-scale peasant insurrection had not been used under similar circumstances prior to 1790. Gustav III's raising of the royalist Swedish peasantry in 1788, however, should not be overlooked. Cf. also *ibid.*, 216–17, 335–36. That F. believed there were limits to the effectiveness of popular insurrections was shown, according to his letter of 6 Dec. 1796 to Sophie, Lövstad arkiv VIII, by the way the French in Italy contained this danger through "severity and even cruelty," which "proves well how one may govern a country."

27. F. to Taube, 5 May, 9, 16 June, 4 July 1797, Taube arkiv III, RA. F. was at the same time concerned over the threat of a French landing in Ireland. F. to Sophie, 17 January 1797, Lövstad arkiv VIII.

28. F. to Taube, 26 Nov. 1796, Taube arkiv III, RA.

29. Sorel, *L'Eur. et la Rév. franç.* IV, 5. Cf. Sayous, *Mémoires de Mallet du Pan* I, 417–18; II, 74–77, 211, 283–84; F. to Taube, 13 Jan. 1797, Taube arkiv III, RA.

30. *Dagbok* II, 296–97, 361, 367, 369, 371–72, 383, 385.

31. *Ibid.*, 328, 347.

32. Godechot, in *Contre-révolution*, 149, notes the general tendency of the counterrevolutionaries to concern themselves with means rather than ends, thereby minimizing their differences.

33. *Dagbok* I, 207–208, 210–11, 306, 328; Sayous, *Mémoires de Mallet du Pan* I, 367, quoting from Mallet's *Considérations*.

34. *Dagbok* I, 360, 368–69.

35. *Ibid.*, 46. Cf. F. to Taube, 2 Mar. 1794, Taube arkiv III, RA.

36. *Dagbok* I, 387, 401, 423; II, 246; F. to Sophie, "ce 21" [apparently 1793], Lövstad arkiv VII.

37. *Dagbok* II, 301, 385; III, 108–109.

38. *Dagbok* II, 376, 456, 522.

39. *Ibid.*, 509–10; *ibid.* III, 31, 351; F. to Taube, 22 Dec. 1795, 23 June 1796, Taube arkiv III, RA; cf. *Dagbok* II, 424n. Discontent with Louis XVIII and his advisers was widespread among French royalists at this time and there was much speculation over replacing him with the Duc d'Angoulême, in which Artois was himself apparently involved. See Sayous, *Mémoires de Mallet du Pan* II, 203–204, 211, 281–84.

40. *Dagbok* II, 452; III, 31, 37.

41. *Dagbok* III, 45. Cf. Godechot, *Contre-révolution*, 304–305.

42. *Dagbok* III, 31, 105.

43. *Ibid.*, 70.

44. F. to Taube, 27 Apr., 12 May 1797, Taube arkiv III, RA; F. to Sophie, 4 Apr. 1797, Lövstad arkiv VIII; cf. *Dagbok* III, 73, 76, 81.

45. *Dagbok* III, 84; F. to Sophie, 23 May 1797, Lövstad arkiv VIII.

46. *Dagbok* III, 86, 99.

47. Concerning the problem of a marriage match for Gustav IV Adolf, see especially Carlsson, *SUPH III:1*; Boëthius, "Förmyndareregering," III, IV; R. Pétiet, *Gustave IV Adolphe et la Révolution française. Relations diplomatiques de la France et de la Suède de 1792 à 1810 d'après des documents d'archives inédits* (Paris, 1914).

48. *Dagbok* II, 406–407, 410, 417; F. to Taube, 10 Nov. 1795, Taube arkiv III, RA. Le Hoc's speech is in *HEC* V, 102.

49. *Dagbok* II, 401, 411, 414, 503–504; F. to Taube, 4, 25 May 1796, Taube arkiv III, RA.

50. F. to Taube, 18 Oct. 1796, 10 Mar. 1797, Taube arkiv III, RA; *Dagbok* III, 70–71, 82.

51. *Ibid.*, 85, 95; Carlsson, *SUPH III:1*, 52–54.

52. *Dagbok* III, 50.

CHAPTER X

1. F. to Sophie, 13 Dec. 1796, 17 Jan. 1797, Lövstad arkiv VIII; *Dagbok* III, 51.

2. Richard Nordin, "En österrikisk diplomat om Sveriges inre förhållanden år 1797," *Historisk tidskrift* (1911), 49–51.

3. On Gustav IV Adolf's earlier foreign policy, see especially Carlsson, *SUPH III:1*; Sten Carlsson, *Gustav IV Adolf. En biografi* (Stockholm, 1946); Sven G. Svenson, *Gattjinatraktaten 1799. Studier i Gustav*

454 COUNT HANS AXEL VON FERSEN

IV Adolfs utrikespolitik 1796–1800 (Uppsala, 1952); J. W. Nilsson, *De diplomatiska förbindelserna mellan Sverige och Frankrike under Gustaf IV Adolf* (Uppsala, 1899). On Taube's influence, Nordin, "Österrikisk diplomat," 41, 44; *HEC* V, 261–62; VI, 3, 7, 84; Bernhard von Schinkel & C. W. Bergman, *Minnen ur Sveriges nyare historia*, 10 vol. (Stockholm, 1852–68), IV, 24–27; Svenson, *Gattjinatraktaten*, 41, 46–50.

4. Söderhjelm, *FMA*, 283–84; F. to Sophie, 12 Mar., 22 Nov. 1796, Lövstad arkiv VII, VIII; same to Taube, 1 Nov. 1792, 26 Feb., 15 Nov., 9 Dec. 1795, 12 Jan., 18 Oct., 26, 29 Nov. 1796, 13 Jan., 9 May 1798, Taube arkiv II, III, RA; *Dagbok* III, 171–72. Cf. Svenson, *Gattjinatraktaten*, 94–95.

5. Carlsson, *Gustav IV Adolf*, 78; Svenson, *Gattjinatraktaten*, 94–96, 98–102; *HEC* VI, 3; *Dagbok* III, 95–96.

6. Carlsson, *SUPH III:1*, 44, 51; Svenson, *Gattjinatraktaten*, 108n.; *Dagbok* III, 48, 145.

7. *Dagbok* III, 48, 51–53, 57–58; F. to Taube, 29 Nov. 1796, Taube arkiv III, RA.

8. *Dagbok* III, 48, 49, 51–52, 57–58, 65–66; Söderhjelm, *FMA*, 361.

9. *Dagbok* III, 58, 77, 98–99, 106–107.

10. *Ibid.*, 94; F.'s accreditation as commissioner, Allm. Fredskongr. LXVII, RA; F. to Sparre, 18 July 1797 (2 ltrs.), *ibid.*

11. Engeström, *Minnen* II, 23–25; Engeström I.F.8., 48, KB; Pétiet, *Gustave IV Adolphe et la Rév. franç.*, 219; *HEC* VI, 77; F. to Sophie, 15 Aug. 1797, Lövstad arkiv VIII; Svenson, *Gattjinatraktaten*, 108n.

12. Sorel, *L'Eur. et la Rév. franç.* V, 156–58. On the Congress of Rastadt, see besides this volume of Sorel, *op. cit.*, especially Heinrich von Sybel, *History of the French Revolution*, 4 vol. (London, 1867), IV. F. arkiv VIII, RA, contains some documents concerning the congress.

13. Richard Nordin, "Fersen och Bonaparte," in *Studier tillägnade Harald Hjärne* (Uppsala, 1908), 508; also the same author's "Sveriges förhållanden till Österrike under tiden närmast före kongressen i Rastadt," *Historisk tidskrift* (1907), 139–40.

14. *HEC* VI, 31; Hochschild, *Memoarer* III, 256, 258, 259.

15. Schinkel-Bergman, *Minnen* IV, 27–34; Söderhjelm in *Dagbok* III, 128–29.

16. Sorel, *L'Eur. et la Rév. franç.* V, 173–74, 231–32; Nordin, "Sveriges förhållanden till Österrike," 146.

17. Ironically, as will be seen, this idea was first suggested by the Austrians, then by L. von Engeström, in the spring of 1797. Nordin, "Sveriges förhållanden till Österrike," 146–47, 153, 155–56; Carlsson, *SUPH III:1*, 57.

18. Hochschild, *Memoarer* III, 260. Cf. Nordin, "Sveriges förhållanden till Österrike," 145, 154; Nilsson, *Diplomatiska förbindelserna*, 22.

19. This is argued convincingly in Svenson, *Gattjinatraktaten*, 107–108. Carlsson, *SUPH III:1*, 56, concurs. Hildebrand, *SBL* XV, 724–25, disagrees, since Bildt had been designated as an alternate for the post. This seems inconclusive since this provision must have derived from F.'s known hesitations over returning to active service. Cf. Nilsson, *Diplo-*

matiska förbindelserna, 22; Arne Stade, "Gustav IV Adolf och Norge 1798 och 1801. Till frågan om den svenska utrikespolitikens karaktär och målsättning 1796–1803," *Historisk tidskrift* (1955), 355n.

20. F. to Gustav IV Adolf, 16 Sept. 1797, Allm. fredskongr. LXVII, RA.

21. *Dagbok* III, 112, 117–18; F. to Gust. IV Ad., 21 Sept. 1797, Allm. Fredskongr. LXVII, RA; *HEC* VI, 252–54; Nilsson, *Diplomatiska förbindelserna*, 23n.; F. to Taube, 14 Oct. 1797, Taube arkiv III, RA; F.'s accreditation as ambassador, 6 Oct. 1797, F. arkiv XVIII, RA; Hildebrand, *SBL* XV, 725.

22. *Dagbok* III, 121, 122; F. to Gust. IV Ad., 28 Oct., 11 Nov. 1797, Allm. Fredskongr. LXVII, RA.

23. Nordin, "Fersen och Bonaparte," 516–17.

24. Emile Dard, "Bonaparte et Fersen," *Revue des Deux Mondes* (1938), 619–20; Söderhjelm, *FMA*, 356–57.

25. Söderhjelm, *FMA*, 361; *Dagbok* III, 114.

26. *Dagbok* III, 109, 112–13, 118–19; F. to Gust. IV Ad., 19 Sept. 1797, Allm. fredskongr. LXVII, RA; Engeström, *Minnen* II, 20–21; Nordin, "Sveriges förhållanden till Österrike," 129, 147n., 153; Nilsson, *Diplomatiska förbindelserna*, 25n.; Svenson, *Gattjinatraktaten*, 99–100, 118–19. An undated copy of a letter from Engeström to Gustav IV Adolf, in F. arkiv XVIII, RA, discusses this exchange plan.

27. Engeström, *Minnen* II, 22–23; cf. Carl Schörbing's "Kort Berättelse om Svenska Ambassaden till FredsCongressen i Rastadt 1797 och 1798 uti Herr Grefve Fersens person," 37–38, in Engeström I.f.8., KB; F. to Gust. IV Ad., 18 Nov. 1797, Allm. fredskongr. LXVII, RA.

28. Engeström, *Minnen* II, 23–25; Svenson, *Gattjinatraktaten*, 120–21. F. first mentions Art. 20 on 15 Nov. 1797, when Schörbing brought him Bildt's message in Karlsruhe. *Dagbok* III, 140–41; cf. F. to Gust. IV Ad., 18 Nov. 1797, Allm. fredskongr. LXVII, RA.

29. See Schinkel-Bergman, *Minnen* IV, 26–36; Flach, *Fersen*, 119–23; Söderhjelm in *FMA*, 363–64, and in *Dagbok* III, 123–38. The older view is disputed in Nilsson, *Diplomatiska förbindelserna*, 22n., 23n., 26n., 27n., 28–29; Nordin, "Fersen och Bonaparte," 518–19; Carlsson, *SUPH* III:1, 56; Svenson, *Gattjinatraktaten*, 99–100.

30. *Dagbok* III, 109, 119, 491–92, 497; F. to Sophie, 26 Sept. 1797, Lövstad arkiv VIII; F. to Taube, 30 May 1792, 1 Sept., 8 Dec. 1793, 2, 23, 30 Mar., 18 May 1796, Taube arkiv II, III, RA; F. to Engeström, 3 Oct., 24 Nov., 2, 22 Dec. 1797, Brev till Lars von Engeström III, KB; Nordin, "Sveriges förhållanden till Österrike," 129–32.

31. See note 29, above.

32. Engeström, *Minnen* II, 23n.; Nilsson, *Diplomatiska förbindelserna*, 22–23; cf. F. to Taube, 26 Sept. 1797, Taube arkiv III, RA; F. to Gust. IV Ad., 18 Nov. 1797, Allm. fredskongr. LXVII, RA.

33. F. to Gust. IV Ad., 14, 28 Oct., 4, 11 Nov. 1797, Allm. fredskongr. LXVII, RA; F. to Sparre, 8 Sept. 1797, *ibid.*; F. to Taube, 18, 25 Nov., 26 Dec. 1797, Taube arkiv III, RA; cf. Nilsson, *Diplomatiska förbindelserna*, 24–25. In these letters, F. expresses apprehension over

French efforts to "republicanize" the left bank of the Rhine and mistrust of Austria vis-à-vis the integrity of the Empire.

34. Nordin, "Fersen och Bonaparte," 509, 513, 532–34; Nilsson, *Diplomatiska förbindelserna,* 35–36; Svenson, *Gattjinatraktaten,* 120–21; C. G. Schulz von Ascheraden (Berlin) to F., 13 Dec. 1797, F. arkiv XVIII, RA; F. to Taube, 16 Dec. 1797, Taube arkiv III, RA.

35. *Dagbok* III, 140–41; F. to Gust. IV Ad., 18 Nov. 1797, Allm. fredskongr. LXVII, RA; Schörbing, "Kort Berättelse," 37–38, Engeström I.f.8., KB. Schörbing's tone is critical of F. for disregarding his warnings, but his account was apparently written well after the events it describes and contains demonstrable errors. Cf. Hildebrand, *SBL* XV, 725. F. meanwhile had a high opinion of Schörbing, as shown by his recommendations for his later service. See F. to Taube, 21 Apr. 1798, Taube arkiv III, RA; F. to Gust. IV Ad., 23 Nov. 1804, F. arkiv II, RA.

36. Cf. Arvid Ahnfelt, *Ur svenska hofvets och aristokratiens lif,* 3 vol. (Stockholm, 1880–81), III, "Ur landshöfdingen friherre J. af Nordins hofkrönika"; Hochschild, *Memoarer* III, 301; Schinkel-Bergman, *Minnen* IV, 35; Schörbing, "Kort Berättelse," 45, Engeström I.f.8., KB; F. to Sophie, 17, 24 Oct. 1797, Lövstad arkiv VIII; Söderhjelm in *Dagbok* III, 127; F. to "M. le baron" (Stockholm), 10 Oct. 1797, Allm. fredskongr. LXVII, RA; memorandum on monthly expenses attached to Schörbing's letter to Sparre, 9 Dec. 1797, *ibid.,* gives details.

37. *Dagbok* III, 141; F. to Gust. IV Ad., 18, 19 Nov. 1797, Allm. fredskongr. LXVII, RA.

38. *Dagbok* III, 142–43; F. to Gust. IV Ad., 19 Nov. 1797, Allm. fredskongr. LXVII, RA.

39. *Dagbok* III, 145–47; F. to Gust. IV Ad., 29 Nov. 1797, Allm. fredskongr. LXVII, RA; Schörbing, "Kort Berättelse," 40, Engeström I.f.8., KB. Cf. Dard, "Bonaparte et Fersen," 622–23; Nilsson, *Diplomatiska förbindelserna,* 119–20.

40. *Dagbok* III, 147–49; Schörbing, "Kort Berättelse," 41, Engeström I.f.8., KB.

41. F. to Gust. IV Ad., 29 Nov. 1797, Allm. fredskongr. LXVII, RA. The version of F.'s report of 29 Nov. 1797 in Nilsson, *Diplomatiska förbindelserna,* 119–22, contains minor errors. Cf. Schörbing, "Kort Berättelse," 40–45, Engeström I.f.8., KB.

42. *Correspondance de Napoléon Ier.,* 32 vol. (Paris, 1858–70), III, 597–98. According to Engeström, Bonaparte later told Sieyès that F. was "disconcerted by my declaration but the politeness I showed him on his departure revived him, which gives me a very slender opinion of him." Engeström I.f.8., KB, 48.

43. *Dagbok* III, 149–53; cf. Söderhjelm, *FMA,* 363; Schörbing, "Kort Berättelse," 43–44, Engeström I.f.8., KB.

44. Ludovic Sciout, *Le Directoire,* 4 vol. (Paris, 1895–97), III, 201–203; Nordin, "Fersen och Bonaparte," 520–22; *Dagbok* III, 151–52.

45. F. to Gust. IV Ad., 2 Dec. 1797, Allm. fredskongr. LXVII, RA; *Dagbok* III, 152. Cf. Nordin, "Fersen och Bonaparte," 522.

46. That Bonaparte used F. to obtain political advantages other than

those his associates in Paris had envisioned and eliminated F. from the congress sooner than they might have wished seems borne out by the strong disapproval Barras—also a close associate of Talleyrand and Staël —expresses in his description of Bonaparte's treatment of F. *Mémoires de Barras*, ed. G. Duruy, 4 vol. (Paris, 1895–96), III, 102–106.

47. Nordin, "Fersen och Bonaparte," 528–29.

48. *HEC* VI, 76–78; Schinkel-Bergman, *Minnen* IV, 31–34; Nilsson, *Diplomatiska förbindelserna*, 38; Dard, "Bonaparte et Fersen," 620; F. to Taube, 23 Dec. 1797, Taube arkiv III, RA.

49. Nordin, "Fersen och Bonaparte," 518–19; Svenson, *Gattjinatraktaten*, 108; Carlsson, *SUPH III:1*, 56; Hildebrand, *SBL* XV, 724.

50. *Memoirs of Count Lavalette* (London, 1894), 150–51.

51. *Moniteur Universel*, Octadi, 18 Frimaire an VI (8 Dec. 1797); *The Times*, 18, 20 Dec. 1797; *Dagbok* III, 167.

52. *Dagbok* III, 151, 153–54, 156, 159–60, 171, 216–17, 234; F. to Gust. IV Ad., 25 Apr., 16 May, 25 July, 9 Aug. 1798, Diplomatica: Germanica IV F (Baden), RA; F. to Taube, 29 Nov. 1797, 16 May, 18 July 1798, Taube arkiv III, RA. F. as early as Feb. 1798 was concerned that "the revolution in Turkey" was due to French intrigues and would permit the spread of "republicanization" through Wallachia and Moldavia into Poland. F. to Gust. IV Ad., 28 Feb. 1798, Allm. fredskongr. LXVII, RA. Cf. also Sorel, *L'Eur. et la Rév. franç.* V, 270, 340–41.

53. *Dagbok* III, 147–48, 151, 154–56; F. to Gust. IV Ad., 29 Nov., 2, 6, 13, 26 Dec. 1797, Allm. fredskongr. LXVII, RA. F.'s own views and recommendations are usually in separate *apostilles* attached to his regular dispatches.

54. *Dagbok* III, 157–58, 160, 164, 167–68.

55. F. to Sophie, 2 May 1797, Lövstad arkiv VIII; F. to Gust. IV Ad., 8 Sept., 14, 24, 28 Oct., 4, 11, 18, 19, 29 Nov., 2, 6, 9, 13, 16, 19, 23, 26, 30 Dec. 1797, 3, 5, 10, 13, 20, 24, 31 Jan., 3, 7, 21, 24 Feb., 28 Mar. 1798, Allm. fredskongr. LXVII, RA; F. to Taube, 9, 26 Sept., 18, 25 Nov. 1797, Taube arkiv III, RA; *HEC* VI, 254; *Dagbok* III, 158–61, 170–71. Cf. Sorel, *L'Eur. et la Rév. franç.* V, 269, 274; Nilsson, *Diplomatiska förbindelserna*, 31–32.

56. F. to Gust. IV Ad., 13, 26, 30 Dec. 1797, 6, 18 Jan. (2 ltrs.) 1798, Allm. fredskongr. LXVII, RA.

57. F. to Gust IV Ad., 18 Nov., 19, 26 Dec. 1797, 5 Jan., 7 Mar. 1798, *ibid.*; same to same, 21 Feb. 1798, F. arkiv II, RA; F. to Taube, 29 Nov. 16, 23 Dec. 1797, Taube arkiv III, RA; *HEC* VI, 245, 257; *Dagbok* III, 141, 161–62, 163, 165, 167, 187, 188, 190; Schörbing, "Kort Berättelse," 45, Engeström I.f.8., KB. Cf. Svenson, *Gattjinatraktaten*, 128n.

58. *Dagbok* III, 171–72, 174, 183, 190, 250, 271. F. learned from Reutersvärd, now legation secretary at The Hague, that both Staël and his own superior, F.'s cousin, F. A. Löwenhielm, had actually intrigued to prevent his acceptance at Rastadt. *Ibid.*, 183, 250. Nilsson, *Diplomatiska förbindelserna*, 37; Dard, "Bonaparte et Fersen," 630.

59. Svenson, *Gattjinatraktaten*, 113–16; Carlsson, *SUPH III:1*, 57–58; Nilsson, *Diplomatiska förbindelserna*, 43–48.

60. *HEC* VI, 256–58; *Dagbok* III, 166; Söderhjelm in *ibid.*, 136–37; Stade, "Gustav IV Adolf och Norge," 360–61.
61. *Dagbok* III, 166, 171–72, 174, 177, 180–81, 183, 184, 186, 188–189, 193, 194, 214, 228; F. to Taube, 7, 14 Feb., 13, 21 Apr. 1798, Taube arkiv III, RA; same to same, 7 Apr. 1798, Handskriftsavdelningen F 567 c., UUB; cf. F. to Sophie, 23 Feb. 1797, Lövstad arkiv VIII.
62. *Dagbok* III, 180–81; cf. diary, 4 Nov. 1797, *ibid.*, 120, in which F. already senses the probability of civil strife in France if the army returns there; F. to Gust. IV Ad., 31 Jan., 28 Feb. 1798, Allm. fredskongr. LXVII, RA; F. to Taube, 31 Jan., 13 Apr. 1798, Taube arkiv III, RA.
63. F. to Gust. IV Ad., 4, 19 Nov., 6, 16 Dec. 1797, 13 Jan., 3 Feb., 10 Mar. 1798, Allm. fredskongr. LXVII, RA; F. Taube, 16 Dec. 1797, Taube arkiv III, RA; *Dagbok* III, 155, 182, 187, 191. Cf. Nilsson, *Diplomatiska förbindelserna*, 24–25; Svenson, *Gattjinatraktaten*, 135–36.
64. F. to Taube, 26 Sept., 14 Oct., 18, 25 Nov. 1797, Taube arkiv III, RA; F. to Gust. IV Ad., 4 Nov. 2 Dec. 1797, Allm. fredskongr. LXVII, RA. Cf. Nilsson, *Diplomatiska förbindelserna*, 24, 31–32; *Dagbok* III, 112–13, 115, 161.
65. F. to Gust. IV Ad., 26, 30 Dec. 1797, 5, 6, 13 Jan., 24, 28 Feb., 10, 24 Mar. 1798, Allm. fredskongr. LXVII, RA; *Dagbok* III, 160–64, 167, 182, 189. Cf. Nilsson, *Diplomatiska förbindelserna*, 31–32; Sorel, *L'Eur. et la Rév. franç.* V, 303.
66. Svenson, *Gattjinatraktaten*, 125–27; Hochschild, *Memoarer* III, 277, 281; F. to Gust. IV Ad., 18 Jan., 3, 21 Feb. 1798, Allm. fredskongr. LXVII, RA; same to same, 21 Feb. 1798, F. arkiv II, RA; F. to Taube, 17 Jan. 1798, Taube arkiv III, RA; *Dagbok* III, 166, 171–72.
67. *Dagbok* III, 186–87, 190, 193–94, 197–98, 201; F. to Gust. IV Ad., 7, 24 Mar. 1798, Allm. fredskongr. LXVII, RA; Svenson, *Gattjinatraktaten*, 127–28.
68. *Dagbok* III, 214. Cf. Svenson, *Gattjinatraktaten*, 128.
69. Stade, "Gustav IV Adolf och Norge," 363; Engeström, *Minnen* II, 24n.; cf. Nilsson, *Diplomatiska förbindelserna*, 55n.

CHAPTER XI

1. *Dagbok* III, 194, 201, 214; Söderhjelm in *ibid.*, 202–203; Dard, "Bonaparte et Fersen," 630.
2. Schinkel-Bergman, *Minnen* IV, 36; Flach, *Fersen*, 122; *Dagbok* III, 194; F. to Taube, 31 Mar. 1798, Taube arkiv III, RA.
3. F.'s dispatches to Gust. IV Adolf, Mar. 1798–Mar. 1799, *passim.*, Germanica IV F (Baden), RA; cf. Nilsson, *Diplomatiska förbindelserna*, 32n.; F. arkiv XVII and XVIII, RA, contain much material on the congress and revolutionary activity throughout Europe.
4. *Dagbok* III, 245–46, 284.
5. See, for instance, F. to Gust. IV Ad., 18 Apr., 16, 30 May, 6, 17, 27, 31 Oct., 14, 28 Nov., 8 Dec. 1798, 26 Jan., 20 Feb. 1799, Germanica IV F (Baden), RA. Cf. Nilsson, *Diplomatiska förbindelserna*, 32–33.

6. *Dagbok* III, 173, 176, 182, 194–97, 219–20, 222–23; Nilsson, *Diplomatiska förbindelserna*, 32n. On the spread of revolution in Italy and Switzerland, cf. for instance, F. to Gust. IV Ad., 23 Dec. 1797, 3, 6, 10, 13, 24, 27 Jan., 3, 7, 21, 28 Feb., 3, 14, 17, 21, 28 Mar. 1798, Allm. fredskongr. LXVII, RA; same to same 4, 14 15, 28 Apr., 5, 9, 12, 16 May 1798, Germanica IV F (Baden), RA.

7. *Dagbok* III, 173, 222–23; cf. F. to Gust. IV Ad., 17 Mar. 1798, Allm. fredskongr. LXVII, RA; same to same, 17 Oct., 14 Nov. 1798, Germanica IV F (Baden), RA.

8. *Dagbok* III, 175, 197, 245, 268, 271, 295, 298; F. to Gust. IV Ad., 2, 13, 19 Sept., 14 Dec. 1798, Germanica IV F (Baden), RA.

9. *Dagbok* III, 155, 224, 234, 268, 291, 293–94; F. to Gust. IV Ad., 17, 27 Oct., 8 Dec. 1798, Germanica IV F (Baden), RA.

10. *Dagbok* III, 97, 105, 107–108, 217, 294, 400; F. to Gust. IV Ad., 27 Oct., 8 Dec. 1798, Germanica IV F (Baden), RA.

11. *Dagbok* III, 223–26, 229; cf. F. to Gust. IV Ad., 31 Oct. 1798, Germanica IV F (Baden), RA; F. to Taube, 9 May 1798, Taube arkiv III, RA.

12. *Dagbok* III, 287; cf. F. to Gust. IV Ad., 27 Oct., 8 Dec. 1798, Germanica IV F (Baden), RA.

13. *Dagbok* III, 216, 221–23, 227, 234, 250, 256, 266, 268. On F. and the Austrians, cf. F. to Gust. IV Ad., 16 May 1798, Germanica IV F (Baden), RA; Schörbing, "Kort Berättelse," 45, Engeström I.f.8., KB.

14. *Dagbok* III, 276, 293–94, 296, 300–301, 307–309, 313; F. to Gust. IV Ad., 13, 31 Oct., 14, 17 Nov., 1 Dec. 1798, Germanica IV F (Baden), RA.

15. See Sorel, *L'Eur. et la Rév. franç.* V, 393–401.

16. *Dagbok* III, 354, 361, 372, 374, 379, 401; F. to Gust. IV Ad., (?) May 1799, F. arkiv II, RA; same to same, 1 July 1799, Germanica IV F (Baden), RA.

17. In Feb. 1798, the French accused F. of dealings with émigrés, apparently to get him out of Rastadt. See F. to Gust. IV Ad., 3 Feb. 1798, Allm. fredskongr. LXVII, RA; same to same, 10 Feb. 1798, Handskriftsavdelningen F 467 b., UUB; *HEC* VI, 257–58; *Dagbok* III, 185.

18. *Dagbok* III, 217, 254.

19. *Ibid.*, 266, 272, 274, 280, 283, 292, 308, 351; IV, 20, 25. In a letter to F. on 9 May 1799, a Baron von Berckheim in Baden describes in some detail a set of regulations devised for the "association." F. arkiv XII, RA; cf. F. to Gust. IV Ad., 11 Sept. 1801, Handskriftsavdelningen F 657 b., UUB. On this episode see also Alma Söderhjelm, "En fascistisk liga i Europa 1798 och 1799," in her *Kärlek och politik*, 121–42. The project is strongly reminiscent of the alleged revolutionary "Club de la Propagande," which so preoccupied F. in 1791–92. See Ch. VI, Sect. 5, above.

20. *Dagbok* III, 254, 292n.; K. Erdmannsdörffer & K. Obser, ed., *Politische Correspondenz Karl Friedrichs von Baden, 1783–1806*, 5 vol. (Heidelberg, 1896), III, xxii–xxiii, 135, 137, 393n., 396–99; IV, lxiii–lxiv, 453–54, 457; V, 36, 51, 140–41, 330, 474–75, 735. The émigré

general in Swedish service, Charles de Suremain, in *Mémoires du lieu-tenant-général de Suremain* (*1794–1815*) (Paris, 1902), 68, gives a few details on "Saint-Geniès," whom he met in 1801, and claims his real name was Varenchon and that he was nothing but a wastrel and a French spy.

21. *Dagbok* III, 266; Erdmannsdörffer, *Politische Correspondenz* III, xxii–xxiv, 134–37, 177; Söderhjelm, *Kärlek och politik*, 125–27. Mallet du Pan wrote of Danican in April 1796, "We had time to form a judgment of him; he has a good heart and a detestable head." Sayous, *Mémoires de Mallet du Pan* II, 228.

22. *Dagbok* III, 280, 284–88; Erdmannsdörffer, *Politische Correspondenz* III, xxxviii–xxxix, 135–36; Söderhjelm, *Kärlek och politik*, 128–34, 136. Cf. F. to Gust. IV Ad., 31 Oct., 14 Nov. 1798, Germanica IV F (Baden), RA; F.'s account book, F. arkiv XXII, RA.

23. *Dagbok* III, 283.

24. *Ibid.*, 285; F. to Gust. IV Ad., 31 Oct., 14 Nov. 1798, Germanica IV F (Baden), RA; "Addition à la note remise à son Excellence le Comte de Fersen, relativement aux troubles qui sont sur le point d'éclater dans le Würtemberg, la Suabe et la Bavière," unsigned, dated 8 Nov. 1798, F. arkiv XVIII, RA. Cf. Söderhjelm, *Kärlek och politik*, 131–33, 135; Heinrich Scheel, *Süddeutsche Jakobiner* (East Berlin, 1962), 401n. Jacques Droz, *L'Allemagne et la Révolution française* (Paris, 1949), 111–34.

25. "Addition à la note," F. arkiv XVIII, RA. In Feb. 1799, Danican, using the pseudonym "Beaumann," attempted through other channels to present essentially the same plan to the duke of Württemberg. Scheel, *Süddeutsche Jakobiner*, 509.

26. *Dagbok* III, 292–93, 305–308, 376. Berckheim wanted funds and assured F. that if he could obtain 100 or 150 *louis*, he could promise ten to fifteen thousand new members in two or three months. Berckheim to F., 9 May 1799, F. arkiv XII, RA. F. to Gust. IV Ad., 26 Jan. 1799, Germanica IV F (Baden), RA; Erdmannsdörffer, *Politische Correspondenz* III, 137, 177–91; IV, 503; V, 740.

27. *Dagbok* III, 284, 288, 352, 376, 399, 401, 415.

28. *Ibid.*, 376; IV, 19–20, 25; Erdmannsdörffer, *Politische Correspondenz* III, xxxix.

29. *Dagbok* III, 111, 119, 139, 143, 145, 187–88, 194–95, 213–15, 249, 276, 302, 316; F. to Sophie, 10 Oct., 10 Nov. 1798. Lövstad arkiv VIII. Queen Fredrika also described to her mother in lurid terms the moral laxity of the Swedish court. She was especially horrified by Duchess Charlotta, whose regular lover was Fabian Fersen, but who was said to possess "all tastes," and Sophie Piper, whom she accused of extreme promiscuity, repeating the gossip of an alleged lover that to satisfy her, "one would have to be Hercules himself." I am indebted for these details, from Korrespondenz (Karl Friedrich) V, Band 20, Gross-herzogliches Familien-Archiv, in the Badensisches Generallarchiv, Karls-ruhe, to Profesor Sten Carlsson and Rector Herbert Lund. Cf. Sten Carlsson, "Fredrika Dorothea Wilhelmina," *Svenskt biografiskt lexikon*

XVI (Stockholm, 1960), 474–78. These comments on Sophie doubtless derived from malicious gossip, for her relationship with Taube evidently was based on mutual fidelity.

30. *Dagbok* III, 285. Cf. *Ibid.*, 139–41, 214–19, 226, 228, 238–41, 244–45, 248–53, 267, 269–70, 277, 285–88, 292–93, 299, 301, 306, 310, 313–14, 319–20; cf. Söderhjelm in *ibid.*, 204–209.

31. *Ibid.*, 211, 240–41, 252–53, 266, 270, 274–76, 298, 302, 315, 319–20.

32. *Ibid.*, 297–98, 301, 312, 342; F. to Gust. IV Ad., 26 Dec. 1798, 9, 16, 20 Feb., 2, 14, 28 Mar., 20 June, 5 Aug. 1799, Germanica IV F (Baden), RA; F. to Ehrenheim, 2 Jan. 1799, *ibid.*; Hochschild, *Memoarer* III, 301. F.'s appointment and compensation as ambassador terminated at the end of January 1799.

33. Cf. Hochschild, *Memoarer* III, 312.

34. *Dagbok* III, 15–18, 49–53, 58, 63, 66–67, 69, 72, 74–75, 77, 90, 92, 96, 105, 163, 228–29, 241, 261–63, 272, 276–77, 281–83, 286, 297; F. to Sophie, 12 May, 4, 28 June 5, 25 July, 16 Aug., 13 Dec. 1796, 3, 24, 31 Jan., 23 Feb., 7 Mar., 4, 11, 18 Apr., 23 May, 18 July, 1 Aug., 5, 12, 19 Sept., 3, 17 Oct., 2 Dec. 1797, Lövstad arkiv VIII; Söderhjelm in *Dagbok* III, 323, 338–41. Cf. Ch. VIII, Sect. I.

35. *Dagbok* III, 299–301, 303–307, 310–12, 319, 342, 344, 347, 353, 401–402, 405, 407; Söderhjelm in *ibid.*, 321, 341; Söderhjelm, *FMA*, 365.

36. Dard, *Rival de Fersen*, 57–58, 90–100; Söderhjelm in *Dagbok* III, 321–38.

37. *Dagbok* III, 194, 284, 291; F. to Gust. IV Ad., 28 Nov. 1798, Germanica IV F (Baden), RA; Svenson, *Gattjinatraktaten*, 134–42.

38. *Dagbok* II, 414; III, 54, 143, 227, 234, 295; F. to Gust. IV Ad., 15 Dec. 1798, Handskriftsavdelningen F 567 b., UUB; Hochschild, *Memoarer* III, 301; Pétiet, *Gustave IV Adolphe et la Rév. franc.*, 230–31; Svenson, *Gattjinatraktaten*, 135–36.

39. *Dagbok* III, 264–65, 267, 292; Engeström, *Minnen* II, 39–41; Svensen, *Gattjinatraktaten*, 101, 204. Taube had regarded Engeström with extreme suspicion and ill-will since the latter's brother, Johan, had been implicated in the conspiracy against Gustav III in 1792. Cf. Taube to F., 5 Oct. 1792, 17 Apr. [1793?], F. arkiv XIV, RA.

40. *Dagbok* III, 267, 276, 343, 357–60, 363–64, 366–72, 395, 398, 401, 408; F. to Gust. IV Ad., 2, 13 June, 22 July 1798, 20 Feb. 1799, Germanica IV F (Baden), RA; same to same, 30 Apr., (?) May 1799, F. arkiv II, RA; Söderhjelm, *Gustaf III:s syskon*, 56–57; Engeström, *Minnen* II, 39–40. Financial claims were also made on Sweden. On 6 July 1798, F. forwarded a number of petitions from persons in Germany, including the Counts von Wittgensteins' request for repayment of debts dating back to the Thirty Years' War. Germanica IV F (Baden), RA.

41. *Dagbok* III, 368–69; cf. Hochschild, *Memoarer* III, 309; Svenson, *Gattjinatraktaten*, 204–209, 211–12.

42. *Dagbok* III, 242–43, 249; F. to Gust. IV Ad., 27 June 1798, F. arkiv II, RA. F. had of course long been concerned about Swedish

462 COUNT HANS AXEL VON FERSEN

Jacobins. On 10 Feb. 1796, he writes of several Swedes in Paris, including a young Baron Funck, "with his hair cut round without powder and who distinguishes himself by his Carmagnole principles." Taube arkiv III, RA. The connection between tonsorial style and political outlook is obviously nothing new.

43. *Dagbok* III, 358–59, 374. F. here includes among the "democratic league" also Engeström, Casström, K.F. Nordenskiöld, and Nils Rosén von Rosenstein. See also F. to Taube, 2 May 1798, Taube arkiv III, RA.

44. *Dagbok* III, 378, 388, 394, 398, 406–408; F. to Gust. IV Ad., 28 Mar., 20 Apr. 1799, Germanica IV F (Baden), RA.

45. *Dagbok* III, 409–10, 412–13; Söderhjelm in *ibid.*, 386; F. to Gust. IV Ad., 6 June, 8 Aug. 1799, F. arkiv II, RA; same to same, 20 June, 5 Aug. 1799, Germanica IV F (Baden), RA; Tegnér, *Armfelt* II, 372–74; Hochschild, *Memoarer* III, 312.

46. *Dagbok* III, 412–13; Engeström, *Minnen* II, 42, 44–46, 155–57; Taube's testament and related documents (mostly in F.'s hand), Taube arkiv IV, RA; Hochschild, *Memoarer* III, 312, 314–15; *Dropmore Papers* VI, 66–67; P. Wieselgren, ed., *DeLaGardiska arkivet. Handlingar ur grefliga DeLaGardiska biblioteket på Löberöd*, 20 vol. (Stockholm, 1831–44), XX, 69; Tegnér, *Armfelt* II, 273.

47. *Dagbok* III, 413, 415, 418.

48. *Ibid.*, 420, 422–25. Cf. F. to Sophie, 13 Sept. 1798, Lövstad arkiv VIII, on F.'s warm relationship with Breteuil and his daughter, Mme. de Matignon, whom he habitually called his "sister."

49. *Dagbok* III, 392–93, 395, 399–400; F. to Gust. IV Ad., 6 June 1799, F. arkiv II, RA; Nilsson, *Diplomatiska förbindelserna*, 123–25; Hochschild, *Memoarer* III, 309; Svenson, *Gattjinatraktaten*, 221–26. The French consul general, Delisle, reported on 14 June 1799 that Gustav IV Adolf's Regensburg Manifesto was dictated by Russia and backed by the "Fersen cabale" against the influence of "the chancellor." Pétiet, *Gustave IV Adolphe et la Rév. franc.*, 230–31.

50. *Dagbok* III, 395, 400, 415; F. to Gust. IV Ad., 22 July 1799, Germanica IV F (Baden), RA; Hochschild, *Memoarer* III, 312.

51. Svenson, *Gattjinatraktaten*, 202–203, 225–27, 244–48, 264–66, 269, 273–74, 288–90, 314–24.

CHAPTER XII

1. *Dagbok* IV, 19–22. Cf. Flach, *Fersen*, 24.

2. *Dagbok* IV, 19, 25. Cf. Svenson, *Gattjinatraktaten*, 332.

3. *Dagbok* IV, 22–23, 26, 27, 43–44; Hochschild, *Memoarer* III, 301; *DeLaGardiska arkivet* XX, 69.

4. *Dagbok* IV, 51, 56–57.

5. *Ibid.*, 20, 25, 34, 36, 53, 67; Söderhjelm in *ibid.*, 10–11; Engeström, *Minnen* II, 46. F. also mistrusted Staël and C.G. Brinkman in Paris, Claës Lagersvärd in Genoa, Carl Bildt in Vienna, F. A. Löwenhielm in The Hague, and Engeström's secretary, S.N. Casström.

6. Nordin, "Österrikisk diplomat," 41–42, 46, 49–51; *Dagbok* IV, 27. Cf. R. Peyre, "Sympathies des états scandinaves pour la Révolution française et pour Bonaparte," *Revue des études napoléoniennes* I (1912), 340–41.

7. [Hans Hierta], *Några tankar om sättet att åter upprätta och befästa den urgamla franska monarkien* (1799); Olof Dixelius, *Den unge Järta. En studie över en litterär politiker* (Uppsala, 1953), 177–78, 276; Svenson, *Gattjinatraktaten*, 332–33.

8. *Dagbok* IV, 37.

9. *Ibid.*, 37–38.

10. *Ibid.*, 39; *Svenska akademiens handlingar* LV (Stockholm, 1877), 266; H.S. Nyberg, *Johan Adam Tingstadius* (Stockholm, 1953), 170–73.

11. *Dagbok* IV, 39–41; Sven G. Svenson, "Studentens klang- och jubeltid. Från Juntan till skandinavism," in *Uppsalastudenten genom tiderna* (Uppsala, 1950), 94–95.

12. *Dagbok* IV, 42–43, 148, 376. On Uppsala University at this time, see the generally favorable descriptions in Joseph Acerbi, *Travels through Sweden, Finland, and Lappland to the North Cape in the Years 1798 and 1799*, 2 vol. (London, 1802), I, 149–56; and Robert Ker Porter, *Travelling Sketches in Russia and Sweden, 1805, 1806, 1807, 1808*, 2 vol. (London, 1809), II, 153–74; and the strongly critical account in E.D. Clarke, *Travels in Various Countries of Scandinavia; including Denmark, Sweden, Norway, Lapland and Finland*, 3 vol. (London, 1838), III, 1–49.

13. *Dagbok* IV, 42–43; *HEC* VI, 245.

14. *Dagbok* IV, 46; Hildebrand, *SBL* XV, 727; G.G. Adlerbeth, *Historiska anteckningar*, ed. Elof Tegnér, 3 vol. (Stockholm, 1892), III, 53–54; F. to Gust. IV Ad., 17 June 1806, F. arkiv II, RA; Kanslersämbetets för Uppsala universitet arkiv: Uppsala universitet, kanslerns koncepter, B 17, B 18, B 19, RA. Cf. *DeLaGardiska arkivet* XX, 111–12.

15. Hans Gabriel Trolle-Wachtmeister, *Anteckningar och minnen*, ed. Elof Tegnér, 2 vol. (Stockholm, 1889), I, 10. H.G. Wachtmeister added Trolle to his name in 1810, but to avoid confusion and to distinguish him from his father, Count C.A. Wachtmeister, I use the later form of his name throughout. *Dagbok* IV, 46.

16. Birger Liljekrantz, *Benjamin Höijer. En studie över hans utveckling* (Lund, 1912), 236, 261–62, 319–20; F. to Consistorium Academicum, 15 May 1800, Kanslerns koncepter B 17, RA; same to same, (?) May 1807, Kanslerns koncepter B 18, RA; same to same, 30 Nov. 1809, Kanslerns koncepter B 19, RA; Svenson, "Studentens klang- och jubeltid," 95–96; K.F. Werner, "Gustav Abraham [Silfverstolpe]," in *Några anteckningar om adliga ätten Silfverstolpe* (Stockholm, 1884), 286. On 21 Mar. 1809, F. himself proposed Höijer as first choice to fill the newly vacant professorship of logic and metaphysics, to the royal council. Protokoll i konseljen och kungl. beredning, 1809, I, RA.

17. *Dagbok* IV, 70–73; chancellor's memorandum, 26 Feb. 1800, Kanslerns koncepter B 17, RA; F. to Rector Magnificus, 6 Mar.

464 COUNT HANS AXEL VON FERSEN

1800, *ibid.*; Svenson, "Studentens klang- och jubeltid," 90–92; Werner, "Gustaf Abraham Silfverstolpe," 257–74; Birger Schöldström, *Förbiskymtande skuggor* (Stockholm, 1883), 63–66.

18. Svenson, "Studentens klang- och jubeltid," 96–99; Werner, "Gustaf Abraham Silfverstolpe," 287–325; Nyberg, *Johan Adam Tingstadius,* 175–79; Schöldström, *Förbiskymtande skuggor,* 59–86; *Dagbok* IV, 147; Söderhjelm in *ibid.,* 147n.; F. to Consistorium Academicum, 24 Sept. 1800, Kanslerns koncepter B 17, RA. L.F. Leijel would appear to have been related to Catherine Leyel, whom F. courted in 1778.

19. *Dagbok* IV, 46–47, 59–60, 74, 147–48, 355, 364, 366, 375–76, 406, 438; Söderhjelm in *ibid.,* 12; chancellor's memoranda, *passim.,* Kanslerns koncepter B 17, B 18, B 19, RA, esp. 9 May 1800, 3 Oct., 20 Nov. 1806, 1 Oct. 1807; Beskow, *Lefnadsminnen,* 40; Flach, *Fersen,* 125–36; M.J. Crusentolpe, *Medaljonger och statyetter* (Stockholm, 1882), 312; cf. Yngve Lövegren, *Naturaliekabinett i Sverige under 1700-talet* (Lund, 1952). On 11 Sept. 1801, F. recommended Pehr Afzelius for a professorship by virtue of his talents, assuring Gustav IV Adolf that the latter had "avowed to me his wrongs and errors." Handskriftsavdelningen F 657 b., UUB.

20. Chancellor's memoranda, 24 Apr. 1804, 10 Mar. 1808, 7 Feb., 6, 30 Apr. 1809, Kanslerns koncepter B 17, B 19, RA; *Dagbok* IV, 389. According to Clarke, *Travels* III, 20, there were not over 300 students at Uppsala in 1799–1800. The English Dr. Fiott Lee spoke of an enrollment of 800 in 1807. *Ibid.,* 20n., 24n.

21. *Dagbok* IV, 148, 375.

22. *Samuel Ödmanns skrifter och brev,* ed. Henning Wijkmark (Stockholm, 1925), II, 230. During F.'s absence on the Continent in 1801–1803, M.J. Brahe assumed his duties as chancellor. Kanslerns koncepter B 17, B 18, B 19, RA; F. to Gust. IV Ad., 11 Sept. 1801, Handskriftsavdelningen F 657 b., UUB; F. to Wetenskaps-Societeten i Uppsala, 7 June 1804, Kanslerns koncepter B 17, RA; Engeström I.f.8., KB; Beskow, *Lefnadsminnen,* 40. Schering Rosenhane, however, claimed in 1800 that F. did not speak Latin with the professors "for fear they might laugh at his Italian accent." *DeLaGardiska arkivet* XX, 112.

23. *Dagbok* IV, 46–47, 202. Cf. Lappmarkens ecklesiastikverk arkiv, RA. This body was established by the estates in 1738 to propagate "the pure evangelical doctrine" among the Lapps. Its protocol shows F. attended 4 meetings between Dec. 1799 and Sept. 1801.

24. On the reorganization of the chancellery, see A. Forsell, "Utrikesförvaltningens historia 1721–1809," in Sven Tunberg, *et al., Den svenska utrikesförvaltningens historia* (Uppsala, 1935), 290–93. On the *Kanslersgille,* see Kanslersgillets arkiv: kanslersgillet till Kungliga Majestetet, RA, Vols. I–IV. On education in Sweden in this period, see Sam Clason, *Karl XIII och Karl XIV Johan* (Stockholm, 1923), 46–48. Primary education, meanwhile appears to have been good. Joseph Acerbi wrote with some exaggeration in 1802, "There is, perhaps, no country in Europe where instruction is so universally

diffused among the very lowest of the people as in Sweden, except Iceland, Scotland, and the small republic of Geneva. All the people in towns, villages, and hamlets, without exception, are taught to read." *Travels* I, 136.

25. On the *Kanslersgille* and the new school ordinance, see O.T. Sjöfors, *Kanslärsgillet och 1807 års skolordning* (Lund, 1919). The protocols show that the *Kanslersgille* normally met two or three times each year and that F. began to attend in Mar. 1803, after returning from the Continent. Kanslersgillets arkiv, RA.

26. Sjöfors, *Kanslärsgillet, passim.*, esp. 36–85; *Dagbok* IV, 535.

27. Hildebrand, *SBL* XV, 731; *Dagbok* IV, 297, 348, 390; Söderhjelm in *ibid.*, 77, 170; cf. Söderhjelm, *FMA*, 125.

28. See *HEC* VI, 243–44; Engeström, *Minnen* II, 224; Hochschild, *Memoarer* III, 303–304, 306–308, 316, 319–23; Adlerbeth, *Hist. anteckn.* III, 30–31, 39–40, 51; Olle Gasslander, "The Convoy Affair of 1798," *Scandinavian Economic History Review* II (1954), 22–30.

29. *Dagbok* IV, 34, 47, 55–62.

30. See Malte Hamnström, *Om realisationsfrågan vid riksdagen i Norrköping år 1800* (Härnösand, 1896), 5–18; *Dagbok* IV, 22–24, 27.

31. Adlerbeth, *Hist. anteckn.* III, 31.

32. *Dagbok* IV, 22–23, 58. Cf. Taube's fears over Gustav III's convening of the Gävle riksdag of 1792. Taube to F., 6 Dec. 1791, F. arkiv XIV, RA.

33. *Dagbok* IV, 61.

34. *Ibid.*, 62, 66–67, 70.

35. *Ibid.*, 64–65; *HEC* VII, 11; Svenson, *Gattjinatraktaten*, 337–38. On Budberg, see *Dropmore Papers* IV, 66; *Dagbok* III, 110.

36. *Dagbok* IV, 62–63, 65–66, 70, 129.

37. *Ibid.*, 64–65, 67. On the Norrköping Riksdag of 1800, see especially Stavenow, *Gustavianska tiden*; Hamnström, *Realisationsfrågan*; Sam Clason, "Några anmärkningar rörande riksdagen i Norrköping år 1800," *Historisk tidskrift* (1897), 1–31; Adlerbeth, *Hist. anteckn.* III; Erik Elinder, "Adolf Ludvig Hamiltons minnesanteckningar från 1800 års riksdag," *Personhistorisk tidskrift* LII (1954), 73–142.

38. *Dagbok* IV, 64, 72; *HEC* VIII, 9.

39. *HEC* VII, 7, 12.

40. *Dagbok* IV, 86–89.

41. *Ibid.*, 62, 65–66, 70, 85–86, 98.

42. *Dagbok* IV, 93–95, 98; Adlerbeth, *Hist. anteckn.* III, 71–72; Elinder, "Hamiltons minnesanteckn.," 104–106; Schöldström, *Förbiskymtande skuggor*, 70–72.

43. On the solution of the financial problem, see Clason, "Några anmärkn.," 10–12; Elinder, "Hamiltons minnesanteckn.," 107–108, 130; Stavenow, *Gustavianska tiden*, 284–85; Hamnström, *Realisationsfrågan*, 67–69, 79–81; *Dagbok* IV, 103–104, 106.

44. *Dagbok* IV, 86–87.

45. *Ibid.*, 84–85, 91. Sten Carlsson, in *Stådssamhälle och ståndspersoner*, 236–37, has shown that most of the so-called "Jacobins" at the

Riksdag of 1800 did not hold positions in the state service and a number were in modest circumstances.
46. *Dagbok* IV, 91.
47. *Ibid.*, 84, 89–91; Söderhjelm in *ibid.*, 78–80.
48. *Ibid.*, 33. Cf. Elinder, "Hamiltons minnesanteckn.," 95.
49. *Dagbok* IV, 95, 97, 99–100, 102, 104, 106, 114, 130.
50. *Ibid.*, 104, 106.
51. *Ibid.*, 107; Hamnström, *Realisationsfrågan*, 91–92, 98–101.
52. *Dagbok* IV, 107. Cf. *HEC* VII, 27–28; Elinder, "Hamiltons minnesanteckn.," 115.
53. *Dagbok* IV, 108–11, 115; Hamnström, *Realisationsfrågan*, 102–104; Clason, "Några anmärkn.," 20–23, 27; Elinder, "Hamiltons minnesanteckn.," 116–23.
54. *HEC* VII, 31; Söderhjelm in *Dagbok* IV, 82; Dixelius, *Den unge Järta*, 328; Elinder, "Hamiltons minnesanteckn.," 115; Svenson, "Studentens klang- och jubeltid," 96.
55. Elinder, "Hamiltons minnesanteckn.," 137.
56. *Dagbok* IV, 116.
57. Söderhjelm, in *ibid*, 77.
58. *Ibid.*, 146, 150, 152–54, 156–57, 189–90; cf. chancellor's memorandum, 17 Dec. 1800, Kanslerns koncepter B 17, RA, concerning Uppsala University's share of the levy.
59. *Dagbok* IV, 195, 391. Cf. J.A. Almquist, *Stockholms stads brandförsakringskontor 1746–1921* (Stockholm, 1921).
60. Cf. Kjell Kumlien, "Axel von Fersens dagbok," *Ord och bild* (1937), 382–84.

CHAPTER XIII

1. *Dagbok* IV, 90.
2. *Ibid.*, 159. For Gustav IV Adolf's foreign policy in this period, see especially Carlsson, *SUPH III:1;* Seved Johnson, *Sverige och stormakterna 1800–1804* (Lund, 1957); the same author's "Neutralitetsförbundet i sitt storpolitiska sammanhang," *Historisk tidskrift* (1953), 313–27; Gasslander, "Convoy Affair."
3. *Dagbok* IV, Cf. Carlsson, *SUPH III:1*, 82; Johnson, *Sverige och stormakterna*, 61.
4. *Dagbok* IV, 160–61, 172, 174–80, 184–85; Söderhjelm in *ibid.*, 170; Adlerbeth, *Hist. anteckn.* III, 86; Hochschild, *Memoarer* III, 334–36; *HEC* VII, 56, 62. The protocols of the council show meetings were normally held once or twice a week with F. in regular attendance, and generally dealt with routine administrative matters. They do not show the part taken in the sessions by those present, other than to note their attendance. Cf. Protokoll i inrikes civilärenden 1800, 1801; Protokoll i krigsärenden 1801; Protokoll i utrikesärenden 1800–1801; all in RA.
5. Cf. Col. H. H. Anckarhielm (Gustafvia) to F., 30 Apr., 15 July 1801, F. arkiv XII, RA, containing a lengthy account of the British occupation of St. Barthélemy.

6. *Dagbok* IV, 180, 194, 200, 201, 204, 220–21.

7. *Ibid.*, 201.

8. *Ibid.*, 189, 191, 193–98; Adlerbeth, *Hist. anteckn.* III, 98, 127–28; *HEC* VII, 67. On the reorganization of the *Kanslikollegium*, see Forsell, "Utrikesförvaltningens historia," 290–94.

9. *Dagbok* IV, 189, 191, 194; *HEC* VII, 67.

10. *Dagbok* IV, 191–92.

11. *Ibid.*, 198, 221.

12. *Ibid.*, 205–206; Hochschild, *Memoarer* III, 343, 345; Adlerbeth, *Hist. anteckn.* III, 109.

13. *Dagbok* IV, 54, 197, 213–14.

14. *Ibid.*, 215, 217–18, 224; F. to Gust. IV Ad., 5 May 1801, Handskriftsavdelningen F 657 b., UUB; *HEC* VII, 67.

15. *Dagbok* IV, 221, 224–27.

16. *Ibid.*, 155, 225, 227–28; F. to Gust. IV Ad., 28 May 1801, Handskriftsavdelningen F 657 b., UUB. On the origins of the office of *riksmarskalk*, see *HEC* VII, 169–70.

17. *Dagbok* IV, 230–32; Hochschild, *Memoarer* II, 345–46; Adlerbeth, *Hist. Anteckn.* III, 106–107.

18. Johnson, *Sverige och stormakterna*, 76–115; Nilsson, *Diplomatiska förbindelserna*, 88–107; Engeström, *Minnen* II, 62.

19. *Dagbok* IV, 43–45, 47–49, 52, 56–57; cf. *HEC* VII, 10, 59. Alma Söderhjelm, in *Dagbok* IV, 126, discerned "the embryo of a more tender attachment" in F.'s interest in Queen Fredrika, though there seems to be no very convincing evidence of this.

20. *Dagbok* IV, 230–32, 236–37, 242; *HEC* VII, 211. Cf. Trolle-Wachtmeister, *Anteckningar* I, 19–20.

21. *Dagbok* IV, 223, 228, 232, 235, 240, 253.

22. See F. W. Morén's review of *Dagbok* IV, in *Historisk tidskrift* (1936), 422–23. Cf. *HEC* VII, 51, 58–59, 117, 127, 133–34, 142, 145–46.

23. *Dagbok* IV, 132, 134, 138–41, 144–45, 148, 155–56, 189, 216, 229–30, 247, 251; Söderhjelm in *ibid.*, 119–25; F. to Gust. IV Ad., 28 May 1801, Handskriftsavdelningen F 657 b., UUB; Gust. IV Ad. to F., 20 Aug. 1801, F. arkiv XI, RA. F. seems to have first mentioned the idea of a journey to Italy with Sophie in his letter to her of 4 Oct. 1796, Lövstad arkiv VIII. F.'s letter register, F. arkiv X, RA, shows a lively correspondence with Marianne in 1801.

24. Söderhjelm in *Dagbok* IV, 255–60. In this, as in certain subsequent sections, she summarizes parts of the diary. Cf. F. to Gust. IV Ad., 28 Oct., 22 Nov., 18 Dec. 1801, Handskriftsavdelningen F 657 b., UUB On Italy at this time, cf. André Fugier, *Napoléon et l'Italie* (Paris, 1947). Lövstad arkiv VIII contains an impressive collection of passports and travel documents for F. and his party.

25. *Dagbok* IV, 261–64, 276–77, 280, 303, 312–13, 334; Söderhjelm in *ibid.*, 277, who considered Ketty the love best suited to F. On her affair with Armfelt, see Tegnér, *Armfelt* II, 89–90, 158. Cf. F. to Gust.

IV Ad., 18 Dec. 1801, 5, 19 Jan. 1802, Handskriftsavdelningen F 657 b., UUB.

26. *Dagbok* IV, 269.

27. *Ibid.*, 275; F. to Gustav IV Adolf, 2, 27 Mar. 1802, Handskriftsavdelningen F 657 b., UUB.

28. *HEC* VII, 536–37. In this connection, young H. G. Trolle-Wachtmeister, who had a reputation in Sweden of being something of a Jacobin, had difficulties in obtaining French permission to travel in Italy two years later, in 1804, when Franco-Swedish relations were again on the decline. Trolle-Wachtmeister, *Anteckningar* I, 38.

29. *Dagbok* IV, 222–23, 239, 243–44, 251, 266, 279; Adlerbeth, *Hist anteckn.* III, 107; *HEC* VII, 115.

30. *Dagbok* IV, 267–71, 275, 282–83, 286–87, 289–90, 297; Söderhjelm in *ibid.*, 269, 272–74; F. to Gust. IV Ad., 4 May 1802, Handskriftsavdelningen F 657 b., UUB. Cf. Trolle-Wachtmeister, *Anteckningar* I, 38–40.

31. *Dagbok* IV, 290, 293, 298, 306.

32. On Naples in this period, see Harold Acton, *The Bourbons of Naples* (London, 1956); R. R. Palmer, *The Age of the Democratic Revolution*, 2 vol. (Princeton, 1959–64), II, 382–91.

33. *Dagbok* IV, 299–300. Cf. Acton, *Bourbons of Naples*, 455–56.

34. *Dagbok* IV, 301.

35. *Ibid.*, 299.

36. Trolle-Wachtmeister, *Anteckningar* I, 40–41.

37. *Dagbok* IV, 293, 298, 300–301, 306. Marie-Caroline had been profuse in her gratitude to F. for all he had done for her sister, Marie-Antoinette. Alma Söderhjelm surmised in *ibid.*, 292, that F. wished to avoid meeting her because of the role she was understood to have played in the white terror of 1799 in Naples. F. wrote to Gust. IV Ad. on 21 Aug. 1802 that he had left Naples, despite the queen's expressed wish to see him, because of Sophie's ill health. Handskriftsavdelningen F 657 b., UUB.

38. *Dagbok* IV, 304, 308–12; Söderhjelm in *ibid.*, 307, 312n. On Hedvig Möllersvärd's affair with Budberg, see also Alma Söderhjelm, "Den verkliga Heddas journal. Vad de Fersenska papperen ha att förmäla i en aktuell historia," *Sydsvenska dagbladet–snällposten*, No. 349, 22 Dec. 1935, p. 14.

39. *Dagbok* IV, 312–14, 318–22; Söderhjelm in *ibid.*, 315–17.

40. Carlsson, *Gustav IV Adolf*, 83; *Dagbok* IV, 33, 336, 338; Söderhjelm, in *ibid.*, 327; Scaevola [K. A. Strömbäck], *Utländska diplomaters minnen från svenska hofvet* (Stockholm, 1885), 516; cf. Pétiet, *Gustave IV Adolphe et la Rév. franç.*, 269; Lodren-Lateran's dispatch, in Grossherzogliches Familien-Archiv, Badensisches Generallarchiv, Karlsruhe. (See Ch. XI, note 29.)

41. *Dagbok* IV, 334–35, 338, 342, 363, 365, 369, 371–73; Söderhjelm in *ibid.*, 165–66, 327–28, 330; Morén, review of *ibid.*

42. *Ibid.*, 335, 353, 366–67, 391.

43. *Ibid.*, 355, 364.

44. *Ibid.*, 334–36, 342–47; *HEC* VII, 200–201, 208–209; Adlerbeth, *Hist. anteckn.* III, 147–48; Johnson, *Sverige och stormakterna*, 127–38.

45. *Dagbok* IV, 338–40, 347–57. Cf. *HEC* VII, 214–28, 497–527; Adlerbeth, *Hist. anteckn.* III, 157–58, 160–63; Trolle-Wachtmeister, *Anteckningar* I, 23–30.

46. *Dagbok* IV, 338; Trolle-Wachtmeister, *Anteckningar* I, 24. On 3 Jan. 1798, F. had written Taube that he had no knowledge of "this Boheman," of whom Taube had written; he considered it impossible that Boheman could have taken any of the French royal family's money out of France, on the basis of his own knowledge of the matter, but did not dismiss the possibility that Boheman might later have acquired some of it through some skullduggery, for which reason F. wanted Taube to advise him whether Boheman himself boasted that his wealth derived from the French king and queen. Taube arkiv III, RA. Boheman told Duchess Charlotta that her friend Sophie Piper's late lover, Baron Taube, was condemned for all eternity to plant potatoes! Though the duchess wanted to bring Sophie into his lodge, Boheman was afraid of Sophie's good sense. Trolle-Wachtmeister, *Anteckningar* I, 26.

47. *Dagbok* II, 291; IV, 338–40, 348–53, 357. In Stockholm in 1800 there were some 60 academies, societies, and orders. *HEC* VII, 404n. The mystical and occultist orders in Sweden, as well as their opponents, are brilliantly treated in Martin Lamm, *Upplysningstidens romantik*, 2 vol. (Stockholm, 1918–20), II, 1–121.

48. *Dagbok* IV, 360; *HEC* VII, 189–90. On the Abborfors crisis, see Johnson, *Sverige och stormakterna*, 151–53, 159–63; Carlsson, *SUPH III:1*, 76–78.

49. *Dagbok* IV, 358–61.

50. *Ibid.*, 361.

51. *Ibid.*, 361–63, 365, 370–71; Johnson, *Sverige och stormakterna*, 159–69. Johnson feels that Gustav IV Adolf and Lagerbjelke might have chosen war, had they felt sure of French assistance. *Ibid.*, 165–69. Queen Fredrika wrote her mother in Karlsruhe on 19 Apr. 1803 that she hoped the threat would pass so that it would not interfere with her projected trip to Germany; she saw no reason for so much fuss over that unfortunate litle bridge at Aborrfors and could not see why the Russians should want it since they already had one twice as large. Grossherzogliches Familien-Archiv, Badensisches Generallarchiv, Karlsruhe. (See Ch. XI, note 29.)

52. *Dagbok* IV, 112, 132, 360, 365, 367–71, 373–74; *HEC* VII, 131–32, 247–48.

53. *Dagbok* IV, 374, 380, 387–88, 425. Protokoll i inrikes-civilärenden, konselj- och kabinettsprotokoll, 1803, 1804, 1805, RA. As chairman of the interim government, F. wrote a number of letters to Lagerbjelke, who accompanied the king, which are quite friendly in tone. Gustaf Lagerbjelke samling XIV, RA.

54. *HEC* VII, 255, 277. On disagreements within the interim government, cf. F. to Gust. IV Ad., 30 Nov. 1803, F. arkiv II, RA.

55. *HEC* VII, 255–56.

56. *Dagbok* IV, 362, 364, 376–80, 405. The official papers of the grand marshals are in the *Riksmarskalksämbetets expedition*, in the royal palace, Stockholm, well arranged and indexed.

57. *Dagbok* IV, 372, 379–80, 400.

58. *Ibid.*, 394, 402, 404–406.

59. *Ibid.*, 364–65, 396, 423.

60. *Ibid.*, 380–84, 390, 411, 423; F. to Gust. IV Ad., 23 Dec. 1803, 10, 18 Feb. 1804, F. arkiv II, RA; cf. *HEC* VII, 139. See also the criticism of F.'s "despotic" strictness in managing the court by a former page in "Memorarer af Hofintendenten von Röök, in Ahnfelt, *Ur svenska hofvets och aristokratiens lif* I, 40–42.

61. *Dagbok* IV, 379, 385–88, 391–92, 401–402, 410–11; Gust. IV Ad. to F., 30 May 1804, F. arkiv XI, RA; F. to Lagerbjelke, 24 Feb. 1804, Lagerbjelke samling XIV, RA; F. to Gust. IV Ad., 28 Oct. 1801, Handskriftsavdelningen F 657 b., UUB, with details on Duke Fredrik; *HEC* VII, 7, 268–71. On Duke Fredrik, see Söderhjelm, *Gustaf III:s syskon*, 67–106.

62. *Dagbok* IV, 336, 356, 407–409, 412–14; F. to Gust. IV Ad., 30 Nov. 1803, 18 Apr., 9 June, 24 July, 31 Aug., 7, 21 Sept. 1804, F. arkiv II, RA; Gust. IV Ad. to F., 13 Aug. 1804, F. arkiv XI, RA; *HEC* VII, 317–19. Cf. Gérard Walter, *Le comte de Provence* (Paris, 1950), 361–72; M. de Barante, ed., *Lettres et instructions de Louis XVIII au comte de Saint-Priest* (Paris, 1845), 168–74.

63. *Dagbok* IV, 413–15, 418; F. to Gust. IV Ad., 31 Aug., 21, 25 Sept., 5, 9 Oct. 1804, F. arkiv II, RA; Gust. IV Ad. to F., 3, 9 Oct. 1804, F. arkiv XI, RA; Daudet, *Histoire de l'émigration* III, 326–56; Walter, *Le comte de Provence*, 368–71.

64. *Dagbok* IV, 414–17; F. to Gust. IV Ad., 10, 17 Oct. 1804, F. arkiv II, RA; "Copie de la lettre à Calmar ce 27 septembre [*sic*] 1804, de Louis XVIII au Comte de Saint-Priest," *ibid.*; Gust. IV Ad., 20 Nov. 1804, F. arkiv XI, RA; *HEC* VII, 317–19, 570–75; Walter, *Le comte de Provence*, 371–72; Barante, *Lettres et instructions*, 177.

65. *Dagbok* IV, 415–16; F. to Gust. IV Ad., 15 Oct., 12 Nov. 1804, F. arkiv II, RA; Gust. IV Ad. to F., 29 Oct. 1804, F. arkiv XI, RA. Cf. *The Diaries and Letters of Sir George Jackson*, ed. Lady Jackson, 2 vol. (London, 1872), I, 216–17; Daudet, *Histoire de l'émigration* III, 340–62; Barante, *Lettres et instructions*, 180. F.'s account of his meeting with the princes disproves Daudet's contention, *op. cit.*, 361–62, that in disagreement with Artois, F. approved the proposed manifesto and urged that it be published without delay so long as it was not dated on Swedish soil. F. was above all interested in encouraging the Bourbons to leave before they caused any complications.

66. *Dagbok* IV, 416–17; Gust. IV Ad. to F., 19 Aug. 1805, F. arkiv XI, RA; *HEC* VII, 416–17; Daudet, *Histoire de l'émigration*, III, 362–81.

67. *Dagbok* IV, 412, 420–21, 429, 433; F. to Gust. IV Ad., 24 Dec. 1804, 11 Jan. 1805, F. arkiv II, RA; Gust. IV Ad. to F., 9 Jan. 1805, F. arkiv XI, RA.

68. *Dagbok* IV, 376, 405, 409, 412, 439.

69. *Ibid.*, 363, 372, 379, 391–92, 409, 417, 429, 433.

70. André Desfeuilles, "Félix Berger, cuisinier d'Axel de Fersen. D'après une correspondance inédite, 1801–1807," *Mémoires de l'Académie de Vaucluse* (Avignon, 1953, pamphlet), 16–17.

71. *Dagbok* IV, 22, 46, 94–95, 141–43, 148, 336, 361, 368, 380, 384–85, 392, 400, 402, 404, 432–34, 439, 529, 534; Söderhjelm in *ibid.*, 531, 536–37. One is reminded of G. J. Ehrensvärd's earlier comment that "in Sweden, what always loses out is the indigenous." *Dagboksanteckningar* I, 144. However, see also similar criticisms of Swedish society and culture by foreigners: Acerbi, *Travels* I, 34–81; Clarke, *Travels* III, 44–45, 66–67; Porter, *Travelling Sketches* II, 118–25, 134–41.

72. *Dagbok* IV, 394, 401, 409. Cf. *HEC* VII, 282–83.

73. *Dagbok* IV, 45, 83, 180, 232, 371, 384, 389, 400, 406, 433, 437–38, 529, 535; Söderhjelm in *ibid.*, 78–80, 529, 535.

74. *Ibid.*, 363, 368, 371–72, 378, 380, 392; Söderhjelm in *ibid.*, 324–27, 531.

75. See Söderhjelm in *ibid.*, 324–25, 327, 329, 331; also diary, *ibid.*, 333.

76. *Ibid.*, 409, 413, 418–19, 422–23, 427–29, 431–32, 434, 437. Cf. *HEC* VII, 336–40; Adlerbeth, *Hist. anteckn.* III, 202–203.

77. *Dagbok* IV, 432, 434–35, 439; *HEC* VII, 358–59.

78. *Dagbok* II, 304, 311; IV, 502–504; *HEC* VIII, 34–35; Trolle-Wachtmeister, *Anteckningar* I, 61–62, 66; Carlsson, *Gustav IV Adolf*, 98. Gustav III's opera house, built in 1782, was replaced in 1891 by the present Stockholm Opera.

79. *Dagbok* IV, 481, 489–90, 501–502, 556–57; Adlerbeth, *Hist. anteckn.* III, 208, 262; *HEC* VIII, 78–79, 337–38; Trolle-Wachtmeister, *Anteckningar*, I, 68, 72, 74, 82.

CHAPTER XIV

1. On Gustav IV Adolf's foreign policy preceding and during the War of the Third Coalition, see especially, Carlsson, *Gustav IV Adolf*; Carlsson, *SUPH III:1;* Johnson, *Sverige cch stormakterna*; Seved Johnson, "Legend och verklighet kring Gustav IV Adolfs brytning med Napoleon," *Svensk tidskrift* XXXVII (1950), 460–66; Herbert Lundh, *Gustav IV Adolf och Sveriges utrikespolitik 1801–1804. Förhistoria till Sveriges deltagande i det tredje koalitionskriget mot Frankrike* (Uppsala, 1926); J. Holland Rose, "Gustavus IV and the Formation of the Third Coalition," *Révue napoléonienne* II (1902), 88–93. On St. Génié, see Pétiet, *Gustave IV Adolphe et la Rév. franç.*, 304.

2. *Dagbok* IV, 395–99, 401; cf. Gust. IV Ad., to F., 17 Mar. 1804, F. arkiv XI, RA; F. to Gust. IV Ad., 6 Apr. 1804, F. arkiv II, RA. F.'s letters to G. Lagerbjelke, who accompanied the king, show F. now well disposed toward Lagerbjelke and, like him, fearful of Sweden's involvement in a larger European conflict. F. to Lagerbjelke, 11 [Aug. 1803], 18, 24 Apr., 6 July, 3 Aug. 1804, Lagerbjelke samling XIV, RA. A sign of F.'s resignation toward the new order on the Continent might be

found in his requests to Lagerbjelke that he arrange for him the purchase in Paris of clothes for his sister and nieces, and of a watch for himself. F. to Lagerbjelke, 5 June, 5 Oct. 1804, *ibid.*

3. *Dagbok* IV, 401–402, 404, 407; F. to Gust. IV Ad., 18 Apr., 18 May 1804, F. arkiv II, RA; F. to Lagerbjelke, 6 Apr., 29 May, 6, 13 July 1804, Lagerbjelke samling XIV, RA.

4. Carlsson, *Gustav IV Adolf*, 131; F. to Lagerbjelke, 6, 18 Apr., 9 June, 29 Dec. 1804, Lagerbjelke samling XIV, RA.

5. *Dagbok* IV, 394, 398; *HEC* VII, 280–83; Adlerbeth, *Hist anteckn.* III, 185; Engeström, *Minnen* II, 46; Pétiet, *Gustave IV Adolphe et la Rév. franç.*, 305.

6. Carlsson, *Gustav IV Adolf*, 132; *HEC* VII, 307–11, which gives the text of the *Moniteur* article; cf. *ibid.*, 315; Pétiet, *Gustave IV Adolphe et la Rév. franç.*, 311–14; *Dagbok* IV, 412; F. to Gust. IV Ad., 7 Sept. 1804, F. arkiv II, RA.

7. On Gustav IV Adolf's relations specifically with Britain, 1804–1809, see especially K. V. Key-Åberg, *De diplomatiska förbindelserna mellan Sverige och Storbrittanien under Gustaf IV Adolfs krig mot Napoleon* (Uppsala, 1890); Raymond Carr, "Gustavus IV and the British Government, 1804–1809," *English Historical Review* LX (1945), 36–66; W. F. Reddaway, "Canning and the Baltic in 1807," *The Baltic Countries* II (1936). *Dagbok* IV, 413.

8. *Dagbok* IV, 435–36. On Sweden's relations with Prussia in this period, see especially C. Grimberg, *De diplomatiska förbindelserna mellan Sverige och Preussen 1804–1808* (Göteborg, 1903); Jackson, *Diaries* I.

9. *Dagbok* IV, 436–37; cf. *HEC* VII, 352. As early as December 1795, F. noted that Gustav Adolf refused to wear the Russian Order of St. Andrew as long as Armfelt, then under a cloud because of his alleged conspiracy the previous year, wore it. *Dagbok* II, 230.

10. *Dagbok* IV, 438.

11. Söderhjelm in *ibid.*, 446–47. Söderhjelm summarizes parts of the diary for 1805–1807. According to *HEC* VII, 382, it was rumored in Stockholm that F. traveled to Germany on a secret diplomatic mission.

12. Söderhjelm in *Dagbok* IV, 448–51; letter register, F. arkiv X, RA.

13. *Dagbok* IV, 451–54; Gust. IV Ad. to F., 6 Aug. 1805, F. arkiv XI, RA; Count von Loos to F., 14 Sept. 1805, Autografssamlingen F, KB; *HEC* VII, 364–66. According to the Danish minister in Jan. 1807, F., who often invited the diplomatic corps to his home, always left out the Saxon chargé d'affaires because of this incident. C. J. Anker & F. U. Wrangel, ed., *Utdrag ur danska diplomaters meddelanden från Stockholm 1807–1808, 1810, 1812–13* (Stockholm, 1897), 3–4. The affair was not forgotten in Paris either. Cf. S. J. Boëthius, ed., *Bihang till Minnen ur Sveriges nyare historia*, 3 vol. (Uppsala, 1880–81), II, 159.

14. On Sweden's part in the War of the Third Coalition, see especially Gustaf Björlin, *Sveriges krig i Tyskland åren 1805–1807* (Stockholm, 1882); Stavenow, *Gustavianska tiden.*

15. Gust. IV Ad. to F., 19 Aug. 1805, F. arkiv II, RA; *Dagbok IV*, 459–60. Cf. Carlsson, *Gustav IV Adolf*, 143.

16. Cf. *HEC* VII, 421.

17. *Dagbok* IV, 130, 264, 296, 304, 306, 356, 392–94, 401. In the spring of 1804, F. granted four months' leave to his cook, Félix Berger, to travel to Paris, in which connection André Desfeuilles, in "Félix Berger, cuisinier d'Axel de Fersen," 10–11, 21–25, speculates that Berger might have been charged with secret political dealings by F. This seems unlikely, in view of F.'s political attitudes by this time, though it is not impossible that he wished to learn something of the fate of some of his old friends in France. Pétiet, in *Gustave IV Adolphe et la Rév. franç.*, 319, is altogether misleading in inferring that Gustav Adolf's entry into the Third Coalition represents F.'s preponderant influence at this time.

18. *Dagbok* IV, 460.

19. Söderhjelm in *ibid.*, 461–62.

20. *Ibid.*, 464–65; *HEC* VII, 421.

21. *Dagbok* IV, 465; Grimberg, *Sverige och Preussen*, 58–62.

22. *Dagbok* IV, 466.

23. *Ibid.*, 466–67.

24. *Ibid.*, 467–68. Cf. Key-Åberg, *Sverige och Storbrittanien*, 58n.

25. *Dagbok* IV, 468–69; Gust. IV Ad.'s circular to foreign envoys, 6 Dec. 1805, F. arkiv II, RA.

26. *Dagbok* IV, 469.

27. *Ibid.*, 469–70.

28. *Ibid.*, 470. C. Armfelt's dispatch from Troppau, 4 Dec. 1805, F. arkiv XIX, RA; Stedingk's dispatch, same date, *ibid.* See also Pétiet, *Gustave IV Adolphe et la Rév. franç.*, 321.

29. *Dagbok* IV, 470–71; dispatches from Count Düben and Baron Armfelt, 14 Dec. 1805, from Teschen and Breslau, F. arkiv III, RA, announcing armistice; F. to Gust. IV Ad., 23 Dec. 1805, F. arkiv II, RA; *Bihang till Journalen för Litteratur och Theater* (6 Sept. 1810), 2. The editor of this journal, P. A. Wallmark, published excerpts from F.'s correspondence with Gustav IV Adolf, Dec. 1805–June 1806, in the original French with parallel Swedish translation, in agreement with Fabian Fersen, who first edited the letters. See Söderhjelm, *Kärlek och politik*, 177–78, which casts some light on this though Alma Söderhjelm did not herself know that Wallmark had published the letters; see also Fabian Fersen to Wallmark, 12 Dec. 1812, Brev till P. A. Wallmark XVI, KB. Wallmark's published version of this correspondence must be used with caution since it does not generally indicate deletions.

30. *Dagbok* IV, 471–72; Björlin, *Sveriges krig i Tyskland*, 94–96; D. Alopaeus to G. af Wetterstedt, 13/25 Dec. 1805, F. arkiv XIX, RA; Gust. IV Ad. to F., 8 Jan. 1806, F. arkiv XI, RA.

31. F. to Gust. IV Ad., 7, 25 Jan. 1806, F. arkiv II, RA; *Bihang till Journalen* (6 Sept. 1810), 3–4.

32. *Dagbok* IV, 479–80, 482; Söderhjelm in *ibid.*, 474–75.

33. *Dagbok* IV, 480–81; Count Münster (Hannover), to Gust. IV

Ad., 8 Feb. 1806 (copy), F. arkiv XIX, RA; *Bihang till Journalen* (29 Sept. 1810), 1–2; *ibid.*(6 Sept. 1810), 5–6, 9; cf. F. to Gust. IV Ad., 12 Feb. 1806, F. arkiv II, RA.

34. French translation of C. J. Fox to Pierrepont, 14 Feb. 1806, F. arkiv XIX, RA; cf. Boëthius, *Bihang till Minnen* II, 35; *Dagbok* IV, 481–83; *Bihang till Journalen* (29 Sept. 1810), 2–5.

35. *Dagbok* IV, 483–84, 493; F. to Gust. IV Ad., 5 May 1806, F. arkiv II, RA.

36. *Dagbok* IV, 481–82, 488–90; Söderhjelm in *ibid.*, 474–75, 481, 488–89, 508; *HEC* VII, 422.

37. Söderhjelm in *Dagbok* IV, 476; *HEC* VII, 404. On Dr. Gall and phrenology, cf. Jackson, *Diaries* I, 277, 283–84; *DeLaGardiska arkivet* XIX, 16–19.

38. *Dagbok* IV, 476–78; Fauche-Borel to F., 21 Dec. 1805, F. arkiv XIX, RA, from which it appears that F. might have met Fauche-Borel shortly thereafter; Moustier to F., 8 Jan. 1806, F. arkiv XIII, RA; F. to Gust. IV Ad., 15 Jan. 1806, F. arkiv II, RA; Gust. IV Ad. to F., 3 Feb. 1806, F. arkiv XI, RA.

39. F. to Gust. IV Ad., 15, 20 Jan. 1806, F. arkiv II, RA; *Dagbok* IV, 478; Söderhjelm in *ibid.*, 476–79; *Handlingar ur Brinkman'ska arkivet på Trolle-Ljungby*, ed. G. Andersson, 2 vol. (Örebro, 1859–65), II, 228–29; *HEC* VII, 422–26; *Dropmore Papers* VIII, 210–11.

40. Adlerbeth, *Hist. anteckn.* III, 221, 223; *Dagbok* IV, 484–85, 487–88, 512–13; cf. *ibid.*, 407 and F. to Gust. IV Ad., 20 July 1804, F. arkiv II, RA.

41. *Dagbok* IV, 485–86; Grimberg, *Sverige och Preussen*, 70–72.

42. *Dagbok* IV, 491–92; Gust. IV Ad. to F., 26 Apr. 1806, F. arkiv XI, RA; *Bihang till Journalen* (29 Sept. 1810), 5–7. The comment on England's "egotistical" policy is omitted in this version, while a marginal notation on the original observes that though F.'s remark is "just," it would at that time be impolitic to print it. Cf. F. arkiv II, RA.

43. *Dagbok* IV, 492–93.

44. *Ibid.*, 493–95; *Bihang till Journalen* (29 Sept. 1810), 8–9; *ibid.* (6 Sept. 1810), 6–7; Gust. IV Ad. to Frederick William III, 21 May 1806, F. arkiv XIX, RA. F. later noted that the king's order could not be carried out since shallow water had generally kept the Swedish fleet too far out at sea. *Dagbok* IV, 495. Gustav Adolf's blockade of Prussian Baltic ports meanwhile caused difficulties for both his British and Russian allies. *Dropmore Papers* VIII, 234, 243-44; note from D. Alopaeus, 5 May 1806, and unsigned Swedish note, 23 May 1806, F. arkiv XIX, RA; Ministerstvo innostrannykh del SSSR, *Vneshnyaya politika Rossii XIX-go i nachala XX-go veka. Dokumenty Rossiiskogo ministerstva inostrannykh del*, series I (1801–15), III (Moscow, 1963), 140–42, 182, 247.

45. Grimberg, *Sverige och Preussen*, 81–82; cf. Jackson, *Diaries*, I, 440–41; Brinkman to F., 30 May 1806, F. arkiv XII, RA.

46. *Dagbok* IV, 497; Söderhjelm in *ibid.*, 497–98; Pierrepont to F., n.d., F. arkiv XIX, RA.

47. *Dagbok* IV, 499; *Bihang till Journalen* (29 Sept. 1810), 9; *ibid.* (6 Sept. 1810), 9.
48. Söderhjelm in *Dagbok* IV, 499–501; diary, *ibid.*, 508; F. to Gust. IV Ad., 10, 17 June 1806, 14 July 1807, F. arkiv II, RA; Gust. IV Ad. to F., 24, 28 July 1806, F. arkiv XI, RA.
49. *HEC* VII, 421–22, 433–34; Trolle-Wachtmeister, *Anteckningar* I, 79. See also Carlsson, "Wachtmeisters dagbok," 59–60. This work contains some useful material not given by E. Tegnér's 1889 edition. F. stated in his diary for 8 Jan. 1808, *Dagbok* IV, 558, that he then received his first letter from the king in two years.
50. F. to Lagerbjelke, 6 July 1804, Lagerbjelke samling XIV, RA.
51. Trolle-Wachtmeister, *Anteckningar* I, 68.
52. *Ibid.*, 47, 64, 79, 83; Carlsson, "Wachtmeisters dagbok," 59–60. Cf. Staf, *Polisväsendet*, 282, 285.
53. Carr, "Gustavus IV and the British Government," 50.
54. Björlin, *Sveriges krig i Tyskland*, 138, 193–94; *Dagbok* IV, 506.
55. *Dagbok* IV, 507–508.
56. See Morén, review of *Dagbok* IV, 423.
57. Adlerbeth, *Hist. anteckn.* III, 220; *HEC* VII, 421, 433, 439; *Corespondance de Napoléon Ier.*, XI, 503; Henrik Schück, ed., *Gustavianska brev* (Stockholm, 1918), 128; *Excellensen A.F. Skjöldebrands memoarer*, ed. Henrik Schück, 5 vol. (Stockholm, 1903–1904), IV, 101–102.
58. For this historiographical dispute, see Sture Bolin, "Gustaf IV Adolf i svensk historisk opinion," *Svensk tidskrift* XXVIII (1941), 323–36; supplemented by Carlsson, *Gustav IV Adolf*, 348–55; and Svenson, *Gattjinatraktaten*, 9–30.

CHAPTER XV

1. Desfeuilles, "Félix Berger cuisinier d'Axel de Fersen," 12–26; Engeström I.f.8., KB, 33, 35; Ture Nerman, *Fersenska mordet* (Stockholm, 1933); 50–52; Stockholm stads mantalslängder 1810, Stockholm stadsarkivet; Stockholm stads taxeringslängder 1810, Stockholm stadsarkivet; *Dagbok* IV, 545; Söderhjelm in *ibid.*, 531, 577; Sture M. Waller, *Georg Carl von Döbeln* (Lund, 1947), 598; Schinkel-Bergman, *Minnen* V, 531–32; Skjöldebrand, *Memoarer* IV, 101. For many details on F.'s household, carriages, liveries, treatment of servants, etc., see accounts, F. arkiv XX, XXI, XXII, XXIV, RA, esp. estate inventory, dated 13 Nov. 1810, F. arkiv XXI, RA; see also Lövstad arkiv XXI.
2. *Dagbok* IV, 548; Söderhjelm in *ibid.*, 514, 526, 537, 542–48. F.'s accounts, F. arkiv XXII, RA, give valuable clues regarding his movements in his last years.
3. F. first mentions Emelie in Feb. 1795, *Dagbok* II, 274; cf. *ibid.* IV, 23, 534. My discussion of their affair is based primarily on Söderhjelm's treatment in *ibid.*, 518–28, 537–49. F.'s friend, Marianne Ehrenström, later maintained that although F. wished to marry Emelie, she doubted that Emelie would have accepted, despite her warm friendship

476 COUNT HANS AXEL VON FERSEN

for him. Henrik Schück, *Den sista gustavianska hofdamen. Ur Marianne Ehrenströms minnen* (Stockholm, 1919), 138. See also F.'s letter register, F. arkiv X, RA, and accounts, F. arkiv XXII, RA. There are documents on F.'s guardianship of the Finspång estate in F. arkiv XX, RA. Schahovskoy-Stretchneff, *Le comte de Fersen*, gives some rather questionable details on this relationship.

4. *Dagbok* IV, 535, 545, 564, 566; Ahnfelt, *Ur svenska hofvets och aristokratiens lif* I, 166, 173n.; protocol for meetings of directors of Swedish East India Company of 27 June, 4 July 1808, Handel och sjöfart IV, Handelskompanier: Östindiska kompaniet III, RA; Schück, *Sista gustavianska hofdamen,* 143; accounts, F. arkiv XXII, RA; Duke Karl to F., 20 June 1807, F. arkiv II, RA; letters from F. on financial details connected with his official duties, in H. E. Lagerheims samling, serie II, B 29, RA; Skjöldebrand, *Memoarer* IV, 102.

5. *Dagbok* IV, 556–58, 561–64, 568–70; *HEC* VIII, 109, 192, 194–95, 231, 295–97, 815; Trolle-Wachtmeister, *Anteckningar* I, 83, 85, 159, 249; Carlsson, "Wachtmeisters dagbok," 60; Engström, *Minnen* II, 62; Carlsson, *Gustav IV Adolf,* 161; Sten Carlsson, *Gustav IV Adolfs fall* (Lund, 1944), 180–82; Forsell, "Utrikesförvaltningens historia," 297–98; Hildebrand, *SBL* XV, 710; F. to Gust. IV Ad., 31 Dec. 1808, regarding Duc de Piennes (last preserved letter from F. to Gustav IV Adolf). Curiously enough, Trolle-Wachtmeister, in *Anteckningar* I, 70–71, claims that in the summer of 1807, the king considered creating four Swedish "princes" *(furstar),* one of whom was to be F.

6. *Dagbok* IV, 552–64; *HEC* VIII, 97–100, 106–107, 109–113, 501–502; Carlsson, *Gustav IV Adolf,* 162.

7. See Söderhjelm in *Dagbok* IV, 548–50, 552. In a letter to Fabian Fersen of 20 Dec. 1810, Professor L. J. Rabenius of Uppsala asked whether F. had not been working on the manuscript of a "larger work," since he had often seen F. "lay the paper, on which he was writing, on top of a large pile of quarto-sized paper. . . ." F. arkiv XXI, RA. Presumably this was F.'s diary, for there is nothing else to suggest a "larger work."

8. *HEC* VII, 421–22; VIII, 681; Trolle-Wachtmeister, *Anteckningar* I, 79, 247; Skjöldebrand, *Memoarer* IV, 101–102; Schinkel-Bergman, *Minnen* V, 231–32.

9. F. to Taube, 6 July 1794, Taube arkiv III, RA; Geffroy, "Lettres," 98–99; Axel Lindvald, ed. *Kong Christian VIII.s Dagbøger og Optegnelser, I: 1799–1814* (Copenhagen, 1943), 94–95; Trolle-Wachtmeister, *Anteckningar* I, 247.

10. On the Russo-Swedish war of 1808–1809, see especially Carlsson, *Gustav IV Adolf*; Carlsson, *SUPH III:1*; Stavenow, *Gustavianska tiden*; Carr, "Gustavus IV and the British Government"; Anders Grade, *Sverige och Tilsit-alliansen 1807–1810* (Lund, 1913).

11. *HEC* VIII, 157.

12. Ahnfelt, *Ur svenska hofvets och aristokratiens lif* I, 164–66, 173n.; Schück, *Sista gustavianska hofdamen,* 106–108. The British chargé

d'affaires at this time was Augustus Foster, son of F.'s old friend, Lady Elizabeth Foster. Stuart, *Dear Bess*, 161.

13. On the coup d'état of 1809, see especially Carlsson, *Gustav IV Adolf;* Carlsson, *Gustav IV Adolfs fall;* Birger Sjövall, *Georg Adlersparre och tronfrågen 1809* (Lund, 1917).

14. Sam Clason & Carl af Petersens, ed. *För hundra år sen. Skildringar och bref från revolutionsåren 1809–1810,* 3 vol. (Stockholm, 1909–10), I, 14; *HEC* VIII, 315, 327n.

15. Carlsson, *Gustav IV Adolf,* 194–97; *HEC* VIII, 315–16, 318; Hildebrand, "Fabian Reinhold von Fersen," 755–56.

16. Cf. the various accounts of the 13 March 1809 in Clason, *För hundra år sen* I.

17. *HEC* VIII, 327; Suremain, *Mémoires,* 139–42. Strangely, Söderhjelm, in *Dagbok* IV, 576, did not know where F. was on 13 March 1809!

18. Cf. Scaevola, *Utländska diplomaters minnen,* 477.

19. See esp. Sjövall, *Adlersparre och tronfrågan.*

20. Carlsson, *Gustaf IV Adolf,* 212–13; Sjövall, *Adlersparre och tronfrågan,* 33–34; *HEC* VIII, 355–58, 399, 781; Trolle-Wachtmeister, *Anteckningar* I, 190–92.

21. Trolle-Wachtmeister, *Anteckningar* I, 199–200, 204, 223, 233. Klingspor's exclusion may have been a quid pro quo for F.'s, in view of the growing rivalry between Adlersparre and Adlercreutz.

22. Clason, *För hundra år sen* I, 242.

23. Schinkel-Bergman, *Minnen* V, 56–57; Trolle-Wachtmeister, *Anteckningar* I, 206, 209; Sture M. Waller, "Bidrag till kännedom om 1809–1810 års riksdags förhistoria och första skede," *Historisk tidskrift* (1953), 58.

24. Beskow, *Lefnadsminnen,* 119–20; *HEC* VIII, 356; cf. *ibid.,* 399; G. Rein, *Karl Johan Adlercreutz. Försök till en levnadsteckning,* 2 vol. (Helsingfors, 1925–27), II, 97, 108–11. Sjövall, in *Adlersparre och tronfrågan,* 59, simply claimed that the whole council except F. was won over to Adlersparre's proposition, without giving any source.

25. Söderhjelm in *Dagbok* IV, 577–78, 580; Clason, *För hundra år sen* I, 130–43; *HEC* VIII, 394–99, 403, 407–408; 1809 års statsrådsprotokoller (april–december 1809), Kammarexpeditionen, RA, 25.

26. Account book, F. arkiv XXII, RA; Clason, *För hundra år sen* I, 171; *HEC* VIII, 380, 392; Skjöldebrand, *Memoarer* IV, 91; Christian Wåhlin, "Anteckningar om riksdagarna 1809–10, 1812 och 1815," *Historiska handlingar* XXV:2 (Stockholm, 1916), 68. The inventories, in F. arkiv XVIII, RA, provide much information of the private wealth of the Vasa family and objects in the possession of Gustav IV Adolf and presumably of Gustav III.

27. Carlsson, *SUPH III:1,* 125–33, 153–54. Cf. F. to Lady Elizabeth Foster, 25 Mar. 1810, Geffory, "Lettres," 99, complaining of the impending break between Sweden and England. Among other things, the loss of Finland meant the loss of F.'s estate at Wuojoki. In Nov.

1809, it was leased to J. M. Gottschalk, then in Apr. 1811, sold *pro forma* by F.'s heirs to their relative by marriage, Baroness Sara Klinckow-ström, née Cuthbert, who was a British subject. Documents in F. arkiv XXI, RA, and Lövstad arkiv XXI.

28. On the Gustavians and their opponents, the "Men of 1809," see especially Sjövall, *Adlersparre och tronfrågan;* Göran Wibling, *Opinioner och stämningar i Sverige 1809–10* (Uppsala, 1954); Staf, *Polisväsendet;* Clason, *Karl XIII och Karl XIV Johan;* Sture Waller, *Rutger Macklean och 1809–1810 års riksdag* (Lund, 1953); Sigfrid Andgren, *Konung och ständer 1809–1812* (Lund, 1933).

29. Geffroy, "Lettres," 99. On Karl August, see Einar Forssberg, *Karl August, gustavianerna och 1809 års män* (Hälsingborg, 1942).

30. Schinkel-Bergman, *Minnen* V, 130, 139–40, 145–47, 231; Clason, *För hundra år sen* II, 43; *HEC* VIII, 477; Anker, *Danska diplomaters meddelanden,* 55; Trolle-Wachtmeister, *Anteckningar* I, 47, 246–49; Söderhjelm in *Dagbok* IV, 581; Wibling, *Opinioner och stämningar,* 190–91; Sjövall, *Adlersparre och tronfrågan,* 360, 363–64; Andgren, *Konung och ständer,* 28–29.

31. Schinkel-Bergman, *Minnen* V, 147–48, 151–53, 157–58n., 167–69, 216, 232; *HEC* VIII, 476, 489–90; Skjöldebrand, *Memoarer* IV, 96–97; Jöns Person Häggman, Anteckningar 1808–16, D. 1048 a., KB, 26–27; Nerman, *Fersenska mordet,* 8, 14; Wibling, *Opinioner och stämningar,* 204; Wåhlin, "Anteckningar," 85.

32. Schinkel-Bergman, *Minnen* V, 154, 231; Clason, *För hundra år sen* I, 194–95; Wåhlin, "Anteckningar," 86; Engeström, *Minnen* II, 143; Häggman, Anteckningar, KB, 24; *HEC* VIII, 493, 496. Skjölde-brand's contention, *Memoarer* IV, 97, that F. had a "very strong ex-change of words" with the prince is unconfirmed and seems question-able. See also M. J. Crusenstolpe, *Carl XIII och Hedvig Elisabeth Char-lotta* (Stockholm, 1861), 440–41.

33. Schinkel-Bergman, *Minnen* V, 158. Cf. Crusenstolpe, *Medaljonger och statyetter,* 310, 312; anonymous "Essai d'un récit historique des événements arrivés à Stockholm pendant l'année 1810," F MID Kant-selyariya 1810-g. D 10815, fol. 46, Central Archive, Moscow, in Ryska filmsamlingen II, Roll 41 (microfilm), RA.

34. Sam Clason, ed., *Handlingar till kronprins Carl Augusts historia,* Historiska handlingar, XXVII:2 (Stockholm, 1925), 226, 234, 236–37. Clason dates this letter sometime in Feb. 1810. It shows the influence on the prince of the Adlersparre faction.

35. Waller, *Döbeln,* 601; Trolle-Wachtmeister, *Anteckningar* I, 247n.; Stafsundssamlingen: Manuskript- och avskriftssamlingen XXI, RA, con-tains a collection of letters and documents on Karl August's reception in Sweden and his death.

36. Clason, *Karl XIII och Karl XIV Johan,* 159; Wibling, *Opinioner och stämningar,* 174–77, 226–27; Sjövall, *Adlersparre och tronfrågan,* 59n.; Clason, *För hundra år sen* I, 220; II, 72–74; *HEC* VIII, 499–500, 563; Schinkel-Bergman, *Minnen* V, 141, 146–47, 164, 166; Häggman,

Anteckningar, KB, 25; Georg Adlersparre, *Handlingar rörande Sveriges äldre, nyare och nyaste historia*, 9 vol. (Stockholm, 1830–33); III, 11–12n.; Otto Sjögren, *Karl August Grevesmöhlen*. *Karaktärsbild från en upprörd tid* (Stockholm, 1882), 46–47; Staf, *Polisväsendet*, 318–19. Staf reports, *ibid.*, 318, 517n., that since Otto Sjögren used the Grevesmöhlen papers at RA in 1882, they can no longer be found.

37. On Karl August's physical condition and death, see A. J. Amnéus, "Om kronprinsen Karl Augusts dödssätt och de rättsmedicinska hufvudpunkterna af rättegången mot Rossi," *Uppsala universitetets årsskrift, 1866 (Medicin)*, 1–88. On van Suchtelen, see A. Ahnfelt, *Två krönta rivaler*, 2 vol. (Stockholm, 1887), I, 9–39.

38. Waller, *Döbeln*, 600–601; Wibling, *Opinioner och stämningar*, 177, 206, 215n., 238–40; Birger Sjövall, *Om partier och paskviller å riddarhuset vid 1809–1810 års riksdag* (Kristianstad, 1922), 22–23; Carlsson, "Wachtmeisters dagbok," 59–60; Trolle-Wachtmeister, *Anteckningar I*, 246–47; Scaevola, *Utländska diplomaters minnen*, 480, 488, 491; Schinkel-Bergman, *Minnen* V, 140, 164–66, 215–16; Häggman, Anteckningar, KB, 26; *HEC* VIII, 535–38, 561–62, 565, 814–15; Skjöldebrand, *Memoarer* IV, 103; [L. F. Norstedt], Brev från Hofkamrer L. F. Norstedt till J. G. Norstedt om Fersenska mordet, Ep. N. 3a., KB; "Essai," fol. 49, Ryska filmsaml., II, RA; Hildebrand, "Eva Sophie von Fersen," 751, and "Fabian Reinhold von Fersen," 755.

39. Gerhard Hafström, "Mordet på Axel Fersen," *Svenskt biografiskt lexikon XV* (Stockholm, 1956), 733–34; Wibling, *Opinioner och stämningar*, 189–90, 204–208, 256n.; Waller, *Döbeln*, 599–600; Schinkel-Bergman, *Minnen* V, 214–16, 224, 231–33; *HEC* VIII 163–64, 528–30. 533–35, 537–38, 561–64, 814–15; Engeström, *Minnen* II, 151–52; Ehrenström, *Hist. anteckn.* II, 605, 607–608; Anker, *Danska diplomaters meddelanden*, 62–66; Suremain, *Mémoires*, 194–95; Skjöldebrand, *Memoarer* IV, 102; Scaevola, *Utländska diplomaters minnen*, 480, 488, 491; Nerman, *Fersenska mordet*, 25; Söderhjelm in *Dagbok* IV, 572–73; accounts, F. arkiv XXII, RA. The last document signed by F. in Riksmarskalksämbetet, Kongl. bref för åren 1806–10, is dated 1 June 1810.

40. Some of these leaflets are contained in Engeström osign. 25, KB, and Norstedt, bref, KB. Excerpts from the Berzelius-Pontin report, often distorted, were widely distributed from hand to hand; Norstedt sent a copy to his brother in Norrköping, for which he paid one *riksdaler*. When Berzelius and Pontin returned to Stockholm in late June, they were invited to the Opinion Club and asked *what kind* of poison had been used on the crown prince; when they denied any basis for such rumors, they were suspected of having been bought off and ostracized. H. G. Söderbaum, *Jacob Berzelius*, 2 vol. (Stockholm, 1929), I, 349–64. Hafström, *SBL* XV, 733–35; Wibling, *Opinioner och stämningar*, 185–86, 194–201, 206–15; Nerman, *Fersenska mordet*, 26, 28; Sjövall, *Partier och paskviller*, 23; Rune Hedman, "Massan vid fersenska upploppet," in Torgny Nevéus, ed., *Historia kring Stockholm. Från frihetstiden till sekelskiftet* (Stockholm, 1967), 37–38; Schinkel-Berg-

man, *Minnen* V, 221, 224–27; Clason, *För hundra år sen* I, 220; II, 179; Trolle-Wachtmeister, *Anteckningar* I, 249–50; Scaevola, *Utländska diplomaters minnen*, 491–92; Ahnfelt, *Två krönta rivaler* I, 106–107; Amnéus, "Karl Augusts dödssätt," 19–31, 57, 66–80.

41. Ehrenström, *Hist. anteckn.* II, 608–609.

42. Wibling, *Opinioner och stämningar*, 67–68, 72, 76–77, 185–86, 194–95, 209–10, 215–33, 249–55; Gerhard Hafström, "Justitiekanslern och Fersenska mordet," in *Festskrift tillägnad Birger Ekeberg* (Stockholm, 1950), 186, 189; Rasmus Nyerup, *Rejser til Stockholm i Aarene 1810 og 1812* (Copenhagen, 1816), 29. *"Räfvarne"* is given in its entirety in Wibling, *Opinioner och stämningar*, 215–20. On the *Nya Posten*, see *ibid.*, 58–81. On Törneblad, see *ibid.*, 76-77, 222–26; cf. *HEC* VIII, 535. Engeström, in *Minnen* II, 153n., and Marianne Ehrenström, in Schück, *Sista gustavianska hofdamen*, 137–38, likewise accused Törneblad, though the latter source mentions that a Herr Holthausen and a Countess d'Albedyhll had also been suspected. A manuscript copy of *"Räfvarne"* in the later Bishop Kullberg's papers, Brevskrivare: Anders Carlsson af Kullberg, Ericsbergsarkivet, RA, bears an anonymous notation, "by von Holthausen?," followed by another, initialed by M. J. Crusenstolpe, "No. Af Kullberg, according to Book Printer Delén's confidential assertion to M. J. C." Another suspect was the journalist Adolf Regnér. Schück, *Gustavianska brev*, 128–29, 533.

43. Waller, *Döbeln*, 597–98; Wibling, *Opinioner och stämningar*, 257–61; *HEC* VIII, 561, 563, 814–15; "Essai," fol. 48, Ryska filmsaml. II, RA; Ehrenström, *Hist. anteckn.* II, 610–12; Nyerup, *Rejser*, 7, 9–11, 14, 17–20, 22; Suremain, *Mémoires*, 204; Norstedt, Bref, KB; J. A. Cronstedt to Karl XIII, 26 June 1810, Landshöfdingars skrivelser till Kungl. Maj:t, Östergötland, vol. 64 (1810), RA. Karl August's faithful Danish adjutant, von Holst, consistently refused to believe that his master could have been poisoned. Clason, *Handlingar till Carl Augusts historia*, 283.

44. Hafström, *SBL* XV, 734–36; Schinkel-Bergman, *Minnen* V, 218, 220–21, 226, 228, 369; Crusenstolpe, *Carl XIII*, 447–48, 451–52; Waller, *Döbeln*, 599; *HEC* VIII, 407, 532, 534–35, 537; Engeström osign. 25, KB; Häggman, Anteckningar, KB, 25–26. Karl XIII, however, was hesitant to push the investigation too far, lest it reveal the complicity of "families with which I am used to associate," as he wrote Engeström, "and besides, what should people abroad think when they observe among us endless conspiracies, revolutions, and murders...." Schinkel-Bergman, *Minnen* V, 220. In this, he recalls his behavior after his brother's assassination in 1792.

45. Hafström, "Justitiekanslern," 184, 203, 207; Hafström, *SBL* XV, 736; Schinkel-Bergman, *Minnen* V, 229–31; Skjöldebrand, *Memoarer* IV, 107; Suremain, *Mémoires*, 198–99; *HEC* VIII, 539; Nerman, *Fersenska mordet*, 37; Silfversparre's own account of his orders in "Underdånig rapport angående det, Onsdagen den 20de. Junii, härstädes före-

fallne oväsende," dated 3 July 1810, Silfversparre arkiv LXVII, Tosterupsamlingen, RA.

46. Schinkel-Bergman, *Minnen* V, 233–35; Skjöldebrand, *Memoarer* IV, 105; Suremain, *Mémoires*, 199; *HEC* VIII, 538; Ahnfelt, *Ur svenska hofvets och aristokratiens lif* I, 171–73; Schück, *Sista gustavianska hofdamen*, 138–39; accounts, F. arkiv XXII, RA; Häggman, Anteckningar, KB, 29–30; Ehrenström, *Hist. anteckn.* II, 609; Ahnfelt, *Två krönta rivaler* I, 107; Wibling, *Opinioner och stämningar*, 211; H. Rosengren, "Fersenska mordet. Några ord med anledning af ett hundraårsminne," *Ord och bild* (1910), 338.

47. Suremain, *Mémoires*, 199; Schinkel-Bergman, *Minnen* V, 231; Ehrenström, *Hist. anteckn.* II, 609–10; Trolle-Wachtmeister, *Anteckningar* I, 251.

48. Nerman, *Fersenska mordet*, 50; Schinkel-Bergman, *Minnen* V, 228, 235; Clason, *För hundra år sen* I, 229; Clason, *Karl XIII och Karl XIV Johan*, 163; Häggman, Anteckningar, KB, 26–28.

49. The material on F.'s assassination is immense, probably greater than that connected with any other episode in his life. The whole affair deserves a full-length scholarly study, which it has thus far not received and which lies beyond the limits of this biography. The best treatment is to be found in Gerhard Hafström's articles, "Justitiekanslern och Fersenska mordet" (1950) and "Mordet på Axel Fersen" (1956), already cited. Also useful is Nerman, *Fersenska mordet* (1933), within the limits set forth in G. Hafström's critiques in *Personhistorisk tidskrift* XXXIV (1933), 146–47, and *Historisk tidskrift* (1934), 124–28. Rune Hedman, "Massan vid fersenska upploppet" (1967) and the same author's more detailed "Massan vid det s.k. fersenska upploppet," *Historisk tidskrift* (1969), 2–71, are most useful, especially for the socioeconomic background. See also Rosengren, "Fersenska mordet"; Rein, *Adlercreutz* II, 285–95; J. P. af Billberg, "Fersenska mordet. En samtida skildring i enskilt brev," *Genealogisk tidskrift* XVI (1961), 35–37. Somewhat less useful is Ola Hansson, "L'assassinat de Fersen," *Revue d'histoire diplomatique* (1911), 195–207. For some of the many contemporary accounts, see, besides the voluminous court investigations in F. arkiv XXXVIII–XLII, RA, Danish minister Dernath in Anker, *Danska diplomaters meddelanden*, 68–72; Leonhard von Hauswolff in Clason, *För hundra år sen* I, 215–29; Salomon Brelin, "Öfverste Brelins anteckningar 1809–18," *Svenska memoarer och bref* I, ed. Henrik Schück & Oscar Levertin, (Stockholm, 1900) 18–34; Suchtelen in Ahnfelt, *Två krönta rivaler* I, 105; "Berättelse af majoren friherre Gustaf von Düben om mordet på RiksMarskalken Grefve von Fersen 20 Junii 1810," in M. G. Crusenstolpe, ed., *Portfeuille*, 3 vol. (Stockholm, 1837–42), I, 218–26; Norstedt, *Bref*, KB; Nils Wilhelm Forsslund, Efterlämnade anteckningar, MS excerpt in custody of *förste arkivarie* Nils F. Holm, RA; anonymous letter, dated Jacobslund, 26 June [1810], and second, undated anonymous account, Brevskrivare: Fersen, Hans Axel von, Ericsbergsarkivet, RA; "Handlingar rörande Fersenska mordet," I. A. Silfversparre

482 COUNT HANS AXEL VON FERSEN

arkiv, LXVII, Tosterupsamlingen, RA; Häggman, Anteckningar, KB, 28–34; *HEC* VIII; Skjöldebrand, *Memoarer* IV; Suremain, *Mémoires*; "Essai," fol. 49–53, Ryska filmsaml. II, RA; *Autentisk Beretning om det der er foregaaet i Sverrig i Anledning af Kronprindsens død . . . oversat af svensk ved M. Hagerup* (Copenhagen, 1810); Hans Friedrich Helwig, *Efterretning om de i Stockholm i Sommeren 1810 forefaldne Revolutions-Optrin og sammes Følger* (Aalborg, 1810).

50. Hafström, *SBL* XV, 373; Nerman, *Fersenska mordet*, 55–56; Brelin, "Anteckningar," 19; Schück, *Sista gustavianska hofdamen*, 139; Suremain, *Mémoires*, 199; Schinkel-Bergman, *Minnen* V, 235–36; *HEC* VIII, 538–39. The threatening letter is given in full in *ibid.*, 559–60; cf. Vallotton, *Marie-Antoinette et Fersen*, 411–12; Wibling, *Opinioner och stämningar*, 247–48.

51. Brelin, "Anteckningar," 18–19; *HEC* VIII, 539; Schinkel-Bergman, *Minnen* V, 228; Wibling, *Opinioner och stämningar*, 247–48.

52. Hafström, *SBL* XV, 737; Nerman, *Fersenska mordet*, 59–60; Staf, *Polisväsendet*, 237–38; Schinkel-Bergman, *Minnen* V, 236–37; Skjöldebrand, *Memoarer* IV, 105–106; Brelin, "Anteckningar," 19–20, 23, 30; *HEC* VIII, 559.

53. Skjöldebrand, *Memoarer* IV, 105–106; cf. Häggman, Anteckningar, KB, 28–29; Nerman, *Fersenska mordet*, 59–60.

54. Hafström, "Justitiekanslern," 185; Nerman, *Fersenska mordet*, 65, 68–69; Suremain, *Mémoires*, 199; Schinkel-Bergman, *Minnen* V, 237; Brelin, "Anteckningar," 19–20; Düben, "Berättelse," 221; anonymous "Berättelse angående Gref: Fersens Mord d. 20 Juni 1810," Silfversparre arkiv LXVII, RA; Norstedt, Bref, KB; Nyerup, *Rejser*, 26.

55. Hafström, "Justitiekanslern," 187, 189–91; Hafström, *SBL* XV, 737; Staf, *Polisväsendet*, 327–28; Hedman, "Massan vid fersenska upploppet," 47–50; Nerman, *Fersenska mordet*, 89, 94–95, 99; *HEC* VIII, 540; Brelin, "Anteckningar,' 23; Häggman, Anteckningar, KB, 29; Düben, "Berättelse," 221; Forsslund, Anteckningar, in custody of N. F. Holm, RA.

56. Hafström, "Justitiekanslern," 187, 190–91, 196; Hafström, *SBL* XV, 737–39; Suremain, *Mémoires*, 199–201; Skjöldebrand, *Memoarer* IV, 107–108; Schück, *Sista gustavianska hofdamen*, 144.

57. Hafström, "Justitiekanslern," 188, 191–92; Hafström, *SBL* XV, 738–39; Forsslund, Anteckningar, in custody of N. F. Holm, RA; Brelin, "Anteckningar," 25; Düben, "Berättelse," 221–22.

58. Hafström, "Justitiekanslern," 193; Skjöldebrand, *Memoarer* IV, 108–109; Brelin, "Anteckningar," 24.

59. Hafström, "Justitiekanslern," 192–95; Hafström, *SBL* XV, 739–40; Nerman, *Fersenska mordet*, 110, 129–30, 140–46; Schinkel-Bergman, *Minnen* V, 239–40; Sköldebrand, *Memoarer* IV, 109, Brelin, "Anteckningar," 26–27; Häggman, Anteckningar, KB, 30; Düben, "Berättelse," 222–24.

60. Hafström, "Justitiekanslern," 186, 195; Nerman, *Fersenska mordet*, 135, 141, 149, 153–59, 344–47; Hedman, "Massan vid fersenska upploppet," 47–51; Skjöldebrand, *Memoarer* IV, 109; Suremain, *Mém-*

oires, 203. Brelin, "Anteckningar," 25; *HEC* VIII, 559, Schinkel-Berg-man's account of F. in his last moments beseeching God's forgiveness for his assassins sounds apocryphal, to say the least! *Minnen* V, 240–41. Cf. Häggman, Anteckningar, KB, 30.

61. Hafström, "Justitiekanslern," 195; Nerman, *Fersenska mordet*, 170–71; Brelin, "Anteckningar," 28; *HEC* VIII, 559; Clason, *För hundra år sen* I, 218, 224, 235. F.'s wallet, containing the aforemen-tioned threatening letter, was also returned a few days later. Nerman, *Fersenska mordet*, 168. A scrap of F.'s black coat, about 1" square, is pinned to one of Norstedt's letters to his brother, Bref, KB. According to the undated, anonymous account in Brevskrivare: Hans Axel von Fersen, Ericsbergsarkivet, RA, pieces of F.'s clothing later sold for 12, 16, and 24 *riksdaler*, the purchasers including "better dressed ladies."

62. Hafström, "Justitiekanslern," 196; Suremain, *Mémoires*, 200–201; Engeström, *Minnen* II, 153; Anker, *Danska diplomaters meddelanden*, 71; *HEC* VIII, 542–46. Silfversparre arkiv LXVII, Tosterupsamlingen, RA, contains Karl XIII's order to Silfversparre, which is, however, signed only by Suremain as "first adjutant to the king, on duty," and the receipt of which Silfversparre noted at 3:30 P.M.

63. Nerman, *Fersenka mordet*, 160–65; Skjöldebrand, *Memoarer* IV, 121.

64. Nerman, *Fersenska mordet*, 141, 185–237, 346–47; Skjöldebrand, *Memoarer* IV, 111–19; Suremain, *Mémoires*, 202; Brelin, "Anteck-ningar," 31–32; *HEC* VIII, 546–47, 559; Norstedt, Bref, KB; Wibling, *Opinioner och stämningar*, 254n. In addition to estimates of casualties in the above, the anonymous letter, dated Jacobslund, 26 June [1810], in Brevskrivare: Hans Axel von Fersen, Ericsbergsarkivet, RA, estimates 15 to 20 dead, 50 wounded on the evening of 20 June 1810. Cf. Hed-man, "Massan vid fersenska upploppet," 50–51. Hedman has found 8 verified deaths, plus some questionable cases. *Ibid.*, 42–43.

65. Hildebrand, "Eva Sophie von Fersen," 752–53; Engeström osign. 25, KB; Norstedt, Bref, KB; Nerman, *Fersenska mordet*, 238–42; *HEC* VIII, 547–51, 555, 561–62; Brelin, "Anteckningar," 29; Schück, *Sista gustavianska hofdamen*, 148–59, 154–62; Ahnfelt, *Ur svenska hofvets och aristokratiens lif* I, 173–74.

66. Engeström osign. 25, KB; Hafström, "Justitiekanslern," 208; Haf-ström, *SBL* XV, 742–43; Rein, *Adlercreutz* II, 296; Engeström, *Minnen* II, 153–54; Nerman, *Fersenska mordet*, 246; Ahnfelt, *Två krönta rivaler* I, 110–12. I am indebted to Professor Gerhard Hafström for sugges-tions in this matter given in an interview in August 1966.

CHAPTER XVI

1. Hafström, "Justitiekanslern," 197; Hafström, *SBL* XV, 735, 741, 743; Nerman, *Fersenska mordet*, 277; Staf, *Polisväsendet*, 319, 324–28; Hedman, "Massan vid fersenska upploppet," 44–45; Hedman, "Massan vid det s.k. fersenska upploppet," 26; *HEC* VIII, 554, 570–71; 616–17; Amnéus, "Karl Augusts dödssätt," 40–57; Söderbaum, *Berzelius* I, 349,

352–63; *Kongl. Maj:ts Nådiga Kungörelse angående . . . KronPrinsen CARL AUGUSTS död. Gifwen Stockholms slott den 9 November 1810* (Stockholm, 1810); *Kongl. Maj:ts och Rikets Svea HofRätts Utslag . . . Stockholm, 5 November 1810* (Stockholm, 1810).

2. Clason, *För hundra år sen* I, 219; Düben, "Berättelse," 220n.; I. C. Drewsen, *Rejsedagbog. Optegnelser fra en Rejse i Sommeren 1838* (Copenhagen, 1941), 150–51, 173–75; Georg Adlersparre, *Handlingar* III, 11–12n.; C. A. Adlersparre, *1809 och 1810. Tidstaflor,* 3 vol. (Stockholm, 1850), II, 3–4, 40–41, 46, 107–11, 143–44, 147–51, 162–63; Tegnér *Armfelt* III, 223; Ehrenström, *Hist. anteckn.* II, 618; Schinkel-Bergman, *Minnen* V, 249; Sjögren, *Grevesmöhlen,* 49; Wibling, *Opinioner och stämningar,* 250–55, 291–92, 295–96. For examples of continued radical propaganda after 20 June 1810, see P. Hanselli, *Ur en samlares papper,* 2 vol. (Uppsala, 1868–69), II, 105–12; cf. C. Grimberg, "Domaren Lynch in Stockholm år 1810," *Dagens nyheter,* No. 62, 5 Mar. 1922. In 1818, the rumor circulated that Hedvig Elisabeth Charlotta had tried to poison King Karl XIV Johan but had died of her own poison. Cf. Schück, *Sista gustavianska hofdamen,* 193; Drewsen, *Rejsedagbog,* 151, 174–75. The poison usually mentioned in such rumors was the diabolical *aqua tofana,* which was supposed to kill after a considerable delay. Cf. *Dropmore Papers* VI, 66–67.

3. Söderhjelm in *Dagbok* IV, 586–90; Nerman, *Fersenska mordet,* 179–82, 272–74; *HEC* VIII, 616–18, 621–22; 624–30; Ehrenström, *Hist. anteckn.* II, 612–13; Clason, *För hundra år sen* I, 237, 244–47; Scaevola, *Utländska diplomaters minnen,* 523–24; Anker, *Danska diplomaters meddelenden,* 74; Flach, *Fersen,* 170–71; Engeström osign. 25, KB; Norstedt, Bref, KB; Häggman, Anteckningar, KB, 30–31. For Sophie Piper's correspondence with Karl XIII at this time, cf. Brevskrivare: Fersen, Eva Sophie (Piper), Ericsbergsarkivet, RA, and Armfeltska samlingen XII, RA. For other correspondence by her on these matters, Lövstad arkiv XX, XXI. F. arkiv XXI, RA, contains details on F.'s funeral and burial. On 12 Nov. 1810, Karl XIII accepted the resignation from royal service of most members of the Fersen family. Riksmarskalksämbetet, Kongl. bref för åren 1806–10, Royal Palace. Until his death, Bernadotte, who became Karl XIV Johan, bore on his chest the tattoo, "mort à roi" [*sic*]. *Dagens nyheter,* 25 Sept. 1966, 8.

4. "Fersiaden," MS, i:Vt. 128, KB. I have used this version in preference to the slightly different one printed in Hanselli, *Ur en samlares papper* II, 128–31. Cf. L. J. Rabenius, *Officium Parentale viro . . . Axelio von Fersen die XXI Martii MDCCCXI nomine Academiae Upsaliensis* (Uppsala, 1811). According to *fil. kand.* Rune Hedman of Uppsala, there are a number of handwritten copies of the "Fersiad" in different Swedish manuscript collections, indicating that it was widely distributed and known at the time. Cf. also "Ord afsjungna vid parentationen i Upsala öfver akademiens kansler, h.e. grefve Axel Fersen," and "Parodi på föregående parentation," in Hanselli, *Ur en samlares papper* II, 124–27.

5. Gustaf Murray, *Personalier öfver . . . Grefve Herr Hans Axel von Fersen, upläste vid dess jordfästning* . . . *den 4 december 1810* (Stockholm, 1811), 30; Häggman, Anteckningar, KB, 30, which expresses the same idea; Clason, *Karl XIII och Karl XIV Johan*, 165; *HEC* VIII, 532; Trolle-Wachtmeister, *Anteckningar* I, 253n.; Tegnér, *Armfelt* III, 236; Ahnfelt. *Två krönta rivaler* I, 343; Boëthius, *Bihang till Minnen* II, 232–35. Söderhjelm in *Dagbok* IV, 532, wrongly attributes the quoted passage to *juris professor* L. J. Rabenius's eulogy at Uppsala in March 1811.

6. Waller, *Döbeln*, 272; Nerman, *Fersenska mordet*, 31–32; Scaevola, *Utländska diplomaters minnen*, 493; Tegnér, *Armfelt* III, 224–25; Söderhjelm in *Dagbok* IV, 582–84; anonymous handwritten leaflet, dated Stockholm, 21 June 1810, G. Andersson samling XXXIII, Lund universitetsbibliotek; Nyerup, *Rejser*, 28–29; cf. Häggman, Anteckningar, KB, 30.

7. Skjöldebrand, *Memoarer* IV, 109; Brelin, "Anteckningar," 18–19; *DeLaGardiska arkivet* XX, 84–86; Ehrenström, *Hist. Anteckn.* II, 608; Anker, *Danska diplomaters meddelanden*, 72–73; Ahnfelt, *Två krönta rivaler* I, 107; Nerman, *Fersenska mordet*, 344–47; Waller, *Döbeln*, 598–99; Wibling, *Opinioner och stämningar*, 247–48.

8. *HEC* VIII, 555, 559, 721; Trolle-Wachtmeister, *Anteckningar* I, 250–51, 253n. (Napoleon's comments); Scaevola, *Utländska diplomaters minnen*, 480; Häggman, Anteckningar, KB, 28; C. A. Adlersparre, *1809 och 1810* II, 165–66, 182; Tegnér, *Armfelt* III, 225n.; Waller, *Döbeln*, 292, 599–600.

9. Andersson, *Handlingar ur Brinkman'ska arkivet* II, 365 (Ehrenström's letter); Wibling, *Opinioner och stämningar*, 67–71, 231–38, 283–86; Waller, *Döbeln*, 292; Hedman, "Massan vid fersenska upploppet," 51–52; Porter, *Travelling Sketches* II, 118–19; 124–25; *HEC* VIII 557, 563; Söderhjelm in *Dagbok* IV, 572, 575, for Sophie Piper's comments. For an anecdote indicating F.'s consideration toward members of the Stockholm working class in 1809, see Forsslund, *Efterlämnade anteckningar*, in custody of N. F. Holm, RA. The element of loyalty to the Vasas of the Stockholm lower classes is indicated by Häggman's assertion, Anteckningar, KB, 29, that some of the crowd in the Hultgren house accused F. of having taken part in the assassination of Gustav III and the deposition of Gustav IV Adolf. In an anonymous "Song," appended to the "Fersiad," F. is accused of being in league with the betrayer of Sveaborg, C. O. Cronstedt, the regicide of 1792, C. P. Lilliehorn, the Finnish separatist, G. M. Sprengtporten, and by implication, with G. M. Armfelt. Hanselli, *Ur en samlares papper* II, 131–33.

10. Waller, *Döbeln*, 601; Wibling, *Opinioner och stämningar*, 69–70, 73–75, 206, 220–48, 283–86, 290; Andgren, *Konung och ständer*, 93; *HEC* VIII, 494, 496–98, 535–36; "Essai," fol. 41–42, 46, 48, Ryska filmsaml. II, RA. This source claims F. and his "party," though disillusioned in their "proud hopes" of managing Karl August, held "an even greater hatred" for Gustav Adolf and his family. *Ibid.*, fol. 42, 47.

486   COUNT HANS AXEL VON FERSEN

Dagbok IV, 22; Clason, *För hundra år sen* I, 221. Häggman recounts that F. was murdered on the same spot where Countess Brahe pleaded in vain for her husband's life to F. A. von Fersen after the abortive royalist coup of 1756, "a proof, that is, of God's divine retribution. *Nemesis divina.*" Häggman, Anteckningar, KB, 31. For somewhat similar speculations, see Crusenstolpe, *Medaljonger och statyetter*, 305–306.

11. Anker, *Danska diplomaters meddelanden*, 71–73; Ahnfelt, *Två krönta rivaler* I, 107; Ehrenström, *Hist. anteckn.* II, 603–604; Waller, *Döbeln*, 598–99; Hedman, "Massan vid fersenska upploppet," 52–54.

12. Nerman, *Fersenska mordet*, 277–341, 347, gives personal details on persons indicted in the case; Wibling, *Opinioner och stämningar*, 76–77; Skjöldebrand, *Memoarer* IV, 125; Hedman, "Massan vid det s.k. fersenska upploppet," 57, 69.

13. Hafström, *SBL*, XV, 741–42; Staf, *Polisväsendet*, 328.

14. Hafström, *SBL* XV, 742; Hedman, "Massan vid det s.k. fersenska upploppet," 26; Nerman, *Fersenska mordet*, 277; Trolle-Wachtmeister, *Anteckningar* I, 251–52; *HEC* VIII, 720–22, 760–61, 828; Staf, *Polisväsendet*, 321–28. Staf maintains that Gen. Skjöldebrand apparently withheld certain reports from the investigation, containing "unverified accusations by anonymous persons," which he had burned when they were rediscovered nearly twenty years later. *Ibid.*, 324–25.

15. Hafström, *SBL* XV, 741; Trolle-Wachtmeister, *Anteckningar* I, 250–51; Wåhlin, "Anteckningar," 121; Düben, "Berättelse," 226; Schinkel-Bergman, *Minnen* V, 222–23, 250–51; cf. August Gynther, "Fersenska mordet. Vilka buro det största ansvaret?", *Göteborgs handels- och sjöfarts-tidning*, 22 Sept. 1934, supplement, 4, 7. On the role of crowds in later eighteenth-century politics, see George Rudé, *The Crowd in History* (New York, 1964). For Gustav III's use of the crowd, see Staf, *Polisväsendet*, 328–29.

16. Clason, *Karl XIII och Karl XIV Johan*, 165; Schinkel-Bergman, *Minnen* V, 216–17, 222, 250–51; Anker, *Danska diplomaters meddelanden*, 61–62; *HEC* VIII, 532–33, 573–75; Suremain, *Mémoires*, 194–95; Wåhlin, "Anteckningar," 121; Engeström, osign. 25, KB. Kunstler's statement, *Le secret de Fersen*, 344–45, that the inquest proved the plot intended to "get rid of Count Fersen and overthrow the king," is entirely misleading.

17. *HEC* VIII, 534–38; Suremain, *Mémoires*, 203; C. A. Adlersparre, *1809 och 1810* II, 166; Schinkel-Bergman, *Minnen* V, 232–33; Crusenstolpe, *Carl XIII*, 457; Drewsen, *Rejsedagbog*, 150–51, 173–75.

18. Trolle-Wachtmeister, *Anteckningar* I, 250–51; *HEC* VIII, 555; Schinkel-Bergman, *Minnen* V, 222; Clason, *Karl XIII och Karl XIV Johan*, 165.

19. Hafström, *SBL* XV, 741; Suremain, *Mémoires*, 198.

20. Boëthius, *Bihang till Minnen* II, 223; cf. C. A. Adlersparre, *1809 och 1810* II, 182.

21. Waller, *Döbeln*, 599; Schinkel-Bergman, *Minnen* V, 251; Brelin, "Anteckningar," 26; Suremain, *Mémoires*, 203; Scaevola, *Utländska*

diplomaters minnen, 493. H. D. Clarke wrote in 1808 that the honesty and sincerity of the Swedes could degenerate into a "great credulity," so that "The *Swedes* are always open to imposition, and ready to follow the dictates of any leader, however sinister his designs may be." *Travels* III, 48.

22. Hafström, "Justitiekanslern," 202–203; Trolle-Wachtmeister, *Anteckningar* I, 251; Nerman, *Fersenska mordet*, 260–61. The military were evidently further inhibited by the example of the so-called Ebel Riot of 1793, which, at the insistence of Duke Karl and against the objections of his advisers, the commanding general adjutant had succeeded in dispelling through persuasion and without violence. Cf. C. A. Adlersparre, *1809 och 1810* I, 22–23n.

23. Brelin, "Anteckningar," 32–33; Nerman, *Fersenska mordet*, 231–37, 319–39; Waller, *Döbeln*, 599.

24. *HEC* VIII, 554, 562–64, 612, 721, 760–61, 828; Skjöldebrand, *Memoarer* IV, 108–10; Suremain, *Mémoires*, 198–201; Trolle-Wachtmeister, *Anteckningar* I, 251; Schinkel-Bergman, *Minnen* V, 239; Crusenstolpe, *Carl XIII*, 452–54; Tegnér, *Armfelt* III, 224–25; Rein, *Adlercreutz* II, 295–96; Wibling, *Opinioner och stämningar*, 176.

25. *HEC* VIII, 574–75; Schinkel-Bergman, *Minnen* V, 228–31, 235; Troll-Wachtmeister, *Anteckningar* I, 250–52, 253n.

26. C. A. Adlersparre, *1809–1810* II, 165–66, 182, 192–95; III, 80, 101; *HEC* VIII, 721, 760–61; Clason, *För hundra år sen*, I, 241; Düben, "Berättelse," 223n.; Nerman, *Fersenska mordet*, 258–61; Hafström, "Justitiekanslern," 197–209; Hafström, *SBL* XV, 741–43; Hafström, reviews of Nerman, *op. cit.*, in *Personhistorisk tidskrift*, 147, and *Historisk tidskrift*, 127; interview with Professor Hafström, 1966. Cf. Sam Clason, "Ett dystert hundraårsminne. Fersenska mordet den 20 juni 1810," *Sydsvenska dagbladet–snällposten*, No. 163, 19 June 1910, 4. Also Silfversparre's account of the events of 20 June 1810 in his "Underdånig rapport" of 3 July 1810, and his letter to Karl XIII of 24 Mar. 1811, justifying his behavior on that occasion, both in Silfversparre arkiv LXVII, Tosterupsamlingen, RA. Silfversparre's version differs markedly from the main body of evidence and must be used with caution. See also summary of Adlercreutz's report to the king of 25 June 1810, Rein, *Adlercreutz* II, 300–301; cf. Staf, *Polisväsendet*, 320–21.

27. *HEC* VIII, 401–402, 570–71, 612; Trolle-Wachtmeister, *Anteckningar* I, 190–91, 206.

28. *HEC* VIII, 535–37, 552, 721; C. D. Hamilton, *Anteckningar af en gammal gustavian* (Linköping, 1855), 114; Tegnér, *Armfelt* III, 225n.; Clason, *För hundra år sen* I, 221, 247; Schinkel-Bergman, *Minnen* V, 221–23; Crusenstolpe, *Carl XIII*, 456–58; Waller, *Döbeln*, 292, 599–600.

29. *HEC* VIII, 535–37, 552–53, 721; Trolle-Wachtmeister, *Anteckningar* I, 250–51; Schinkel-Bergman, *Minnen* V, 216–18. Cf. Erik Fahlbeck, *Lars August Mannerheim* (Lund, 1969), 164–67.

30. Tegnér, *Armfelt* III, 225n.; Wibling, *Opinioner och stämningar*,

174. Cf. Werner, "Gustaf Abraham Silfverstolpe," 333. *Dagbok* II, 285–86; Crusenstolpe, *Carl XIII*, 446.

31. *HEC* VIII, 476, 511, 523, 552; F. to Taube, 24 June, 15 July 1792, Taube arkiv II, RA; Taube to F., 15 May, 8 Aug. 1792, n.d. (c. Mar. 1793), F. arkiv XIV, RA.

32. Hamilton, *Anteckningar*, 114, 142; Engeström, *Minnen* II, 153 (on Wetterstedt). On Engeström, see Hafström, "Justitiekanslern," 205; Staf, *Polisväsendet*, 316–18; Ahnfelt, *Ur svenska hofvets och aristokratiens lif* I, 170–71 (M. Ehrenström's assertion); cf. Engeström, *Minnen* II, 152, 155–56. F. apparently considered himself on reasonably good terms with Engeström, since he wrote to him on 30 Sept. 1809 to solicit his influence in obtaining a position in the foreign office for his nephew—Sophie's son—Charles Piper. Brev till Lars von Engeström VII (1809), KB. On Järta, see below. Adlercreutz was also on the council. Cf. the diary of Councillor G. G. Adlerbeth's son, Jakob, excerpted in Henrik Schück, "Före det Fersenska mordet," *Aftonbladet*, 22 June 1907, 6.

33. Engeström, *Minnen* II, 151–53; Boëthius, *Bihang till Minnen* II, 216–20.

34. "Essai," fol. 47, Ryska filmsaml. II, RA; Häggman, Anteckningar, KB, 28; Tegnér, *Armfelt* III, 223–24, 225n.; Ehrenström, *Hist. anteckn.* II, 618; Düben, "Berättelse," 220n.; Schinkel-Bergman, *Minnen* V, 147, 152–53, 214–15, 223, 228n.; C. A. Adlersparre, *1809 års revolution och dess män*, 2 vol. (Stockholm, 1849), and *1809 och 1810*, esp. II, 46, 148–51; III, 17–18; G. Adlersparre, *Handlingar* III, 11–12n.; Crusenstolpe, *Carl XIII*, 456, which takes Schinkel-Bergman to task for not making their accusations more clearly; G. Adlersparre to Silfversparre, 24 June 1810, Silfversparre samling LXVII, Tosterupsamlingen, RA; Daniel Toijer, ed., *Brinkman och Adlersparre. En brevväxling från Karl Johanstiden* (Stockholm, 1962), 50, 237; Trolle-Wachtmeister, *Anteckningar* I, 233–35; *HEC* VIII, 352–53, 528, 530, 532–33, 552; Sjövall, *Partier och paskviller*, 3–5; Waller, *Döbeln*, 600; Clason, *Karl XIII och Karl XIV Johan*, 159–60; Theodor Tufvesson, "Adlersparre och Fersenska mordet," *Personhistorisk tidskrift* XX (1920), 66–68.

35. Engeström, *Minnen* II, 151; Trolle-Wachtmeister, *Anteckningar* I, 250; cf. Schinkel-Bergman, *Minnen* V, 223; interview with Professor Hafström, 1966. According to Staf, *Polisväsendet*, 325, Järta offered to serve as acting vice-governor of Stockholm to conduct the investigation of 20 June, which was refused "at the highest level," presumably because he knew too much. Järta wrote to B. von Beskow in 1836 that he knew who the real organizers were. *Ibid.*, 325. On Järta's position vis-à-vis the various revolutionary factions, see Beskow, *Lefnadsminnen*, 102–105.

36. Tegnér, *Armfelt* III, 225; Schinkel-Bergman, *Minnen* V, 141, 146–47, 166, 222, 232, 249; Crusenstolpe, *Carl XIII*, 448; Sjögren, *Grevesmöhlen*, 47–49; Skjöldebrand, *Memoarer* IV, 126–29; Staf, *Polisväsendet*, 329–30; Nerman, *Fersenska mordet*, 312–13; Sjövall, *Partier och paskviller*, 8, 22–23; Rosengren, "Fersenska mordet," 350; interview

Notes and References 489

with Professor Hafström, 1966; Jöran Wibling, "Carl August Greves-möhlen," *Svenskt biografiskt lexikon* XVII (Stockholm, 1967), 267–69; Wibling, *Opinioner och stämningar*, 13–16, 58, 234, 238–48; Hedman, "Massan vid fersenska upploppet," 42. For the April leaflet and van Suchtelen's dispatches, see Wibling, *Opinioner och stämningar*, 238–40. I am obliged to Dr. Wibling for a copy of the late Anders Larson's unpublished article, "Grevesmöhlen, Fersenska mordet och Bernadottes val" (written in 1956–57) in revised page proofs.

37. Erik Lönnroth, "Revolution för en dag," *Dagens nyheter*, 20 June 1960. Wibling, "Grevesmöhlen," 268, notes some deterioration in Grevesmöhlen's relations with government circles when during the spring of 1810 he came to be increasingly feared as a very dangerous man, and believes he "very likely acted largely on his own initiative" in June.

38. Wibling, *Opinioner och stämningar*, 282–317; Wibling, "Grevesmöhlen," 267–70; Lönnroth, "Revolution för en dag"; cf. Erik Lönnroth, "Press och agitation i Sverige 1809–1810," *Dagens nyheter*, 2 Mar. 1955; Hedman, "Massan vid fersenska upploppet," 54; Suremain, *Mémoires*, 194–204.

39. Scaevola, *Utländska diplomaters minnen*, 480; Clason, *För hundra år sen* I, 228.

40. Scaevola, *Utländska diplomaters minnen*, 480.

41. Cf. E. D. Clarke's pessimistic prognosis of Sweden's situation, written at about this time, in *Travels* III, 155, concluding, ". . . he must indeed be sanguine who can hope to see *Sweden* regenerated and her glory restored."

42. Norstedt, Bref, KB; Anker, *Danska diplomaters meddelanden*, 72–73; *DeLaGardiska arkivet* XX, 84–86; *HEC* VIII, 519, 552–53, 559; Nyerup, *Rejser*, 28–29; Scaevola, *Utländska diplomaters minnen*, 493; Tegnér, *Armfelt* III, 223–25; Carl von Bonsdorff, *Gustav Mauritz Armfelt. Levnadsskildring*, 4 vol. (Helsingfors, 1939–40), II, 615–18; Clason, *Karl XIII och Karl XIV Johan*, 165, 268; Söderhjelm in *Dagbok* IV, 582, 584; Nerman, *Fersenska mordet*, 31–32; Waller, *Döbeln*, 292, 599; Wibling, *Opinioner och stämningar*, 255–72.

43. Häggman, Anteckningar, KB, 35; "Essai," fol. 48–50, Ryska filmsaml. II, RA.

44. Anker, *Danska diplomaters meddelanden*, 73; Andgren, *Konung och ständer*, iii, 118–21; Wibling, *Opinioner och stämningar*, 261, 300–302; Clason, *Karl XIII och Karl XIV Johan*, 176, 216–17; Alrik Gustafson, *A History of Swedish Literature* (Minneapolis, 1961), 155–56.

45. C. A. Adlersparre, *1809 och 1810* II, 165–66, 182; III, 80, 101; M. J. Crusenstolpe, *Skildringar ur det inre af dagens historia*, 2 vol. (4th ed., Stockholm, 1837), I, 174–76n.; Crusenstolpe, *Carl XIII*, 443–58; Crusenstolpe's editorial note to Düben, "Berättelse," 223n.

46. Suremain, *Mémoires*, 221; Trolle-Wachtmeister, *Anteckningar* I, 251, 253; Schinkel-Bergman, *Minnen*, V, 26. This source even alleges that F. himself, on learning of Karl August's death, held that "nothing less than the election of one of Napoleon's marshals can save us." *Ibid.*, 191.

490 COUNT HANS AXEL VON FERSEN

47. Tegnér, *Armfelt* III, 225–26, 236–37; Bonsdorff, *Armfelt* II, 431, 615–18; Ehrenström, *Hist. anteckn.* II, 619, 625.

48. Trolle-Wachtmeister, *Anteckningar* I, 254. Napoleon himself in 1816 considered Bernadotte "one of the chief causes of our ruin." J. Christopher Herold, ed., *The Mind of Napoleon* (New York, 1961), 175.

49. Morris, *Diary* I, 271.

50. Holmberg, "Riddare av det förgångna."

51. Albert Guérard, *France in the Classical Age: The Life and Death of an Ideal* (New York, 1965), 310.

52. Bouillé, *Mémoires*, 314.

53. Klinckowström I, 87.

54. Söderhjelm, *FMA*, 152; *Dagbok* II, 56, 213. Spinoza quoted in David Maland, *Europe in the Seventeenth Century* (New York, 1966), 20. Cf. Arnaud-Bouteloup, *Rôle politique*, 351.

55. Crusenstolpe, *Medaljonger och statyetter*, 310; F. to Gust. IV Ad., 4 Nov. 1797, Allm. fredskongr. LXVII, RA; F. to father, 9 June 1789, FAF arkiv IX, RA.

56. See, for instance, Engeström, *Minnen*, II. Fogelqvist, *Typer och tänkesätt*, 253.

57. On Breteuil's ideal of reform through enlightened despotism, see Chaumié, *Le réseau d'Antraigues*, 37–38, 341n. Cf. Godechot, *Contrerévolution*, 21. Godechot writes of the leading counterrevolutionary ideologues that they were themselves for the most part "revolutionaries in their own ways." *Ibid.*, 2.

58. Crusenstolpe, *Medaljonger och statyetter*, 309.

59. Holmberg, "Riddaren av det förgånga"; Lönnroth, "Revolution för en dag"; Fogelqvist, *Typer och tänkesätt*, 253; F. to Taube, 16 Dec. 1797, Taube arkiv III, RA.

60. Skjöldebrand, *Memoarer* IV, 101–102; Crusenstolpe, *Medaljonger och statyetter*, 310; Beskow, *Lefnadsminnen*, 40.

61. Cf. Kjell Kumlien, "Axel von Fersens dagbok," *Ord och bild* (1937), 382–84, in which he emphasizes F.'s likenesses with his father in respect to conscientiousness, thoroughness, sense of order, and duty.

62. Tegnér, *Armfelt* II, 374.

Bibliography

The bibliography which follows consists of works actually used in preparing this study; it nevertheless does not include a considerable number of works providing background or general reference, or which are cited only once in the footnotes. In one respect, however, there is some deviation from this principle: in the case of materials dealing specifically with Fersen, it has seemed appropriate to provide as complete a list as possible, even though many of the published works were of no use to the present study.

Documents are cited, where possible, in their best published versions. To save space, however, they are identified individually only when unpublished, not when taken from printed works. It should be borne in mind that the distinction between works classified here as published sources and as secondary studies respectively is arbitrary at best. For instance, the published edition of Fersen's diary, Alma Söderhjelm, *Axel von Fersens dagbok*, 4 vol. (Stockholm, 1925–36), is naturally listed under published sources, but it contains much commentary by the editor; where this is referred to rather than the diary itself, I have so indicated in my footnotes. Similarly, Professor Söderhjelm's *Fersen et Marie-Antoinette* (Paris, 1930) though basically a secondary study, contains very extensive documentary material; indeed, most of my citations from this important work are to the documents it includes, rather than to the author's discussion. I have, for example, preferred to cite from this source diary entries, when contained therein, in preference to the *Dagbok*, since they are here given in the original French. A number of other secondary works likewise contain valuable documentation.

A detailed discussion of much of the Fersen bibliography, including both published and unpublished materials, is appended to Bengt Hildebrand, "Hans Axel von Fersen," in *Svenskt biografiskt lexikon* XV (Stockholm, 1956), 743–50.

In alphabetizing this bibliography, the Swedish letter *å* is considered equivalent to *aa*, *ä* to *ae*, and *ö* to *oe*. The following abbreviations are used:

491

Arneth, *MAJL* = Alfred, Ritter von Arneth, *Marie-Antoinette, Joseph II und Leopold II. Ihr Briefwechsel* (Leipzig, 1866).

Dagbok = Alma Söderhjelm, ed., *Axel von Fersens dagbok*, 4 vol. (Stockholm, 1925–36).

Dropmore Papers = Great Britain. Historical Manuscripts Commission. *The Manuscripts of J. B. Fortescue Preserved at Dropmore*, 10 vol. (London, 1892–1927).

F. arkiv = Stafsundssamlingen. Hans Axel von Fersens arkiv, Riksarkivet, Stockholm.

FAF arkiv = Stafsundssamlingen. Fredrik Axel von Fersens arkiv, Riksarkivet, Stockholm.

FAF, HS = R. M. Klinckowström, ed., *Riksrådet och fält-marskalken m.m. Fredrik Axel von Fersens historiska skrifter*, 8 vol. (Stockholm, 1867–71).

Feuillet de Conches = F. Feuillet de Conches, ed., *Louis XVI, Marie-Antoinette et Madame Élisabeth. Lettres et documents inédits*, 6 vol. (Paris, 1864–73).

HEC = *Hedvig Elisabeth Charlottas dagbok*, ed. Carl Carlsson Bonde & Cecilia af Klercker, 9 vol. (Stockholm, 1902–42).

KB = Kungliga biblioteket (The Royal Library), Stockholm.

Klinckowström = R. M. Klinckowström, ed., *Le comte de Fersen et la cour de France*, 2 vol. (Paris, 1877–78).

LUB = Lunds universitetsbibliotek.

RA = Riksarkivet (The Swedish State Archives), Stockholm.

SBL = *Svenskt biografiskt lexikon* (Stockholm, 1907–).

Söderhjelm, *FMA* = Alma Söderhjelm, *Fersen et Marie-Antoinette* (Paris, 1930).

Söderhjelm, *SOFR* = Alma Söderhjelm, *Sverige och den franska revolutionen*, 2 vol. (Stockholm, 1920–24).

SUPH = Nils Ahnlund et al., *Den svenska utrikespolitikens historia*, 5 vol. (Stockholm, 1951–61).

UUB = Uppsala universitetsbibliotek.

I. PRIMARY SOURCES: UNPUBLISHED

Badensisches Generallandsarchiv, Karlsruhe:
Grossherzogliches Familien-Archiv. Korrespondenz (Karl Friedrich), V, Band 20. Korrespondenz mit Gustaf IV Adolf. (From notes by Professor Sten Carlsson from notes by Rector Herbert Lundh.)
Kungliga biblioteket, Stockholm. (KB)
Autografsamlingen:
Brev från generalen Hans Axel von Fersen.
Lars von Engeströms samling:
Ep. E. 10:1–26. Brev erhållna åren 1786–1823, III, VII.
I. f. 8. Anteckningar rörande ätten von Fersen och riksmarskalken grefve Axel von Fersen.
Osign. 25. Brev till E....., aktstycken jämte anmärkningar av E..... angående H. A. von Fersen och upploppet 20/6.

[Fersen]:
H. f. 1. Anteckningar rörande friherrliga och grevliga ätterna Fersen.
[Fersen, Axel von]:
i:Vt. 128. Anonymous, "Fersiaden."
[Häggman, Jöns Person]:
D. 1048 a. Häggman, Jöns Person: Anteckningar 1808–16.
[Norstedt, L. F.]:
Ep. N. 3 a. Brev från hofkamrer L. F. Norstedt till J. G. Norstedt
  om fersenska mordet.
[Wallmark, P. A.]:
Ep. V. 4:6. Brev till P. A. Wallmark.
Vadstena landsarkiv, Vadstena.
Lövstad arkiv:
VII, VIII. Brev från Axel von Fersen d. y. till Sophie Piper, 1770–
  1795, 1796–1802.
XII, XX. Diverse handlingar rörande franska revolutionen.
XXI. Diverse papper.
Lunds universitetsbibliotek, Lund. (LUB).
G. Anderssons samling, XXII.
Riksarkivet, Stockholm. (RA).
Armfeltska samlingen:
III. Brev till G. M. Armfelt, F-K.
XII. Brev.
Börstorpssamlingen:
X. Brev till Fredrik Sparre.
Sam Clasons samling:
CIII. Avskrifter från Moskva tagna 1925, I.
  "Stockholm 1810." [folder.]
Diplomatica:
Allmänna fredskongresser:
LXVII. Ambassadör Axel von Fersens depescher 1797–98.
Gallica:
Vol. 499. Generalmajor Axel von Fersens depescher 1791–92.
Vol. 500. Generalmajor Axel von Fersens depescher 1793–94.
Germanica:
(Kejsaren) B:1 (1791). Axel von Fersens depescher från Wien
  och Prag 1791.
F. IV (Baden). Axel von Fersens depescher från Karlsruhe
  1798–99.
Direktionen över Lappmarkens ecklesiastikverk arkiv; Koncepter 1799–
  1801.
Ericsbergsarkivet:
Brevskrivareserie.
Forsslund, Nils Wilhelm:
Nils Wilh. Forsslunds efterlämnade anteckningar. (Excerpts in
  possession of *förste arkivarie* Nils F. Holm.)

494 COUNT HANS AXEL VON FERSEN

Handel och sjöfart:
Handlingar angående 1731 års Östindiska kompaniet 1800–13 och odat. LV.
Kanslersgillets arkiv [1801–1809].
Kanslersgillets protokoll, I–IV.
Kanslersämbetets för Uppsala universitetet arkiv:
Uppsala universitetskanslerns koncept, B 17, B 18, B 19.
Gustaf Lagerbjelke samling:
XIV. Brev.
H. E. Lagerheims samling 1805–8:
Serie II: B 29. Brev.
Landshövdingars skrivelser till Kungliga Majestätet: Östergötland, LXIV.
Protokoll:
Inrikes-civila ärenden.
Konseljen och kungliga beredningen, 1809.
Krigsärenden.
Rådsprotokoll och föredragningslistor.
1809 års statsrådsprotokoller, april-december. Kammerexpeditionen.
Reuterholm samling, 1789–95:
VIII. Brev till G. A. Reuterholm.
Ryska filmsamlingen II:
Roll 41. MID Kantselyariya 1810-g., d. 10811. [Chancellor's instructions to Ambassador van Suchtelen, 1810.] Fol. 51–85.
d. 10815, "Essai d'un récit historique des événements arrivés à Stockholm pendant l'année 1810." Fol. 40–53.
Stafsundssamlingen:
Hans Axel von Fersens samling:
I. Kopier och koncept av brev till Gustav III, 1783–92, till hertigen-regenten Karl, 1792–94, och till Gustav IV Adolf, 1792.
II. Koncept av brev till Gustav IV Adolf 1793–1808.
III. Koncept av brev till rikskanslern, svenska diplomater, m.m.
IV–IX. Dagböcker 1770–79, 1791–1808.
X. Brevregister, 1783–1801, 1802–1808.
XI. Brev från furstliga personer.
XII–XIV. Brev från enskilda personer.
XV. Osignerade brev och brevavskrifter. Svenska och utländska bulletiner.
XVI. Handlingar rörande 1788–1790 års krig.
XVII. Handlingar rörande de franska förbindelserna och revolutionen.
XVIII. Handlingar rörande Gustav IV Adolfs giftermål. Fersens beskickningshandlingar från kongressen i Rastadt, m.m.
XIX. Handlingar angående konungens resa i Tyskland och kampanjen i Pommern 1805–6.
XX. Personliga förhållanden.
XXI. Handlingar rörande Fersens död och begravning. Bouppteckning. Arvskifteshandlingar.

XXII–XXXVII. Räkenskaper.
XXXVIII–XLII. Handlingar angående mordet på riksmarskalken Axel von Fersen.
Fredrik Axel von Fersens samling:
VIII–IX. Brev från Axel von Fersen d.y. till sin far.
XI. Brev till kamreraren Eric Nortun.
XXXIV. Axel von Fersens [d.ä.] och hans hustrus testamenten, boupptecknings- och arvskifteshandlingar.
Manuskript- och avskriftssamlingen:
XXI. Brev och handlingar rörande kronprinsens Carl Augusts mottagande och död.
Evert Taubes samling:
I. Brevväxling.
II–III. Brev från Axel von Fersen d.y.
IV. Testamente och arvskifteshandlingar.
Tosterupsamlingen:
I. L. Silfversparres papper.
LVII. Brev.
LXVII. Brev och handlingar rörande revolutionen 1809, f.d. konungens vistelse i Sverige, samt fersenska mordet.
Slottsarkivet, Royal Palace, Stockholm: Riksmarskalksämbetets arkiv.
Stockholms stadsarkiv, Stockholm.
Stockholm stads mantalslängder.
Stockholm stads taxeringslängder.
Samfundet för Svenskt biografiskt lexikons utgivande, Stockholm.
Personregister till *Axel von Fersens dagbok,* I–IV, utg. av Alma Söderhjelm. (n.d., typescript.)
Uppsala universitetsbibliotek, Uppsala. (UUB).
Handskriftsavdelningen: [Brev från Axel von Fersen d.y.]:
Brevskrivare: F 647 e.; B 273.; G 70.; F 818 b.; F 501.; F 657 b.;
G 103.; G 231 c.; F 830 c.; F 653 a.; F 520.; F 657 c.; G 300 i.;
W 814.; G 360.; X 241. (von Fersen).
In private ownership of *Ingeniör* Arne Forslund, Stockholm.
Brev fran Axel von Fersen d.ä. till Johan Jacob Forslund 1770–82.

II. PRIMARY SOURCES: PUBLISHED

[Anonymous]. *Historia om Riksmarskalken Axel von Fersens mord, utanför Rådhuset i Stockholm, den 20 juni 1810* (Stockholm, 1844).
Acerbi, Joseph. *Travels through Sweden, Finland, and Lappland to the North Cape in the Years 1798 and 1799,* 2 vol. (London, 1802).
[Adlerbeth, G. G.]. *Gustaf III:s resa i Italien. Anteckningar af Gudm. Göran Adlerbeth,* ed. Henrik Schück. Svenska memoarer och bref, V (Stockholm, 1902).
———. *Historiska anteckningar,* ed. Elof. Tegnér, 2 vol. (Stockholm, 1892).
Adlersparre, Georg. *Handlingar rörande Sveriges äldre, nyare och nyaste historia samt historiska personer,* 9 vol. (Stockholm, 1830–33), III.

Ahnfelt, A. *Ur svenska hofvets och aristokratiens lif*, 7 vol. (Stockholm, 1880–83).

Alin, O. *Tronföljarvalet 1810*, Historiska handlingar XVII (Stockholm, 1899).

Andersson, G., ed. *Handlingar ur Brinkman'ska arkivet på Trolle-Ljungby*, 2 vol. (Örebro, 1859–65).

Anker, C. J., ed. *Utdrag ur danska diplomaters meddelanden från Stockholm 1807–1808, 1810 och 1812–13*, trans. F. U. Wrangel (Stockholm, 1898).

Arneth, Alfred, Ritter von, ed. *Joseph II und Leopold von Toscana. Ihr Briefwechsel von 1781 bis 1790*, 2 vol. (Vienna, 1872), I.

————. *Marie Antoinette, Joseph II und Leopold II. Ihr Briefwechsel* (Leipzig, 1866).

Autentisk Beretning om det der er foregaaet i Sverrig i Anledning af Kronprindsens død . . . oversat af svensk ved M. Hagerup (Copenhagen, 1810).

Bachaumont, Louis Petit de. *Mémoires secrets pour servir à l'histoire de la République des lettres en France*, 36 vol. (London, 1784–89).

Bacourt, M. A. de, ed. *Correspondance entre le comte de Mirabeau et le comte de La Marck pendant les années 1789, 1790 et 1791*, 3 vol. (Paris, 1851).

Barante, M. de, ed. *Lettres et instructions de Louis XVIII au comte de Saint-Priest* (Paris, 1845).

Bertrand de Moleville, A. F. de. *Mémoires particuliers pour servir à l'histoire de la fin du règne de Louis XVI*, 2 vol. (Paris, 1816).

Beskow, Bernhard von. *Lefnadsminnen* (Stockholm, 1870).

Biörnstierna, M.F.F. *See* Stedingk, Curt von.

Boëthius, S. J., ed. *Bihang till Minnen ur Sveriges nyare historia*, 3 vol. (Stockholm, 1880–83).

[Bonde, Carl]. "Öfverste kammarjunkaren friherre Carl Bonde till Gustaf IV Adolf från en beskickning till Napoleon 1801–2," *Historisk tidskrift* (1885), 355–67.

Bouillé, François-Claude-Amour, marquis de. *Mémoires du marquis de Bouillé*, ed. M. F. Barrière (Paris, 1859).

[Bouillé, Louis-Joseph-Amour, marquis de]. *Mémoire du marquis de Bouillé (comte Louis), lieutenant-général, sur le départ de Louis XVI au mois de juin 1791*, S. A. de Berville & M. F. Barrière, ed., *Collection des mémoires rélatifs à la Révolution française*, XLI (Paris, 1823).

[Brelin, S.]. *Överste Brelins anteckningar. Svenska memoarer och bref*, ed. H. Schück & O. Levertin, I (Stockholm, 1900).

Brown, J. *Memoirs of the Courts of Sweden and Denmark during the Reigns of Christian VII of Denmark and Gustavus III and IV of Sweden*, 2 vol. (London, 1913). Originally published 1818.

Campan, Jeanne Louise Henriette (Genest). *Mémoires sur la vie privée de Marie-Antoinette*, 3 vol. (Paris, 1822).

Carlsson, Sten. "Hans Gabriel Wachtmeisters dagbok 1807–1809," *Vetenskaps-Societeten i Lund, Årsbok 1943* (Lund, 1944), 43–75.

Clarke, E. D. *Travels in Various Countries of Scandinavia; including Denmark, Sweden, Norway, Lapland and Finland*, 3 vol. (London, 1838), II.

Clason, Sam., ed. *Handlingar till kronprins Carl Augusts historia*, Historiska handlingar, XXVII:2 (Stockholm, 1925).

Clason, Sam, & af Petersens, Carl, eds. *För hundra år sen. Skildringar och bref från revolutionsåren 1809–1810*, 3 vol. (Stockholm, 1909–10).

Closen, Baron Ludwig von. *The Revolutionary Journal of Baron Ludwig von Closen, 1780–1783*, ed. Evelyn M. Alcomb (Chapel Hill, 1958).

Coxe, William. *Travels into Poland, Russia, Sweden and Denmark*, 4 vol. London, 1787).

Dardel, H. L. von. *Fältmarskalken von Stedingks tidigare levnadsöden skildrade efter brev till överståthållaren Carl Sparre* (Örebro, 1922).

Desfeuilles, André. "Félix Berger, cuisinier d'Axel de Fersen. D'après une correspondance inédite, 1801–1807," *Mémoires de l'Académie de Vaucluse* (Avignon, 1953). Pamphlet.

[Drewsen, I. C.]. *I. C. Drewsens Rejsedagbok. Optegnelser fra en Rejse i Sommeren 1838*, udgivd ved Højesteretssagfører Stein (Copenhagen, 1941).

[Düben, Gustaf von]. "Berättelse af majoren friherre Gustaf von Düben om mordet å RiksMarskalken Grefve von Fersen 20 Junii 1810," in M. G. Crusenstolpe, ed., *Portfeuille*, 3 vol. (Stockholm, 1837–42), I, 218–26.

Dumas, Count Mathieu. *Memoirs of His Own Time*, 2 vol. (London, 1839), I.

[Ehrenström, J. A.] *Statsrådet Johan Albert Ehrenströms efterlemnade historiska anteckningar*, ed. S. J. Boëthius, 2 vol. (Stockholm, 1883).

[Ehrensvärd, Gustaf Johan]. *Dagboksanteckningar förda vid Gustaf III:s hof*, ed. E. V. Montan, 2 vol. (Stockholm, 1877–78).

Elinder, Erik. "Adolf Ludvig Hamiltons minnesanteckningar från 1800 års riksdag," *Personhistorisk tidskrift*, LII (1954), 73–142.

[Engeström, Lars von]. *Minnen och anteckningar*, ed. Elof Tegnér, 2 vol. (Stockholm, 1876).

Erdmannsdörffer, K., and Obser, K., eds. *Politische Correspondenz Karl Friedrichs von Baden, 1783–1806*, 5 vol. (Heidelberg, 1896).

[Esterhazy, comte Valentin d']. *Mémoires du comte Valentin d'Esterhazy*, ed. Ernest Daudet (2nd ed., Paris, 1905).

[Fersen, Hans Axel von]. "La Guerre d'Amérique (1780–1783) par le comte Jean Axel de Fersen," *Bibliothèque de souvenirs et récits militaires*, édité par Henri Gautier, XX (n.d., n.p.).

[Fersen, Hans Axel von]. *Rettet die Königin: Revolutionstagebuch 1789–1793*, ed. and trans. Anni Carlsson (Munich, 1970).

[Fersen, H. A. von]. [Drafts of letters to Gustav IV Adolf, 1805–1806], *Bihang till Journalen för Litteratur och Theater*, 6, 29 September 1810.

Feuillet de Conches, F., ed. *Louis XVI, Marie-Antoinette et Madame Élisabeth. Lettres et documents inédits*, 6 vol. (Paris, 1864–73).

France. Commission des archives diplomatiques, *Recueil des instructions données aux ambassadeurs et ministres de France depuis les traités de Westphalie jusqu'à la Révolution française*, 25 vol. (Paris, 1884–1929), II (*La Suède*); IX (*La Russie*).

Geffroy, Auguste, ed. "Lettres du comte Axel Fersen à Milady Elizabeth Foster, Devonshire House, à Londres. (Collection d'autographes à La Haye)," *Revue d'histoire diplomatique*, II (1888), 91–99.

Geijer, E. G., ed. *Konung Gustaf III:s efterlemnade och femtio år efter hans död öppnade papper*, 2nd ed., in *Erik Gustaf Geijers samlade skrifter*, supplement I. (Stockholm, 1876).

Great Britain. Historical Manuscripts Commision. *The Manuscripts of J. B. Fortescue Preserved at Dropmore*, 10 vol. (London, 1892–1927).

Hamilton, C. D. *Anteckningar af en gammal gustavian* (Linköping, 1855).

Hanselli, P. *Ur en samlares papper*, 2 vol. (Uppsala, 1868–69).

[Hedvig Elisabeth Charlotta]. *Hedvig Elisabeth Charlottas dagbok*, ed. Carl Carlsson Bonde & Cecilia af Klercker, 9 vol. (Stockholm, 1902–42).

Heidenstam, O. G. de. *Marie-Antoinette, Fersen et Barnave. Leur correspondance* (Paris, 1913). Undependable. Also English translation (N.Y., 1927).

Helwig, Hans Friedrich. *Efterretning om de i Stockholm i Sommeren 1810 forefaldne Revolutions-Optrin og sammes Følger* (Aalborg, 1810).

Hennings, Beth, ed. *Ögonvittnen: Gustav III* (Stockholm, 1960).

Hermelin, Baron Samuel Gustaf. *Berättelse om Nordamerikas Förenta stater 1784. Bref till kanslipresidenten* (Stockholm, 1894).

[Hochschild, R. F.]. *Memoarer*, ed. H. Schück, 3 vol. (Stockholm, 1908–1909).

[Holland, Elizabeth (Vassall) Fox, Lady]. *The Journal of Elizabeth Lady Holland*, ed. the Earl of Ilchester, 2 vol. (London, 1908), I.

[Holland, Henry Richard Vassall Fox, Baron]. *Foreign Reminiscences*, ed. by his son, Henry Edward, Lord Holland (2nd ed., London, 1851).

Holmes, Georgina, trans. "The French Army in the Revolutionary War. Count de Fersen's Private Letters to his Father, 1780–81," *Magazine of American History*, XXV (1891), 55–70, 156–73.

Hutton, James, ed. *Selections from the Letters and Correspondence of Sir James Bland Burges, Bart., Sometime Under-Secretary of State for Foreign Affairs with Notices of his Life* (London, 1885).

[Jackson, Sir George]. *Diaries and Letters of Sir George Jackson*, ed. Lady Jackson, 2 vol. (London, 1872).

Klinckowström, R. M. *Le comte de Fersen et la cour de France*, 2 vol. (Paris, 1877–78).

———, ed. *Riksrådet och fält-marskalken m.m. Fredrik Axel von Fersens historiska skrifter*, 8 vol. (Stockholm, 1867–72).

La Rocheterie, Maxime de, and Marquis de Beaucourt, eds. *Lettres de Marie-Antoinette*, 2 vol. (Paris, 1895–96).

Lauzun, Duc de. *Mémoires* (Paris, 1929).

Legran, W. [pseud. for F. U. Wrangel]. *Ur arkivens gömmor* (Stockholm, 1912).

Léouzon le Duc, L. A., ed. *Correspondance diplomatique du baron de Staël-Holstein, ambassadeur de Suède en France, et de son successeur comme chargé d'affaires, le baron Brinkman. Documents inédits sur la Révolution (1783–1799) recueillés aux archives royales de Suède* (Paris, 1881).

Lescure, Mathurin A. F. de. *Correspondance secrète inédite sur Louis XVI, Marie-Antoinette, la cour et la ville*, 2 vol. (Paris, 1866).

Lévis, Gaston Pierre Marc, Duc de. *Souvenirs et portraits, 1780–1789* (Paris, 1813).

Limon, M. de. *La vie et le martyre de Louis XVI* (London, 1793).

[Malouet, Baron]. *Mémoires de Malouet*, publiés par son petit-fils, le baron Malouet (Paris, 1868).

Ministerstvo inostrannykh del SSSR. *Vneshnyaya politika Rossii XIX-go i nachala XX-go veka. Dokumenty rossiiskogo ministerstva inostrannykh del*, first series, vol. III (Moscow, 1963).

Moniteur universel.

[Montslosier, Comte de]. *Souvenirs d'un émigré, 1791–98*, eds., Comte de Larouzière-Montlosier and Ernest d'Hauterive (Paris, 1951).

[Morris, Governeur]. *A Diary of the French Revolution*, ed. Beatrix Cary Davenport, 2 vol. (Boston, 1939).

Murray, Dr. Gustaf. *Tal vid Hans Excellence RiksMarskalken, Högvälborne Grefve Herr Axel von Fersens begrafning . . . den 4 december 1810* (Stockholm, 1811).

—————. *Personalier öfver . . . Grefve Herr Hans Axel von Fersen, upläste vid Dess Jordfästning i Riddarholms-Krykan den 4 december 1810* (Stockholm, 1811).

[Napoleon I]. *Correspondance de Napoléon I*er*.*, 32 vol. (Paris, 1858–70).

Nordin, Richard. "En österrikisk diplomat om Sveriges inre förhållanden år 1797," *Historisk tidskrift* (1911), 37–51.

Nyerup, Rasmus. *Rejser til Stockholm i Aarene 1810–1812, eller hans paa disse Rejser holdte Dagbøger, med tilhørende Bilag* (Copenhagen, 1816).

[Piper, Sophie]. [Letters to an unknown correspondent in Germany and to Lars von Engeström, 1810]. *Die Zeiten oder Archiv für die neueste Staatengeschichte und Politik*, XXIV (Leipzig, 1810), 137–53.

Porter, Robert Ker. *Travelling Sketches in Russia and Sweden, 1805, 1806, 1807, 1808*, 2 vol. (London, 1809), II.

Rabenius, L. J. *Officium Parentale viro Axelio von Fersen die XXI Martii MDCCCXI nomine Academiae Upsaliensis* (Uppsala, 1811).

Rydén, S., ed. *Miranda i Sverige och Norge 1787* (Stockholm, 1950).

[Saint-Priest, Comte de]. *Mémoires des règnes de Louis XV et de Louis XVI*, ed., Baron de Barante, 2 vol. (Paris, 1929), II.

Sayous, A., ed. *Mémoires et correspondance de Mallet du Pan*, 2 vol. (Paris, 1851).

Scævola [K. A. Strömbäck], ed. *Utländska diplomaters minnen från svenska hofvet* (Stockholm, 1885).

Schinkel, Bernhard von. *Minnen ur Sveriges nyare historia*, ed. C. W. Bergman, 10 vol. (Stockholm, 1852–68).

Schlitter, Hanns, ed. *Briefe der Erzherzogin Marie Christine Statthalterin der Niederlande an Leopold II. Nebst einer Einleitung: Zur Geschichte der französischen Politik Leopolds II.* Fontes Rerum Austriacarum, II. Abteilung: Diplomataria et acta, XLVIII:1 (Vienna, 1896).

[Schröderheim, Elis]. *Skrifter till konung Gustaf III:s historia jämte urval ur Schröderheims brefväxling*, ed. Elof Tegnér (2nd ed., Stockholm, 1892).

Schück, Henrik, ed. *Den sista gustavianska hofdamen. Ur Marianne Ehrenströms minnen* (Stockholm, 1919).

————. *Gustavianska brev* (Stockholm, 1918).

[Skjöldebrand, A. F.]. *Excellensen A.F. Skjöldebrands memoarer*, ed. Henrik Schück, 5 vol. (Stockholm, 1903–1904).

Söderhjelm, Alma, ed. *Axel von Fersens dagbok*, 4 vols. (Stockholm, 1925–36).

————. "Les débuts de Fersen d'après son journal intime," *Bibliothèque universelle et revue de Genève* (mai 1929), 556–68.

————. ed. *Marie-Antoinette et Barnave. Correspondance secrète (juillet 1791–janvier 1792)* (Paris, 1934).

[Stedingk, Curt von]. *Mémoires posthumes du feld-maréchal comte de Stedingk, rédigés sur des lettres, depêches et autres pièces authentiques*, ed. Count M. F. F. Biörnstierna, 2 vol. (Paris, 1844–47).

[Suremain, Charles de]. *Mémoires du lieutenant-général de Suremain (1794–1815)* (Paris, 1902).

Tegnér, Elof, ed. *Konung Gustaf III:s bref till friherre G.M. Armfelt*, Historiska handlingar XII:3 (Stockholm, 1883).

Thompson, J. M., ed. *French Revolutionary Documents, 1789–94* (Oxford, 1933).

Tilly, Comte Alexandre de. *Mémoires du comte Alexandre de Tilly pour servir à l'histoire des mœurs à la fin du 18e. siècle*, 2 vol. (Paris, 1828), II.

The Times.

Toijer, Daniel, ed. *Brinkman och Adlersparre. En brevväxling från Karl Johans-tiden* (Stockholm, 1962).

[Trolle-Wachtmeister, Hans Gabriel]. *Anteckningar och minnen*, ed. Elof Tegnér, 2 vol. (Stockholm, 1889), I.

Vivenot, Alfred, Ritter von, ed. *Quellen zur Geschichte der deutschen Kaiserpolitik Oesterreichs während der französischen Revolutionskriege, 1790–1801*, 5 vol. (Vienna, 1873–93), I, II.

Vivie, Aurélien, ed. *Lettres de Gustave III à la comtesse de Boufflers et de la comtesse au roi*, Actes de l'Académie nationale des sciences, belles-lettres et arts de Bordeaux. 3e. série -60e année, 1898. (Paris, 1898).

Wieselgren, P., ed. *DeLaGardiska arkivet. Handlingar ur grefliga DeLa-Gardiska bibloteket på Löberöd*, 20 vol. (Stockholm, 1831–44).

Wormeley, Katherine P., ed. *Diary and Correspondence of Count Axel de Fersen* (London, 1902).

[Wåhlin, Christian]. "Anteckningar om riksdagarna 1809–10, 1812 och 1815," in Axel Brusewitz, ed., *Handlingar rörande riksdagarna 1809–15*, Historiska handlingar XXV:2 (Stockholm, 1916).

[Washington, George]. *Writings of George Washington*, ed. John C. Fitzpatrick, XXI (Washington, 1937).

Wrangel, F. U., ed. *Lettres d'Axel de Fersen à son père pendant la guerre de l'indépendance d'Amérique* (Paris, 1929).

III. SECONDARY WORKS, SPECIFICALLY ON AXEL VON FERSEN

[Anonymous]. "Fersens arkiv i stekarhus," *Svenska dagbladet*, 14 January 1954.

Arnaud-Bouteloup, Jeanne. "Le roman d'Axel Fersen et Marie-Antoinette (à propos du livre d'Alma Söderhjelm)," *Revue hebdomaire*, VII (1930), 400–13, VIII (1930), 39–58.

Austin, Paul Britten. *Famous Swedes* (London, 1962). Section on Fersen.

Baumann, Émile. *Marie-Antoinette et Axel Fersen* (Paris, 1931).

Bellissent, G. "Le comte de Fersen, créancier de Louis XVI," *Revue historique de la Révolution française*, XV (1923), 353–66.

Billberg, J. P. af. "Fersenska mordet. En samtida skildring i enskilt brev," *Genealogisk tidskrift*, XVI (1961), 35–37.

Bonde, Carl Carlsson, "Fersenska mordet," Meddelat af Carl C:son Bonde. Skildrat af drottning Hedvig Elisabeth Charlotta i hennes dagboksanteckningar för år 1810. *Personhistorisk tidskrift*, I (1899), 1–15.

Bord, Gustave. *Autour du Temple, 1792–1795*, 2 vol. (Paris, 1912), II, Ch. II, "Fersen et Craufurd."

Bordeaux, Henry. *Amitié ou amour. Marie-Antoinette et Fersen. Pauline de Beaumont et Chateaubriand*, etc. (Paris, 1932), 27–80.

————. *Châteaux en Suède* (Paris, 1928), Ch. IV, "Le secret du comte Fersen," (same as chapter on subject in author's *Amitié ou amour*, above).

Bülau, Friedrich, "Graf Axel Fersen," *Geheime Geschichten und rätselhafte Menschen*, VII (Leipzig, 1856), 368–75; VIII (1857), 501.

Cajumi, Arrigo. "Tilly, Fersen e Maria Antonietta," *La Cultura*, IX (1930), 425–41.

Carlsson, Sten. "Axel von Fersen den yngre," *Svenska dagbladet*, 7 April 1957, 17.

Carnegy. *A Queen's Knight: The Life of Count Axel de Fersen* (London, 1911).

502 COUNT HANS AXEL VON FERSEN

Castelot, André. "Les vingt juin du comte Axel de Fersen," *Historia*, No. 163 (1960), 661–68.

Clason, Sam. "Fersenska mordet," *Sydsvenska dagbladet-snällposten*, No. 163, 19 June 1910.

Contenson, Ludovic de. "Marie-Antoinette, Barnave et Fersen," *Revue d'histoire diplomatique*, XLIX (1935), 28–42.

Coryn, Marjorie. *Marie Antoinette and Axel de Fersen* (London, 1938).

Coussanges, Jacques de. "Fersen d'après son journal," *Mercure de France*, CLXXXVIII (1926), 56–79.

Dard, Émile. "Bonaparte et Fersen," *Revue des Deux Mondes* (1938), 614–31.

Dardel, H. von. Review of *Axel von Fersens dagbok*, ed. A. Söderhjelm, II, *Personhistorisk tidskrift*, XXIX (1927), 174–75.

Durand, R. Review of A. Söderhjelm, *Fersen et Marie-Antoinette*, in *Revue critique d'histoire et littérature* (1930), 457–59.

Erdman, Nils. "Ädlingen från l'Ancien régime," *Nya dagligt allehanda*, 28 July 1937.

Fersen, H. von, *Graf Axel Fersen. Ein Lebensbild* (Berlin, 1896).

Fitz-James, Duchesse de. "Marie-Antoinette et Fersen," *La vie contemporaine* (1894).

Flach, F. F. *Grefve Hans Axel von Fersen. Minnesteckning jemte utdrag ur hans dagbok och brefvexling* (Stockholm, 1896).

Fogelqvist, Torsten. *Typer och tänkesätt* (Stockholm, 1927). Essay entitled "Drottningens vän," 231–54.

Forstrand, C. "Ur 1810 års minnen. C. Forstrand: två kronprinsar—Fersenska mordet. Frih. G. A. von Dübens berättelse," *Vinterbloss* (1909), 10–15.

Furumark, Agneta. *Från Axel von Fersens tid. Skatter från Lövstad* (Norrköping, 1967). Exihibition catalog.

Gaulot, Paul. *Un ami de la reine* (Paris, 1892). Also in English (N.Y., 1893).

––––––. "M. de Fersen et Marie-Antoinette," *Revue politique et littéraire* (*Revue bleue*), L, No. 19–20, 582–90, 624–31, 660–66.

Geffroy, Auguste. [Studio sopra Maria Antonietta e Fersen, sopra di "Communicazioni e letture,"] Accademia dei Lincei, Roma, *Atti*, ser. III (1878–79), 99.

Gélis, F. de. *Un ami de la reine Marie-Antoinette. Le comte de Fersen grand maréchal de Suède* (Paris, 1935).

Gonzalez Ruiz, Nicholas. *Axel de Fersen. El romántico amor de María Antonietta* (Fourth ed., Madrid, 1968).

Granath, W. *Fersenska mordet. Historisk roman* (Stockholm, 1904).

Grimberg, C. "Domaren Lynch i Stockholm år 1810. Då Stockholms befolkning spelade hämnande mordängel. Nya detaljer om det Fersenska mordet och dess miljö," *Dagens nyheter*, No. 62, 5 March 1922, Sunday supplement.

Gurnell, Rachel. "The Count de Fersen," *Gentleman's Magazine*, new ser., XLVIII (1892), 295–306.

Gynther, August, "Fersenska mordet. Vilka buro ansvaret?", *Göteborgs handels- och sjöfartstidning*, 22 September 1934.

Hafström, Gerhard. "Justitiekanslern och fersenska mordet," *Festskrift tillägnad Hans Excellens Riksmarskalken juris doctor Birger Ekeberg den 10 Augusti 1950* (Stockholm, 1950), 183–209.

––––––. "Mordet på Axel Fersen," *Svenskt biografiskt lexikon*, XV (Stockholm, 1956), 733–43.

––––––. Reviews of T. Nerman, *Fersenska mordet*, in *Personhistorisk tidskrift*, XXXIV (1933), 146–47, and *Historisk tidskrift* (1934), 124–28.

Hallsten, Harald. "Axel von Fersen i Nordamerika," *Östgöte correspondent*, 8 August 1970.

Hansson, Ola. "L'assassinat de Fersen (20 juin 1810)," *Revue d'histoire diplomatique* (1911), 195–207.

Hausser, H. Review of A. Söderhjelm, *Fersen et Marie-Antoinette*, in *Revue historique*, CLXIV (1930), 177–79.

Hedman, Rune. "Massan vid fersenska upploppet 1810," in Torgny Nevéus, ed., *Historia kring Stockholm. Från frihetstiden till sekelskiftet* (Stockholm, 1967), 35–54.

––––––. "Massan vid det s. k. fersenska upploppet," *Historisk tidskrift* (1969), 2–71.

Heidenstam, O.-G. de. "Fersen et Marie-Antoinette," *Revue de Paris*, III (1912), 472–94.

Hesekiel, Georg. "Graf Axel Fersen," in *Gemischte Gesellschaft. Biografische Skizzen* (Berlin, 1867), 55–73.

Hildebrand, Bengt. "von Fersen," *Svenskt biografiskt lexikon*, XV (Stockholm, 1956), 644–54.

––––––. "Hans Axel von Fersen," *Svenskt biografiskt lexikon*, XV (Stockholm, 1956), 703–33, and bibliography, 743–47.

Holmberg, Olle. "Riddaren av det förgånga," *Dagens nyheter*, 16 March 1952.

Hüe, G. "Comte de Fersen, de dernier fidèle de Marie-Antoinette (1755–1810)," *Les contemporains* (n.d.), 16 pp.

Karmin, O. "Le trésor de Marie-Antoinette et le comte de Fersen," *Revue historique de la Révolution française*, XV (1923), 121–45.

Krumhansl, Bernice. "Side by Side with Washington," *American Swedish Monthly* (November 1966), 26–27.

Kumlien, Kjell. "Axel von Fersens dagbok," *Ord och bild* (1937), 382–84.

Kunstler, Charles. *Fersen et son secret* (Paris, 1947).

––––––. *La douceur d'aimer. Le roman de Fersen* (Paris, 1951).

––––––. *Fersen et Marie-Antoinette* (Paris, 1961).

La Rocheterie, Maxime de. "Le comte de Fersen et la cour de France," *Revue des questions historiques*, XXV (1879), 201–13.

Larson, Anders. "Grevesmöhlen, Fersenska mordet och Bernadottes val" (unpublished article, written 1956–57, in corrected page proofs. Copy provided by *Landsarkivarie* Jöran Wibling, Härnösand).

Lauzel, A. "Count Fersen," *Nation*, XXVII (1878), 128–29, 142–43.

Lescure, M. de. "Le comte de Fersen et Marie-Antoinette. D'après des documents nouveaux," *Le correspondant*, CX (1878), 5–31, 238–52, 404–29.

Lewenhaupt, Ebba L. *Den natten* (Stockholm, 1957). Historical novel.

Lundberg, Gunnar W. "Un portrait d'Axel de Fersen dernier colonel du régiment Royal-Suédois," *Bulletin historique du Royal-Suédois*, I (1946).

Lundberg, Gunnar, and F. E. F. Desfeuilles. "Les comtes de Sparre et le comte de Fersen colonels du Royal-Suédois (1694–1717 et 1742–1791), *Revue internationale d'histoire militaire comparée*, I (1939), 33–62.

Mariecourt, André de. "Fersen et la guerre d'Amérique," *France États-unis*, XL (1924), 57–59.

Mathiez, Albert. "Les papiers de Fersen," *Annales historiques de la Révolution française*, VII (1930), 557–59.

Maury, Lucien. "Staël et Fersen," *Revue politique et littéraire (Revue bleue)*, CXIV (1932), 372–74.

Moeschlin, Felix. *Den vakre Fersen* (Stockholm, 1940). Historical novel.

Morén, F. W. Review of *Axel von Fersens dagbok*, ed. A. Söderhjelm, IV, *Historisk tidskrift* (1936), 422–23.

Nerman, Ture. "Domaren Lynch i Stockholm. Ett reportage i kämnärs-rättens 3,400 sidor vittnesmål av fersenska mordet," *Dagens nyheter*, 15 October 1933.

————. *Fersenska mordet. Ett historiskt reportage från Stockholm den 20 juni 1810* (Stockholm, 1933).

Nion, F. de. "Un héros de roman: le comte Axel de Fersen," *Revue hebdomaire*, I (1920), 469–88.

Nordén, Arthur. "Var Fersen drottningens älskare?", *Stockholms-Tidningen Stockholms-Dagblad*, 17 January 1932. Sunday supplement.

Nordenfalk, E. *Axel von Fersen. Ett 200-års minne* (Norrköping, 1955). Exhibition catalog.

Nordin, Richard. "Fersen och Bonaparte," in *Studier tillägnade Harald Hjärne* (Uppsala, 1908), 507–34.

Pfeiffer, Sara (pseud. "Sylvia"). *Axel Fersen och Marie-Antoinette. Historisk romantisk skildring* (Stockholm, 1885).

Pilon, Edmond. "L'Amitié de Fersen et de Lauzun," *Bulletin historique du Royal-Suédois*, IX (1943), 133–35.

Rosengren, H. "Fersenska mordet. Några ord med anledning af ett hundraårsminne," *Ord och bild* (1910), 337–52.

Sahlberg, Gardar. *Fersenska mordet* (Stockholm, 1974). Appeared while this book was in press.

Schahovskoy-Stretchneff, Princess. *Le comte de Fersen, Charles Gustave de Lilienfeld, la princesse Zémire* (Paris, 1910).

Schück, Henrik. "Före det fersenska mordet," *Aftonbladet*, No. 143, 22 June 1907.

Simpson, Evan John. *The King's Masque* (New York, 1941). Fiction.

Söderhjelm, Alma. *Fersen et Marie-Antoinette. Correspondance et journal intime inédits du comte Axel de Fersen* (Paris, 1930).

————. "Lettres et journal intime du comte Axel de Fersen," *Revue de Paris*, XXXVI (1929), 79–105, 379–409.

————. "När Axel Fersen träffade Napoleon," *Åbo underrättelser*, 6 May 1928.

————. "Vem har gjort strykningarna i Marie-Antoinettes brev till Fersen?" *Aftonbladet*, 29 January 1933.

Sorg, Roger. "Le vrai visage d'Axel Fersen," *Revue de France* XIII (1933), 525–40.

Spens, Willy de. *Fersen le bien aimé* (Paris, 1961).

Staël von Holstein, Lage. "Kring Fersen och Marie-Antoinette," *Sydsvenska dagbladet-snällposten*, 11 April 1932.

Strömberg, Kjell. "Fersen, la reine et... Louis XVII," *Nouvelle Revue des Deux Mondes* (January 1974), 100–13.

————. *Mänskligt högvilt i närbild* (Stockholm, 1973).

————. "Vackra Fersen–ridderlig Tristan eller cynisk don Juan?" *Stockholms-Tidningen Stockholms-Dagblad*, 30 May 1933.

Tesson, L. "L'hôtel dit des Fersen, 17 rue Matignon," Ville de Paris. Commission municipale du vieux Paris, *Procès-verbaux, 1921* (Paris, 1921), 37–40.

Thompson, J. M. "The Fersen Papers and their Editors," *English Historical Review*, XLVII (1932), 73–85.

Tufvesson, T. "Adlersparre och fersenska mordet," *Personhistorisk tidskrift*, XX (1918–19), 66–68.

Vallotton, Henry. *Marie-Antoinette et Fersen* (Paris, 1952).

Vauflart, Albert. "La maison du comte de Fersen, rue Matignon," *Extrait des mélanges Émile Le Senne* (Paris, 1916), 283–317.

Versen, F. von. *Geschichte des Geschlechtes von Versen und von Fersen*, 2 vol. (Berlin, 1909).

Vest, Eliel. "Grefve Hans Axel von Fersen. En minnesteckning," *Atheneum* (Helsingfors), I (1898), 89–112.

Wahlström, Lydia. "A Queen's Knight," *American Scandinavian Review* (1931), 748–55.

————. Review of *Axel von Fersens dagbok*, ed. A. Söderhjelm, III, *Personhistorisk tidskrift*, XXX (1929), 159–61.

Wallis, Ernst. "Fersenska mordet," *Folk-kalendern Svea*, L (1893), 131–41.

Warburg, K. "Fersenska mordet. Ett hundraårsminne," *Göteborgs Handels– och sjöfartstidning*, 18 June 1910.

IV. SECONDARY WORKS, OTHER

Åkeson, Nils. *Gustaf III:s förhållande till den franska revolutionen* (Lund, 1887).

Acton, Harold. *The Bourbons of Naples* (London, 1956).

Adlersparre, C. A. *1809 och 1810. Tidstaflor*, 3 vol. (Stockholm, 1850).

Ahnfelt, A. *Två krönta rivaler*, 2 vol. (Stockholm, 1887), I.

Aimond, Charles. *L'énigme de Varennes* (Paris, 1936).

Amnéus, A. J. "Om kronprinsen Karl Augusts dödsätt och de rättsmed-

506 COUNT HANS AXEL VON FERSEN

icinska hufvudpunkterna af rättegången mot Rossi," *Upsala universitets årsskrift 1866* (*medicin*), (Uppsala, 1866), 1–88.

Andgren, Sigfrid. *Konung och ständer 1809–1812* (Lund, 1933).

Arnaud-Bouteloup, Jeanne. *Le rôle politique de Marie-Antoinette* (Paris, 1924).

Bain, R. Nisbet. *Gustavus III and his Contemporaries*, 2 vol. (London, 1894).

————. "The Assassination of Gustavus III of Sweden," *English Historical Review* (1887), 543–52.

Barton, H. Arnold. "Sweden and the War of American Independence," *William and Mary Quarterly*, 3rd ser., XXIII (1966), 408–30.

————. "The Origins of the Brunswick Manifesto," *French Historical Studies*, V (1967), 146–69.

————. "Gustav III of Sweden and the Enlightenment," *Eighteenth-Century Studies*, VI (1972), 1–34.

————. "Late Gustavian Autocracy in Sweden: Gustaf IV Adolf and His Opponents, 1792–1809," *Scandinavian Studies*, XLVI (1974), 265–84.

————. "Russia and the Problem of Sweden-Finland, 1721–1809," *East European Quarterly*, V (1972), 431–55.

————. "The Swedish Succession Crises of 1809 and 1810, and the Question of Scandinavian Union," *Scandinavian Studies*, XLII (1970), 309–33.

————. Review of Stanley Loomis, *The Fatal Friendship*, in *The American-Scandinavian Review*, LX (1972), 312, 314.

Benson, Adolph B. *Sweden and the American Revolution* (New Haven, 1926).

Beskow, Bernhard von. *Om Gustaf den tredje såsom konung och menniska*, Svenska akademiens handlingar ifrån 1796, XXXII, XXXIV, XXXVII, XLII, XLIV (Stockholm, 1860–69).

Bimbinet, Eugène. *La fuite de Louis XVI à Varennes*, 2 vol. (Paris, 1868).

Björlin, G. *Sveriges krig i Tyskland åren 1805–1807* (Stockholm, 1882).

Boberg, Stig. *Gustav III och tryckfriheten* (Stockholm, 1951).

Boëthius, S. J. "Gustaf IV Adolfs förmyndareregering och den franska revolutionen," *Historisk tidskrift* (1888), 95–130, 177–230; (1889), 1–44, 275–322.

Bolin, Sture. "Gustaf IV Adolf i svensk historisk opinion," *Svensk tidskrift*, XXVIII (1941), 323–36.

Bonsdorff, Carl von. *Gustav Mauritz Armfelt. Levnadsskildring*, 4 vol., Skrifter utgivna av svenska litteratursällskapet i Finland (Helsingfors, 1939–40).

Brückner, A. "Schweden und Russland 1788," *Historische Zeitschrift*, XXII (1869), 314–402.

Brunot, Ferdinand. *Histoire de la langue française des origines à 1900*, 40 vol. (Paris, 1905–53), VIII.

Brusewitz, Axel. "Till frågan om Gustaf III:s sista författningsplaner," *Historisk tidskrift* (1912), 210–16.

––––––. Critique of published edition of *Hedvig Elisabeth Charlottas dagbok, Scandia,* XIV (1941), 165–78.

Carlsson, Sten. "Fredrika Dorothea Wilhelmina," *Svenskt biografiskt lexikon,* XVI (Stockholm, 1966), 474–78.

––––––. *Gustav IV Adolf. En biografi* (Stockholm, 1946).

––––––. *Gustav IV Adolfs fall* (Lund, 1944).

––––––. *Ståndssamhälle och ståndspersoner 1700–1865* (Lund, 1949).

––––––. *Den svenska utrikespolitikens historia,* III:1, *1792–1810* (Stockholm, 1954).

––––––. *Svensk historia. Tiden efter 1718* (Stockholm, 1961).

Carlyle, Thomas. *The French Revolution, A History* (Modern Library ed., New York, 1934).

Carr, R. "Gustavus IV and the British Government," *English Historical Review,* LX (1945), 36–66.

Castelot, André. *Queen of France* (New York, 1957).

Castrén, Gunnar. *Gustav Philip Creutz* (Stockholm, 1917).

Castries, Duc de. *Les émigrés, 1789–1814* (Paris, 1962).

[Château de Versailles]. *Marie-Antoinette, archiduchesse, dauphine et reine,* Éditions des musées nationaux (Paris, 1955). Exhibition catalog.

Chaumié, Jacqueline. *Le réseau d'Antraigues et la contre-révolution, 1791–1793* (Paris, 1965).

––––––. *Les relations diplomatiques entre l'Espagne et la France de Varennes à la mort de Louis XVI* (Bordeaux, 1957).

Clapham, J. H. *The Causes of the War of 1792* (Cambridge, 1899).

Clason, Sam. "Några anmärkningar rörande riksdagen i Norrköping år 1800," *Historisk tidskrift* (1897), 1–31.

––––––. *Karl XIII och Karl XIV Johan 1809–1844,* Sveriges historia till våra dagar, XI (Stockholm, 1923).

Crusenstolpe, J. J. *Carl XIII och Hedvig Elisabeth Charlotta* (Stockholm, 1861).

––––––. *Medaljonger och statyetter* (Stockholm, 1882).

Crüwell, G. A. *Die Beziehungen König Gustafs III. von Schweden zur Königin Marie Antoinette von Frankreich* (Berlin, 1897).

Dard, Émile. "Bonaparte et Fersen," *Revue des Deux Mondes* (1938), 614–31.

––––––. *Un rival de Fersen. Quentin Craufurd* (Paris, 1947).

Daudet, Ernest. *Histoire de l'émigration pendant la Révolution française,* 3 vol. (Paris, 1905–1907).

––––––. "Un drame d'amour à la cour de Suède, 1784–1795," *Revue des Deux Mondes,* X (1912), 344–77, 669–700.

Delbèke, F. *La franc-maçonnerie et la République française et autres essais sur le dixhuitième siècle* (Antwerp, 1938).

Dixelius, Olof. *Den unge Järta. En studie över en litterär politiker* (Uppsala, 1953).

Droz, Jacques. *L'Allemagne et la Révolution française* (Paris, 1949).

––––––. "La légende du complot illuministe et les origines du romanticisme politique en Allemagne," *Revue historique*, vol. 226 (1961), 313–38.

Echeverria, Durand. *Mirage in the West: A History of the French Image of American Society to 1815* (Princeton, 1957).

Elfstrand, Percy, ed. *Svensk historisk bibliografi 1951–56*, LXXII–LXXVII (Stockholm, 1952–58).

Elgenstierna, G. *Den introducerade svenska adelns ättartavlor*, 9 vol. (Stockholm, 1925–36).

Elovson, Harald. "De svenska officerarna i nordamerikanska frihetskriget," *Scandia*, II (1929), 314–27.

––––––. *Amerika i svensk litteratur 1750–1820* (Lund, 1930).

Flammermont, Jules. *Négotiations secrètes de Louis XVI et du baron de Breteuil avec la cour de Berlin, décembre 1791–juillet 1792* (Paris, 1885).

Forsell, A. "Utrikesförvaltningens historia 1721–1809," in Sven Tunberg, *et al., Den svenska utrikesförvaltningens historia* (Uppsala, 1935), 261–98.

Fournel, Victor. *L'événement de Varennes* (Paris, 1890).

––––––. "La fuite de Louis XVI," *Revue des questions historiques*, V (1868), 107–88, 426–84.

Fugier, André. *Napoléon et l'Italie* (Paris, 1947).

––––––. *La Révolution française et l'empire napoléonien*, Histoire des relations internationales, IV (Paris, 1954).

Gabriel, Charles-Nicolas. *Louis XVI, le marquis de Bouillé et Varennes* (Paris, 1874).

Gasslander, Olle. "The Convoy Affair of 1798," *Scandinavian Economic History Review*, II (1954), 22–29.

Geffroy, Auguste. *Gustave III et la cour de France*, 2 vol. (Paris, 1867).

Godechot, Jacques. *La Contre-révolution: doctrine et action, 1789–1804* (Paris, 1961).

Grimberg, C. *De diplomatiska förbindelserna mellan Sverige och Preussen 1804–1808*, Göteborgs högskolas årsskrift 1903 (Göteborg, 1903).

Gustafson, Alrik. *A History of Swedish Literature* (Minneapolis, 1961).

Hamnström, Malte. *Om realisationsfrågan vid riksdagen i Norrköping år 1800* (Härnösand, 1896).

Hastier, Louis. "Une amie de Marie-Antoinette–la Baronne de Korff," *Revue des Deux Mondes* (15 August 1961), 524–44.

Heidrich, Kurt. *Preussen im Kampfe gegen die französische Revolution bis zur zweiten Teilung Polens* (Stuttgart & Berlin, 1908).

Hennings, Beth. *Gustav III* (Stockholm, 1957).

––––––. "Det gustavianska enväldet. Gammalsvensk anda och europeisk kultur," in Evert Wrangel, ed., *Svenska folket genom tiderna*, VII (Malmö, 1938), 11–50.

Herold, J. Christopher. *Mistress to an Age: A Life of Madame de Staël* (New York, 1958).

Hildebrand, Bengt. "Fabian Reinhold von Fersen," *Svenskt biografiskt lexikon*, XV (Stockholm, 1956), 754–58.

————. "Eva Sophie von Fersen," *Svenskt biografiskt lexikon*, XV (Stockholm, 1956), 750–54.

Hildebrand, Ingegerd. *Den svenska kolonin S:t Barthélemy och Västindiska kompaniet fram till 1796* (Lund, 1951).

Hjärne, Erland, "Gustav III och franska revolutionen," *Svensk tidskrift*, XIX (1929), 502–22.

Jägerskiöld, Olof. "Fredrik Axel von Fersen," *Svenskt biografiskt lexikon*, XV (Stockholm, 1956), 686–708.

————. *Den svenska utrikespolitikens historia*, II:2 *1721–1792*, (Stockholm, 1957).

Jägerskiöld, Stig. "Tyrannmord och motståndsrätt, 1792–1809," *Scandia* (1962), 113–66.

Johnson, Amandus, *Swedish Contributions to American Freedom, 1776–1783*, 2 vol. (Philadelphia, 1953–57).

Johnson, Seved. "Legend och verklighet kring Gustav IV Adolfs brytning med Napoleon," *Svensk tidskrift*, XXXVII (1950), 460–66.

————. Review of Svenson, *Gattjinatraktaten 1799*, in *Historisk tidskrift* (1954), 341–49.

————. *Sverige och stormakterna 1800–1804* (Lund, 1957).

Key-Åberg, K. V. *De diplomatiska förbindelserna mellan Sverige och Storbrittanien under Gustaf IV Adolfs krig emot Napoleon intill konventionen i Stralsund den 7 september 1807* (Uppsala, 1891).

Kjellin, Gunnar. " 'Hvilke äro de sannskyldige jacobinerne?'—sengustavianska opinioner och stämningar," *Historisk tidskrift* (1963), 188–96.

Krusius-Ahrenberg, Lolo. *Tyrannmördaren C. F. Ehrensvärd* (Helsingfors, 1947).

Lacour-Gayet, Robert. "Qu'esperaient les émigrés?", *Revue de Paris*, LXX (1963), 96–109.

Lamm, Martin. *Upplysningstidens romantik*, 2 vol. (Stockholm, 1918-20).

Landberg, Georg. *Gustav III i eftervärldens dom* (Stockholm, 1945).

La Rocheterie, Maxime. *The Life of Marie-Antoinette*, trans. Cora Hamilton Bell, 2 vol. (London, 1893).

Lefebvre, Georges. *La Révolution française* (Paris, 1951).

————. *Napoléon* (fourth ed., Paris, 1953).

Lenotre, G. (pseud. for Gosselin, G.). *Le drame de Varennes* (Paris, 1908).

Lenz, Max. "Marie Antoinette im Kampf mit der Revolution," *Preussische Jahrbücher*, LXXVIII (1894), 1–28, 255–311.

————. "Die Vorbereitungen der Flucht Ludwigs XVI. (Oktober 1790 bis Juni 1791.) Ein Beitrag zur Kritik der französischen Memoirenliteratur," *Historische Zeitschrift*, LXXII (1894), 1–43, 213–46.

Lesch, Bruno. *Jan Anders Jägerhorn. Patriot och världsborgare, separatist och emigrant. En tidsskildring.* Svenska litteratursällskapet i Finland, CCLXXXVIII (Helsingfors, 1941).

Lestapis, Arnaud de. "Royalistes et monarchiens," *Revue des Deux Mondes* (1960), 271–83, 501–13.

Levertin, Oscar. "Den armfeltska konspirationen," *Samlade skrifter*, X:1 (Stockholm, 1907), 165–74.

510   COUNT HANS AXEL VON FERSEN

——. "Hertiginnans dagbok," *Samlade skrifter*, X:1 (Stockholm, 1907), 89–114.

Liljekrantz, Birger. *Benjamin Höijer. En studie över hans utveckling* (Lund, 1912).

Lönnroth, Erik. "Press och agitation i Sverige 1809–1810," *Dagens nyheter*, 2 March 1955.

——. "Revolution för en dag," *Dagens nyheter*, 19 June 1960.

Loomis, Stanley. *The Fatal Friendship* (New York, 1972).

Lundh, Herbert. *Gustav IV Adolf och Sveriges utrikespolitik 1801–1804* (Uppsala, 1926).

Mallet, Bernard. *Mallet du Pan and the French Revolution* (London, 1902).

Malmström, Carl Gustaf. "Axel von Fersen som memoarförfattare," in his *Smärre skrifter rörande sjuttonhundratalets historia* (Stockholm, 1889), 209–40.

Morén, F. W. "Några problem i samband med tronföljdsfrågan 1809," *Historisk tidskrift* (1938), 46–56.

Nilsson, J. W. *De diplomatiska förbindelserna mellan Sverige och Frankrike under Gustaf IV Adolf* (Uppsala, 1899).

Nordin, Richard. "En blick på Sveriges förhållanden till Österrike under tiden närmast före kongressen i Rastadt," *Historisk tidskrift* (1907), 129–56.

Norrlin, Lennart. *Anders Fredrik Reutersvärd. Biografisk studie* (Stockholm, 1953). Pamphlet.

Nyberg, H. S. *Johan Adam Tingstadius*, Svenska akademiens minnesteckningar (Stockholm, 1953).

Nylund, Martin. *G. A. Reuterholm under förmyndaretiden 1792–96* (Uppsala, 1917).

Odelberg, Wilhelm. *Viceamiral Carl Olof Cronstedt* (Stockholm, 1954).

Odhner, C. T. "Ett bidrag till Anjalaförbundets historia," *Historisk tidskrift* (1882), 70–76.

——. *Sveriges politiska historia under konung Gustaf III:s regering*, 3 vol. (Stockholm, 1885–1905).

Palme, S. U. "Fredrik Axel von Fersens memoarer. Ett meddelande rörande deras tillkomsttid och tillkomstsätt," *Personhistorisk tidskrift*, XXXVII (1936), 173–81.

Palmer, Robert R. *The Age of the Democratic Revolution*, 2 vol. (Princeton, 1959–64).

Palou, Jean. "Autour de la fuite du roi," *Annales historiques de la Révolution française*, XXXIII (1962), 187–92.

Paris. Bibliothèque nationale, Départment des imprimés. *Répertoire de l'histoire de la Révolution française: travaux publiés de 1800 à 1940*, ed. Gérard Walter, 2 vol. (Paris, 1941–51).

Pétiet, R. *Gustave IV Adolphe et la Révolution française. Relations diplomatiques de la France et de la Suède de 1792 à 1810 d'après des documents d'archives inédits* (Paris, 1914).

Peyre, R. "Sympathies des états scandinaves pour la Révolution française et pour Napoléon," *Revue des études napoléoniennes,* I (1912), 335–48.

Praviel, Armand. "La maîtresse de Fersen: variété inédite," *Les œuvres libres,* vol. 166 (1935), 207–60.

Reddaway, W. F. "Canning and the Baltic in 1807," *The Baltic Countries,* II (1936).

Rein, G. *Karl Johan Adlercreutz. Försök till en levnadsteckning,* Svenska litteratursällskapet i Finland, 2 vol. (Helsingfors, 1925–27), II.

Roberts, Michael. "Sweden," in Albert Goodwin, ed., *The European Nobility in the Eighteenth Century* (London, 1953), 136–53.

Rose, J. Holland. "Gustavus IV and the Formulation of the Third Coalition," *Revue napoléonienne,* II (1902), 88–93.

Ross, Steven T. "The Military Strategy of the Directory: The Campaigns of 1799," *French Historical Studies,* V (1967), 170–87.

Scheel, H. *Süddeutsche Jakobiner. Klassenkämpfe und republikanische Strebungen im deutschen Süden am Ende des 18. Jahrhunderts* ([East] Berlin, 1962).

Schöldström, Birger, *Förbiskymtande skuggor* (Stockholm, 1883).

Sciout, Ludovic. *Le Directoire,* 4 vol. (Paris, 1895–97).

Setterwall, Kristian. *Svensk historisk bibliografi 1771–1874* (Stockholm, 1937).

————. *Svensk historisk bibliografi 1901–1920* (Uppsala, 1923).

Sjöfors, O. T. *Kanslärsgillet och 1807 års skolordning* (Lund, 1919).

Sjögren, Otto. *Karl August Grevesmöhlen. Karaktärsbild från en upprörd tid* (Stockholm, 1882).

Sjögren, Paul. *Svensk historisk bibliografi 1921–35* (Uppsala, 1956).

Sjövall, Birger. *Georg Adlersparre och tronfrågan 1809* (Lund, 1917).

————. *Om partier och paskviller å riddarhuset vid 1809–1810 års riksdag.* Bilaga till Kristianstads högre allmänna läroverks årsredogörelse 1921–22 (Kristianstad, 1922).

Söderbaum, H. G. *Jacob Berzelius,* 3 vol. (Uppsala, 1929), I.

Söderhjelm, Alma. *Gustaf III:s syskon* (Stockholm, 1945).

————. *Kärlek och politik* (Stockholm, 1933).

————. *Marie Antoinettes stora hemlighet* (Stockholm, 1934).

————. *Revolutionärer och emigranter* (Stockholm, 1918).

————. *Spel och verklighet* (Stockholm, 1941).

————. *Den stora revolutionen,* 2 vol. (Stockholm, 1927–29).

————. *Sverige och den franska revolutionen,* 2 vol. (Stockholm, 1920–24).

————. "Den verkliga Heddas journal. Vad de fersenska papperen ha att förmäla i en aktuell historia," *Sydsvenska dagbladet-snällposten,* 22 December 1935.

Sorel, Albert. *L'Europe et la Révolution française,* 8 vol. (Paris, 1885–1904).

————. "La fuite de Louis XVI et les essais d'intervention en 1791: Varennes et Pillnitz," *Revue des Deux Mondes,* III (1886), 314–46.

Stålhane, Henning. *Gustaf III:s resa till Italien och Frankrike* (Stockholm, 1953).

Stade, A. "Gustaf IV Adolf och Norge, 1798 och 1801," *Historisk tidskrift* (1955), 353–83.

Staf, Nils. *Polisväsendet i Stockholm 1776–1850* (Uppsala, 1950).

Stavenow, Ludvig. *Den gustavianska tiden 1772–1809*, Sveriges historia till våra dagar, X (Stockholm, 1925).

Stenström, Stig. "Gustaf III:s divertismenter och de sista gustavianska riddarspelen," *Kungliga livrustkammaren*, XIV (1946), 99–120.

––––––. "Gustaf III:s riddarspel 1776 och 1777,' *Kungliga livrustkammaren*, XIV (1946), 26–64.

Ström, Å. V. "Gustav IV Adolf och vilddjuret," *Svenska dagbladet*, 31 January 1937.

Strömbom, Sixten, ed. *Index över svenska porträtt 1500–1850*, 3 vol. (Stockholm, 1935–43), I.

Stuart, D. M. *Dear Bess: The Life and Times of Lady Elizabeth Foster* (London, 1955).

Svanström, R., and C. F. Palmstierna. *Short History of Sweden* (Oxford, 1934).

Svenson, Sven G. *Gattjinatraktaten 1799. Studier i Gustav IV Adolfs utrikespolitik 1796–1800* (Uppsala, 1952).

––––––. "Studentens klang- och jubeltid. Från Juntan till skandinavism," in *Uppsalastudenten genom tiderna* (Uppsala, 1950), 73–194.

Tegnér, Elof. "Folkväpningen i Sverige 1788. Anteckningar ur Gustaf III:s och G.M. Armfelts efterlemnade papper," *Historisk tidskrift* (1881), 213–46.

––––––. *Gustaf Mauritz Armfelt. Studier ur Armfelts efterlämnade papper samt andra handskrifvna och tryckta källor*, 3 vol. (Stockholm, 1883–87).

Thompson, J. M. *The French Revolution* (Oxford, 1944).

Waller, Sture M. *Georg Carl von Döbeln. Studier i Sveriges militäriska och politiska historia 1808–1813* (Lund, 1947).

Walter, Gerard. *Le comte de Provence roi des émigrés* (Paris, 1950).

Wandruszka, Adam. *Leopold II*, 2 vol. (Vienna, 1963–65), II.

Werner, K. F. "Gustaf Abraham [Silfverstolpe]," in *Några anteckningar om adliga ätten Silfverstolpe* (Stockholm, 1884), 248–360.

Westrin, Theodor. "Om G. M. Sprengtportens tillämnade deltagande i Nordamerikanska frihetskriget," *Studier utgifna af svenska litteratursällskapet i Finland*, IX (1887–8), 34–41.

Wibling, Jöran. "Carl August Grevesmöhlen," *Svenskt biografiskt lexikon*, XVII (Stockholm, 1967), 266–71.

––––––. *Opinioner och stämningar i Sverige 1809–10* (Uppsala, 1954).

Wrangel, Ewert, ed. *Den gustavianska kulturen*, Svenska folket genom tiderna, VII (Malmö, 1938).

Wrangel, F. U. *Blasieholmen och dess inbyggare* (2nd ed., Stockholm, 1914).

––––––. *Origines et débuts du Royal-Suédois* (Paris, 1914).

Zweig, Stefan. *Marie-Antoinette: The Portrait of an Average Woman* New York, 1933).

Index

The Swedish letters å, ä, ö, and the German ü, are alphabetized as aa, ae, oe, and ue, respectively.

513

COUNT HANS AXEL VON FERSEN

tions with Gustav III, 40, 42-47 passim., 50-59 passim., 80-81, 86-87, 155, 159, 315, 398, 400, 422-n60, 429n35, 445n5, 447n41; proprietary colonel of the Royal-Suédois regiment, 47, 58, 65, 74-75, 82, 84, 202, 203, 208, 415n34, 422n46; visits to Sweden between *1784* and *1788*, 48, 51 74; considered by Gustav III for foreign minister, 48, 193; serves in Swedish-Russian war, *1788*, 51-59, 66; secret visit to Paris (*Feb., 1792*), 67-68, 70, 144, 146-48, 155, 162, 435n41; as Swedish ambassador at Congress of Rastadt, *1797-98*, 70, 182, 234-57 passim., 259, 264, 265, 266, 278, 299, 309, 400, 456-n42, 456-57n46, 457n58, 459n17, 461n32; periods in France, *1784-88*, 74; views on the nature of the French Revolution, 78, 81-83, 86-93, 102, 104-106, 147, 149-50, 222, 253, 257-58, 398-99; on the press and public opinion, 78, 167, 168, 173, 191, 195-96, 197, 219, 221, 224, 260, 261, 298; in "October Days" (*5* and *6 Oct. 1789*), 83-84, 96, 111; seeks appointment as Gustav III's ambassador to France, 85-86, 94-95, 109, 141, 155, 180, 223; becomes Gustav III's special agent in Paris, *1790*, 87-88, 94, 169; fear of the spread of revolution, 87, 92, 107, 110-11, 150-51, 168-69, 191, 196, 198-99, 204, 241, 253, 256-58, 262, 268, 269-70, 274, 284-95 passim., 300, 312, 321, 390, 429-n36, 452n20, 455-56n33, 457n52, 461-62n42; ideas and projects to combat the French Revolution, 88-93, 100-111, 128-29, 132-33, 135, 137, 140-50, 159-65, 161, 163-65, 218-27, 241, 252-53, 257-64, 297, 317, 400, 452n26; plans for flight of the French royal family from Paris, 89, 91, 96, 97, 106-17, 126-27, 160; involvement in Brunswick Manifesto, *1792*, 92, 159-65, 179, 219; loans to the French royal family, 114, 186-87, 208, 429n43, 430n44, 445n11,

449n76, 450n84, 450n85; gets royal family out of Paris, *June 1791*, 117-24; remains Gustav III's special agent for French affairs after flight to Varennes, 126, 131, 133, 138, 176; also remains secret advisor to Marie-Antoinette and Louis XVI, 126, 131, 133, 138, 156, 176, 400; mission to Vienna, *1791*, 130-37; relations with Duke Karl of Södermanland (from *1809*, Karl XIII, King of Sweden), 155, 176, 177, 192-94, 197, 368-69, 438n7, 438n8, 442n58, 442-n62; Duke Karl secretly accredits as minister, later ambassador, to French king, 156, 158, 167, 174, 175-76, 181; disapproval of French policy of regency of Duke Karl, 158-59, 166, 171, 173, 177, 192, 197-99, 220, 229; views on War of the First Coalition, 159, 164-65, 167, 173-78 passim., 180, 211-12, 215-23, 227-28, 257; projects to protect or save the French royal family after their imprisonment, 165-81 passim.; intrigues against, in Swedish government, 170-71, 193, 252, 255, 271, 274, 344, 383, 385-92, 393, 394; end of personal involvement in French affairs, 181, 182, 191, 444n92; case of the *1,500,000 livres*, 186-88, 204-209, 449-50n81; in Sweden, *1794-95*, 188, 193-202; and the Armfelt Conspiracy, 189-92, 202; reluctance to accept official positions, 193, 202, 233-35, 267, 271, 299, 329, 446n36, 454n19; relations with Gustav IV Adolf, 195, 231-33, 260, 264, 265, 267, 271-75, 286, 288, 291, 294-95, 297-300, 303-305, 309-10, 315, 328-44 passim., 349-50, 354, 399, 400, 447n41, 462n49, 473n17, 473n29, 475n49, 476n5, 485n10; personal observations and criticisms of Gustav IV Adolf, 195, 303-305, 310-13, 323-47 passim., 350; purchases Breteuil's plantation on Santo Domingo, 203-204; in Vienna, *1795-96*, 205-206, 210-12; views on French succession